YELLOWSTONE
& GRAND TETON
NATIONAL PARKS

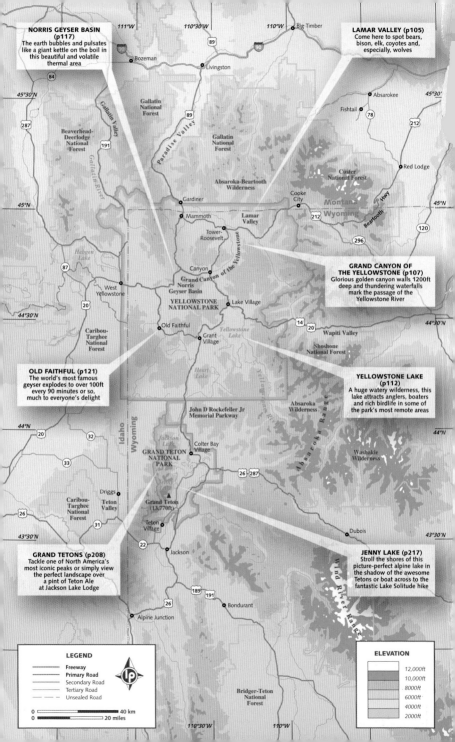

NORRIS GEYSER BASIN (p117)
The earth bubbles and pulsates like a giant kettle on the boil in this beautiful and volatile thermal area

LAMAR VALLEY (p105)
Come here to spot bears, bison, elk, coyotes and, especially, wolves

GRAND CANYON OF THE YELLOWSTONE (p107)
Glorious golden canyon walls 1200ft deep and thundering waterfalls mark the passage of the Yellowstone River

OLD FAITHFUL (p121)
The world's most famous geyser explodes to over 100ft every 90 minutes or so, much to everyone's delight

YELLOWSTONE LAKE (p112)
A huge watery wilderness, this lake attracts anglers, boaters and rich birdlife in some of the park's most remote areas

GRAND TETONS (p208)
Tackle one of North America's most iconic peaks or simply view the perfect landscape over a pint of Teton Ale at Jackson Lake Lodge

JENNY LAKE (p217)
Stroll the shores of this picture-perfect alpine lake in the shadow of the awesome Tetons or boat across to the fantastic Lake Solitude hike

Big Timber
Bozeman
Livingston
Absarokee
Fishtail
Red Lodge
Gallatin National Forest
Beaverhead-Deerlodge National Forest
Paradise Valley
Gallatin Valley
Gallatin River
Gallatin National Forest
Absaroka-Beartooth Wilderness
Custer National Forest
Gardiner
Cooke City
Montana
Wyoming
Beartooth Hwy
Mammoth
Lamar Valley
Tower-Roosevelt
Hebgen Lake
Canyon
Grand Canyon of the Yellowstone
West Yellowstone
Norris Geyser Basin
YELLOWSTONE NATIONAL PARK
Lake Village
Wapiti Valley
Old Faithful
Yellowstone Lake
Grant Village
Shoshone National Forest
Caribou-Targhee National Forest
Heart Lake
Absaroka Wilderness
Yellowstone River
Absaroka Range
John D Rockefeller Jr Memorial Parkway
Idaho
Wyoming
Jackson Lake
Colter Bay Village
Washakie Wilderness
GRAND TETON NATIONAL PARK
Driggs
Teton Valley
Grand Teton (13,770ft)
Teton Village
Caribou-Targhee National Forest
Dubois
Jackson
Wind River Range
Alpine Junction
Bondurant
Bridger-Teton National Forest

LEGEND
Freeway
Primary Road
Secondary Road
Tertiary Road
Unsealed Road
0   40 km
0   20 miles

ELEVATION
12,000ft
10,000ft
8000ft
6000ft
4000ft
2000ft

111°W   110°30'W   110°W
45°30'N
45°30'
45°N
45°N
44°30'N
44°30'N
44°N
44°N
43°30'N
43°30'N
110°30'W   110°W

YELLOWSTONE & GRAND TETON NATIONAL PARKS

Yellowstone and Grand Teton National Parks offer such a wonderful breadth of pleasures that each person's highlights will be unique. It might be the first time you see a moose or go camping with the kids, the bison that passes just a few feet from your car or the thrilling sight of a geyser in action.

There's no 'right way' to explore the parks. Beyond the sights listed in this section, our best advice is to slow down and get out of the car – you'll only come to grips with the park on foot. As John Muir once said, 'Nothing can be done well at a speed of 40 miles a day.' Let alone 45mph.

Thermal Features

It's hard to grasp the epic scale of the Yellowstone supervolcano, but it's the fuel behind Yellowstone's incredible thermal features. Towering geysers such as Old Faithful and Giant are the crowd pleasers, belching mud pots the comedians and the turquoise hot springs the beautiful assistants in Yellowstone's 'steam-operated freak show.'

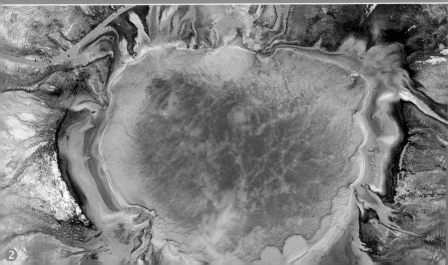

Author Tip

Get the latest timings or activity reports from Old Faithful Visitor Center to see which of the big geysers is scheduled to erupt during your visit. Try to visit at least one backcountry thermal feature, away from the boardwalks. Enjoy a legal hot spring soak at Boiling Springs near Mammoth, 'the park's worst-kept secret.'

① Old Faithful

In the Upper Geyser Basin view the world's most famous geyser (p121) from different angles – from the main boardwalk, from the Old Faithful Inn balcony and from the side of Observation Hill.

② Grand Prismatic Spring

The rainbow colors fringing this huge spring (p124) make it the park's most beautiful thermal feature. Get the best views from the lava hill across the river on the Fairy Falls Trail.

③ Norris Geyser Basin

Rare acidic geysers, jet blue springs, the world's tallest geyser (Steamboat Geyser) and the beautiful Porcelain Basin (p117) make this our favorite collection of thermal features.

④ Mammoth Terraces

Hot water cascades over surreal travertine terraces in this beautiful group of hot springs and multicolored channels (p101). Come and see what happens when a mountain turns itself inside out.

⑤ Morning Glory Pool

This gloriously clear turquoise pool (p123) in the Upper Geyser Basin epitomizes the beauty and fragility of Yellowstone's thermal features.

⑥ Shoshone Geyser Basin

The largest backcountry geyser basin (p146) is a long day or an overnight hike away, by the shores of remote Shoshone Lake.

Watching Wildlife

Once the geysers have subsided and you've snapped the Yellowstone Canyon from the requisite six viewpoints, it's the primeval wildness of Yellowstone that will keep you coming back for more. The haunting early-morning howl of a wolf and the glimpse of a grizzly lumbering across a valley floor will make the hairs stand up on your neck.

Author Tip
Dawn and dusk are the only times for serious wildlife-watchers. Get to the most popular turnouts early, as they fill up quickly in summer. Bring a big zoom lens, a decent pair of binoculars or, better still, bring a spotting scope. Understand animal psychology for the best chance of spotting something memorable. Just driving the Grand Loop almost guarantees you a view of bison and elk.

Lamar Valley
The 'American Serengeti' (p105), this wide-open plain is home to wolves, bison, elk, grizzlies, coyotes and the wild complex forces of nature that link them.

Hayden Valley
This valley is the park's second viewing site (p111) for bears, coyotes, bison and hawks, especially in spring.

Mammoth
Elk graze the manicured lawns here year-round, but it's the September rut that is most memorable, as bucks fill the park with their high-pitched bugles and herd their harems into Mammoth Junction (p99).

Antelope Creek
Several pullouts (p107) offer some of the best views over prime grizzly habitat.

Mt Washburn
Haul yourself up to the top of Mt Washburn (p138) and you'll be rewarded with close-up views of bighorn sheep grazing the nearby crags. There's also a good chance of spotting black bears and even grizzlies, who flock to the mountain in August.

Oxbow Bend
Riparian wildlife at its finest: elk, moose, sandhill cranes, blue herons, trumpeter swans and pelicans flock to this ultra scenic stretch of the Snake River (p216).

8

Activities

The best way to experience Yellowstone is in the backcountry. Head off the road and you'll lose 90% of the crowds; continue a mile or more and you'll lose another 5%; overnight in the backcountry and you'll join a minority of 1%. Whether it's a silent paddle on a glassy lake or the adrenaline rush of a whitewater ride, these activities will help you unlock the parks' best secrets.

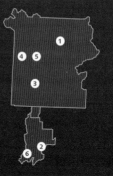

Author Tip
Yellowstone is a great place to learn an activity, from a fly-fishing clinic to a rock-climbing course. Outfitters lead adventurous trips on horseback through the region's wilderness. Get insider tips and route advice from the region's gear-rental shops (p287).

❶ Take a Day Hike
There are literally dozens of hikes to choose from. Our favorite? Mt Washburn (p138) – a hike that climbs to the top of the 10,243ft peak for some of the park's best views.

❷ Experience the Snake River
Meander through the wilderness on a picturesque sunset float down the Snake River, or get the blood pumping on a white-water rafting trip (p233).

❸ Paddle Shoshone Lake
Yellowstone's largest backcountry lake, the remote and tranquil Shoshone Lake (p158) is the perfect spot to dip your paddle on a multiday canoe trip.

❹ Fly-Fish a Blue-Ribbon River
Pack some spare wholly buggers or iris caddis and spend a few unforgettable days casting your lures on the Madison River, or the Gibbon, Gallatin and Yellowstone Rivers (p49).

❺ Backpack the Teton Crest Trail
Savor the region's most stupendous alpine scenery on this multiday, high-altitude trek (p227).

❻ Climb Grand Teton
Buck the trend and look *down* on the Tetons on a guided climb with Exum Mountain Guides (p232). One-day mountaineering courses are available.

Unnatural Wonders

After a few days of sleeping in a tent and eating beans out of a can, you might just start missing those urban comforts. If it's raining or you just need to feel carpet between your toes again, head into the surrounding gateway towns for some Wild-West culture.

Author Tip

The combined museums of Cody are the region's best and would have made Buffalo Bill proud (and the nighttime rodeo is a hoot, too). The ghosts of Calamity Jane and Butch Cassidy still haunt Livingston and Red Lodge. Bozeman and Jackson rank as our favorite towns in the region.

① Draper Museum of Natural History

Goldilocks never browsed so boldly: peek inside a naturalist's cabin and a field-station classroom to learn some tools of the trade. It's part of the fantastic Buffalo Bill Historical Center (p188).

② Museum of the Rockies

Everyone loves a Montanan dinosaur and this fantastic and family-friendly museum and planetarium (p195) is the place to see them.

③ Old Faithful Inn

Possibly the world's grandest log cabin and the best example of classic Yellowstone 'parkitecture,' the inn's lobby offers comfy seats and acres of rustic charm (p166).

④ Jackson

Welcome to the new West in the region's most sophisticated shopping and dining center. Looking for a special souvenir? Try 'The Deuce,' a rabbit-fur jockstrap and a booming bestseller at the Alaska Fur Gallery (p243).

⑤ Museum of the Yellowstone

Meet the snarling Snaggletooth: this great stuffed grizzly once haunted the dumpsters of West Yellowstone; sadly he's now the museum's most popular attraction (p171).

⑥ Jackson's Antler Archway

Take your picture under this goofy downtown landmark crafted from 2000 elk antlers or, heck, just charge it: at a recent Boy Scout auction (p245) one sold for over $50,000.

Winter

Winter is perhaps Yellowstone's most
beguiling season. The park is covered
by up to 15ft of snow, Yellowstone Lake
freezes to a depth of 2ft and the park's
geysers seem twice as powerful in the
frigid air. The animals congregate in the
warmer valleys and so are easier to spot;
bison warm themselves in the park's geyser
basins; and the silence is awesome.

Author Tip

It's trickier to go it alone in winter so consider signing up for an activities package or a snowcoach tour, especially if you want to visit Old Faithful or Canyon. Plan your schedule around skier shuttles and free ranger snowshoe hikes. And bring some extra hot chocolate.

① Upper Geyser Basin

Yellowstone's thermal features seem grander when gliding past on a pair of skinny skis (p160).

② Grand Canyon of the Yellowstone

Watch the Upper Falls tumble into a frozen canyon beside a giant snow cone of frozen spray. For a treat, stay at a yurt in the giant whiteness of the surrounding backcountry (p161).

③ Mystic Falls & Fairy Falls

Snowshoe or ski out to either of these frozen backcountry waterfalls (p130 and p129) on this fine day trip from Old Faithful.

④ West Yellowstone

This is Yellowstone's snowmobiling epicenter. You can also sign up for a snowcoach tour or learn to cross-country ski on the region's most extensive network of groomed trails (p173).

⑤ Big Sky

One of the West's best ski resorts (p197), Big Sky is an hour from the park's northwest corner (where there are some great cross-country routes). The downhill is superb, as is the cross-country at Lone Mountain Ranch.

⑥ Cottonwood Creek

When the Grand Teton park road closes, take to the trails and enjoy fabulous views of the Teton Range: a dusting of powder makes this a fun one (p235).

Family Fun

Greening the planet is a red-hot topic, but when it comes to wilderness, today's kids get less and less of the real thing. In fact, untamed, unfettered wild space might scare us a little. Fear not, Yellowstone and Grand Teton offer marvels for every age: the rainbow shock of Prismatic Spring, the sheer force of a geyser erupting or a grizzly ambling across a meadow.

Author Tip

Exploring the backcountry as a family offers an opportunity to make discoveries and learn skills. Adventure can have a tangible goal: route finding, reaching a landmark or completing a junior ranger badge requirement. But it is equally important to teach safety and caution – returning to the trailhead at a reasonable hour, keeping an eye on the weather and respecting the space and privacy of wildlife.

❶ Geyser Country

Explore the strange world of scenery that gurgles, burps and spurts on walks like Lone Star Geyser (p132), Artist Paint Pots (p118) and Monument Geyser Basin (p142).

❷ Rodeo Roundup

In Cody, the self-proclaimed Rodeo Capital of the World, pros wrestle steers and ride bucking broncs at the Cody Stampede or the Cody Nite Rodeo (p191).

❸ Teton's Alpine Lakes

Ease into overnighting by backpacking the flat trail to Bearpaw Lake (p222), where an icy dip is followed by an evening of eyeballing the constellations.

❹ Western Cookout

Fresh corn, flame-broiled steaks, beans and coffee that will curl your hair are classic open-air Western fare. Dine cowboy-style on the trail at Tower-Roosevelt Junction (p167).

❺ Wild West reenactment

Hey mister, is that a real handlebar mustache? Get a taste of the old Wild West on a summer visit to Cody for daily gunslinger showdowns (p192).

❻ Family-Friendly Hiking

Kit up the kids with boots and hat, and give them a taste of nature while exploring one of the gentle trails that abound in Yellowstone National Park (p57).

Wildflowers in full bloom in Grand Teton National Park

Contents

Yellowstone & Grand
Teton National Parks   3

The Authors   19

Destination Yellowstone
& Grand Teton
National Parks   21

Planning Your Trip   23

Itineraries   31

Activities   39

Kids & Pets   56

Environment   63

History   81

Yellowstone
National Park   91

SIGHTS   99
Mammoth Country   99
Roosevelt Country   103
Canyon Country   107
Lake Country   112
Norris   116
Geyser Country   119
Bechler Region   127
HIKING   128
Easy Hikes   128
Day Hikes   133
Backcountry Hikes   143
BIKING   153
Mammoth Country   154
Canyon Country   154
Lake Country   155
Geyser Country   155
DRIVING   156
OTHER ACTIVITIES   157

Horseback Riding   157
Boating   157
Fishing   158
Cross-Country Skiing
& Snowshoeing   160
SLEEPING   160
Mammoth Country   161
Roosevelt Country   163
Canyon Country   164
Lake Country   165
Geyser Country   165
Bechler Region   166
EATING & DRINKING   166
Mammoth Country   167
Roosevelt Country   167
Canyon Country   167
Geyser Country   167
Lake Country   168

Around
Yellowstone   169

GATEWAY TOWNS   170
West Yellowstone   170
Gardiner   175
Cooke City   178
BEARTOOTH ROUTE   180
Billings   180
Red Lodge   181
Beartooth Highway   183
Chief Joseph Scenic
Highway   187
WAPITI ROUTE   188
Cody   188
GALLATIN VALLEY ROUTE   194
Bozeman   194
Gallatin Valley   196
Hebgen Lake Area   201
PARADISE VALLEY ROUTE   203
Livingston   203
Paradise Valley   205

Grand Teton
National Park   208

SIGHTS   214
Colter Bay Region   214
Central Tetons   217
The Eastern Slopes   219
John D Rockefeller
Jr Memorial Parkway   220
HIKING   221

Day Hikes   221
Backcountry Hikes   226
BIKING   **228**
DRIVING   **230**
OTHER ACTIVITIES   **231**
Rock Climbing
& Mountaineering   231
Horseback Riding   232
Boating   232
Fishing   234
Winter Activities   234
SLEEPING   **235**
Colter Bay Region   236
Central Tetons   237
John D Rockefeller
Jr Memorial Parkway   238
EATING & DRINKING   **238**
Colter Bay Region   238
Central Tetons   239
John D Rockefeller
Jr Memorial Parkway   239

Around
Grand Teton   **240**
Jackson   241
Jackson Hole   249
Upper Wind River Valley   253
Idaho's Teton Valley   253

Directory   **258**
Accommodations   258
Business Hours   262
Climate Charts   263
Courses   263
Discount Cards   263
Festivals & Events   264
Food & Drink   264
Holidays   264
Insurance   264
International Visitors   264
Internet Access   265
Money   265
Post   265
Showers & Laundry   265
Telephone   266
Time   266
Tourist Information   266
Tours   267
Travelers with
Disabilities   267
Volunteering   268
Women Travelers   268
Work   269

Transportation   **270**
Health & Safety   **276**
Clothing
& Equipment   **285**
Glossary   **290**
Behind the Scenes   **292**
Index   **298**
World Time Zones   **310**
Map Legend   **312**

Regional Map Contents

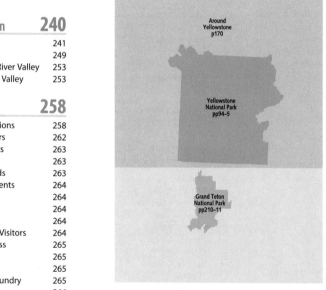

The Authors

BRADLEY MAYHEW

More at home trekking through the remoter parts of inner Asia than dodging lines of bison-watching SUVs in Wyoming, Bradley has written Lonely Planet guides to *Tibet, Central Asia, Bhutan, Nepal, Mongolia, China, Shanghai, Jordan* and *Pakistan*, as well as the first edition of this guide. He has also worked on guides for Odyssey, Insight Guides and Dorling Kindersley. An expat Brit, Bradley has called Montana home for the last seven years and heads for the Beartooths as often as he can.

My Yellowstone National Park

My favorite moment on this trip was on the Cascade Lake (p139), just a few miles from Canyon Junction. Out of the corner of my eye I spotted a large bull elk trotting along the forest line, followed by five young elk. Except they weren't elk, they were wolves and for the next two hours I stood transfixed as the white and gray wolves circled the elk like ghosts. At one point they got him down, but the elk stood firm, swiping at the nearest wolves with a crack of his huge antlers. Eventually I continued the hike to Observation Peak, but when I got back down they were still there, the elk bugling now and then, both the wolves and elk casting me occasional glances. It was a wild, powerful, stripped-down few hours that comes to me whenever I think of the park.

Cascade Lake

CAROLYN MCCARTHY

Author and journalist Carolyn McCarthy has spent the last nine years traveling the Americas from Alaska to Tierra del Fuego writing about travel, culture and the environment. In her outdoor pursuits, she has scaled peaks in the Rockies and Andes and worked as a hiking guide in Patagonia. This trip to Yellowstone and the Tetons re-inforced her admiration for wilderness, hot springs and wild things. A frequent contributor to newspapers and magazines, she has written about Chile, Ecuador, Costa Rica and El Salvador for Lonely Planet. Visit her blog at www.carolynswildblueyonder. blogspot.com.

My Grand Teton National Park

Places like the Tetons should be savored not tamed. The wildlife looks right through you, weather shifts the landscape, and marvelous sights and smells prickle your skin.

For starters, you can find solitude on the Idaho side. I recommend hiking Alaska Basin (p254), where high plateaus pocked with snow sprout wildflowers at the same time. Ease back into civilization at Drigg's honky-tonk Knotty Pine (p255).

The thin trail twisting into the granite-walled depths of Death Canyon (p225) presents another fun excursion. Good navigators can extend the trip by bagging Static Peak (named for its many lightning strikes). On lazy days, nothing beats a delicious swim in Leigh Lake (p222), followed by dripping dry on its unspoiled beaches.

Leigh Lake
Alaska Basin
Static Peak
Knotty Pine
Death Canyon

CONTRIBUTING AUTHOR

David Lukas is a professional naturalist whose travels and writing take him around the world, but he always returns to his home landscape of the American West. He has contributed environment and wildlife chapters to about 15 Lonely Planet guides.

LONELY PLANET AUTHORS

Why is our travel information the best in the world? It's simple: our authors are independent, dedicated travellers. They don't research using just the Internet or phone, and they don't take freebies in exchange for positive coverage. They travel widely, to all the popular spots and off the beaten track. They personally visit thousands of hotels, restaurants, cafés, bars, galleries, palaces, museums and more – and they take pride in getting all the details right, and telling it how it is. For more, see the authors section on www.lonelyplanet.com.

Destination Yellowstone & Grand Teton National Parks

There's nowhere in the world quite like Yellowstone. From its raging geysers to its free-roaming herds of bison, the land stands as one last remaining pocket of a wild, primeval America. Here you will find the country's largest collection of elk (30,000), the continent's largest wild bison herd (3000) and the world's densest collection of geysers and fossilized forests, set in a land roamed by wolves, grizzlies, lynx, moose and antelope. As the world's oldest national park and part of the world's largest intact temperate mountain ecosystem, Yellowstone has transcended even this landscape to become synonymous with environmental protection worldwide.

The park is probably most famous for its geysers and hot springs – nature's crowd pleasers – whose magical explosions and graceful beauty still capture the visitor's imagination as they did 150 years ago. Yellowstone is a landscape created by grinding glaciers and volcanic eruptions, a place of fire and brimstone where the very earth breathes, belches and bubbles like a giant kettle on the boil. The sensual blast of hot steam followed by cold air, the aroma of rotten eggs and the belching sound of a hot spring are memories that you will forever associate with Yellowstone. The park's highways traverse these geysers, through meadows and forests, past roadside wildlife and campsites aromatic with pine needles and family campfires.

Each region of the park boasts its own character. To the northwest, Mammoth offers ornate terraces and colorful pools. Roosevelt is a wilder land of wolves and bison. Canyon holds one of the park's great draws in the 1200ft-deep Grand Canyon of the Yellowstone. Further south, Yellowstone Lake is a huge wilderness of water that shelters the park's most remote reaches. Geyser holds the majority of the park's geothermal wonders.

South of Yellowstone is Grand Teton National Park, probably the most famous natural skyline in the United States. These vertical peaks, reflected in a string of gorgeous glacial lakes, come close to most people's picture-postcard image of alpine splendor and will send a shiver of excitement down the spine of even the least vertically inclined.

Opportunities to venture into the backcountry abound in both parks, whether on foot, horseback, boat, ski or snowshoe. Buckle up and climb the Tetons, canoe around Shoshone Lake, mountain bike to the summit of Mt Washburn or hike for days through the remote backcountry – the choice is yours.

Raw nature is rarely this accessible. In Yellowstone even the most sedentary couch potato can be at eye level with a mountain peak or hike around a glacial lake. Drive the Beartooth Highway, the northeast gateway to the park, and you'll find yourself at 10,000ft without even unbuckling your seatbelt. Only around Old Faithful does the wilderness give way in places to theme-park chaos. Elsewhere, it is still surprisingly easy to lose the crowds. Park the car and head off down a trail, if only for a mile or two, and the park will reveal its true beauty.

'The park is probably most famous for its geysers and hot springs – nature's crowd pleasers'

Yellowstone's wonders don't stop at its boundaries. The two parks and their surrounding seven national forests and three national wildlife refuges form a larger, interconnected area six times the size of Yellowstone: the Greater Yellowstone Ecosystem. Here you'll find the blue-ribbon trout streams and hiking routes of the Gallatin and Madison Rivers, the awesome 10,000ft-high Beartooth Plateau and the Shoshone National Forest, which encompasses one of the largest tracts of wilderness in the lower 48.

Created by the *Yellowstone National Park Act* (1872) as a 'public park or pleasuring-ground for the benefit and enjoyment of the people,' this mother of all national parks straddles a tense line between preservation and recreation, access and excess. To snowmobile or not to snowmobile? To suppress natural fires or let them burn? To promote greater access or restrict large areas of wilderness to protect animal habitat? Park planners face these dilemmas on a daily basis. For all its controversies, Yellowstone has come to epitomize the very best and worst of the national park system.

'Park the car and head off down a trail, if only for a mile or two, and the park will reveal its true beauty'

These days the park attracts up to 30,000 visitors daily and more than three million visitors annually, processing visitors on a scale that writer Edward Abbey termed 'industrial tourism.' When bison or elk graze by the Grand Loop Rd, the result is close to a mob scene, with traffic backing up for hundreds of yards. Debate rages over how best to manage this influx. Ironically, the park's great appeal threatens to destroy the very features that attract such numbers.

Yellowstone is many things to many people: a natural Eden, a paradise lost, an extreme sports playground or the world's biggest petting zoo. From Yogi Bear's Jellystone Park (smarter than the average bear!) to iconic Old Faithful, Yellowstone has gone beyond its physical landscape to become an integral part of the American national consciousness. But all pigeonholing falls short. Yellowstone has a depth and breadth of beauty that requires repeated visits to fully appreciate its complexities and wonder.

Despite all the controversies, the traffic jams and the crowds, Yellowstone and Grand Teton still deliver. Nowhere else in mainstream America can you simply step out of the car and step into the raw forces of nature. Watch a moose trawl for food in a secluded pond, hike to magnificent Teton views, fish for trout under a golden sunset and reinvigorate yourself in two of America's greatest natural wonders.

Planning Your Trip

So, you've finally decided to take that long overdue Yellowstone vacation – cascading waterfalls, roaming bison, exploding geysers...oh yes, and three million other tourists. If you are reading this section for the first time in your RV halfway to Wyoming, then pull over, read the colour section that opens this book and the Itineraries chapter (p31), come up with a rough plan and book some accommodations. Even the most nonchalant, laid-back traveler will find that a small amount of planning greases the wheels of Yellowstone travel.

The golden rule when planning your vacation is to avoid being too ambitious. Don't try to cover the entire region in one military-style maneuver. If you have only a short time, then choose one area to explore. Don't be afraid to leave some things out – you'll have an excuse to return! Yellowstone and Grand Teton are places that reward many visits at different times of the year.

Some ultra-organized travelers book their accommodations a year in advance. Others just turn up at the park, grab a first-come, first-served campsite, and base themselves there for a week. The deciding factor is how flexible you can be. If your deadlines are tight (and most people's are), then book at least a few nights' accommodations well in advance. There's nothing worse than driving around, tired and cranky, looking for the park's only vacant campsite, only to face a 40-mile drive back out of the park.

So if you've promised your kids a hike with a llama, or your sweetie a secluded lakeshore cabin, then preplan and prebook – there are simply too many other visitors to leave things to chance. If you've decided to just drive into the wild blue yonder, that can work too, but you'll have to opt for remote campsites in secluded areas and more time in the surrounding national forests. And these just may end up being the highlights of your trip.

WHEN TO GO

For most travelers, the Yellowstone region is a summer destination, when the weather is most forgiving and there are more services. But the area offers draws in any season. Winter offers several unique attractions and is becoming increasingly popular.

See the climate charts (p263) for more information.

The weather is notoriously unpredictable in the Rockies. Freak storms can bring snow in high summer, and chinook winds can temporarily raise temperatures by 25°F in midwinter. Annual rainfall has more to do with park topography than seasonal variations, ranging from 10in in the north to about 80in in the southwest. Local residents will tell you that, unlike elsewhere, Yellowstone has only three seasons: July, August and winter. The parks' peak summer season runs from Memorial Day (last Monday in May) to Labor Day (first Monday in September), peaking in July and August. Outside school summer holidays it's noticeably quieter. May and mid-September to the end of October are considered the shoulder season.

Spring

Average high temperatures in April and May range from 40°F to 50°F, with low temperatures ranging from 0°F to -20°F. In late May and June average high temperatures are from 60°F to 70°F. Snow lingers into April and May.

Despite boasting 950 miles of backcountry trails and 97 trailheads, only 5% of visitors to Yellowstone hike more than a mile away from the road.

May and June are usually quite rainy, and this, combined with snowmelt, means that spring rivers and waterfalls are at their peak. This is a good time for wildlife viewing, with giftshop-sized baby elk and bison finding their feet, but many hiking trails are boggy, and there is still snow at higher elevations. In June wildflowers start to bloom at lower elevations.

Summer

It starts to feel like summer in the Rocky Mountains around June, and the warm weather lasts until about mid-September. High temperatures at lower elevations are usually around 70°F and occasionally reach 80°F, with nighttime lows ranging from 40°F to 30°F. Temperatures in the parks are at least 10°F cooler than down on the plains around Cody and Billings. July and August are the driest months, but afternoon thunderstorms are common, especially in the Tetons, which create their very own microclimate.

As visitor numbers peak, moose and elk retreat into the backcountry to avoid both the heat and the tourists. Mosquito season kicks in until mid-August. Daylight remains until about 9:30pm, allowing ample time for late-afternoon and evening excursions. August is a prime hiking month, when wildflowers are in full bloom at higher altitudes.

High summer is also the time of greatest traffic, so you'll need to secure your campsite early and budget extra time to get round the parks.

Fall

The weather becomes increasingly unreliable into fall. While winter weather doesn't usually settle in until late November, snowstorms can start hitting the mountain areas as early as September, and snow starts piling up by mid-October.

COPING WITH THE CROWDS

Come July, Yellowstone braces for the summer tourist invasion. If you are traveling during this peak season, be prepared to share the park's wonders, as well as its campgrounds, parking spots and hiking trails. It may not be quite the wilderness experience you were hoping for. British writer Rudyard Kipling's reaction to the considerably fewer crowds around Old Faithful in 1889 was forthright: 'Today I am in the Yellowstone National Park and I wish I were dead.'

That's perhaps a tad harsh, but traveling in the off-season certainly offers many rewards: you don't have to contend with crowded roads, shops or visitor centers, and places to stay offer more affordable rates. The downside is that tours and guided activities have limited schedules, restaurants are sometimes shut for the season, and campgrounds become unreliable. The best off-season time is just after Labor Day, from the middle of September through October, as the weather usually stays warm and services aren't yet totally shut down. The campgrounds are also quieter, as most kids have gone back to school.

If you have to travel in July and August, don't panic – it's still surprisingly easy to avoid the worst of the mayhem. You'll lose 90% of the tourists simply by walking a mile from the road. Follow the example of the park animals and get up early, rest at lunchtime and stay out late. Be at the trailhead at 8am for the best light, the fewest tourists and the most parking spaces. Get active during the hour just before sunset; the land basks in gorgeous light, the tourists are rushing back to set up their campsites and the wildlife is back out again.

To avoid the worst of the cafeteria lines, get used to eating meals outside of set times. Have lunch at 2pm and you are guaranteed a seat. Bear in mind that roads are generally busiest between 11am and 3pm.

Finally, if it gets too much, head out of the park. While the Gallatin National Forest may not have the same sexy ring as Yellowstone National Park, the hikes are just as superb and the mountains just as breathtaking – and you'll probably have the trail to yourself.

September is a particularly good month to visit. Elks bugle during the fall rut, and the aspens and cottonwoods turn golden, especially in Grand Teton, which boasts the most impressive fall colors. Nights can be cold if you are camping, but you should be able to negotiate off-season discounts at many hotels. Hiking and fishing are excellent. On the downside, ranger programs start to peter out after Labor Day, campsites start to close some of their services in September and the days begin getting shorter.

Winter

The park's winter season runs from late December to March, with daytime temperatures ranging from 0°F to 20°F. Night-time temperatures often drop below zero. Mammoth is the warmest corner of the park, with daytime temperatures averaging between 25°F and 45°F. The park's average winter snowfall is 150in, with 200in to 400in at higher elevations.

Park Opening Dates
YELLOWSTONE

Yellowstone's opening schedule is fiendishly complicated. The north entrance at Gardiner is open year-round, as is the north road from Gardiner to Cooke City via Mammoth and Tower-Roosevelt Junction.

The first of the other roads to open, in mid- to late-April, are the West Entrance Rd and the western sections of the Grand Loop Rd: Mammoth Hot Springs to Norris, Norris to Madison, and Madison to Old Faithful.

The south and east entrance approach roads, and the Grand Loop Rd over Craig Pass (8262ft) between West Thumb Junction and Old Faithful, typically open in early May.

The Grand Loop Rd between Tower and Canyon Junctions over Dunraven Pass (8859ft) is the last to open, usually by Memorial Day. It is also the first to close. Once open, entrances stay open 24 hours.

All park roads close on the first Monday in November, except for the Gardiner–Cooke City road. The Beartooth Hwy (Hwy 212) between Red Lodge and Cooke City is blocked by snow from mid-October to around Memorial Day.

Entrances open to snow vehicles (snowmobiles) from the third Wednesday in December through to mid-March, when spring plowing starts. Roads out of Norris are the first to close. All roads are closed again by the second Monday in March, except for the Gardiner–Cooke City road, which is open all winter.

GRAND TETON

Grand Teton National Park is open year-round, though some roads and most services close in winter.

In winter you can drive along US 26/89/191 to Flagg Ranch but no further. Teton Park Rd is closed to motorized vehicles from Taggart Lake Trailhead to Signal Mountain from November 1 to May 1, as is the unpaved portion of the Moose-Wilson road inside the park. Grassy Lake Rd is closed by snow from mid-November to late May.

RESERVATIONS

Almost all accommodations, except for National Park Service (NPS) campsites, can be reserved. It's possible to reserve around half of Yellowstone park's campsites with Xanterra (p161) and some Forestry Service campsites around the parks (see p260).

If you're planning to take one of the most popular backpacking routes, consider booking your backcountry sites by April for Yellowstone (see

Over three million people visit Yellowstone in summer; just 140,000 arrive in winter.

PLANNING YOUR TRIP

p96) and from January 1 in Grand Teton (see p213). Yes, you even need reservations in the wilderness! Even park activities like horseback riding and cookouts should be reserved a couple days in advance. Remember the golden rule: the more specific a plan you have, the earlier you need to book. The more interesting and upscale accommodation options (such as the cabins at Jackson Lake Lodge; p237) start taking bookings in November for the following year. Xanterra accommodations start booking a year in advance.

COSTS & MONEY

The cost of your Yellowstone vacation will be largely decided by whether you spend your nights round the campground fire or at the lobby bar. Campsites inside the parks range from $12 to $17, and you can prepare your own food for a song, especially if you stock up on supplies outside the park. Once you've paid your park entry fee, all sights inside the park are free, as are most ranger programs. There's no charge to hike or for backcountry permits. Outside the parks, many national forests even offer free dispersed camping. RV sites cost around $35 with hookups.

Costs rise faster than the Tetons as soon as you check into the park's hotels. The cheapest cabins in Yellowstone start at around $55, and most hotel rooms start at $100. You can shave a bit off this by staying outside the parks in the gateway towns, but even here you're going to have to shell out $70 for even a budget motel room in summer. Restaurants aren't a bad value in the park, and you can eat fairly well from $10 per head per meal. Gas in the park is 20% pricier than elsewhere in Wyoming and Montana.

Activities can also mount up – a Wild West cookout for a family of four will set you back more than $200 for two hours of fun. On the bright side, you can hike for days for little more than the cost of a few granola bars.

FESTIVALS & EVENTS

The National Park Service rarely lets its hair down, but there are some excellent events in the surrounding communities that are well worth attending.

One oddity is Yellowstone's **Christmas in August** (August 25), which dates back to the turn of the last century, when a freak August snowstorm stranded a group of visitors in the Upper Geyser Basin. Old Faithful Inn is decked out with Christmas decorations and carol singers. It's surreal.

In Yellowstone's gateway communities, rodeo is the major cultural event of the year. Cody's nightly summer rodeo (June to August) is well worth attending. The **Cody Stampede** is the region's biggest July 4 weekend rodeo, but there are also smaller rodeos at this time in Livingston and Red Lodge. More rodeos pull into Gardiner in mid-June and West Yellowstone in mid-August (http://yellowstonerodeo.com).

Yellowstone's history of 'mountain man rendezvous' resulted from trade and social interactions between trappers, settlers and Native Americans in the mid-19th century. Reenactments are held in late July at Red Lodge's **Mountain Man Rendezvous** and West Yellowstone's **Burnt Hole Rendezvous** in August. The latter is a reenactment of the 1859 gathering and includes tomahawk-throwing competitions, black-powder marksmanship contests and lots of teepees.

The region's Native American culture is celebrated in the **Annual Plains Indian Powwow**, held in mid-June at Cody's Buffalo Bill Historic Center (p188); July's **Native American Festival Show & Dance** in Teton Village; and the **Crow Fair** (www.crow-fair.com) in the Crow Agency, west of Billings, on the third weekend in August, which features Native American dances, rodeo and snacks.

Music lovers can choose between Cody's **Yellowstone Jazz Festival** or the excellent **Grand Teton Music Festival** (www.gtmf.org) in Teton Village, both in July, or the regionally famed **Targhee Bluegrass Festival**, held in August at Grand Targhee Ski Resort in Idaho's Teton Valley.

Entrance Fees & Passes

The entry fee for Yellowstone (currently $25 but expected to rise) also covers Grand Teton and is valid for seven days, so keep your receipt for re-entry. An annual pass for both parks costs $50.

Several flavors of annual passes grant unlimited access to national parks. The passes admit a private vehicle and its passengers, or the pass holder, spouse and children, at parks where per-person fees are imposed. You'll need a photo ID to purchase and use the pass.

The 'America the Beautiful – National Parks and Federal Recreational Lands Pass' is a clumsily named Interagency Pass (IAP; $80) that gives access to any fee-paying site administered by the NPS, US Forest Service (USFS), US Fish & Wildlife Service (USFWS) or Bureau of Land Management (BLM).

A lifetime seniors' pass covering the same areas costs a one-off fee of $10 and allows US residents 62 years and older (and accompanying passengers in a private vehicle) unlimited entry to all sites, with a further 50% discount on camping and other fees.

The free access pass offers the same benefits to US residents who are blind or permanently disabled (proof is required). If you have an old Golden Age or Golden Access pass, there's no need to replace it with the new pass.

You can buy the passes at all park entrances or purchase one online at http://store.usgs.gov/pass. For more information see www.nps.gov/fees_passes.htm.

BOOKS

The following books are our pick of the general books on Yellowstone, and most are available in park bookstores or the **Yellowstone Association** (www.yellowstoneassociation.org). For specific titles on Yellowstone's environment, history, activities and wildlife, see those chapters in this book.

Lost in My Own Backyard, by Tim Cahill, is the one to bring if you only have space for one book. It's a warm homage to the park by a long-time resident of the Yellowstone region, and as with all of Cahill's writings, it's extremely engaging. Chapters lead you along the Mt Washburn and Fossil Forest hikes, through the Thorofare and Bechler regions and up into Monument Geyser Basin.

For travel with an environmental slant, *Walking Down the Wild: A Journey Through the Yellowstone Rockies,* by Red Lodge resident Gary Ferguson, is one naturalist's account of his 500-mile trek through the Greater Yellowstone region. Ferguson is also the author of *Hawk's Rest: A Season in the Remote Heart of Yellowstone,* an account of his three-month stay in the Thorofare, Yellowstone's remotest corner. Ferguson's main ire focuses on the outfitters who he believes treat the region like a private fiefdom. Hawk's Rest is the name of the cabin he lived in.

Teewinot, by mountain guide Jack Turner, is a climber's ode to the Tetons. Peppered with Zen philosophy, it describes a year in the life of the mountains. An ardent conservationist, Turner describes the park as the 'most compromised…in the national park system.' It will get you as close to the Teton peaks and their changing seasons as you are likely to get.

Death in Yellowstone, by Lee Whittlesey, the park's archivist, is a morbidly fascinating chronicle of 'accidents and foolhardiness' in the park over the last century or more. The more than 300 post mortems range from the horrifying (boiled alive in a hot spring, disemboweled by a grizzly) to the ridiculous (backing a car accidentally over the edge of the Yellowstone canyon, death from wild parsnips).

PLANNING YOUR TRIP

HOW MUCH?

Hotel room in the park $60-180

Park campsite $14-18

Lunch in the park $8

Dinner in the park $25

Yellowstone & Grand Teton entry fee $25

See also Lonely Planet Index, inside back cover.

Jellystone's Yogi Bear, Ranger Smith and Boo-Boo were all inspired by Yellowstone National Park, with a little help from baseball star Yogi Berra.

A River Runs Through It, by Norman Maclean, is the story of two brothers who share a love of fly fishing. It's required reading for armchair anglers. The movie of the same name starring Robert Redford and Brad Pitt was filmed largely in the Gallatin Valley south of Bozeman.

Yellowstone Trivia, by Janet Spencer and Vince Moravek, is just perfect for driving your family mad with endless fascinating little factoids – did you know Gary Cooper worked as a park guide for four summers? Did you know that the Trout Jacuzzi is an underwater geyser off the coast of West Thumb? You know you want it.

Another one good for boring people silly is *Yellowstone Place Names,* by Lee Whittlesey, which details the stories, both mildly interesting and extremely dull, behind every place name in the region. Perfect for the obsessive-compulsive in your life.

Ring of Fire: Writers of the Yellowstone Region, edited by Bill Hoagland, is an anthology of Greater Yellowstone writings, with selections from Tim Cahill, Gary Ferguson, Paul Schuller and others. For a sampler of Wyoming life dip into Annie Proulx's *Close Range: Wyoming Stories,* which includes the short story *Brokeback Mountain.*

Letters from Yellowstone, by Diane Smith, is a first novel that pieces together in letter form a fictional 1898 botanical expedition into Yellowstone Park, from the perspective of the team's sole female member. It's the perfect summer park read.

MAPS

The NPS hands out good park maps at entrance stations, but these are only for general orientation. A good topographic map is essential for any hiking trip. Both National Geographic's Trails Illustrated and Earthwalk Press offer waterproof maps of Yellowstone and Grand Teton, with 80ft contour intervals. Both maps indicate areas burned in the 1988 fires, but Earthwalk Press' map divides these into canopy and mixed burns.

Trails Illustrated's *Yellowstone National Park* has a scale of 1:168,500 and is good for general navigation and trail-choosing. Four separate smaller scale maps (1:63,360) cover Mammoth Hot Springs, Old Faithful, the Tower/Canyon area and Yellowstone Lake, and are good for anyone attempting a longer hike or an overnighter. They also produce a 1:78,000 *Grand Teton National Park* map, with a 1:24,000 inset of the Grand Teton climbing area.

Earthwalk produces a 1:106,250 *Hiking Map & Guide: Yellowstone National Park* and a 1:72,500 *Hiking Map & Guide: Grand Teton National Park,* with 1:48,000 blow-ups of the popular central regions.

FIVE FILMS TO GET YOU IN THE MOOD

- *A River Runs Through It* (1992) – Directed by Robert Redford and starring Brad Pitt and Craig Scheffer. Filmed partly in the Gallatin and Paradise Valleys and Livingston.

- *The Horse Whisperer* (1998) – Directed by Robert Redford and starring Robert Redford and Kristin Scott Thomas. Filmed partly in Livingston.

- *Shane* (1953) – Directed by George Steven. Classic western starring Alan Ladd. Shot in the Tetons.

- *Yellowstone* – Imax big screen movie that shows daily at the Imax theatre at West Yellowstone and is available on DVD.

- *Silence and Solitude* (2003) – Follow photographer Tom Murphy (p148) into the Yellowstone backcountry in the depths of winter in this Emmy-nominated Montana PBS documentary.

For a different perspective, the *Yellowstone National Park Panoramic Hiking Map* is a hand-drawn picture map showing the major geographical features and hiking trails. It's of little use as an actual trail guide, but it's a great visual aid to planning a hike.

Getting to backcountry trailheads outside the parks can be a trying tangle of switchback roads and unmarked USFS roads. If you are going to be hiking outside the park, get a topographic map or a USGS map of the area.

For tips on using maps to navigate while on hikes, see p288.

USGS MAPS

The United States Geological Survey (USGS) publishes detailed 1:24,000 topographic maps, known as 'quads,' covering the entire Greater Yellowstone region. Due to their large scale, quads reproduce topographic detail quite accurately, but having to use numerous maps – especially for longer hiking routes – is cumbersome and expensive. Also, many quads have not been revised for decades, so infrastructure such as trails, roads or buildings may be shown incorrectly.

To order a USGS map index and price list, phone ☎ 888-ASK-USGS (888-275-8747) or visit the USGS website at http://mapping.usgs.gov. Forestry Service ranger district offices, park visitor centers and outdoor stores in regional towns usually sell hiking maps and some USGS quads.

Digital Resources

CD-ROMs containing hundreds of digitized USGS 1:24,000 quads and 1:100,000 topographic maps that cover entire states are widely available from around $50. Trails Illustrated's *National Parks of the USA* ($20) focuses on 15 parks, including Yellowstone, Grand Teton and Glacier, and will work out elevation profiles for chosen trails and print custom topo maps. It's also GPS compatible.

Companies like **iGage** (www.igage.com) and **Maptech** (www.maptech.com) sell software that allows hikers using a GPS receiver to plot their exact route on their computers.

For something even snazzier the **Virtual Tour Guide** (☎ 877-SELF TOUR; www.virtualtourguide.net; 116 Grizzly Ave, West Yellowstone) is a rentable GPS unit with a touch screen that gives you directions to points of interest and offers tips to spot wildlife. You can rent it at any of Yellowstone's gateway towns and drop it off at another, but it's not cheap at around $50/90 for one/two days.

Several webcams offer interesting peeks into the park. Watch Old Faithful erupt online at www.nps.gov/yell/oldfaithfulcam.htm (refreshed every 30 seconds) and check out the amazing 360-degree panoramas at www.virtualguidebooks.com/Wyoming/Wyoming.html.

INTERNET RESOURCES

Online you can research specific hikes, find average temperatures, book hotel rooms, make campground reservations, buy wilderness maps, take online tours, watch Old Faithful erupt on a web cam and download park podcasts. Hell, you almost don't need to go to the park!

This section offers a roundup of the top sites for the Greater Yellowstone area. For other specific websites, see the relevant sections of this guide. Some of the best sites belong to the state tourist offices (p266) and the neighboring national forests (p267).

Lonely Planet's own **website** (www.lonelyplanet.com) is also a great resource; it's home to the Thorn Tree bulletin board, where you can ask fellow travelers for their tips and share your own when you get back.

PLANNING YOUR TRIP

Yellowstone is 80% forest, 15% grassland and 5% water. Around 96% of the park territory is in Wyoming, 3% is in Montana and 1% in Idaho.

YELLOWSTONE IN YOUR IPOD (& OTHER NEAT GADGETS)

You can use a combination of MP3 players and your car stereo to liven up the drive to the parks. If nothing else, it solves the festering debate over whose music to listen to!

You can get the free NPS podcasts *Yellowstone in Depth* or *Inside Yellowstone* from the Photos & Multimedia section of the park **website** (www.nps.gov/yell). The private website www.yellowstonepark .com also offers a couple of free podcasts. You can also get these through iTunes, as well as podcasts from the Greater Yellowstone Coalition.

Another option is an audio book. Tim Cahill's *Lost in My Own Backyard* (see p27) is available on audio CD or MP3, read by the author, or try the audio version of *Lost in Yellowstone: Truman Everts' 37 Days of Peril* (see p102).

The company **Tourcaster** (www.tourcaster.com) sells hour-long downloadable audio tours of both Yellowstone and Grand Teton parks for $12, or try the AutoTour CD by Fireside Productions.

Use your cell phone to listen to a historical guide (p219) to Menor's Ferry at Grand Teton or download the audio files to your MP3 player.

AllYellowstonePark.com (www.yellowstoneparknet.com) This detail-rich site has a snappy grid organization and covers both the park and surrounding communities, though many of the 'hot sites' feel like paid advertising. See also www.westyellowstonenet.com and www.jacksonholenet.com.

Grand Teton Lodge Company (www.gtlc.com) Information on campsites, dining and activities in Grand Teton National Park from the main park concessionaire.

Grand Teton National Park (www.nps.gov/grte) The official site offers similar information and resources to its big brother.

Great Outdoor Recreation Pages (GORP; www.gorp.com) Excellent general resource on outdoor activities, both in the parks and beyond.

Greater Yellowstone Coalition (www.greateryellowstone.org) Podcasts, environmental news and information on such touchy subjects as winter use, wolves and the delisting of grizzlies.

The Total Yellowstone Page (www.yellowstone-natl-park.com) Every so often a personal website morphs into a reputable source for public information. Such is the case with Yellowstone fan John Uhler's site, which offers extensive information on park lodging and activities. He also offers www.grand.teton.national-park.com.

Windows into Wonderland (www.windowsintowonderland.org) Fun and educational electronic field trips for kids, young and old.

www.yellowstonepark.com Wyoming-based publisher that features monthly news, decent links, itinerary builders and lots of interactive polls and trivia. It also publishes the *Yellowstone Journal* magazine.

Wyoming Tourism (http://wyomingtourism.org/yellowstone) Section of the state tourism website that focuses on Yellowstone, with inspirational slideshows and video.

Xanterra Parks & Resorts (www.travelyellowstone.com) The online home for Yellowstone's concession services group, which oversees all lodging, restaurants, stores, tours, activities and transportation within Yellowstone. Details, prices, opening hours and online reservations.

Yellowstone National Park (www.nps.gov/yell) The labyrinthine official park website should be your first port of call for everything from bear updates to backcountry permit requirements. There are downloadable brochures and podcasts, plus trip planners, online tours, videos, park panoramas and a helpful list of outfitters within the park. Best of all, you can download current issues of the park newspaper for a rundown of daily programs and opening schedules.

Yellowstone National Park.com (www.yellowstonenationalpark.com) This attractive and easy-to-navigate site is an amalgam of sorts, featuring photography, plenty of geyser info, and good camping and hiking information (with trail descriptions).

Yellowstone Net (www.yellowstone.net) Extensive site that will quickly inspire, with videos, online tours, games and lots of information. The forum is a great place to get insider tips on the park.

Yellowstone Net Newspaper (www.yellowstone.net/newspaper) Browsing the Yellowstone Net News is a good way to survey the scene from a safe distance. Catch up on news with links from regional papers.

Itineraries

YELLOWSTONE IN A DAY – THE NORTHERN LOOP   One Day

- Head straight to the **Lamar Valley** (p105) around dawn to spot wolves, coyotes or bison.
- Grab a Hiker's Breakfast at Roosevelt Lodge then walk the **Yellowstone Picnic Area Hike** (p128) for crowdless views into The Narrows.
- Cross **Dunraven Pass** (p106), keeping an eye out for wildlife at Antelope Creek or Washburn Hot Springs Overlook.
- Take three to four hours to hike up **Mt Washburn** (p138) for the park's best views.
- Picnic amid the pines at shady **Cascade Lake Trail** (p139) picnic area, followed by a short stroll along the nearby trail.
- Gawp at the **Grand Canyon of the Yellowstone** (p110) from Uncle Tom's Trail, before taking in more views from Artist Point.
- Drive across the Solfatara Plateau to the superheated **Norris Geyser Basin** (p117).
- Stroll the boardwalks to surreal Palette Springs and Canary Springs at **Mammoth Hot Springs** (p101).

This route through the north of the park takes in some premier wildlife-watching, views of the Grand Canyon and an assortment of geysers and hot springs. You can join this loop anywhere.

ITINERARIES

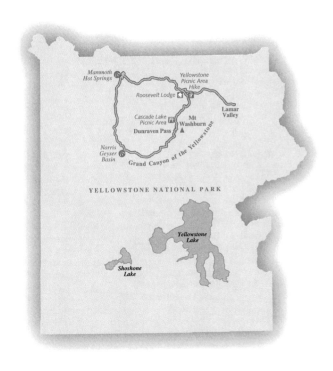

YELLOWSTONE IN A DAY – THE SOUTHERN LOOP   One Day

The southern loop takes in epic Yellowstone Lake, the park's greatest geysers (including Old Faithful) and a swim in the Firehole River. As in the previous itinerary, you can join this loop anywhere.

- Wake up early by **Yellowstone Lake** (p112) and join the birdlife for a lakeshore stroll at dawn.
- Drive west from West Thumb up over the **Continental Divide** (p127) before descending into Geyser Country.
- Stake out Upper Geyser Basin to catch **Old Faithful** (p121) and, if you're lucky, a biggie like Riverside or Daisy.
- Head north to Midway Geyser Basin and admire our favorite thermal feature, **Grand Prismatic Spring** (p124).
- Splash about with the kids in the thermally heated **Firehole Swimming Area** (p126).
- Photograph the tumbling Gibbon Falls and continue north to the **Porcelain Basin** (p117) hot springs.
- Savor views of the **Grand Canyon of the Yellowstone** (p110) from Uncle Tom's Trail and Artist Point.
- Swing south to the **Hayden Valley** (p111) for some sunset wildlife-watching before returning to Yellowstone Lake.

TETON IN A DAY

One Day

- Start at **Dornan's Chuckwagon** (p239) with a hot stack of flapjacks at wooden picnic tables.
- Explore the historic **Menor's Ferry** (p219) with a cell-phone tour.
- Hike the ragged hills to glacial moraines cupping **Taggart and Bradley Lakes** (p224).
- Photograph the Teton's toothy Cathedral group at the scenic **Schwabacher's Landing** (p220).
- Spread your blanket at the edge of the pines and picnic by the **Log Chapel of the Sacred Heart** (p217).
- Check out the incredible Native American beadwork at the **Indian Arts Museum** (p214).
- Enjoy a huckleberry margarita with stunning panoramic views at the Blue Heron, part of **Jackson Lake Lodge** (p238).
- Train your binoculars on **Willow Flats** (p216) to find moose munching in the dusky light.

Starting at Moose Junction, cruise the valley north for a sense of place but find a trail for a sense of splendor. Less is more. For a more in-depth experience, take in a few of the above attractions.

ITINERARIES

Indian Arts Museum
Jackson Lake Lodge
Willow Flats Turnout
Jackson Lake
Log Chapel of the Sacred Heart
GRAND TETON NATIONAL PARK
Schwabacher's Landing
Taggart Lake Trailhead
Menor's Ferry
Dornan's Chuckwagon

BILLINGS TO LIVINGSTON, THE LONG WAY

Four Days

The road to scenic beauty is rarely a direct one, so take this looping 'U' for the park's most impressive approach roads, the park's northern highlights and a drive through paradise.

- Make the short but steep hike up to **Glacier Lake** (p182), a turquoise lake set in a high, peak-fringed bowl.
- Reward yourself with the region's best chocolate malt at the **Red Box Car** (p183) in historic Red Lodge.
- Drive America's most scenic 70 miles, the **Beartooth Hwy** (p183).
- Hike and overnight at **Beauty Lake** (p186), high in the heart of the lake-strewn Beartooth plateau.
- Enter the park at the northeast entrance and hunt for petrified trees on **Fossil Forest Trail** (p137).
- Head south to Canyon and take the short afternoon walk to **Ribbon Lake** (p140) and overnight in Canyon Village.
- Visit the canyon in the morning, then head west to overnight at quiet **Indian Creek Campground** (p162).
- Stroll the travertine terraces at **Mammoth** (p99) and take a guided walk through historical Fort Yellowstone.
- Head north out of the park through the Paradise Valley, looking for bighorns by the **Devil's Slide** (p206).
- Soak in the hot springs and savor the gourmet dinner at **Chico Hot Springs** (p205).
- Drink with the ghost of Calamity Jane at the **Livingston Bar & Grille** (p204).

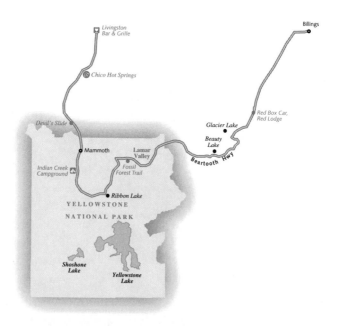

YELLOWSTONE & GRAND TETON   One Week

- Take a morning to climb **Bunsen Peak** (p134) for fantastic views over Mammoth, the hoodoos and Gardner's Hole.
- Stop at **Willow Park** (p103) for a picnic and some relaxing moose-spotting.
- Drive south to Madison Junction to fly-fish the **Madison River** (p126) and spot elk and bison in the surrounding meadows.
- Hike from bikeable **Fountain Freight Rd** (p156) to either Fairy Falls or Sentinel Meadows for backcountry geysers and bison.
- Overnight at historic **Old Faithful Inn** (p124) and catch the Upper Geyser Basin in the moonlight.
- Pause at **Isa Lake** (p127) to watch the waters drain off both sides of the Continental Divide.
- Drive south into Grand Teton and search for Canada geese, trumpeter swans and herons at **Oxbow Bend** (p220).
- Linger on **Jenny Lake Drive** (p217), stopping for awesome views of the Cathedral Group of the Central Tetons.
- Stroll the forested shoreline of **String and Leigh Lakes** (p222).
- Join the crowds for Grand Teton's most popular day hike: around Jenny Lake and up Cascade Canyon to **Lake Solitude** (p223).
- Cycle around **Mormon Row** (p229) for some classic shots of barns and bison before heading south to Jackson.

Add on the above attractions to the previous itineraries for a rewarding weeklong tour of the park's highlights.

ITINERARIES

YELLOWSTONE & GRAND TETON ADVENTURE   Two Weeks

With two weeks you can combine the earlier itinerary highlights with some multiday backcountry trips. Then budget at least a day to recover from it all!

- Gem up on the delights awaiting you with a Yellowstone Imax film or a visit to Grizzly & Wolf Discovery Center in the gateway town of **West Yellowstone** (p171).
- Overnight at **Madison** (p126), near the alleged birthplace of the national park system, and spot elk in the surrounding meadows.
- Hike or bike out to **Lone Star Geyser** (p132) to catch a backcountry eruption.
- Explore stunning **Shoshone Lake** p158) on a multiday backcountry trip, either on foot or by canoe.
- Trek out to **Heart Lake** (p150) for thermal features, a serene lake and views from atop Mt Sheridan.
- Take a break with a backcountry soak in the **Huckleberry Hot Springs** (p228) near Flagg Ranch.
- Head down to the Grand Tetons, rent a sea kayak from Signal Mountain Marina and embark on a multiday paddle around **Jackson Lake** (p232).
- Ogle the Tetons through the 60ft windows of the **Jackson Lake Lodge** (p216) before returning to the terrace for some moose spotting over a well-deserved Teton Ale.
- Take in symphony under the stars at the acclaimed annual **Grand Teton Music Festival** (p250).
- Soar over herds of elk at dawn while splurging on a **hot-air-balloon ride** (p244).
- Leave on a natural high by walking the classic **Teton Crest Trail** (p227).

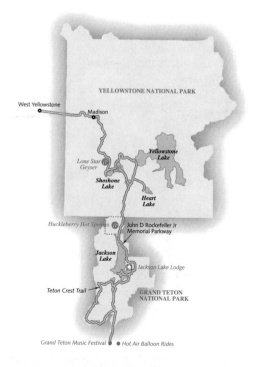

YELLOWSTONE NATIONAL PARK

West Yellowstone

Madison

Yellowstone Lake

Lone Star Geyser

Shoshone Lake

Heart Lake

Huckleberry Hot Springs

John D Rockefeller Jr Memorial Parkway

Jackson Lake

Jackson Lake Lodge

Teton Crest Trail

GRAND TETON NATIONAL PARK

Grand Teton Music Festival   Hot Air Balloon Rides

TETON & SOUTHERN YELLOWSTONE   One Week

- Roam the gut-turning and gravelly **Grassy Lake Road** (p220) with your fishing pole in tow.
- Embark on a backpacking odyssey, traversing remote terrain via the wild **Bechler River Trail** (p152).
- Slough off the mud and soak your cares away at **Ferris Fork backcountry hot springs** (p153).
- Catch a double feature at the **Spud Drive-In Theatre** (p255), an all-Americana experience.
- Stare the Grand Teton square in the face, after a long slog up **Table Mountain** (p253).
- Grab a burrito at Picas then get jiggy to live music at the **Stagecoach Bar** (p252).
- Shake off the trail dust with a sound night's sleep at the exclusive **Jenny Lake Lodge** (p237).
- Kayak the cobalt expanse of **Jackson Lake** (p232), exploring the quiet coves and beaches.
- Scan **Oxbow Bend** (p216) for signs of elk, moose and bald eagles in a prime wildlife habitat.
- Summit **Signal Mountain** (p217) by car for the stunning views that put it all into perspective.

Dare to leave it all behind. First tackle the remote Bechler Corner and the Teton's western slope. Loop back to the front side to end your sojourn in style.

ITINERARIES

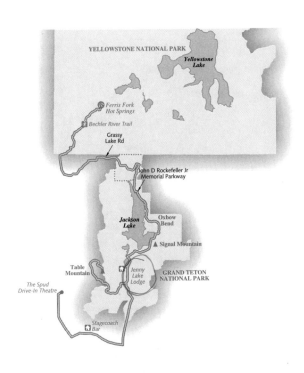

JACKSON HOLE & THE TETONS   **Four Days**

Location, location, location. With Jackson as your launch pad, you can explore the best the valley has to offer and be back in time for a little nightlife.

- Start with a breakfast of pan-fried trout at the classic **Nora's Fish Creek Inn** (p253).
- Saddle your road bike to ride the **Hole in One loop** (p229) – extra points for starting from Wilson.
- Opt for a Zonker Stout at the award-winning **Snake River Brewing Company** (p248).
- Hike up to **Inspiration Point** (p219) and return by ferry across Jenny Lake.
- Detour to **Moose Ponds** (p219) to snag a glimpse of its namesake ungulates.
- Rumble your pickup along the dirt roads and main corridors of the **Plains & Panoramas route** (p230).
- Splash, paddle and back-paddle on an adrenaline-soaked white-water raft trip down **Snake River Canyon** (p244).
- Join the locals powering up **Jackson Peak** (p243) for a quick adrenaline fix.
- Take in some local theater at the new **Center for the Arts** (p241).
- Try wine tasting on the deck sampling the lauded collection at **Dornan's Wine Shoppe** (p239) with killer views.
- Treat yourself to wild arugula with strawberries and a T-bone steak at **Old Yellowstone Garage** (p248).

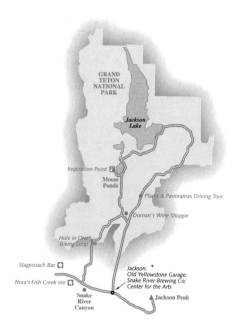

GRAND TETON NATIONAL PARK

Jackson Lake

Inspiration Point

Moose Ponds

Plains & Panoramas Driving Tour

Dornan's Wine Shoppe

Hole in One Biking Loop

Stagecoach Bar

Nora's Fish Creek Inn

Jackson:
Old Yellowstone Garage;
Snake River Brewing Co;
Center for the Arts

Snake River Canyon

Jackson Peak

Activities

Alive, sweeping and often stunning, this wilderness is a playground for the outdoor enthusiast. And play – not gawping from the car – is the way to discover what's on offer. Just feast your eyes, and your pulse will accelerate. Ranging from the Tetons' ragged spires to Yellowstone's vast meadows, this natural refuge is home to the highest concentration of thermal features in the world – plus marauding wolves, bison herds and cutthroat trout. Wildlife is prolific and often present when visitors undertake quieter sports like fishing, hiking and canoeing. Thrill-seekers can go white-water rafting, climb, paraglide or kayak.

In summer access to high-country destinations improves: roads open, snowfields melt and the sun shines. Increased wildlife activity means taking the usual precautions and staying a respectful distance away, but even during peak season, you can find some solitude on the trail.

A carefully planned shoulder-season visit can take advantage of fall and spring's cooler weather and good access without the trademark crowds of summer. Know before you go which roads are open, where the hunting grounds are (in fall) and what you will do if the weather turns nasty.

Yellowstone's most magical time might be winter, when just getting there requires a ride in a snowcoach or cross-country skiing. The main road through Grand Teton National Park closes and becomes a mecca for skiers and snowshoers. World-class ski resorts offer long and luxuriant powder runs as well as Nordic terrain and skating.

With no shortage of recreation on tap, enthusiasm is essential, but so are experience and know-how. If trying some of these activities for the first time, it pays to start slow and get a guide or instructor if necessary.

'There is no better way to escape the crowds and appreciate alpine vistas...than on the trails'

SUMMER ACTIVITIES

Every animal that burrowed and snoozed the long winter away snaps to life at the prospect of a Yellowstone summer, and we should be no exception. It's time to lace up your boots and rekindle your friendship with the wild. In spite of – or because of – inconveniences, it's well worth setting aside a few nights in the backcountry; camping equipment is readily available throughout the region (see p287). When your hiking boots get battered, saddle up, stargaze or try the region's water sports.

HIKING & BACKPACKING

There is no better way to escape the crowds and appreciate the alpine vistas – cascading waterfalls, charismatic wildlife and hyperactive thermal areas – than on the trail.

Yellowstone National Park offers 92 trailheads, leading to more than 900 miles of maintained trails and 300 designated backcountry campsites. According to the National Park Service (NPS), less than 1% of park visitors sleep out in the backcountry. Here, more than in most national parks, the backcountry is yours for the taking.

Be prepared for seasonal conditions. Fire outbreaks or bear activity can close trails without warning at any time. At the higher elevations, trails may be snow-covered until late July. August and September are the driest months, and May and June are the wettest. Ticks proliferate on low elevation trails between mid-March and mid-July, so wear

ACTIVITIES

TOP 10 ACTIVITIES IN GREATER YELLOWSTONE

Hiking – Stroll back in geologic time on the Fossil Forest Trail (p137) or scramble the heights of Avalanche Peak (p141).

Climbing – Scale the sheer granite of the Grand Teton (p231) for heart-thumping valley views.

Stargazing – Recline and find Orion on a moonless night (p165).

Nature walks – Trek with a ranger to score the inside scoop on wildlife (p112).

Canoeing – Paddle the placid waters of Jackson Lake (p244).

Fishing – Land the big one (p158) while wading in one of Yellowstone's famous rivers.

Wildlife-watching – Observe wolves on the prowl (p105) or bears at play (p111).

Horseback riding – Kick up trail dust on an equestrian tour (p157) of the backcountry.

Snowboarding – Carve a path through the powder at great resorts like Big Sky (p197) and Jackson Hole (p250).

Cross-country skiing – Glide through the alabaster landscape of winter (p159).

---

insect repellent and long pants. Mosquitoes are most intense in June and July, petering out by mid-August. September is an excellent month for hiking.

Peruse Grand Teton National Park's sublime alpine scenery via its 200 miles of hiking trails. Popular campsites like Bradley Lake, Surprise Lake, Upper Paintbrush, Holly Lake, Phelps Lake, Cascade Canyon, Marion Lake and Leigh Lake fill up fast, so plan in advance or keep your itinerary flexible; see p234 for more information. Higher elevations often remain snow-covered until late July, and high passes such as Paintbrush Divide and Hurricane Pass remain under snow as late as mid-August. Become familiar with using an ice tool; it may be necessary in early summer.

Tracing the watershed divide 3100 miles from New Mexico to Canada, the **Continental Divide Trail** (CDT; www.cdtrail.org) bisects beautiful sections of the Teton Wilderness and Yellowstone. This is a great option for hearty thru-hikers who want to extend their trip beyond the boundaries of the parks. The nonprofit organization's website has helpful maps, trip planning and volunteer opportunities. From the Idaho side, the CDT crosses the spine of the region, taking in Summit Lake, the Shoshone Geyser Basin, Heart Lake and the Thorofare, all in Yellowstone Park, and then Two Ocean Pass and North Buffalo Fork in the Teton Wilderness before continuing on to Brooks Lake on the Dubois–Grand Teton road. Useful guidebooks to the trail include *Wyoming's Continental Divide Trail: The Official Guide*.

Backcountry permits are required for overnight trips in Yellowstone and Grand Teton. These can be acquired at visitor centers and ranger stations; see p93 and p212. In Yellowstone, backcountry campers must watch a bear-safety video and review regulations with a ranger before obtaining a permit (waived if you can prove you've done a trip in the same year).

Also, don't neglect the hiking options, of various difficulty levels, listed in the Around Yellowstone and Around Grand Teton chapters.

Difficulty Level

There are hikes for every ability level in Greater Yellowstone. The duration for hikes listed in this guide refers to walking time only and doesn't include breaks. Our trail descriptions follow these guidelines:

Easy Manageable for nearly all walkers, an easy hike is under 4 miles, with fairly even, possibly paved terrain and no significant elevation gain or loss.

Moderate Fine for fit hikers and active, capable children, moderate hikes have a modest elevation gain.
Difficult For very fit and experienced hikers only. Trails might be strenuous, long and even indistinct in places. Expect significant elevation gain and scrambling may be necessary.

Easy Hikes

If you want a few hours in the fresh air or the opportunity for kids to trek without too many obstacles, easy hikes are a good bet. Those listed in the Yellowstone chapter (p128) are less than 4 miles and traverse fairly even terrain with almost no elevation gain or loss. Where possible, we have indicated which hikes are paved and wheelchair accessible.

Day Hikes

Almost every part of the Greater Yellowstone region offers outstanding hiking. Don't overlook the longer trails – you can fashion short day hikes by following the first couple miles of a longer trail.

Travelers with little hiking experience will appreciate the well-marked and well-maintained trails, often with rest room facilities at either end. Some less-frequented trails are not maintained. In some forested areas these trails may be marked by a series of blazed trees; in Yellowstone trees bear orange metal tags; on rocky moraines look for cairns.

The **Hole Hiking Experience** (☎ 866-733-4453; www.holehike.com) offers privately guided hikes and snowshoe trips in Jackson Hole and the Teton Valley. See p133 and p221 for more information on day hikes in Yellowstone and Grand Teton.

Backcountry Hikes

For the independent-minded, the wonders and solitude of the remote backcountry are well worth hauling in overnight gear. Both parks offer backpacking trips to meet the needs of every hiker's abilities. Overnight trips require backcountry permits, available from visitor centers or ranger stations; see p93 and p212.

If you're not used to hiking with a pack, start with one of the easier options. Backcountry campsites like those at Yellowstone's Ribbon Lake (p140) or Grand Teton's Leigh and Bearpaw Lakes (p222), are less than a two-hour hike from the trailhead.

The 150-mile Howard Eaton Trail, named for a famous Bighorn Mountain guide, is Yellowstone's longest trail. The remote southwest wilderness offers some interesting hiking and kayaking combinations.

Outside Yellowstone's eastern entrance, the wild and largely inaccessible Absaroka Range (part of the Shoshone National Forest) offers fine extended backcountry hikes into Yellowstone. The Thorofare Region, southeast of Yellowstone Lake, offers Yellowstone's most remote terrain, ideal for committed, self-sufficient backpackers. These remote wildernesses – also the habitat of grizzlies – are favored by horse packers, as the distances are large, the terrain rugged and the trails seldom used. Hunters frequent these areas in late September and early October, so wear orange clothes and expect sites to fill up.

ACTIVITIES

BEST BACKCOUNTRY BOOKS

A Climber's Guide to the Teton Range The bible of Teton Mountaineering.
Mountaineering, the Freedom of the Hills An ultimate primer for backcountry behavior.
Nols Cookery Camp cuisine beyond the ramen noodle.

HIKING IN YELLOWSTONE NATIONAL PARK

Name	Hike type	Region	Round-trip distance	Duration	Difficulty
Avalanche Peak	day	Lake Country	4 miles	3½-5hr	difficult
Beaver Ponds Trail	day	Mammoth Country	5 miles	2½hr	easy-moderate
Bechler Meadows & Falls	day	Bechler Region	8 miles	3½hr	easy-moderate
Bechler River Trail	backcountry	Bechler Region	28 miles	4 days	moderate
Black Canyon of the Yellowstone	backcountry	Mammoth Country	18.5 miles (one way)	1-2 days	moderate
Bunsen Peak (& Osprey Falls)	day	Mammoth Country	10.2 miles	6-7hr	moderate-difficult
Cache Lake	day	Mammoth Country	11.2 miles	6hr	easy-moderate
Cascade Lake & Observation Peak	day	Canyon Country	10.4 miles	4-5hr	moderate
DeLacy Creek Trail	easy	Geyser Country	6 miles	2½-3½hr	easy
Fairy Falls & Twin Buttes	easy	Geyser Country	6 miles	3-4hr	easy
Fossil Forest Trail	day	Roosevelt Country	3.5 miles	2½-3½hr	moderate-difficult
Heart Lake & Mt Sheridan	backcountry	Lake Country	16 miles	1-2 days	easy-moderate
Lone Star Geyser	easy	Geyser Country	4.8 miles	1½-2½hr	easy
Mt Washburn	day	Canyon Country	6.4 miles	4hr	moderate
Mt Washburn & Sevenmile Hole	backcountry	Canyon Country	15.6 miles	2 days	moderate-difficult
Mystic Falls & Biscuit Basin	easy	Geyser Country	3 miles	1½-2hr	easy
Pelican Valley	day	Lake Country	16 miles	6-8hr	easy-moderate
Ribbon Lake	day	Canyon Country	6.4 miles	3-4hr	easy
Sentinel Meadows & Queen's Laundry Geyser	easy	Geyser Country	3.2 miles	2½hr	easy
North Shoshone Lake & Shoshone Geyser Basin	backcountry	Geyser Country	20 miles	2 days	moderate
Yellowstone River Picnic Area Trail	easy	Roosevelt Country	4 miles	1½-2hr	easy

🐾 Wildlife Watching 🏙 View 👪 Great for Families 🌊 Waterfall ♨ Thermal Features 🎣 Fishing 🚲 Bicycles 🚻 Restrooms

Responsible Backcountry Use

These backcountry environments are fragile and cannot support careless activity, especially in the wake of heavy visitation. Be familiar with the **Leave No Trace** (www.lnt.org/programs/lnt7/index.html) ethic and practice it.

HIKING

To prevent further erosion, always stay on the trail and don't create shortcuts, especially when hiking up or down mountain switchbacks.

Elevation change	Features	Facilities	Description	Page
2100ft			Suddenly steep, this peak ascent offers unparalleled views of the Absaroka Range & Yellowstone Lake	141
350ft			Rolling hike from the facilities of Mammoth Junction through sagebrush to secluded ponds	133
negligible			A solitary walk through lush forest, with big falls & wildlife-watching opportunities	143
1100ft			A wild backcountry traverse filled with rivers, cascades, hot springs & prolific wildlife	152
1250ft descent			Classic early-season shuttle trek along the Yellowstone River	143
2100ft			Uphill climb to mountain-top views & then a steep descent into a canyon for up-close views of a little-visited waterfall	134
720ft			Three-quarter-day hike past moose habitat to a secluded mountain lake	135
1400ft			Wet hike through meadows & grazing bison, then up the side of a mountain for expansive views	139
200ft			Short hike through meadows to the shores of the park's largest backcountry lake	132
negligible			Flat stroll through lodgepole forest to a 197ft waterfall & a little-visited geyser	129
800ft			Steep unmaintained trail to several 50-million-year-old petrified trees & fine views	137
345/ 3145ft			Solitude at this backcountry lake near thermal features; challenge-seekers can climb Mt Sheridan (3145ft)	150
negligible			Bike or stroll along an old service road to a fine backcountry geyser that erupts every three hours	132
1400ft			The park's most popular trail, offering epic views of Yellowstone caldera, and a mountain-bike route option	138, 154
2800ft			Shuttle hike from mountain peak to canyon floor through the heart of grizzly country	149
700ft			Loop hike from a colorful geyser basin & hot springs to a pretty waterfall, with a more challenging return option	130
negligible			Bird-watchers favor this rolling stroll through meadows & sagebrush in the heart of bear country	140
negligible			Fine family hike or a first overnighter to moose habitat & views of Yellowstone Canyon	140
negligible			Loop hike past bison & hot springs to an historic backcountry geyser, with some off-trail sections	131
600ft			Part of the Continental Divide Trail to a remote geyser basin & stunningly silent backcountry lake	146
350ft			Crowdless views of the lower Yellowstone Canyon, a must for amateur geologists	128

Ranger Station   Backcountry Campsite   Picnic Sites   Wheelchair Accessible

Staying on the trail even when it's muddy will prevent damage to the surrounding terrain.

CAMPSITES

To preserve the environment, use old campsites instead of clearing new ones. Camp at least 200ft from the nearest lake, river or stream. If you have to share a common camping area with other hiking parties, pitch your tent a respectful distance from them and avoid intrusive noise.

HIKING IN GRAND TETON NATIONAL PARK

Name	Hike type	Region	Round-trip distance	Duration	Difficulty
Avalanche Canyon & Lake Taminah	day	Central Tetons	11 miles	6-7hr	difficult
Death Canyon	day	Central Tetons	8-10 miles	5hr	moderate
Garnet Canyon	day	Central Tetons	12 miles	9hr	difficult
Hermitage Point	day	Colter Bay Region	9.2 miles	4hr moderate	easy-
Lake Solitude	day	Central Tetons	14.4 miles	6-7hr difficult	moderate-
Leigh & Bearpaw Lakes	day	Central Tetons	7.4 miles	3½hr	easy- moderate
Paintbrush Divide	backcountry	Central Tetons	17.8 miles	2-3 days	moderate
Surprise & Amphitheater Lakes	day	Central Tetons	9.6 miles	5-6hr	difficult
Taggart & Bradley Lakes	day	Central Tetons	5.9 miles	3hr	easy- moderate
Two Ocean Lake & Grand View Point	day	Colter Bay Region	6.4 miles	3½hr	easy- moderate

Wildlife Watching | View | Great for Families | Restrooms | Backcountry Campsite | Boat Shuttle | Picnic Sites

CAMPFIRES

For many hikers, the campfire is almost synonymous with a wilderness experience; however, campfires can cause major environmental degradation in heavily used backcountry areas. They are now restricted in many parts of Yellowstone, Grand Teton and surrounding national forests. During a long dry spell, a local campfire ban may be imposed on public lands. All hikers should carry and use a lightweight stove.

MEET THE RANGERS

Emissaries of the parks, resource people, law enforcers and rescuers, these men and women sweating it out in the trademark taupe campaign hats and polyester duds do a diverse and often thankless job. In addition to patrolling, rangers give over 4000 programs yearly (mostly June to Labor Day). Don't be shy about taking advantage of the best they have to offer:

Ranger adventure hikes – experience Yellowstone backcountry on a challenging day hike (ranging from 3 miles to 7 miles and up to six hours in duration) with an experienced ranger. This fee **program** (adult/child $15/5) is ideal for solo travelers or those eager for an interpretive angle, with destinations from the wildlife-rich Hayden Valley to the challenging Avalanche Peak. Reserve in advance (see also p141).

Ranger programs – stargaze, learn to track or explore the workings of hot-water wilderness with an insider at these free, short outings (lasting about one hour). Campers shouldn't miss the nightly wheelchair-accessible Campfire Talks in the campgrounds. Programs last about an hour and, like the visitor center lectures, cover cool topics like entertaining creature-features or local Native American history.

Park newspapers *Yellowstone Today* and *Teewinot* (Grand Teton National Park) list all events and schedules.

Elevation change	Features	Facilities	Description	Page
2300ft			This challenging hike runs the gamut of good stuff: lake swims & killer views	225
1360ft			An ethereal river valley flanked by granite climbing walls	225
4800ft			This climbers' route hauls the heartiest hikers into a world of rock & ice	224
negligible			A wild & windswept point facing the multifanged Mt Moran	221
2240ft			Alpine scenery & altitude gain: this ultrapopular grind scales to a mountain lake via a gradual climb	223
negligible			A fun, flat family outing skirting forest-clad, crystal-clear swimming hole	222
3775ft			This pretty grind lifts you up into the alpine scenery above tree-level	226
3000ft			One of the park's oldest trails, the crowds love this classic leg-burner with valley views	223
560ft			Glacial lakes set in wildflower meadows & thick pine forest	224
400ft			A fresh alternative with lush forest, wildflowers & good bird-watching	221

If there already is a fire ring, use only dead and downed wood. Keep the fire at least 9ft away from flammable material (including grass and wood), watch it at all times, and douse it thoroughly with water or dirt before going to sleep or leaving the site – always be sure it is fully out.

WATER & TOILETS
Water contaminated by careless or irresponsible hikers is a common cause of illness in the backcountry. Always use toilets established at trailheads, campgrounds or along trails, regardless of the stink factor. Where no toilet exists, bury human waste in a 6in-deep 'cat hole' at least 300ft from the nearest lake or watercourse. Pack out toilet paper in a sealed plastic bag.

Avoid using soaps and detergents – sand or a kitchen scouring pad clean pots remarkably well. In high-altitude lakes even biodegradable soap may not degrade. Tip dishwater far from streams and remove residue food from dishes and discarded water with a small basin or strainer. Put these residuals in the trash – discarding it on the ground or leaving your dishes dirty might attract bears.

ACCESS
Some hikes outside the national parks are accessed via private property, which may extend well beyond the trailhead. Roads or trails through freehold land are not automatically a right of way, and the goodwill of local landholders depends on the continuing cooperation of all visitors. Please do not camp (or collect firewood) on private land without permission, and leave stock gates as you find them.

Top Trails Yellowstone & Grand Teton National Parks by Andrew Dean Nystrom (Wilderness Press) and *A Rangers Guide to Yellowstone Day Hikes* by Roger Anderson and Carol Shively Anderson will help you choose between the region's many hiking options.

ACTIVITIES

TETON RESCUE RANGER

Meet Drew Hardesty, avalanche expert, accomplished climber and Jenny Lake Rescue Ranger.

What's the job like? Primarily we're there to be ranging – really a lost art since money has been siphoned away from the national parks. On the clock, three to four days a week, we are climbing or doing a long traverse through the range. It keeps us in shape and out there where the public is for safety.

Any bear stories? At Mary Lake some people left their backpacks for just five minutes and a bear came and got the food. It's so silly. It's not a bear problem: it's a human problem.

Do climbers often get in over their heads? A really strong climber in the gym must deal with altitude, weather and a pack in the alpine environment. We try to get people to tone down the routes they choose.

How are the Tetons different from other parks? As the birthplace for American mountaineering; they bring people from all over the country and the world – people with a really similar stoke on the outdoors and life. There's a sense of freedom and good community that's hard to find these days. Plus, the BlackBerry doesn't get any reception.

Safety

Hikers and campers must reckon with the elements and their own frame of mind. Be prepared for Yellowstone's unpredictable weather – you may go to bed under a clear sky and wake up under two feet of snow, even in mid-August. Afternoon weather is particularly volatile in the Tetons, so get an early start. Check the latest weather forecast before setting off, and keep watch on the weather.

Before attempting to scale anything, read A Climber's Guide to the Teton Range, the bible of Teton mountaineering.

The most cautious safety measures suggest never hiking alone. Regardless, always let someone know where you are going and how long you plan to be gone. Use sign-in boards at trailheads or ranger stations. Travelers who are looking for hiking companions can inquire or post notices at ranger stations, outdoor equipment stores, campgrounds and hostels. Don't rely on your cell phone for emergency contact, as coverage may be spotty.

Those with little hiking or backpacking experience should not attempt to do too much too soon. Know your limitations, know the route you plan to take, and pace yourself accordingly.

For information about animal encounters and other issues, consult the Health & Safety chapter (p276).

ROCK CLIMBING & MOUNTAINEERING

American mountaineering was born in the Tetons when Paul Petzoldt built the country's first guiding school here in 1929. These huge granite faces continue to be among America's premier climbing destinations. Excellent short routes abound, as well as the classic longer summits like Grand Teton (p231), Mt Moran and Mt Owen, along famous routes like the Upper Exum Ridge and Owen-Spalding route. The best season for climbing is mid-July through August.

The ultimate primer for backcountry behavior is Mountaineering, the Freedom of the Hills by Steven M Cox and Kris Fulsaas.

If you're a novice you will definitely want quality instruction and guidance. **Exum Mountain Guides** (☎ 307-733-2297; www.exumguides.com) at Jenny Lake or **Jackson Hole Mountain Guides** (☎ 307-733-4979, 800-239-7642; www.jhmg .com) in Jackson are well-established and reputable guide services also offering instruction. Both offer one-day mountaineering courses ($150) for beginners and intermediates. A course or previous experience is necessary to attempt Grand Teton on a guided climb (two-day Owen Route $515 to $645 per person). The most popular climbs are day-long climbs of South (12,514ft) and Middle Teton (12,804ft), and two-day ascents of Grand Teton (13,770ft).

The best ice climbing in the region is found at the South Fork of the Shoshone River, 40 miles southwest of Cody. The season runs from November to April, with the coldest weather providing the best conditions. For details contact the climbers' nerve center east of Yellowstone, **Bison Willy's Bunkhouse** (☎ 307-587-0629; www.bisonwillys.com).

A prime resource for climbers in the Tetons during summer is the American Alpine Club's **Climbers' Ranch** (☎ 307-733-7271; www.americanalpineclub .org). In addition to serving as a hostel for climbers and hikers (p231), the organization's extensive library and knowledgeable staff prove excellent resources. Look for slideshows and educational events in summer and information about June's volunteer week. If you plan to rely heavily on the expertise of the Climbers' Ranch, membership is recommended.

ROAD & MOUNTAIN BIKING

Bicycling is recommended from late April to October, when the parks' roads, topping out at 8860ft, are probably free of snow. Cyclists will find campsites reserved for hikers and cyclists at almost all campgrounds in Yellowstone National Park.

Cyclists may ride on all public roads and a few designated service roads but are not allowed on any trails or backcountry areas. Most park roads are rough and narrow and do not have shoulders: expect careless drivers with one eye on the bison and another on the map. Snowbanks cover many roadsides through June, making cycling more challenging.

The *Bicycling in Yellowstone National Park* brochure has a map with suggested routes, and some information is available on the park website. For recommended rides in Yellowstone and Grand Teton National Park, see p153 and p228. Bicycle repairs and parts are not available inside the park; it's typically 20 to 30 miles between services. Xanterra rents bikes at Old Faithful. In spring, Yellowstone National Park opens its roads exclusively to cyclists (see p284); it's a great time to pedal the park.

The annual fall **Cycle Tour** (www.cycleyellowstone.com; per person $45), organized by the Chamber of Commerce in West Yellowstone, offers a van-supported ride to destinations within the park that change yearly. **Teton Mountain Bike Tours** (☎ 307-733-0712; www.tetonmtbike.com) offers family-friendly guided mountain-bike tours of Grand Teton and Yellowstone. Half-day tours cost around $60 and include transportation, bike hire and helmet. **Wilderness Ventures** (☎ 307-733-2122; www.wildernessventures.com) leads multisport trips for teens.

Riding can be more diverse and less stressful outside the park, away from the RV parades. Bikes are restricted from entering designated wilderness areas, but may otherwise ride on national-forest trails. Trail etiquette requires that cyclists yield to other users. Helmets should always be worn to reduce the risk of head injury, but they are not mandated by law.

A bike path system totaling 41 miles is planned to parallel the Teton Park Rd in Grand Teton National Park. Check for updates at a park visitor center. Nine miles of paths are planned from the park's south boundary to Antelope Flats Rd, 15 miles of path between North Jenny Lake and Colter Bay, 10 miles along Teton Park Rd from Moose Junction to North Jenny Lake Junction, and 3 miles along the Moose–Wilson Rd from Granite Canyon entrance station to the Rockefeller Preserve.

The ski areas of Big Sky (p197) and Grand Targhee (p255) offer lift-serviced trails, while Snow King Resort's (p247) trails may only be accessed with private outfitter **Hoback Sports** (☎ 307-733-5335; 520 W Broadway Ave;

'Riding can be more diverse and less stressful outside the park, away from the RV parades'

ACTIVITIES

(🕑 9am-7pm) in Jackson. West Yellowstone offers an excellent network of trails both inside and outside Yellowstone National Park, including the Rendezvous Ski Trails (p173). There is also good single track in the Absaroka and Gallatin Ranges, accessible from Paradise Valley (p207). Bozeman is Montana's mountain-biking hub, largely due to its young and fearless population. Jackson is the major hub for rides around Jackson Hole.

HORSEBACK RIDING & PACK TRIPS

If you're eager to break in your Wranglers on a saddle, consider the wide range of options available, starting from two-hour rides to multiday cattle drives, and rustic operations where guests sweep the stables to ritzy guest ranches with hot tubs and umbrella drinks.

Horseback riding satisfies a primal romantic notion: you can mosey along through beautiful countryside, crossing rivers and ascending steep slopes that would have cost dearly on foot. Overnights have an added element of adventure; essentially you are backpacking but without carrying a load. After a day's work, horses are tethered, kept in a separate area and, if in national parks, fed pellet food (hay carries invasive species). Depending on your experience and comfort level, you may be allowed to help care for your animal.

For the casual rider, horseback riding is pricey, as visitors end up subsidizing the cost of feeding these hay burners through the winter. Rates for recreational horseback riding start at around $25 to $35 an hour, $60 to $70 for a half day and $75 to $130 for a full day. Guided trips usually require a minimum of two people. Backcountry pack trips cost upward of $200 per person per day and usually involve some related activity, such as fly-fishing. If you're an experienced rider, and want a peppier steed, let the guides know in advance.

In Yellowstone Park there are corrals at Mammoth, Roosevelt and Canyon Junction. Grand Teton has rides from Jackson Lake Lodge and Colter Bay (p232). Ranches in the Wapiti (p194) and Gallatin (p200) Valleys operate horseback rides for nonguests.

Check out the **Dude Ranchers' Association** (www.duderanch.org) for helpful information and links. The following state organizations provide information for licensed outfitters:

Idaho Outfitters & Guides Association (☎ 208-342-1919, 800-494-3246; www.ioga.org; 711 N 5th St, Box 95, Boise, ID 83701)

Montana Outfitters & Guides Association (☎ 406-449-3578; www.moga-montana.org; 2 North Last Chance Gulch, PO Box 1248, Helena, MT 59624)

Wyoming Outfitters & Guides Association (☎ 307-527-7453; www.wyoga.org; 1716 8th St, Cody)

Those people planning private horseback trips should arrange their stay through the backcountry office at park visitor centers and consult the parks' online planning information for pack trips.

RAFTING

Cold water, adrenaline and stunning scenery make rafting a prime summer draw. It's a great group activity; teens in particular will be ever grateful for trading in the minivan for a splashier ride. Commercial outfitters in Grand Teton and outside the parks offer options ranging from inexpensive half-day trips to overnight and multiday expeditions. More sedate float or tube trips are also available (see p233).

White-water trips through Paradise Valley run down the Yellowstone River, America's longest free-flowing river, from Gardiner (p176). Trips on

Keen paddlers can prepare for a boating assault on Greater Yellowstone by turning the pages of *Paddling Yellowstone and Grand Teton National Parks* by Don Nelson.

the exciting Gallatin River (p199) start near Big Sky. The Snake River has white-water trips between Hoback Junction and Alpine south of Jackson. Scenic floats through Grand Teton National Park down Snake River are popular with families, with wildlife viewing best at dusk and dawn. The Shoshone River west of Cody flows through the scenic Absaroka Range.

Paddlers can choose from large rafts for 12 or more people, or smaller rafts for six; pick the latter if you prefer paddling, otherwise your full-time job is 'holding on.' Full-day trips run from $50 to $90 depending on location, and overnight trips can cost $100 to $200 per person.

White-water trips are not without risk. It's not unusual for participants to fall out of the raft in rough water, although serious injuries are rare and the vast majority of trips are without incident. All trip participants are required to wear US Coast Guard–approved life jackets, and even nonswimmers are welcome. All guides are trained in lifesaving techniques.

River classifications vary over the course of the year, depending on the water level. Higher water levels, usually associated with spring runoff, make a river trip more challenging.

CANOEING & KAYAKING

Exploring the wilderness on water offers another perspective on the breadth of beauty and solitude beyond the roads. Yellowstone offers exciting opportunities for paddlers: families can take a load off little legs and cool off, while romantics can paddle up to hidden camp on a remote beach.

One stunning destination is the pine-rimmed Shoshone Lake (p158), the largest backcountry lake in the lower 48. It's popular with boaters who arrive via the Lewis River Channel and also visit the remote Shoshone Geyser Basin. The vast Yellowstone Lake offers access to remotest reaches of the park, where you can hike into the rarely visited southeast corner. Inquire at Bridge Bay Marina on Yellowstone Lake about boat charters or potential shuttles to the southeast corner.

Grand Teton's Jackson Lake offers scenic backcountry paddling (see p232), with several islands to explore and hiking in the little-visited northwest corner. Novice and family paddlers favor String and Leigh Lakes (see p233), and Lewis Lake in Yellowstone. Wildlife-watching is most superlative on Two Ocean Lake.

At Colter Bay in Grand Teton you can rent canoes (p232), but they can't go far, as trips are limited to the bay. For a longer trip, it's best to rent from an outdoor shop such as **Dornan's** (☎ 307-733-2522; www.dornans.com) at Moose.

Kayakers can paddle the Snake River (see p233), with sections appropriate for a range of abilities and top-notch wildlife-watching. Kayak rentals and instruction are available in Jackson (p244).

FISHING

Boasting some of the country's best rivers, Greater Yellowstone takes fly-fishing very seriously, particularly in Montana. The craze for recreation in rubber waders was boosted by Robert Redford's *A River Runs Through It*, filmed on the Gallatin and Madison Rivers.

Yellowstone offers more than 400 fishable waters where you'll find seven species: cutthroat, rainbow, brown, brook and lake (Mackinaw) trout; Arctic grayling; and mountain whitefish. Fishing season runs from the Saturday of Memorial Day weekend, near the end of May, to the first Sunday in November, except on Yellowstone Lake, which opens June 15. Bait angling is generally banned. Catch and release is standard in many areas and has played a major part in boosting fish stocks. Pick up a copy of the relevant state or park fishing regulations (p97) before you head out.

'Pine-rimmed Shoshone Lake is the largest back-country lake in the lower 48'

ACTIVITIES

The park's best fishing streams are the Gibbon, Madison and Yellowstone Rivers, though you can't really go wrong anywhere – see p158 for more information. Slough Creek has gained a reputation as angling heaven. The Madison, Gibbon and Firehole Rivers in Yellowstone are fly-fishing only.

In Grand Teton National Park, Leigh and Jenny Lakes both offer good fishing and are stocked with lake, brown, brook and Snake River cutthroat trout. One of the best fishing spots is on the Snake River just below the Jackson Lake dam (with parking on both sides of the river). Ice fishing is growing in popularity, although spring and fall offer the best fishing.

Outside the parks, the Madison is the region's most acclaimed river, though it's also the most mobbed, especially during early July's salmon fly hatch. The Henry's Fork of the Snake River in Island Park is another prime spot.

Fishing shops offering equipment and guides, and float trips proliferate around the region's prime fishing areas. Hit them up for tips on where to fish and what flies to pack. Fly 'afishionados' shouldn't miss Livingston's Fly Fishing Discovery Center (p204).

Whet your angling appetite with *Fishing Yellowstone National Park: An Angler's Complete Guide to More than 100 Streams, Rivers, and Lakes* by Richard Parks.

Fishing Licenses

A Yellowstone National Park fishing permit is required to fish in the park. Anglers 16 years of age and older must purchase a $15 three-day permit, a $20 seven-day permit or a $35 season permit. To fish in Grand Teton National Park, only a Wyoming fishing license is required (with a $10.50 conservation stamp for all but one-day licenses).

Outside the parks, Wyoming generally offers year-round fishing. Fishing licenses are daily (nonresident/resident $11/4) or yearly (nonresident/resident $76/19). For details contact the **Wyoming Game & Fish Dept** (☎ 307-777-4600; http://gf.st ate.wy.us).

To get a Montana fishing license, you must first have a conservation license (nonresident/resident $10/8) – good for the rest of your life and available where fishing licenses are sold. A seasonal license (nonresident/resident $60/18) is good for one year; a two-day stamp costs $15. Contact the Bozeman division of **Montana Fish, Wildlife & Parks** (☎ 406-994-4042, 24hr information 406-994-5700; www.fwp.state.mt.us; 1400 South 19th, Bozeman, MT 59718).

Local vendors and the **Idaho Dept of Fish & Game** (☎ 208-334-3700; www.state .id.us/fishgame) issue fishing licenses. Daily licenses cost $12 for the first day and $5 for additional consecutive days; or purchase a full season license (nonresident/resident $82/26).

SWIMMING & SOAKING

When summer temperatures soar, nothing beats taking to the water. Yellowstone and Grand Teton are blessed with crystalline lakes and rivers, ranging from deep cobalt to rusted greens, some so private that skinny dipping is *de rigueur*. Pull over and spend a lazy afternoon on the fine beaches at Sedge Bay (p116) on Yellowstone Lake and Leigh Lake (p222) in Grand Teton. A long soak in the hot springs of Chico (p205) in Paradise Valley or Boiling River (p101) in Yellowstone National Park washes away even the longest drive. If you have the bucks, consider pampering yourself in the spas at Chico or Teton Valley.

For safety reasons, visitors are not allowed to go directly into hot springs, but swimming where hot springs empty into a non-thermal river is allowed. Today there are only a couple of places where swimming is tacitly allowed (though not advertised) in Yellowstone: the Boiling River just north of Mammoth and the Firehole River (p126) in Geyser Country.

> **TOP PHOTO OPS**
>
> ▪ **Schwabacher's Landing** (p220), Grand Teton
>
> ▪ **Oxbow Bend** (p216), Grand Teton
>
> ▪ **Mormon Row** (p229), southeast Grand Teton
>
> ▪ **Artist Point** (p110), Grand Canyon of the Yellowstone
>
> ▪ **Grand Prismatic Spring** (p124), Midway Geyser Basin

Backcountry hikers will be rewarded with some of the world's best soaks in the Bechler Region and on the hike to Heart Lake. Other backcountry soaks are whispered about furtively in local bars; try these at your own risk.

For more on the inherent dangers in hot-spring soaking see the Health & Safety chapter (p281).

Other prime spots for a soak include Granite Hot Springs (p252) southeast of Jackson, and Huckleberry Hot Springs (p228) near Flagg Ranch in the Rockefeller Parkway. In Grand Teton, String Lake (p222) and Taggart Lake (p224) are popular places for a dip.

PHOTOGRAPHY

Photo opportunities are plentiful in the parks: it's not worth causing a traffic pile-up just to get a shot. The best light coincides with peak hours for animal-watching: early morning and late afternoon. Try to settle yourself into a prime spot at this time and keep disturbances to a minimum. In bright conditions it is best to have the sun behind you over your left shoulder. Thermal features are best captured during the middle of the day, when they produce less steam; polarizing filters help a great deal. To give a sense of scale, include the boardwalks or a human figure. Be careful not to get geyser splashes on your lens, as it forms silica on the glass and is difficult to remove.

For information on wolf-watching, see p105.

You'll need a 300mm lens and a tripod to get good wildlife shots and a macro lens to capture wildflowers. The Yellowstone General Stores have photo supplies and machines that allow you to make digital prints.

Always ask permission to photograph someone close up. Since you can't ask wildlife, simply never crowd them. For more advice on picture-taking, see Lonely Planet's *Travel Photography*.

Xanterra runs early-morning photo safaris that depart daily from Lake Yellowstone Hotel (p165), Old Faithful Inn (p124) and Mammoth Hot Springs Hotel (p162). And Yellowstone photographer par excellence Tom Murphy runs photography tours of Yellowstone through his **Wilderness Photography Expeditions** (☎ 406-222-2986; www.tmurphywild.com). You could also hone your skills via a photography course with the **Yellowstone Institute** (www.yellowstoneassociation.org).

WINTER ACTIVITIES

While the grouse roost in snowdrifts and bison huddle in frosted masses, visitors are likely to spend their winter time intentionally spending calories. The options of skiing, snowshoeing and wildlife-watching are just too good. An increasingly popular season, winter still only attracts a fraction of summer's numbers. The season for winter sports runs from the end of November to April, depending on weather, though February and March generally offer the best snow conditions. In Yellowstone

ACTIVITIES

and Grand Teton National Parks, winter activities include cross-country skiing, backcountry skiing, skate skiing (with short skis on groomed hardpack trails), snowshoeing and snowmobiling. See also p159.

Most park trails are not groomed, but unplowed roads and trails are open for cross-country skiing. Backcountry trips require extra caution, as streams and geothermal areas can be hidden by snow: Carry a map and compass when you venture off designated trails or roads. Some roads are groomed for snowmobiles and other snow vehicles; exercise caution if you are a skier sharing the road.

In Grand Teton National Park the **Craig Thomas Discovery & Visitor Center** (☎ 307-739-3300; ☼ 8am-7pm summer, 8am-5pm rest of year, closed Christmas day) is the winter-activity hub, offering information on weather, road, ski and avalanche conditions. All park campgrounds closed in winter, but there is limited tent and RV camping near the **Colter Bay Visitor Center** (☎ 307-739-3594; ☼ 8am-5pm early May–mid-May, 8am-7pm Jun-early Sep, 8am-5pm Sep-early Oct). Teton Park Rd is plowed from Jackson Lake Junction to Signal Mountain Lodge (p237) and from Moose to the Taggart Lake Trailhead.

Jackson and Big Sky sit pretty among the Rockies' most popular ski destinations. Both are equipped with modern lift technology, snow-grooming systems, child care, rental equipment and facilities. They are also the springboard for many other activities. Nonskiers can take scenic chairlift rides at Grand Targhee and Big Sky.

Lift tickets for major ski areas cost anywhere from $45 to $75 for a full day or about two-thirds that for a half day (usually after 1pm). Three-day or weeklong lift passes are more economical, especially if they do not need to be used on consecutive days. Trip planners should look at early season, weekend or weeklong resort packages that include lodging, meals and equipment rental.

For a more economical yet equally adventuresome activity, check out the cross-country and backcountry skiing options. If you need a guide, dozens of outfitters offer ski and snowmobile trips. West Yellowstone is the major base for organized winter activities into Yellowstone. Rental equipment (including warm outerwear) is easily found in the area (p287).

For one unforgettable journey, take a snowcoach to the Old Faithful Snow Lodge (p166) and spend a few days skiing around the kaleidoscope-hued geyser basins, around the Grand Canyon of the Yellowstone and up Mt Washburn.

Information

For information on snow and avalanche conditions in national forests, contact the **Backcountry Avalanche Hazard & Weather Forecast** (☎ recorded information 307-733-2664; www.jhavalanche.org). **Mountain Weather** (www.mountainweather .com) presents Jackson Hole snow and weather reports and links to other resorts and webcams at Grand Targhee. You may also find www .mtavalanche.com, the website of the Gallatin National Forest Avalanche Center, a useful source of information.

Most national forests supply free winter-use travel maps. Get the Montana Winter Guide at www.wintermt.com.

DOWNHILL SKIING & SNOWBOARDING

With impressive snowfalls and wild and lovely terrain, the northern Rockies are a premier downhill destination. Most resorts offer other onsite winter activities as well as top-notch ski and snowboard instruction. Those willing to risk less-than-peak conditions should look for cheaper early-season or late-season package deals in November or from March to April.

Hike the Continental Divide at www.cdtrail .org.

Scope out Cody's winter sports at www.coldfear .com.

ACTIVITIES

World-class terrain and heart-thumping views breed fanatics at **Jackson Hole** (www.jacksonhole.com), Wyoming's largest resort, in Teton Village. The town of Jackson's own miniresort, **Snow King** (☎ 307-733-5200, 800-522-5464; www.snowking.com; 400 E Snow King Ave), and **Grand Targhee** (☎ 307-353-2300, 800-827-4433; www.grandtarghee.com) in Alta, Idaho, offer an intimate atmosphere that's great for families.

Montana's premier resort is **Big Sky** (www.bigskyresort.com), 33 miles south of Bozeman, with a gondola, nine chairlifts, 80 miles of runs and 4180ft of vertical drop, in addition to a booming second-home community. The nearby **Moonlight Basin** (www.moonlightbasin.com), on the 11,166ft Lonesome Peak, has become the locals' favorite; this northern slope gets 400in of light, dry powder per season. **Red Lodge Mountain** (☎ 800-444-8977, ski reports 406-446-2610; www.redlodgemountain.com; lifts adult $45, child $15-39; ☒ end Nov-early Apr) is increasing in popularity; besides sitting astride a party town, it offers excellent cross-country opportunities.

CROSS-COUNTRY & BACKCOUNTRY SKIING

Nothing approximates heaven more than gliding through snow-covered wilderness under a sharp, blue sky. Nordic (or cross-country) skiing offers a great workout in stunning settings, and saves bucks on lift tickets. The national park and forest services maintain summer hiking trails as cross-country trails during winter, offering terrific solitude and wildlife-watching opportunities.

Backcountry skiing takes skiers to more difficult terrain than regular nordic gear can handle. The equipment, either telemark (single-camber skis with edges and free-heel bindings) or rondonee (an alpine hybrid system allowing for free-heeled ascents), fitted with climbing skins for ascents, allows skiers to travel cross-country and down steep slopes.

SNOWMOBILE WARS

The early 1960s saw a boom in in the number of snowmobiles descending upon Yellowstone. At their peak, up to 1600 snowmobiles traveled through Yellowstone and Grand Teton daily, their emissions creating pollution levels greater than those in the city of Los Angeles. Concern about the environmental impact led to a long-term analysis of the situation.

In 2004, a temporary decision was made to allow 720 snowmobiles per day in Yellowstone, all of them professionally guided, with a further 140 snowmobiles allowed in Grand Teton. The three-year trial period was considered a success by the National Parks Service: moving violations decreased by 84% because of commercial guiding and BAT (Best Available Technology) requirements on snowmobiles resulted in cleaner emissions.

In 2007 the park service finally announced a long-term winter use plan, to replace the temporary ruling. From December 2008, the number of snowmobiles allowed into the park will be reduced to 540 (300 from West Yellowstone, 170 from Jackson Hole, 30 from Cody and 20 from Gardiner). All must be commercially guided and meet strict limits on noise and pollution emissions. The number of snowcoaches allowed into the park will rise to 83 per day. Snowmobilers will be able to access the park through the eastern Sylvan Pass park entrance, but only when there is no avalanche threat.

In Grand Teton snowmobiles will banned from the Moran Junction–Flagg Ranch section of the Continental Divide Snowmobile Trail. A total of 25 per day will be allowed on Grassy Lake Rd (guides not required here) and 40 per day on Jackson Lake (to provide access to ice fishermen).

Local communities and snowmobile manufacturers remain bitter over the economic impacts of restricted snowmobiling, while some environmentalists wish to ban all motorized oversnow travel in the park, citing the impact of snowmobiling on bison during their most critical survival season. With neither side content with compromise, this chilly debate is bound to rumble on, most likely in the courts.

Newcomers to the sport should take a lesson (available at most ski resorts) and get in some resort runs before tackling the backcountry. In addition, backcountry skiers must be well versed in avalanche safety.

Land controlled by the NPS, US Forest Service, Bureau of Land Management and private owners supports hundreds of miles of cross-country trails. In Yellowstone (see also p160) there is one maintained ski trail that parallels the road from the West Entrance to Madison to Old Faithful and Shoshone. Stay off the groomed roads meant for motorized travel. Otherwise, skiers will find ungroomed backcountry trails with orange markers. Although many resorts offer cross-country facilities adjacent to alpine slopes, most Nordic skiers avoid the downhill crowds by visiting dedicated Nordic areas and backcountry trails. The best of these are Rendezvous Trail System (p173) in West Yellowstone, with 18.5 miles of dedicated and groomed Nordic paths (Rendezvous is the winter training ground for the US Nordic team).

Held in late November, the West Yellowstone Ski Festival (p173) brings Nordic skiers from around the world and offers demos and clinics. West Yellowstone is also the jumping-off point for cross-country trails in Yellowstone's extreme northwest corner. The Fawn and Bighorn Pass Trails connect to form a loop of around 10 miles through elk wintering areas.

In Grand Teton (see also p234) winter backcountry trails are usually marked with orange flags, although funding problems may change this. Trails are not machine groomed but frequent use keeps the trails packed down. Good skiing routes include the 5 miles up Signal Mountain Rd, the trail from the Taggart Lake parking area to the Jenny Lake overlook, and the uphill route up and around Two Ocean Lake. Avalanches are a major hazard in the canyons and upper areas of the Tetons.

Lone Mountain Ranch (p199) at Big Sky has 46.5 miles of privately groomed trails, and nearby Mountain Meadows Guest Ranch has a further 15.5 miles. Red Lodge Nordic Center (p182) has 9 miles of trails.

One great trip is the ski run from Wind River Lake (p253) at Togwotee Pass to Brooks Lake Lodge for lunch. Bear Creek Rd, starting from Jardine (5 miles from Gardiner), has 6.5 miles of occasionally groomed trail.

> 'Most Nordic skiers avoid the downhill crowds by visiting dedicated Nordic areas and backcountry trails'

SNOWSHOEING

In Yellowstone and elsewhere you can generally snowshoe anywhere – the problem is getting to the trailhead. Try not to mark groomed cross-country trails with your snowshoes, though; stay a few paces from any groomed areas. You can access trails from the Mammoth–Cooke City road all winter, and ski shuttles run to snowbound parts of the park from Mammoth and Old Faithful. Most resorts and hotels rent snowshoes. **Skinny Skis** (☎ 307-733-6094; 65 W Deloney Ave) in Jackson can offer good recommendations on where to go. For more information, please see p287.

Rangers lead snowshoe hikes from West Yellowstone's Riverside trail (BYO snowshoes) and Grand Teton's Discovery Center (snowshoes provided). Lone Mountain Ranch (p199) at Big Sky has exclusive snowshoe trails. See also p160 and p234.

SNOWMOBILING

In 2007 snowmobiling numbers were reduced in Yellowstone and Grand Teton National Parks (see the boxed text, p53), but the issue remains a live one. However, even if snowmobiles are eventually banned from the parks, the surrounding national forests still offer hundreds of miles of trails.

West Yellowstone is the 'snowmobile capital of the world.' Here you can legally drive snowmobiles in town and attend March's **World Snowmobile**

Expo (www.snowmobileexpo.com). There are over 1000 miles of snowmobile trails between West Yellowstone and Targhee National Forest in neighboring Idaho. One is the popular 34-mile Two Top Mountain Loop, the country's first National Recreational Snowmobile Trail. Flagg Ranch Resort (p238) is the southern snowmobiling gateway to Yellowstone (for commercial tours only). The West Yellowstone **Chamber of Commerce Information Center** (☎ 406-646-7701; www.westyellowstonechamber.com; Canyon St) offers a free *Winter Guide to Yellowstone Country* map with hundreds of miles of snowmobiling routes.

Create your own adventure at www .trails.com.

Yellowstone's snowmobile travel season runs from the third Wednesday in December to early March. All roads except for the North Entrance through the Northeast Entrance (open only to wheeled vehicles) are groomed for oversnow vehicles. Snowmobilers should know that the road from the West Entrance to Madison to Old Faithful is shared with cross-country skiers; ride with caution. The road from Cody through Sylvan Pass may be closed to snowmobilers in 2008; check for updates with the park service.

Speed limits are generally 45mph. Snowmobiles are not allowed in any wilderness areas. If you are new to snowmobiling, bear in mind that it's much more comfortable to ride solo than to double up. When renting, check the cost of clothing rental and insurance, and whether the first tank of gas is free. Backrests and heated handgrips are desirable extras.

In Grand Teton National Park snowmobiling is allowed on Grassy Lake Rd and the **Continental Divide Snowmobile Trail** (☎ trail conditions 307-739-3612). The 360-mile Continental Divide Snowmobile Trail connects Dubois to Togwotee Pass, Grand Teton and Yellowstone. Check ahead for **Wyoming snowmobile trail conditions** (☎ 800-225-5996; http://wyotrails.state.wy.us /snow). The frozen surface of Jackson Lake is open to snowmobiles for fishing access only. Entrance fees for snowmobilers are $15 for one day and $20 for seven days for Grand Teton. All snowmobiles in both parks must meet best available technology standards. Cooke City (p178) is another regional hub for snowmobiling activity.

SNOWCOACH TOURS

Pioneered in Canada, snowcoaches are essentially converted vans on snow tracks. These heated vehicles are used for transportation in and around the park in winter. Snowcoach tours depart daily from West Yellowstone (p173), Flagg Ranch Resort (p238), Wapiti Valley and Mammoth; most stop at Old Faithful and all stop for wildlife-watching opportunities. Vehicles may also be available to charter. **Xanterra** (www.travelyellowstone.com), the Yellowstone concessionaire, operates tours ranging from $50 to $120. Operators based in gateway towns are listed in the Around Grand Teton and Around Yellowstone chapters.

DOGSLEDDING

Speeding through snowy forests with a pack of dogs at your call – could anything be more romantic? Dogsledding is possible outside the parks in national forest areas. If you have always wanted to travel by paw power, several companies offer day and half-day trips (adult $110 to $185, child under 10 $85 to $129). In Big Sky, **Spirit of the North** (☎ 406-682-7994; www .huskypower.com) offers 8-mile half-day adventures with you in the driver's seat. In Jackson, **Continental Divide Dogsled Adventures** (☎ 800-531-MUSH; www .dogsledadventures.com) runs day trips or overnight trips in yurts (Central Asian–style circular tents).

ACTIVITIES

Kids & Pets

If Yellowstone's wonderland of spurting geysers, gurgling mud pots and wild animals turns adults into kids, then imagine its impact on young ones antsy to explore. In addition, Grand Teton's mountain attractions can be easily scaled down for little legs – and offer ample rewards in the form of picnics and lake swims. It is telling that a number of returning visitors first fell in love with the parks as children.

Piling your loved ones into the car for a summer sojourn to the parks can yield some unforgettable family moments. Though traveling with kids and pets requires more advanced planning, it can offer great rewards.

For kids there is heaps to do in the parks. Simply exploring the surroundings and snuggling into tents offers a complete departure from the humdrum everyday routine. Your dog will thank you for the introduction to all these new sights and smells, but consider carefully before taking your dog along. It is no fun having Rover in tow only to find out he is limited to the paved parking lots and picnic areas.

This guide aims to make your visit with kids and pets as hassle-free and fun as possible.

BRINGING THE KIDS

The national parks are as kid-friendly as a destination gets, though the wilderness must be treated with respect. The National Park Service (NPS) looks after its young visitors well, with fun outings, education programs and kid-focused presentations. Children under 12 stay free in park accommodations and most restaurants offer kid menus. Activities ranging from horseback riding to white-water rafting offer a thrill for all members of the family. For a rundown of the best family hikes, see Best Hikes for Little Legs (opposite).

Fun Stuff for Families
TRIP PLANNING

Who Pooped in the Park? by Gary D Robson is a fun illustrated storybook that explores scat and tracks found in Yellowstone.

Active, adventurous and environmentally aware parents are often eager to have their kids develop similar interests, but be careful not to turn the fun stuff into a chore. Confiscating Gameboys at the park gate is one thing, but having kids memorize 20 types of rock before they can toast their marshmallows could leave scars.

Keep the kids in mind as you plan your itinerary or include them in the trip planning from the get-go. If they have a stake in the plan, they will be more interested when they arrive, or so the theory goes. Kids tend to thrive with structured activities that can give them a purpose in the park. Lonely Planet's *Travel with Children*, by Cathy Lanigan, provides good information, advice and anecdotes.

On long-distance road trips, break up car time with ice-cream stops, short hikes or picnics. Visitor centers have lots of child-oriented exhibits and can divert kids' attention through children's books, coloring books and jigsaw puzzles while you furtively check out the maps.

Mix up natural scenery with the contrasting attractions of towns like West Yellowstone (p170) and Jackson (p241). Spend some time at places that both kids and adults can enjoy, such as the Draper Museum of Natural History in the Buffalo Bill Historical Center (p188) in Cody, the tram (p250) in Teton Village, the ropes course at Grand Targhee Resort (p255) or the alpine slide at Jackson's Snow King Resort (p247).

And don't forget that most towns have good libraries, as well as movie houses, for that rainy day.

For winter suggestions, see p51.

GEAR UP

Most car-rental agencies can add a child's car seat for a nominal fee, but it is best to inquire while making your reservation. Strollers may be harder to come by, so it is best to take yours with you or consider a baby backpack, handy for getting beyond the boardwalk and onto the trails with tots or babies over six months old.

Before your trip, make sure the kids have adequate hiking shoes – this could be anything from broken-in sneakers to waterproof boots, depending on the range of terrain you'll cover. Near Jackson, Dornan's (p212) in Moose rents children's bikes with helmets. As well, kids' gear can be found at Skinny Skis (p250) in Jackson, Sierra Trading Post (p289) in Cody and other locations.

HIKING

Don't be overly ambitious. Let them set the pace, and realize that you're not likely to make it to the top of Grand Teton on this trip. Try to pick a route that offers an easy out. A cool destination, like a lake or falls, offers extra incentive. Choosing a shorter route gives kids a chance to slow down and explore. Outfitting kids with a mini backpack (with snacks and lunch) and a small hiking stick helps them feel part of the expedition.

Kids love splashing about in the warm water springs of Boiling (p101) and Firehole Rivers (p126) or the tiny beaches at Leigh Lake (p222), so bring swimsuits and towels or a change of clothes.

PARK PROGRAMS

Yellowstone National Park runs the popular **Junior Ranger Program** (www .nps.gov/yell/planyourvisit/juniorranger.htm; book $3; ☺ Jun-Labor Day), in which children can earn a very cool badge. Kids complete the Nature Paper, an activity book with questions and games, as well as activities such as attending a ranger talk and completing a hike. The program can be completed in two days and is aimed at five- to 12-year-olds (although adults can enjoy it, too). Grand Teton has a similar program called the **Grand Adventure** (www .nps.gov/grte/forkids/index.htm); inquire about it at any visitor center.

Families should take advantage of Yellowstone's ranger-led activities; half-hour programs presented at the visitor centers. Several campgrounds run family-oriented campfire programs with lectures or live music in

---

BEST HIKES FOR LITTLE LEGS

If you're hiking with young children, try the following destinations, all within 2 miles of a road:

- Wraith Falls (p102), on the Mammoth to Tower-Roosevelt road
- Ribbon Lake (p140), near the Grand Canyon of the Yellowstone
- Trout Lake (p105), in the park's northwest corner
- String and Leigh Lakes (p222), in Grand Teton National Park
- Natural Bridge Trail (p142), near Bridge Bay
- Mystic Falls (p130), in Upper Geyser Basin
- Artist Paint Pots (p118), near Norris Junction
- Storm Point Trail (p116), on the north side of Lake Yellowstone

the early evenings. See the park newspapers for details. Grand Teton's campfire program is based in Colter Bay.

For more in-depth experiences, the **Yellowstone Association** (☎ 307-344-2289; www.yellowstoneassociation.org) offers a range of excellent year-round family programs. The most popular is Yellowstone for Families, where a qualified naturalist takes families (with children aged from eight to 12 years old) animal tracking, exploring and wildlife-watching in the park. Other fun stuff includes painting at Artists' Point or taking wildlife photos.

One-hour stagecoach rides from Roosevelt Lodge travel the sagebrush flats. Trips go several times per day and run from early June to August. Reserve with **Xanterra** (☎ 307-344-7311; adult/child over 2 $10/8). Yellowstone Buddies at Old Faithful Inn is an interpretive program for six to 11 year olds. The cost is $22 for a three-hour morning with lunch or $15 for a two-hour evening. Xanterra runs the program Monday to Thursday from July until mid-August.

Ranger adventure hikes (child/child under 7 $5/free) can be a good challenge and a chance to meet other kids. Grand Teton's Junior Ranger hikes take kids eight to 12 years old (chaperoned with a parent) on a 2-mile hike. They run several times a week from June to early August. Reserve ahead at the visitors centers.

Find the mystery animal, embark on an e–field trip or take the first steps toward the Junior Ranger badge at the official Grand Teton site (www .nps.gov/grte/forkids /index.htm).

TEENS

The Tetons and Yellowstone offer tons of things for teens to do. If your teens do not have much outdoor experience, it may be wise to enroll them in a course. Bike rentals are available in all gateway towns. Climbing gyms usually have short beginner courses appropriate for teens and ski resorts often have mountain biking or alpine slide options. Readers suggest white-water rafting and swimming – there are plenty of alpine lakes that become divine retreats when the temperatures soar. Teens of every skill level can have a blast exploring ski and snowboard runs at area resorts. All hikes included in this guide are appropriate for fit teens.

OUTSIDE THE PARKS

Camping under a starry sky, fishing for cutthroat trout and toasting marshmallows over a hot campfire are rites of passage for kids. Families should take advantage of national forest campsites, which can be less crowded than their national park counterparts.

Daytime adventures in hiking, paddling, rafting, fishing and horseback riding offer an opportunity for families to share time, and have some

THE COOLEST CAMPS

Field Learning (www.tetonscience.org) Make inquiries through GPS scavenger hunts or ecology expeditions. The Teton Science School offers outstanding programs for small fries, high schoolers and families.

Mini Mountaineers (www.jhmg.com/school/kids/index.php) The Kids Rock program offers kids six to 10 years old a chance to get vertical (with parents in tow) in a safe and fun outing run by mountain pros. Teens can choose programs that expand on climbing technique and teamwork. Most kids' fave? Tramping through snowfields in summer.

Rock Star Treatment (www.jhrocknrollcamp.com) Rock & Roll camp means jamming in day or overnight programs under the tutelage of a professional musician. Budding Claptons and the like must have a year's instrument instruction under their belts. Of course, camp culminates in a live performance.

SEVEN RAINY DAY REFUGES

- Public libraries in the gateway communities
- The indoor climbing wall at Core Mountain Sports (p190) in Cody
- The kids' workshops at Cody's Buffalo Bill Historical Center (p188)
- The IMAX theater (p171) in West Yellowstone
- The Grizzly & Wolf Discovery Center (p171) in West Yellowstone
- The kids' art studio at Jackson's National Museum of Wildlife Art (p241)
- Jackson's movie theaters (p249)

---

fun. In general children must be at least eight years old for horseback riding (and at least 4ft tall) and six years old for scenic floats. Canoes can be rented at **Dornan's** (☎ 307-733-2522; www.dornans.com) for lazy days on the Tetons' lakes. Kids can fish for free at the pond at Jackson Hole.

Newcomers to the west will be as riveted watching bucking broncs as the wildlife. Summer rodeos, the **Buffalo Bill Stampede** (www.codystampederodeo .com) in Cody and the **JH Rodeo Company** (☎ 307-733-2805; www.jhrodeo.com) in Jackson offer affordable family rates and activities. In Jackson, kids 14 and up can grab a lasso and join the 'calf scramble,' a chaotic mass of children roping calves. Both Jackson (7pm on the square) and Cody (6pm at Irma's Hotel) have daily staged gunfights – perhaps not much of an educational tool but still popular with families.

The ski areas are often open in the summer with activities ideal for families and with day-care services, too. In winter they are a haven for families: if yours doesn't ski, consider tubing, snowshoeing or an inexpensive cross-country outing. For more information see p51.

Visitor centers stock a wide range of children's activity books and games, including child-oriented wildlife-spotting guides. Outside the parks, kids will enjoy the interactive exhibits of the Draper Museum at Cody (part of the Buffalo Bill Historic Center; p188) and the make-your-own-art studio at the National Museum of Wildlife Art (p241) in Jackson, as well as the huge dinosaur skeletons at Bozeman's Museum of the Rockies (p195).

Bugling Elk and Sleeping Grizzlies, by Shirley Craighead, teaches about the ecology of Yellowstone and the Tetons.

Keeping It Safe

Of course, no parents deliberately leave behind sunscreen and water when embarking on a 5-mile hike, but it does happen more often than you would expect. Never underestimate the misery of a thirsty, sunburned, bitten and exhausted child with a 3-mile hike still ahead. It's helpful to have a checklist of supplies needed for hikes, including sufficient water or iodine tablets, sunscreen and a packable heat blanket that only weighs a few ounces.

When hiking with children, make sure they carry a flashlight and whistle, and know what to do if they get lost. Some families carry small walkie-talkies as an emergency backup, although in case of a bear encounter you should keep your children within sight on the trail.

Be particularly careful of children if you stop by the road to watch wildlife; everyone is likely to be watching the bison, not the traffic. Forays to overviews like the Grand Canyon of the Yellowstone or the Yellowstone River Picnic Area hike require extra attention, as some areas without guardrails present sheer drops. Thermal areas are another potential danger, as kids often don't comprehend just how hot the water is. More than one child has been burned while testing the waters of a hot spring.

IF BART SIMPSON DISCOVERED NATURE...

Ten-year-old Wilton Springer lives in Grand Teton National Park, where his dad is a rescue ranger in summer.

What's Yellowstone like? Cool. There's Old Faithful, all the geysers that go *pflap!* And hot springs you can throw a snowball into and it will melt in, like, two seconds. If you walked in one, you'd probably die.

What should kids do in the Tetons? I'd say go hiking. Go to the Jenny Lake boat dock and go across the lake. Go to Hidden Falls. Sometimes we take our canoe out and catch trout. There's cutthroat, brook, rainbow and some other kind that I don't remember.

What are your favorite animals? Picas, marmots and ermine weasels. Picas make little squeaky sounds. They are really cool. During the summer they collect grasses to eat over the winter. Their piles, I've only seen them two feet tall, but they can be up to five feet. When they do that they over-prepare for winter.

It's a good idea to run through together the kinds of situations you might encounter before leaving home. A short pretrip outing could help kids who don't normally hike know what to bring and expect while getting excited about the trip. Do your research and let your kids know the proper way to handle an animal encounter, in addition to the Leave No Trace ethics that reinforce minimizing impact, taking only photographs, packing out trash and respecting wildlife.

BRINGING THE PETS

While your vacation time loyalty to your furry friend is admirable, national parks are no place for pets. If you are already traveling with your pet, one alternative is to take advantage of national forest trails where dogs are allowed on a leash; there's a lot near Yellowstone and the Tetons. Service animals such as seeing eye dogs are welcome in national parks. To prevent misunderstandings with rangers and others, service animals should always wear their vests.

See Spot Run

Shoshone National Forest, Bridger Teton National Forest, Gallatin National Forest and Caribou-Targhee National Forest all allow dogs on leashes. In Jedediah Smith Wilderness dogs must be under voice control at all times. A glance at an atlas reveals the city parks, rivers and lakes that can offer Fido a refreshing dip. Once there, check sign postings for new restrictions and local leash laws and, more importantly, keep an eye out for wildlife before your retriever exercises its instincts.

Wilderness areas and some town parks may allow dogs off the leash if they respond promptly to voice command. Make sure your dog is responsive before testing this (especially in the presence of wildlife or children). Owners may be ticketed and fined for irresponsible stewardship.

Some hotels (indicated throughout the text) will allow pets for an extra fee, but these are few, particularly in Jackson. Your best bet is to reserve a spot well in advance given the shortage of these kinds of accommodations. Yellowstone's official site gives tips and regulations for pets at www.nps.gov/yell/pla nyourvisit/pets.htm.

Kennels

Kennels can be found in most gateway towns. Wherever possible, they are listed throughout the book. If traveling through an area where you don't see one, ask for the local veterinary clinic. Their staff will usually have a good lead on the best local kennels or private dog-sitting services.

Look for kennels that are ABKA (American Boarding Kennel Association) certified. When choosing a kennel, ask for a walk through. Consider the following factors: the size of the sleeping space, the presence of outdoor yards or play spaces, the number of daily walks or play sessions, the size and attentiveness of the staff and the kennel's certifications. Some even have webcams, so brooding pet parents won't miss a whimper. Facilities that always keep dogs separate might keep your teacup poodle out of a tussle or prevent it from catching an illness from another dog. Some prefer some canine company to pass the time (in this case, ensure it is well supervised). Kennels may also provide lodgings for cats, birds and fish.

BOZEMAN, MT
Doggie Daycare & Motel (☎ 406-763-5585; www.doggiedaycareandmotel.com; 421 Garnet Mt Way) is an ABKA-certified kennel offering dog and cat boarding, and a full grooming facility, 11 miles south of Bozeman.

CODY, WY
A full-service facility with climate-controlled indoor/outdoor boarding with exercise in large courtyards, **Chinook Boarding Kennels** (☎ 307-587-3379; www.woofyproducts.com; 134 E Cooper Ln) has a certified groomer, private training and pet sitting. Reservations are required as space is limited.

DRIGGS, ID
Trail Creek Pet Center (☎ 208-354-2571; 180 S 150 East; ⊗ 8am-6pm) is an AKBA-certified boarding facility with grooming and an outdoor exercise center for pets. Offers pet pick-up and drop-off.

JACKSON, WY
Happy Trails Pet Resort (☎ 307-733-1606; www.springcreekanimalhospital.com; 1035 W Broadway) is an AKBA-accredited veterinary clinic with modern kennels for up to 35 dogs, as well as cat condos for daycare or overnight stays. Deluxe suites have webcams and televisions.

Scavenge for clues about Yellowstone's explosive past, play with the jackelopes and explore the park through puzzles and games at the official Yellowstone site (www.nps.gov/yell/forkids/index.htm).

DOGGIE DOS & DON'TS

The tight restrictions on pets in Yellowstone and Grand Teton National Parks mean you're probably better off giving Fido a squeeze goodbye and leaving him at home. In the parks pets must be leashed at all times and are not allowed on any boardwalks or backcountry trails, or more than 100ft from roads or paved paths.

Sound difficult? It is.

Finding accommodations is another challenge. Pets are allowed in Yellowstone's cabins, but not in the hotels. Most campgrounds allow dogs but do not permit them to go loose. What can you do when you go hiking? Check the pet into a kennel, since it's illegal to leave any unattended pet (known as bear bait) tied to objects in the parks. If the temperatures are cool, it may stay inside a ventilated vehicle. Needless to say, you will have to clean up after your beloved.

Like people, animals need conditioning for the outdoors. That bijon frieze sitting pretty in the condo window may longingly gaze outside, but it is probably not in prime condition to summit peaks or swim currents. Break your pet in slowly with easier treks where allowed.

Adequate food, shelter and water should always be handy (but never left out where it can attract wild animals). Bring a stash of plastic bags to clean up after your dog and have a water dish (an old frisbee works). Never let your pet get near thermal features – they won't know it's hot until it's too late.

PARADISE VALLEY, MT

Kennels at the Smith Family Ranch (☎ 406-848-7477; www.paradisevalleyvacation .com; 1828 Old Yellowstone Trail South) is a working ranch between Gardiner and Emigrant that can accommodate up to six dogs.

Querencia Kennels (☎ 406-333-4500; www.querencia.com; 55 Querencia Dr, Emigrant) is a lodge in the Paradise Valley that also offers canine accommodations with ample room to romp.

Horse Trails & Equestrian Facilities

Kids and curious adults can test their sleuthing skills and explore park puzzles at the fun national parks. Webrangers site (www .nps.gov/archive /webrangers).

Private stock is allowed in the park only after July 1, due to snowy and wet springtime conditions. While horses are not allowed in front country campgrounds, some backcountry sites accommodate them. Bechler Corner has a number of sites and is a favorite of horseback riding groups. For more information, contact the **backcountry ranger office** (☎ 307-344-2160).

Bringing a horse or pack animal with you requires extensive advance planning. The appropriate backcountry stock rules and grazing information can be downloaded from www.nps.gov/yell/planyourvisit/horseride .htm for Yellowstone National Park and at www.nps.gov/grte/planyour visit/horserides.htm for Grand Teton National Park.

In Grand Teton National Park late snows sometimes prevent the openings of backcountry stock campsites: consult with the **parks permit office** (☎ 307-739-3309). Often stock users choose to camp in the national forest and travel in on day trips. Outside the park, stock camping areas in the John D Rockefeller Jr Memorial Parkway (along the unpaved road between Flagg Ranch and Grassy Lake) do not require a permit. For stock camping in the Bridger-Teton National Forest, consult the **supervisor's office** (☎ 307-733-5500).

Inside Grand Teton National Park, Death Canyon Trailhead Rd boasts the only stock campsite accessible by vehicle. Permits can be obtained from the Craig Thomas Discovery & Visitor Center (p212). Backcountry stock camping is allowed in the north fork of Granite Canyon, Death Canyon, the south fork of Cascade Canyon, Paintbrush Canyon and Berry Creek. Backcountry permits are required.

Xanterra offers one- to two-hour **horseback riding** (☎ 307-344-7311) trips at Mammoth, Tower-Roosevelt and Canyon. In addition, their wagon rides take visitors on an arduous pilgrimage to a BBQ steak dinner. Guided, multiday stock trips using horses or llamas are available through licensed stock operators at www.nps.gov/yell/planyourvisit/stockbusn.htm and www.nps.gov/grte/planyourvisit/horserides.htm) for Yellowstone and Grand Teton National Parks, respectively.

Environment

Yellowstone is a spectacular landscape shaped by volcanoes and glaciers – fire and ice – on a mind-boggling scale. The park's geysers, hot springs and steam vents are some of the premier geothermal features found anywhere in the world and they offer both geologists and visitors a vivid peek into the center of the earth. From acidic soils to waterlogged valleys, the environment on this superheated plateau affects the lives of the plants and animals that call this park home and makes it one of the leading wildlife destinations in North America.

THE LAND

THE YELLOWSTONE HOT SPOT

If you're already in the park, take a moment to consider that you're standing on a thin piece of crust floating atop a huge 125-mile-deep plume of molten rock. You have, in essence, journeyed to a supervolcano atop one of the foremost hot spots on the earth.

Hot spots are places where buoyant molten rock, heated by magma deep under the earth's crust, has risen through the upper mantle close to the earth's surface. Similar hot spots have created island chains like Hawaii and Iceland. Although hot spots don't move, the crust of the earth over a hot spot does, and as the crust moves, it forms a line of progressively newer volcanoes. Because the crust of the North American plate is moving southwest at an inch a year, the Yellowstone hot spot has burned a chain of volcanoes across the American West from southeastern Oregon (where it was active 16 million years ago) to northern Wyoming (where it was last active 600,000 years ago). After a few million years, the Yellowstone hot spot will slide over to North Dakota.

However, the Yellowstone region has been sitting atop this hot spot for about two million years now, resulting in massive supervolcanic eruptions roughly every 650,000 years. The last three eruptions (dated at two million, 1.3 million and 600,000 years ago) have been centered on Island Park, Henry's Fork and Yellowstone, respectively.

The most recent explosion formed the 1000-sq-mile Yellowstone caldera, which dominates the center of the park. In an eruption 1000 to 2000 times as powerful as the Mt St Helens eruption in 1980, the explosion spat out magma and clouds of 1800°F liquid ash at supersonic speeds, vaporizing everything in its path. Ash billowed into the sky, traveling thousands of square miles in a matter of minutes, and suffocating the land in blisteringly hot ash flows. The crater roof and floor then imploded and dropped thousands of feet, creating a smoldering volcanic pit 48 miles by 27 miles wide. Ash landed as far away as the Gulf of Mexico, and smaller fragments circled the globe many times, causing a volcanic winter by reducing the amount of solar heat reaching the earth.

The awesome energy unleashed by the forest fires of 1988 is utterly insignificant compared with even the smallest of Yellowstone's many eruptions. Visitors may be surprised that Yellowstone is not more mountainous; the reason quite simply is that the mountains were either blown away by the explosion or sank into the caldera.

Since the explosion, at least 30 subsequent lava flows, dating from 150,000 to 70,000 years ago, have filled in and obscured the caldera, and forests have mostly reclaimed the area, though you can still make out the caldera in numerous places. Turnouts on the road south of Dunraven Pass

For a unique perspective check out the aerial photographs of Norris Geyser Basin at http://volcanoes.usgs .gov/yvo/2007/balloon .html.

provide excellent views of the northern part of the caldera, and much of the caldera's outline can be seen from the summit of Mt Washburn (p138).

Many of Yellowstone's volcanic and geothermal features highlight the silica-rich nature of the rocks that underlie the region and give character to the lava and heated waters that rise to the surface. Silica colors the pink to gray rhyolitic lava that dominates the landscape of the park. When dissolved in superheated water, silica (in a form called 'sinter' or 'geyserite') leaves a white crust around the mouths of geysers and hot springs, or clogs up narrow steam vents to create powerful geyser explosions.

YELLOWSTONE'S THERMAL FEATURES

Fueled by its underground furnace, Yellowstone bubbles like a pot on a hot stove to produce over 10,000 geothermal features – more than all other geothermal areas on the planet combined. This isn't all that surprising: magma, the earth's molten rock, is closer to the surface here than anywhere else on Earth – just 3 miles to 5 miles underground – and the average heat flow from the region is 40 times the global average.

But heat isn't everything. Essential to Yellowstone's thermal features is the addition of water, falling onto Yellowstone as rain or, more often, snow. This surface water may seep down as deep as 2 miles before it drains through the side channels of geysers, hot springs and underground aquifers. The water that eventually comes to the surface through a hot spring or geyser may have fallen as snow or rain up to 500 years ago.

Yellowstone's geothermal features and their 'plumbing' are constantly in flux, and what seem like permanent features to us are mere blips on the geologic timescale. Geysers suddenly erupt, or dry up; hot springs gradually appear, or explode so violently that they destroy themselves.

Scientists are only beginning to fathom these complex underground systems, but it's clear that this is a threatened landscape unless the broader region is safeguarded thoughtfully. Yellowstone protects about half of the world's geysers, but in areas like Iceland and New Zealand, where geothermal features have been developed as energy sources, geysers and geothermal activity may be altered or cease altogether.

Geysers

Only a handful of Yellowstone's thermal features are active geysers (from the Icelandic *geysir,* meaning 'to gush or rage'), but these still comprise about 50% of the global total, making the park a globally significant resource.

How geysers form is one of the primary questions asked by first-time visitors to the park. Geysers form as snowmelt percolates into the hot rock beneath the park, where it is superheated. This heated water begins to rise, creating convection currents. The earth acts like a giant pressure cooker, keeping the water liquid even though it reaches temperatures of over 400°F. As the water rises, it dissolves silica trapped in the surrounding rhyolite rock base. At the surface this silica is deposited as the mineral sinter (geyserite), creating the familiar ash-colored landscape that characterizes Yellowstone's thermal basins.

What gives geysers their 'oomph' is the sinter seal that junks up the escape valves in geyser chambers. This temporary blockage causes an intense buildup of gas until the seal breaks and releases the accumulated pressure. As the superheated water rushes toward the surface, water pressure drops and the water expands more than 1500 times in a violent chain reaction as it flashes into steam and explodes into the sky. Geysers require walls of hard rock like rhyolite (the limestone in areas like

Mammoth can't stand the pressure), part of the reason why Yellowstone's geysers are concentrated in the southwest of the park.

If you are out geyser hunting, an eruption is often signaled by an overflowing cone or pool, though this can go on for hours. Some eruptions surge hundreds of feet into the air; others shoot gracefully across rivers. Some erupt every few years; others are in perpetual torment.

Geysers and hot springs are often connected in complex and delicate underground networks and affect each other in ways we don't yet understand.

Hot Springs

Hot springs occur when there is a gradual rather than explosive release of hot water. The remarkable colors are a combination of mineral content, which affects the absorption and reflection of light, and water temperature, which supports a range of algae communities. The fact that algae or thermophiles are very temperature-specific leads to beautiful concentric bands of colors. Blue pools are the hottest pools and absorb all color except blue. Green pools result when the blue is mixed with small amounts of yellow sulfur. The smallest springs rage away like hot oil in a deep fat fryer, and larger springs churn like giant washing machines. Yet others remain completely still.

Mud Pots

Mud pots, a sort of hot spring of viscous bubbling mud, are created when rock is dissolved by the sulfuric acid in groundwater to create kaolinite, a form of clay. Mud pots are generally above the water table, higher than geysers, where less water is available. Most mud pots derive their water directly from rain, snow and condensation, so the mud consistency depends on climatic conditions. Mud pots are generally quite watery in spring and thicker toward the end of the summer. The bubbling of the mud makes them appear as if they are boiling, but this is actually the release of steam and gas. The mud is often colored by minerals such as sulfur and iron, giving rise to the nickname 'paint pots.'

Fumaroles

These are essentially dry geysers, bursting with heat but without a major water source, so water boils away before reaching the surface. These steam vents also give off carbon dioxide and some hydrogen sulfide (the

---

LIVING WITH THE HEAT

Given that Yellowstone, with its 10,000 geothermal features, is the world's foremost source of heated water, it comes as no surprise that heat-loving (thermophilic) micro-organisms were first discovered in the park's boiling hot waters in 1966. Further investigation has proven that a huge variety of microbes and bacteria find their homes in these extreme waters, where they tolerate not only the heat but also extremely acidic or alkaline conditions and toxicity of various minerals. The study of these organisms increased dramatically in 1985 after one of the species yielded an important enzyme that allows scientists to run DNA fingerprinting tests (p90). Other research is revealing important clues about the origins of life on earth and survival of life in outer space.

Much of this activity occurs on a microscopic scale, but visitors will still appreciate these remarkable lifeforms because they produce brilliant colors in nearly every body of water. Each species lives in a highly specific temperature and chemical zone, so they produce rings and patches of different colors. These color patterns give the park's hot springs and pools their unique character.

'rotten egg' smell), often with a hiss or roaring sound. Roaring Mountain (p103) on the Mammoth–Norris road is a huge collection of fumaroles.

Travertine Terraces

The limestone rock of the Mammoth region contrasts with the silica-rich rhyolite found elsewhere in the park. Here, carbon dioxide in the hot water forms carbonic acid, which then dissolves the surrounding limestone (calcium carbonate). As this watery solution breaks the surface, some carbon dioxide escapes from the solution and limestone is deposited as travertine (as opposed to the geyserite), forming beautiful terraces. These terraces can grow up to an inch per day and are in constant flux.

Yellowstone Lake

One of the world's largest alpine lakes, Yellowstone Lake was formed by the collapse of the Yellowstone caldera and was then shaped by glacial erosion. Over time, the lake has drained west into the Pacific Ocean, north to the Arctic Ocean and now into the Atlantic Ocean via the Gulf of Mexico.

Between 1923 and 1984 the Yellowstone caldera rose 3ft (and then started to drop). This caused the lake's north shore to rise, creating beaches, and the south shore to drop, causing inundation.

Hydrothermal explosions have further shaped the shoreline, creating the inlets of West Thumb (which is a smaller caldera within the larger caldera), Mary Bay and nearby Indian Pond. All the thermal features normally found in geyser basins can also be found beneath Yellowstone Lake. Recent underwater robotic cameras have revealed underwater geysers, 20ft-high cones, rows of thermal spires and more than 200 vents and craters, some the size of football fields, on the lake floor. Mary Bay and the lake floor canyon west of Stevenson Island are the hottest parts of the lake, due to numerous hot springs and vents.

In addition to the 137-sq-mile Yellowstone Lake, the park is also the source of several of North America's largest rivers, contributing to both the Mississippi River system via the Missouri River, and to the Columbia River system via the Snake River.

OTHER GEOLOGIC FEATURES
Grand Canyon of the Yellowstone

This canyon, one of the park's premier attractions, was formed as the land lifted higher due to rising magma and the Yellowstone River cut down

---

GEOLOGIC WONDERS

Grand Prismatic Spring (p124) The park's most beautiful geothermal feature.

Grand Teton (p208) Molten dikes, fault scarps and those peaks!

Hebgen Lake (p201) Ponder the awesome earthquake of 1959.

Mammoth Hot Springs (p101) Graceful travertine terraces.

Mud pots Head to Mud Volcano (p112) south of Canyon; Artist Paint Pots (p118) south of Norris; or Fountain Paint Pot (p125) in the Lower Geyser Basin.

Norris Geyser Basin (p117) The region's hottest geothermal area, featuring Echinus Geyser, the park's second-most-popular geyser, and Steamboat Geyser, the world's largest.

Obsidian Cliff (p103) Dark volcanic glass from the interior of a cooled lava flow.

Petrified forests Hike up Specimen Ridge (p137) in Yellowstone or take the interpretive walk at Tom Miner Basin (p205) in Paradise Valley.

Sheepeater Cliffs and Calcite Springs (p103 & p106) Hexagonal basalt columns near Tower Falls.

Upper Geyser Basin (p121) Old Faithful, Morning Glory Pool and other gems.

through an area of rhyolite that had been weakened by thermal activity (think of how a potato becomes softer when it is baked). The fledgling canyon was temporarily blocked up to three times by glaciers (18,000 to 14,000 years ago), and the subsequent glacial flooding created a classic V-shaped (river-eroded) canyon. The canyon reached its present form only about 10,000 years ago.

Like many of Yellowstone's waterfalls, the Lower Falls of the Yellowstone tumble over the junction of hard lava bedrock and softer rock, in this case rhyolite and thermal areas. The spectacular colors of the canyon walls are created as hot waters percolate through the rhyolite picking up iron oxides that stain the walls many different colors.

Petrified Forests

Petrified forests are found throughout the region, particularly in the Gallatin Forest (p206) and at Specimen Ridge (p137) in Yellowstone. What remains are trees that were rapidly buried by lava and mudflows. The wood cells have been gradually replaced with silica derived from the volcanic ash. In many areas subsequent forests grew in the fertile volcanic soil, as quickly as 200 years after an eruption, only to have later eruptions cover them in ash and lava. In Yellowstone's Specimen Ridge, this has resulted in up to 27 petrified forests layered on top of each other. The ridge contains more than 100 types of petrified vegetation and is believed to hold the word's largest collection of petrified trees.

The petrified trees we see today are around 50 million years old and have been exposed by erosion. Studies have revealed that these trees include subtropical redwoods and oaks, which point toward moister and warmer prehistoric climatic conditions.

The Teton Fault

The Tetons are mere geologic toddlers. Surrounding ranges like the Gallatins and Beartooths were formed 55 to 80 million years ago by volcanic action, as part of the east end of the Basin and Range region that dominates western USA. At this time Jackson Hole was still a high plateau. The Tetons started to rise only 13 million years ago as the earth's crust stretched apart. At that time the current peaks of the Tetons were still some 6 miles underground.

The key to the Teton's breathtaking profile is the 40-mile-long Teton Fault, which runs along the base of the range. Land on the east side of the fault has fallen, over millions of years, as the west block has hinged and angled upward. The east block has in fact dropped four times further than the peaks have risen. The range was essentially created by a succession of several thousand major earthquakes and slippages. Several of these scarps are visible near Jenny Lake.

As high as the Tetons appear, this vertical distance is actually only a third of the fault's total displacement. Gradual erosion of the peaks, combined with sedimentation in the Jackson Hole valley, has diminished the scale of the Tetons by up to two-thirds.

The very tops of the Tetons consist of limestone, deposited by an ancient sea 360 million years ago. Over time these relatively soft sedimentary rocks have largely eroded, exposing the more resistant granite. Freezing ice wedged and shattered this crystalline rock along its weakest joints, creating today's impressive pinnacles.

One result of the Teton's angled faulting is that the entire Jackson Hole valley tilts westward. The west half of Jackson Lake is three times deeper than the east, due to both tilting and glacial scouring. Oddly, the land

Learn more about Yellowstone's fascinating geology with *Windows into the Earth*, by Robert B Smith and Lee J Siegel.

west of the Teton peaks is drained to the east; that is, the peaks don't define the drainage systems as in most other mountain ranges.

Glaciation

The other major formative influence on the Yellowstone environment has been glaciation. As if supervolcanic activity weren't enough, sheets of ice up to 4000ft thick periodically covered Yellowstone and the Tetons, leaving only the tips of the highest mountain peaks visible. The most recent ice sheet, known as the Pinedale Glaciation, covered about 90% of Yellowstone National Park and melted about 13,000 years ago.

As glacial ice built up and moved downhill, it sharpened peaks, carved out glacial valleys, scoured walls, and created ridges of debris (moraines) and lakes. The piedmont lakes lining the base of the Tetons were formed just in this way, with lakes dammed up behind moraines like glacial footprints as the glaciers melted. Research has shown that the Snake River once flowed south out of Jackson Lake, until blocked and diverted by glacial moraines (it now flows east). Grand Teton's popular hike, the Cascade Valley, lies in a classic U-shaped glacial valley, which contrasts dramatically with the V-shaped river erosion found in Yellowstone Canyon. South of Jackson Lake, huge blocks of melting glacial ice formed the depressions known as The Potholes. In Yellowstone's Geyser Basin, ice melted so quickly that large mounds of glacial debris were deposited to form low ranges such as the Porcupine Hills, while deposits of glacial debris beneath today's thermal features act as water reservoirs for the various geysers and hot springs. Glaciers have largely retreated today, and the region's largest glaciers are now found in the Wind River Mountains, which have the largest glaciers in the lower 48.

Grasshopper Glacier, outside Cooke City, was named for millions of extinct grasshoppers entombed in its ice. However, most of the grasshoppers have decomposed as the glacier melts due to global warming.

Yellowstone's Future

The Yellowstone region has been geologically stable for about 10,000 years now, but the land remains restless. Continued tension in the earth's crust and earthquakes make this one of the most seismically active areas in the USA, with 1000 to 3000 earthquakes occurring each year.

In 1925 the entire mountainside flanking the Gros Ventre River collapsed, forming a dammed lake that held for two years, until the dam finally broke and tore downstream, killing six people in the settlement of Kelly.

In 1959 a 7.5-scale earthquake occurred in the Hebgen Lake region just west of the park and created Quake Lake (see the boxed text, p202). Three hundred of Yellowstone's geysers spontaneously erupted in the aftermath of this quake.

Although a 6.1 scale earthquake rocked the Norris Geyser Basin in 1975, geologists don't expect large earthquakes in Yellowstone National Park because underground heat softens the bedrock and makes it less likely to fracture.

Yellowstone is rising or falling as much as an inch a year, moving 65ft with each slow motion 'breath,' particularly at Mallard Lake Dome just east of Old Faithful, and Sour Creek Dome, east of the Hayden Valley. These movements in the earth's crust are probably due to the withdrawal of molten rock from twin magma chambers on the rim of the Yellowstone caldera.

No one knows for sure what will happen if (or when) Yellowstone's slumbering giant awakens. The last major Yellowstone eruption dwarfed every other volcanic eruption on the earth's surface for the past several million years, and such an explosion remains beyond human experience.

The bulging of magma chambers on the rim of the Yellowstone caldera indicates that another eruption is likely but, scientists agree, not for at least another 10,000 years. A major eruption would undoubtedly destroy the park as we know it, and cause major climate change that would affect human activity around the world.

Until then, enjoy the wondrous spectacle of Yellowstone's thermal features, and as you gaze up at Old Faithful or down through a hot spring into the bowels of the earth, remember the awesome forces at work below these surface expressions of Yellowstone's true grandeur.

WILDLIFE

The 2.5 million acres of wilderness within Yellowstone and Grand Teton National Parks constitute the biological heart of what is increasingly referred to as the Greater Yellowstone Ecosystem – the earth's largest intact temperate ecosystem. Greater Yellowstone radiates out from its untamed core into 18 million acres of surrounding federal lands and private property, forming a vast wilderness that is arguably one of the world's premier wildlife-viewing areas (see also p99), especially for larger mammals.

For a leg up on spotting wildlife carry a field guide such as Watching Yellowstone & Grand Teton Wildlife *by Todd Wilkinson.*

Animals and plant communities within Yellowstone are shaped by the region's legacy as a geologic and geothermal 'hot spot.' Not only has the uplift of the land over an underground magma chamber made the park a high-elevation landscape, but the leaching of rhyolite volcanic deposits has created acidic soils that favor the lodgepole pine forests that cover 60% of Yellowstone's main plateau. The park's elevation also led to extensive glaciation during the ice ages, which left behind impermeable deposits that create waterlogged landscapes in places like Hayden Valley.

Charismatic species of Yellowstone include the lynx, bald eagle, grizzly bear, whooping crane and a reintroduced gray wolf population. Featured below are some species visitors are most likely to see – or would most like to see.

Animals

LARGE MAMMALS

The prospect of seeing 'charismatic megafauna' is one of the region's biggest draws. Yellowstone National Park alone harbors 60 resident mammal species, including seven native species of ungulates (hoofed mammals). Much of the wildlife mentioned below also ranges beyond the parks' boundaries into surrounding areas.

Bears

The black bear roams montane and subalpine forests throughout Greater Yellowstone. It's an adaptable, primarily vegetarian forager that sporadically hunts smaller animals. About half of black bears are black in color; the anomalies are brown or cinnamon. Black bears are somewhat smaller than grizzlies and have more tapered muzzles, larger ears and smaller claws. Although they are generally more tolerant of humans and less aggressive than grizzlies, black bears should always be treated as dangerous.

Like grizzlies, black bears hibernate in a den over winter and conserve energy by reducing their metabolism. During the tourist season, they are often spotted in Yellowstone National Park around Tower and Canyon.

The endangered grizzly bear once ranged across the western US. Today its population in the lower 48 has been reduced to less than 1200, with 400 to 600 grizzlies inhabiting the Greater Yellowstone region. Federal

ENVIRONMENT

WILDLIFE-WATCHING

Yellowstone's megafauna is one of its greatest attractions for young and old alike. Bison never fail to impress, and you'll cherish the first time you see a moose grazing a lakebed, while fewer things get your heart pumping faster than a bear sighting.

If you are serious about spotting wildlife, invest in some good binoculars. If you are really serious, get a spotting scope. A good-quality telephoto camera lens will also work quite well for observing wildlife at a safe distance.

Different seasons each offer their own highlights; spotted wapiti calves and baby bison are adorable in late spring, while the fall rut brings the sounds of bugling elk to the park. In general, spring and fall are the best times to view wildlife. In summer you need to head out around dawn and dusk, as most animals withdraw to forests to avoid the midday heat. Always pack a drink and a snack for yourself, in case you come across something exciting and want to sit and watch for a while.

The park's northeastern Lamar Valley (p105) has been dubbed the 'Serengeti of North America' for its large herds of bison, elk and the occasional grizzly or coyote. The valley is by far the best place to spot wolves, particularly in spring. If you are interested in wolves, get a copy of the park's wolf observation sheet, which differentiates the various packs and individual members, or consider signing up for a wolf-watching class with the **Yellowstone Association Institute** (www .yellowstoneassociation.org/institute). The observation sheet is posted at campgrounds at Pebble and Slough Creeks (p163), which make the best wolf-watching bases.

The central Hayden Valley (p111) is the other main wildlife-watching area, and its pullouts can get crowded with spotters around dusk. The valley is a good place to view large predators like wolves and grizzlies, especially in spring when thawing winter carcasses offer almost guaranteed sightings. Coyotes, elk and bison are all common. The tree line is a good place to scan for wildlife. The more you know about animals' habitat and habits, the more likely you are to catch a glimpse of them.

If all else fails, you are guaranteed a grizzly sighting at West Yellowstone's Grizzly & Wolf Discovery Center (p171).

Follow the proper etiquette when watching wildlife:

- Animals have the right of way; allow animals (generally bison) to cross the road freely and in their own time.
- Don't chase animals.
- If you cause an animal to move, you are too close.
- Never position yourself between an animal and its young.
- It's illegal to be within 100yd of bears or 25yd of all other animals.
- Don't feed the animals!

delisting of the grizzly as a threatened species in April 2007 and the implementation of an ecosystem-wide conservation strategy are among the region's hottest topics.

Male grizzlies reach up to 8ft in length (from nose to tail) and 3.5ft in height at the shoulder (when on all fours) and can weigh more than 700lb at maturity. Although some grizzlies are almost black, their coats are typically pale brown to cinnamon with a 'grizzled' look. They can be distinguished from black bears by their concave (dish-shaped) facial profile, smaller and more rounded ears, prominent shoulder hump and long, nonretractable claws.

If you find some bear tracks, you might notice that the toe pads of a black bear are widely spaced and form a strong arc, while grizzly bear tracks show closely spaced toes in a fairly straight line, along with impressions from their very long claws.

Omnivorous opportunists and notorious berry eaters, grizzlies have an amazing sense of smell – acute enough to detect food miles away. Grizzlies enjoy a wide range of food sources, which varies seasonally. After bears emerge from hibernation between early March and late May, they feed mostly on roots and winter-killed carrion, turning to elk calves and then spawning cutthroat trout in late June. A feast of army cutworm moths lures bears to higher elevations in early September. Fall signals the buildup to hibernation, and consumption of whitebark nuts and the raiding of squirrels' pinecone stashes become obsessions. Before hibernation, bears can eat up to 100,000 berries in a single day. Scientists are concerned that falling levels of cutthroat trout in Yellowstone Lake and the spread of blister rust fungus, which kills whitebark pines, will have an increasingly detrimental effect on grizzly food supplies in the park.

Male grizzlies generally live alone, require over 800 sq miles of territory, and live for up to 30 years. Females have one to four cubs every three years and are fiercely protective of the cubs, which stay by their mother's side for two years.

Grizzlies are most active at dawn and dusk in open meadows and grasslands near whitebark and lodgepole pines. They can become extremely agitated and aggressive if approached or surprised, but otherwise they do not normally attack humans. However, they viciously defend carcasses and can outrun a horse when provoked, thus trails are often closed when a grizzly is feeding nearby on a bison, elk or moose. For tips on what to do if you encounter a bear, see p278.

'Before hibernation, bears can eat up to 100,000 berries in a single day'

Coyotes, Foxes & Wolves

The cagey coyote (locally pronounced 'kye-oat') is actually a small opportunistic wolf species that devours anything from carrion to berries and insects. Its slender, reddish-gray form and nocturnal yelps soon become familiar to hikers. Coyotes form small packs to hunt larger prey such as elk calves or livestock, for which ranchers detest them. While wide-scale coyote eradication programs have had no lasting impact, the reintroduction of wolves (which fill a similar ecological niche) is estimated to have reduced the region's coyote population by 50%.

The small, nimble red fox grows to 3.5ft, weighs up to 15lb and has a brilliant red coat. Foxes have catlike pupils, whereas wolves and coyotes have round pupils. Foxes favor meadows and forest edges and are primarily nocturnal. Although widely distributed, the red fox is not as abundant as the coyote, perhaps because the latter is such a strong competitor.

The gray wolf (see also p105), aka timber wolf, was once the Rocky Mountains' main predator, but relentless persecution has reduced its territory to a narrow belt stretching from Canada to the northern Rockies. Its successful reintroduction continues to spark much controversy. Wolves look rather like a large, blackish German shepherd and roam in close-knit packs of five to eight animals ruled by a dominant 'alpha' male and female pair. The alpha pair are the only members of a pack to breed (normally in February), but the entire pack cares for the pups. Between four and six pups are born in April or May, and denning lasts into August.

Wolves eat meat only and, in Greater Yellowstone, tend to focus their predation on elk. Packs communicate via facial expressions, scent markings and long, mournful howls that can be heard from miles away.

Packs currently roam the Greater Yellowstone region as far afield as the Washakie Wilderness, Spanish Peaks, Beartooth Mountains, and the Teton and Gros Ventre National Forests. In Yellowstone itself packs go

ENVIRONMENT

CALL OF THE WILD

Wolves ranged widely throughout North America in pre-Columbian times. They flourished in the West until the late 19th century, when homesteaders' livestock replaced bison herds in the Great Plains ecology. Poaching and predator control greatly reduced their population in the early 1900s. The creation of the National Park Service (NPS) in 1916 paradoxically led to the wolf's extinction in the park within a few years under misguided predator-control policies that allowed big game populations to increase to unsustainable levels.

Recognizing their mistake, federal agencies worked more than 20 years on plans to reintroduce gray wolves. Ranchers were predictably suspicious, claiming that this alpha-predator would diminish game populations and that adequate compensation for wolf-killed livestock was unlikely. They also argued that wolves had already returned to the region, though some reported sightings may have been mistaken. The gray wolf, 26in to 34in high at the shoulder, 5ft to 6ft long (from nose to tail) and weighing 70lb to 120lb, is more imposing than the smaller coyote, but inexperienced viewers could easily confuse the two from a distance.

Federal wildlife managers proposed a compromise, revising the wolves' status from 'endangered' to 'threatened,' thereby granting ranchers the right to shoot wolves caught attacking livestock. In February 1995, 14 captured Canadian wolves were released into acclimation pens in Yellowstone's Lamar Valley, and more than a decade later there are 300 wolves in Yellowstone and well over a thousand in the surrounding area. Since 1995 about 1000 sheep and cattle have been reportedly killed, with many of the ranchers compensated for their losses, while at the same time 'wolf watching' has become an extremely popular activity that brings about $35 million a year into the local economy. For additional info you might consult Douglas Smith and Gary Ferguson's *Decade of the Wolf: Returning the Wild to Yellowstone* or Hank Fischer's *Wolf Wars*.

by names like Mollie (the upper Lamar Valley), Druid (Lamar Valley), Slough (the northeast corner), Leopold (southeast of Mammoth) and Cougar (the central plateau).

Ungulates

Greater Yellowstone's most abundant large mammal, elk (aka wapiti or red deer in Europe) can weigh 700lb and stand up to 5ft tall at the shoulder. Their summer coats are golden-brown, and the males (bulls) have a darker throat mane. Each year bulls grow impressive multipoint antlers (up to 5ft long, weighing up to 30lb) for the fall rut (mating season), when they round up harems of up to 60 females (hinds) and unleash resonant, bugling calls to warn off other males. Although elk populations were decimated in the 19th century, their numbers have largely recovered – beyond sustainable levels say some. Elk are cautious and elusive, and prized by trophy hunters who covet the massive rack of antlers that male elk briefly carry each fall.

Yellowstonewolves.org (www.yellowstone wolves.org) is a project that allows school children to track the activities of individual wolves or wolf packs via the internet.

Elk graze along forest edges; the largest herd in Yellowstone National Park beds down in the meadows west of Madison Campground. September to mid-October is the rutting season. Irresistibly cute calves drop in May to late June. An estimated 30,000 elk from seven to eight different herds summer in Yellowstone National Park and 17,000 in Jackson Hole. In winter, large herds migrate south to the National Elk Refuge (p243) in Jackson Hole. Winter counts of elk have dropped 50% since wolves were reintroduced, but scientists can't agree whether these declines are due to wolves, several years of drought or intense pressure from hunters.

The continent's largest land mammal, the American bison – commonly called 'buffalo' – once roamed the American West in vast numbers (60 million), often migrating to Greater Yellowstone's high plateaus during summer. Greater Yellowstone is the only region where wild bison have

ENVIRONMENT

lived since primitive times. By 1902 there were only 23 wild bison living in the Yellowstone region. The park's current population was effectively bred back from the brink of extinction. Today, numerous herds exist throughout the Greater Yellowstone Ecosystem (an increasing number on private ranches), with three distinct herds ranging in Yellowstone National Park and another in Grand Teton National Park.

A truly majestic animal, full-grown male (bull) bison may stand more than 6ft high at the shoulder, have a total length of 12ft and weigh 2000lb. Bison have a thick, shaggy light brown coat and a high, rounded back. Both sexes have short black horns that curve upward.

Despite their docile, hulking appearance and 'aloof' manner, bison are surprisingly agile. They become increasingly uneasy when approached. A raised tail indicates one of two subsequent events: a charge or discharge. Statistically speaking, bison are much more dangerous than bears. Every year several visitors are gored and seriously injured, and some are even killed.

Bison roam three main areas of Yellowstone National Park: Lamar Valley, Pelican Valley at the north end of Yellowstone Lake, and along the Mary Mountain corridor between Hayden Valley and Lower Geyser Basin beside the Firehole River. August is rutting season – keep your distance to avoid becoming an unwilling rodeo clown.

The bacterial disease brucellosis (below) is one of the ecosystem's hottest issues. Management plans call for intense monitoring of bison populations, with a goal of reducing the herd to 3000 animals and maintaining Montana's 'brucellosis class-free' status.

The largest of the world's deer species, moose typically stand up 5ft to 7ft at the shoulder, can reach 10ft in length and weigh as much as 1000lb. They have a brownish-black coat and a thick, black horselike muzzle. The male (bull) has massive, cupped antlers, each weighing up to 50lb, which are shed after the fall rut. Moose mainly browse aspen and willows, but also feed on aquatic plants. They are superb swimmers and can dive to depths of 20ft. Moose may become aggressive if cornered or defending

---

BISON & BRUCELLOSIS

A national symbol long revered by Native Americans, Yellowstone's hybrid mountain-plains bison are some of the USA's last free-roaming herds. Despite protection within national parks, their existence is threatened. Harsh winters force bison to stray north outside the parks toward Gardiner, Montana, and west toward West Yellowstone, Montana, in search of desperately needed food.

During the 1996–97 winter, Montana ranchers slaughtered more than 1100 bison (one-third of the herd) that strayed outside the park, ostensibly to prevent the spread of brucellosis, a bacterium that causes domestic cows to abort their calves. Brucellosis spreads from the region's abundant elk population to the bison, which are themselves unaffected by the bacteria. Whether or not brucellosis can actually spread from bison to cattle is questionable, as scientific studies are inconclusive. But public outrage soared upon viewing footage of the slaughter, filmed by the Missoula, Montana–based group Cold Mountain, Cold Rivers.

No policy to halt the continuing bison slaughter has been implemented, but a long-term management plan is being considered that would allow bison to move outside the park into designated safe foraging areas, limit the maximum number of bison inside the park or vaccinate bison against brucellosis. Yellowstone's bison specialists doubt that brucellosis can be eradicated, however, due to the overpopulation of elk.

Snowmobiling also affects winter bison movement and is being studied as part of the equation. For updates on this volatile issue, contact the West Yellowstone–based **Buffalo Field Campaign** (☎ 406-646-0070; www.buffalofieldcampaign.org).

calves and may strike out with powerful blows from their front hooves. An estimated 1000 moose are found in Yellowstone National Park, where they favor marshy meadows like those found in Willow Valley, just south of Mammoth Springs, or on the east side of Lamar Valley.

Arguably the animal that best symbolizes the Rocky Mountains, bighorn sheep are robust, muscular beasts, colored grayish brown with a white muzzle tip, underbelly and rump patch. Males (rams) grow up to 6ft long, stand almost 4ft at the shoulder and weigh more than 300lb. Their ideal habitat is alpine meadows or subalpine forests fringed by rocky ridges, which allow them to easily escape predators. Rams have thick, curled horns (weighing up to 40lb), which they use during the fall rut (from mid-September to late October) in fierce head-butting bouts with rivals. Discreet hikers can often closely observe bighorn herds around ridges or alpine valleys; try looking for them on rocky crags between Mammoth and Gardiner.

For Everything There Is a Season, by Frank C Craighead, is a delightful account of wildlife through the seasons by one of Yellowstone's legendary naturalists.

Introduced to Montana for sports-hunting, nonnative mountain goat expanded their range into Yellowstone in 1990, where they are raising concern that they might impact fragile mountains meadows. Surefooted and confident in even the most precipitous terrain, the mountain goat is highly adapted to the harsh environment of the upper subalpine and alpine zones. It has a shaggy, snow-white coat that includes a thin beard and narrow, almost straight, black horns. Mountain goats can reach 5ft, stand 4ft at the shoulder and weigh up to 300lb. Beware where you pee: goats crave salt and will gnaw down vegetation (and anything in their way) in order to slake their hankering.

Cats

The solitary, mostly nocturnal, bobcat is a handsome feline (a scaled-up version of the domestic tabby) with a brown-spotted, yellowish-tan coat and a cropped tail. It mainly eats birds and rodents, but when easier prey is scarce it may take small deer or pronghorn. Bobcats are thought to be widespread in the region, and it's not unusual to see one darting across a meadow or into a willow thicket. Surveys in 2001 confirmed the presence of at least one lynx in Yellowstone. This threatened cat is similar in appearance to the bobcat, but can be recognized by its entirely black tail tip.

North America's largest cat, the mountain lion (aka cougar) prefers remote, forested areas of the park. With a size and shape similar to that of a smallish (African) lioness, the mountain lion may reach 7.5ft from nose to tail and can weigh up to 170lb. Even backcountry biologists who study it rarely encounter this solitary and highly elusive creature. It typically preys on mule deer, elk and small mammals, and in summer it follows these animals as they migrate to higher ground. While curious mountain lions are known to 'stalk' people without harmful intent, they occasionally attack humans.

In 1999 a female mountain lion with three cubs set up den on Millar Butte, in full view of Elk Refuge Rd, just south of Grand Teton National Park, and stayed there for six weeks. Around 15,000 people visited the area to see the cougar family during its brief stay.

BIRDS

Boasting 316 recorded winged species (of which 148 stay to nest), Greater Yellowstone offers a delightful birdwatching experience. The American Bird Conservancy recently recognized Yellowstone National Park as a 'globally important bird area.' Noteworthy large birds include common ravens, resurgent peregrine falcons, reclusive sandhill cranes, honking

Canadian geese and American white pelicans. Smaller birds like pesky black-billed magpies and yellow-headed blackbirds are common sights.

Birds of Prey

This group of birds (aka raptors) includes eagles, falcons, hawks and harriers. Sweeping across lakes, forests or plains in search of fish or small game, they are some of the most interesting and easily watched birds in the area.

The iconic bald eagle is a large raptor, with a wingspan up to 8ft. It has brown plumage and a distinctive 'bald' white head. Bald eagle pairs mate for life, building their nest close to water. The size of the nest grows with each breeding season to become a truly massive structure up to 12ft in diameter. The bald eagle takes fish (or harasses an osprey until it drops its catch), but also preys on other birds or smaller mammals. Nesting eagles are extremely sensitive to human disturbance.

The true 'king of the Rockies,' the gracious golden eagle is sometimes spotted riding thermals high above craggy ridges. This majestic mountain bird was venerated by Native Americans, who fashioned headdresses from its golden-brown plumage. The golden eagle is marginally smaller but heavier than the bald eagle and typically nests on rocky cliff ledges that afford a bird's-eye view of potential prey and predators. The golden eagle's diet is also more varied, and it will swoop down on anything from fish and rodents to deer fawns.

The great horned owl is mottled gray-brown with prominent, 'horned' ear tufts and a white throat. It's found throughout the Rockies, although its camouflage is so effective that few hikers even notice when they pass one. Asleep during the day, it preys on nocturnal rodents but also feasts on grouse and other birds. It has a deep, resonant hooting call.

The large, black turkey vulture is a clumsy creature, but once airborne it's a superb glider with a wingspan up to 6ft. Although its featherless red face should be enough to scare animals to death, the turkey vulture prefers to scavenge already dead animals.

The fish-eating osprey haunts larger lakes and rivers, nesting in shore-line treetops. Its upper wings and body are dark brown, and its underside is white on the body and inner wings, and speckled brown-white on the outer wings. This well-adapted hunter has efficient water-shedding feathers and clamplike feet with two pairs of opposing toes to better grasp slippery, wriggling fish.

'Nesting eagles are extremely sensitive to human disturbance'

Waterfowl

A vast number of waterfowl visit the many lakes, marshes and rivers of Greater Yellowstone, while other birds like coots, cranes, gulls and some ducks stay in the area to nest.

The spectacular trumpeter swan, North America's largest wild fowl, is hardy enough to winter here, primarily in the Henry's Fork and Red Rock Lakes region west of the park. In 1932 only 69 swans remained alive in the lower 48 states, all of them in Greater Yellowstone. Since then numbers have climbed to around 2500, but their numbers are declining again. It has proven difficult to wean them from winter feeding and get them to find their own wild foods, and cantankerous Canadian trumpeter populations continue to crowd them out.

Long-legged great blue herons and red-capped sandhill cranes may be seen striding gracefully in wet meadows and along the edges of water, where they use their long bills to capture fish, snakes, frogs and rodents. In the fall and spring, cranes gather into large noisy flocks.

On larger bodies of water the common loon may be quite prevalent, and its beautiful mournful wail can be heard echoing across tranquil backcountry lakes. Up to 35in long, it has a black-green head with a speckled upper body and white underparts. The loon's dense body mass enables it to dive to depths of 150ft but also necessitates a long runway for takeoff, which limits it to larger lakes.

Smaller Birds

The boisterous Clark's nutcracker, a member of the crow family, is light gray with black wings and a white tail. It patrols subalpine forests, feeding largely on conifer nuts, which it breaks open with its long, black beak.

The diminutive mountain chickadee is a playful and gregarious year-round resident of subalpine forests. It has a black cap and throat bib, and its onomatopoeic name describes its distinctive call, 'chick-a-dee-dee.'

The red-naped sapsucker is a woodpecker species with a black back, white stripes above and below each eye, and a red chin and forehead. It bores into tree bark (preferably aspen or willow), discharging gooey sap that traps insects, both of which it devours. Despite the damage it causes to the trees, the bird's activity helps control the even more destructive bark beetle and other noxious insects.

The striking blue Steller's jay has a black crest, head and nape. Its grating 'ack-ack-ack' call is also distinctive, if less attractive. Although its diet consists of pine nuts, berries and insects, it's also an incorrigible scavenger and frequently raids camps for unattended scraps.

FISH

Yellowstone Lake is at the heart of one of North America's most significant aquatic wildernesses, which is home to 21 gilled species. There are 2650 miles of running water, with more than 220 lakes and at least a thousand streams covering 5% of the park's surface area. Fish provide critical forage for bears, waterfowl, otters and raptors throughout the ecosystem.

When Yellowstone became a national park, 40% of its waters were fishless. Introduction of nonnative species and stocking of some 310 million fish drastically altered the aquatic environment. Today 40 of the park's lakes are fishable. In 2001, National Parks Service (NPS) fishing regulations changed to require the release of all native sport fish caught in park waters. Fish-watching is an increasingly popular pastime around the outlet of Yellowstone Lake at Fishing Bridge and LeHardy's Rapids, where cutthroat trout spawn in spring.

Current major threats to Yellowstone's near-pristine aquatic ecosystem include the illegal introduction of predatory lake trout into Yellowstone Lake; increased cutthroat mortalities from parasitic whirling disease; and the invasion of New Zealand mud snails, which have been found in densities of ½ million snails per square yard and crowd out native aquatic insects.

Six nonnative species live in the Yellowstone area: tasty rainbow trout, big brown trout, diminutive brook trout, tyrannical lake trout (the biggest culprits in the decline of endangered native cutthroat), lead-colored lake chub and a cutthroat-rainbow trout hybrid.

Plants

Flora from the surrounding mountains, deserts, montane forests, arctic tundra and Great Plains all converge in Greater Yellowstone, where they are grouped into five distinct vegetation zones – riparian, foothills, montane, subalpine and alpine. Yellowstone National Park's herbarium

'Fish provide critical forage for bears, waterfowl, otters and raptors throughout the ecosystem'

has inventoried 1717 species (counting 190 nonnative species), including nonvascular plants such as mosses, fungi, liverworts and 186 species of lichen. Seven percent of these species are considered rare.

TREES

While flowers rise and fade with ephemeral beauty, trees maintain their majesty for centuries and are thus an ideal study for the budding nature enthusiast. With a few simple tips in hand, it's possible to identify prominent species and appreciate the full sweep of trees cloaking the landscape. The harsher climatic conditions at higher elevations strongly favor hardy conifers. With the exception of aspen, eight conifers dominate Greater Yellowstone's forests, which make up 60% of the region's total vegetation. Pines are especially well represented, with two-, three- and five-needle species.

In Yellowstone National Park, Douglas firs, quaking aspens, shrubs and berry bushes blanket the mixed forests from 6000 to 7000ft between Mammoth Hot Springs and Roosevelt Junction. Lodgepole pine forests, which range from 7600 to 8400ft, cover 60% of the park's broad plateaus. At elevations above 8400ft the forests are predominantly Engelmann spruces and subalpine firs, interspersed with lodgepole pines. Above the tree line (10,000ft) is alpine tundra that supports lichen, sedges, grasses and delicate wildflowers like alpine buttercup and phlox.

The beautiful quaking aspen has radiant silver-white bark and rounded leaves that 'tremble' in the mountain breezes. Aspen foliage turns a striking orange-gold for just a few weeks in fall. As a regeneration species, it tends to reproduce by sending out root runners rather than by seeding. A stand of aspen is likely to consist mainly of clones from an original parent tree.

Not a true fir at all, Douglas fir is a tall, adaptable and extremely widespread tree that ranges from the foothills to the subalpine zone and from very dry to quite moist locations. Douglas fir has flattened, irregularly arranged needles, 4in-long cones with distinctive three-toothed bracts protruding between the scales, and thick, corky bark that protects it from fire.

True firs bear a superficial resemblance to spruces, but can be easily differentiated by their flat, blunt needles and cones that point upward on their upper branches. Easily the Rockies' most abundant and widespread fir species, the subalpine fir is usually found in close association with Engelmann or blue spruce. Subalpine fir has characteristic silvery-gray bark with horizontal blister scars that often become cracked on older trees.

Lodgepole pine forests extend well into the montane zone. Many lodgepoles are dependent on periodic forest fires to melt the resins that seal their cones shut, ensuring that their seeds disperse only when fire has prepared a fertile bed of ash, while other lodgepoles disperse their seeds each fall like regular pine trees. Lodgepoles sport needles in bunches of two and straight, narrow 'polelike' trunks that make for dense stands in recently regenerated forests.

Found in subalpine zones, the five-needled whitebark pine has smallish, almost round cones that remain purple until maturity. Its seeds provide crucial autumnal forage for grizzly bears. Large individuals of this species stand near Dunraven Pass in Yellowstone and South Cascade Canyon in Grand Teton National Park.

Engelmann spruce is a towering, cold-tolerant conifer capable of withstanding winter temperatures of -50°F. It tends to dominate subalpine

Plants of Yellowstone and Grand Teton National Parks, by Richard J Shaw (Wheelwright Press, 2000), is a well-illustrated introduction to the region's rich vegetation.

ENVIRONMENT

forests. Like other spruce species, Engelmann has round, slightly pointed needles and pendant cones that hang off the branch. Its resonant wood is used to make piano sounding boards.

SHRUBS

The term 'shrub' is a somewhat arbitrary label that designates a woody plant with many stems. These small woody plants may grow as heaths, form thickets or stand as single bushes on slopes and in meadows.

Shrubby cinquefoil grows in meadows from the foothills to the tundra, sometimes in association with sagebrush. All summer long this multi-branched bush (up to 4ft high) is covered in yellow, buttercuplike flowers with five petals. Both livestock and native mammals, such as deer and bighorn sheep, browse the foliage only when no other food is available, so nibbled cinquefoil bushes are one indication of overgrazing.

Several dozen species of small willows are found in Greater Yellowstone, but their diversity makes precise taxonomical classification impossible. Willows can be identified by their distinctive fluffy, silky 'catkin' flowers, which resemble small bottlebrushes. Dwarf willows, such as the tiny arctic willow, only reach a few inches in height and creep along heat-storing alpine rocks to form 'mats.' Shrub willows, including the common gray-leafed willow, form thickets along subalpine and alpine stream basins.

The scrumptious blueberry genus includes species locally known as bilberry, cranberry, grouseberry, huckleberry and whortleberry. Almost all produce small, round fruits of bright red to deep purple that sustain bears and other wildlife throughout the Rockies. One of the most common species is the dwarf blueberry, which typically grows among lodgepole pines. Its low mats emit an enticingly fruity fragrance.

Junipers are aromatic, cedarlike conifers that generally thrive in dry, well-drained areas. Rocky Mountain juniper can approach the size of a small tree, and older shrubs (which may reach 1500 years) are typically gnarled and knotted. Birds feed on juniper 'berries,' allowing the seed to sprout by removing its fleshy covering.

Strongly aromatic sagebrush thrives on foothills and drier montane meadows. Grazing mammals shun the bitter foliage, so overgrazing tends to favor the spread of sagebrush. Hikers, on the other hand, enjoy the rich fragrance of a sagebrush meadow in the wake of afternoon thundery showers.

WILDFLOWERS

A breathtaking variety of native (and exotic) wildflowers are found throughout Greater Yellowstone. Blooms peak from June to July, although some species (like gentians) tend to be at their best in August.

There are more than a dozen species of gentian (usually pronounced 'jen-shun') in Greater Yellowstone. Most have trumpetlike flowers that are at least partially blue or purple. They tend to bloom later than most other Rockies wildflowers. Found above 10,000ft, the pretty arctic gentian has greenish-white flowers with purple stripes and prefers moist, open sites like alpine bogs.

Columbines come in variants of blue, red, white and yellow and are typically found at the edges of small, shaded clearings up to 9000ft. The especially attractive Colorado columbine has blue-white flowers with delicate long spurs, resembling a bird in flight. The nectar in the spur tips attracts butterflies and hummingbirds.

Fireweed is a perennial that grows as a single stem up to 6ft tall, crowned by clusters of pink, four-petaled flowers about an inch in

'A breath-taking variety of native (and exotic) wildflowers are found throughout Greater Yellowstone'

jumps) were the weapons of choice in the Rockies and Great Plains, respectively. Obsidian from Yellowstone (see p103) made such durable spear and arrow tips that they were traded for hundreds of miles.

Early suggestions that Native Americans were too frightened to visit the Yellowstone plateau were unfounded. The Tukudika (or Sheepeaters) – a Shoshone-Bannock people who hunted bighorn sheep in the mountains of Yellowstone – were the region's only permanent inhabitants before white settlement, though surrounding tribes such as the Crow/Absaroka (to the northeast), Shoshone (east), Bannock (south and west), Blackfeet/Siksikau (north) and Gros Ventre (south) hunted, traded and traveled seasonally through the region.

The Sheepeaters never acquired horses or iron tools and are often portrayed as a shy, simple and undeveloped people, but they were proficient tanners whose composite bows were powerful enough to send an arrow straight through a bison (it's thought the Sheepeaters made the sheep horns more pliable by soaking them in Yellowstone's boiling hot springs). The Sheepeaters, who never numbered more than about 400, spent the summers in camps of *wikiups* (teepee-like frames of leaning lodgepole branches), using dogs to transport their gear. The last of the Tukudika were hustled off the new park territory into the Wind River Reservation in the early 1870s to come under the control of the Shoshone chief Washakie.

One of the region's most extraordinary modern episodes involving Native Americans was the 1877 flight of the Nez Percé, led by Chief Joseph, who fled their ancestral lands in Oregon to escape persecution by the US Army (opposite). Today, the National Park Service recognizes formal affiliations with 25 modern tribes.

TRAPPERS, TRADERS & TOURISTS

The first Europeans to come in contact with Native Americans in Greater Yellowstone were French fur trappers from eastern Canada who encountered the Crow (who called the Yellowstone the Elk River) and Sioux in the late 1700s while exploring the upper Missouri River tributaries in search of beaver. These lonesome French-speaking trappers gave the Tetons their name – they dubbed the three most prominent peaks Les Trois Tetons for their ostensible resemblance to female breasts. (As one writer wryly noted, that's what happens when you let French fur trappers name mountains!)

The USA's Louisiana Purchase of present-day Montana, most of Wyoming, and eastern Colorado from the French in 1803 led President Thomas Jefferson to commission the famous Lewis and Clark Corps of Discovery in 1804–06. The Shoshone and Nez Percé told the expedition's

diameter. As its name suggests, fireweed is a vigorous opportunist that colonizes recently burned areas.

Succulent shoots of Indian hellebore (aka corn lily) emerge from melting snowbanks in early summer and quickly develop into proud 7ft-high stalks with large leathery leaves crowned by maizelike flower tassels. This plant, found mainly on moist subalpine slopes, contains poisonous alkaloids – Native Americans used it as an insecticide.

The delicate, yellow glacier lily (aka dogtooth violet or fawn lily) is a perennial subalpine to alpine species that thrives where winter snow lingers. In early summer the bulb produces several bright-yellow flowers with six upward-curled petals. These lilies often blanket entire tundra slopes, which bears eagerly dig up to extract the edible bulbs.

Another member of the lily family, beargrass is limited to the southern part of Yellowstone National Park and the northern reaches of the Tetons. It's a hardy perennial found in well-drained montane and subalpine clearings. Fragrant white starlike flowers cluster around a central 4ft-high stalk. The waxy, bladelike leaves are favored spring forage among grizzly bears.

The most commonly observed flower in the Tetons may be the bright red Indian paintbrush. Its complex, leaflike flower is a favorite food source for hummingbirds.

ENVIRONMENTAL ISSUES

As is often the case, environmental issues and controversies haunt even a pristine park like Yellowstone. While issues such as mining, logging, increasing development, and air pollution lurk on the horizon, other topics boil closer to the surface and sometimes erupt into full-blown battles.

Given Yellowstone's mandate to protect wildlife, it's not surprising that some of the fiercest battles are fought over questions of how to manage wildlife. The slaughter of disease-carrying bison that wander out of the park is a particularly vexing topic (see the boxed text, p73). No less troubling is the question of how to protect top-level predators like grizzly bears and gray wolves when they leave the park and run into conflict with local ranchers. The environmental values that attract visitors from all over the world are not necessarily appreciated in the same way by local folks who have to make a living from the land, and resolution is unfortunately hard to come by because both sides often overstate their cases.

An example of one highly public issue was the park's handling of wildfires that blackened 30% of the park in 1988. In 1972 the NPS decided to switch from a strategy of suppressing wildfires to a 'let-burn' policy. Small prescribed burns might have restored the natural balance over time, but several hundred lightning strikes in one day during the dry, windy summer of 1988 ignited major infernos that blazed until the first snows in September finally put them out.

The 1988 fires were more a public relations disaster than an environmental catastrophe, and the controversy turned into front-page news all across the country. Only a few large mammals, mostly elk, died. Small mammals, on the other hand, perished in large numbers because they were unable to outrun the fires and proved more vulnerable to predators in the fires' aftermath due to reduced habitat. Tourism operators in gateway communities, which suffered short-term losses from decreased visitation, unfairly criticized the essentially sound NPS policy of allowing natural fires to burn.

The Greater Yellowstone Coalition (www.greater yellowstone.org) works on behalf of every major issue affecting the Yellowstone region.

7–08	1827	1829	1834	1835–9
winter Greater the first o travel wstone	First written account of Greater Yellowstone published in a Philadelphia newspaper, detailing trapper Daniel Potts' trip along the Tetons and the shore of Yellowstone Lake	Bill Sublette names Jackson Hole ('hole' means valley) after fellow trapper David Jackson; trapper Joe Meek stumbles upon Norris Geyser Basin	Warren Ferris is the first 'tourist' to Yellowstone and the first person to use the word 'geyser' in describing Yellowstone's thermal features	Trapper Osbourne Russell travels through Yellowstone three times

To this day, one of the more troubling issues is the policy of allowing hundreds of noisy, smog-creating snowmobiles a day into the park during the winter. Out of 350,000 people who commented on this policy, 75% wanted snowmobiles out of the park entirely, and numerous environmental organizations have taken a firm stance on this issue. However, a much anticipated plan to scale back snowmobile traffic was reversed when the Bush administration changed its mind under pressure from industry groups. Because of this reversal, expect to hear the noise of snowmobiles 70% of the time if you visit popular spots in winter.

SUSTAINABILITY

When Yellowstone approached its 125th anniversary in 1997, the park began thinking about how it could best protect its features for the next 125 years. The small size of the park's infrastructure and the limited scale of its gateway communities meant it could not undertake all of the sustainable practices it wanted to. But the park still developed a plan for making Yellowstone more green. The plan includes strategies for reducing traffic congestion, promoting alternative fuels and energy sources, improvements to existing buildings, and a comprehensive recycling and waste management program.

The park's recycling seems particularly innovative. By working together with surrounding communities that don't have the resources to single-handedly start their own recycling programs, this co-op handles the recycling needs of a 35,000-sq-mile area that would otherwise have no other options but to dump waste. The park remains committed to its impressive goal of diverting 90% of all solid waste by 2008.

Although the park doesn't have shuttle buses and visitors must use their own cars to traverse the park's vast open spaces, visitors can still help out by recycling their waste and hiking or biking as much as possible.

'Visitors can still help out by recycling their waste and hiking or biking as much as possible'

History

As the world's oldest national park, Yellowstone holds a key place in both the historical development of the US National Park Service and the spread of protected wilderness areas across the globe. This is hallowed ground to both environmentalists and tourists, and the tensions between the two form the major theme of the past, present and doubtless the future of Yellowstone and Grand Teton.

FIRST PEOPLES

Recent archaeological evidence unearthed near Pinedale, Wyoming, and excavations from Osprey Beach on Yellowstone Lake (forensically dated bison blood residue from chert and obsidian projectile points) suggest that human inhabitation of the Greater Yellowstone region began soon after the Pinedale Glaciation period ended, between 12,000 and 14,000 years ago. Only a few thousand years before that, the Yellowstone region was almost completely covered in glaciers.

Archaeologists divide Greater Yellowstone's first inhabitants – ice-age hunter-gatherers who chased spectacular megafauna such as bear-sized beavers, enormous camels, gigantic moose, massive mastodons and 20ft-tall bison – into two distinct cultures, Clovis and Folsom, based on the uniquely shaped stone spearheads they fashioned.

Rising global temperatures about 9000 years ago caused rapid melting of the North American ice sheet. The combination of a warmer, drier climate and overhunting by humans triggered a collapse of the ice-age ecosystem, wiping out a majority of the large game species on which these cultures depended. Hunters continued their reliance on the modern bison, but around 5500 BC some peoples began hunting smaller game and foraging for plants.

There's little evidence that these early inhabitants were truly at home in the Rocky Mountains' high ranges – the winter was simply too harsh. Rather, tribes from the surrounding plains established summer camps in sheltered foothill valleys and made lengthy forays into the high mountain to hunt or collect food and medicinal plants.

The human presence in Greater Yellowstone increased dramatical 1500 to 2000 years ago, coinciding with a more favorable climate, resurge large mammal populations and development of the bow and arrow, whi replaced the *atlatl* (spear-thrower). Sheep traps and *pishkum* (buff

TIMELINE

9000 BC–AD 1870	early 1700s	1797	1803	180
Native American inhabitation of area now known as Greater Yellowstone	The arrival of the horse revolutionizes Native American lifestyles	French map makes first reference to the 'R. des Roches Jaunes,' or Yellow Stone River	Louisiana Purchas doubles US territo for $15 million; France cedes Gre Yellowstone to	John Colter' journey into Yellowstone, 'white man' through Yell

THE FLIGHT OF THE NEZ PERCÉ

The discovery of gold in 1877 spurred the United States government to forcibly relocate the Nez Percé (Nimi'ipuu in their language) from Oregon's Wallowa Valley. After an initial skirmish, the Nez Percé (pronounced 'Nez Purse') set off on what would become an epic 1100-mile flight from the US Army. The route of their journey is now a national historic trail. For more info see www.fs.fed.us/npnht.

By August 23, 1877, 700 of the Nez Percé (of whom only 250 were braves), led by Chief Joseph, crossed the Targhee Pass and entered Yellowstone Park along the Madison River, crossing the Firehole River at modern-day Nez Percé Creek (p156). At that time only 25 tourists were visiting the park, and the Nez Percé somehow managed to bump into all of them, taking six hostage, killing one, and releasing the others near Mud Volcano. Just before reaching Pelican Creek, a band of braves diverted General Howard's men up into the Hayden and Lamar Valleys (at one point camping at Indian Pond) while the bulk of the tribe hurried up Pelican Creek and out of the park's northeast corner. You can visit the spot of two of the group's river crossings at Nez Percé Creek (p156) and the Nez Percé Ford (p113).

In September they progressed through Crandall Creek into the Clarks Fork of the Yellowstone with US forces pressing hard on their heels, and troops led by General Sturgis blocking routes ahead. Sturgis' son had been killed by Indians the year before at the Battle of Little Bighorn, and one can only imagine that he was itching for revenge. The Percé once again pulled off a brilliant escape. A group of braves diverted Sturgis' troops while the Nez Percé slipped through the net, passing out of the valley through a gorge thought impassable by the US Army.

Believing they were in Canada, the Nez Percé slowed down just 30 tragic miles before the border, where US troops under General Nelson Miles finally caught up with them at the Battle of Bear Paw. After a 1500-mile, 3½-month chase that included four battles, the 87 men, 184 women and 47 children surrendered on October 5, 1877, with Chief Joseph's words: 'From where the sun now stands, I will fight no more forever.' It was the end of a fight they had not sought. Joseph was never allowed to return to his homeland and died in 1904, allegedly of a broken heart.

leaders about a 'thundering volcano to the south' that made the earth tremble, though the expedition only made it as far south as the lower Gallatin Valley (which they named) and the area along the Yellowstone River, east of Livingston, Montana.

As knowledge of the American West grew, so did interest in its exploitable resources. Most sought after was the beaver, whose 'plews' (pelts) were so sought after that they became known among the trappers as 'hairy dollars.' John Colter, a member of the Lewis and Clark expedition, returned to explore the Yellowstone area during the winter of 1807–08 to try his luck as a trapper. Colter headed south from the Bighorn River into the Absaroka Mountains, into Jackson Hole, over the Tetons (in winter!) and then north

1840	1864	1868	1869	1870
Last mountain man rendezvous held in Pinedale, Wyoming	Montana Territory created; gold discovery at Virginia City attracts settlers	Wyoming Territory created; its boundaries match those of the modern state of Wyoming	Folsom-Cook-Peterson month-long expedition into park takes them as far south as Shoshone Lake	Washburn-Langford-Doane expedition leads to the legend of the founding of Yellowstone National Park

past Yellowstone Lake. His epic 500-mile loop hike made him the first white man to visit the Yellowstone region, though it's not thought he saw any of the region's geysers. Colter sent reports about his extensive travels (and travails) to Missouri Territory governor William Lewis, who published a map of Colter's route in 1814. Colter lent his name to Colter's Hell, a series of thermal features along the Shoshone River outside Cody.

After the War of 1812, renewed demand for furs propelled another generation of trappers westward. Legendary 'mountain men' like Jedediah Smith, Jim Bridger, David Jackson (after whom Jackson Hole is named), William Sublette, Kit Carson, Jim Beckwourth (a free African American) and Thomas Fitzpatrick came to know the rugged Rockies' backcountry better than anyone except the Indians, with whom many of the men formed beneficial relationships, often learning the languages and taking Indian wives. Annual summer rendezvous – huge trading fairs attended by suppliers, Natives Americans and even tourists – began in 1825 at the headwaters of Wyoming's Green River. The last mountain man rendezvous was in 1840, as the fur trade hit the skids and silk hats replaced beaver as the must-have accessory of the season.

The romantic image of the mountain man, however, is an exaggeration; rather than rugged individualists selling their catch to the highest bidder, most of the trappers were salaried company men who were often advanced a year's supplies and ended the year in debt (many a mountain main blew his entire year's income on women and liquor during a two-week-long rendezvous binge). The lasting contribution of the mountain men was their local knowledge of the terrain and the opening up of the routes across the mountains, which paved the way for later immigrants and explorers. After the decline in the beaver trade, many mountain men become army or tourist guides.

OFFICIAL EXPLORATIONS

The US defeat of Mexico in the 1846–48 Mexican War yielded a bounty of new Western territory to explore. The immediate aftermath of the Civil War and ongoing Indian skirmishes further delayed government-sponsored territorial exploration. The US Corps of Topographical Engineers, guided by ex-trapper Jim Bridger, attempted to explore the Yellowstone Plateau from the south in 1860, but impassable snow-covered mountain passes put the kibosh on their journey.

In the fall of 1869 the private three-member Folsom-Cook-Peterson expedition headed south from Bozeman, Montana, for a month to explore the divide between the Gallatin and Yellowstone Rivers. They made it past the Grand Canyon and Yellowstone Lake as far south as Shoshone Lake

---

Colter's most famous exploit was when he was captured by Blackfoot, stripped naked and forced to run for his life. He managed to elude the Blackfoot by hiding in a valley and walked 300 miles back to civilization, living off berries and roots.

Osborne Russell's autobiography, *Journal of a Trapper*, offers a classic insight into the life of a trapper in the 1840s, with modern notes by former park historian Aubrey Haines. Also worth a read is *John Colter: His Years in the Rockies* by Burton Harris.

1871	1872	1877	1883	1890
Hayden expedition to Yellowstone, with photographer William H Jackson and artist Thomas Moran; James Stevenson becomes the first person to sail on Yellowstone Lake	President Ulysses S Grant signs the *Yellowstone National Park Act* on March 1; Nathanial Langford claims to have climbed Grand Teton	Philetus W Norris becomes park superintendent and builds the first roads; the Nez Percé, led by Chief Joseph, flee the US Army through Yellowstone National Park	Railroad spur line finished to Cinnibar, near north entrance of Yellowstone National Park; Great Plains bison pronounced extinct east of Continental Divide; first bicycle tour of the park	First tourist guidebook to Yellowstone published; Wyoming becomes the 44th state of the USA

and returned in fine fettle to write a popular magazine article that refueled interest in exploration among scientists and the Eastern establishment. Upon witnessing a 150ft eruption of Great Fountain Geyser in the Firehole Lake region, the team wrote: 'We could not contain our enthusiasm; with one accord we all took off our hats and yelled with all our might!'

With considerable foresight, Cook wrote: 'We knew that as soon as the wonderful character of the country was generally known outside there would be plenty of people hurrying in to get possession, unless something was done.'

Folsom, Cook and Peterson gained enough notoriety to be invited along for the landmark 1870 Washburn-Langford-Doane expedition, bankrolled primarily by the Northern Pacific Railroad, which was seeking a route across the Montana Territory and publicity to attract investors and tourists. The 19-man party, led by former Montana tax collector Nathaniel Langford and Montana Surveyor-General Henry Washburn, was given a military escort by Lt Gustavus Doane from Fort Ellis (near present-day Bozeman). They successfully traced the route of the 1869 expedition, named many thermal features (including Old Faithful) and returned to the East Coast 40 days later. They received a hero's welcome from the national media, which finally began to take seriously their reports of a landscape 'so grand as to strain conception and stagger belief.' One of Langford's lectures about Yellowstone caught the attention of Dr Ferdinand Hayden, director of the newly formed US Geological Survey (USGS). Hayden soon persuaded congress, with substantial lobbying muscle from Northern Pacific supporters, to appropriate $40,000 for the first federally funded scientific expedition to the Greater Yellowstone region.

PROSPECTING VS PROTECTION

The epic California gold rush of 1848 started a new era of Western resource extraction. After the passing of the *Homestead Act* of 1862, veins of the glittering, rich yellow metal were unearthed by prospectors all around the periphery of Greater Yellowstone: in 1863, at Alder Gulch near Virginia City, Montana, and at Crevice Creek in 1867, just beyond the future north boundary of Yellowstone National Park. The region's last significant strike occurred in 1870, at the New World Mining District near present-day Cooke City, just outside Yellowstone's northeast entrance.

In 1871 the 34-man Hayden Expedition set out from Fort Ellis with a full cavalry escort. Hayden's scientific work was fairly pedestrian, but two members of his party, landscape painter Thomas Moran and photographer William Henry Jackson, produced works of art that offered proof of the region's amazing sights and ultimately led to the designation

---

For an overview of the mountain men, try *The Mountain Men* by George Laycock, which gives individual portraits of John Colter, Jim Bridger, Jedediah Smith and others, as well as the craft of trapping.

Yellowstone Park's Heritage & Research Center (p176) in Gardiner is home to the park's archives and boasts 90,000 photographic prints and negatives, 20,000 books and 35,000 archeological artifacts. Tours are available by reservation.

1894	1902	1903	1904	1905
Lacey Act passed by congress, prohibiting hunting in Yellowstone National Park	Only 25 bison remain in Yellowstone National Park	President Theodore Roosevelt dedicates Yellowstone National Park North Entrance Arch; Northern Pacific Railroad line reaches Gardiner	Old Faithful Inn completed; Fort Yellowstone completed	Final section of the Grand Loop Rd completed, between Tower-Roosevelt and Canyon over the Dunraven Pass

of Yellowstone as a national park in 1872 – in large part because the politicians were convinced that preservation of the remote, uncivilized region would do 'no harm to the material interests of the people.' Thus began the ongoing struggle to preserve nature while maximizing the 'multiple uses' of the nation's natural resources.

You can see examples of Jackson and Moran's iconic artwork at Mammoth's Albright Visitor Center, p96.

THE NATIONAL PARK IDEA

Portrait artist George Catlin is credited with originally suggesting the idea of a 'national park' during an 1832 trip through the wild Dakota Territory. The US's first nationally protected area was created a few months later at Hot Springs, Arkansas. For decades the park service promoted the notion that the idea of a Yellowstone national park was born at Madison junction by the members of the Hayden expedition, though this has been called into question in recent years – see the boxed text, p126.

In 1872, President Ulysses S Grant signed the landmark *Yellowstone National Park Act*, setting aside 'the tract of land in the Territories of Montana and Wyoming, lying near the headwaters of the Yellowstone River,' and 'all timber, mineral deposits, natural curiosities, or wonders …in their natural condition.' The proclamation put a box on the map around what was thought to be the extent of the region's thermal areas but neglected to appropriate any management funds. The park's first superintendent, one Nathaniel Langford (he of the 1870 expedition), was unpaid and only visited the park twice in his five-year tenure! Federal legislators incorrectly assumed that leases granted to private concessionaires would produce enough revenue to sustain the park until the railroad (and mass tourism) arrived. This lack of funding led early park administrators to seek private business partners, such as the railroads, to develop infrastructure and promote tourism.

www.nps.gov/history /museum/exhibits /moran offers an online exhibition of paintings by Thomas Moran.

The most important legacy of the National Park Service (NPS) is much greater than simply preserving a unique ecosystem. That the national park and preservation idea has spread worldwide is a testament to the pioneering thinking of early US conservationists.

THE US ARMY & EARLY STEWARDSHIP

A decade of rampant squatting, wildlife poaching, wanton vandalism of thermal features and general lawlessness in Yellowstone National Park preceded an 1882 visit by Civil War hero General Philip Sheridan. Sheridan persuaded congress to appropriate $9000 to hire 10 protective assistants to aid the park's staffless superintendent. But park regulations still didn't allow for any substantial punishments beyond expelling

1908	1910–11	1915	1916	1918
Union Pacific Railroad spur line arrives in West Yellowstone; first dude ranch opens in Jackson Hole	Jackson Lake dam built for irrigation for Idaho potato farmers	First car (a Model T Ford) allowed into Yellowstone National Park; car entry fees cost the modern equivalent of $93 per vehicle	National Park Service (NPS) created under the presidency of Woodrow Wilson, after 15 national parks had already been established	National Park Service assumes management of Yellowstone from US Army, which had governed the park since 1886

trespassers. The jurisdiction of Wyoming territorial law was extended into the park in 1884, but poaching remained rampant.

After a series of political scandals in the early 1880s involving land-grab attempts by a string of shady park superintendents (widely perceived to be in the pocket of railroad interests, who wanted a monopoly on lodging and transportation in the park), Congress flatly refused to fund the park's civilian administration in 1886. Public opinion was divided as to whether the park should preserve the 'curiosities' and 'freaks and phenomena of nature' or avoid getting into 'show business' entirely. A few prominent senators even insisted that the park be returned to the public domain. With no budget forthcoming, the Secretary of the Interior had little choice but to call in the US cavalry from nearby Fort Custer to provide protection.

In the absence of park rangers, the army patrolled the park from 1886 until the handoff to the newly created NPS in 1918. At first, troops were stationed in a makeshift fort at Mammoth Hot Springs called Camp Sheridan. Construction of nearby Fort Yellowstone (present-day park headquarters) began in 1891. By the early 1900s, mounted troops were stationed year-round throughout the backcountry. Fighting fires, building roads, protecting desirable wildlife (bison and elk) from poaching and predators, entertaining visitors and preserving the park's natural features were the soldiers' primary duties. Predator control, such as poisoning coyotes, was common, but under the army's rule Yellowstone's environmental status quo was largely maintained. Of the 16 original soldier stations, three remain – at Norris (now a museum), Tower and Bechler.

By 1916 the Department of the Interior was responsible for 14 parks and 21 monuments, but lacked a centralized management structure. During its formative years, the park service in Yellowstone poisoned predators, shot wolves, stocked fisheries with nonendemic species, destroyed habitat in the name of development and arranged bear-feeding displays, all of which contributed to the development of an artificial and ultimately unsustainable ecology. Modern managers now openly admit that early efforts to exterminate predators were misguided.

> www.yellowstone-online.com/history/yhtwo.html is an online history of Yellowstone place names by Jim Macdonald.

RAILROADS, AUTOMOBILES & MASS TOURISM

The Northern Pacific Railroad arrived in Livingston, Montana, in 1883, the same year Congress allocated funds to begin construction of the Grand Loop Rd in Yellowstone National Park. A spur line was extended south from Livingston to Cinnabar, just outside the park's north entrance, and the Union Pacific completed spur lines to Cody and West Yellowstone in 1901 and 1908. These concurrent developments ushered in the era of modern mass tourism in Greater Yellowstone.

1923	1926	1929	1932	1936
Meeting at cabin of Maude Noble to try to establish Grand Teton National Park; the last gray wolf den in Yellowstone National Park is destroyed by park rangers	Rockefeller travels through the Yellowstone and Teton region, encouraged by the park superintendent	Congress creates Grand Teton National Park; the east and northwest extents of Yellowstone National Park are extended by President Hoover	Winter wildlife range near the north entrance added to Yellowstone National Park by President Hoover	Beartooth Hwy opens at cost of $2.5 million

ROCKEFELLER, ROOSEVELT & THE TETONS

Despite the precedent set by Yellowstone, transformation of the Tetons into a national park was no easy matter, as commercial ranching and hunting interests stubbornly resisted attempts to transfer private and USFS (United States Forest Service) lands to the NPS. At its creation in 1929, Grand Teton National Park included only the main part of the Teton Range and the lakes immediately below. Distressed at Jackson Hole's commercial development, John D Rockefeller Jr surreptitiously purchased more than 55 sq miles of land to donate to the park (but retained rights to all park concessions), but political bickering prevented the philanthropist's tax write-off until President Franklin D Roosevelt interceded.

Rockefeller's 32,000-acre bequest finally came under NPS jurisdiction when Roosevelt declared Jackson Hole a national monument in 1943. With post-WWII tourism booming in 1950, legislation conferred national park status and expanded the boundaries to include most of Jackson Hole. Today, the Rockefeller-owned Grand Teton Lodge Company is the park's major concessionaire, and the curious park is the only one outside Alaska that permits hunting and the only one with a commercial airport.

The railroad's grand plans to monopolize public access to the park were thwarted by lobbying efforts of politically influential hunting groups, like Theodore Roosevelt's Boone & Crockett Club, which fervently opposed the railroad's proposals for spur lines through big-game wildlife corridors and geyser basins. Ultimately, the army's construction of wagon roads and the arrival of the automobile would scuttle the railroad's bid for domination of concession and transportation interests.

National interest in wilderness recreation grew rapidly during the early decades of the 20th century, thanks largely to increased prosperity and higher automobile ownership. More than 80% of Yellowstone's 52,000 visitors in 1915 arrived via railroad. By 1940 nearly all of Yellowstone's half million visitors would enter the park in private automobiles.

In 1905, completion of the skeleton of what is known today as the Grand Loop Rd by the US Army Corps of Engineers established the blueprint of the standardized Yellowstone tourist experience. Lobbying by motoring clubs persuaded the NPS to admit automobiles in 1915. Constant clashes between cars and stagecoaches over right-of-way on the narrow one-way roads led to the banishment of horse-drawn wagons in 1916.

Establishment of the USFS and the Yellowstone Timber Reserve (part of today's Shoshone and Bridger-Teton National Forest) in 1891, Jackson's National Elk Refuge in 1912 and Grand Teton National Park in 1929 opened up Greater Yellowstone's south flank to public visitation. East Coast philanthropist John D Rockefeller's 200,000-acre land grant in

www.nps.gov/archive /yell/slidefile/index .htm is a fantastic online archive of historic and current images of the park, including some fine photos by William Henry Jackson.

1941	1943	1948	1950	1955
Last bear-feeding shows at Canyon Village in Yellowstone National Park	President Franklin Roosevelt creates Jackson Hole National Monument, with Forest Service and Rockefeller's land	Yellowstone National Park receives one million visitors in a single year for the first time	Jackson Hole National Monument becomes part of Grand Teton National Park; Mission 66 launched to radically boost the park's tourist infrastructure	Rockefeller's Grand Teton Lodge Company opens Jackson Lake Lodge

1949 added the final pieces of Grand Teton National Park and marked the tipping point in Greater Yellowstone's transition from a resource-based region to a tourist-driven economy.

Modern intensive development of a small area (about 1%) of Yellowstone National Park for tourism, however, continues to raise controversy. Fewer in-park accommodations and a significantly shorter network of roads are struggling to support bigger and bigger RVs and an ever-increasing number of visitors. The park's 370 miles of narrow roads are overcrowded, and some view the more than 2000 buildings as an artificial distraction from the park's natural splendor. The NPS sees it as meeting public demand. Historian Richard White has argued that rather than being a vestige of wild America, Yellowstone is 'a petting zoo with a highway running through it.'

Herein lies possibly the biggest challenge facing Greater Yellowstone today – is it possible for swarms of wildness- and wildlife-seekers to enjoy solitude and appreciate nature en masse?

MANAGING NATURAL RESOURCES

Beginning in 1959 with pioneering ecological studies of Yellowstone grizzly bears, the NPS emphasized scientific study of its natural resources. The landmark Leopold Report, published in 1963, suggested that 'a national park should represent a vignette of primitive America.' The report concluded that a more passive 'natural regulation' regime should replace past policies biased toward hands-on resource manipulation.

Soon after the transition to natural regulation, landmark federal environmental laws such as the *Wild & Scenic Rivers Act* (1968), *National Trails System Act* (1968), *National Environmental Policy Act* (1969), *Endangered Species Act* (1973), *Clean Water Act* (1977) and *Clean Air Act* (1977) all reflected the nation's growing environmental awareness. In 1976 Yellowstone became a UN biosphere reserve, and in 1978 it was designated a World Heritage Site.

Yellowstone's most famous recent event was the summer fire season of 1988, when one-third of the park went up in smoke as 25 fires raged through the park for 3½ months. Over 25,000 firefighters were drafted in to battle the flames at a cost of $120 million as TV anchors proclaimed the death of Yellowstone National Park. The event cast a critical spotlight on the park service's policy of letting natural fires burn. Twenty years on, a mosaic of meadows and new-growth forest has rejuvenated the park. Regardless of our instinctive desire to protect the park, fire is in fact essential to replenish the poor soils of the Yellowstone plateau, and Yellowstone is a healthier place for it.

Read up on Yellowstone's history at www.nps.gov /history/history/online _books/haines1, which features the online text of *Yellowstone National Park: Its Exploration and Establishment* by Aubrey L Haines.

1959	1963	1967	1970	1972
Huge 7.5-scale earthquake hits the Hebgen region, creating Earthquake Lake and causing the eruptions of several Yellowstone geysers	First snowmobiles enter Yellowstone National Park	NPS turns to 'natural management' of Greater Yellowstone wildlife	New bear management plan; last of the bear-feeding garbage dumps closed	50-millionth visitor to Yellowstone National Park in first century of the park – the next 50 million arrive by 1992; John D Rockefeller Jr Memorial Parkway is established, linking the two parks

MILLION-DOLLAR MICROBES

In 1966 microbiologist Dr Thomas Brock isolated a unique enzyme in a thermophilic micro-organism called *Thermus aquaticus*, or 'Taq,' which he extracted from the 158°F+ Mushroom Pool in Yellowstone's Lower Geyser Basin. Coupled with the perfection of the polymerase chain reaction (PCR) process, Brock's discovery ultimately facilitated the replication of DNA for finger-printing and genetic engineering, and sparked an ongoing debate about 'bioprospecting' and the commercialization of public domain resources.

The NPS continues to issue around 50 free research permits per year to scientists studying microbes. 'Extremeophiles' harvested for free have generated hundreds of millions of dollars of revenue for patent holders. The Taq enzyme alone generates over $100 million a year. Until recently, no legal mechanism existed for the NPS to receive royalty payments for such scientific discoveries, but in 1997 a California-based biotechnology corporation called Diversa signed the first benefits-sharing agreement with the NPS, which ensures that a portion of future profits from research in the park will go toward resource preservation.

Not all research efforts are strictly commercial. For example, the National Aeronautic and Space Administration (NASA) is studying the biogeochemical signature of cyanobacteria found around hot springs using spectral satellite imaging. The hope is to match this signature with a similar signature on Mars, which would help to decide where to land on the red planet when attempting to confirm the existence of ancient volcanoes and hot springs.

Other startling discoveries include the DNA sequencing analysis of an organism found in a hot spring in the Hayden Valley. This revealed what is considered to be the living entity most closely related to the primordial origin of life.

Researchers estimate there are at least 18,000 active thermal features in YNP, and that as many as 99% of species present in Yellowstone's extreme environments have yet to be identified. And with more thermophiles estimated to live in one square inch of a hot spring than the number of people living on earth, there's plenty of room for research.

For Teton history, the park website www.nps.gov/history/history/online_books/grte2/hrs.htm offers the online text of the book *A Place Called Jackson Hole*.

Apart from fire management, other current resource management flashpoints include: the ongoing bioprospecting debate triggered by the biologically (and financially) significant 1966 discovery of the *Thermus aquaticus* microbe in a Yellowstone hot spring (above); questions about overgrazing by ungulates on the Northern Range; ongoing bear management experiments with the recently delisted grizzly population; the threat of mining and hydrothermal energy development adjacent to Yellowstone; controversies surrounding management and hazing of the park's bison herd (p73); and heated debates about the appropriateness and ecological impact of winter snowmobile use. Born out of the contradictions inherent in its mandate of both preservation and utilization, Yellowstone's controversies are likely to twist and turn for some time to come.

1988	**1992**	**1993**	**1995**	**2007**
Much-publicized wildfires sweep through the Greater Yellowstone region, burning one-third of the park; entire park closed on August 20 for first time in history	Winter visitation of Yellowstone National Park exceeds 140,000	Over 100 million people have by this time visited Yellowstone National Park	Gray wolf reintroduced to Yellowstone National Park; Yellowstone joins the list of World Heritage Sites in danger	Grizzly bear delisted from endangered species list, giving control over numbers to state not federal authorities and opening up the possibility of hunting

Yellowstone National Park

Yellowstone National Park is the crown jewel of the Greater Yellowstone Ecosystem and the destination of nearly every visitor to the region. More than three million people a year are drawn to its fantastic geysers, waterfalls, canyons, wildlife and lakes. A journey to the park isn't just a vacation – it's a modern pilgrimage to one of America's most admirable and enduring national landmarks.

Yellowstone offers several distinct regions, and it's worth investing time to visit at least a couple to get a feel for the park's diversity. The two greatest draws are the Grand Canyon of the Yellowstone and the geysers around Old Faithful, followed by the geothermal terraces at Mammoth, the vast Yellowstone Lake and the wildlife-rich Lamar Valley.

Your interests will dictate how you spend your time in the park. All areas offer superb fishing, hiking and wildlife-watching. Whichever you choose, reserve a little free time. The crowds and traffic will seem twice as bad if you're in a rush, and you'll appreciate the extra time if you have a surprise encounter with a moose or bison.

Yellowstone's spectacular roadside sights are reward enough, but your fondest memories may well be the precious moments of calm and beauty at the beginning and end of each day. From geysers and gorges to golden lakeshore sunsets or dawn mists rising over a steaming geyser basin, Yellowstone's beauty is both spectacular and subtle.

HIGHLIGHTS

- Feeling the tension build as you wait for an eruption of **Old Faithful** (p121) – not the biggest or most frequent, but easily the most iconic geyser in the park
- Finding a private spot to contemplate the gigantic scale of the **Grand Canyon of the Yellowstone** (p107) and its thundering Lower Falls
- Marveling at the ethereal floating rainbow colors of **Grand Prismatic Spring** (p124), Yellowstone's most beautiful thermal feature
- Wandering the colorful travertine mounds of the Lower Terrace and watching elk wander among the historic buildings in **Mammoth** (p99)
- Feeling the hair stand up on the back of your neck as you spot your first wild wolf or grizzly in the **Lamar Valley** (p105)
- Sniffing the sulfur dioxide and feeling the ground beneath you bubble and pulsate on a boardwalk tour of **Norris Geyser Basin** (p117), home to the world's tallest geyser, Steamboat

FAST FACTS

- **Area** 3472 sq miles
- **Highest elevation** 11,358ft
- **Average high/low January temperature** 29/9°F
- **Average high/low July temperature** 80/40°F

When You Arrive

When the park is open (early May to early November and late December to mid-March), all park entrances are open 24 hours daily. Entry reservations are not necessary, but a park entrance permit is.

Entry permits, available at all five park entrance stations (credit cards accepted) and valid for seven days for both Yellowstone and Grand Teton National Parks, cost $25 per private (noncommercial) vehicle, $20 per motorcycle/snowmobile and $12 per person for individuals entering by bicycle or on skis or foot. Keep the entrance fee receipt for reentry to the park. An annual Yellowstone and Grand Teton National Parks pass costs $50. For more details on park passes see p27.

Park admission is free on August 25, the anniversary of the founding of the National Park Service (NPS).

Upon entry, visitors receive a free map and copy of the park's seasonal newspaper, *Yellowstone Today,* which has a useful orientation map and schedule of ranger-led activities, special events, opening hours and educational activities.

Orientation

Seven distinct regions comprise the 3472-sq-mile park (starting clockwise from the north): Mammoth, Roosevelt, Canyon, Lake and Geyser Countries; the Norris area; and remote Bechler region in the extreme southwest corner.

A clockwise drive from the North Entrance begins at Mammoth Hot Springs in the dry, low-elevation northwest corner of the park. East of here is Tower-Roosevelt Junction. Further east is Roosevelt Country, the wildest part of the park accessible by road and home to wolves and bison in the Lamar Valley. From Tower-Roosevelt Junc-

tion the mountain highway heads south past Mt Washburn (10,243ft) and over Dunraven Pass (8859ft) to Canyon Junction, offering awesome views of the Absaroka (pronounced 'Ab-sor-kee') Range.

Continue south along the Yellowstone River through wildlife-rich Hayden Valley to Fishing Bridge Junction (7792ft). This is Lake Country, beloved by grizzlies and dominated by the liquid wilderness of Yellowstone Lake.

The Grand Loop Rd skirts the lake's northwest shore to West Thumb Junction, then heads west over the Continental Divide at Craig Pass (8262ft) to Old Faithful in the heart of Geyser Country, home to the park's richest collection of geothermal features. South of here is remote Shoshone Lake.

Turning north from Old Faithful, the Grand Loop Rd follows the Firehole River past several beautiful geyser basins to Madison Junction (6806ft) and the popular fly-fishing stretches of the Madison and Gibbon Rivers. From here a road leads west out of the park to the gateway town of West Yellowstone. The Grand Loop Rd continues northeast up the Gibbon River canyon to Norris Junction, home to the park's second most impressive collection of geysers. From here the road heads past views of the dry Gallatin Range back to Mammoth Hot Springs.

The Bechler region, in the far southwest, is only accessible by road from Ashton, Idaho, from the John D Rockefeller Jr Memorial Parkway, or by a four-day hike from the Old Faithful region.

GETTING AWAY FROM IT ALL

Shhh...don't tell anyone about these five seldom-visited Yellowstone sights:

Bechler region (p143) The bone-crushing drive deters most visitors from this lush wilderness area, home to dozens of waterfalls.

Fossil Forest Hike (p137) An unmarked turnoff and path leads up to fine views and several petrified tree stumps.

Imperial Geyser (p130) Lose the crowds just 10 minutes past popular Fairy Falls.

Pocket Basin (p126) Lose the boardwalks in this collection of off-trail hot springs and mud pots.

Upper Geyser Basin (p121) Geyser eruptions seem even eerier during a full moon.

YELLOWSTONE IN ONE DAY, TWO DAYS OR FOUR DAYS

If we've been unable to persuade you to stay in Yellowstone for longer than 12 hours, check out the two Yellowstone in a Day itineraries starting p31. You'll need to start out early and stay out late. For a two-day trip combine the northern and southern loop options to take in most of the park's roadside highlights.

If you have four days in the park, throw in some wildlife viewing in the Lamar or Hayden Valleys (p105 and p111), preferably first thing in the morning or just before dusk, and make at least one hike, perhaps the Yellowstone River Picnic Area (p128), Beaver Ponds (p133) or Mt Washburn (p138) trails. The weeklong Billings to Livingston Trail (p34) and Yellowstone & Grand Teton (p35) itineraries both spend around four days in the park, so pick and mix some sights from those. Figure on one day in Mammoth and Roosevelt countries, a day seeing the sights of Canyon and Norris Geyser Basin, a full day in Geyser Country, and a day hiking and then getting out of the park.

ENTRANCE STATIONS

The park has five entrance stations. The historic arched North Entrance Station (5314ft), on US 89 near Gardiner, Montana, is the only one open year-round. The other four are typically open from mid-April or early May to late October, weather permitting. They are the Northeast Entrance (7365ft), on US 212 near Cooke City, Montana; the East Entrance (6951ft), on US 14/16/20 at the head of the Wapiti Valley; the South Entrance (6886ft), on US 89/191/287 north of Grand Teton National Park; and the West Entrance (6667ft), on US 20/191/287 near West Yellowstone, Montana. Notice boards at entrances indicate which campgrounds are full or closed. See p25 for opening dates.

MAJOR ROADS

Conceived by Lt Daniel C Kingman in 1886 and named by writer Harry W Frantz in 1923, the 142-mile, figure-eight Grand Loop Rd passes most of the park's major attractions. The 12-mile Norris–Canyon road links Norris and Canyon Junctions, dividing the Grand Loop Rd into two shorter loops: the 96-mile Lower (South) Loop and the 70-mile Upper (North) Loop.

Information

BOOKSTORES

The nonprofit Yellowstone Association operates **bookstores** (www.yellowstoneassociation.org) at the park's visitor centers and information stations, and at Norris Geyser Basin. Hiking maps and guidebooks are usually available. Members get a 15% discount.

The park produces a series of informative pamphlets (50¢) on Yellowstone's main attractions; these are available at visitor centers and in weatherproof boxes at the sites.

MEDICAL SERVICES

There are clinics at Mammoth, Old Faithful and Lake Village – see p277.

MONEY

There are 24-hour ATMs at Canyon Lodge, Canyon General Store, Fishing Bridge General Store, Grant Village General Store, Lake Yellowstone Hotel, Old Faithful Inn, Old Faithful General Store, Old Faithful Snow Lodge, Mammoth General Store and Mammoth Hotel.

POST OFFICES

The only year-round post office is at Mammoth. Seasonal post offices operate at Canyon, Lake Village, Grant Village and Old Faithful.

SHOWERS & LAUNDRY

Canyon Village, Fishing Bridge RV Park and Grant Village provide laundry and showers. Old Faithful Lodge, Mammoth Hot Springs Hotel and Roosevelt Lodge offer showers only; and Lake Lodge and Old Faithful Snow Lodge have laundry only. All facilities close in winter. Showers cost $3.25, plus $1 for a towel.

VISITOR CENTERS & RANGER STATIONS

Yellowstone's visitor centers and information stations are usually open 9am to 6pm, with extended hours from 8am to 7pm in summer. Most are closed or open reduced hours Labor Day to Memorial Day; the Albright Visitor Center in Mammoth is open

Yellowstone National Park

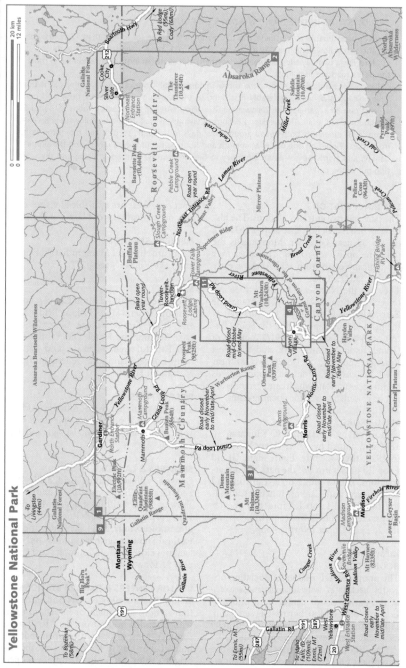

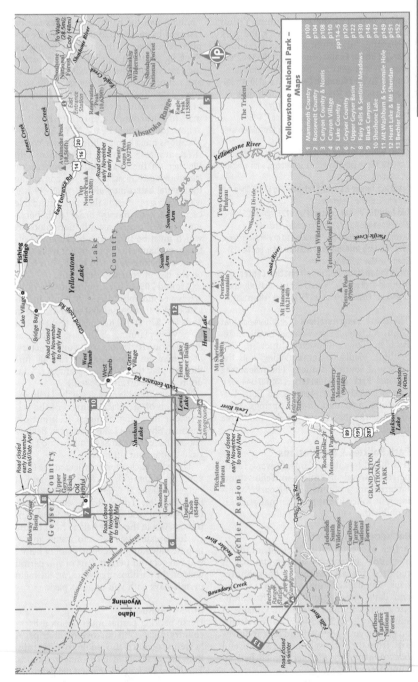

Yellowstone National Park – Maps

1	Mammoth Country	p100
2	Roosevelt Country	p104
3	Canyon Country & Norris	p108
4	Canyon Village	p110
5	Lake Country	pp114–5
6	Geyser Country	p120
7	Upper Geyser Basin	p122
8	Fairy Falls & Sentinel Meadows	p130
9	Black Canyon	p145
10	Shoshone Lake	p147
11	Mt Washburn & Sevenmile Hole	p149
12	Heart Lake & Mt Sheridan	p151
13	Bechler River	p152

year-round, and the Old Faithful Visitor Center is open in winter. Check the park newspaper for current hours of operation.

Albright Visitor Center (Map p100; ☎ 307-344-2263) Open year-round, with videos and displays on park history.

Canyon Visitor Education Center (Map p110; ☎ 307-242-2550) Open late May to mid-October, with a backcountry office. Displays Yellowstone geology.

Fishing Bridge Visitor Center (Map pp114-15; ☎ 307-242-2450) Open late May to late September, with bird exhibits.

Grant Village Visitor Center (Map pp114-15; ☎ 307-242-2650) Open late May to late September, with exhibits on wildfires.

Madison Junior Ranger Station (Map p120) Open early June to late September.

Old Faithful Visitor Center (Map p122; ☎ 307-545-2750) Open late April to early November, and mid-December to mid-March, with videos and geyser predictions.

West Thumb Information Station (Map pp114–15) Open late May to late September.

West Yellowstone Visitor Information Center Open mid-April to early Nov, mid-Dec to mid-March, in the Chamber of Commerce (Map p172) in West Yellowstone.

There are **ranger stations** (🕑 8:30am-5pm) at Grant Village, Lake Village, Lewis Lake, Bechler, Tower-Roosevelt Junction, Old Faithful, Madison, Lamar Valley, and the West and South Entrances. The **Yellowstone National Park headquarters** (☎ 307-344-7381; www.nps.gov/yell; 🕑 9am-6pm) is at Fort Yellowstone in Mammoth Hot Springs. Most of the park's brochures are downloadable from its website.

Park Policies & Regulations

It is illegal to collect plants, flowers, rocks, petrified wood or antlers in Yellowstone. Firearms are prohibited in the park. Swimming in water of entirely thermal origin is prohibited.

BACKCOUNTRY PERMITS

A free backcountry-use permit, available at visitor centers and ranger stations, is required for all overnight backcountry trips. The backcountry-use permit is site- and date- specific and states the campsite where you must overnight. Outside of summer call ☎ 307-344-7381 for details on getting your permit. Send for (or download from the park website) the very useful *Backcountry Trip Planner*, which lists all campsites.

About half the backcountry sites can be reserved by mail; a $20 reservation fee applies regardless of the number of nights. Booking starts on April 1, when all existing reservations are dealt with at random, and continues up to 48 hours before your start date. Reservations can be made in person at a ranger center or through the mail to Backcountry Office, PO Box 168, Yellowstone National Park, WY 82190. Applications must be on a Trip Planner Worksheet, available with the Backcountry Trip Planner on the **NPS website** (www.nps.gov/yell/planyourvisit/publications.htm) or by contacting the **central backcountry office** (☎ 307-344-2160; yell_bco@nps.gov). Send the nonrefundable cash, check or money order with booking. You will receive a confirmation notice, which must be taken to a backcountry office to exchange for a permit not more than 48 hours before your trip but before 10am on the day of your trip departure.

Around 20% of backcountry-use permits are issued no more than 48 hours in advance on a first come, first served, walk-in basis (no $20 fee). This means that you can leave your planning to the last minute, as long as you are flexible with your itinerary. (You may, for example, have to walk further one day than you had planned if your desired site is already booked.)

The most popular areas are the Hellroaring region of the Black Canyon of the Yellowstone in spring, Slough Creek in early summer, Shoshone Lake in August, Bechler region in August and September, and Heart Lake throughout summer.

There are backcountry offices at the Canyon and Mammoth visitor centers and at ranger stations at Grant Village, Lake Village, Bechler, Tower-Roosevelt Junction, Old Faithful, and the West and South Entrances. Get to the office half an hour before closing because you have to watch an 18-minute video on backcountry safety before you can get your permit. Part of you permit goes on the dashboard of your car; the main permit stays with you on your pack.

HORSE PACKING

Horse-packing parties must obtain a backcountry-use permit for overnight trips. A horse-use permit is also required for day trips. Both are available at most ranger stations. The *Horse Packing in Yellowstone* pamphlet lists regulations. Pack animals include horses, burros, mules, ponies and llamas.

Some backcountry trails are closed to stock, and those that are open may be temporarily closed in spring and early summer due to wet conditions. Overnight pack trips are not allowed until July 1. Stock can only be kept at designated campsites. Hay is not permitted at the trailhead or in the backcountry.

FISHING

Yellowstone's 634 lakes and ponds constitute one of the most significant aquatic ecosystems in the United States. Anglers come from all over to spend afternoons casting in golden sunlight for cutthroat trout, grayling and mountain whitefish. These species, among 11 that are native to the park, are catch-and-release only. Some areas (such as the Gibbon River below Gibbon Falls) are open to fly-fishing only. Lead weights are prohibited; only nontoxic alternatives are sanctioned.

The useful *Fishing Regulations* pamphlet details the park's complex rules and regulations. Fishing season usually runs from the Saturday of Memorial Day weekend to the first Sunday in November, except for streams that flow into Yellowstone Lake and some tributaries of the Yellowstone River, which open July 15. Other rivers are permanently closed to fishing, including a 6-mile stretch of the Yellowstone River in the Hayden Valley; some may close during the season due to bear activity.

A Yellowstone Park (not a Wyoming state) fishing permit is required for anglers aged 16 and older. These cost $15 for three days, $20 for seven days or $35 for the season; nonfee permits are required for unsupervised anglers aged 15 and under. Permits are available from ranger stations, visitor centers and Yellowstone general stores. A boating permit is required for float tubes, which are allowed only on the Lewis River between Lewis and Shoshone Lakes.

BOATING

Boating is permitted May 1 to November 1, although some areas may close during the season. Motorized vessels are allowed only on Lewis Lake and parts of Yellowstone Lake. Sylvan, Eleanor and Twin Lakes, plus Beach Springs Lagoon, are closed to boating. All streams in the park and the Yellowstone River are also closed to boating, except on the Lewis River between Lewis and Shoshone Lakes, where hand-propelled vessels are allowed. Launching is permitted only at Bridge Bay, Grant Village (open mid-June) and Lewis Lake. Hand-carried vessels may launch at Sedge Bay. Study the *Boating Regulations* pamphlet before embarking.

A boating permit is required for all vessels, including float tubes. Permits for motorized vessels cost $10 per week or $20 per year and are available from Canyon Visitor Center, Bridge Bay Marina, Grant Village Visitor Center, Lake Village Ranger Station, Lewis Lake Ranger Station and the South Entrance. Permits for nonmotorized vessels cost $5 per week or $10 per year and are available from the above-mentioned offices, as well as the Albright and Mammoth Visitor Centers, Old Faithful Backcountry Office, Northeast Entrance and Bechler Ranger Station.

Unpredictable weather and high wind on Yellowstone Lake's open water can easily capsize a small vessel. Be cautious and

---

REELING IN AQUATIC INVADERS: LAKE TROUT

Lake (or Mackinaw) trout were introduced to Yellowstone Lake illegally (although the park itself had stocked Lewis and Shoshone Lakes with them earlier). Since they have no natural predators, their Pac-Man-like presence has wreaked havoc on native cutthroat trout. In a year, one lake trout can eat 41 cutthroats, sushi dinners normally destined for feeding grizzlies and bald eagles. If the trend continues, the native trout population may fall to 10% of historic highs and affect the overall ecological balance.

With a fishing rod and free time you could help redress the situation. Regulations encourage anglers to catch lake trout. The **Volunteer Fly Fishing Program** (www.nps.gov/yell/naturescience /vol_fishing.htm) puts anglers on the park's 2650 miles of streams and 150 lakes to help collect biological data through catch-and-release techniques.

remember that hypothermia sets in quickly in these 45°F waters. The best place for information is the Backcountry Ranger Station by the Conoco at Grant Village.

Unlike Grand Teton, waterskiing and jet skis are prohibited in Yellowstone. Personal flotation devices (PFDs) are required for all craft.

For information on guided trips, rentals and regulations, see p157.

Dangers & Annoyances

Yellowstone is grizzly country. Bears that associate humans with food quickly become a problem, a danger and then a target, so keep all your food packed away in campgrounds or strung up on a bear pole in the backcountry – see p278 for more on bears and p46 for advice on hiking safely.

For all the focus on grizzlies, more people are injured by park bison (and even moose) each year than bears. The golden rule is to keep your distance – 100 yards from bears and 25 yards from anything taller than a chipmunk.

The other main wildlife-related danger comes from slamming into the car in front of you while staring at a photogenic herd of roadside elk. Exercise caution whenever the desire to rubberneck becomes irresistible, and if you must stop, make sure you pull completely off the road (see p283).

Theft from trailhead parking lots is not common but it's not unheard of. Always lock your car and keep valuables out of sight.

Getting Around

Unless you're part of a guided bus tour, the only way to get around is to drive. There is no public transportation within Yellowstone National Park, except for a few ski-drop services during winter.

DRIVING

The speed limit in most of the park is 45mph, dropping to 25mph at busy turnouts or junctions. In the words of writer Tim Cahill, anything faster than this is 'both illegal and silly.'

Gas and diesel are available at most junctions. Stations at Old Faithful and Canyon are open whenever the park is open to vehicles. The Roosevelt station closes at the beginning of September, Fishing Bridge in mid-September, Grant Village in late Sep-

tember and Mammoth in early October. Stations are manned from around 8am to 7pm and offer 24-hour credit-card service at the pump.

Towing and repair services and basic car parts are available at Conoco stations at **Old Faithful** (mid-April to early November), **Grant Village** (late May to mid-September), **Fishing Bridge** (late May to early September) and **Canyon** (☎ breakdown service 307-242-7644; ☺ May–early Oct).

Dial ☎ 307-344-2114 to check road and weather conditions prior to your visit, as road construction, rock or mudslides, and snow can close park entrances and roads at any time. See the Planning chapter p25 for details on road opening and closing schedules.

ORGANIZED TOURS

Xanterra (☎ 307-344-7311; www.travelyellowstone.com) runs a slew of daily tours, all of which offer discounts for children aged 12 to 16 and are free for kids under 12. The ambitious eight-hour **Yellowstone in a Day** (☺ Jun–late Sep) departs from Gardiner (adult/child 12–16 $62/31) or Mammoth Hot Springs ($60/30).

The similar length **Circle of Fire** ($55/27.50; ☺ mid-May–mid-Oct) departs Old Faithful Inn, Grant Village, Lake Yellowstone Hotel, Fishing Bridge RV Park, Canyon Lodge and Bridge Bay Campground and takes in the lower loop, including the geyser basins and Canyon.

The half-day **Washburn Expedition** (☺ Jun–early Oct) departs Bridge Bay Campground, Lake Yellowstone Hotel and Fishing Bridge RV Park ($34/16) or Canyon Lodge ($28/16) and takes in the upper loop, including Mammoth and Norris.

Less grueling three- to four-hour **Lamar Valley wildlife excursions** (from Canyon $43/21.50, from other destinations $36/18; ☺ mid-Jun–mid-Aug) depart at about 4pm from four locations (Bridge Bay Campground, Lake Yellowstone Hotel, Fishing Bridge RV Park and Canyon Lodge).

Daily two-hour **sunset tours** ($30/15; ☺ mid-Jun–mid-Sep) run from Lake Yellowstone Hotel and Fishing Bridge RV Park along Lake Yellowstone's north shore to the Lake Butte Overlook. Early morning **photo safaris** ($58) depart daily from Lake Yellowstone Hotel, Old Faithful Inn or Mammoth Hotel.

There are dozens of other tours, ranging from daily tours of the Tetons and weekend excursions to the Beartooth Mountains to hour-long local tours that don't require reservations. Most of these tours are on the wonderful Old Yellow Buses, a refurbished fleet of classic convertible 19-seater touring cars that plied the park's roads between 1936 and 1956, only to return to the park in 2007. They are guaranteed to add a touch of class to your sightseeing. See the Things to Do section of www.travelyellowstone.com for details on all Xanterra tours.

SIGHTS

MAMMOTH COUNTRY

Mammoth Country is renowned for its graceful geothermal terraces and the towering Gallatin Range to the northwest. As the lowest and driest region of the park, it's also the warmest and a major base for winter and early- or late-season activities.

The region's Northern Range is an important wintering area for wildlife, including the park's largest herds of elk,

---

BEST PLACES TO SPOT WILDLIFE

■ Lamar Valley (p105) in Roosevelt Country, the 'American Serengeti,' for wolves, bison and trumpeter swans; Antelope Creek (p107) for grizzlies

■ Mammoth Country elk trimming the lawns at Mammoth (right), wildfowl at Blacktail Ponds (p102) and moose at Willow Park (p103) and Glen Creek (p135)

■ Lake Country birdlife at Sedge Bay (p116); bison, moose, marmots and waterfowl at Storm Point (p116); springtime grizzlies at Pelican Creek (p140)

■ Norris Elk Park (p118) for, well, elk, as well as bison

■ Hayden Valley (p111) in Canyon Country for bison, coyotes and bears; ospreys in the canyon; south of Mud Volcano (p112) for bison

■ Mt Washburn (p138) for bighorn sheep, black bears and grizzlies

■ Fountain Paint Pot (p125) in Geyser Country for bison

---

pronghorn, mule deer and bighorn sheep. Some 15,000 elk – around half the park's population – winter here, attracted by the lower temperatures and lack of snow on many south-facing slopes (due to the sun and prevailing wind). The poorly aerated and drained soil supports scant vegetation, creating 'dry desert' conditions and raising concerns about whether the land can support the elk population.

ORIENTATION

For visitors (and most elk) the focal point of the Mammoth region is Mammoth Junction, 5 miles south of the park entrance, which contains the region's main services, including food, accommodation, gas and a general store. Showers are available in the Mammoth Hot Springs Hotel from 7am to 10pm. Just south of the junction is Mammoth Hot Springs, the area's main thermal attraction. From here roads go south to Norris (21 miles) and east to Tower-Roosevelt Junction (18 miles).

Mammoth

Mammoth Junction (6239ft) is on a plateau above Mammoth Campground. Attached to the campus-like historic and administrative heart of the park is the Albright Visitor Center. (Horace Albright was park superintendent between 1919 and 1929 and director of the National Park Service from 1929 to 1933.) Elk regularly graze the manicured lawns, bringing traffic to a standstill, and the high-pitched cries of bugling elk echo around the region in fall.

FORT YELLOWSTONE

Mammoth Hot Springs was known as Fort Yellowstone from 1886 to 1918, when the US Army managed the park. The **Mammoth Visitor Center Museum** (☎ 307-344-2263) in the Albright Visitor Center was formerly the army's bachelor quarters, but now features reproductions of 19th-century watercolors by Thomas Moran (1837–1926) and B&W photographs by William Henry Jackson, both of whom accompanied the 1871 Hayden expedition. There are also displays on the park's early visitors, lots of stuffed animals and two 20-minute videos on the parks, starting on the hour and half-hour. Don't miss the fine photographs of former superintendent Norris in his trademark

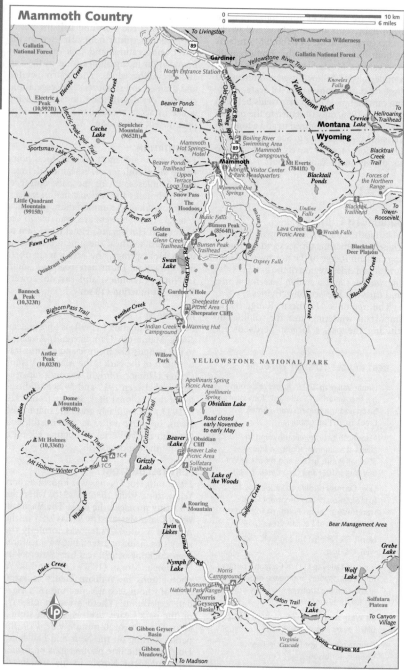

Mammoth Country

0 — 10 km
0 — 6 miles

Gallatin National Forest

To Livingston

89

Gardiner

North Entrance Station

North Absaroka Wilderness

Gallatin National Forest

Yellowstone River Trail

Knowles Falls

To Hellroaring Trailhead

Electric Creek

Reese Creek

Beaver Ponds Trail

Old Gardiner Rd

North Entrance Rd

Yellowstone River

Crevice Lake

Montana

Wyoming

Electric Peak (10,992ft)

Electric Peak Spur Trail

Cache Lake

Sepulcher Mountain (9652ft)

Boiling River Swimming Area

Mammoth Hot Springs Hotel

89

Mammoth Campground

Rescue Creek

Mt Everts (7841ft)

Blacktrail Ponds

Blacktrail Creek Trail

Sportsman Lake Trail

Gardner River Trail

Beaver Ponds Trailhead

Mammoth

Albright Visitor Center & Park Headquarters

Forces of the Northern Range

To Tower-Roosevelt

Little Quadrant Mountain (9915ft)

Upper Terrace Loop Trail

Snow Pass

The Hoodoos

Mammoth Hot Springs

Undine Falls

Blacktrail Trailhead

Fawn Pass Trail

Rustic Falls

Bunsen Peak (8564ft)

Lava Creek Picnic Area

Wraith Falls

Blacktrail Deer Plateau

Fawn Creek

Quadrant Mountain

Golden Gate

Glenn Creek Trailhead

Bunsen Peak Trailhead

Sheepeater Canyon

Osprey Falls

Lupine Creek

Blacktrail Deer Creek

Bannock Peak (10,323ft)

Bighorn Pass Trail

Gardner River

Swan Lake

Grand Loop Rd

Gardner's Hole

Sheepeater Cliffs Picnic Area

Sheepeater Cliffs

Lava Creek

Panther Creek

Antler Peak (10,023ft)

Indian Creek Campground

Warming Hut

Willow Park

YELLOWSTONE NATIONAL PARK

Indian Creek

Dome Mountain (9894ft)

Apollinaris Spring Picnic Area

Apollinaris Spring

Obsidian Lake

Trilobite Lake Trail

Grizzly Lake Trail

Road closed early November to early May

Mt Holmes (10,336ft)

Beaver Lake

Obsidian Cliff

Beaver Lake Picnic Area

Mt Holmes-Winter Creek Trail

1C4

1C5

Grizzly Lake

Solfatara Trailhead

Lake of the Woods

Solfatara Creek

Winter Creek

Roaring Mountain

Bear Management Area

Grebe Lake

Duck Creek

Twin Lakes

Grand Loop Rd

Nymph Lake

Norris Campground

Museum of the National Park Ranger

Wolf Lake

Solfatara Plateau

Howard Eaton Trail

Ice Lake

Norris Geyser Basin

To Canyon Village

Gibbon Geyser Basin

Virginia Cascade

Norris Canyon Rd

Gibbon Meadows

To Madison

buckskins and mountain man Jim Bridger bearing an uncanny resemblance to country singer Willie Nelson.

If you're particularly interested in park history, pick up the *Fort Yellowstone Historic District Tour Guide* brochure (50¢) for a self-guided tour of the fort's original buildings. The tour takes in the former jail, barracks, granary and stables, most of which have been converted to employee residences. If you are here on a Sunday morning, pop into the lovely English-style church (1913), whose stained-glass windows depict Old Faithful and Yellowstone Falls. You can even get married here for a $100 reservation fee (☎ 307-344-2003). Rangers lead hour-long history walks daily at 6pm, departing from the visitor center.

There are fine views over the hot springs from Capital Hill, just in front of the church.

MAMMOTH HOT SPRINGS

The imposing **Lower** and **Upper Terraces** of Mammoth Hot Springs are the product of dissolved subterranean limestone (itself originally deposited by ancient seas), which is continually deposited as the spring waters cool on contact with air. As guidebooks love to say, the mountain is in effect turning itself inside out, depositing over a ton of travertine (limestone deposits) here every year. The colored runoff of the naturally white terraces is due to the bacteria and algae that flourish in the warm waters. See p66 for more details on the construction of the terraces.

Two hours' worth of boardwalks wend their way around the Lower Terraces and connect to the Upper Terraces Loop. The rutting Rocky Mountain elk that sometimes lounge on Opal Terrace in fall are a favorite photo opportunity.

Surreal **Palette Springs** (accessed from the bottom parking lot) and sulfur-yellow **Canary Springs** (accessed from the top loop) are the most beautiful sites, but thermal activity is constantly in flux, so check the current state of play at the visitor center. The famously ornate travertine formations that characterize the terraces of **Minerva Spring** have been dry since 2002 but are still beautiful. At the bottom of the terraces, by the parking area, is the phallic, dormant 36ft-high hot spring cone called **Liberty Cap**, ap-

parently named after hats worn during the French Revolution. The former spring must have had particularly high water pressure to create such a tall cone over its estimated 2500-year life span. Across the road, **Opal Spring** is slowly converging on a century-old residence designed by Robert Reamer (the architect of the Old Faithful Inn and Roosevelt Arch). Park strategists have to decide which to preserve – the architecture or the spring.

A less stimulating 1.5-mile paved one-way road loops counterclockwise around the Upper Terraces; no vehicles longer than 25ft are permitted. The overlook affords impressive views of the Lower Terraces and Fort Yellowstone and offers access to **Canary Springs** and **New Blue Spring**. Highlights further around the loop include the sponge-like **Orange Spring Mound** and the perfectly named **White Elephant Back Terrace**. The loop joins the main road near the large **Angel Terrace**.

Ninety-minute ranger walks leave from the Upper Terraces parking lot daily at 9am.

BOILING RIVER

One of the few places where you can take a soak in Yellowstone is Boiling River. See p281 for the potential dangers of soaking in hot springs.

The turnoff to the parking area is along the Montana–Wyoming border, by a sign that marks the 45th parallel (halfway between the equator and the North Pole). A trail leads 0.5 miles (about 15 minutes) along the river to a point where an underground boiling river surfaces from below a limestone overhang. There are several pools along the riverside.

Bring a towel and flip-flops. The only changing area is the vault toilet at the parking lot. Swimming is allowed only during daylight hours, and food, pets, alcohol and nudity are prohibited. The pools are closed during high river levels (most commonly in spring).

The turnouts north of here are good places to spot pronghorn in the summer and bighorn sheep and elk in the winter.

Mammoth to Tower-Roosevelt

The 18-mile road to Tower-Roosevelt Junction heads east from Mammoth over the Gardner River Bridge, where the Gardner

TRUMAN EVERTS

Everts Ridge, northwest of Mammoth, is named after Truman Everts, a member of the 1870 Washburn-Langford-Doane expedition and a notable early tourist disaster story.

Separated from his group on the southern shores of Yellowstone Lake in September 1870, the 54-year-old tax inspector soon lost his bearings and promptly broke his glasses. His horse then bolted, taking all Everts' equipment with it save for a penknife and a pair of opera glasses (not quite as useless as they sound – they helped him make fire!). He kept warm at night by cuddling up to hot springs near Heart Lake, until he ended up badly burning himself. At one point he spent the night in a tree, as a pacing mountain lion stalked him from below.

After 37 days lost in the wilderness, Everts was finally discovered, shoeless, frostbitten, emaciated, delirious and raving like a madman…but alive.

River meets the Yellowstone River. By the roadside, just over 2 miles from Mammoth, is pretty **Undine Falls**, aptly named for an alluring folkloric water spirit.

The easy 1-mile round-trip walk to **Wraith Falls** is a good family hike through pretty meadows and fire-burn patches. The trail begins at the pullout east of Lava Creek Picnic Area, 5 miles from Mammoth, and follows Lupine Creek for 15 minutes to the base of a 79ft cascade.

Just past **Blacktail Ponds** (good for spotting muskrats and waterfowl) is the Blacktail Trailhead, which leads down into the Black Canyon of the Yellowstone and Gardiner.

Two miles past here, the 0.5-mile **Forces of the Northern Range Self-Guiding Trail** is an accessible boardwalk that teaches kids about the environmental forces of this part of the park. Kids will get a kick from placing their hand on a wolf print.

The 6-mile one-way **Blacktail Plateau Dr** detours off the main highway to offer glimpses of gorgeous summer wildflowers (June and July) and golden fall colors (September). The road follows part of the Bannock Trail, a hunting route taken by Bannock Indians in the mid-19th century. The trail originated in Idaho, crossed the Yellowstone Valley at the Bannock Ford (see p128) and continued through the Lamar Valley to Soda Butte Creek before leaving what is now the park at its northeast corner and continuing to Bighorn Valley. Along the second half of this drive, near Crescent Hill, is the spot where Truman Everts was finally discovered after wandering lost in the park for 37 days (see the boxed text, above). RVs and trailers are not allowed down the rough, unpaved road.

Instead of taking Blacktail Plateau Dr, you continue east on the main Grand Loop Rd. You'll pass **Phantom Lake** (one of three interconnected lakes that are normally dry by July) and an unsigned **scenic overview** of Hellroaring Mountain, Garnet Hill, and the Yellowstone River and Hellroaring Creek Valleys. A couple of miles further is the **Hellroaring Trailhead**, a short drive down a dirt road and popular with horse trips. Half a mile past here, **Floating Island Lake** is dense with vegetation, making it a good place to spot birds.

Just before you reach Tower-Roosevelt Junction is the 0.25-mile turnoff (no RVs or trailers) to the heavily visited **Petrified Tree**, surrounded by a fence like a priceless work of art. The tree is worth a quick look if you've never seen one before, but the parking lot can be cramped and busy. A better way to visit the tree is on an early morning hike from Roosevelt Lodge on the Lost Lake loop (p129).

Mammoth to Norris

The 20-mile road from Mammoth to Norris passes the Upper Terraces and enters a jumbled landscape of **hoodoos**, formed when the travertine deposits of nearby Terrace Mountain slipped down the hillside, breaking into boulder-like fragments. The road climbs to the cantilevered road of the Golden Gate, named after the light-colored rock formed from cooled ash flows. The sprouting knob of rock on the outside of the road was actually pulled down and then replaced when the road was widened! Shortly afterwards a pullout offers views of tiny **Rustic Falls**, a natural funnel that was probably used by Sheepeater Indians to trap bighorn sheep.

The peak rising to the left is **Bunsen Peak** (8564ft), a plug of solidified magma that formed inside a long since eroded volcanic cone. A hiking and biking trail heads up and around Bunsen Peak from the busy Bunsen Peak Trailhead (p134 and p154). Further along on the right, delightful **Swan Lake** in the middle of Gardner's Hole offers good bird-watching (look for trumpeter swans in winter and early spring) and views of the Gallatins. A board helps identify the various peaks.

Two miles further south, turn off for the **Sheepeater Cliffs**, an amazing collection of half-million-year-old hexagonal basalt columns, stacked like building blocks. You'll find a scenic picnic area and walks along the river to more formations (no buses, trailers or RVs allowed). The Sheepeaters, also known as the Tukudika, were a sub-tribe of the Shoshone and the park's earliest year-round inhabitants.

The road passes a nice fishing spot and wintertime warming hut near Indian Creek Campground, then continues to a pullout at **Willow Park** 2 miles further south (a good place to look for moose) and then a pleasant picnic spot at **Appolinaris Spring**, once a popular stagecoach stop in the 1880s for parched travelers headed to Norris.

Obsidian Cliff, to the left of the road, exposes the interior of a 180,000-year-old lava flow. Rapid cooling prevented the formation of crystals and fused the lava into this form of volcanic glass. Obsidian, used for spearheads and arrowheads, was widely traded by Native Americans and was one of the major reasons early peoples visited the Yellowstone region. The park service was forced to remove the cliffside trails of this National Historic Landmark due to pilfering of the obsidian – leave it alone!

Just 1 mile further, the **Beaver Lake** picnic area offers a fine spot for a picnic and some wildlife-watching. Just past here, isolated fumaroles, hot springs and other thermal features start to appear by the side of the road, heralding the approach of the thermally active Norris region.

Roaring Mountain is a huge bleached hillside pockmarked with hissing fumaroles. During its heyday around the turn of the last century, visitors could hear the roar of the fumaroles from over 4 miles away. The activity is much reduced today.

From here the road passes pretty **North** and **South Twin Lakes** and descends to beautiful **Nymph Lake**. The lake's bubbling pools, bleached white shoreline and steaming geysers lend the area a powerfully primeval air; something out of the landscapes of Tolkien or the age of the dinosaurs. Just south of here is the unsigned but superbly named Devil's Frying Pan springs. The smell of sulfur stays with you as the road quickly descends into the Norris Geyser Basin.

ROOSEVELT COUNTRY

President Theodore Roosevelt visited this rugged area in the park's northeast corner during a two-week jaunt through the park in 1903, lending his name to the rustic Roosevelt Lodge by Tower-Roosevelt Junction that opened three years later. Fossil forests, the wildlife-rich Lamar River Valley and its tributary trout streams, and the dramatic and craggy peaks of the Absaroka Range are the highlights in this remote, scenic and undeveloped region. The rustic cabins, stagecoach rides and Western cookouts of the Roosevelt Lodge add to the region's frontier feel. The region is the birthplace of the park's current bison and wolf populations and one of the park's great wildlife-viewing areas.

The 29-mile Northeast Entrance Rd passes from Cooke City through the Lamar Valley to Tower-Roosevelt Junction (6270ft) and then continues west for 18 miles to Mammoth Hot Springs. This is the only road in the park that remains open year round. From Tower-Roosevelt junction the Grand Loop road heads south to Canyon Junction, over the high Dunraven Pass.

For details of the road between Tower-Roosevelt and Mammoth, see p101.

INFORMATION

Roosevelt Lodge has lodging, food, showers, a grocery store and a nearby Conoco gas station. Tower Ranger Station just west of Tower-Roosevelt Junction is the place to get your backcountry permits.

> **TIP**
>
> The historic Roosevelt Lodge (p164) is well worth a stop. There are several hiking trails behind the hotel, and the small store is a good place to refuel. The rocking chairs on the porch are a great spot to take a break or read a book on a rainy day.

Roosevelt Country

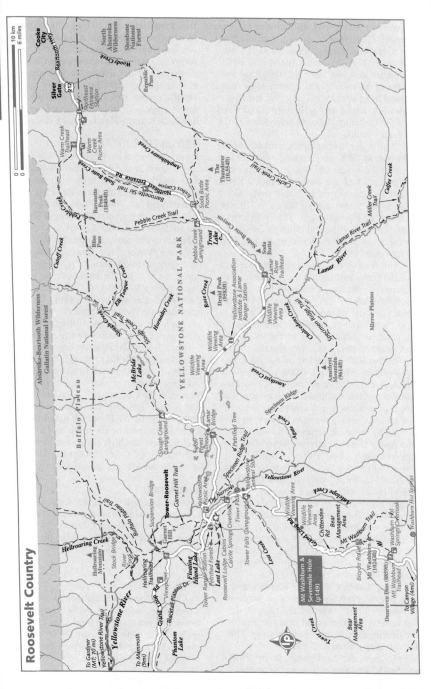

Northeast Entrance to Tower-Roosevelt

It's 29 miles from the Northeast Entrance to Tower-Roosevelt. A couple of miles inside the Northeast Entrance the road enters Wyoming and follows Soda Butte Creek, offering fine views of the craggy ridgeline of towering Barronette Peak (10,404ft) to the west. It was Jack Baronet who rescued Truman Everts (p102) for a promised $600 reward; not only did he not get the reward, but the park misspelled the peak they named after him! Near Pebble Creek Campground at tiny Icebox Canyon, the lovely valley warms up and opens wide. Southeast is a ridgeline known as the Thunderer (10,554ft), after the frequent storms that gather here.

Two miles past Pebble Creek is the trailhead for the short 0.5-mile walk through fir forest and summer wildflowers to scenic **Trout Lake,** named after the abundant cutthroats who spawn here in early summer. The 10-minute uphill hike to the pretty lake is steep enough to leave you puffing, but this is still one of the park's best short family hikes. It's popular also with anglers, who are allowed to keep their catch of rainbow (but not cutthroat) trout.

Further along the road watch (and sniff) for the whitish-yellow travertine cone of **Soda Butte,** the only thermal feature in this part of the park.

The road now joins the mixed sage and grasslands of the **Lamar Valley,** one of the park's premier wildlife viewing areas. The roadside turnouts between Pebble and Slough (pronounced 'slew') Creek campgrounds, particularly the stretch between Lamar River Trailhead and the Lamar Canyon, are prime places to spot wolves from the nearby Druid pack (named after nearby

---

WATCHING WOLVES Carolyn McCarthy

You sit. You watch. You wait. Unlike Old Faithful, wolves don't operate on schedule. The closest thing is to track reported sightings. Then you race to the nearest lookout. And watch. And wait.

We rolled out of bed at 4am, without a peep from the bluebirds, who probably still snoozed. What followed bordered on asinine: driving around mountain-pass pullouts in the dusky light, setting up spotting scopes in blustery winds, only to dismantle them minutes later. False alarm. We nestled into a steep overlook on Chittenden Rd, where others had already set up their post in the chill of daybreak: couples snuggled with spotting scopes while roaming children still wore pajamas. We asked the group if they had seen anything. They shrugged. 'Just grizzlies.'

Watching wolves is all about expectation. Call it the excitement of waiting for something so wild that only few ever witness. A Native American story says the white man rose from the hair of a dead wolf. Mongols revered them and shamanic Turks believed them to be their ancestors while Europeans crafted suspenseful fairy tales using their tufted shadows and sharp incisors. But what was the reality?

Wolves were hunted to the brink of extinction in the United States. In 1995, under much controversy, they were reintroduced into Yellowstone. At last count there were 136 wolves, and numbers are growing.

On Chittenden Rd, someone spotted an elk cow wandering dazed on the edge of the forest deep below us. The elk circled around, as if she was looking for something. It turned out to be her calf.

The calf was limp in the grip of the wolf, but the stunned mother elk stood her ground. What followed was dazzling. She kept charging, but the wolf kept returning to the carcass. It was not unlike a dance. But this wasn't Wild Animal Kingdom. This was happening at my feet. Sure, a mile away, but real and live in the frosted morning air.

The elk cow was brave, resilient. The wolf was patient. An alpha female wearing a radio collar, she was not young. Her fur was flecked with grey. She finally, decisively, snatched the carcass, likely off to feed the litter.

In moments, the onlookers packed up their spotting scopes. As the sky brightened, the regular traffic started flowing, people clueless to the dramas of the wild that had played out while they slept.

To join a wolf course, contact the **Yellowstone Association** (www.yellowstoneassociation.com).

Druid Peak). Both elk and large herds of bison also make the broad Lamar Valley their winter range, occupying independent ecological niches alongside coyotes, pronghorns and bears.

Also here is the former **Buffalo Ranch**, which almost single handedly raised Yellowstone's buffalo herds between 1907 and 1960. The buildings are now home to the excellent Yellowstone Institute (see p263).

About 6 miles before Tower-Roosevelt Junction a dirt road turns off north to Slough Creek Campground, offering fishing and hiking access. Further along the main road are several glacially formed 'kettle' ponds, which are periodically closed to protect nesting trumpeter swans. Just before Tower the road passes the popular Yellowstone Picnic Area and bridges the Yellowstone River. For details on the Mammoth to Tower road see p101.

CALCITE SPRINGS OVERLOOK

This worthwhile overlook 1.5 miles south of Tower-Roosevelt Junction offers vertiginous views of a section of the Grand Canyon of the Yellowstone known as the Narrows. A short trail leads to views north of the gorge's sulfuric yellows and smoking sides. All around are vertical basalt columns, part of a 25ft-deep lava flow that covered the area 1.3 million years ago. Below the basalt are glacial deposits; above the basalt are layers of volcanic ash. More hexagonal basalt columns hang above the roadside a little further along the main road, though parking here is very limited.

You'll find dramatic (and crowd-free!) views of Calcite Springs and the Narrows from the Yellowstone River Picnic Area Trail (see p128).

TOWER FALL

Two-and-a-half miles south of Tower-Roosevelt Junction, Tower Creek plunges over 132ft Tower Fall before joining the Yellowstone River. The fall gets its name from the volcanic breccia towers around it, which are like a demonic fortress and earn it the nickname The Devil's Den. Local storytellers claim that prominent Minaret Peak gets its name from one Minnie Rhett, the girlfriend of an early park visitor, but that sounds to us like one of Jim Bridger's tall tales. Iconic landscape painter Thomas Moran created one of his most famous paintings here.

From a scenic overlook beside the Yellowstone General Store, a 1-mile round-trip trail descends 200 vertical feet to the base of the falls for the best views. Stop in for well-deserved ice cream on the way back. Note that the busy parking lot often fills up in the middle of the day.

Tower Fall Campground is just across the road from the parking area. The potholed and narrow section of road between Tower Fall and Tower-Roosevelt Junction is one of the worst in the park.

Tower-Roosevelt to Canyon

It's 19 miles from Tower-Roosevelt to Canyon. The Grand Loop Rd starts to climb from Tower Fall on its way to **Dunraven Pass**

THE TALLEST TALES IN THE WEST

Jim Bridger is famed as a mountain main and trapper who explored the Yellowstone region in the 1830s, but he was also the West's consummate teller of tall tales. Level-headed lowlanders may have dismissed his outrageous stories with a patronizing slap on the back, but as with most enduring stories, most of the fiction was actually based in fact.

Bridger's most famous tales told of Yellowstone's petrified trees (fact, though he couldn't resist upping the ante to 'peetrified birds singing peetrified songs'), a 'mountain of glass' that acted as a giant telescope (fiction, but based on the volcanic glass of Obsidian Cliff), a river that flowed so fast that friction made it hot on the bottom (actually thermal runoff on the Firehole River) and a spot on Yellowstone Lake where you could throw out a line and reel in a cooked fish (fact, a technique proved by early tourists at Fishing Cone, with the help of an underwater geyser).

He also told of a place where fish could cross the Rocky Mountains, actually Two Ocean Plateau just south of the park, where a stream atop the Continental Divide branches into two, one stream leading to the Atlantic, the other to the Pacific. (Lake Isa does the same thing between Old Faithful and Yellowstone Lake but has no fish.)

(8859ft), the highest part of the Grand Loop Rd and named after the British earl who traveled here in 1874 (it was Dunraven's travelogue *The Great Divide* that popularized the park in Europe). East of the road is **Antelope Creek**, prime grizzly habitat and thus closed to visitors. Several turnouts offer popular wildlife-watching opportunities here.

Named after Hiram Chittenden, one of park's early road engineers and historians, Chittenden Rd branches off to the left just before the pass. The road is a popular hiking and mountain-biking trail to the summit of **Mt Washburn** (10,243ft). A second, hiking-only trail leads to the peak from Dunraven Pass, 5 miles further south. See p138 for details of the hike to Mt Washburn and p154 for details of the bike route.

Just below Dunraven Pass is the **Washburn Hot Springs Overlook**, where an interpretive sign describes the hot springs and the surrounding Yellowstone caldera. This is also a good wildlife-watching area; in summer 2007 the star of the show was a grizzly sow and her four cubs, all of whom would make an almost daily appearance in the meadows below the turnout.

CANYON COUNTRY
The Canyon area is the second-most-heavily visited part of the park after Old Faithful, due largely to the scenic grandeur of the Grand Canyon of the Yellowstone, but also due to the junction's central location and its concentration of visitor services. The Grand Canyon of the Yellowstone is the star of the show and a series of scenic overlooks and a network of trails along the canyon's rims and interiors highlight its beauty from a dozen angles.

ORIENTATION & INFORMATION
Canyon Village and Visitor Information Center lie just east of Canyon Junction along North Rim Dr. Canyon Village has accommodation, three restaurants, a general store, the Yellowstone Adventures outdoor gear store and an ATM.

The campground area has **showers** (☻7am-1:30pm, 3pm-9:30pm), a **laundry** (☻7am-9pm) and an ice machine. Canyon Ranger Station is inside the Visitor Information Center.

Canyon Visitor Education Center
This new visitor center (p96), opened in 2007, is well worth a visit for its innovative and interactive displays on Yellowstone's geology. The highlight is a room-sized relief model of the park, on which you can trace the terrain of your upcoming hike. There's a sobering map of recent earthquakes in the park (an average of 2500 each year!), scratchy B&W videos of Old Faithful through the years, a huge satellite map of the park and a computer animation booth that details the annual bison migrations through the parks. One surprise is the artist's impression of what the park may have looked like 20,000 years ago – covered in a 4000ft-thick layer of ice. Twenty-minute movies play on the hour and half hour.

Grand Canyon of the Yellowstone
After its placid meanderings north from Yellowstone Lake through the Hayden Valley, the Yellowstone River musters up its energy and suddenly plummets over **Upper Falls** (109ft) and then the much larger **Lower Falls** (308ft), before raging through the 1000ft-deep Grand Canyon of the Yellowstone. More than 4000ft wide at the top, the canyon snakes for 20 miles as far as the Narrows near Tower-Roosevelt Junction. The only way to reach the canyon floor is via the Sevenmile Hole Trail (see p149).

Much of the canyon's beauty comes from its subtle range of colors, from egg white to salmon pink, a byproduct of iron oxidization in the rock (and not, as many assume, of sulfur deposits). As park publications note, the canyon is in effect rusting. Whiffs of steam still rise from vents in the canyon wall, hinting at the thermal activity that played a major role in the creation of the Yellowstone canyon (by weakening the rhyolite rock). The canyon is relatively recent in geological terms, carved out not by glacial erosion but by water supplied by ice dams that melted and flooded the region during the recent ice age. See p66 for more on the formation of the canyon.

The Lower Falls are twice the height of Niagara and are most impressive in spring, when the water volume can be up to 12 times that of fall. The eye-catching green notch indicates a patch of deeper and less

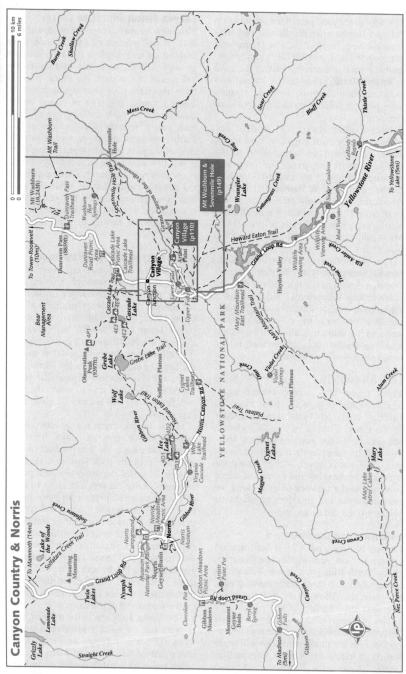

Canyon Country & Norris

turbulent water. At the base of the falls the reds and creams of the canyon walls turn to a mossy green, fed by the thundering spray of the river. Bring binoculars to spot ospreys that nest in the canyon from late April till early September. The falls are perhaps most spectacular in winter, when the spray freezes into a giant cone in front of the falls.

Rangers lead hikes daily at 9am from the parking lot above Uncle Tom's Trailhead and give short talks four times a day (10am for kids) at Artist Point.

In 2007 and 2008 South Rim Drive was upgraded, with access closed to Artist Point and beyond. From 2008 attention will turn to the North Rim, and you may find parts or all of the North Rim Drive closed. Eventually the current one-way traffic system on that road will be reversed. Check with the park website in advance and the visitor education center once you arrive.

NORTH RIM

Three popular scenic overlooks line the 2.5-mile North Rim Dr (one way beyond Canyon Village): Inspiration, Grandview and Lookout Points.

Most visitors drive between the viewpoints, but you can also hike the **North Rim Trail**, which connects all three. The trail parallels the road from Inspiration Point to the Upper Falls Overlook (2.5 miles) and then continues 0.75 miles further to Chittenden Bridge on South Rim Dr, where it links up with the South Rim Trail. The only disadvantage to this route is that it's one-way, so you'll have to either retrace your steps or arrange a designated automobile driver to pick you up.

The one-way drive turns off the main road near Canyon Campground. Take a left to reach busy **Inspiration Point**, which offers an overview of the length of the canyon and a small section of the lower falls. There are a few steps to descend. There used to be more, before the old lookout point fell (literally) victim to the canyon's relentless erosion.

Just before Inspiration Point is a huge granite boulder scooped up from the Beartooth Mountains by a glacier and deposited here 80,000 years ago. The **Glacier Boulder Trail** starts here for the 5-mile hike to Sevenmile Hole (see p149). An easy, one-hour

(2-mile) round-trip hike takes you along this trail, through forest and past intermittent canyon vistas to views of **Silver Cord Cascade**, the park's highest falls (or rather series of falls). This is a particularly fine late-afternoon hike, but keep a tight rein on the kids, as there are no barriers between them and the sheer canyon dropoffs.

The one-way road continues to **Grandview Point**, which offers views north of the colorful smoking canyon walls, and then popular **Lookout Point**. Lookout Point offers the best views of the Lower Falls, while an adjacent 0.5-mile trail drops 500ft to **Red Rock** for even closer views. The average age of the crowd plummets with the elevation (it's hard on the knees). The trails here can be very slippery so watch your step. It was around here that iconic early painter Thomas Moran made the sketches for his famous painting of the canyon, allegedly weeping over the lack of colors in his palette.

Half a mile beyond Lookout Point, a steep 0.75-mile trail descends 600ft to the **Brink of the Lower Falls** for exciting close-up views of the tumbling white water as it rushes over the lip of the falls. Heading back up isn't half as much fun as going down.

The less dramatic **Upper Falls Viewpoint** is also accessible by road: the turnoff is south

---

YELLOW STONE

The name Yellowstone was not inspired by the technicolor walls of the Grand Canyon as many people think, but rather the yellowish-tan bluffs near the confluence of the Yellowstone and Missouri Rivers in western North Dakota (though some sources also suggest the bluffs near Billings). In 1798 British fur trader David Thompson anglicized the phrase 'R des roches Jaunes,' which means 'Yellow Rock (or Stone) River,' and which was used on a French map to describe the area near the Mandan villages of the upper Missouri. The French had for their part simply translated the Minetaree Indian name for the river, Mi tsi a da zi (Rock Yellow River).

In the region of the upper Yellowstone, near what is now the park, the Crow Indians knew the river as the Elk, but Elk National Park just doesn't have the same ring to it…

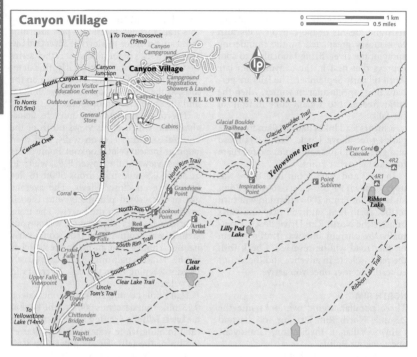

Canyon Village

0 — 1 km
0 — 0.5 miles

To Tower-Roosevelt (19mi)

Canyon Campground

Canyon Junction

Canyon Village

Norris Canyon Rd

Campground Registration, Showers & Laundry

Canyon Visitor Education Center

To Norris (10.5mi)

Outdoor Gear Shop

Canyon Lodge

YELLOWSTONE NATIONAL PARK

General Store

Cabins

Glacial Boulder Trailhead

Glacier Boulder Trail

Cascade Creek

Yellowstone River

Silver Cord Cascade

4R2

Grand Loop Rd

North Rim Trail

Point Sublime

4R1

Corral

Grandview Point

Inspiration Point

Ribbon Lake

North Rim Dr

Lookout Point

Red Rock

Artist Point

Lilly Pad Lake

Lower Falls

South Rim Trail

Crystal Falls

South Rim Drive

Clear Lake

Clear Lake Trail

Ribbon Lake Trail

Upper Falls Viewpoint

Uncle Tom's Trail

To Yellowstone Lake (14mi)

Upper Falls

Chittenden Bridge

Wapiti Trailhead

---

of Canyon Junction and Cascade Creek on the main Grand Loop Rd to Fishing Bridge. A short walk to the right (south) leads to the Brink of the Upper Falls, though the best views of the falls are actually from the Uncle Tom's parking area across the gorge. A five-minute walk north along the North Rim Trail (a former stagecoach road) leads to an overview of the much smaller but graceful **Crystal Falls**, the 'Hidden' or 'Third' waterfall of the Canyon region.

SOUTH RIM

South Rim Dr passes the Wapiti Trailhead en route to the canyon's most spectacular overlook, at Artist Point. The 3.25-mile **South Rim Trail** follows the canyon rim from Chittenden Bridge to Point Sublime via Artist Point.

Uncle Tom's Trail is one of the region's largest parking areas and offers the best views of the Upper and Lower Falls. The viewpoint across the river to the Upper Falls is close to the parking lot. Uncle Tom's Trail itself is a steep route that descends 500ft to the base of the Lower Falls. The

trail was constructed in 1898 by early park entrepreneur Uncle Tom Richardson, who would lead tourists across the river and down a series of trails and rope ladders for views of the falls and a picnic lunch. Sadly the rope ladders are now a thing of the past (Tom's permit was rescinded in 1903), but the 328 metal steps still descend three quarters of the way into the canyon.

In 1889 the park service wisely turned down an application to build an elevator here that would whisk tourists down to the canyon floor, though you may wish they had changed their mind as you make the tough return climb. Rangers lead a 1-mile stroll from here twice a day, as well as a longer 3-mile walk in the morning.

The Clear Lake Trail heads from the parking lot across South Rim Dr and offers an alternative route to Clear and Ribbon Lakes (see p140).

Artist Point is probably the most famous of the canyon's viewpoints. It was not, as many people assume, named for the spot where Thomas Moran sketched his famous

Lake Country

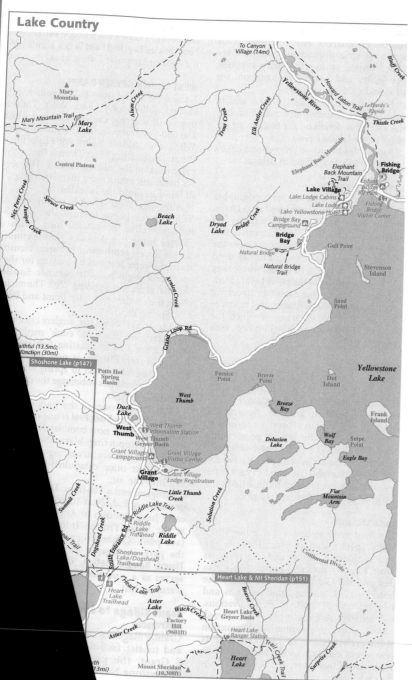

landscape of the falls (a copy of which is on display in the Canyon Visitor Education Center). It was actually named by the park photographer FJ Haynes for its superlative scenic views. Rangers give short talks here seven times a day.

From Artist Point a trail leads 1 mile to **Point Sublime** for more fabulous views of the canyon walls. The trail was due to be renovated in 2008, so check that it is open. The 4-mile (two-hour) round-trip hike to Ribbon Lake (see p140) branches off from here.

Canyon to Lake

South of Canyon Junction, the Grand Loop Rd winds down 16 miles to Lake Yellowstone via the excellent wildlife-watching opportunities of the Hayden Valley and the interesting Mud Volcano.

HAYDEN VALLEY

The Yellowstone River is broad and shallow as it meanders gently through the vast grasslands of Hayden Valley, named after the expedition leader whose 1871 survey led to the establishment of the park the following year. This former lakebed was formed in the last ice age when a glacial outburst flooded the valley, turning the region into an arm of Yellowstone Lake. The fine silt-and-clay soil of the former lake bed prevents water from percolating into the ground, making the area marshy and impenetrable to most trees. This supports the rich shrubs and grasses favored by bison.

Hayden Valley is one of the park's premier **wildlife-viewing** areas. With patience you're likely to see coyotes, springtime grizzlies, elk and lots of bison. Bird-watching is equally good, including white pelicans

---

THE WILDLIFE BIOLOGIST

Nathan Varley is about as native as the cutthroat trout. He grew up in Yellowstone as the son of a fisheries biologist and is now a course instructor, backcountry guide and wildlife biologist specializing in wolves.

How can people take better advantage of their time here? A general answer is to recognize that there is a whole lot more here than they've heard about. Yellowstone is a 2-million acre wilderness, not just a few road stops. The backcountry is a whole different experience.

Could one say after 30-odd years, 'Ah, Yellowstone. Been there. Done it'? It is a challenge to make it new and fresh every day. The people help since it's new to them. You can feed off that enthusiasm.

What are some gems? There are three or four trails in the Gallatin Mountains that don't get overused: Fawn Pass, Bighorn Pass and the Sportsman Lake Trail take you into some amazing mountainous wilderness where wildlife is everywhere. You see elk and moose and bears on the west side of the park. The central part of the park, Pelican Valley and upper Broad Creek trail systems, have a lot of campsites which sit empty every night. It's spectacular because you have a lot of wildlife, it's very scenic and there are also thermal areas – pots of boiling mud.

Tell us about the glamorous field of wolf research. You spend a lot of time behind a computer; an expensive piece of equipment handles data for you, and you may never handle a wolf with a radio collar or even see it. I might when I am guiding, but as a scientist it doesn't matter.

How do guiding and teaching fit in? What gets me more in touch with the wolf is my work taking people out or teaching a class. There we see the wolves and that helps my data on how to interpret them.

Any favorite wolf moment? One time I saw an adult male try to lead the yearlings across the road. They were afraid of it because of the cars and people. The male would lead them on down, cross and they would get to the edge of the pavement and turn and walk away. So we watched that happen three or four times. The male was getting frustrated. Then he started to play. He would pounce on one of the yearlings then start running away with his tail tucked so they would chase him, and when he got them chasing him, he would subtly turn direction toward the road. A couple of times they realized what was going on and so they'd put on the brakes and skid back. You could see this total moment of confusion on their faces. He eventually got them to cross with this technique that I just thought was so innovative on the part of an animal – to figure out how to get them to overcome their fear and do it.

and trumpeter swans, sandhill cranes (also at Alum Creek), ospreys, bald eagles and Canada geese. There are popular viewing areas 1 mile north of Sulfur Cauldron and 1.5 miles north of Trout Creek. Set up your spotting scope early, as the pullouts fill with cars an hour or two before dusk.

Rangers lead midweek walks in the Hayden Valley three times a week at 7am.

MUD VOLCANO
One of the park's most geologically volatile regions, this thermal area 10 miles south of Canyon Junction and 6 miles north of Fishing Bridge Junction contains an assortment of mud pots and other gurgling sulfurous pits. It's also a favorite grazing ground for bison and elk. The nearby Sour Creek resurgent dome is the fuel that superheats the mud volcanoes. During a series of earthquakes in 1979 the mud pots developed enough heat and gases to literally cook lodgepole pines and grasses on neighboring hillsides. One mud pot was recently discovered underneath the parking lot.

Mud Volcano itself has not erupted since the 1871 Langford-Washington-Doane expedition first encountered it. A crater is all that remains of the original cone. **Dragon's Mouth Spring** gets its name from the roaring and crashing that emanates from a hidden lair and is constantly in flux. In 1999 the pool cooled and its color changed from green to white and now gray.

The easiest way to see the other sights is to follow the 2.3-mile loop boardwalk (there are some steps) clockwise, past Mud Geyser and up Cooking Hillside. Halfway up, **Churning Cauldron** is a favorite. The dark colors of this and other pots are due to the presence of iron sulfides.

Black Dragon's Cauldron appeared in 1948 in a crack in the earth and has since moved south 200ft along the crack to produce an elliptical pool. The rolling motion of the water is actually due to rising gases rather than boiling water. Nearby **Sour Lake** is as acidic as battery acid. Further downhill, **Grizzly Fumarole** changes throughout the year from a fumarole to a mud pot and even a muddy spring, according to the amount of moisture in the ground.

Sulfur Cauldron, just a few hundred yards north, by a pullout in the road, is one of the most acidic springs in the park, at pH

1.3. Other thermal areas, visible across the Yellowstone River, can only be reached by hiking the Howard Eaton Trail.

Rangers lead 90-minute hikes daily at 3:30pm to **The Gumper**, a huge seething mud pot off the boardwalk behind Sour Lake. Visitors are not allowed to leave the boardwalk unguided.

South of Mud Volcano is a great area to spot bison.

LAKE COUNTRY
Yellowstone Lake (7733ft) is Lake Country's shimmering centerpiece, one of the world's largest alpine lakes, with the largest inland population of cutthroat trout in the US. Yellowstone River emerges from the north end of the lake and flows through Hayden Valley to the Grand Canyon of the Yellowstone. The lake's south and eastern borders flank the steep Absaroka Range marking the border of the park's remote and pristine Thorofare region.

ORIENTATION & INFORMATION
A 22-mile section of the Grand Loop Rd hugs Yellowstone Lake's shoreline between Fishing Bridge Junction to the north and West Thumb Junction to the west. Visitor centers and convenience stores are available at Fishing Bridge, Bridge Bay and Grant Village. Grant and Lake Village offer the most visitor services, including dining. At Bridge Bay Marina, **Xanterra** (www.travelyellow stone.com) offers one-hour lake cruises and rents outboard motorboats and rowboats.

Yellowstone Lake
The largest high-altitude lake in North America, the deep cobalt Yellowstone Lake (136 sq miles) has been a human draw for millennia; artifacts found along the lakeshore date back 12,000 years. Traditionally this was only a summering spot for native groups. The lake remains frozen almost half the year, from January to early June, though its average depth is 140ft (maximum 390ft), and even though parts of the lake floor boil with underwater hot springs.

In addition to excellent fishing and boating, the lake also offers prime birdwatching and wildlife-watching. Early summer visitors shouldn't miss an amazing display of spawning cutthroat trout at Fishing Bridge and LeHardy's Rapids, 3

miles north of the bridge. As crucial food sources for grizzlies and waterfowl, some spawning areas around the lakeshore are closed during spring and early summer. For fishing and boating information, see p158 and p157 respectively.

Thermal activity rings the lake, and in cold weather steaming thermals blur into the water. For details on the fascinating geology of the lake see p66.

Rangers lead tours of Yellowstone Lake's shoreline daily from Fishing Bridge.

LEHARDY'S RAPIDS
These rapids are named after topographer Paul LeHardy, whose raft overturned here, spilling guns, provisions and bedding but sparing his life. Rock uplift created this steplike cascade, which formally marks the end of Yellowstone Lake. Cutthroat trout are plentiful in late springtime, where they can be seen resting in the pools before hurling themselves up the rapids to spawning grounds near Fishing Bridge. Just north of here are three picnic areas, of which the Nez Percé Ford picnic site is the nicest, with riverside tables.

FISHING BRIDGE
There has been a bridge at Fishing Bridge since 1902, but it closed to fishing in 1973 to protect spawning cutthroat trout to the benefit of resident grizzlies. Because of heavy grizzly activity, there is continuing pressure to close the area to protect this crucial habitat. The **visitor center** was built here in 1931 as an information station for the first automobile tourists. The center contains displays on local birdlife (look for the great skulls on the candelabra).

LAKE VILLAGE
The buttercup-yellow Lake Yellowstone Hotel (p165), dating from 1891, is the park's oldest building and certainly it˥ most elegant. Robert Reamer (who aˀ designed the Old Faithful Inn) rebuilˀ hotel in 1903, adding Ionic columˀ false balconies. Despite recent renoˀ old hallways reveal a crooked tiˀ and expansive, this southern-style ˥ is the perfect setting for classical concˀ and sunset cocktails in the waterfront sun room. Hotel tours start at 5:30pm on summer weekdays.

You'll find several spots to picnic and/or fish between Lake Village and West Thumb. Near Bridge Bay, **Gull Point Dr** is a scenic picnic spot and popular fishing area.

WEST THUMB GEYSER BASIN
Named for its location in the near hand-shaped Yellowstone Lake, West Thumb is a small volcanic caldera spawned some 150,000 years ago inside the much larger Yellowstone caldera. Yellowstone Lake filled the crater, creating West Thumb Bay, a circular inlet on the lake's west end. The geyser basin still pours more than 3000 gallons of hot water into the lake daily.

Although West Thumb is not one of Yellowstone's prime thermal sites, its 0.ˀ mile shoreline boardwalk loop (witɦ shorter inner loop) passes through than a dozen geothermal features. ˥ its underwater features by lookinɡ spots or a slight bulge in summˀ thermal areas surrounding Weˀ clude the roadside Pumice Pˀ Hot Spring Basin.

At famous **Fishing Cone**, ˀ the infamous 'hook 'nˀ prepare their catch, ˀ boiling water. Fishiˀ Fluctuating lake levˀ summer sometimˀ Lakeshore Geyseˀ

Abyss Pool isˀ springs. Nearˀ tiest, thougˀ years of ˀ **Thumb Pˀ energyˀ 25ft ˀ rˀ dˀ

Yellۥ.

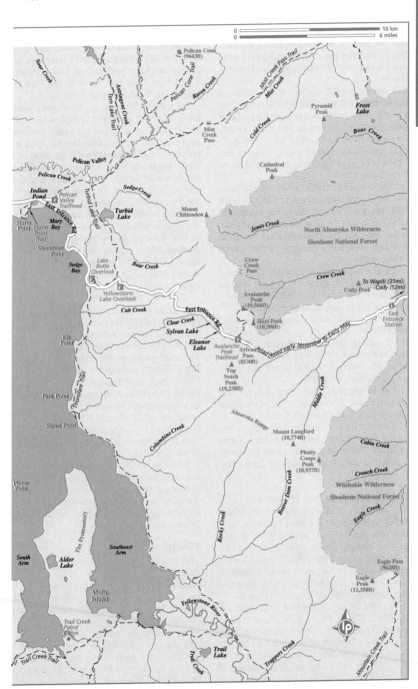

The **visitor center** offers an exhibit on fire and an hourly 20-minute video entitled *Ten Years After the Fire*. Evening presentations at the amphitheater are geared toward families.

From Grant Village the road climbs to the **Continental Divide** (7988ft) and drops into a burn area, past several trailheads. **Lewis Lake**, the third largest in the park, comes into view here, and several lake-view pullouts offer nice picnic spots. Boaters use Lewis Lake as the gateway to remote Shoshone Lake.

When you hit traffic south of the lake, you have probably arrived at the 30ft **Lewis Falls**. Walk a little way along the north side of the falls for the best views or along the south side for the closest access. In good weather, look for a glimpse of the Tetons to the south.

To the west, the Pitchstone Trailhead cuts over the pitchstone (ash tuft) plateau to Grassy Lake Rd. Its roadside meadows are excellent places to spot moose.

A major burn area signals the start of **Lewis Canyon**. There are lots of pullouts along the roadside, but the southernmost offers the best views. Volcanic rock that dates from an eruption 70,000 years ago comprises the canyon walls.

Just before the South Entrance, a small pullout beside a bridge offers access to small Moose Falls and Crawfish Creek.

The entrance station is adjacent to the Snake River Picnic Area. From here it's 18 miles to Colter Bay and 43 miles to Moose Visitor Center, both in Grand Teton National Park.

Fishing Bridge to East Entrance

Off the lake's northeast shore, lush **Pelican Valley** ranks among the park's prime grizzly habitats. At Pelican Creek Bridge, 1 mile east of Fishing Bridge Visitor Center, an easy 1-mile loop trail winds through lodgepole forest. Keep an eye out for moose in the wetlands. The lakeside ponds south of the highway offer great bird-watching.

Formed by a giant steam (not lava) explosion, Storm Point, 1.5 miles further east, juts into the north end of the lake. The 2-mile **Storm Point Trail** begins near Indian Pond, strolling through diverse wildlife habitats including meadows, shoreline and old forest. Wildlife is particularly active around dusk and dawn. Try spotting bison, moose, marmots and waterfowl. The trail closes in late spring and early summer due to bear activity. Just east of Storm Point, a dirt road branches north to the Pelican Valley Trailhead (see p140).

Like West Thumb, crater-shaped **Mary Bay** is the result of a thermal explosion. Both Mary Bay and neighboring Sedge Bay are peppered with underwater thermal areas, of which roiling **Steamboat Point** is the most obvious. **Sedge Bay** beach is a launching point for canoe or kayak trips south along the lake's east shoreline. Bird-watchers flock to the bay's southeast corner.

As the East Entrance Rd turns away from the lake, a mile-long paved road (no buses or trailers) branches north to the **Lake Butte Overlook**, which offers grand views of Yellowstone Lake. In the winter it hosts intrepid skaters and skiers. Further east is the less impressive Yellowstone Lake Overlook.

The main road gradually climbs up the west slope of the remote Absaroka Range past lovely **Sylvan Lake** (with a picnic area and catch-and-release fishing), Eleanor Lake and the Avalanche Peak Trailhead (p141). The road peaks at the slide area of **Sylvan Pass** (8530ft), dominated by 10,238ft Top Notch Peak to the south. East of the pass the landscape becomes turns more rugged and impressive. The high barren walls of Mt Langford (10,774ft) and Plenty Coups Peak (10,937ft) rise to the south. Middle Creek, with several good fishing spots, parallels the south side of the road.

The East Entrance marks the boundary between Yellowstone National Park and Shoshone National Forest. On this road travelers can reach Cody via the Wapiti Valley. For details about the Buffalo Bill Scenic Byway, see p192.

NORRIS

The Norris area was a former US Army outpost. The historic log Norris Soldier Station (1908), one of only three left from the era of army control of the park, now houses the **Museum of the National Park Ranger** (☎ 307-344-7353; ☷ 9am-5pm end May-end Sep), often staffed by retired NPS employees. The museum's exhibits detail the evolution of the ranger profession from its military origins, including a fun mock-up of an old ranger cabin. Norris is named after Philetus

W Norris, the park's second superintendent (1877–82), who is notable for constructing some of the park's first roads and for the shameless frequency with which he named park features after himself.

The Gibbon River flows through meadows in front of the building, making it a pleasant place to look for wildlife. Norris Campground is right next door.

ORIENTATION & INFORMATION

Norris sits at the junction of roads from Madison (14 miles), Canyon (12 miles) and Mammoth (20 miles) Junctions. There's not much in the way of facilities here – bring water, as the stuff in the campground spigots is putrid. North of the junction is Norris Campground; west is Norris Geyser Basin, with busy bathrooms, an information station and a bookstore. A pleasant 1-mile trail (no bikes) connects the basin and the campground.

Norris Geyser Basin

North and west of Norris Junction, the Norris Geyser Basin is North America's most volatile and oldest continuously active geothermal area (in existence for some 115,000 years). It's also the site of Yellowstone's hottest recorded temperatures, where three intersecting faults underlain by magma rise to within 2 miles of the surface. Barely 1000ft below the surface, scientific instruments have recorded temperatures as high as 459°F. The basin was temporarily closed in 2003 due to a rise in the surrounding rock temperature. Norris is also home to the majority of the world's acidic geysers, fed by the basin's abundant supplies of sulfur. In Norris the earth sighs, boils and rages like nowhere else on earth.

Norris' geothermal features change seasonally, most commonly in August or September: clear pools transform into spouting geysers or mud pots and vice versa. Thermal activity is also affected by mysterious disturbances, which generally last only a few days before things revert to 'normal.'

Norris Geyser Basin features two distinct areas: Porcelain Basin and Back Basin. Overlooking Porcelain Basin is the tiny **Norris Museum** (☎ 307-344-2812; ☼ 9am-5pm late May-end Sep), which opened as the park's first in 1930. There are ranger-led 90-minute walking tours of the basin at 10am daily, as well as at 4pm three times a week and there are short talks at 2:30pm.

The area's only bathrooms are in the parking lot. The parking area and toilets can get crowded, so try to schedule a visit early or late in the day.

PORCELAIN BASIN

One mile of boardwalks loop through open Porcelain Basin, the park's hottest exposed basin. (The name comes from the area's milky deposits of sinter, also known as geyserite.) The bleached basin boils and bubbles like some giant laboratory experiment and the ash-white ground actually pulsates in places. Check out the overviews from **Porcelain Terrace Overlook**, near the Norris Museum; views that in the words of Rudyard Kipling made it look 'as though the tide of desolation had gone out.'

Trails descend from the museum past the continually blowing fumarole of **Black Growler Steam Vent**, which has shifted location several times in recent years. As with most fumaroles, this vent is higher than the basin floor and is thus without a reliable supply of water. Below here is the large but currently inactive Ledge Geyser.

Going clockwise, the boardwalk heads left past **Crackling Lake** and the **Whale's Mouth**, a gaping blue hot spring, to the swirling waters of **Whirligig Geyser**. This geyser became dramatically acidic in 2000, helping support the green cyanidium algae and yellow cyanobacteria that create many of the stunning colors in its drainage channels. The color of these bacterial mats indicates the relative temperatures of the water, from very hot blues and whites (up to 199°F) to cooler yellows and greens (144°F) and even cooler beiges and dark browns (130°F to 80°F). Nearby **Constant Geyser** erupts every 20 minutes or so, but blink and you'll miss the brief eruptions.

Up a side path, **Congress Pool** appeared in 1891, the year scientists convened in Yellowstone for a geologic congress. The footpath to Norris Campground leads off beside Nuphar Lake.

BACK BASIN

Two miles of boardwalks and gentle trails snake through forested Back Basin. **Emerald Spring** combines reflected blue light with yellow sulfur deposits to create a striking blue-green color.

Steamboat Geyser, the world's tallest active geyser, infrequently skyrockets up to an awesome 400ft. The geyser was dormant for half a century until 1961 and quiet again for most of the 1990s, but erupted twice in 2002 and most recently in 2005. At the time of research the geyser was splashing with minor bursts only.

Nearby **Cistern Spring** is linked to the geyser through underground channels and empties for a day or two following Steamboat's eruptions. The spring is slowly drowning its surroundings in geyserite deposits.

Dramatic **Echinus Geyser** (e-*ki*-nus), the park's largest acidic geyser, erupted every couple of hours until fairly recently, with spouts reaching up to 60ft and sometimes continuing for more than an hour, but these days it's pretty quiet. It's a crowd favorite when it is active. You can get closer to the action here than at almost any of the park's other geysers, and if you sit in the grandstand, you may well get wet during an eruption (kids love it). The water air-cools to safe temperatures and isn't that acidic (pH 3.5, like vinegar or lemon juice) but will harm glasses and camera lenses. Furious bubbling signals an imminent eruption. Echinus is named for its spiny geyserite deposits (echinoderms include sea urchins), characteristic of acidic solutions.

After deposits sealed its tiny 2in-wide vent, **Porkchop Geyser** exploded in 1989, blowing huge lumps of geyserite 200ft into the air. Recent rises in the ground temperature forced the park service to reroute the boardwalk around the back of Porkchop Geyser for safety purposes.

Nearby **Pearl Geyser** is one of the park's prettiest. Punsters love the British pronunciation of **Veteran Geyser** – 'Veteran Geezer.' **Minute Geyser** is a victim of early visitor vandalism and sadly no longer erupts every 60 seconds, despite its constant bubbling.

Norris to Madison Junction

The 14-mile Norris to Madison Junction road passes the easily missed Chocolate Pots, a brown-tinged hot spring. The spring is just over 3 miles from Norris Junction, by a turnout past Elk Park. The aptly named **Elk Park** is a fine place to spot elk and bison

and you'll likely have to navigate a car jam here.

Just under 5 miles south of Norris Junction an easy 1-mile trail leads through burned forest to the fun mud pots and springs of **Artist Paint Pots**. The best mudpots are in the far right-hand corner.

The road crosses the Gibbon River three times, past the trailhead to Monument Geyser Basin (see p142) and the pretty blue-green **Beryl Spring** (where the rolling action of the water comes from escaping gases rather than boiling water).

As the road and river descends off the Solfatara Plateau, you pass **Gibbon Falls**, one of the park's prettiest. For the best views of the falls you'll have to park and walk downhill along the road. Like so many of Yellowstone's waterfalls and cascades the falls flow over hard rhyolite and mark the edge of the Yellowstone caldera (see p63).

Five miles further west a parking area on the right gives access to **Terrace Spring**, a large pool with a rolling geyser in the corner. Two lovely hot springs above form the namesake terrace. You could safely miss both Terrace and Beryl Springs if you are tight on time.

From here the road drops down to Madison Junction, with its campground and junior ranger station. The station is a good place to stop if you have kids; there are plenty of kid-friendly activities, bear skins to stroke and talks every half hour. Spotting scopes offer a close-up look at the elk that frequent the Madison Valley. For details of the road heading west to West Yellowstone, see p126.

Norris to Canyon

The 12-mile Norris–Canyon road connects the two parts of the Grand Loop Rd across the cooled lava flows of the Solfatara Plateau. Just past the junction the **Norris Meadows Picnic Area** offers some fine birdwatching over the plain of the meandering Gibbon River.

About 2 miles into the drive a one-way side road branches off past **Virginia Cascade**, which like Gibbon Falls lies on the caldera boundary. One story goes that the superintendent wanted to name the falls after his wife, Virginia, but the NPS was against naming park features after living people, so they compromised by naming the fall after the state of (ahem…) Virginia. The 2.5-mile road is closed to buses, trailers and RVs.

Back on the main road a small boardwalk trail marks the spot where a freak tornado ripped through the plateau in 1984. This was also the spot of the fiercest of 1988's wildfires.

Ice Lake Trail leads 0.5 miles to the peaceful namesake lake, with a handicapped-accessible backcountry site (4D3) on its southern shore. In his book *Lost in My Own Backyard*, writer Tim Cahill wrote of the lake: 'Is this a great country or what? Where else would the wilderness – or one lovely part of it – be made accessible in such a way that the disabled can spend entire sleepless nights worried about being eaten by a bear, just like any able-bodied hiker?' Excellent. Sites 4D1 and 4D2 are just a mile or so from the road and make a great first backcountry site for young families. Camping here feels like owning your own private lake. Trails continue northeast along the border of a major burn area to Wolf Lake (3 miles) and Grebe Lake (another 1.5 miles). For details on longer hike options to Cascade Lake, see p139.

Further down the Norris–Canyon road, you'll pass the Cygnet Lakes and then the Grebe Lake and Cascade Creek Trailheads, which offer an alternative route through burned forest to Grebe and Cascade Lakes.

GEYSER COUNTRY

Yellowstone's Geyser Country holds the park's most spectacular geothermal features, (over half the world's total) concentrated in the world's densest concentration of geysers (over 200 spouters in 1.5 sq miles). It is Geyser Country that makes the Yellowstone plateau utterly and globally unique.

The majority of the geysers line the Firehole River, the aquatic backbone of the basin, whose tributaries feed 21 of the park's 110 waterfalls. Both the Firehole and Madison Rivers offer superb fly-fishing, and the meadows along them support large wildlife populations.

Budget at least half a day here to see the area around Old Faithful, and a whole day to see all the geyser basins, though you could easily spend a day or two more if you catch the geyser-watching bug. If time is tight, concentrate on Upper and Midway Geyser Basins and skip Biscuit and Black Sand Basins.

The most famous geysers always attract a crowd, but sometimes it's the smaller features that are the most interesting. The smaller geysers make up for their lack of size with great names, such as North Goggles, Little Squirt, Gizmo, Spanker, Spasmodic, Slurper and Bulger (aliases the seven dwarfs might adopt to form a criminal gang).

Historian Daniel Boorstin has suggested that Yellowstone Park's enormous appeal is 'due to the fact that its natural phenomena, which erupt on schedule, come closest to the artificiality of "regular" tourist performances.' So grab some popcorn and check show times on the visitor-center board.

ORIENTATION & INFORMATION

The Old Faithful area boasts a visitor center, two gas stations, three hotels and several general stores, including the original 1897 knotty pine Hamilton Store, the oldest structure still in use in the park. The Yellowstone General Store next to the Snow Lodge has the park's best selection of groceries and sells fishing flies, spotting scopes and fishing permits.

The combined ranger station, backcountry office and medical clinic are set back from the main parking area, across the west parking lot from the visitor center. The Old Faithful Snow Lodge gift shop offers bike rentals in the summer and snowshoe and ski rentals in winter.

TIP

The first thing to do when you arrive at Old Faithful is to check the predicted geyser eruption times at the visitor center and then plan your route around these. Predictions are made for the region's six main geysers – Old Faithful, Grand, Castle, Riverside, Daisy and the Lower Geyser Basin's Great Fountain – and these are also posted at Old Faithful Lodge, Old Faithful Inn and the Madison Junior Ranger Station.

Remember, though, that geysers rarely erupt on schedule, so take some snacks and sunblock for the wait. Riverside runs to within 30 minutes of predictions, but Grand is only reliable within two or three hours. Still, there's always something erupting in Upper Geyser Basin, and if you're really lucky you'll catch a biggie like Beehive or Daisy.

lonelyplanet.com

YELLOWSTONE NATIONAL PARK

Geyser Country

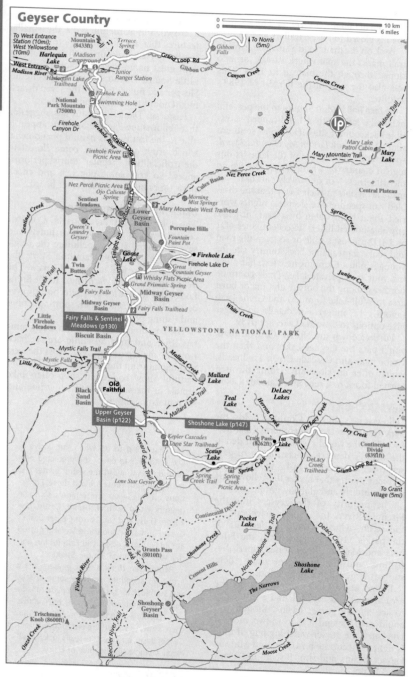

0 _____ 10 km
0 _____ 6 miles

To West Entrance Station (10mi); West Yellowstone (10mi)

Purple Mountain (8433ft)

Terrace Spring

Gibbon Falls

To Norris (5mi)

Harlequin Lake

West Entrance Rd

Madison Campground

Grand Loop Rd

Madison River

Harlequin Lake Trailhead

Junior Ranger Station

Gibbon Canyon

Canyon Creek

Cowan Creek

National Park Mountain (7500ft)

Firehole Falls

Swimming Hole

Maggie Creek

Firehole Canyon Dr

Grand Loop Rd

Firehole River

Plateau Trail

Mary Lake Patrol Cabin

Mary Lake

Firehole River Picnic Area

Mary Mountain Trail

Mary Lake

Nez Percé Picnic Area

Ojo Caliente Spring

Culex Basin

Nez Perce Creek

Central Plateau

Sentinel Meadows

Morning Mist Springs

Mary Mountain West Trailhead

Spruce Creek

Lower Geyser Basin

Queen's Laundry Geyser

Porcupine Hills

Sentinel Creek

Fountain Paint Pot

Goose Lake

Firehole Lake

Fountain Freight Rd

Firehole Lake Dr

Juniper Creek

Twin Buttes

Great Fountain Geyser

Whisky Flats Picnic Area

Fairy Creek Trail

Fairy Falls

Grand Prismatic Spring

Midway Geyser Basin

White Creek

Little Firehole Meadows

Midway Geyser Basin

Fairy Falls Trailhead

YELLOWSTONE NATIONAL PARK

Fairy Falls & Sentinel Meadows (p130)

Biscuit Basin

Mystic Falls Trail

Mallard Creek

Mystic Falls

Little Firehole River

Mallard Lake

DeLacy Lakes

Black Sand Basin

Old Faithful

Mallard Lake Trail

Teal Lake

Herron Creek

DeLacy Creek

Upper Geyser Basin (p122)

Shoshone Lake (p147)

Dry Creek

Kepler Cascades

Lone Star Trailhead

Craig Pass (8262ft)

Isa Lake

Continental Divide (8391ft)

Howard Eaton Trail

Scaup Lake

Spring Creek

DeLacy Creek Trailhead

Grand Loop Rd

Lone Star Geyser

Spring Creek Trail

Spring Creek Picnic Area

To Grant Village (5mi)

Continental Divide

Pocket Lake

Shoshone Lake Trail

Shoshone Creek

North Shoshone Lake Trail

Shoshone Lake

Delacy Creek Trail

Grants Pass (8010ft)

Cement Hills

Firehole River

The Narrows

Summit Creek

Bechler River Trail

Shoshone Geyser Basin

Trischman Knob (8600ft)

Ouzel Creek

Moose Creek

Lewis River Channel

Public **showers** (⏱ 6:30am-11pm) are available in the reception area at Old Faithful Lodge. There are no campgrounds in the Old Faithful area.

For details of the drive from Madison Junction to Old Faithful, see p156.

Upper Geyser Basin

This heavily visited basin holds 180 of the park's 200 to 250 geysers, the most famous of which is geriatric **Old Faithful**. Boardwalks, footpaths and a cycling path along the Firehole River link the five distinct geyser groups, the furthest of which is only 1.5 miles from Old Faithful.

The **Old Faithful Visitor Center** (⏱ late Apr–early Nov & mid-Dec–mid-Mar) offers a bookstore and information booth and shows films 30 minutes before and 15 minutes after an eruption of Old Faithful. The center closes at 7pm in summer, but an information window stays open until 8pm. Rangers give a geology talk outside the visitor center six times a day and offer an evening presentation at 7:30pm. There's a short talk for kids at 10am. Daily geology walks depart at 5:30pm from Castle Geyser and at 8:30am from the visitor center. At the time of research, the center was in a temporary location awaiting the completion of a new and improved center by 2010.

The best loop around the Upper Geyser Basin follows the paved road one way and the boardwalk the other for a total of 3 miles. To this you can add a small hike up to Observation Point for views over the basin. There is a smaller loop around Geyser Hill, but you'll miss many of the best geysers if you limit yourself to this.

You can combine the central geyser loop with surrounding thermal areas by hiking out to Biscuit and Black Sand Basins or biking past many of the geysers on the way to Biscuit Basin and back.

OLD FAITHFUL

Erupting every 90 minutes or so to impatient (preliminary hand clapping is not uncommon) visitors' delight, Old Faithful spouts some 8000 gallons of water up to 180ft in the air, though the last time we checked, the old salt was in need of a dose of Viagra. Water temperature is normally 204°F and the steam is about 350°F. It's worth viewing the eruption from several

different locations – the geyser-side seats, the balcony of the Old Faithful Inn and from a distance on Observation Hill.

Though neither the tallest nor most predictable geyser in the park, Old Faithful is considered the tallest predictable geyser. For over 75 years the geyser faithfully erupted every hour or so, one reason for the name the Washburn expedition gave it in 1870. The average time between shows these days is 90 minutes and getting longer, though this has historically varied between 45 and 110 minutes. The average eruption lasts around four minutes. The longer the eruption, the longer the recovery time.

Scientists have worked out that the length of time until the next eruption is mathematically linked to the duration of the last eruption. A two-minute eruption takes 55 minutes to recover from; a 4.5-minute eruption takes 90 minutes. Rangers correctly predict eruptions to within 10 minutes about 90% of the time. And no, Old Faithful has never erupted on the hour.

After years of studying the geyser, we have our own method of calculating exactly when an eruption of Old Faithful is imminent. Just count the number of bored people seated around the geyser – the number of tourists is inversely proportional to the amount of time left until the next eruption.

OBSERVATION HILL

For a pre- or post-eruption overview of the entire basin, follow a branch trail from the Firehole River up a couple hundred vertical feet to Observation Point for an alternative view of the Old Faithful eruption. From here you can descend to Solitary Geyser to rejoin the boardwalk for a 1.1-mile loop.

Solitary Geyser started off as a hot spring until it was diverted into a swimming pool in 1915 (the pool was dismantled in 1950). The lowering of the water level turned the spring into a geyser, triggering eruptions that continue to this day, even though water levels have returned to normal. Small eruptions occur every four to eight minutes.

GEYSER HILL

Not far from Old Faithful is the unmarked **Chinese Spring**, named after an Asian (actually Japanese) laundry that once operated here. Dirty clothes were put into the spring along with soap, and the owners waited for

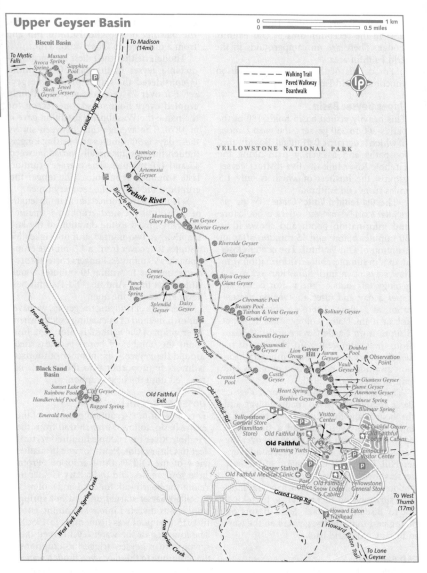

Upper Geyser Basin

the clothes to fly out, apparently clean, in an induced eruption. Don't try a repeat performance, unless you want a citation.

Nearby, riverside **Blue Star Spring** was the site of a macabre incident in winter 1996–97, when a young bison fell into the boiling waters and died, causing the pool to smell like beef soup for days.

Consistent seepage from **Giantess Geyser** and **Vault Geyser** have created geyserite terraces that look like scaled relief maps. Giantess springs to life between two and six times a year, though when active the geyser erupts twice hourly for up to 40 hours. The surrounding area shakes from underground steam explosions just before it erupts. Vault

Geyser was inactive for a decade until bursting back into life in 1998.

Doublet Pool is known for its deep blue color, scalloped geyserite border and the occasional thumping that emanates from collapsing steam and gas bubbles deep underground. **Aurum Geyser** is thought somehow to be connected to water deposits in the meadow behind it.

The **Lion Geyser** group is a gathering of four interconnected geysers (two lions and two cubs), whose eruptions are preceded by a roar, hence the name. **Heart Spring** is said to resemble the shape of a human heart.

Beehive Geyser erupts twice a day, up to 190ft through its 4ft-high cone-shaped nozzle, and is the second or third tallest regularly active geyser in the park. Beehive has an 'indicator' – a smaller vent that when active signals the main eruption.

Erupting every 20 minutes, **Plume** is one of the easiest geysers to catch. It's also one of basin's youngest geysers, created by a steam explosion in 1922. Interestingly, its eruptions seem to have different phases at night and day. Nearby **Anemone Geyser** erupts every 15 minutes or so.

Rangers lead 90-minute walks of Geyser Hill daily at 8:30am.

THE MAIN LOOP

Along the tarmac trail west of the Old Faithful Inn is **Castle Geyser**, whose huge cone, resembling a bleached sandcastle, attests to its status as the oldest geyser in the region, somewhere between 5000 and 15,000 years old (and built atop an even older spring). Castle goes off every 13 hours or so and can be predicted to within an hour; the water eruption is followed by a noisy 30-minute steam phase, as the heat and steam energy long outlast the water supply. Nearby 42ft-deep **Crested Pool** is almost constantly boiling. This is one of the best places to get overviews of the basin.

The predictable **Daisy Geyser** lets loose at an angle up to 75ft every three hours or so and can be predicted to within 45 minutes, except when nearby Splendid Geyser erupts. Splendid is one of the largest in the region but erupts irregularly – apparently sometimes triggered by a change in atmospheric pressure, which slightly reduces the pool's boiling point. Don't confuse Daisy with the larger constantly splashing cone

of **Comet Geyser**. All three geysers are linked by underground chambers.

Grotto erupts every eight hours for up to 10 hours. The cone takes its weird shape from trees that have been encased in the geyserite. Increased activity in Grotto generally means less activity in Giant Geyser. The picturesque **Riverside Geyser** puts on an amazing show when a 75ft column of water arcs over the Firehole River, often capped by a rainbow. Twenty-minute outpourings occur about every six hours; water spilling over the cone signals an imminent eruption.

Across the Firehole River, nearby **Fan** and **Mortar Geysers** erupt infrequently but in unison, with Fan bursting water out of 17 individual jets.

A steamy favorite, which is well worth the walk, is beautiful **Morning Glory Pool**, named after the flower. Unfortunately, the pool is slowly changing temperature and, therefore, color, due to the tons of trash thrown into the pool by past visitors (the main access road to Old Faithful passed beside the pool until 1971). The refuse diminishes circulation and accelerates heat loss. As the pool cools, orange bacteria spreads from its sides, replacing the gorgeous blue tones. In 1950 park staff induced an eruption to empty and clean the spring, pulling out $86.27 in pennies, 76 handkerchiefs, several towels, socks, shirts and even women's underwear!

From Morning Glory, hardcore geyser gazers can follow a walking trail to several minor features such as **Artemisia Geyser**, named for its similarity to the color of sagebrush (*Artemisia*), and **Atomizer Geyser**, named for the large amounts of steam that follow its minor eruptions.

Back toward Old Faithful, a boardwalk branches off the cycle path to **Giant Geyser**, which produces stupendous 250ft eruptions but may be dormant for decades. It currently erupts every three to 10 days (with eruptions that last an hour), reaches heights of 180ft to 250ft and expels an astonishing one million gallons of hot water with each eruption. The cessation of otherwise continuous **Bijou Geyser** nearby signals an imminent eruption of Giant Geyser.

The strikingly colorful **Chromatic Pool** and **Beauty Pool** are linked, so when one drops, the other rises.

Next is **Grand Geyser**, ranking as the world's tallest predictable geyser (150ft to

180ft). It spews in bursts every eight hours or so and lasts about 12 minutes. It will often pause after nine minutes and then restart after a minute or so; the subsequent bursts are typically the most spectacular. Grand is a fountain geyser, not a cone like Old Faithful. Nearby **Turban Geyser** acts as a trigger for Grand and, along with **Vent Geyser**, continues to rage for one to two hours after Grand subsides.

Sawmill Geyser is in eruption about 30% of the time, but its extents are highly variable. Water spins violently in its crater like a circular saw. Nearby **Spasmodic** is also in eruption a third of the time and erupts from more than 20 vents.

Rangers lead 90-minute walks of the Upper Geyser Basin daily at 5:30pm.

OLD FAITHFUL INN

Seattle architect Robert C Reamer designed the enchanting Old Faithful Inn (1904), a national historic landmark and one of the world's largest log buildings. It's the only building in the park that looks like it actually belongs here. The log rafters of its seven-story lobby rise nearly 90ft, and the chimney of the central fireplace (actually eight fireplaces combined) contains more than 500 tons of rock. It's definitely a worthwhile visit, even for nonguests. Be sure to check out the Crow's Nest, a wonderful top-floor balcony where musicians used to play for dancers below (it hasn't been used since 1959). The 2nd-floor observation deck offers the chance to enjoy fine views of Old Faithful geyser over the beverage of your choice, and the lobby hosts occasional talks by regional authors.

Free 45-minute Historic Inn tours depart from the fireplace at 9:30am, 11am, 2pm and 3:30pm. For a review of accommodation options at the inn, see above.

Black Sand Basin

This geyser basin, 1 mile northwest of Old Faithful, has a few interesting features. The eponymous black sand is derived from weathered volcanic glass (obsidian).

Cliff Geyser is named for the geyserite wall that separates the geyser from Iron Spring Creek and is a frequent splasher. Nearby **Ragged Spring** frequently joins in the action with 12ft bursts. **Emerald Pool** looks like an exquisite flower with a lovely orange lip and gets its pretty color from yellow bacteria

that blend with blue reflected from the sky. **Rainbow Pool** is connected to nearby Sunset Lake and is one of the more colorful in the park. The ground under the boardwalks here is literally boiling.

Unsigned **Handkerchief Pool**, just to the south of Rainbow Pool, was once one of Yellowstone's most famous features. Visitors would place a handkerchief in the pool and watch it get sucked down and then spat out 'clean' through a side vent. The pool stopped functioning in the 1920s, after one dimwit jammed logs into the opening, but it has since restored itself. Today it's illegal to throw anything into any of Yellowstone's thermal features.

You can access Black Sand Basin by car or, better, by foot from Daisy Geyser. Rangers lead hour-long walks here daily at 1pm.

Biscuit Basin

Two miles further north, Biscuit Basin was named for biscuitlike deposits that surrounded stunning **Sapphire Pool**, but these were destroyed during violent eruptions that followed the 1959 Hebgen earthquake (see p202). If you're low on time, this is one basin you could safely miss.

The main features here are deep **Jewel Geyser**, which erupts every 10 minutes or so, with lovely yellow run-offs, and **Shell Geyser**, which is shaped like a clamshell and linked underground. **Mustard Spring** is named for its iron-oxide-induced dark-yellow color.

A 0.5-mile hiking and biking trail leads from across the highway to Upper Geyser Basin's Daisy Falls and a hiking path crosses the road to lead to Artemisia and Atomizer geysers in the Upper Geyser Basin.

The Mystic Falls Trail starts here – see p130 for details. There are free daily ranger-led hikes to the falls at 9am from Avoca Spring.

Midway Geyser Basin

Five miles north of Old Faithful and 2 miles south of the Firehole Lake Dr entrance is Midway Geyser Basin. The algae-tinged indigo waters of the 370ft-wide **Grand Prismatic Spring**, the park's largest and deepest (121ft) hot spring, is the key sight here and probably the most beautiful thermal feature in the park. The spring drains into **Excelsior Pool**, a huge former geyser that blew itself out of existence in the 1880s with massive

300ft explosions of water. The last eruptions here were in 1985, when the pool erupted almost continuously for 46 hours, before lulling itself back into a deep sleep. The pool continually discharges an amazing 4000 gallons of boiling water a minute into the Firehole River; according to T Scott Bryan's *The Geysers of Yellowstone*, that's enough to fill 300,000 automobile gas tanks every day! More water is expelled here in a single day than Old Faithful releases in two months. You can admire the colorful yellow and orange runoff as you approach the basin over the bridge.

The features are linked by a 0.5-mile accessible boardwalk; budget about 30 minutes here.

For the most dramatic photos of Grand Prismatic Spring, drive south to Fairy Falls Trailhead, walk for 1 mile, and then take a faint path up the side of the fire-burned ridge (itself a lava deposit from the west rim of the caldera). From above, the spring looks like a giant blue eye, weeping exquisite multicolored tears.

Lower Geyser Basin

Separate roads access the three main sections of this sprawling thermal basin: the main Grand Loop Rd passes Fountain Paint Pot; the one-way Firehole Lake Dr loops off the main road to Great Fountain and other geysers; and Fountain Flat Dr offers access to hiking trails and minor thermal features.

FIREHOLE LAKE DRIVE

Firehole Lake Dr is a one-way, 3-mile road starting 2 miles north of Midway Geyser Basin and about 1 mile south of the Fountain Paint Pot parking lot. It passes several pretty pools and large geysers, including huge **Great Fountain Geyser**, which soars up to 200ft in a series of wide staccato bursts every 11 hours or so. Eruption times are predicted by the visitor center at Old Faithful to within a couple of hours, and you'll often find people waiting with a picnic lunch and a good book. The crater begins to overflow 90 minutes before an eruption and violent boiling signals an imminent eruption. Eruptions can last one hour.

The nearby 30ft cone of **White Dome Geyser** usually erupts every half hour or so. The geyser is the symbol of the Yellowstone Association, whose decal really should decorate the windshield of your car (see the inside front cover of this book). Nearby **Pink Cone Geyser** gets its color from manganese dioxide deposits. A road was built right across the side of this cone in the 1930s.

Firehole Lake is a large hot spring ringed by several small geysers, including the raging waters of Artemisia Geyser and the sensuous smoothness of Young Hopeful.

Across the road, **Hot Lake** (also known as Black Warrior Lake) offers more geysers and even a small cascade of boiling water. **Steady Geyser** is in continual eruption through one of two vents.

FOUNTAIN PAINT POT

Roughly midway between Madison Junction and Old Faithful, Fountain Paint Pot Nature Trail takes in four types of thermal features along a 0.5-mile boardwalk loop. **Fountain Paint Pot** itself is a huge bowl of plopping goop that ranks as one of the biggest in the park. The action is sloppiest in spring, with some mud pots drying up by August. The area around the thermal features is slowly being drowned in deposits, while, beyond, a grassy basin supports the park's largest bison herd.

The **mud pots** are the top-billed comedians of the show. **Red Spouter** is particularly interesting, since it acts like a muddy hot spring in early summer, only to become a mud pot and then a fumarole later in the year. It only appeared after the huge Hebgen Earthquake of 1959. Morning and Fountain Geysers are impressive but infrequent gushers; the latter drains into Spasm Geyser.

Clepsydra Geyser has erupted almost constantly since the Hebgen Lake earthquake in 1959 (see p202). The geyser was named Clepsydra (Greek for 'water clock') at the time when it used to go off every three minutes on the button. **Jelly Geyser** does indeed look like an upside-down bowl of Jell-O.

In 1981 **Celestine Pool** was the site of one of the park's most famous accidents, when a young Californian man dived headfirst into the hot spring to save his dog who had controversially decided to cool off in the enticing pool. (It's hard to know which of the two ranks as the more stupid, the one who jumped in or the one who jumped in after him.) Sadly both died as a result of their burns.

For a map of Fountain Paint Pot and Firehole Lake Dr pick up the park-service trail guide (50¢). Rangers lead tours here three times a week at 9am.

FOUNTAIN FLAT DRIVE

This former freight road turns off the Grand Loop Rd at pleasant Nez Percé Picnic Area and continues south for 1.5 miles to a hiking and biking trailhead. From here the road is accessible to bikers and hikers all the way to Fairy Falls Trailhead, 4 miles away. The trail is wheelchair accessible for 2.2 miles to the Goose Lake (OD5) campsite.

Just beyond a parking lot is the **Ojo Caliente Hot Spring**, which empties into the river (Ojo Caliente means 'Hot Spring' in Spanish). Just south of the bridge is the trail to Sentinel Meadows (see p131).

Two trails on either side of the bridge over the Firehole River offer access to the little-visited **Pocket Basin** (Map p130), a miniature caldera created by a hydrothermal explosion that must have been on the scale of an atomic bomb. The northern trail leads past the mud pot of Grotto Spring and inviting Baby Bathtub Spring to the River Group, a collection of four or five geysers and hot springs that includes Cavern Spring, Bath Spring, Azure Spring, Diadem Spring and Cone Spring. Over the ridge is one of the park's largest collections of mud pots. Across the river is Mound Spring, which erupts every half hour or so. The basin isn't on the scale of the more famous thermal features further south, but this is one place you can explore away from the boardwalks and parking lots. Remember to take the normal precautions when approaching any thermal feature.

Firehole Canyon Dr

The one-way Firehole Canyon Dr leaves the Grand Loop Rd just south of Madison Junction. The road passes 40ft-high **Firehole Falls** at the foot of towering dark rhyolite cliffs, but the main attraction here is the lukewarm **Firehole Swimming Area** (no fee), one of the few locations in the park that's open for swimming. The kids will love it. There are two toilets here but limited parking.

Madison to West Yellowstone

Madison Junction sits at the confluence of the Firehole, Madison and Gibbon Rivers. Towering above the small information station is **National Park Mountain** (7500ft), which commemorates the spot where in 1870 the idea of preserving Yellowstone was allegedly first mentioned (see the boxed text, below).

The Madison Valley is of interest mainly to anglers and wildlife-watchers, though all will appreciate the sublime afternoon light and active herds of deer, elk and bison. Due to the long snow-free season many elk live in the valley year-round, while bison migrate through the valley en route between winter habitat near the park's western boundary and summer grazing in the Hayden Valley. The 14-mile road to West Yellowstone is also one of the park's busiest tourist corridors.

Two miles east of Madison, the family-friendly Harlequin Lake Trailhead leads 0.5

THE GREAT NATIONAL PARK SERVICE MYTH

The story, and it's a good one, goes that on September 19, 1870, towards the end of the Langford-Washburn-Doane expedition, three men sat down at the junction of the Firehole and Gibbon Rivers by present-day Madison Junction to discuss what they had seen and to ruminate on its future. One suggested that there was money was to be made from the region's wonders but it was Montanan attorney Cornelius Hedges who suggested that the Yellowstone region be made into a national park. And thus the seeds of the National Park Service were sown.

But was it really this simple? The idea of protecting the area had been suggested beforehand, by artist George Caitlin in 1833 (though not in direct reference to Yellowstone), by Montanan Governor Thomas Meagher in 1865 and by David Folsom during his expedition of 1869. Over the years park historians began to question the altruistic version of history, and today the notion that the national park idea stemmed from one specific man on one specific day has been largely debunked.

The park service originally ran with the myth, going as far as staging annual recreations of the event between 1957 and 1964, and has been reluctant to ditch the tale. As more than one former park superintendent has noted, it's such a compelling story that had it not happened, the park service would have been forced to invent it.

miles north to a pond. The trailhead is also a fine place to spot wildlife in the lovely valley to the south. Elk often lie in the meadows here, with only their heads poking up above the long grass. From here the road threads between volcanic bluffs, with towering Mt Haynes (8235ft) on the left and Mt Jackson on the right, past several excellent fly-fishing spots, before the valley opens up to views of the distant Gallatin Range.

Halfway along the road the Seven Mile Bridge marks the Madison River Picnic Area, popular with fly-fishers, and the Gneiss Creek Trailhead. The area south of the road here is closed to protect trumpeter swan habitat. A couple of miles later, vehicles are not allowed to stop for a quarter-mile stretch of the main road to protect bald eagle habitat. In 1988 this section of the park was engulfed in the North Fork fire, the largest of that summer's giant blazes.

Four miles further, Riverside Dr is a 1-mile, two-way road that's useful for fishing access and perhaps some family biking. Three miles later the Two Ribbons Trail is a 0.75-mile wheelchair-accessible trail that offers a fairly dull loop or point-to-point stroll through some fire burns.

Shortly after you enter Montana, about 2 miles before West Yellowstone, a side road to the north accesses several more fishing spots. And then suddenly, just like that, you are out of the wilderness and in the middle of bustling West Yellowstone (see p170).

Old Faithful to West Thumb

Three miles into the 17-mile drive between Old Faithful and West Thumb is **Kepler Cascades**, where a wooden platform offers fine views of the 125ft falls. Just past the cascades turnout is the parking area for the worthwhile hike or bike ride to **Lone Star Geyser** (p132 and p155). The road climbs past Scaup Lake, the Spring Creek Picnic Area (site of the park's biggest stagecoach robbery in 1908) and the Continental Divide Trailhead before reaching **Isa Lake** at Craig Pass (8262ft).

Craig Pass is an unassuming spot of deep significance. Lily-choked Isa Lake sits astride both the road and the **Continental Divide** and in spring drains (or rather seeps) into both the Atlantic and Pacific drainages. The west side of the lake drains year-round into the Firehole River, which flows into the Missouri and Mississippi before finally reaching the Atlantic *to the east;* the east side (in spring only) flows into Shoshone Lake and then the Lewis, Snake and Columbia rivers and thus the Pacific Ocean *to the west.* Imagine the water particles eagerly anticipating which trip they'll get to make. The lake was named after Isabelle Jelke, the first park tourist to visit the lake, and freezes solid in winter under around 15ft of snow.

From the pass, the road descends to the DeLacy Creek Picnic Area and Trailhead (see p132) and shortly afterward offers a tantalizing sliver of a view towards remote Shoshone Lake. From here the road ascends back across the Continental Divide (8391ft), before finally descending to excellent views of Yellowstone Lake and the turnoff to West Thumb. See the Lake Country section, p112, for routes onward from here.

BECHLER REGION

Visitors must go out of their way to find the Bechler region. Located in the remote southwest area of the park, it cannot be reached via the main entrance points or loops. Known for its numerous waterfalls and the park's highest rainfall, the remote Bechler (*Beckler*) region, also known as Cascade Corner, is largely the preserve of hardy backpackers, outfitters and horseback riders who brave flooded streams, monster mosquitoes and boggy marshland to access beautiful backcountry with the park's largest waterfalls and outstanding thermal soaking springs. The 8000-hectare meadow is home to diverse wildlife, including sandhill cranes, moose and coyotes. Bring adequate repellent – mosquitoes are often brutal along the river until the end of July.

Visitors en route to a hike in the region or traveling Grassy Lake Rd might want to pay a visit to the Cave Falls cascades and swimming hole (see p143). For details on Grassy Lake Rd and its day hikes to Beula Lake and Union Falls, see the Around Yellowstone chapter (p256).

ORIENTATION & INFORMATION

Bechler is accessed via Bechler Ranger Station or Cave Falls Trailhead, both off the mostly unpaved Cave Falls Rd via US 20 from Ashton, Idaho, a two-hour drive from West Yellowstone, Montana, via ID Hwy 47 and Marysville Rd. Alternative approaches include coming from Driggs, Idaho, to the south (joining US 20) or the brutal, unpaved Grassy Lake Rd/Reclamation Rd, from the turnoff just north of Flagg Ranch, part of John D Rockefeller Memorial Parkway, 2 miles south of Yellowstone's South Entrance; allow at least two hours from Flagg Ranch.

HIKING

Easily the best way to get a close-up taste of Yellowstone's unique combination of rolling landscape, wildlife and thermal activity is on foot, along the more than 900 miles of maintained trails. Hiking is also the best way to escape the crowds. Only 10% of visitors step off the road or boardwalks and only 1% overnight in the backcountry. It's one thing to photograph a bison from your car, but it's quite another thing to hike gingerly past a snorting herd out on their turf.

So pick up a map, pack some granola bars and work into your Yellowstone itinerary at least a couple of the following great hikes. Note that the park uses a three character code (eg 2K7) to identify both trailheads and specific backcountry campsites, and we have included these wherever useful.

EASY HIKES

For a rundown of our personal definitions of what is an easy, moderate and difficult hike, see p40.

Roosevelt Country

Hikes in this region lead to petrified forests, meadows of wildflowers and excellent places to spot bison and bighorn sheep.

YELLOWSTONE RIVER PICNIC AREA TRAIL

Duration 1½–2 hours
Distance 4-mile round-trip or loop
Difficulty easy
Elevation Change 350ft
Start/Finish Yellowstone River Picnic Area (2K7; Map p104)
Nearest Town/Junction Tower-Roosevelt
Summary A lovely stroll that offers crowdless vistas over the Narrows, offering much historical and geological interest.

Popular with picnicking families, this scenic stroll offers fantastic views into the eroded

towers and basalt formations of the Narrows and Calcite Springs, and possible glimpses of osprey and bighorn sheep: bring your binoculars. To get to the trailhead, take the Northeast Entrance Rd across the bridge from Tower-Roosevelt to the picnic area parking lot, 1.5 miles east of the junction. There's no formal parking, so you'll have to park in one of the picnic sites.

Several unofficial dirt trails climb the slopes behind the picnic area but the official (signed) trail leads off from the picnic site left of the vault toilets to ascend a couple hundred feet and deposit you puffing on the rim of the **Yellowstone canyon**. En route the trail passes a large erratic boulder, deposited in the valley over 10,000 years ago from the Beartooth Mountains by slow-moving glaciers. You'll notice along this hike how many of the Douglas firs have prospered in the moist, protective shade of these huge boulders. The hike traces the canyon's north rim for a couple of miles, providing unobscured views down past the cooked canyon walls to the **Yellowstone River** and north and east beyond rolling ridges to the peaks of the Absaroka Range.

The trail stays in open country on the ridgeline 800ft above the canyon floor for the whole route. About 20 minutes from the trailhead you may smell sulfur, a sign that you are about to pass 180-degree views of the Calcite Springs thermal area across the canyon. Ten minutes further and there's fine views of the breccia spires of the Narrows. Look out for bighorn sheep below the basalt columns at **Overhanging Cliff**.

The trail abruptly ends at a bald **hilltop lookout** that offers views down on the site of the Bannock Indian ford, used by the Bannock to cross the Yellowstone River during their annual hunting trips across the park (see p102). You can also see the Tower Falls region (but not the falls themselves) to the right and the fire tower atop Mt Washburn in the distance.

From here you can retrace your steps to investigate the views of the canyon for a second time, or alternatively take the trail left (northeast) for a few minutes to the three-way junction with the **Specimen Ridge Trail**. Take a left at this junction to return downhill back to the road and the picnic area. (If you have some excess energy, you could ascend the trail up the to the top of

Specimen Ridge for fine views over the Lamar Valley.)

Just before reaching the road, branch left at the trail register and cut cross-county back to the trailhead, paralleling the road to join the large erratic boulder mentioned at the start of the hike. Otherwise you'll have to hike along the road, an unpleasant end to a lovely hike.

LOST LAKE

Duration 2 hours
Distance 3.3-mile loop
Difficulty easy
Elevation Change 600ft
Start/Finish Tower-Junction (2K2), Roosevelt Lodge (Map p104)
Nearest Town/Junction Tower-Roosevelt
Summary A peaceful early-morning hike to a secluded lake and a petrified tree – perfect for families and anyone staying or dining at Roosevelt Lodge.

The Lost Lake Loop trail begins behind Roosevelt Lodge (take the right fork), climbing about 300ft past Lost Lake to a petrified tree, from which the trail climbs onto a plateau and then descends to the Tower Ranger Station. Before you even start the hike, warm up with a quick 10-minute detour left at the trailhead to the small but pretty **Lost Creek Falls**.

From the trailhead the trail switchbacks surprisingly steeply for the first 10 minutes onto the ridge. Look out for mule deer here in the early morning. Take a right at the junction (left leads to Tower Fall Campground 2.9 miles away) and you'll come to the meadows surrounding **Lost Lake**, about 30 minutes from the trailhead. The trail traverses the length of the lake, past lily pads and dragonflies, to a good potential picnic spot at the end of the lake. If you're lucky, you might spot moose here.

From here the trail descends through meadows thick with spring wildflowers to reach the parking lot of the **Petrified Tree** (p102). Take a couple of minutes to appreciate the 50-million-year-old stone redwood (there used to be three such trees here but early tourists chipped away the other two). If you started the hike early, you'll have the place to yourself; later in the day the parking lot will be jammed with reversing SUVs.

The trail back to Roosevelt Lodge follows the orange markers up the hill from the edge of the parking lot and ascends to an open sagebrush plateau, offering fine views ahead to Junction Butte, Specimen Ridge and the Absaroka Range to the east. The trail then descends to the **Tower Ranger Station**. You'll likely see mule deer grazing in the meadows here; at the very least you'll see a John Deere parked by the ranger station. Cross the wooden bridge by the orange trail marker and in two minutes you'll be back at the cabins of Roosevelt Lodge, where breakfast will be waiting.

Geyser Country

Even the short hikes described below will get you away from the crowds at Old Faithful to some spectacular backcountry waterfalls and geysers.

FAIRY FALLS & TWIN BUTTES

Duration 3–4 hours
Distance 6 miles
Difficulty easy
Elevation Change negligible
Start/Finish Fairy Falls Trailhead (OK5; Map p120)
Nearest Town/Junction Old Faithful
Summary A short jaunt to one of the most accessible backcountry cascades, with fine views over several thermal features.

Tucked away in the northwest corner of the Midway Geyser Basin, 197ft Fairy Falls receives relatively few visitors, even though it's only a short jaunt from Old Faithful. Beyond Fairy Falls the lollipop loop trail continues to a hidden thermal area at the base of the Twin Buttes, two conspicuous bald hills severely charred in the 1988 fires. The geysers are undeveloped, and you're likely to have them to yourself – in stark contrast to the throngs around Grand Prismatic Spring.

The Fairy Falls (Steel Bridge) Trailhead is just west of the Grand Loop Rd, 1 mile south of the Midway Geyser Basin turnoff and 4.5 miles north of the Old Faithful overpass. Use the north side of Trails Illustrated's 1:63,360 map No 302 *Old Faithful*.

Fairy Falls & Sentinel Meadows

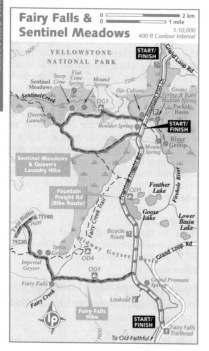

and clumps of raspberries and fireweed flourish around a pretty pool, which makes for a fine swimming hole on a hot summer day.

After crossing a footbridge, the trail continues 0.7 miles northwest toward the prominent **Twin Buttes** and several conspicuous plumes of rising steam. Cross several marshy patches with the aid of log bridges and head for the closest plume emanating from **Spray Geyser**, erupting frequently to a height of 6ft to 8ft. Return a little way along the trail, then continue west, following the outlet from **Imperial Geyser**, which is lined with orange algae. Imperial plays almost perpetually, projecting blasts of water up to 20ft into its large rainbow pool. If you care to climb onto the buttes, head across the open slopes behind Imperial Geyser. After discovering the collection of little pools hidden in a hollow between the two summits, you can continue to either summit without much difficulty. Views to the east encompass the Lower and Midway Geyser Basins, while to the west the trail-free Madison Plateau stretches off toward the park boundary. Retrace your steps to the Fairy Falls Trailhead.

The trail is closed until the last Saturday of May, due to the presence of bears.

Cross the **Firehole River** on the silver trestle bridge, then head northwest along Fountain Flat Dr, which is now a wide gravel biking and hiking path. After 1 mile you'll notice multicolored steam rising from **Grand Prismatic Spring** on the right. You can't reach the boardwalk from this trail, but you can scramble up the unofficial trails to your left for an astonishing bird's-eye view of Yellowstone's most beautiful thermal feature. Continue 0.33 miles to a trail junction and turn left onto the narrower **Fairy Creek Trail**. The trail, which winds 1.6 miles past backcountry campsite OD1 through lodgepole forest burned in the 1988 fires, is uninteresting at first, but as you near Fairy Falls you'll find a variety of lush foliage growing on the damp ground amid blackened stumps.

At 197ft, **Fairy Falls** is the park's seventh-highest waterfall, but the volume of water is hardly on a par with the falls on the Yellowstone River. Still, patterned streaks of white water blanket the dark lower rocks,

MYSTIC FALLS & BISCUIT BASIN

Duration 1½–2 hours
Distance 3-mile loop
Difficulty easy
Elevation Change 700ft
Start/Finish Biscuit Basin (OK4; Map p120)
Nearest Town/Junction Old Faithful
Summary A short family-friendly stroll from an interesting thermal basin to a 70ft waterfall, with the option for a longer loop hike.

The shorter, out-and-back option to the base of the falls is relatively flat and thus popular with families. Due to a lack of shade, the longer loop hike to the overlook is best done in the morning or late afternoon. The trail is closed until the last Saturday of May due to the presence of bears.

The Biscuit Basin turnoff is 2 miles north of the Old Faithful overpass and 14 miles south of Madison Junction, on the west side of Grand Loop Rd. Use the north side of Trails Illustrated's 1:63,360 map No 302 *Old Faithful*.

From the parking area, head west across the Firehole River bridge. Follow the **Biscuit Basin boardwalk** loop 0.3 miles around to the left past several notable geysers and hot springs (see p124). Just west of Avoca Spring, the wide, sandy **Mystic Falls Trail** (blazed but unsigned) ducks into burned lodgepole forest dotted with wildflowers.

The undulating trail parallels, but does not cross, the **Little Firehole River**. Soon you'll reach the signed Summit Lake/Little Firehole Meadows junction. From here it's 0.7 miles to the left on the most direct route to the falls, saving the longer overlook loop – visible on a cliff to the right – for the return trip. Heading upstream into the canyon, the path can be muddy where seeps cross the trail. After 10 to 15 minutes the trail arrives at the bottom of the 70ft **Mystic Falls**, 1.2 miles from Biscuit Basin, where orange hot spring bacterial seeps are in abundance. A series of switchbacks lead to the top of the falls.

Retrace your steps to complete this family-friendly hike. If you're fit or traveling without children, you can choose instead to complete the loop (which adds 1 mile and a sweaty 500ft elevation gain) by continuing 0.5 miles through more burned lodgepoles to the Fairy Creek/Little Firehole Meadows Trail junction. Turn right and descend to the **Biscuit Basin Overlook** for an expansive bird's-eye view of the Upper Geyser Basin and the 1988 wildfire aftermath. Follow the switchbacks downhill to rejoin the Mystic Falls Trail, then retrace your steps to Biscuit Basin.

SENTINEL MEADOWS & QUEEN'S LAUNDRY GEYSER

Duration 2½ hours
Distance 3.2 miles
Difficulty easy
Elevation Change negligible
Start/Finish Freight Rd Trailhead (OK6), Fountain Flat Drive (Map p120)
Nearest Town/Junction Madison Junction
Summary Some off-trail exploring to a little-visited geyser basin, with a good chance of spotting bison.

This trail (Map p130) is a good choice if you fancy a bit of simple off-route trailfinding. It's flat and easy but requires some basic navigational skills. Park at the end of **Fountain Flat Drive**, just off the main Grand Loop Rd, 6 miles south of Madison Junction and 13 miles north of Old Faithful. From the parking lot it's 0.3 miles along the dirt road to the **Ojo Caliente Spring** and the bridge over the Firehole River, which is where the Sentinel Meadows Trail branches west off the gravel road. You can bike this first section and chain your bike to the bridge for your return.

Turning onto the Sentinel Meadows Trail, the trail swings away from the Firehole River, passing underneath telephone lines. The soil quickly turns to white, hinting at the thermal features lying ahead. Fifteen minutes into the hike you pass backcountry campsite OG1. The trail climbs a small hill to offer views of the valley, its three smoking thermal features and a probable scattering of bison. **Mound Spring** is the closest and most expansive of the springs; **Steep Cone** is the tallest, and **Flat Cone** is the furthest, across the creek. The trail ascends a second small hill, before skirting around a patch of new-growth forest, 1.7 miles from the trailhead.

This is where things get tricky. As the main trail bends to the left to hook around the forested hill, look to the right to see the steam of **Queen's Laundry Geyser** – this is your destination. Look out for a faint trail that parallels the main path as it swings to the south (a post in the ground makes a rough marker). This faint trail heads northwest, skirting the forest, and after 100 yards curves right over a rough log bridge. The trail peters out here and the ground gets boggy, so trace a large arc counterclockwise to the right of the bog, staying on dry ground to get to the far northern side of the geyser, by a **ruined wooden cabin**. The cabin is a former bathhouse, built in 1881 by Park Superintendent Norris as the first park building designed solely for public use. The geyser gets its name from the bathing costumes that used to hang up to dry on strings beside the bathhouse. The deep blue geyser drains past the bathhouse into a wide cascade. Don't get too close to the geyser – act as if the normal boardwalks and warning signs were in place.

Back at the junction you can return to the Sentinel Meadows Trailhead. Alternatively, continue on the main trail as it curves east, past a pond, across a bridge, over a small rise and then along the edge of a new forest, beside an open plain favored by bison. The characteristic Twin Buttes are visible to the south near Fairy Falls. After 20 minutes you'll see the orange trail marker pointing across the boggy plain. Ignore this and continue straight (east) along the forest edge until you see a cliff-like butte straight ahead. As the trail peters out, continue east across the plain towards the right side of the hill. Take a minute to investigate **Boulder Spring**, a perpetual spouter that looks as if it's coming straight out of the hill. Several creekside pools offer potential soaking sites here.

Cross the makeshift bridge to the right and head straight under the telephone poles to rejoin the Fountain Freight Rd. The trailhead is a five-minute walk to the left and the parking lot is 10 minutes further. If you fancy some more exploration, check out the off-trail geysers of **Pocket Basin**, accessed from two unmarked trails on either side of the Firehole Bridge (see p126).

LONE STAR GEYSER

Duration 1½–2½ hours
Distance 4.8-mile round-trip
Difficulty easy
Elevation Change negligible
Start/Finish Lone Star Trailhead (OK1; Map p120)
Nearest Town/Junction Old Faithful
Summary An easy level stroll along a former service road to one of the park's largest backcountry geysers.

This paved and pine-lined hike is popular with both day hikers and cyclists (p155), yet is quite a contrast to the chaotic scene around Old Faithful. Isolated Lone Star erupts every three hours for between two and 30 minutes and reaches 30ft to 45ft in height, and it's definitely worth timing your visit with an eruption. Check with Old Faithful Visitor Center (p96) for predicted eruption times and bring a book or a packed lunch for the wait. If the parking lot at Lone Star Trailhead is full, park at the neighboring Kepler Cascades turnout.

From Lone Star Trailhead, above **Kepler Cascades** (where the Firehole River speeds through a spectacular gorge), take the old

paved road (closed to cars) past a tiny weir that diverts water to Old Faithful village.

The road crosses the Firehole River bridge and follows the upper Firehole River, heading upstream past the Spring Creek Trail junction (1.6 miles) to end at the steepsided, 9ft-tall **Lone Star Geyser**, after an easy 2.4 miles. Check the NPS logbook (in the wooden information box in front of the geyser) to gauge exactly when the next eruption might occur; if you catch an eruption, fill in the log for future visitors. If you have time to kill, consider following a section of the trail to **Shoshone Lake** to check out the minor thermal areas along the Firehole River.

To completely avoid the crowds, consider taking the quieter but hillier **Howard Eaton Trail** (OK2) from 1 mile south of the Old Faithful overpass, as an alternative (if slightly longer) 3.2-mile route. The trail joins the Shoshone Lake trail 0.3 miles beyond Lone Star geyser. You could take one route in and the other out if you can arrange a vehicle shuttle.

For nearby backcountry campsites and the overnight trip to Shoshone Lake, see p146.

DELACY CREEK TRAIL

Duration 2½–3½ hours
Distance 6 miles
Difficulty easy
Elevation Change 200ft
Start/Finish DeLacy Creek Trailhead (7K2; Map p147)
Nearest Town/Junction Old Faithful, West Thumb
Summary An easy hike through meadows and forest to the gravel shores of the park's largest backcountry lake.

The DeLacy Creek Trail offers the quickest access to Shoshone Lake, one of the park's largest and loveliest lakes (in fact, Shoshone Lake was originally called DeLacy Lake). The trailhead is on the Grand Loop Rd, east of Craig Pass near the DeLacy Creek Picnic Area, halfway between Old Faithful and West Thumb Junction. The parking area is on the north side of the road, the trail on the south.

June and July bring lovely wildflowers along the route but also plenty of biting insects, so bring bug repellent before August. The **meadows** are good habitat for moose, elk, mule deer, coyote and sandhill cranes. DeLacy Creek is the last section of the North Shoshone Lake Trail, described on p146.

The trail leads through forest for 20 minutes to a classic oxbow bend in the creek, before continuing through forest into open meadows. Ten minutes later you climb to a small hill for your first views of the lake and the valley. About 30 minutes later, just after passing the meandering lily-choked creek, you'll get to the gravelly shore of the huge **Shoshone Lake**. Enjoy a picnic on the beach and then return the way you came.

Lake Country

Lake Country is best known for its boating opportunities, but its great hikes are also worth getting to know. Bear activity cuts short the hiking season: check trail openings if you are coming in early summer, and always hike with others.

ELEPHANT BACK MOUNTAIN

Duration 1½–2 hours
Distance 3.5-mile loop
Difficulty easy–moderate
Elevation Change 800ft
Start/Finish Elephant Back Trailhead (Map pp114–15)
Nearest Town/Junction Lake Village
Summary This easy ascent follows a well-trodden path and rewards you with lake views near the top.

This popular ascent is a great family picnic option. The trailhead is 1 mile south of Fishing Bridge Junction and 0.5 miles north of the Lake Village turnoff on the Grand Loop Rd. From Lake Hotel it is 0.25 miles one way through the woods past Section J of the hotel's cabins. Use the north side of Trails Illustrated's 1:83,333 map No 305 *Yellowstone Lake*.

The start of this lollipop loop trail parallels Grand Loop Rd for a hundred yards, then abruptly ducks into the forest. A few minutes from the road it passes the old **Lake Village waterworks**, then crosses beneath a power line and begins a steady climb. The forest floor here is thick with wildflowers, wild berries and fungi. Watch for deer and moose.

After passing through 1 mile of lodgepole pines, the trail reaches a junction.

Both trails lead to the **panoramic overlook** (8600ft) of Yellowstone Lake and Stevenson Island, Pelican Valley and the Absaroka Range. The trail to the left (0.8 miles) is steeper than the trail to the right (0.9 miles). Hike clockwise up the steep one and down the easier one for an easy-on-the-knees loop. You can picnic with a view at the wooden benches at the top. Looking out, Pelican Valley's meadows lie to the left, Stevenson Island sits in the lake ahead, and the Absaroka Range outlines the horizon in the distance.

DAY HIKES
Mammoth Country

Hikes in the relatively low-elevation area around the park's North Entrance highlight scenic canyons, panoramic peaks, and numerous lakes, streams and waterfalls, all under the backdrop of the Gallatin Range. This is one of the park's hottest regions in summer, so consider hiking later in the season or outside of midday.

BEAVER PONDS TRAIL

Duration 2½ hours
Distance 5 miles
Difficulty easy–moderate
Elevation Change 350ft
Start/Finish Sepulcher Mountain/Beaver Ponds Trailhead (1K1; Map p100)
Nearest Town/Junction Mammoth
Summary An enjoyable loop hike, perfect if you're overnighting at Mammoth, that climbs to five ponds and offers a good chance of spotting moose and waterfowl.

This 5-mile loop, with gentle climbs and lots of wildlife, begins between Liberty Cap and a private house next to the bus parking lot at Mammoth. The trail ascends through the fir and spruce forests along **Clematis Creek** and in 2.5 miles reaches a series of five ponds amid meadows, where beavers and moose emerge in the mornings and evenings.

Before you get started, it's worth pausing at trailside **Hymen Terrace**, named after the Greek god of marriage and one of the prettiest of Mammoth's many hot spring terraces. The trail is clearly signposted and follows the Sepulcher Mountain trail for the first 0.7 miles, taking a right at the first junction over a wooden bridge. Follow the trail as it starts to switchback up the hill and about 20 minutes into the hike you reach the signed junction. Turn right for the **Beaver Ponds Loop** (left for the Sepulcher Mountain Trail).

As the path flattens, it passes through patches of forest and open sagebrush before a small side trail reveals fine **views** over Mammoth. Ten minutes later the trail crosses a 4WD service track leading up to a hilltop radio transmitter, before passing a patch of quaking aspens and descending through forest to the first of several beaver-dammed ponds (one hour from the trailhead). The fifth and final pond offers fine views of Sepulcher Mountain in the background and is a good place to spot moose, elk and pronghorn. Cross the outlet at the far end of the lake and ascend to a small ridge.

From here, the trail continues across an open **sagebrush plateau**, offering views down on Gardiner town and both the modern and former stagecoach roads to the park, until you reach a ridge with fine views over the orderly buildings and manicured green lawns of Mammoth. Continue right for more views or descend to the employee parking lot and the 4WD road to Gardiner that leads off behind the Mammoth Hot Springs Hotel. Grab a well-deserved ice cream at the general store before returning to your vehicle. You've earned it!

BUNSEN PEAK (& OSPREY FALLS)

Duration 2½ hours (6–7 hours including falls)
Distance 4.2-mile round-trip (10.2 miles including falls)
Difficulty moderate–difficult
Elevation Change 1300ft (2100ft with side trip)
Start/Finish Bunsen Peak Trailhead (1K4; Map p100)
Nearest Town/Junction Mammoth
Summary A short but steep hike up the side of an ancient lava plug for superb views, with the option of descending to an impressive canyon waterfall.

Bunsen Peak (8564ft) is a popular family day hike, and you can extend it to a more demanding day hike by continuing down the mountain's gentler eastern slope to the Bunsen Peak Rd and then *waaay* down (800ft) to the base of seldom-visited Osprey Falls. It's also possible to bike 'n' hike out to Osprey Falls (see p154). The initial Bunsen Peak Trail climbs east out of Gardner's Hole to the exposed summit of Bunsen Peak, offering outstanding panoramas of Mammoth, the Gallatin Range, Swan Lake Flats and the Blacktail Deer Plateau.

Bunsen Peak's trails (especially along the south slope) are free of snow much earlier than those on most other peaks in the park and thus can be negotiated as early as May with some mild glissading. Be prepared for frequent afternoon thunderstorms, which bring fierce winds and lightning year-round.

Bunsen Peak was named by the 1872 Hayden Survey for German scientist Robert Wilhelm Eberhard von Bunsen (after whom the Bunsen burner was also named), whose pioneering theories about the inner workings of Icelandic geysers influenced early Yellowstone hydrothermal research. The mountain is actually an ancient lava plug, whose surrounding volcanic walls have partially eroded away.

From the Mammoth Visitor Center, head 4.5 miles south on Grand Loop Rd, cross the **Golden Gate Bridge**, and turn left into the unpaved parking area on the east side of the road, just beyond the Rustic Falls turnout. The parking lot is small and fills up quickly, so get here early.

From 7250ft, the well-trodden single-track dirt trail begins behind a barricade on the left (north) side of unpaved **Bunsen Peak Rd**. The trail climbs immediately through sagebrush interspersed with wildflowers, then enters a heavily burned Douglas fir and lodgepole pine mosaic. You'll get early **views** of the Golden Gate below and to the left, and the ash-colored jumble of the hoodoos to the north. About half an hour from the trailhead a series of meadows offer views southwest to Swan Lake Flats, Antler Peak (10,023ft) and Mt Holmes (10,336ft). Five minutes later, at one of the many switchbacks, you'll gain a great **view** of the eroded sandstone cliffs and spire of Cathedral Rock, with views down to the red roofs and bleached travertine mounds of Mammoth. The layered sandstone-and-shale mountain of Mt Everts (7841ft) to the north, offers proof that the area was underwater 70 to 140 million years ago. Beyond the Cathedral Rock outcrop, the switchbacks get steeper on the north side of the mountain and the exposed dome-shaped peak comes into view. Keep your eyes peeled for bighorn sheep.

The trail passes under electricity wires before radio communications equipment marks the first of three small summits, 2.1 miles (one hour) from the trailhead. Continue east along the loose talus ridge to the exposed easternmost summit for the best southern panoramas. Electric Peak (10,992ft), one of the largest in the Gallatin Range, looms largest to the northwest, marking the park's northern boundary, with the Absaroka Range to the northeast.

Either retrace your steps down the west slope or wind around the peak to descend the east slope (see side trip) to the Osprey Falls Trail.

SIDE TRIP: OSPREY FALLS & SHEEPEATER CANYON
3–4 hours, 6 miles, 800ft ascent
From the south side of the third summit, the trail descends east through the burnt forest and volcanic talus of Bunsen Peak's eastern flank. It's 1.9 miles (one hour) downhill to the Bunsen Peak Rd. After about 45 minutes, just after you catch sight of the Bunsen Peak Rd, look for the orange marker that points you left along a subtrail to the **Osprey Falls Trailhead**.

From the marked trailhead, the 1.4-mile Osprey Falls trail wanders along the cliffs for 10 minutes before dropping like a stone into the **Sheepeater Canyon**, losing 800ft in a bit less than a mile via a series of narrow, rocky switchbacks. Finally the trail levels out by the Gardner River to reach the base of the impressive, little-seen 150ft **Osprey Falls**, set below an impressive basalt cliff and spire. You're more likely to see marmots or water ouzels in the canyon than the namesake bighorn sheep or osprey, which now prefer to nest along the Yellowstone River. The falls are a refreshing spot to linger over a packed lunch and contemplate the relentless chaos and synergy of the park's natural forces.

Retrace your steps back out of the canyon and haul yourself back up 45 minutes to Bunsen Peak Rd, from where it's a fairly dull 3.2-mile (1¼ hour) trudge along the abandoned dirt road back to the Bunsen Peak Trailhead. After 20 minutes look for a pair of antlers by the side of the trail shortly before views of the upper Gardner River. In the early morning and evening, hikers often spot wildlife (elk, bison, waterfowl and otters) in the meadows and ponds of **Gardner's Hole**, near the parking area. Look for muskrats in the roadside pond.

CACHE LAKE

Duration 6 hours
Distance 11.2 miles
Difficulty moderate
Elevation Change 720ft
Start/Finish Glen Creek Trailhead (1K3; Map p100)
Nearest Town/Junction Mammoth
Summary A gentle climb through a variety of habitat to a secluded mountain lake, with a good chance of spotting moose en route.

Long enough to give you a workout but not hard enough to wipe you out, Cache Lake is a satisfying three-quarter-day hike that leads into the park's northeastern corner. Park in the Bunsen Peak Trailhead 4.5 miles south of Mammoth, across the road from the Glen Creek Trailhead, and get here early as it fills up quickly. The turnout further south is reserved for horse trailers.

Trails Illustrated's 1:63,360 map No 303 *Mammoth Hot Springs* covers the route. Otherwise, use the USGS 1:24,000 quads: *Mammoth* and *Quadrant Mountain*.

The wide and signed trail crosses open sagebrush country, with **views** ahead to Electric Peak. Just 100 yards into the trail a horse track joins from the left – you'll likely pass an outfitter stock party somewhere on this hike. After 30 minutes you'll cross a small rise and descend past a meandering stream. Just before the telephone lines, be sure not to take the unsigned path beside a small cairn that branches right towards Snow Pass. The trail marker underneath the telephone wires marks the junction of the Snow Pass (right) and Fawn Pass (left) trails; continue straight and then straight through a second similar junction.

The trail then enters a dark, wooded valley and climbs above a thin, lush valley, where

OTHER HIKES

Mammoth Country

There are several other cardio hikes in the Mammoth area. West of Mammoth is **Sepulcher Mountain** (9652ft). The loop hike via Howard Eaton Trail climbs 3400ft to its summit and returns via Snow Pass (11 miles).

Alternatively, the 19-mile trail to **Mount Holmes** (10,336ft) begins south of Indian Creek at Willow Flats Picnic Area and heads west to the summit. It's a long day hike with an elevation gain of 3000ft. Alternatively, make camp at 1C4 or 1C5 and take radial hikes to the peak and nearby Grizzly and Trilobite Lakes.

Three longer east–west backpacking routes begin west of Mammoth and lead to US 191 in Montana: the 19.5-mile **Bighorn Pass Trail** begins from Indian Creek Campground, and the 21-mile **Fawn Pass Trail** and 23-mile **Sportsman Lake Trail** to its north both begin at Glen Creek Trailhead south of Mammoth.

An appealing shorter hike is the 12.5-mile **Blacktail Deer Creek Trail**, 7 miles east of Mammoth. It descends 1100ft from the trailhead north into the Black Canyon of the Yellowstone to join the Black Canyon of the Yellowstone hike (p143). After crossing the river, it continues downstream (northwest) to Gardiner, Montana, necessitating a vehicle shuttle.

Roosevelt Country

From the stagecoach road just north of Tower-Roosevelt Junction, the 7.5-mile **Garnet Hill Trail** is an easy three-hour loop north of the Grand Loop Rd. The trail heads northwest along Elk Creek and then loops around Garnet Hill to return to Roosevelt Lodge. For an extension, take a left at the Garnet Hill junction, a right to cross the suspension bridge over the Yellowstone River, then drop down to Hellroaring Creek (add 2.5 miles). You can also reach the trail from Hellroaring Trailhead, 3.5 miles west of Tower-Roosevelt Junction.

The **Slough Creek Trail**, which begins 0.5 miles before Slough Creek Campground, is a pleasant overnight hike along a popular fishing stream. It's possible to head east up Elk Tongue Creek, cross Bliss Pass (8 miles from the trailhead) and descend Pebble Creek to the namesake campground for a total hike of 21 miles. Bliss Pass may be snowbound until mid-July, and fording Pebble Creek can be tricky early in the season. This is a popular horse trail. The first part of the hike follows a historic wagon trail still used by the Silver Tip Ranch; though it lies just outside the north boundary, the trail is only accessible from the park and enjoys a historic right of access. Backcountry sites along Slough Creek are limited to a maximum stay of three nights between mid-June and mid-September.

If you're only up for a day hike, try the first part of the Slough Creek Trail. Head uphill past the patrol cabin to where the trail rejoins the river at the first meadow (4-mile round-trip), or continue to the second meadow or nearby McBride Lake (cross Slough Creek) for a 6-mile round-trip hike. Be sure to take the right branch at the junction with the trail that continues up to the Buffalo Plateau. There's also nice hiking along the fishing trails that head up Slough Creek from the campground.

Pebble Creek Trail to Warm Creek Trailhead (3K4) is a scenic 12-mile hike that requires a vehicle shuttle. The trail heads up Pebble Creek for 10 miles through burns and lovely wildflowers, crosses a pass, then drops down to the Warm Creek Trailhead and a nearby picnic area on the Northeast Entrance Rd.

Specimen Ridge Trail is a popular but long 19-mile hike up and along the ridge, past Amethyst Mountain, then down into the Lamar Valley. Check with rangers beforehand that the Lamar River ford is traversable.

An extensive trail network branches off the upper Lamar Valley from the Lamar River Trailhead (3K1), 4.7 miles southwest of Pebble Creek Campground. The main trail is the **Lamar River Trail**, which offers good early-morning wildlife-watching. Other trails lead off this one, heading west after 1.4 miles to join the Specimen Ridge Trail, east to Cache Creek after 3.1 miles, or east to Miller Creek after 9.3 miles. The **Miller Creek Trail** eventually climbs up either Bootjack Gap or the sculptured peaks of the Hoodoo Basin for an ambitious multiday expedition into the Sunlight Basin (p187) of Shoshone National Forest. The main trail continues south along the Lamar River, leading toward Wapiti Valley via the Frost Lake Trail, or to Yellowstone Lake via the prime grizzly habitat of Mist Creek.

dozens of birds flit around the trail. Cross a side stream and climb 100 yards to the junction with the Sepulcher Mountain Trail (keep going straight) and keep an eye out for moose grazing in the lush meandering valley below; there are normally at least a couple chomping away here in the mornings. If you've just come to spot moose, you could turn back here for a total 2½ hour return hike.

The trail pulls away from the creek and crosses patches of old forest and open meadows for about 45 minutes to the final junction, which leads right to **Cache Lake** and left to **Electric Peak** and **Sportsman Lake**. From the junction it's a 20-minute uphill climb to the lovely lake, ringed by golden meadows and thick forest, with impressive 10,992ft Electric Peak looming to the right, just over the border in Montana. It's about 2½ hours to the lake from the trailhead. Budget some time to savor the lake before retracing your steps.

Roosevelt Country

This remote area of the park is a bonanza for fans of ancient petrified trees.

FOSSIL FOREST TRAIL

Duration 2½–3½ hours
Distance 3.5 miles
Difficulty moderate–difficult
Elevation Change 800ft
Start/Finish unmarked trailhead (Map p104)
Nearest Town/Junction Tower-Roosevelt Junction
Summary A must for amateur geologists, this unmaintained trail climbs to several petrified trees and offers fine views. Listen out for howling wolves in the early morning.

This hike leads to a couple of isolated patches of petrified forest scattered along Specimen Ridge, thought to hold the word's largest collection of petrified trees. The forests were buried suddenly in ash around 50 million years ago or turned to stone by a vengeful Crow medicine man, depending on your beliefs. See the p67 for more on how trees became petrified. Paleodendrochronologists (scientists who date fossilized trees, a niche profession indeed!) have identified dozens of different species of trees here, including tropical avocado and breadfruit, with dozens of ancient petrified forests stacked atop even older petrified forests!

Please don't pocket any of the petrified wood here or elsewhere in the park. If you are desperate for a petrified wood souvenir, then get a permit from the **Gallatin National Forest Gardiner District Office** (☎ 406-848-7375; 805 Scott St; ✆ closed weekends) and head to Tom Miner Basin (p205) in the Paradise Valley.

This trailhead isn't easy to find, so be sure not to confuse it with the Specimen Ridge Trail a couple of miles further west. The parking area is marked 'Trailhead' and is just a few hundred yards west of the Lamar Canyon bridge, 5 miles east of Tower-Roosevelt Junction and about 1 mile southwest of the turnoff to Slough Creek Campground. Look for the wheelchair-accessible parking spot. A Yellowstone Institute bus is often parked nearby.

The trail is not formally maintained by the park service, so it isn't as easy to follow as most other trails in the park and you won't find any trail information at all. There is no water along the trail. Keep an eye out for the weather; the exposed ridge is definitely not the place to be during a lightning storm.

From the **unmarked trailhead** the fairly clear path starts off following a dirt double track (a former service road to the nearby Crystal Valley) and then veers right after 100 yards to head up the hillside for 45 minutes, through meadows of wildflowers (in July) and past buffalo wallows to a small patch of forest. Branch right along the steeper path and after 10 minutes' uphill climb you'll reach your first petrified tree stump by a bend in the trail, about 40 minutes from the trailhead. Five minutes later comes the second stump, with a third piece lying by the side of the trail. From here it's more uphill, past a volcanic outcrop enclosing another fossilized tree and onto the ridgeline, where a side path offers a steeper alternate route down to the main loop road.

The main trail continues up the ridge and after a couple of minutes branches right on a subtrail, skirting and then traversing a small patch of forest to the stump of a **petrified giant redwood**. This fabulous tree would once have topped out at 200ft in height! Below the huge stump are two thinner but taller upright trees and views back up towards the redwood's petrified roots. Dozens more fossilized trees lie scattered along the steep forested slopes but they are dangerous to reach on the crumbling cliff face. The **views** over the Lamar and Yellowstone valleys are simply superb.

The subtrail continues up the hillside to join the main trail just before a small cairn; continue for 20 minutes uphill along the ridge to the summit of **Specimen Ridge**, marked by a cairn. There are wonderful views from here of bison herds in the valley below, birds of prey riding the thermals, and the Grand Canyon of the Yellowstone River in the distance. Return the way you came – the views west are stunning.

Canyon Country

Though the surrounding backcountry draws far less attention than does the Grand Canyon of the Yellowstone, it is every bit as interesting. Abundant wildlife, good camping, mesmerizing cascades and great vistas await.

MT WASHBURN

Duration 4 hours
Distance 6.4 miles
Difficulty moderate
Elevation Change 1400ft
Start/Finish Dunraven Pass Trailhead (4K9; Map p108)
Nearest Town/Junction Canyon
Summary Yellowstone's most popular day hike offers unsurpassed 360-degree mountain-top views, with the chance of spotting bighorn sheep and black bears.

This popular out-and-back hike climbs gradually to the fire lookout tower on the summit of 10,243ft **Mt Washburn** (Map p149) for some of the park's best views. Over 10,000 people hike this trail annually, so head out early to avoid the crowds. Teenagers should be able to do the hike.

Mt Washburn is all that remains of a volcano that erupted some 640,000 years ago, forming the vast Yellowstone caldera (see p63). Interpretive displays in the lookout tower help point out the caldera extents, making this a memorable place to get a sense of the awesome scale of the Yellowstone supervolcano. The peak is named after

Montana Surveyor-General Henry Washburn, who rode up the peak for a panoramic view during the Washburn-Langford-Doane expedition of 1870.

The suggested route starts from Dunraven Pass (8859ft) on the Grand Loop Rd, 4.8 miles north of Canyon and 14.2 miles south of Tower. Alternatively, begin from the larger Chittenden parking area (5 miles north of the pass) for a marginally shorter but more exposed hike (and bike trail) to the summit. Use the south side of Trails Illustrated's 1:63,360 map No 304 *Tower/ Canyon*. Two USGS 1:24,000 quads also cover the route: *Canyon Village* and *Mount Washburn*.

The Washburn Bear Management Area, immediately east of the trail on the mountain's east slope, is closed annually from August 1 to November 10 and open May 10 to July 31 only by special permit from the Tower Ranger Station, so avoid wandering off-trail. Keep in mind that grizzlies flock to Mount Washburn's east slopes in large numbers during August and September in search of ripening whitebark pine nuts.

Snow often obstructs the Dunraven Pass approach through the end of June. Wildflower displays in July and August are legendary. Frequent afternoon thunderstorms bring fierce winds and lightning, so pack a windbreaker even if the weather looks clear and be ready to make a quick descent if a storm rolls in.

The wide trail follows a rough, disused road (dating from 1905) and so makes for a comfortable, steady ascent, following a series of long ribbonlike loops through a forest of subalpine firs. After 20 minutes the views start to open up. The fire tower appears dauntingly distant, but the climb really isn't as painful as it looks! Continue northeast up broad switchbacks, then follow a narrow ridge past a few stunted whitebark pines (look out for bears) to the gravel Chittenden Rd at the Mt Washburn Trail junction. At the junction the road left leads up to the three-story **fire-lookout tower**, about two hours from the trailhead. The side trail right at the junction leads down the Washburn Spur Trail to Canyon Junction (see the Alternative Route following).

The viewing platform and ground-level public observation room has restrooms, a calling-card-only pay phone, a public 20x

Zeiss telescope, displays on the Yellowstone caldera and graphics to help you identify the peaks and valleys surrounding you. The fire tower was built in the 1930s and is still staffed from June to October. The majestic panoramas (when the weather is clear) stretch across the Yellowstone caldera south to Yellowstone Lake, Canyon and the Hayden Valley and north to the Beartooth and Absaroka Ranges. Below you are the smoking Washburn Hot Springs. Keep your eyes peeled for marmots and bighorn sheep basking near the summit. If the crowds get too much, you can always head five minutes down the Washburn Spur Trail for some peace and quiet. From the summit return the way you came.

ALTERNATIVE ROUTE: MT WASHBURN SPUR TRAIL TO CANYON
3 hours, 8.1 miles, 2340ft descent

If you can arrange a shuttle, consider hiking the 5.4-mile **Mt Washburn Spur Trail** to the junction with the Sevenmile Hole Trail and then on to the **Glacial Boulder Trailhead** in Canyon, an 11.3-mile hike through the heart of grizzly country and past the **Washburn Hot Springs**. For an excellent overnight option, head down into the Sevenmile Hole – see p149 for details of both of these options. These hikes can be done in reverse, but this adds 850ft of ascent.

CASCADE LAKE & OBSERVATION PEAK

Duration 4–5 hours
Distance 10.4 miles
Difficulty moderate
Elevation Change 1400ft
Start/Finish Cascade Lake Trailhead (4K5; Map p108)
Nearest Town/Junction Canyon
Summary There's plenty of flexibility here for all levels, mixing an easy hike to Cascade Lake with fine views atop Observation Peak.

There's something for everyone on this trail, which starts just a couple of minutes' drive north of Canyon Village. The full hike climbs 1400ft to Observation Peak (9397ft), but the easier turnaround at Cascade Lake gives a hike of only 4.4 miles. You can also add on a 4-mile return side trip to Grebe Lake, should you want. If you can arrange a car shuttle, it's also possible to hike in

from Cascade Lake Trailhead and hike out south to the slightly further Cascade Creek Trailhead, on the Canyon–Norris road.

Start the hike at the **Cascade Lake Trailhead**, 1.5 miles north of Canyon Junction, or the nearby picnic area of the same name. July is a great time for wildflowers along this route, but the trail can be wet early in the season.

The path from the trailhead quickly joins the trail from the picnic area and continues past the trailhead board to enter an open valley frequented by bison. The double-wide track crosses several creeks before swinging into forest to follow a meandering creek. Thirty minutes into the hike you'll hit the Cascade Creek Trail that leads here from the Canyon–Norris road. Take the right branch to **Cascade Lake**.

Ten minutes from the junction, the path leads into a wide valley, past backcountry site 4E4 on the left to the trail junction at the west end of the lake, less than an hour from the trailhead. The right branch leads to backcountry site 4E3 and Observation Peak; straight ahead takes you to the eastern part of the lake and on to Grebe Lake 2 miles away. The last time we did this hike we stood transfixed here for over two hours as a pack of six wolves attempted to take down a bull elk by the edge of the forest.

The lake itself opens to meadows on the west and backs on to a ghost forest of burnt snags. The lake is worth exploring for its wildfowl and occasional moose. Bison often graze the meadows to the east. The lake's waters drain down Cascade Creek, eventually to plunge into the Yellowstone River in the form of Crystal Falls (see p109).

The hike up to **Observation Peak**, part of the Washburn Range, takes about 1¼ hours and gains 1400ft in 3 miles. After 30 minutes the trail crests a saddle and curves to the left, opening up views of the peak ahead. It loops further to a ridge line, giving you time to catch your breath before the final 20-minute climb to 4P1, one of the park's most unusual backcountry campsites, in a forested hollow just below the main peak. The site makes a fine place to enjoy dusk and dawn views, but there's no water here, so you'll have to haul up everything you need.

The views from the peak are superb; Cascade and Grebe Lakes sit below you, smoking Norris Geyser Basin is to the west and the Hayden Valley yawns to the south. Temporarily hidden below to the left are views of the Yellowstone Canyon. To the north is the Washburn Bear Management Area, classic grizzly country. The ranger hut at the summit is normally boarded up. The descent back to Cascade Lake takes about one hour, from where you return to the trailhead the way you came.

EXTENSION

From Cascade Lake you can continue west onto the Solfatara Plateau to join the Grebe Lake Trail, which passes Grebe and Wolf Lakes; these are also accessible from trailheads on the Norris–Canyon road. This is a popular area for easy overnight hikes, with campsites at all four lakes (Cascade, Grebe, Wolf and Ice). Grebe Lake offers the nicest campsites. These trails can be wet and buggy mid-June to mid-July.

RIBBON LAKE

Duration 3–4 hours
Distance 6.4 miles
Difficulty easy
Elevation Change negligible
Start/Finish Uncle Tom's Parking Lot (Map p110)
Nearest Town/Junction Canyon Village
Summary Views of the Yellowstone Canyon lead to several backcountry lakes, where you might just spot a moose.

Southeast of the Yellowstone Canyon's South Rim, a network of trails meanders through meadows and forests and past several small lakes. This loop links several of these and makes a nice antidote to only seeing canyon views framed by the windshield of your car.

Park at Uncle Tom's Parking Area on the Canyon's South Rim Drive and, after checking out the views of the Upper Falls and the Lower Falls from Uncle Tom's Trail (p110), take the **South Rim Trail** east from Uncle Tom's Trail, along the rim of the canyon to Artist Point for some of the finest views of the Grand Canyon of the Yellowstone.

From **Artist Point** take the trail east toward Point Sublime and turn off right halfway along the trail, past **Lily Pad Lake** for 0.3 miles

to another junction. Branch left here and descend to **Ribbon Lake**, a lovely forested pond with a good chance of spotting moose. For a close-up view of **Silver Cord Cascade**, continue on the path to the canyon rim, then head left along the canyon wall to the small falls. A faint path connects to the main trail at a small footbridge. This is the furthest point of the hike, 3.4 miles from the start.

Two secluded backcountry sites by the lake make for an easy overnighter less than 2 miles from the trailhead (4R1 is right on the lake; 4R2 is on the main trail and less private). Mosquitoes can be a problem here before mid-August, so pack some spray.

From Ribbon Lake head back to the junction with Lily Pad Lake and instead of returning the way you came, continue straight, past several minor fumaroles and hot springs to the acidic, spring-fed waters of **Clear Lake**, 1.5 miles from Ribbon Lake. Continue along the Clear Lake Trail and at the next unsigned junction take the right branch for the final 0.7 miles back to Uncle Tom's Parking Area. The left branch continues to the **Wapiti Lake Trailhead**, 1.5 miles away.

Lake Country

Boating, fishing and watching wildlife are the most popular activities in this region. The following hikes either put you in a position to do one of these activities (away from the crowds) or lead you to grand panoramas.

PELICAN VALLEY

Duration 6–8 hours
Distance 16-mile loop
Difficulty easy–moderate
Elevation Change negligible
Start/Finish Pelican Valley Trail (5K3; Map pp114–15)
Nearest Town/Junction Fishing Bridge
Summary Bird-watchers favor this rolling stroll through meadows and sagebrush in the heart of bear country.

Rangers recommend a minimum party of four hikers for this popular lollipop loop, among the most concentrated grizzly country in the lower 48 states. Backcountry camping is not allowed anywhere in the valley. Bring plenty to drink and a hat, since there's no shade along the trail. Hiking in the morning

---

ADVENTURE HIKES

If you prefer to hike in a group, experienced rangers lead **Adventure Hikes** (adult/child $15/5) from Old Faithful to Shoshone Lake, Lone Star Geyser and Pocket Basin. There are other adventure hikes in the Mammoth (Beaver Ponds, Snow Pass), Canyon (Hayden Valley) and Lake (Avalanche Peak) regions. Hikes leave once or twice a week between June and early September and require reservations. See the park newspaper for details and buy tickets at visitor centers.

---

or late afternoon on overcast, rainy, or even snowy days offers the best chance to catch a glimpse of charismatic wildlife.

Pelican Valley is closed for bear activity from April 1 to July 3 and is open for day use only (9am to 7pm) from July 4 to November 10. The July 4 opening is typically the busiest day in the valley, when animals are likely to be most skittish. Off-trail travel is prohibited on the first 2.5 miles of the trail.

The trailhead sits at a gravel parking lot on the east end of an old service road. It is off the north side of the East Entrance Rd, 3.5 miles east of Fishing Bridge and 23.5 miles west of the East Entrance. The lot is across the road from the trailhead for Storm Point and Indian (ex-Squaw) Pond. Use the north side of Trails Illustrated's 1:63,360 map No 305 *Lake Yellowstone*.

The **Pelican Valley Trail** follows the abandoned Turbid Lake service road due east for a few minutes, then veers north along the forest edge to an overlook, which provides the first sight of the Pelican Creek drainage, a couple of miles away. Look for pelicans at the mouth of the creek. The trail descends through open meadow to the valley floor, passing through boggy sections. Near the poorly marked Turbid Lake Trail junction, scan the forest edge (and trail) for signs of coyotes, bison, elk and grizzlies.

A mile further the trail passes the rickety remains of the **Pelican Creek Bridge**, near which you may spot cutthroat trout. Make the easy ford and climb a terrace for 1.5 miles to the bridge over **Astringent Creek**, just before another junction. The marshy area around a group of thermal springs just south of the trail offers good wildlife-watching.

Continue east along the forest edge, scanning the clover patches for bear scat.

Follow the old service road northeast for 1.5 miles to another easy ford of Pelican Creek and the Upper Pelican Creek Trail junction. Stay in the meadows to the right for 0.33 miles to the Pelican Cone Trail junction, where a small stream provides the valley's best drinking water. The ill-defined trail cuts south away from the valley edge, crossing meadows to ford **Raven Creek**. Search carefully for a shallow spot. There are plenty of waist-deep swimming holes here.

Beyond Raven Creek, the poorly defined trail heads southeast through sagebrush-interspersed meadows. The trail passes through a dormant thermal area with sulfurous odors. After a patch of unburned forest, follow through rolling sagebrush hills to the **Pelican Springs Patrol Cabin** and the Mist Creek Pass Trail junction. From here, it's a well-defined, undulating 5 miles back to the Pelican Bridge junction along the forested south edge of the valley.

AVALANCHE PEAK

Duration 3½–5 hours
Distance 4-mile loop
Difficulty difficult
Elevation Change 2100ft
Start/Finish Avalanche Peak Trailhead (5N2; Map pp114–15)
Nearest Town/Junction Fishing Bridge
Summary Suddenly steep, this challenging peak ascent offers unparalleled views of the Absaroka Range and Yellowstone Lake.

This thigh-burner is infrequently used but well maintained (by Sierra Club volunteers). Steep sections make it unsuitable for baby backpacks. Check for closures; in early fall the trail is frequented by grizzlies foraging whitebark pine nuts.

During the late-spring snowmelt, subalpine wildflowers peak and midsummer means a profusion of high alpine butterflies. From midsummer on get an early start since afternoon lightning storms are common. Regardless of the season, pack your hiking poles and a shell jacket for protection against gusty winds and afternoon thundershowers. You will find snowfields above the tree line through mid-July, even on the trail's south-facing slopes.

The trailhead sits off the East Entrance Rd, 0.5 miles west of Sylvan Pass, 19 miles east of Fishing Bridge Junction, and 8 miles west of the park's East Entrance. Park in the paved lot on the south side of the road by Eleanor Lake's west side picnic area. Use the north side of Trails Illustrated's 1:63,360 map No 305 *Yellowstone Lake*.

From the signed **trailhead** (8466ft), the trail climbs steeply through lush forests of spruce and fir along a small unnamed stream. Thirty minutes from the road the trail crosses the stream and traverses west across an old avalanche chute, then east again into mature **whitebark pine forest**. Signs mark revegetation areas where an abandoned trail used to climb straight up the chutes.

A little over a mile from the road the trail levels out and emerges at the base of a huge amphitheater-like bowl. Here, the third signed revegetation area marks a junction: a steeper, more exposed route heads off to the left (west) and a more gradual unmaintained route veers off to the right around the back side of the bowl. The main trail to the left climbs along open talus slopes to arrive at the mountain's south ridge.

Above the glacial cirques, panoramic views extend north to the Beartooths and south to the Tetons. Thousands of acres just west of the peak were burned in the summer of 2003 after a lightning strike. The true **summit** (10,566ft) sits to the northeast along the narrow ridge beyond a series of talus wind shelters. After a summit picnic, either retrace your steps or follow a steep, unstable talus trail down the east arm of the peak to the saddle shared with jagged **Hoyt Peak** (10,506ft), at the Shoshone National Forest boundary. The latter is only for the sure-footed.

Descend through a series of sparsely forested rolling hills to rejoin the main trail at the foot of the bowl.

Norris

Check out Monument Geyser and drink in fine views on this challenging hike.

MONUMENT GEYSER BASIN TRAIL

Duration 2½–3½ hours
Distance 3–4 miles
Difficulty moderate–difficult
Elevation Change 800ft
Start/Finish Monument Geyser Trailhead (Map p108)
Nearest Town/Junction Norris
Summary A steep but rewarding climb to a little-visited thermal feature, with five views over Gibbon Meadows.

The dormant cones of Monument Geyser Basin are among the park's tallest. There's little active thermal action here these days, but you'll likely have them all to yourself.

OTHER HIKES – LAKE COUNTRY

A section of the 150-mile **Howard Eaton Trail** follows the Yellowstone River north from the parking lot east of Fishing Bridge for 3.5 miles to LeHardy's Rapids. Experienced hikers may choose to continue to Artist Point in Canyon on a 15.5-mile shuttle hike that travels past thermal features, but the trail is not maintained. This is prime grizzly habitat, so consult with rangers about closures.

The 3-mile (1.5-hour) round-trip **Natural Bridge Trail** is perfect for families with small kids. See the biking section (p155) for details. Two short hikes leave from the parking lot of the West Thumb Geyser Basin. The 2-mile round-trip **Yellowstone Lake Overlook Trail** climbs 400ft through meadows to outstanding views of the lake and the Absaroka Range. The trailhead is on the south side of the parking lot (to the right as you drive in). The shorter 1-mile **Duck Lake Trail** is on the other side of the lot. Though scarred from the 1988 fires, it offers views of Yellowstone Lake.

Marshy meadows surround **Riddle Lake**, a favorite of moose. The trailhead is off the South Entrance Rd 3 miles south of Grant Village. The 5-mile round-trip trail traverses the Continental Divide and drops down to the lake. Bear activity closes the trail from April 30 to July 15.

Shoshone/Dogshead Trailhead offers two ways of getting to the lovely Shoshone Lake, the biggest backcountry lake in the lower 48. Popular with anglers, the 6.5-mile **Shoshone Lake (Lewis River Channel) Trail** follows the north shore of Lewis Lake, along the Lewis River Channel, to Shoshone Lake. Return the same way or via the shorter (4.7 miles) forested **Dogshead Trail**.

The short but steep cardio-hike follows the **Gibbon River** for 0.5 miles, then heads uphill for another 0.5 mile, offering fine views of Gibbon Meadows en route. The most prominent feature in the bleached basin is **Monument Geyser** (also known as Thermos Bottle Geyser), which still lets off a bit of steam now and then, unlike the other cones, which have sealed themselves up over the centuries. Budget around 45 minutes up, half an hour down and 30 minutes to explore.

Bechler Region

Bechler boasts the highest concentration of waterfalls in Yellowstone and some of the best backcountry hot-spring soaks anywhere. The area's remoteness means it's best suited to experienced hikers taking long backcountry trips. Popular with horse-pack trips, backpackers and anglers, Bechler sees fierce competition for backcountry campsites in August and September. Campsites may only be reserved for dates after July 20. In-person permits may be granted, weather permitting. In early summer trails may be knee-deep in water, so you inquire about conditions at another ranger station before driving all the way out to Bechler.

BECHLER MEADOWS & FALLS

Duration 3½ hours
Distance 8-mile loop
Difficulty easy–moderate
Elevation Change negligible
Start/Finish Bechler Ranger Station (9K1)
Nearest Town/Junction Driggs, Idaho
Summary A solitary walk through lush forest, with big falls and wildlife-watching opportunities.

Bechler Meadows' extensive wetlands are a wildlife magnet. Grizzlies and black bears as well as rare waterfowl such as gray owls and great blue herons are often spotted. Add substantial cascades to an already spectacular mix by starting from the Cave Falls Trailhead or by taking the Bechler Falls side trip.

This route avoids all fords, so there's no need to inquire about river levels before departing. Use the south side of Trails Illustrated's 1:63,360 map No 302 *Old Faithful*.

From **Bechler Ranger Station**, follow the Bechler Meadows Trail 3 miles northeast

past the Boundary Creek Trail junction through lodgepole pine forest to the Bechler River/Rocky Ford cutoff junction.

If it's not too buggy, hike an extra 0.5 miles north to **Bechler Meadows**. You will across a wooden suspension bridge over Boundary Creek past campsite 9B1. It's an ideal spot to look for sandhill cranes and moose, or angle around the waters for rainbow trout (permit required). See the Bechler River Trail (p152) for a suggested one- to three-day extension.

Retrace your steps to the cutoff southeast 0.7 miles past campsite 9C1 to the wide **Rocky Ford** at the Bechler River Trail junction. Instead of fording the river, trace the river's west bank south for 2 miles to the next junction, where a cutoff leads west 2 miles through forest back to the ranger station.

SIDE TRIP: BECHLER FALLS & CAVE FALLS

30–45 minutes, 3 miles, elevation change negligible
Finish your hike with a 3-mile sidetrip to **Bechler Falls** and **Cave Falls**. An out-and-back hike, it will reward you with a refreshing dip in the swimming hole just past Cave Falls. This worthwhile detour heads 0.5 miles downstream from the Bechler River/Ranger Station cutoff to Bechler Falls, one of Bechler's widest and most voluminous waterfalls. Continue east on the riverbank trail 0.5 miles to the broad-spanning Cave Falls (20ft).

BACKCOUNTRY HIKES
Mammoth Country

Follow the Yellowstone River past waterfalls and meadows on this famed overnight hike.

BLACK CANYON OF THE YELLOWSTONE

Duration 1–2 days
Distance 18.5 miles one way
Difficulty moderate
Elevation Change 1250ft descent
Start/Finish Hellroaring Trailhead/Gardiner (2K8)
Nearest Town/Junction Tower-Roosevelt
Summary One of Yellowstone's classic hikes, following the Yellowstone River through some prime fishing spots and an early season favorite.

Despite the absence of thermal activity, Black Canyon is among Yellowstone's most

REGENERATION – AFTER THE FIRE

Catastrophic wildfires swept across 1.4 million acres of the Greater Yellowstone Ecosystem in the summer of 1988 and torched one-third of Yellowstone National Park. More than 25,000 firefighters battled 51 fires during the driest summer in 112 years. The fires jumped roads, rivers and even the Grand Canyon of the Yellowstone.

Twenty years later, the aftermath of the fires is still very much in evidence. But scientific researchers have closely monitored the long-term effects and the subsequent regeneration of the forests. Far from marking a disaster, many observers now describe the fires as a natural event heralding a new cycle of growth.

Many plants and trees depend on high temperatures to trigger the release of their seeds, and surveys estimated that there were as many as one million seeds per acre on the ground during the fall of 1988. It was also found that only 390 large mammals (less than 1% of the park's total) perished in the fires, the vast majority being elk (and six bears). The year after the fires, the populations of all grazing and browsing mammals flourished thanks to succulent new vegetative growth. Birds thrived on the increased numbers of insects living on dead wood. Ten years later grasses, wildflowers and shrubs were clear winners, aided by increased sunlight and soil nutrients.

For hikers, Yellowstone's scenery has been affected to a certain degree, but not all in a bad way and certainly not to the apocalyptic degree described by the media at the time. Wildflowers are blooming, many views are now unimpeded and it's now easier to see the wildlife thanks to the burns and richer grazing. Smokey the Bear would be proud.

popular overnight hikes. From about 0.5 miles down the unpaved Hellroaring gravel-pit service road, the route goes downstream through a little-visited valley, where the Yellowstone River alternately meanders, surges into rapids and plunges over waterfalls. The route is best approached as a day hike from either end or as a moderate overnight trip, preferably starting from the uphill end to take advantage of the 1250ft descent. It's possible to do as a long day hike. A shuttle is required.

You may extend the trip to 22 miles by starting from the Tower Junction Trailhead (2K2) or shorten it to a more manageable 12-mile day hike by starting at Blacktail Creek Trailhead (1N5), 6.8 miles east of Mammoth.

There are 18 backcountry campsites near or along the route, so a number of overnight trip variations are possible. The 10 riverside sites from 1R2 to 1Y1 are all excellent choices, though none allows campfires – site 1Y7 (roughly halfway) is the suggested stopping point. Avid anglers often spend a week along the trail when the hatch is on.

This route traverses the lowest elevations of any trail in the park and should be free of snow by early June. The Hellroaring Creek ford can be dangerous in anything but low water.

The section near Gardiner crosses steep and eroded slopes that are slippery during spring runoff. The meadows at the start of the route, with thigh-high grasses in places, offer haven to a range of insects, including ticks. Bring bug spray, long pants and patience.

The Hellroaring Trailhead (2K8) turnoff is 3.5 miles northwest of Tower and 14.5 miles east of Mammoth, off the Mammoth–Tower road. Follow the gravel service road 0.5 miles north to the parking area.

In Gardiner the trail ends behind the private Rocky Mountain Campground, on the first road heading east from town on the north side of the Yellowstone River bridge. The trail is not posted from the road, and there's no parking at the campground, but campground staff can advise on suitable parking nearby.

DAY 1: HELLROARING TRAILHEAD TO CAMPSITE 1Y7

3½–4½ hours, 9 miles, 800ft descent

The trail begins by descending 700ft (via switchbacks) during the first mile through scattered trees to a sturdy metal suspension bridge that spans a gorge above the mighty **Yellowstone River**. This first impressive encounter with the river is also the last for the next 2½ hours. The trail heads north into rolling sagebrush lowlands for 0.4 miles to **Hellroaring Junction**. The tricky Hellroaring Creek ford is often waist-deep until August and should only be attempted if the water is low. Alternatively, use the **Hellroaring stock bridge** 1.5 miles upstream and add 3 miles to your total distance.

Beyond the ford, a short, steep 400ft climb leads up to a good canyon overlook. The long, gradual descent passes **Little Cottonwood Creek** (and campsite 1R3), the **Wyoming–Montana border** (and campsite 1R2), and **Cottonwood Creek** (and campsite 1R1) 0.1 miles further west, en route to the north bank of the Yellowstone, which is calm and green at this stage. Riverside campsite 1Y9 is an easy 1.6 miles downstream, just over three hours from the trailhead, with campsites 1Y7 and 1Y5 0.6 miles and 1.4 miles further downstream. No wood fires are allowed at any of these sites.

DAY 2: CAMPSITE 1Y7 TO GARDINER
4–5 hours, 9.5 miles, 200ft descent

After a flat stretch along the riverbank, the trail continues with a short climb to another suspension bridge, at the Blacktail Creek Trail junction. Do not cross here, but descend through pine trees to the deep, green oval of **Crevice Lake**, 1.4 miles northwest of 1Y7. The pines shade the lakeshore as far as the footbridge over **Crevice Creek**.

Past campsite 1Y4, the Yellowstone changes character again as it enters a small canyon. The trail climbs high above the canyon, weaving through a boulder field. Switchbacks descend to an overlook of the short but impressive 15ft **Knowles Falls**. A section of flat bank then leads to more continuous rapids, where the trail is forced to make a steep climb over a rocky shoulder as the river thunders along below a steep cliff.

Scattered pines lead down to the riverbank again, before the trail negotiates a rock outcrop via a narrow ledge just past campsite 1Y2. From here it's a gentle climb away from the river past campsite 1Y1 and several park boundary posts.

The trail's anticlimactic homestretch undulates along the dry slopes of **Deckard**

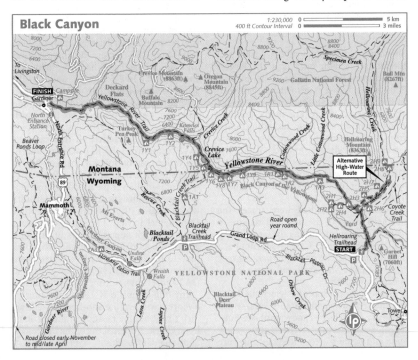

Black Canyon

Flats, crossing Bear Creek on a wooden footbridge. Steep hillsides force the path to contour along a sometimes narrow ledge that is slippery when wet. The town of Gardiner and the Yellowstone–Gardner River confluence eventually come into view around a right-hand bend in the river. Note: the last 0.5 miles of trail crosses private land.

Geyser Country

Lakeside camping and backcountry geysers are the drawcards of this two-day hike.

NORTH SHOSHONE LAKE & SHOSHONE GEYSER BASIN

Duration 2 days
Distance 20 miles
Difficulty moderate
Elevation Change 600ft
Start Lone Star Trailhead (OK1)
Finish DeLacy Creek Trailhead (7K2)
Nearest Town/Junction Old Faithful
Summary Follow the Continental Divide Trail on this easy overnighter that combines a backcountry geyser basin with an unforgettable night by silent Shoshone Lake.

Shoshone Lake is one of the park's real hidden gems. Not only is it the largest backcountry lake in Yellowstone, at over 8000 acres, but it is also the largest lake in the lower 48 states which is not reachable by road. There are many possible routes around the lake, including loops from three directions (Lone Star, DeLacy Creek and Lewis Lake). Much of the first half of this route follows the Continental Divide Trail, which continues along the southern shore of the lake to the Dogshead Trailhead.

The route described here traces the northern shore of the lake and requires a short shuttle or hitch along the Grand Loop Rd. Note that Kepler Cascades turnout is a slightly more secure overnight parking spot than the Lone Star Trailhead, since it sees much more traffic.

Between Lone Star and Shoshone Lake, the trail crosses gentle Grants Pass, which normally isn't clear of snow until late June. The lake is normally frozen until early June and some backcountry campsites are

flooded in early June. Mosquitoes can be an irritant until August.

Use the north side of Trails Illustrated's 1:63,360 map No 302 *Old Faithful*. Two USGS quads also cover the route: *Old Faithful* and *Shoshone Geyser Basin*.

Shoshone Lake is a popular backcountry destination (about one-third of the entire park's backcountry use is concentrated along the shores of the lake), so it's worth reserving sites in advance. Campsite 8R5 in particular gets booked early because of its proximity to the Shoshone Geyser basin. Sites open to hikers along the northern shore include 8T1, 8R5, 8R3, 8R2, 8S3 and 8S2. The latter two sites make a good short overnight trip from DeLacy Creek but are too far north to be convenient for your first night on this trip. 8R2 and 8S2 are mixed hiker- and boat-accessible campsites. All of the lakeshore sites are 'no wood fire' areas.

DAY 1: LONE STAR TRAILHEAD TO 8R2/8R3
6 hours, 11.6 miles, 400ft ascent

For the first 2.4 miles to Lone Star Geyser, see p132. Proceed past the geyser and turn left after 0.3 miles at the junction with the **Howard Eaton Trail** to head southwest. The trail passes the least desirable campsite OA1 (campfires OK) to cross the Firehole River on a footbridge. From here you follow the **Shoshone Lake Trail** 5.8 miles south to the **Shoshone Geyser Basin**. The trail soon passes a small thermal field of scalding hot pools and hissing steam vents (so no, that growling isn't a grizzly bear!). Past OA1 you'll pass the most attractive, off-trail campsite OA2 (campfires OK) in 0.4 miles, and finally the best option for through-hikers, campsite OA3, in another 0.8 miles.

Climb south over the broad rolling ridge to cross the unsigned **Grants Pass** (8010ft), which marks the almost imperceptible Continental Divide. The sandy trail heads down through superb stands of tall, oldgrowth Engelmann spruce and whitebark pine to reach the **Bechler River (Three Rivers) Trail** junction, which is about one hour from OA3 and 1½ miles from the trailhead.

Inviting campsite 8G1 (no campfires) is a short way down the Shoshone Lake Trail, on a rise above the meadows framing Shoshone Creek, 2 miles short of the impressive Shoshone Geyser Basin.

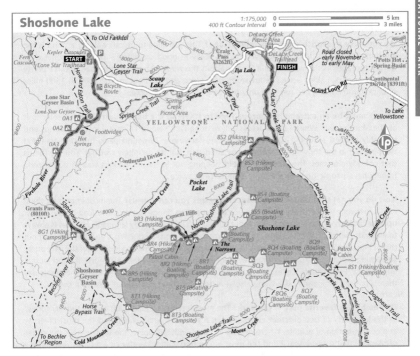

Shoshone Lake

1:175,000   0   5 km
400 ft Contour Interval   0   3 miles

The trail descends through the prime moose and bear habitat of **Shoshone Creek meadows**, occasionally crossing the creek on log bridges. One mile from the Bechler Junction a stock trail branches right over the creek to avoid the marshy geyser basin.

At the North Shoshone Trail junction (8.5 miles from the trailhead, 8.4 miles to DeLacy Creek) it's worth detouring for an hour to explore the geyser basin. Cross the marshy area on wooden logs and take the left branch to dump your pack in one of the bear-proof lockers. Just past here is a small beach, which offers a fine place for a snack overlooking the lake.

Return to the junction and continue straight into the geyser basin for around 0.5 miles. The surrounding meadows are fine places to spot moose and other animals at dusk.

Shoshone Geyser Basin is home to over 80 thermal features and was visited in 1839 by trapper Osborne Russell. The main ones include **Little Great Geyser**, the **Minute Man group**, **Little Bulger** and the **Orion group** further

south, whose **Union Geyser** used to erupt to heights of 100ft. T Scott Bryan's encyclopedic *The Geysers of Yellowstone* details 40 of the basin's geysers, none of which are marked on site.

Back at the North Shoshone Trail junction head northeast along the trail through forest to the backcountry site along the northern shore that you've reserved. Site 8R5 appears after five minutes, while 8R3 and 8R2 are a further hour away. Just before reaching 8R3 you mass an unmarked trail that leads to a ranger patrol cabin. It's around six hours' hiking from the trailhead to here.

DAY 2: 8R2/8R3 TO DELACY TRAILHEAD
4 hours, 7.6 miles, 200ft ascent

From sites 8R3 and 8R2 it's another hour's walk through undulating forest to the northern shoreline. The trail parallels the lovely lake shore for half an hour before dipping back into forest to pass site 8S3. Five minutes further on, a lovely little spit offers a superb place to stop and soak up the silence.

YELLOWSTONE NATIONAL PARK

TOM MURPHY, YELLOWSTONE'S PHOTOGRAPHER LAUREATE

Do you have a favorite season in Yellowstone? The best time to be out walking around is the autumn – there's no insects and everything's really in good condition – but my favorite time for photography is the winter. I'm a fanatic about the winter. You leave the road and it's pretty much your park. I skied across Yellowstone park twice and in about maybe 1000 to 1500 miles of backcountry skiing I've run into only two small groups of people.

Winter must be an extremely rigorous time to travel in the backcountry? Yeah, I refer to it as the Murphy diet. When I skied across Yellowstone Park solo in 14 days, I lost 18 pounds and probably burned around 12,000 calories a day, carrying a 70-pound pack, breaking trail and sleeping out in the snow. It's physically very strenuous, but it's definitely worth it. You see things that nobody else sees. The coldest trip I did sleeping out in the snowbanks was 45 below zero. I rarely have people go with me more than once or twice…

How do you get these wonderful images? Any tips you can give us? The most important thing is to know your subject really well, then you'll start seeing things you never noticed before. I grew up on a cattle ranch, so I learned a lot about animal behavior and body language. My goal is always to illustrate behavior. What's it like to be a coyote? What do they do? What are they thinking out there? Plus, I'm willing to be out there all the time. Spending the time and looking for the exception, something that tells a story, the inner workings of the place, that's the key for me. If I find a great opportunity, like a grizzly feeding on a carcass, I'll go back multiple days and spend the whole day there. I'm still as impatient as anyone else at a stop sign, but I can wait all day for a coyote.

Do you have a favorite part of the park? The most interesting places are mostly the 'ecotones,' at the boundary of two different ecozones, because this is where you'll find the most diversity and concentration of wildlife. Where grassland mixes with subalpine, the timberline – the edges of places – that's where you'll find the most interesting stuff. I like the area around Yellowstone Lake, plus the Lamar and Hayden Valleys. I grew up on the prairie, so I don't really like wandering around in the trees.

Is there a danger of missing stuff by always seeing life through a viewfinder? My experience is exactly the opposite. If I'm trying to capture beauty through my camera, I see a lot more. Maybe it's because I'm not fighting my equipment. It's not about the camera, it's what's in your head, that's what finds the picture. Concentrate on what you see and what you can say about it and you'll get great photographs.

Tom Murphy has published several volumes of Yellowstone photography from his studio in Livingston, Montana, including the award-winning Silence and Solitude. *Check out his images at www.tmurphywild.com.*

Ten minutes later the trail hits site 8S2 and the northern point of the lake as the beach curves to the right in front of large meadows. Follow the beach, looking for the occasional orange metal markers.

Fifteen minutes later the trail cuts inland to join a trail junction at the northeastern point of the lake. From here it's 3 miles along the lily ponds and meadows of **DeLacy Creek** to the end of the hike, about 75 minutes away. The right-hand branch leads 4.2 miles to Dogshead Channel and Lewis Lake.

ALTERNATIVE ROUTES: DELACY CREEK LOOP & DOGSHEAD LOOP
3 & 4 days, 27 & 32 miles, elevation change negligible

There are plenty of other route options, including the 27 miles, three-day lollipop loop of the lake from DeLacy Creek Trailhead or the 32-mile loop of the lake from Dogshead Trailhead near Lewis Lake. You could even do a long day 18-mile return day hike from Lone Star Geyser into the Shoshone Geyser Basin. Thirteen exclusively boat-in sites along both the north and south shores offer those with floating transportation the option of spending weeks here (see p158).

Canyon Country

Take in views of mighty Yellowstone Canyon from a series of lookouts along this trail.

MT WASHBURN & SEVENMILE HOLE

Duration 2 days
Distance 15.6 miles
Difficulty moderate–difficult
Elevation Change 2800ft
Start Dunraven Pass Trailhead (4K9)
Finish Glacial Boulder Trailhead (4K6)
Nearest Town/Junction Canyon Village
Summary Fabulous views, a backcountry thermal feature and a descent into the Yellowstone Canyon that feels like it's 'five miles in and seven miles out.'

This excellent overnight shuttle hike takes you to the top of one of the park's highest peaks and then down, down, down to Sevenmile Hole, a minor hydrothermal area at the bottom of the Grand Canyon of the Yellowstone. It's not a particularly long hike, but it does involve a lot of elevation change (most of it downhill). When the insect hatch is on, the backcountry sites at Sevenmile Hole are very popular, so book your spot well in advance.

DAY 1: MT WASHBURN & SEVENMILE HOLE
6–7 hours, 10.8 miles, 1400ft ascent, 3500ft descent

For details of the first section of this hike up to Mt Washburn, see p138.

From the four-way junction just below Washburn Peak, the **Mt Washburn Spur Trail** drops southeast along an undulating ridge past alpine wildflower meadows. After dipping through a saddle to another little gap at the tree line, bear right and descend 2.6 miles from the summit through small clearings to **Washburn Meadow** and campsite 4E1 (campfires allowed). Keep your wits about you – this is prime grizzly habitat.

The trail descends southwest through boggy grassland grazed by elk and deer to **Washburn Hot Springs**, a small field of boiling mud pots and hissing fumaroles. Proceed past more small thermal areas to the

Sevenmile Hole Trail junction, 2.9 miles from campsite 4E1.

The steep trail switchbacks down 1400ft through Douglas firs, passing a 10ft-high geyser cone before arriving at another, mostly dormant thermal area. Anglers who frequently make the hike claim it feels like 'five miles in and seven miles out.' Weave amid the bubbling pools and small geysers past campsite 4C1, then cross a small thermal stream to campsite 4C2 beside the **Yellowstone River**. Large springs emerge from the reddish chalky cliffs on the river's east bank. To reach campsite 4C3, ford narrow **Sulphur Creek**, then follow the riverbank past a tiny hot pool. Stock animals and wood fires are not allowed at any of the campsites.

Mt Washburn & Sevenmile Hole

Unattended food must be out of reach of bears – if you are day tripping down here hang (don't dump) your pack at the junction.

DAY 2: SEVENMILE HOLE TO GLACIAL BOULDER TRAILHEAD
4 hours, 5 miles, 1400ft ascent

Back at the junction after the hard ascent, heading southwest, the trail is broader and leads along the north rim of the 1200ft-deep **Grand Canyon of the Yellowstone** for the final 2.7 miles, passing through lodgepole forest carpeted with fragrant, low-lying grouseberry shrubs. The views are increasingly spectacular as you pass the unsigned overlook of long, thin **Silver Cord Cascade**, which drops nearly 1000ft to the canyon floor. The amazing technicolor columns of the canyon's eroding sides stretch another 1 mile to the Glacial Boulder Trailhead. **Canyon Village** is 1.5 miles west along paved Inspiration Point road.

ALTERNATIVE ROUTE: GLACIER BOULDER TO SEVENMILE HOLE
2 days (9 hours), 11 miles, 1400ft ascent/descent

An alternative route into Sevenmile Hole starts at the Glacial Boulder Trailhead just before **Inspiration Point**. This out-and-back hike is 11-mile round-trip and drops 1400ft in 1.5 miles; as always, the hard part is the return trip.

Lake Country

Shimmering lakes and talus-covered peaks lend this region its unique character.

HEART LAKE & MT SHERIDAN

Duration 1–2 days
Distance 16-mile round-trip
Difficulty easy–moderate
Elevation Change 345ft (3145ft with side trip)
Start/Finish Heart Lake Trailhead (8N1)
Nearest Town/Junction Grant Village
Summary A backcountry geyser and thermals, the opportunity to peak-bag or fish the lake bestow myriad options onto this straightforward hike.

While the shores of Heart Lake suffered damage from the 1988 fires, it remains a beautiful and rewarding destination. An extensive thermal field extends from the northwest shore of this 2160-acre lake, showcasing boiling hot pots and a large geyser. Heart Lake provides rich habitat for waterfowl, and there are plentiful stocks of cutthroat and elusive but record-setting lake (Mackinaw) trout.

The highest summit in the Red Mountains, Mt Sheridan (10,308ft) rises high above Heart Lake's west shore, providing terrific panoramas. While the extremely fit can knock off Heart Lake and climb Mt Sheridan in a long, uncomplicated day hike, it's worth spending a night (or two) along the lakeshore to relax, watch the bald eagles and osprey, and explore.

Heart Lake trail is closed from April 1 to June 30 due to bear activity: reconfirm the opening date with a backcountry office. Elk carcasses from winter hardship tend to pile up here, leading to an early-season grizzly fiesta.

All west shore campsites have a two-night limit from July 1 to September 1. Heavy snow persists along the trail up to Mt Sheridan until mid-July or later.

Use the south side of Trails Illustrated's 1:63,360 map No 305 *Yellowstone Lake*. Two 1:24,000 USGS maps also cover the route: *Heart Lake* and *Mount Sheridan*. The trailhead is 5.3 miles south of Grant Village and 16.7 miles north of the South Entrance, off South Entrance Rd. There's a toilet at the trailhead.

DAY 1: HEART LAKE TRAILHEAD TO HEART LAKE
3–5 hours, 8 miles, 345ft ascent

Follow the sandy, mostly single-track trail southeast through strewn trunks and new growth **lodgepole forest**. After a few miles, the trail rises slightly over a minor watershed to the first group of smoking fumaroles at the north foot of bald-topped **Factory Hill** (9607ft), 1½ to two hours from the trailhead. Heart Lake, 2 miles downhill, comes into view.

Wind your way down into the intensely active **Heart Lake Geyser Basin**. Numerous spurting springs and boiling pools sit a short way off to the right. The trail crosses warm Witch Creek several times to reach the Heart Lake patrol cabin, just off the lake's north shore (7450ft).

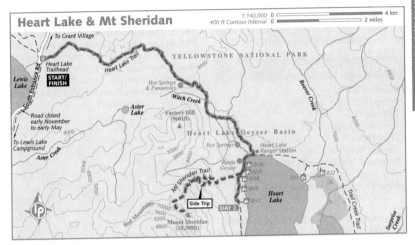

Heart Lake & Mt Sheridan

1:140,000
400 ft Contour Interval

Witch Creek is a prime spot for bathing, near thermal spots. You can inquire about this and current fishing conditions at the log cabin **ranger station** (which is staffed in summer).

Trail Creek Trail departs left (east) around the lake's northeast shore; it's a popular jumping-off point for stock users bound for the Thorofare region.

Heart Lake Trail continues right, first following the gray sand beach to cross the Witch Creek inlet on a log bridge, and then tracing the lake's west shore to reach campsite 8H6. This is the first of five sites alongside firs and spruces fringing the shoreline.

Follow the steam along an often-overgrown trail behind 8H6 to another fascinating thermal area. Here, you will spot the azure **Columbia Pool**. The **Rustic Geyser** spouts up to 50ft at irregular intervals, while other springs bubble up into large calcified bathtubs.

The main trail continues past campsite 8H5 to the junction with the Mt Sheridan Trail, then proceeds about another mile south past campsites 8H4 and 8H3 to 8H2 – only 8H2 and 8H3 allow campfires. The secluded campsite 8J1, which boasts views of Mt Sheridan, is the most coveted campsite.

There are good **views** across the 180ft-deep lake east to Overlook Mountain (9321ft) and southeast to flat-topped Mt Hancock (10,214ft). In the evenings, pairs of grebes often dive and court each other with mellow, lilting voices.

There are six additional campsites surround Heart Lake: 8J1 (two-night limit) and 8J2 (two-night limit, stock parties only) on its northeast side, 8J4 and 8J6 on the southeast shore, 8J3 nearby along Surprise Creek, and 8H1 at the lake's southwest corner. All sites except 8H1 allow campfires.

SIDE TRIP: MT SHERIDAN
4–6 hours, 6 miles, 2800ft ascent

The **Mt Sheridan Trail** crosses over open meadows briefly before its spiraling ascent along a steep spur largely covered in whitebark pines. Bring plenty of water; there is none available on the trail.

You will come to a saddle flanked by wind-battered firs. Continue left (southeast) up the narrowing tundra ridge over old snowdrifts to reach the 10,308ft talus-covered summit. The fire lookout (staffed in summer but otherwise locked) scans 360 degrees from Pitchstone Plateau to the west, Shoshone Lake to the northwest, Yellowstone Lake to the northeast and the jagged Tetons to the south. Snowdrifts often persist through mid-July.

DAY 2: HEART LAKE TO HEART LAKE TRAILHEAD
3–5 hours, 8 miles, 680ft ascent

Retrace your steps from Day 1 back to the start.

Bechler Region

Remote, boggy, beautiful Bechler is a magnet for backcountry enthusiasts.

BECHLER RIVER TRAIL

Duration 4 days
Distance 28-mile round-trip
Difficulty moderate
Elevation Change 1100ft
Start/Finish Bechler Ranger Station (9k1)
Nearest Town/Junction Driggs, Idaho
Summary Traverses wild backcountry filled with rivers, cascades and wildlife, but most come for the soaking opportunities.

Near the head of Bechler Canyon, the Ferris Fork side stream is home to several hidden waterfalls and an outstanding hot springs soak. Anglers will be attracted by the rainbow trout. Sandals and hiking poles are extremely useful for river crossings.

While securing a permit at the backcountry office at any ranger station, ask about river ford and trail conditions – high water and swarms of bugs typically persist along this route through mid- to late July. All of the campsites mentioned here (except 9B9) limit stays to one night.

Use the south side of Trails Illustrated's 1:63,360 map No 302 *Old Faithful*. Three USGS 1:24:000 quads also cover the route: *Trischman Knob*, *Cave Falls* and *Bechler Falls*.

DAY 1: BECHLER RANGER STATION TO CAMPSITE 9B4

3–4 hours, 6.5 miles, elevation change negligible
See the Bechler Meadows & Falls Trail description (p143) for directions from Bechler Ranger Station to Rocky Ford. The extremely wide crossing of the Bechler River is tricky even in low water (around mid-July) and may be completely impassable after heavy rains.

The less interesting, slightly shorter alternative is **Bechler Meadows Trail**, which requires a shorter, knee- to thigh-high ford near campsite 9B2 (no campfires) and treading some boggy terrain.

Beyond the ford, the Bechler River Trail heads east past the Mountain Ash Creek Trail junction. It then cuts north through forested patches and open grassy plains beside the meandering river to campsite 9B3, at the edge of a broad clearing 7 miles from the trailhead. For the first night's stay, the semiprivate, hiker-only campsite 9B4 (no campfires), located 0.5 miles further at the mouth of Bechler River Canyon, is recommended.

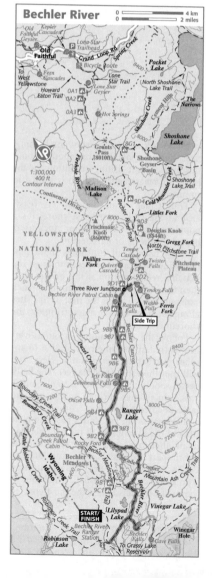

Bechler River

DAY 2: CAMPSITE 9B4 TO THREE RIVER JUNCTION

3½–4½ hours, 7.5 miles, 600ft ascent

The trail continues to parallel the river, climbing through fir and spruce forests, birch trees and boulder fields bordering meadows thick with raspberries, thimbleberries and huckleberries. After 1.8 miles, a marked side trail descends 300yd to a scenic overlook of **Colonnade Falls**, where the Bechler River plunges 85ft in two stages. The trail steepens, passing damp campsite 9B5 to reach the spectacular **Iris Falls**, a 40ft curtain of water spraying thick rainbow-filled mist.

The trail ascends through more old fir and spruce forest past gliding cataracts with picturesque islets and riverside campsite 9B6 to another major ford (a 50ft-wide, waist-deep wade). Upstream, the trail sees many muddy moments as it crosses several cold minor side streams before trailside campsite 9B7. A mile upstream, just before campsite 9B8 (and a pit toilet), is the last, less-serious ford, below a patch of burned forest.

Another mile on, the trail passes several algae-rich thermal areas fringing **Three Rivers Meadow**, then passes inviting campsite 9B9 (no campfires and a two-night limit), with a hiker-only site tucked away on the east side of the canyon near the base of a thundering waterfall that descends from towering **Batchelder Column**. The 9B9 stock-only campsite and an NPS patrol cabin lie across a bridge on the opposite riverbank.

It's worth the steep extra mile slog up out of the lovely river flats to the canyon's wild upper valley, where hidden campsite 9D1 (no campfires) awaits beyond a footbridge over the **Bechler's Ferris Fork**. It doesn't get any lovelier than this: camp perched on a peninsula near **Three River Junction**, overlooking the Gregg, Ferris and Phillips Forks' tumbling confluence.

DAY 3: CAMPSITE 9D1 TO FERRIS FORK HOT SPRINGS

3–4 hours, 4 miles, 500ft ascent

Having made it all this way, you will be giddy if you have booked an extra day in the Three River Junction. When booking your trip, if you reserve another campsite in the 9B group, you can spend a day exploring.

Beyond 9D1, the trail switches back uphill 0.5 miles past 45ft **Ragged Falls** to an unsigned (but well-trodden) turnoff on the east side of the trail for **Ferris Fork Hot Springs**.

The springs' submerged thermal source emanates from the middle of a 45ft-diameter, waist-deep soaking pool, where it mixes with chilly water from the stream's main channel, creating a royal, five-star soak.

After checking out the surrounding thermal features, you might choose to hike another 0.5 to 1.5 miles upstream along the Ferris Fork to explore a quintuplet of seldom-seen waterfalls: 33ft **Tendoy Falls**, 20ft **Gwinna Falls**, 35ft **Sluiceway Falls** and 28ft **Wahhi Falls**.

Retrace your steps down into Bechler Canyon to your chosen 9B series campsite. If you are unable to reserve a campsite for the final night, it's a lengthy but manageable 13.5-mile descent back to the ranger station.

DAY 4: BECHLER RIVER CANYON TO BECHLER RANGER STATION

4–5 hours, 8–12 miles, 800ft descent

Retrace your steps down the canyon to the Bechler Ranger Station via Bechler Meadows Trail, the most direct route, or the more scenic Bechler River Trail.

BIKING

Biking in Yellowstone requires taking precautions. The roads are narrow and the RVs wide: in essence, you can't underestimate the threat of a rear-view mirror. For this reason, it is best to cycle on the main loops between dawn and 9am, before the traffic starts to snarl. Entering the park in the evening or leaving in the morning has you traveling against the flow of traffic.

Another alternative is to bike early or late season before the crowds of late June and after their departure in early September. Of course, your ability to bike in the early season will depend on the weather that year. On a heavy winter snow year, spring travel can be a challenge: check the park road conditions for plowing information.

Yellowstone has very few trails on which mountain biking is allowed, among them are the service road to Lone Star Geyser, Natural Bridge and the Bunsen Peak Rd double-track. For further tips on biking, see the Activities chapter (p47) and Health & Safety (p284).

Note that from mid-March to the third Thursday in April park roads between West Yellowstone and Mammoth in Yellowstone National Park are open to only nonmotorized travel, creating a vehicle-free playground for cyclists and rollerbladers.

Driving Tours (p156) are also suitable for road biking.

MAMMOTH COUNTRY

The Old Gardiner Rd between Mammoth and Gardiner was the late-19th-century stagecoach route into the park. After an initial uphill the dirt road then descends 1000ft in 5 miles. It's not a stunning ride but does offer a rare opportunity to bike in peace inside the park. You'll have to arrange a car shuttle or face a long uphill back. From Gardiner you can continue along dirt roads up into Paradise Valley (see p205). From May to October the road is open to motorized traffic (no RVs or trailers) one-way to Gardiner.

Unpaved Blacktail Plateau Dr (Map p104) offers a challenging ride, though there can be a fair amount of vehicle traffic.

BUNSEN PEAK ROAD (& OSPREY FALLS)

Duration 1 hour cycling plus a 90-minute strenuous hike to Osprey Falls
Distance 6.8 miles
Difficulty easy
Elevation Change negligible (800ft descent on foot to Osprey Falls)
Start/Finish Bunsen Peak Trailhead (1K4; Map p100)
Nearest Town/Junction Mammoth
Summary An easy ride on a former service road, best combined with the strenuous hike down to Osprey Falls.

Now closed to motor vehicles, 6-mile **Bunsen Peak Road** is a dirt road popular among family bikers. Probably the best option is to combine the bike ride with a hike to Osprey Falls (see p134). To do this, lock your bike at a rack by the **Osprey Falls Trailhead**, 3.4 miles into the ride. From here it's best to

return the way you came. It's a largely flat section of gravel road, with a few minor ups and downs, and offers a good family trip (though the descent and return to Osprey Falls is much harder).

From the **Osprey Falls junction** it's possible to continue to downhill to a service road and park vehicle maintenance depot just before Mammoth, from where you can descend along the main road and then a walking trail beside the corral to Mammoth Junction, but you'd have to arrange a car shuttle for this. Biking back up the main road to the Bunsen Peak Trailhead isn't recommended due to the gradient, traffic and lack of a bicycle lane.

CANYON COUNTRY

Two very different routes offer a white-knuckle ride or quality wildlife-watching.

MT WASHBURN

Duration 3 hours
Distance 5.6 miles
Difficulty difficult
Elevation Change 1400ft
Start/Finish Mt Washburn North (2K6; Map p149)
Nearest Town/Junction Canyon Village
Summary This is the park's toughest mountain-bike trip, offering fabulous views from the peak and a thrilling descent.

Mt Washburn is accessed by two former service roads; the southern route from Dunraven Pass is open only to hikers (see p138) but the northerly Chittenden Rd is open to hikers, bikers and the occasional park vehicle delivering supplies to the fire tower atop **Mt Washburn**. This isn't an easy jaunt you can attempt on a $50 bike from Wal-Mart (as we did), but rather a serious high-elevation climb for well-conditioned bikers who have the luxury of plenty of low gears to choose from. The large trailhead is just over 1 mile off the main **Grand Loop Rd** and has a vault toilet.

Access the old service road by the side of the metal gate that blocks the road to cars. The service road was originally open to early motor vehicles, though the early Model T Fords that attempted the route back then had to reverse all the way up the mountain because the engines didn't yet come with fuel pumps! The only traffic you'll see today is tourists and the occasional grizzly bear. The wonderful 1400ft descent is back along the same road. Watch out for hikers and other bikers on the tarmac-and-gravel downhill run, as there are several blind corners. This is also prime grizzly summer habitat, so keep your eyes open for bears.

See p138 for details of the view and facilities atop the peak.

BUFFALO BYWAY

Duration 1½–2 hours
Distance 16 miles one way
Difficulty moderate
Elevation Change 310ft
Start/Finish Canyon Village/Fishing Bridge Junction (Maps p108 & pp114–15)
Nearest Town/Junction Canyon Village; Fishing Bridge Junction
Summary Expect a wildlife-watching bonanza riding through the diverse habitats of Hayden Valley.

The road has a narrow shoulder, so stay attuned to the traffic around you. It is best to set off early. If you start biking at Canyon, you will lose altitude and enjoy the downhill on the first half of the ride (which you pay for in the second half).

Start by detouring left to North Rim Dr to skirt incredible views of the **Lower Falls** of the Yellowstone River. Be aware of herding tour buses on this curvy, potholed detour. After rejoining the main road, you will drop down into **Hayden Valley**, once an enormous glacial lake eventually drained by the Yellowstone River. The lake left silty marshes and fertile soil for grasses favored by wildlife. The ride through this wide open terrain affords views of the river, teeming with geese, trumpeter swans and osprey. Grizzlies can be seen wandering the sagebrush between meadow and forest, where coyotes hunt and bison graze.

At mile 9.5 you will notice a reeking stench. That's **Mud Volcano** and **Sulfur Cauldron**, concentrated pits of sulfur, acids and clay. Pedal on through rolling hills (the last by far the greatest) to finish at **Fishing Bridge Junction**. See p111 for more information on this route.

LAKE COUNTRY

Pack a picnic, grab the kids and take off on an easy jaunt to Natural Bridge.

NATURAL BRIDGE

Duration 45 minutes
Distance 3-mile round-trip
Difficulty easy
Elevation Change 110ft
Start/Finish Bridge Bay Marina (Map pp114–15)
Nearest Town/Junction Bridge Bay
Summary A family-friendly ride to an interesting natural feature.

An excellent family biking trail follows an old stagecoach road that once linked West Thumb to Lake Village. The paved road starts opposite the northbound turnoff to Gull Point Dr, just south of the Bridge Bay turnoff, but parking is found at the Bridge Bay Marina. It is 1.5 miles to **Natural Bridge**, joining the hiking trail en route. The flat route leads to rhyolite cliffs forming a natural bridge 51ft above **Bridge Creek**. You can hike the steep trail to the top but not across the fragile bridge. The trail is closed from late spring to early summer due to bear activity.

GEYSER COUNTRY

In the Upper Geyser Basin bikes are allowed on the road (not the boardwalk) between Old Faithful and Morning Glory Pool (1.3 miles), and between Daisy Geyser and Biscuit Basin (1.3 miles).

You can hire bikes in the Old Faithful Snow Lodge gift shop for $25/35 for a half/full day, with kids bikes at $15/22.50. Bike trains (a kid's bike that hooks on the back of an adult bike) and trailers are also available. Rentals come with a helmet and a lock.

In addition to the Fountain Freight Rd route described following, the former service road to Lone Star Geyser makes for a fine (and flat) 5-mile, round-trip bike ride, though you'll have to dismount for the last few yards to the actual geyser. There's a bike stand at the end of the trail, where you can lock your bike. See p132 for a description of the route and geyser. Take a packed lunch for the geyser wait. Park in the Lone Star Geyser lot next to Kepler Cascades.

FOUNTAIN FREIGHT ROAD

Duration 1 hour cycling (up to 4 hours with excursions)
Distance 7.4 miles
Difficulty easy
Elevation Change negligible
Start/Finish Fairy Falls/Steel Bridge Trailhead (0K5; Map p130)
Nearest Town/Junction Old Faithful
Summary An easy flat bike ride on a gravel road that allows lots of stops and detours on foot – perfect for families.

The 4-mile Old Fountain Freight Rd between Fountain Flat Dr and Fairy Falls Trailhead offers an opportunity to combine some pedaling with a hike to Fairy Falls and an exploration of the Pocket Basin backcountry thermal area.

Park your car at the busy **Fairy Falls Trailhead** (which can fill up in summer) and cycle over the steel bridge (sometimes called Soldier Bridge). After 0.5 miles you'll see the blue blur of **Grand Prismatic Spring** to the right. Park the bike here and make the short but steep hike up the volcanic hillside to the left (look for the trails) for fantastic aerial views over the spring.

From here it's another 0.5 miles to the turnoff to **Fairy Falls**. You can't bike this side trail, but you can park your bike at the rack and make the 3.2-mile return detour to the waterfalls on foot (see p129).

From the turnoff to Fairy Falls, pedal north along the gravel road for 1.2 miles to **Goose Lake**, whose northern shore makes for a good picnic spot, either now or on the way back. Continue north, past the Imperial/Sentinel Meadows Trailhead to the bridge over the Firehole River. Park your bike at the bridge and check out the **Ojo Caliente** hot spring on the north bank. It's also well worth making the short hike along the unmarked trail east on the north side of the river to the hot springs and geysers of little-visited **Pocket Basin** (see above), just 10 minutes from the bridge. The two-hour **Sentinel Meadows and Queen's Laundry Geyser** hike also departs from here (see p131).

From the bridge turn back and cycle the 3.7 miles back to your car. If one member of your group is happy driving down to Old Faithful, the rest of you could continue south from the parking lot for 2.6 miles along the busy Grand Loop Rd to **Biscuit Basin**, where you'll find a 1.3-mile bikeable trail to **Daisy Geyser** and on to **Old Faithful**, another mile away. This makes for a 5-mile extension.

DRIVING

There's hardly a mile of highway on Yellowstone's 142-mile Grand Loop Rd that can't be called scenic. The views are always great, whether it's the panoramic views from Dunraven Pass, lakeshore views across Yellowstone Lake or open valley views across meandering rivers and lodgepole forests. All the main route descriptions of the park in this chapter make for excellent drives.

GEYSER TRAIL

Route Madison to Old Faithful
Distance 25 miles
Speed Limit 45mph, sometimes dropping to 35mph; 25mph approaching Old Faithful area

The northern approach to Old Faithful offers lots of possible stops so don't expect to cruise this route in one hit. The drive parallels the Firehole River and there are dozens of potential fly-fishing spots along this route.

Drive south from Madison Junction, past the junior ranger station, and after 2 miles take the Firehole Canyon Drive to the right. This 2-mile side road takes you past rhyolite cliffs and rapids, the **Firehole Falls** and the popular **Firehole swimming area**.

Back on the main road it's another 3 miles south to Fountain Flat Dr, which branches right to give access to the pleasant Chief Joseph Picnic Area, the Sentinel Meadows hike (p131), Pocket Basin backcountry geyser area (p126) and the bikeable Fountain Freight Rd (left).

Back on the main road, 1 mile south, the road crosses **Chief Joseph Creek**, where an interesting pullout details the flight of the Nez Percé Indians, who crossed this creek in August 1877 fleeing the US Army. For details of the two-week flight of the Nez Percé (pronounced 'Nez Purse') through Yellowstone, see p83.

From here on you'll get your first views of the amazing thermal features ahead. A **pullout** 1 mile ahead offers a fine view of the smoking geysers and pools of Midway Geyser Basin to the right and Firehole Lake Basin on the left, as well as the meandering Firehole Valley and the occasional bison – a classic Yellowstone vista.

Just 1 mile further, take a right into Fountain Paint Pot (p125). Another 1.5 miles south take the left on Firehole Lake Dr (p125) and make the leisurely 3-mile drive past **Great Fountain Geyser** and **Firehole Lake** to see what's on the boil.

Next stop is **Midway Geyser Basin** (p124), which is worth a stop. As you continue south, you'll see the colorful runoffs from **Excelsior Pool** flowing into the Firehole River.

Two miles further is busy Fairy Falls Trailhead, a popular starting point for hikes to Fairy Falls (p129), **views** over Grand Prismatic Spring and bike rides along the gravel Fountain Freight Rd. You'll also likely see bison and fly-fishers in this vicinity.

It's a further 2 miles to the minor thermal sites of **Biscuit Basin** and **Black Sand Basin**, from where bikers can get out and cycle to **Old Faithful**, 1.5 miles away.

OTHER ACTIVITIES

HORSEBACK RIDING
Roosevelt Country
The park concessionaire, **Xanterra** (☎ 307-344-7311), operates all activities listed below. Reservations are recommended and can be made by phone or at activities booths at most hotels. All the activities below operate from early June to early September.

Daily **stagecoach rides** (adult/child under 11 $9.35/7.50) depart from Roosevelt Lodge three to five times daily and last around 45 minutes. For a treat, ask for the tallyho seat.

Old West cookouts are a fun family trip, either on horseback (one-hour trips adult/child $63/53, two-hour trips $75/65) or by horse-drawn wagon ($53/43 per person); reservations are required. Trips depart daily in the late afternoon and travel to the former site of Uncle John Yancey's Pleasant Valley Hotel (1884–87), one of the park's earliest accommodations, for a gut-busting, all-you-can-eat chow-down

of steak and beans accompanied by campfire music. The excursion lasts for about three hours.

Corrals next to Roosevelt Lodge offer one/two-hour **trail rides** ($35/54), four times a day, through sagebrush country. Two-hour rides run just once a day, so reserve ahead. Children must be over eight years old. Rides can be cancelled after rain.

Other Regions
Xanterra also offers one/two hour trail rides for $35/54 at corrals just south of Canyon (seven times a day, mid-June to mid-August) and one-hour rides from corrals just north of Mammoth (five times a day, mid-May to mid-August), in the shadow of Bunsen Peak. Once again, the two-hour ride departs just once a day, so reserve ahead.

BOATING
Yellowstone Lake
The vast Yellowstone Lake just begs for extended kayak, boat and sailboat exploration, but it is important to plan your outing carefully. Water temperatures are very cold, averaging only 45°F in the summer. Moreover, sudden winds can quickly churn up 3ft to 5ft waves, so it's preferable to paddle in the early morning or late afternoon and avoid open-water crossings. Prevailing winds come from the southwest, so if you're headed south, you'll need to set off around dawn.

The **backcountry ranger office** (☎ 307-242-2609; ☉ 8am-5pm) by the Conoco station at Grant Village is an excellent resource. It distributes the **Backcountry Trip Planner** (www .nps.gov/yell/planyourvisit/backcountrytripplanner.htm) describing Yellowstone Lake campsites in detail, with GPS coordinates, photos and mileage from the nearest boat put-ins. Some sites have restrictions on docking, hiking etc. You may also need fishing, boating and backcountry permits (all lake campsites require a backcountry permit).

From Grant Bay, the closest campsites are at Breeze Bay (8 to 10 miles away), some of which are for first- and last-night use only. The canoe and kayak put-in at Sedge Bay (Trailhead 5K4) is the closest point from which to access the lake's Southeast Arm (21 miles), from which you can hike to the park's remote reaches.

There are docks around the lake at Wolf Bay, Eagle Bay and Plover Point, plus several anchor-only sites, including two at Frank Island. The Grant Village marina is nearby, opposite the Conoco station.

Bridge Bay Marina (☎ 307-242-3880; 🕑 8am-8pm) offers dock slip rentals ($17 to $23 per night) and hourly rowboat ($9.50/43 per hour/day) and outboard ($45 per hour) rentals.

Watch for eagles and ospreys on north Yellowstone Lake during one-hour **sightseeing cruises** (adult/child under 2/child $11.25/free/7) that travel to Stevenson Island. They operate at least five times daily from June to mid-September.

BOATING REGULATIONS

The speed limit on the main lake is 45mph. The limit on the south arms is 5mph, while the southernmost inlets are closed to motorboats. Landing is not allowed on the thermally affected shore between Little Thumb Creek and the south end of the West Thumb thermal area.

Certain shorelines are off-limits due to wildlife protection. Frank Island and the south end of Stevenson Island are closed from May 15 to August 15 to protect nesting ospreys and bald eagles. A 0.5-mile closure around Molly Island protects breeding pelicans. The south and east shorelines of the lake are off-limits May 15 to July 14 to prevent bear disturbance.

Boating regulations handbooks are available at all visitor centers. General boating information is at www.nps.gov/yell/plan youryvisit/boating.htm.

Shoshone Lake

The largest backcountry lake in the lower 48, Shoshone Lake (Map p147) spells paradise for hikers and kayakers. The serene lake is closed to motorized vessels and is lined with a dozen secluded boater-only campsites. On its far western edge, Shoshone Geyser Basin's pools, thermals and mud pots comprise the largest backcountry thermal area in the park. One-third of all of Yellowstone's backcountry use takes place along its shores, only open to hikers and hand-propelled boats.

Boaters access the lake up the channel from Lewis Lake. From mid-July to August the channel requires portage of up to 1 mile in cold water (bring appropriate footwear), though in spring you can often paddle through.

Of 20 lakeshore campsites, 13 sites are reserved for boaters, five for hikers and three are shared. All have pit toilets. Rangers claim the nicest campsites are 8Q4, 8R4 and 8R1. Wood fires are not allowed along the lakeshore.

Most boaters make their first camp on the south shore (campsites nearest to the channel are reserved for first- and last-night use only). If you need to cross the lake, do so early in the morning and at the Narrows in the center of the lake. The lake is icebound until mid-June, when flooding is possible at shoreline campsites. Backcountry boating campsites at Shoshone Lake cannot be reserved before July 1 or 15, depending on the site.

For information on hiking to Shoshone Lake, see p146.

FISHING

Yellowstone is justly famous for its fly-fishing. Where else can you cast your line in sight of a grazing bison or a steaming geyser? See p49 for general information on fishing in the region and p97 for park fishing regulations. The park concessionaire Xanterra offers full- or half-day fly-fishing guide services, as well as rod and reel rental.

Yellowstone Lake

Yellowstone Lake is stocked with cutthroat trout, longnose dace, redside shiners, longnose suckers and lake chub. Illegally introduced lake trout are rapidly upsetting the lake's ecosystem. Anglers can help the park by joining the **Volunteer Fly-fisher Program** (www.nps.gov/yell/naturescience/vol_fishing.htm) to collect biological data.

Fishing is not allowed on Pelican Creek from its outlet to 2 miles upstream or on the Yellowstone River from 0.25 miles upstream of Fishing Bridge to its outflow from Yellowstone Lake. Hayden Valley is closed to fishing except for two short catch-and-release stretches.

Popular shore or float-fishing spots include Gull Point, Sand Point Picnic Area, Sedge Bay, Mary Bay and Steamboat Point.

Reserve with **Bridge Bay Marina** (☎ 307-344-7311) for guided Yellowstone Lake **fishing trips** (per 4½ hours $315; 🕑 mid-Jun–mid-Sep), Prices are for up to six people, and include three rods and reels. The marina also has a tackle shop

YELLOWSTONE'S WINTER WONDERLAND

Winter is a magical time to visit Yellowstone. The falls turn to frozen curtains of ice, the geysers spurt taller and steamier than normal and surrounding 'ghost trees' are covered in frozen steam sculptures. The warm thermal areas around Old Faithful, Norris and Mammoth become winter refuges for elk and bison, and the thermally heated (and thus still flowing) rivers attract plenty of waterfowl.

The winter season runs from the late December to mid-March, and activity centers on Mammoth Hot Springs Hotel (p162) and Old Faithful Snow Lodge (p166), the only two accommodations open in the park. Independent travel is more difficult in winter, and most people sign up for a lodging and activity package, which often works out cheaper than arranging things yourself. The **Yellowstone Institute** (☎ 307-344-2294; www.yellowstoneassociation.org/institute) runs excellent winter programs.

Accessing the park is an adventure in itself. The only road open year-round is the northern Mammoth–Cooke City road via Tower-Roosevelt Junction, plus an extension to Mammoth's Upper Terraces. The long-term future of Yellowstone winter use lies in mass-transit snowcoaches. During the season, **Xanterra** (☎ 307-344-7311) operates one-way snowcoach tours once daily between Old Faithful and Mammoth ($64), West Yellowstone ($51) and Flagg Ranch ($64). Trips inside the park include day tours to Canyon from Old Faithful ($118) and Mammoth ($113), half-day tours to Norris from Mammoth ($51) and three-hour tours from Old Faithful to the Firehole Basin ($29.50). A one-way/return express from West Yellowstone to Old Faithful costs $51/80; a day trip gives you about six hours at Old Faithful. Most other snowcoach companies offer only return day trips from West Yellowstone.

For information on winter facilities, see p161.

Activities

Once in the park, use skier shuttles to get to and from trailheads, where you can take a trail or just ski back. Shuttles operate from Mammoth to the Bunsen Peak Rd and Indian Creek ($14.50 round-trip, five per day); from Old Faithful Snow Lodge to Fairy Falls or Divide Trailheads ($13.50 one way; you must ski back) and from West Yellowstone to Sevenmile Bridge/Madison Junction ($15/30 one way).

Three-hour guided **snowshoe tours** ($22, $27 with shoe rental) depart from Old Faithful on Thursday and Sunday. Half-day guided **ski tours** ($41) leave at noon from Old Faithful to Fairy Falls (Saturday) and DeLacy Creek (Wednesday).

Combined snowshoe and ski tours run from Mammoth and Old Faithful to Canyon ($125) once or twice a week. You can ice skate in Mammoth and Old Faithful (free skate rental). Cross-country ski ($16 per day, includes equipment) and snowshoe ($12) rentals are available, as are snowmobiles ($185 per day, plus the shared cost of a guide) and ski instruction ($20 for two hours, $30 with equipment).

Rangers lead free guided snowshoe walks around Mammoth Hot Springs (2pm Sundays) and from West Yellowstone Chamber of Commerce (1:30pm weekends). For more on cross-country ski and snowshoe trails, see p160.

Regulations

The park service enforces a daily cap of 540 snowmobiles into the park, and snowmobilers must be accompanied by a commercial guide. It would be wise to check current regulations before heading out on a snowmobile vacation.

Snowmobiles are banned from all the park's side roads, including the Lake Butte Overlook, Firehole Canyon Dr and a section of the Grand Loop Rd from Canyon to Tower. All other roads are groomed for oversnow travel. The Canyon to Washburn Hot Springs Overlook section of this road is open to Nordic skiers. Snowmobile operators must carry a valid state driver's license. The speed limit between the West Entrance and Old Faithful is 35mph; elsewhere it is 45mph. Roads are only open 7am to 9pm and off-road snowmobiling is prohibited.

Safety

There are obvious dangers involved in winter travel. Visitors (especially snowmobilers) should carry extra clothing, matches, a flashlight, a whistle and backup food. Snowmobilers should also carry a toolkit. All winter visitors need to be particularly careful around thermal areas, as snow can mask potentially lethal pools. Don't approach wildlife during winter; any unnecessary movement will cost them calories they can ill afford.

and offers good fishing information. The marina area itself is closed to fishing.

Detailed fishing information can be found at www.nps.gov/yell/plan yourvisit /fishing.htm.

Geyser Country

The Madison and Gibbon Rivers offer some of the park's best and most scenic fly-fishing. The Firehole (between Biscuit and Midway Geyser Basins), Madison and Gibbon (downstream from Gibbon Falls) Rivers are open for fly-fishing only. During hot summers the Firehole is often closed completely to fishing because of the high water temperatures.

The pullout beneath Mt Haynes on the Madison River between Madison Junction and West Yellowstone (see p126) offers a good, wheelchair-accessible, riverside fishing spot.

Roosevelt Country

Slough Creek is the sweetest fishing spot in the northeast (closely followed by Pebble Creek and Soda Butte Creek), which is one reason why the park's Slough Creek Campground is regularly the first to fill up. Ensure that you make your backcountry reservations early if you want to overnight in any of the Slough Creek backcountry campsites.

CROSS-COUNTRY SKIING & SNOWSHOEING

All backcountry trails are marked with orange markers, so you can ski or snowshoe most of the backcountry trails described in the Hiking section.

See p159 for details on ski shuttles and drops.

Mammoth & Roosevelt Country

The north of the park remains logistically easier to visit in winter because the road between Mammoth and Cooke City remains open year-round.

Around the Mammoth region it's possible to ski from Indian Creek Campground to Sheepeater Cliffs and then along a backcountry trail to Bunsen Peak Trail and left to the Mammoth–Norris road (5 miles) or right down the Bunsen Peak Rd to Mammoth. There are also marked loops around Indian Creek (2.2 miles) and part way along the Bighorn Trail (5.5 miles).

The groomed 1.5-mile Upper Terrace Loop Trail follows the Upper Terrace road (see p101) and is a good place to test out your Nordic legs.

A side trail from here follows an old wagon track to Snow Pass and then along Glen Creek back to the Bunsen Peak Trailhead (4.2 miles).

In the park's northeast corner a popular ski trail parallels the Northeast Entrance road below Barronette Peak (10,404ft) between the Soda Butte Creek bridges (3.5 miles). The 2-mile Bannock Trail runs east out of the park from the Warm Creek picnic area along an old mining road to Silver Gate.

Around Tower-Roosevelt, the 8-mile Blacktail Plateau Trail follows the unplowed road of the same name and is a popular shuttle option. The trail climbs gently to The Cut and then descends for 2 miles to the main Mammoth–Cooke City road.

Geyser Country

The area around Old Faithful has the most trails and facilities in winter. Upper and Midway Geyser Basins both make for some fine ski trips. You can ski or snowshoe from Old Faithful to Black Sand Basin via Daisy Geyser (4 miles) or to Biscuit Basin via Morning Glory and Atomizer Geyser (5 miles, with a possible extension to Mystic Falls). The Frozen Fairy Falls hike (p129) is a popular ski day trip – get dropped off at the southern end of Fountain Freight Rd, visit the falls and ski back to Old Faithful (11 miles).

The 9-mile return Lone Star Geyser Trail takes you from Old Faithful Snow Lodge along the Mallard Lake Trail and parallel to the main road, to cross it at Kepler Cascades. The trail then follows the same route as the hike to Lone Star Geysers (see p132). A ski shuttle will allow you to take the 8-mile Spring Creek Trail (a former stagecoach road) to Lone Star Geyser.

SLEEPING

Although competition for campsites and lodging may be fierce, there's nothing quite like falling asleep to the eerie sounds of bugling elk and howling wolves and waking to the sulfur smell of the earth erupting and bubbling in the area.

Camping

Most of Yellowstone's campsites are in natural junctions, areas once frequented by Native Americans as well as early trappers, explorers and the US Army. There are around 2200 formal campsites in the park, plus well over 100 backcountry sites.

Aside from backcountry campsites (which require a hike to reach), camping inside the park is allowed only in 12 designated campgrounds (see p162) and is limited to 14 days from July 1 to Labor Day and 30 days the rest of the year. Check-out time is 10am. See Park Policies & Regulations at the start of this chapter (p96) for regulations on backcountry camping.

Some campsites are reserved for backpackers and cyclists at all campgrounds except Slough Creek and Canyon. Slough Creek fills early due to popularity with anglers and wolf watchers. Canyon is popular because of its central location. Boaters favor Grant Village and Bridge Bay; canoeists and anglers often base themselves at Lewis Lake. The Madison Campground is closest to Old Faithful, though Grant Village isn't far off. Fishing Bridge is always full of RVs in midsummer, and reservations are essential.

Xanterra runs five of the park's 12 campgrounds, and these are a few dollars pricier than the national park campgrounds. They feature flush toilets, cold running water and vending machines. You can reserve sites through **Xanterra** (☎ 307-344-7311; www.travelyellowstone.com; ⏰ May-end Aug 7am-6pm, other months 8am-5pm). The National Park Service has seven campgrounds available on a first come, first served basis only.

Call ☎ 307-344-2114 for recorded NPS campsite information.

Lodging

Of the cabin options, rustic Lake Lodge is the most peaceful, and Roosevelt Lodge offers the most authentic Western experience. Lake Yellowstone Hotel and Old Faithful Inn provide the park's most atmospheric accommodations. For reservations and information call **Xanterra** (☎ 307-344-7311; www.travelyellowstone.com).

Rooms are priced here at double occupancy, but most lodges have rooms that sleep up to six for an extra $10 per person. All Yellowstone hotel rooms are nonsmoking.

MAMMOTH COUNTRY
Camping
NPS CAMPGROUNDS

Mammoth Campground (Map p100; sites $; ⏰ year-round) The park's most exposed campground, this is a barren, dusty, sagebrush-covered area with sparse shade. On a hairpin bend in the road below Mammoth Hot Springs, it gets some road noise – the inner road sites are quietest – but its relatively low elevation makes it the warmest campground and a good choice for early- or late-season visits. Showers and other facilities are in Mammoth, 1 mile south, or Gardiner, 5 miles north by the North Entrance. When staffed,

---

YELLOWSTONE'S WINTER FACILITIES

Mammoth Hot Springs Hotel and Old Faithful Snow Lodge and their restaurants are the only places open, though there is limited (and cold!) winter camping at Mammoth Campground. In theory, you can snow camp anywhere in the park (including in the vicinity of Old Faithful) with a backcountry permit, but winter camping conditions are for specialists only.

Both hotels rent snowshoes, cross-country skis and winter attire, and they also offer skiing instruction and snowmobile tours. After a day on a snowmobile you'll need a dip in Mammoth Hotel's hot tubs or a massage from the Old Faithful Snow Lodge.

There are no public accommodations in Canyon, but **Yellowstone Expeditions** (☎ 800-728-9333; www.yellowstoneexpeditions.com) runs a winter yurt camp there for its cross-country ski and snowshoe tour clients. Four-day tours from West Yellowstone cost around $865 per person, including transportation, accommodations, food and a guide.

Visitor centers at Old Faithful and Mammoth are open during the winter season. There are winter warming huts at Mammoth, Indian Creek, Old Faithful (in yurts), West Thumb, Fishing Bridge, Madison and Canyon; the latter two have fast food. All except Mammoth and Old Faithful are open 24 hours. Snowmobile fuel is available at Canyon, Fishing Bridge, Old Faithful and Mammoth. Mammoth Clinic (p277) is open weekdays and Old Faithful Clinic (p277) is open periodically.

YELLOWSTONE NATIONAL PARK CAMPGROUNDS

Campground	Location	No of sites	Elevation	Open
Bridge Bay	Lake Country	425	7800ft	late May–mid-Sep
Canyon	Canyon Country	272	7734ft	early June–early Sep
Fishing Bridge RV Park	Lake Country	112	7800ft	mid-May–late Sep
Grant Village	Lake Country	400	7800ft	late May–late Sep
Indian Creek	Mammoth Country	75	7300ft	Jun–mid-Sep
Lewis Lake	Lake Country	85	7800ft	mid-Jun–early Nov
Madison	Geyser Country	280	6806ft	early May–late Oct
Mammoth	Mammoth Country	85	6239ft	year-round
Norris	Norris	116	7484ft	mid-May–late Sep
Pebble Creek	Roosevelt Country	36	6800ft	end May–late Sep
Slough Creek	Roosevelt Country	29	6400ft	late May–end Oct
Tower Falls	Roosevelt Country	32	6650ft	mid-May–late Sep

* Reservations possible through **Xanterra** (☎ 866-439 7375, 307-344-7311)

🔥 Fireplace 🥤 Drinking Water 🚻 Flush Toilets 👫 Ranger Station Nearby ♿ Wheelchair Accessible 🏪 Grocery Store Nearby

the registration office accepts credit cards and offers change if you're paying cash. There are several wheelchair-accessible and hiker/biker sites, and a concessionaire sells firewood between 6pm and 8:30pm. Join one of the ranger talks at the amphitheater at 9pm.

Indian Creek Campground (Map p100; sites $; ☯ Jun–mid-Sep) This low-key spot is probably the park's most underused campground – most people speed by between Mammoth and Old Faithful – which is one reason we like it. Plus, it's often the last in the park to fill up. Set in open forest on a low rise and surrounded by moose territory, there are several hiking trails nearby – to Indian Creek, along the former stagecoach road, or part way along the Bighorn Pass Trail (look for a handout detailing campground trails). Generators are not allowed, but firewood is sold. The site is 8 miles south of Mammoth Junction.

Norris Campground (Map p100; sites $; ☯ mid-May–late Sep) Nestled in scenic open forest on an idyllic, sunny hill overlooking the Gibbon River and bordering meadows, this is one of the park's nicest sites. There are fishing and wildlife-viewing opportunities nearby, Solfatara Creek Trailhead is in the campground and there's a 1-mile trail from near the campground (just over the bridge) to Norris Geyser Basin. The few riverside sites get snapped up very quickly. Campfire talks are held at 7:30pm and firewood is sold between 7pm and 8:30pm.

Lodging

Mammoth Hot Springs Hotel (Map p100; d & cabins $$-$$$, ste $$$$; ☯ early May-early Oct & mid-Dec–early Mar; ♿) A classy vibe, a good variety of accommodations (112 rooms) and a useful location make this one of the park's most popular accommodations. In the evenings there are video and slide presentations in

Reservations required?	Facilities	Description	Page
yes*		A multiple-loop megacomplex appealing to boaters & anglers	164
yes*		A huge 11-loop site slap-bang in the center of the park	164
yes*		A reservations-essential, RV-only spot, well located	165
yes*		A spacious & shady multiloop complex with conveniences & the lake nearby	163
no		Quiet, small, secluded & woodsy	165
no		A shady, quiet campground close to backcountry trails & lake	165
yes*		Lovely riverside location & the closest campground to Old Faithful	163
no		Fairly barren spot near the northern entrance but the warmest site in spring & fall	163
no		Quiet site with a walking trail to the nearby geyser basin	163
no		Fairly cramped site popular with wolf-watchers in the nearby Lamar Valley	163
no		A favorite with anglers, this site fills up the earliest in high season	163
no		Small site that fills up quickly, with several hiking trails	164

RV Dump Station   Payphone

the Map Room to the side of the lobby, where you can check out the huge wall map of the United States assembled from 15 types of wood from around the world.

The main accommodation choice is between hotel rooms in the main building or cabins out back. The cheaper options come with a sink and communal bathrooms, either down the hall in the hotel block or in a separate block out back by the budget cabins.

The main hotel en suite rooms echo the historic feel of the hotel with antique-style bathroom fittings, clawfoot tubs and old B&W photos on the walls. The cabins (closed in winter) are mostly duplex units, with a porch to sit on, but if you value your privacy you can request a detached cabin. The cabins are a bit cheaper than the hotel rooms but don't come with a phone.

Frontier cabins come with a private bathroom, shower and two double beds. Some come with a queen bed and private outdoor hot tub, enclosed in a privacy fence, for an extra $80 or so. The hotel suites have a living room and bedroom, cable TV and a fridge, and can sleep four in two queen beds.

ROOSEVELT COUNTRY
Camping
NATIONAL PARK SERVICE CAMPGROUNDS
Pebble Creek Campground (Map p104; sites $; ☾ late May–late Sep) The park's remotest ground is surrounded on three sides by the rugged cliffs of the Absaroka Range. It's along the banks of a creek in grizzly habitat and is popular with hikers and wolf-watchers, though the sites are a bit cramped. The Pebble Creek hiking trail (p136) starts nearby. Generators are not allowed. Most sites are pull-through. The site is 10 miles from the Northeast Entrance at the lower end of Icebox Canyon. The nearest showers and supplies are at Tower-Roosevelt Junction and there's good fishing at nearby Soda Butte Creek.

Slough Creek Campground (Map p104; sites $; late May-end Oct) This remote, peaceful site, 2.2 miles up an unpaved road, is in grizzly habitat along a prime fishing stream. A couple of walk-in sites are available, and there's easy access to the Slough Creek Trail. Generators are not allowed. The campsite is 10 miles northeast of Tower-Roosevelt Junction. An anglers' paradise, this ground fills up by 11am in high season.

Tower Falls Campground (Map p104; sites $; mid-May–late Sep) This small site is high above Tower Creek in an open pine forest. There are hiking trails nearby and groceries at nearby Tower Falls. It's 3 miles southeast of Tower-Roosevelt Junction. There are hiker/biker sites. Generators are not allowed.

Lodging

Founded in 1906 as a tented camp, present-day **Roosevelt Lodge** (Map p104; Roughrider cabins $$, Frontier cabins $$$; early Jun-early Sep;) was built in 1919 and retains an Old West feel, offering 80 cabins, horseback rides and a Wild West cookout in the heart of sagebrush country.

For groups, families or couples traveling together, the Roughrider cabins are among the park's greatest bargains, because the price is the same for cabins with one, two or three beds, meaning you can cram six people in here for under $20 a head! The pleasant wooden cabins come with a log-burning stove, though the one-bed (and some two-bed) cabins are cramped (because it's the same price, book a larger cabin). There are no en suite bathrooms and not even running water in the room, but the three communal wash blocks have hot water and showers, and are perfectly adequate for your needs.

Frontier cabins are nicely decorated and come with private bathroom, electric heating and two or three double beds. There are two handicapped-accessible cabins with private bathroom.

The Frontier cabins should be booked several months in advance in high season since numbers are limited; the Roughriders should be booked at least a month or two in advance, though you might find a room free on the off chance. There are a limited number of outdoor grills if you want to cook your own food.

There's good hiking nearby; the hike to Lost Lake starts from just behind the lodge – see p129.

CANYON COUNTRY
Camping
XANTERRA CAMPGROUNDS

The huge **Canyon Campground** (Map p110; sites $; early Jun-early Sep) is the most densely forested in the park, but it's also the largest (11 loops!) and one of the most cramped, which makes staying here feel a bit like being churned through a Pink Floyd–style tourism meat grinder. Still, thanks to its central location next to Canyon Village, it's a very popular ground, so book at least a couple of days ahead in summer.

There are pay showers and laundry on site, and the restaurants and supplies of Canyon Village are nearby. Canyon also offers the most tent-only sites (four out of 11 loops) of any campground. Head to the amphitheater at 9pm or 9:30pm for the nightly campfire programs.

Lodging

The enormous **Canyon Lodge** (Map p110; ☎ 307-242-3900; lodge d $$$, Pioneer/Frontier/Western cabins $$/$$/$$$; rooms Jun–mid-Sep, cabins close earlier;) complex has 609 rooms and is set in thick forest. It dates from the opening of the park to mass tourism in the 1950s and 1960s – a drive around the multiple low-rise loops is like a drive back in time to a classic Middle American suburb.

The three types of cabins date from the 1950s and are laid out barracks-style, grouped into blocks of four, six or eight. The simple Pioneer cabins haven't been updated since Yogi Bear last wandered into the park and come with two single beds and a shower only (no tub). The Frontiers are similar but have been renovated. Modern Western cabins come with two queen beds, a coffeemaker and tub/shower, and some are wheelchair accessible. These cabins are slowly being renovated. Cabins can sleep up to four for an extra $10 per person. Loop 'P' generally has the most secluded locations.

The modern Dunraven Lodge and Cascade Lodge both offer modern hotel rooms that were built in the 1990s, some with forest views. Both have coffeemakers and some wheelchair-accessible rooms but no telephone.

LAKE COUNTRY
Camping

The following campgrounds all feature dump stations, but only Fishing Bridge has full sewer and electrical hookups.

A megacomplex adjacent to the marina, 3 miles southwest of Lake Village, **Bridge Bay Campground** (Map pp114-15; sites $; [☿] late May–mid-Sep) appeals to fishing and boating enthusiasts. Tent campers will appreciate the more desirable forested tent-only loops (E and F). Some lower sites offer lake views, but the more private ones are in the upper section. There are a few hiker and biker sites. Showers and laundry facilities are 4 miles away at Fishing Bridge.

Along the north shore of Yellowstone Lake, 1 mile east of Fishing Bridge Junction, **Fishing Bridge RV Park** (Map pp114-15; RV sites $; [☿] mid-May–late Sep) only allows hard-shelled RVs because of heavy bear activity. Rates are for up to four people and include electrical, water and sewerage hookups; all sites are back-ins. Reservations are essential in July and August. Public facilities here include a pay laundry and showers.

Along the west shore of Yellowstone Lake, 22 miles north of the South Entrance, **Grant Village Campground** (Map pp114-15; sites $; [☿] late May-late Sep) is the sole campground on Yellowstone Lake. It's an enormous forested site that has a nearby boat launch, an RV dump station and three loops of tent-only sites. Nearby facilities include showers, laundry and groceries. You'll find lovely spots for lakeshore strolls nearby.

NATIONAL PARK SERVICE CAMPGROUNDS

The forested **Lewis Lake Campground** (Map pp114-15; sites $; [☿] mid-Jun–early Nov) is at the south end of Lewis Lake, about 10 miles north of the South Entrance. A nearby boat launch that provides easy access to Lewis Lake and the Lewis River channel. Snow often remains here through June because of its high elevation and shaded location, so it may not be the best early-season campground, but as a park-run site it is cheaper than most. Bring repellent. A few walk-in and tent-only sites are available and generators are not allowed.

Lodging

The 186 rooms at **Lake Lodge** (Map pp114-15; Pioneer/Western cabins $$/$$$; [☿] early Jun-late Sep) offer a lackluster budget choice. Western cabins are spacious if plain, with faux wood interiors; some in the A and B loops boast lake views and French windows. Cramped cabins recall the 1920s, with exposed boilers and dated decor quickly approaching retro status. The best feature is the rustic main lodge with rockers creaking on the porch, roaring fires inside, a dining hall and a laundromat.

ourpick On the lake, **Lake Yellowstone Hotel** (Map pp114-15; hotel d $$$$, annex d $$$, Frontier cabins $$$; [☿] mid-May–early Oct; [♿]) is a buttercup behemoth that sets romantics aflutter. It harks back to a bygone era, though the 296 rooms that cost $4 in 1895 have appreciated. Rooms feature wicker and floral designs, some sleeping up to six in three queen beds. Main lodge lakeside rooms cost extra, but don't guarantee lake views. The comfortable Frontier cabins are boxed in neat suburban rows. The annex offers limited wheelchair accommodations.

The 300 condo-like boxes, with standard hotel interiors, at **Grant Village** (Map pp114-15; motel r $$$; [☿] late May-end Sep; [♿]) were once dismissed by author Alston Chase as 'an inner-city project in the heart of primitive America, a wilderness ghetto.' They do happen to be the closest lodging to the Tetons for those getting an early start.

GEYSER COUNTRY
Camping
XANTERRA CAMPGROUNDS

In a sunny, open forest in a broad meadow above the banks of the Madison River, **Madison Campground** (Map p120; sites $; [☿] early May-late Oct) is the nearest campground to Old Faithful and the West Entrance. Bison herds and the park's largest elk herd frequent the meadows to its west and it's a great base for fly-fishing the Madison. Tent-only sites are ideally placed along the river. The campground is just west of Madison Junction, 14 miles east of the West Entrance and 16 miles north of Old Faithful. The nearest showers are at Old Faithful. Vending machines offer ice, soft drinks and newspapers. The good *Stars Over Yellowstone* interpretive program runs on Friday and Saturday nights between June and August at the campground's amphitheater, and ranger talks take place other nights. Unfortunately the natural riverside hot springs, 100 yards from the edge of the campground, are now off-limits.

Lodging

our pick The lobby of the historic **Old Faithful Inn** (Map p122; ste $$$$$, d with bathroom $$$-$$$$, d without bathroom $$; ☺ mid-May–mid-Oct; ♿) is a bit of a zoo during the day, but the day-trippers quickly disappear with the sun. The building is full of charm, with 327 rooms, a lovely balcony, library-style desks, and a pianist and singer at lunch and dinner. A stay here is a quintessential Yellowstone experience, but book in advance or you'll find there's no room at the inn. For more on the hotel, see p124.

The hotel has a vast variety of rooms, including some wheelchair-accessible rooms. The cheapest old-wing rooms hold the most atmosphere, with original old copper-top furniture, but the bathrooms are down the hall. Beware also that you can hear every footstep through the creaking wooden ceiling and the radiator heat can be noisy early and late in the season. Easily the best rooms of this kind are off the 3rd-floor lobby.

Families might like the two connecting rooms that can sleep five, either with private bathroom or with bathroom down the hall (around $30 less). Rates for these rooms are per room, regardless of the number of people.

The only rooms that have a view of Old Faithful are a couple of 'premium' rooms on the front side of the east wing; these get snapped up a year in advance. Back rooms in the east wing cost $10 less and have no view. Even if you face Old Faithful, you'll find that the pine trees block most of the view.

The west wing has comfortable 'frontside' rooms – those on the upper floor have decent views of the geyser basin. The high-range rooms are a bit of a misnomer, since they are considered standard hotel rooms. These rooms vary considerably for the same price (rooms with two beds are noticeably larger). Midrange rooms are $30 cheaper. Both have bathrooms (most midrange rooms have only tubs) and can sleep up to four.

The only bum rooms in the hotel are the high-range rooms in the 1000 room number series, as these are below the ground floor. Staff refer to these affectionately as the 'dungeon rooms.' Request a higher floor.

Glummer than its glamorous cousin, the 132-cabin **Old Faithful Lodge** (Map p122; cabins $$-$$$; ☺ mid-May–mid-Sep; ♿) was built in 1923 and has its historical roots in Yellowstone's turn-of-the century tent camps. It's definitely a notch down in atmosphere, though the rooms themselves are fine. The remodeled Frontier cabins come with a private bathroom but no telephone and vary in size, with some very small. Budget cabins have sinks with hot water, but the toilets and showers are in outside blocks. Most cabins are in blocks of twos or fours, though a few are detached. Some north-facing cabins on the north side have views of Old Faithful from the back porch.

The park's most recent accommodation, **Old Faithful Snow Lodge** (Map p122; lodge r $$$, Frontier/Western cabins $$/$$$; ☺ early May–early Nov & mid-Dec–early Mar; ♿) was built in 1999 in a 'New Western' style and offers the only winter accommodations available at Old Faithful. The main lodge has a stylish lobby decorated in bear and elk motifs and 134 comfortable, cozy but bland modern hotel rooms, with two double beds, a hair dryer and a coffeemaker. The pine-walled Frontier cabins are fairly simple but come with bathrooms and a coffeemaker. The modern Western cabins are more spacious, with two double beds, and are warmer in winter. They are $50 cheaper than the hotel rooms.

BECHLER REGION

Camping

Cave Falls Forest Service Campground (☎ 208-524-7500; sites $) Situated in the Caribou-Targhee National Forest, just down the road from Bechler's trailheads, these pleasant woodsy sites line a river cliff offering a slight breeze to ward off mosquitoes. Sites feature picnic tables, fire rings and grills. Vault toilets, bear boxes and water are available.

EATING & DRINKING

Food in the park is split between campfire cuisine, cafeteria food, a couple of fast-food choices and the more pleasant dining rooms of the park's historic inns. The park concessionaire, Xanterra, runs most dining options, so don't be surprised if you get a serious dose of déjà vu every time you open a menu. Most places are a pretty good value, considering the prime real estate. You can get a sneak preview of park menus at the **Xanterra website** (www.travelyellowstone.com).

The park's cafeterias are bland but convenient, and resonably economical for families. All places serve breakfast and most offer an all-you-can-eat buffet that can quickly wipe out even the best-laid hiking plans. Kids' menus are available almost everywhere.

There's also fast food at major junctions, plus snack shops and grocery supplies in the Yellowstone General Stores. Mediocre lunches are reasonably priced but it can be crowded at peak times of the year. Dinners are considerably more expensive but offer rather more culinary adventure. The Grant Village, Old Faithful Inn and Lake Hotel dining rooms all require dinner **reservations** (☎ 307-344-7311).

MAMMOTH COUNTRY

our pick **Mammoth Hot Springs Dining Room** (meals $-$$; ☾ early May-early Oct & mid-Dec–early Mar) There are a few surprises in this elegant place, including the smoked trout starter. Dinner is a more serious affair, with pistachio and parmesan-crusted trout, bison bangers and mash, or squash couscous with saffron coconut cream – the latter a rare vegetarian find. If you're lucky, the daily special will be the great huckleberry Brie chicken. There's a kids' menu here. The breakfast buffet is pretty good for around $10. Reservations are recommended in winter only.

Line up at the fast-food MacYellowstone-style **Mammoth Terrace Grill** (meals $; ☾ 8am-9pm) for ¼lb burgers, chili cheese fries and ice cream, along with some breakfast foods.

The hotel lobby's **Espresso Cart** (☾ 7-9am, 4-9pm) will help you kick-start the day.

ROOSEVELT COUNTRY

Roosevelt Lodge Dining Room (lunch & breakfast $, dinner $$-$$$; ☾ 7:30-10:30am & 11:30am-3pm & 5-9pm early Jun-early Sep) Although popular for its BBQ Western-style ribs and fried chicken, this dining room boasts a menu that stretches to linguine with artichoke hearts, mushrooms and garlic. Take a post-lunch or predinner stroll up to the Lost Creek Falls, a 10-minute walk behind the Roosevelt Lodge. The porch rockers are a fine place for a nightcap.

Old West cookout ($$$$; ☾ depart 5pm early Jun-Labor Day) The Roosevelt Lodge activities center offers this fun cookout, with steak, beans and the kind of cowboy coffee you have to filter through your teeth. Kids will love it. Reservations are required. See p157 for details. Limited groceries are available at the small Yellowstone General Store.

CANYON COUNTRY

Don't expect too much from Canyon's restaurants; a single kitchen prepares all meals – up to 5000 per day!

Cafeteria (meals $; ☾ 6:30-11am, 11:30am-3pm & 4:30-9:30pm Jun–mid-Sep) There are no surprises at this huge and echoing cafeteria, but it's cheap and easy, serving up steak, Santa Fe chicken and a mean bison sausage sandwich, with the same menu as the Old Faithful Lodge Cafeteria. Oatmeal and fruit salads are among the lighter options.

Picnic shop (sandwiches $; ☾ 11am-6pm) Has prepackaged deli sandwiches, yogurt with granola, and ice cream, with a couple of outdoor seats in the sun.

Yellowstone General Store (www.visityellowstonepark.com; meals $; ☾ 7:30am-8:30pm) Has an old-fashioned soda fountain churning, not to mention burgers, chili dogs and root-beer floats, plus an ice cream and espresso stand. Breakfasts include blueberry flapjacks with sausage. A $4 souvenir cup gets you free soda refills at general stores throughout the park, which is quite a deal. Hours can be shortened out of season.

Canyon Lodge dining room (breakfast & lunch $, dinner $$; ☾ 7-10am, 11:30am-2:30pm & 5-10pm) This eatery has a dated casino/steakhouse lounge feels to it, the kind of place you might spot a 1970s-era Joe Pesci in a perm and a leisure suit, but it will do. Lunch features epic build-your-own burgers (including salmon burgers), but the restaurant only truly spreads its chicken wings for dinner, with tasty options like macadamia nut and coconut-crusted tilapia with pineapple salsa. The all-you-can-eat soup and salad bar option is low-grade but refreshing. The good wine and beer list is shared with the bar (open 3:30pm to 11pm). The breakfast menu has some lighter options, such as yogurt with fresh fruit, as well as a full breakfast buffet.

GEYSER COUNTRY

All of the food options in Geyser Country are clustered around Old Faithful.

Bear Paw Deli (meals $; ☾ 10:30am-7:30pm) Next door to Old Faithful Inn, Bear Paw sells fairly unappetizing prewrapped sandwiches, salads and ice cream.

ourpick **Old Faithful Inn Dining Room** (☎ 307-545-4999; breakfast & lunch $, dinner $$-$$$; ⏰ 6:30-10:30am, 11:30am-2:30pm & 5-10pm mid-May–mid-Oct) This buzzing dining room serves good-value steaks, salads and pasta, as well as breakfast, lunch and dinner buffets. Dinners are heavier fare, with pan-seared elk medallions and the staff-recommended pork osso bucco (pork shank in red wine). Try a 'Yellowstone caldera' for dessert – a warm chocolate truffle torte with a fittingly molten center. The huge fireplace and wagon-wheel chandelier add to the rustic atmosphere. Make dinner reservations in the morning or, better, the day before (up to 60 days in advance) or you'll end up eating dinner after 9:30pm.

ourpick **Obsidian Dining Room** (☎ 307-344-7311; dinner $$-$$$; ⏰ 6:30-10am & 5-10pm early May–mid-Oct, mid-Dec–early Mar, lunch in winter only) A quieter affair, the Old Faithful Snow Lodge serves up a few unexpected dishes (such as the steamed mussels and the warm goat-cheese salad with pine nuts), alongside such gamey exotica as grilled antelope sausages with bacon and onions, and bison ribs (the bison are farmed outside the Yellowstone ecosystem). A breakfast buffet is available.

Geyser Grill (meals $; ⏰ 7am-7pm early May–mid-Oct & mid-Dec–early Mar) Nearby Geyser Grill is a fast-food place with burgers, breakfasts, sandwiches, bagels and beer. It closes early.

Old Faithful Lodge Cafeteria (mains $-$$; ⏰ 11am-9pm late May–mid-Sep) It's factory-style functionality rather than fine cuisine, but this is a good-value place, churning out solid standards like meatloaf and prime rib alongside lighter fare like the chicken pesto wrap. The Greek salad ($6) is a lifesaver if you've been living off canned goods for too long. Try to get here early before the buffet-style food gets too stewed. Most noteworthy are the views of Old Faithful from the side window. The cafeteria does not serve breakfast.

Bake Shop (⏰ 7-11am) For quick eats visit the Bake Shop in the lobby. It offers fried chicken, pretzels, cookies and cinnamon rolls, and there's an ice-cream stand.

Yellowstone General Stores (www.visityellowstonepark.com; mains $; ⏰ 7:30am-8:30pm) The two general stores serve up snacks. The original store near Old Faithful has a '50s-style diner counter, complete with original soda fountain stools, that serves up burgers, malts and sandwiches. The store near the Snow Lodge offers individual pizzas, paninis, salads, breakfast biscuits and prepackaged sandwiches in a cafeteria-style setting.

For postgeyser or après-ski cocktails, try the **Bear Pit Bar** (⏰ from 11:30am) in the Old Faithful Inn or the **Firehole Lounge** (⏰ winter) in the Old Faithful Snow Lodge, where the fireside seats get snapped up quickly in winter.

Old Faithful **espresso cart** (⏰ 6:30am-10pm) serves the best coffee in the park.

LAKE COUNTRY

Save your one unwrinkled outfit to dine in style at the **Lake Hotel Dining Room** (meals $$$; ☎ 307-344-7311; ⏰ late May–mid-Oct) in the Lake Yellowstone Hotel. Lunch options include Idaho trout, salads and gorgonzola sandwiches. Dinner ups the ante with rack of lamb, bison prime rib, pastas or a *prix fixe* menu ($39). The kid's menu surprises with healthy sides (but rewards with hot fudge sundaes).

The hotel's **deli** (⏰ 10:30am-9pm) offers fresh sandwiches and soup. The nearby **Lake Lodge Cafeteria** (⏰ from 6:30am; mains $) offers hearty breakfasts and family fare like pot roast, stuffed turkey and pastas.

The smoky BBQ aroma emanating from **Grant Village Restaurant** (☎ 307-344-7311; lunch $, dinner $$; ⏰ 6:30-10am, 11:30am-2:30pm & 5pm-10pm Jun–mid-Sep) could draw a grizzly, though the food turns out to be just good enough. Lunch offers light fare like Reubens and deli sandwiches; dinners includes prime rib and farm-raised trout. Dinner reservations are required.

Grab a stool at the tiny Seven Stool Saloon for a cold brew.

Head to the **Lake House** (⏰ 7am-10:30am & 5-9pm; meals $-$$) for cafeteria-style pizza and pasta and romantic sunsets over the lake. Walk down from the main parking area or gain access from the marina. It's closed for lunch.

Around Yellowstone

The 43,750-sq-mile Greater Yellowstone Ecosystem doesn't suddenly end at the park fence. Enveloping the park kernel is a protective cushion of national forests and wilderness areas, forested mountain ranges and high plateaus that offer almost as much scenic splendor and as many outdoor opportunities as the parks themselves, but without the crowds. Try to allocate at least a couple of days to explore this exceptional area.

Latched limpetlike onto Yellowstone Park's northern boundaries, three towns serve as visitor hubs, where you can stock up on groceries and gas, check email and bed down for the night. None offers an overdose of charm, but they can be useful places to base yourself, especially if you haven't made park reservations. West Yellowstone to the west offers the most commercial services and is the winter hub. Gardiner to the north is the oldest gateway to Yellowstone. To the northeast is Cooke City, the most isolated and rustic of the four gateways, with fewer visitors and less obvious tourist trappings. It's the favorite of many visitors for these very reasons.

North of Yellowstone, the airports of Bozeman and Billings offer convenient access to the park, with young and active Bozeman offering more to visitors. As the gateway to Paradise Valley, Livingston has been entertaining Yellowstone-bound tourists for 120 years and is a must for fly-fishing enthusiasts. The charming outdoors town of Red Lodge to the east is the springboard to the fantastic Beartooth Hwy. East of Yellowstone, the Wyoming town of Cody is the region's premier Wild West town.

Plan your itinerary to combine the Beartooth and Gallatin routes, or the Beartooth, Wapiti and Chief Joseph Scenic Hwy, and you have the ultimate add-on to a classic Yellowstone trip.

HIGHLIGHTS

- Gripping the steering wheel extra tight as you climb the spaghetti loops of the **Beartooth Highway** (p183), America's most scenic road, *waaay* above the treeline
- Blowing off some steam at the **night rodeo** (p191) after a day exploring the ghosts of the Wild West at the **Buffalo Bill Historical Center** (p188) in Cody
- Sucking down an extra large chocolate malt at the **Red Box Car** (p183) after a hard hike in the mountains around Red Lodge
- Staring open-mouthed into the open jaws of the world's largest T Rex skull at Bozeman's **Museum of the Rockies** (p195)
- Hitting the slopes at stylish **Big Sky** (p197), site of the region's best white stuff

GATEWAY TOWNS

WEST YELLOWSTONE

☎ 406 / pop 1500 / elev 6600ft

Seated a scant quarter-mile from Yellowstone National Park, the old rail town of West Yellowstone is a buzzing commercial outcrop. It's tiny as towns go but offers its own brand of diversity: from endless variations on the burger joint and souvenir shop to stuffed grizzlies, live wolves, RV villages, taxidermy clinics and snowmobile shops. As one-stop shopping for those refueling for the park, it's both convenient and fairly complete. You can expect a quality bison burger, as well as award-winning local brews and double licks of tart huckleberry ice cream. Linger an extra day or two and you will find out why most locals stay.

Open wilderness abounds. Ride a bike, paddle a canoe, fly-fish or click on skis – even at the height of tourist season, you can have the serpentine waterways, cool lakes and trails mostly to yourself. Although 'West' bustles in the high seasons (June to September and mid-December to mid-March), its lulls offer laid-back recreation.

West Yellowstone is the regional hub for snowmobiling, as well as a launch pad for snowcoach and ski tours. Most locals battled the National Park Service's proposed ban on snowmobiling in Yellowstone National Park (see the boxed text, p53), and some are still not happy with limits imposed in 2007. Outside the park, unrestricted snowmobiling continues.

History

In the early 1900s the Union Pacific Railroad built a rail line to the western edge of the park to access Geyser Country. The town, then known as Riverside, was at the end of the line. In 1908, Eagle's General Store – still on Yellowstone Ave today – was established. The Madison Hotel was built in 1912 after its owners arrived from a difficult trek to Yellowstone on foot. With rail, food and lodging, the frontier-style town, now called Yellowstone, became a hub of activity, with the Union Pacific at its helm.

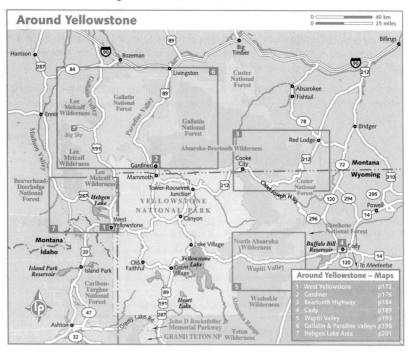

Around Yellowstone

Around Yellowstone – Maps	
1 West Yellowstone	p172
2 Gardiner	p176
3 Beartooth Highway	p184
4 Cody	p189
5 Wapiti Valley	p193
6 Gallatin & Paradise Valleys	p198
7 Hebgen Lake Area	p201

Yellowstone National Park's tourist boom supported services cropping up alongside Union Pacific. With the growth of automobile travel, these independent operations soon overshadowed the railroads. The entrepreneurial spirit ruled: during Prohibition, barrels of feed corn came into town and left as potent 'Yellowstone Spring Water.'

In 1920 the community changed its name to West Yellowstone to avoid confusion between the town and the park.

Orientation & Information

US 191 (from Bozeman) and US 287 (from Ennis) meet 8 miles north of West Yellowstone and continue through town as Canyon St (the main street) then turn east at Yellowstone Ave to enter the park. US 20 leaves Firehole Ave to head west into Idaho.

Book Peddler (☎ 406-646-9358; 106 Canyon St; ☯ 8am-10pm summer) For good general selection, come here. Also serves espresso.

Bookworm Books (14 Canyon St; ☯ 9am-11pm summer) Visit for the best regional selections and bookish expertise.

Canyon Street Laundry (312 Canyon St; ☯ 7am-10pm) Has coin-operated machines, drop-off service and slightly rundown public showers ($2 for six minutes).

Chamber of Commerce Information Center (☎ 406-646-7701; www.westyellowstonechamber.com; Canyon St) In a parking lot south of Yellowstone Ave, it provides friendly traveler assistance. There's a ranger-staffed information desk, free wi-fi and brochures with discount coupons for local attractions.

Gallatin National Forest Service Headquarters (☎ 406-646-7369; Canyon St) Two blocks north of Firehole Ave.

Madison Hotel (☎ 406-646-7745, 800-838-7745; 139 Yellowstone Ave; ☯ closed Oct-late May) Internet access for $5 per hour.

West Yellowstone Public Library (☎ 406-646-9017; 23 Dunraven St; ☯ closed Sun & Mon) Tiny library with free internet (30 minutes maximum). It books up quickly, so phone ahead to reserve time.

West Yellowstone Web Works (27 Geyser) Internet access for $5 per hour.

www.destinationyellowstone.com A rich source of West Yellowstone information.

Sights

Newcomers can attend a free **orientation talk** (☯ 9:30am) at the chamber of commerce. Ranger talks are given daily at 2pm at either the Grizzly & Wolf Discovery Center or

Museum of the Yellowstone. In winter, rangers lead snowshoe hikes along the Riverside trail. Bring your own snowshoes.

Offering an afterlife to 'pest' grizzlies facing extermination, the **Grizzly & Wolf Discovery Center** (☎ 406-646-7001; www.gizzly discoveryctr.org; 201 S Canyon; adult/child 5-12 $8.50/4; ☯ 8am-dusk) inadvertently condemns these magnificent creatures to life sentences of taunting by school children. The concept here is to educate travelers about the nature of bears and wolves. The wolves (a pack of four) were born in captivity. The indoor exhibits are quite good, and there is an information wall with unedited clippings of all the bear encounters in recent times. There are also twice weekly ranger-led slide shows at 7pm.

Next door, the **Yellowstone IMAX Theater** (☎ 406-646-4100; www.yellowstoneimax.com; 101 S Canyon; adult/child $9/6.50; ☯ hourly showings 9am-9pm May-Sep, 1-9pm Oct-Apr) shows *Yellowstone*, *Bears* and *Wolves*, and other films on a screen six stories high.

Housed in the 1909 Union Pacific depot, the small **Museum of the Yellowstone** (☎ 406-646-1100; 124 Yellowstone Ave; adult/child $5/3; ☯ 9am-9pm mid-May–mid-Oct) explores early stagecoach and rail travel. There are also displays on the 1988 fires, wildlife and earthquakes. Rail buffs can check out the well-preserved 1903 **Oregon Short Line Rail Car** in the Holiday Inn.

Churning out light musicals, melodramas and comedies for 40 years, the **Playmill Theater** (☎ 406-646-7757; www.playmill.com; 29 Madison Ave; tickets $15; ☯ Memorial Day-Labor Day; ♿) is a local institution. Reserve your tickets in advance. It also offers a summer theatre camp for ages 12 to 18.

Activities

West Yellowstone is host to a range of cultural and sporting events, from summer rodeo and mountain man rendezvous to the Spam Cup, a series of ski races in which the lucky winner receives a free can of preserved pork products.

SUMMER

Both the Rendezvous and Riverside trail systems offer great **mountain biking** and **trail running** when the snow melts. The chamber of commerce sponsors a spring and fall **cycle tour** (www.cycleyellowstone.com; fee $45) in the park with part of the proceeds going to charity.

AROUND YELLOWSTONE

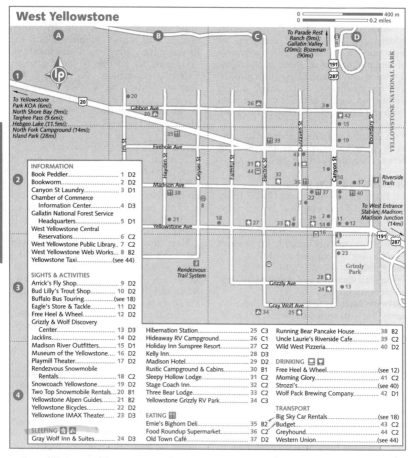

West Yellowstone

0 — 400 m
0 — 0.2 miles

To Parade Rest
Ranch (9mi);
Gallatin Valley
(20mi); Bozeman
(90mi)

To Yellowstone
Park KOA (6mi);
North Shore Bay (9mi);
Targhee Pass (9.6mi);
Hebgen Lake (11.5mi);
North Fork Campground (14mi);
Island Park (28mi)

YELLOWSTONE NATIONAL PARK

Riverside
Trails

To West Entrance
Station; Madison;
Madison Junction
(14mi)

Grizzly
Park

Rendezvous
Trail System

Gibbon Ave
Firehole Ave
Madison Ave
Yellowstone Ave
Grizzly Ave
Gray Wolf Ave

INFORMATION	
Book Peddler	1 D2
Bookworm	2 D2
Canyon St Laundry	3 D1
Chamber of Commerce Information Center	4 D3
Gallatin National Forest Service Headquarters	5 D1
West Yellowstone Central Reservations	6 C2
West Yellowstone Public Library	7 C2
West Yellowstone Web Works	8 B2
Yellowstone Taxi	(see 44)

SIGHTS & ACTIVITIES	
Arrick's Fly Shop	9 D2
Bud Lilly's Trout Shop	10 D2
Buffalo Bus Touring	(see 18)
Eagle's Store & Tackle	11 D2
Free Heel & Wheel	12 D2
Grizzly & Wolf Discovery Center	13 D3
Jacklins	14 D2
Madison River Outfitters	15 D1
Museum of the Yellowstone	16 D2
Playmill Theater	17 D2
Rendezvous Snowmobile Rentals	18 C2
Snowcoach Yellowstone	19 D2
Two Top Snowmobile Rentals	20 B1
Yellowstone Alpen Guides	21 B2
Yellowstone Bicycles	22 D2
Yellowstone IMAX Theater	23 D3

SLEEPING	
Gray Wolf Inn & Suites	24 D3

Hibernation Station	25 C3
Hideaway RV Campground	26 C1
Holiday Inn Sunspree Resort	27 C2
Kelly Inn	28 D3
Madison Hotel	29 D2
Rustic Campground & Cabins	30 B1
Sleepy Hollow Lodge	31 C2
Stage Coach Inn	32 C2
Three Bear Lodge	33 C2
Yellowstone Grizzly RV Park	34 C3

EATING	
Ernie's Bighorn Deli	35 B2
Food Roundup Supermarket	36 C2
Old Town Café	37 D2

Running Bear Pancake House	38 B2
Uncle Laurie's Riverside Cafe	39 C2
Wild West Pizzeria	40 D2

DRINKING	
Free Heel & Wheel	(see 12)
Morning Glory	41 C2
Strozzi's	(see 40)
Wolf Pack Brewing Company	42 D1

TRANSPORT	
Big Sky Car Rentals	(see 18)
Budget	43 C2
Greyhound	44 C2
Western Union	(see 44)

These fully supported trips (with van and repair assistance) are a lot of fun and geared toward a range of abilities.

For outstanding mocha lattes, maps, gear and trail savvy, **Free Heel and Wheel** (406-646-7744; www.freeheelandwheel.com; 40 Yellowstone Ave; 9am-8pm Mon-Sat, 9am-7pm Sun) is the place. In addition to renting mountain bikes ($25 per day), skis ($20) and snowshoes ($15), it offers touring and skate-ski lessons and organize free women's rides.

In the former one-room school house, **Yellowstone Bicycles** (406-646-7815; 132 Madison Ave) rents out mountain and road bikes from $20 a day, including recumbent machines, which are best described as a La-Z-Boy on wheels. The owner is a knowledgeable cyclist.

Bud Lilly's Trout Shop (406-646-7801; www.bud lillys.com; 39 Madison Ave) rents fishing equipment and offers one-day float and walk trips from $220 per person. **Arrick's Fly Shop** (406-646-7290; www.arricks.com; 37 Canyon St), **Jacklins** (406-6467336; www.jacklinsflyshop.com; 105 Yellowstone Ave) and **Madison River Outfitters** (406-646-9644; www.madisonriveroutfitters.com; 117 Canyon St) are all good places for fishing information, equipment and guides, while **Eagle's Store & Tackle** (406-646-9300; Yellowstone Ave) sells backpacking supplies.

Nine miles from West Yellowstone, **Parade Rest Ranch** (406-646-7217; www.paraderestranch .com) offers horseback rides from one to four hours ($35 to $60 per person, daily except Sunday), including sunset rides and corral rides for kids under seven. It offers Western cookouts overlooking Hebgen Lake on Monday and Friday evenings (adult/child $35/15).

WINTER

Thanksgiving week heralds the **Yellowstone Ski Festival** (www.yellowstoneskifestival.com), a great time for ski buffs and newcomers to the sport. Highlights include ski clinics (for kids, too) and gear demos.

In November the world-class **Rendezvous Trail System** becomes the training ground for US Olympic cross-country ski teams, with 30 miles of groomed skiing and skating trails. Grooming goes through March, when the Rendezvous Marathon Ski Race draws hundreds of skiers. There are also special kids' loops. For more information, visit Free Heel and Wheel (opposite).

Less developed but incredibly scenic, the **Riverside Trails** cut through 1.5 miles of fir and pine to emerge on old National Park Service (NPS) roads and other trails alongside the Madison River. Catch a link to the trail on the east side of Boundary St between Madison Ave and Firehole Ave.

Cross-country ski in the park and camp in heated yurts with the highly recommended **Yellowstone Expeditions** (☎ 800-728-9333, 406-646-9333; www.yellowstoneexpeditions.com; 4 days & 3 nights $865). It also offers snowshoe excursions. Trips range from four to eight days.

Many of the hotels rent snowmobiles and offer winter lodging and rental packages. Two of the many snowmobile rental agencies are **Rendezvous Snowmobile Rentals** (☎ 406-646-9564; www.yellowstonevacations.com; 415 Yellowstone Ave) and **Two Top Snowmobile Rentals** (☎ 800-522-7802, 406-646-7802; www.twotopsnowmobile.com; 646 Gibbon Ave). Agencies rent snowmobiles for $114 to $164 per day.

Organized Tours

In summer **Buffalo Bus Touring Company** (☎ 800-426-7669, 406-646-9353; www.snowcoachyellowstone.com/tours/buffalobustours.htm; 415 Yellowstone Ave; adult/child $55/42) picks up from local campgrounds and motels for a full-day tour of park highlights.

In winter **Yellowstone Alpen Guides** (☎ 800-858-3502, 406-646-9591; www.yellowstoneguides.com; 555 Yellowstone Ave; adult/child $99/79) runs 10-person snowcoach tours to Old Faithful, departing daily from mid-December through mid-March. Guided or independent skiing and

snowshoeing options are also available, as are summer van tours of the park and multiday tours.

Snowcoach Yellowstone (☎ 800-426-7669; www.snowcoachyellowstone.com; 415 Yellowstone Ave; adult/child $99/79) run full-day guided snowcoach tours to Old Faithful and Canyon in the park.

Powder hounds can go backcountry with **Hellroaring Ski Adventures** (☎ 406-570-4025; www.skihellroaring.com). For $150 to $250 per person (depending on the number in your group), you get a shuttle, guide, meals (take off $50 if you supply your own food), avalanche rescue equipment, climbing skins, hut accommodations and excellent terrain in the Centennial Mountains. Hut rental, for a minimum of four experienced people, costs $30 per person per night.

Driving

Ditch the wheels along this route for great hiking and a soak in a hot spring.

GALLATIN GALLOP

Route West Yellowstone to Big Sky
Distance 51 miles (one hour)
Speed Limit 45–65mph

This paved route also makes a great bike ride; it is less traveled and notably less crowded than the main park loops. Leave West Yellowstone heading north on Hwy 191, a broad-shouldered highway splitting through pine forest. After passing the junction with Hwy 287 (a scenic detour to Hebgen Lakes), about 12 miles in, there are views of the Madison Valley to the east and Madison River and Hebgen Lake to the west. The road climbs, following the contours of Grayling Creek.

Enter Yellowstone National Park (there is no entry booth here) and pass the headwaters of the **Gallatin River**, where trickles merge from the surrounding springs and high mountain ranges. The meandering river features some outstanding fishing spots (permits necessary). Also keep an eye out for moose frequenting the river willows, as well as elk and deer. The landscape is open – trees were felled by western budworm disease and the 1988 fire. On the east side of the road, **Bighorn Pass** and **Fawn Pass Trails** offer good hiking and hot-springs soaks.

AROUND YELLOWSTONE

The Madison Range and Taylor Peaks lie to the west. Further north, **Specimen Creek Trailhead** leads to Gallatin's **petrified forest**, created 50 million years ago when lava, ash and mudflows swallowed trees and other vegetation, but left them so intact that botanists can still identify the species.

Tight curves wind along the Gallatin River as you leave the park and enter **Gallatin Canyon**. Good hiking trails abound, but remember this is grizzly country. The canyon narrows and steep, rocky cliffs hem the road in. Glimpses of the Gallatin River reveal lively white-water. The land is a patchwork of private and public land: look for signs that announce forest or fishing access, where anglers cast for brown and rainbow trout.

At the entrance to **Big Sky** the valley opens up again, the road skirts beneath broad green hills and stands of Douglas fir. Find a spot to picnic and savor the panorama capped by the snow-dusted Lone Mountain.

If you are continuing on to Bozeman, it is under an hour's drive away (44 miles).

Sleeping

Considering the number of motel signs, there is precious little variety in accommodations. During the off-season (October, November, and mid-March–June), the few places that remain open, including the Stagecoach Inn, Hibernation Station and Kelly Inn, offer excellent discounts.

CAMPING

Tent camping in town means cramming between powered-up RVs – not exactly a picture of serenity. With so much great national forest nearby, tent campers would be well advised to drive out to the Lonesomehurst USFS campground. See the Hebgen Lake information (p203) for details on out-of-town campgrounds.

Most campgrounds are clustered on US 20 at the west end of town.

Yellowstone Grizzly RV Park (☎ 406-646-4466; www.grizzlyrv.com; 210 S Electric St; RV & tent site $; cabins $$-$$$) This RV metropolis hums with activity. Guests like the professional, friendly service, which includes help with tours and rentals. Facilities include showers, laundry, cable TV and a recreation room.

Hideaway RV Campground (☎ 406-646-9049; cnr Gibbon Ave & Electric St; RV & tent site $; 🖳) A quiet mom-and-pop set-up, Hideaway has showers, lockers, toilets and electric hookups.

Rustic Campground & Cabins (☎ 406-646-7387; 624 US 20 & Gibbon Ave; RV & tent site $) Rustic has cable TV hookups, but the charge for tent camping is twice that of USFS campgrounds and is comparatively cramped.

Yellowstone Park KOA (☎ 406-646-7606; RV & tent sites $; 🕙 mid-May–end Sep; 🖳) A large campground 6 miles west of town on US 20, this offers an indoor pool, a hot tub, a games room and nightly BBQ. The passing traffic on US 20 can be bothersome.

LODGING

Madison Hotel (☎ 406-646-7745, 800-838-7745; 139 Yellowstone Ave; hostel $, r $-$$; motel $$-$$$; 🕙 closed Oct-late May; 🖳) Though it's hard to picture Clark Gable snuggled in a potpourri-scented log room, part of the reason to stay at the historic hotel is to revel in its storied past. Hostel rooms are a good value, with sinks, towels, and quilts on rough-hewn log beds. Rooms sit behind a labyrinth of souvenir bric-a-brac; detour to find a cozy lounge with retro armchairs and stuffed animal heads on the wall.

Three Bear Lodge (☎ 406-646-7353, 800-646-7353; 217 Yellowstone Ave; www.three-bear-lodge.com; main lodge d $$$, motel d $$; 🖳) Decked in pine, this friendly lodge offers a range of options and deep discounts in the off-season. Ask for a refurbished queen room (with flat-screen TV and quilted bedcovers) for a considerable upgrade for the same price.

Sleepy Hollow Lodge (☎ 406-646-7707; 124 Electric St; r with kitchen $$-$$$) Tucked into a city lot, this lodge offers immaculate log cabins popular with anglers. It also provides guiding and a fly-tying bench.

Stage Coach Inn (☎ 406-646-7381, 800-842-2882; 209 Madison Ave; r $$$) A longtime hub, Stage Coach has a comfortable reading area, indoor hot tubs, and a good restaurant and saloon. Rooms are decked in wood grain and masculine colors.

Holiday Inn Sunspree Resort (☎ 800-646-7365; www.yellowstoneholidayinn.com; 315 Yellowstone Ave; d $$$; 🖳) Scrubbed but static Holiday Inn is considered the best lodging in town: to prove it, staff wears badges that say 'constant caring friend.' Sheesh.

Hibernation Station (☎ 406-646-4200, 800-580-3557; 212 Gray Wolf Ave; cabins $$$-$$$$) If you love theme parks, Hibernation Station may satisfy that deep-seated Wild West fantasy. These cozy log homes are dolled up in carved cowboy scenes, hot tubs and fireplaces that flame with the flick of a switch. Pets are welcome in some cabins for a $10 fee.

Side by side, facing Grizzly Park, the popular **Kelly Inn** (☎ 406-646-4544, 800-259-4672; 104 Canyon St; r $$$; 🏊) and **Gray Wolf Inn & Suites** (☎ 406-646-0000, 800-852-8602; www.graywolf-inn .com; 250 Canyon St; r $$$-$$$$; 🏊) offer somewhat generic but immaculate accommodations. Both places have a pool, spa and free continental breakfast, plus deep discounts in low season.

Eating & Drinking

our pick **Uncle Laurie's Riverside Café** (Electric & US 20; meals $; 🕐 7am-2pm Mon-Sat) A casual gourmet eatery, Uncle Laurie's serves espresso, excellent vegetarian options stacked with cheese and pesto, and healthy lunchboxes to go. The atmosphere, with lunching rangers and local families, is straight out of Mayberry.

Oversized sandwich maker **Ernie's Bighorn Deli** (US 20; lunch $), on the highway between Geyser and Hayden Sts, is popular and cheap. Grab a stool or booth at the vigorously local **Old Town Café** (☎ 406-646-0126; 128 Madison Ave; meals $) and feast on frothy milkshakes, chicken-fried steak or the perfect burger. Locals also like the cool and cavernous **Wild West Pizzeria** (☎ 406-646-4400; 14 Madison Ave; pizzas $$), adjacent to the divey but fun **Strozzi's Bar** (☎ 406-646-7259; 14 Madison Ave; 🕐 10am-late). Live rock packs the place on Fridays and Saturdays in summer, and there's a pool table.

Wolf Pack Brewing Co (☎ 406-646-7225; 139 Canyon St; burgers $; 🕐 noon-8pm) pours frothy pints of gold- and silver-medal homebrew – we're partial to Wapiti Wheat and the Chocolate Rye. For a strong shot of that other kind of brew, hit the **Morning Glory** (☎ 406-646-7071; 129 Dunraven; 🕐 6am-3pm) coffee roasters or **Free Heel and Wheel** (☎ 406-646-7744; www.freeheelandwheel.com; 40 Yellowstone Ave; 🕐 9am-8pm Mon-Sat, 9am-7pm Sun). The **Running Bear Pancake House** (☎ 406-646-7703; cnr Madison Ave & Hayden St; 🕐 7am-2pm) serves up small and large stacks, eggs and sausage links – a family favorite.

Stock up at the **Food Roundup** (cnr Madison Ave & Dunraven St; 🕐 7am-9pm) supermarket.

Getting There & Away

Greyhound buses accessing Bozeman and Idaho Falls stop at the **Western Union office** (☎ 406-646-0001; 132 Electric St), also the home of **Yellowstone Taxi** (☎ 406-646-1111).

Budget (☎ 406-646-7882; 131 Dunraven St & Yellowstone Airport) and **Big Sky Car Rentals** (☎ 800-426-7669; 415 Yellowstone Ave) offer car rental from $50 a day.

GARDINER
☎ 406 / pop 800 / elev 5134ft

A quintessential gateway town founded and fed on tourism, Gardiner, Montana, is the only entrance to Yellowstone National Park open to automobile traffic year-round. The park starts just where the souvenir stores peter out at the south end of town. Mammoth Hot Springs are only 5 miles away.

The town is named after Johnson Gardner, an 'illiterate and brutal trapper' who worked the area in the 1830s. Gardiner only made it onto the map, misspelled, in the 1880s when the Northern Pacific Railroad unveiled its Park Branch Line from Livingston to nearby Cinnabar. Stagecoaches ferried passengers on the last leg of the journey to the park, and Gardiner grew as a transit stop. By 1883 the town's 200 thirsty residents could stagger between 21 saloons.

These days the friendly and unpretentious town sticks to its ranching, mining and outfitting roots. The **rodeo** still pulls into town five times during the summer, and the plaid shirts and pickups haven't yet given way to microbrews and art galleries.

Orientation & Information

Gardiner is 53 miles south of Livingston via US 89, which is known as Scott St where it parallels the Yellowstone River and 2nd St where it turns south to cross the river. The Yellowstone River divides the town in two.
Chamber of Commerce (☎ 406-848-7971; www .gardinerchamber.com; 220 W Park St; 🕐 9am-6pm Mon-Fri, 9am-5pm Sat, 1-5pm Sun) Offers tourist information, free coffee and a public bathroom.
First Interstate Bank (Scott St W) Has an ATM.
Flying Pig Camping Store (☎ 406-848-7510; Scott St W) Stocks all kinds of gear (including bear pepper spray) but closes for the season by mid-September.
Gallatin National Forest Gardiner District Office (☎ 406-848-7375; www.fs.fed.us/r1/gallatin; 805 Scott St W; 🕐 closed weekends) Provides campground and hiking information.

AROUND YELLOWSTONE

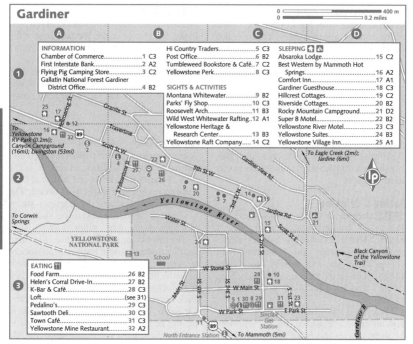

Gardiner

INFORMATION
Chamber of Commerce.....................1 C3
First Interstate Bank.........................2 A2
Flying Pig Camping Store..................3 C2
Gallatin National Forest Gardiner
    District Office..............................4 B2
Hi Country Traders...........................5 C3
Post Office.......................................6 B2
Tumbleweed Bookstore & Café........7 C2
Yellowstone Perk.............................8 C3

SIGHTS & ACTIVITIES
Montana Whitewater.......................9 B2
Parks' Fly Shop..............................10 C3
Roosevelt Arch..............................11 B3
Wild West Whitewater Rafting......12 A1
Yellowstone Heritage &
    Research Center........................13 B3
Yellowstone Raft Company............14 C2

SLEEPING
Absaroka Lodge.............................15 C2
Best Western by Mammoth Hot
    Springs....................................16 A2
Comfort Inn..................................17 A1
Gardiner Guesthouse......................18 C3
Hillcrest Cottages...........................19 C2
Riverside Cottages.........................20 B2
Rocky Mountain Campground........21 D2
Super 8 Motel...............................22 B2
Yellowstone River Motel.................23 C3
Yellowstone Suites.........................24 B3
Yellowstone Village Inn..................25 A1

EATING
Food Farm....................................26 B2
Helen's Corral Drive-In..................27 B2
K-Bar & Café.................................28 C3
Loft...(see 31)
Pedalino's....................................29 C3
Sawtooth Deli...............................30 C3
Town Café....................................31 C3
Yellowstone Mine Restaurant.........32 A2

Hi Country Traders (☎ 406-848-7707; W Park St)
Offers espresso and internet access.

Sinclair Gas Station (☎ 406-848-7501; Scott St W)
Sells Montana state fishing licenses.

Tumbleweed Bookstore & Café (☎ 406-848-2225;
Scott St W; ☼ 8am-8pm) Espresso, wraps, and internet
access at 15¢ per minute, in addition to a good stock of
local-interest books.

Yellowstone Perk (☎ 406-848-2240; Scott St W) Offers
espresso and internet access.

Yellowstone RV Park (Scott St W) Offers public
showers, just west of town.

Sights

Gardiner's most photographed sight is the
park's **Roosevelt Arch**, dedicated by Teddy
Roosevelt himself on April 25, 1903, and
inscribed with congress' words 'for the
benefit and enjoyment of the people.'

The grand new **Yellowstone Heritage &
Research Center** (☎ 307-344-2664; www.nps.gov
/yell/historyculture/collections.htm; ☼ 8am-5pm Mon-Fri,
library 9am-4pm Tue-Fri) holds the park's abundant
archives (over 5 million items and growing)
and serves mainly as a research facility,
though visitors can view the lobby displays

on early park tourism and visit the library.
One-hour public tours operate at 10am on
Tuesday and Thursday (Memorial Day to
Labor Day) and take you into the museum
and photo archives. The tour is limited to 10
people, so reserve ahead of time.

Activities

On the Yellowstone River, rafting trips run
through the Class II to III rapids of Yankee
Jim Canyon (7 miles), one of Montana's
more famous white-water spots. The **Yellowstone Raft Company** (☎ 406-848-7777; www
.yellowstoneraft.com; 406 Scott St W) is in its 30th
year of running half-day white-water trips,
($35/25 adult/child). Full-day tours cost
$78/58 including lunch. It also has half-day
kayaking lessons on the river for $59.

Wild West Whitewater Rafting (☎ 406-848-
2252; www.wildwestrafting.com; Scott St W) does
similar floats, as well as gentler scenic floats
in the upper Paradise Valley north of Chico
Hot Springs and full-day horseback-riding/
rafting combos for $85/75.

Montana Whitewater (☎ 406-848-7398; www
.montanawhitewater.com; 603 Scott St W) rents canoes

and float tubes in addition to raft trips on the Yellowstone and Gallatin.

Several outfitters run fishing trips, horseback riding and pack trips into Yellowstone and other nearby mountain areas, though all are primarily hunting operations. Outfitters include **Hell's A-Roarin' Outfitters** (☎ 406-848-7578; www.hellsaroarinoutfitters .com), **Rendezvous Outfitters** (☎ 800-565-7710; www.yellowstoneroughriders.com) and **North Yellowstone Outfitters** (☎ 406-848-7651; www.northyellow stoneoutfitters.com). Rides start at around $25 per hour, $90 per half day and $150 per full day.

Parks' Fly Shop (☎ 406-848-7314; www.parksfly shop.com; 202 S 2nd St) sells flies, rents gear and offers float trips. Owner Richard Parks is the author of the much-respected *Fly Fishing Yellowstone National Park* (Falcon Press). In winter the action switches to cross-country ski ($12.50 per day) and snowshoe rental.

For back-road biking routes north of Gardiner, see the Paradise Valley section in this chapter (p205). For the backdoor route out of Yellowstone Park, see p154.

Organized Tours

The park concessionaire, **Xanterra** (☎ 307-344-7901; www.travelyellowstone.com) runs its tour **Yellowstone in a Day** (adult/child under 12/child 12-16 $62/free/31) from Gardiner from June to late September, taking in all the major park sights in an exhausting eight hours.

Sleeping

CAMPING & RV

Eagle Creek Campground (sites $; ☯ year-round) This woodsy USFS campground, 2 miles northeast of Gardiner on unpaved Jardine Rd, has 16 sites and pit toilets but no water. Further along the dirt road, 10 miles from Gardiner and 4 miles past Jardine, is Timber Camp. Another 2 miles is Bear Creek Campground. These two offer free dispersed camping with a toilet but no water and are open mid-June to the end of October, depending on snowfall. There are fine hiking options from Bear Creek Trailhead.

Yellowstone RV Park (☎ 406-848-7496; RV & tent sites $; 🖳) At the northwest end of town, this RV park has 48 fairly cramped riverside sites with full hookups, plus showers and a laundry.

Rocky Mountain Campground (☎ 877-534-6931; www.rockymountaincampground.com; 14 Jardine Rd; tent & RV sites $, cabins $-$$; ☯ mid-Apr–mid-Oct; 🖳) A friendly campground overlooking the river from Jardine Rd, it offers showers, laundry, full hookups and fine panoramas of Yellowstone, but little shade. Ask about the simple one- or two-room cabins that can sleep up to six.

LODGING

About half of Gardiner's accommodation closes in the winter and those that remain cut their rates by around 50%.

Gardiner Guesthouse (☎ 406-848-9414; www .gardinerguesthouse.com; 112 E Main St; d with breakfast $$) 'We aim to please' is the attitude at this homey B&B. Kid-friendly, pet-friendly and pretty much everyone-friendly, it offers two rooms with shared bath and one suite available in the main house, as well as a rustic cabin in the back – perfect for anglers hooking up with owner Richard Parks at the next-door fly-fishing shop.

Yellowstone River Motel (☎ 406-848-7303; www .yellowstonerivermotel.com; 14 E Park St; d $$; ☯ May-Oct; 🖳 ♿) This is one of the better-run motel places, clean and friendly with picnic tables and a BBQ area overlooking the river. The newer units come with a fridge and microwave. Six-sleeper apartments are available.

Absaroka Lodge (☎ 800-755-7414; www.yellow stonemotel.com; S 2nd St; r $$-$$$; 🖳) This modern but surprisingly unobtrusive place offers excellent-value doubles, some with kitchenette and all with a fine balcony overlooking the rushing Yellowstone River. Book this one early.

Hillcrest Cottages (☎ 406-848-7353; www.hillcrest cottages.com; 200 Scott St W; d $$, 3-bed cottages $$$; ☯ May-Sep) This mini-village features a variety of pleasant cottages, most with kitchenettes, that sleep two to seven. May, June and late September bring discounts of 40%.

Riverside Cottages (☎ 406-848-7719; www .riversidecottages.com; 521 Scott St W; r $$-$$$; 🖳) Has a collection of functional but not stylish rooms, from cheaper 'efficiencies' that can squeeze in three to larger roadside suites with kitchens that sleep up to six. Most rooms come with bunk beds. The weekly rates are a good deal, as is the hot tub overlooking the river.

Yellowstone Village Inn (☎ 800-228-8158; www .yellowstoneinn.com; 1102 Scott St W; d/ste $$/$$$; 🖳 🖳) Standing alone at the entrance to Gardiner, this quirky '70s motel is pretty good value, with a few family and kitchenette suites.

Yellowstone Suites (☎ 406-848-7937; www.yellow stonesuites.com; 506 S 4th St; d $$$; 🖳) There's plenty of privacy in this well-appointed, four-room 100-year-old B&B, which makes a nice antidote to motel overload. There are cozy sitting spaces and views of Electric Peak, but only two rooms have attached bathrooms. Get a deal by renting an entire floor (two rooms). The breakfasts peter out at the beginning and end of summer.

Best Western by Mammoth Hot Springs (☎ 406-848-7311; Scott St W; d/family ste $$$/$$$$; 🖳) It's not 'by Mammoth Hot Springs' (5 miles away), but once you get past that tiny fib this is a solid choice, with spacious modern rooms. Pay $10 more for a mountain or riverside view, or $20 more for a hot tub in your room. After a hard day in the park, the kids can attack the indoor pool while the adults relax in the sauna. Winter discounts of 50%.

Other chain places include the **Comfort Inn** (☎ 406-848-7536; www.yellowstonecomfortinn.com; d $$; 🖳), and the **Super 8 Motel** (☎ 406-848-7401; d $$; 🖳 🖳), both with free Continental breakfast.

Eating

To fill up on supplies, head to the **Food Farm** (☎ 406-848-7524; Scott St W; ⏱ 7am-8pm), across from the Super 8 Motel. For a quick meal join the locals at the **Sawtooth Deli** (☎ 406-848-7600; 220 W Park St; mains $), which serves hot and cold subs and decent breakfasts.

Helen's Corral Drive-In (☎ 406-848-7627; Scott St W; meals $) is an old-style malt-and-greasy-burger stand that's been clogging arteries since 1960. But really, where else are you going to find a half-pound elk burger?

The **Town Café** (☎ 406-848-7322; E Park St; mains $-$$), next to the Town Motel on Park St, is an old-fashioned (read slightly dingy) family-style spot with breakfast, lunch and dinner year-round. The pricier upstairs **Loft** (⏱ 6-9pm Tue-Sat) has a fine view into the park and a good selection of grilled fish, plus a soup and salad bar.

Also open year-round is the unpretentious **K-Bar & Café** (☎ 406-848-9995; cnr S 2nd & W Main Sts), with pizza and daily lunch specials.

Probably the best restaurant in town, **Pedalino's** (☎ 406-848-9950; W Park St; mains $$; ⏱ 5-9pm Sun-Fri) serves up fine Italian dishes in a casual pine-overdosed dining room. Try the whipped brie and lox with crostini and pomegranate drizzle.

The **Yellowstone Mine Restaurant** (☎ 406-848-7336; Scott St W; mains $$-$$$; ⏱ 6-11am, 5-9:30pm) is dark and gloomy, but the food is generally good, with a good range of steak and fish, including salmon à l'Oscar, broiled on alder wood and topped with crab, asparagus and hollandaise sauce. There's little for vegetarians, though.

COOKE CITY
☎ 406 / pop 85 / elev 7800ft

Set between two forested ridges of the Beartooth Mountains, just four miles from Yellowstone's northeast entrance, this one-street Montana town (population 85 in winter, 350 in summer) gets a steady flow of summer visitors en route between the scenic splendors of the Beartooth Highway and the national park. There's not much here in the way of shops, sights or even trailheads, but this isolated town has a backwoods feel that's more laid-back and less commercial than the park's other gateway towns, and a year-round population that's as rugged as the surrounding peaks.

Cooke City's isolation is due to geography and the lack of a railroad link. Citizens lobbied to bring the railroad to the original mining town of Shoo-Fly, even going so far as to rename the town in 1880 after the Northern Pacific Railroad's Jay Cooke, but even this blatant flattery failed to overcome hard economics. Oddly, this enclave of Montana can only be accessed from Wyoming.

In winter the road from Yellowstone is only plowed as far as Cooke City, so visitors – mostly backcountry skiers and snowmobilers – tend to check in and stay awhile. Gas prices are the highest in the Yellowstone region, but there's not a whole lot you can do about it.

Information

Bearclaw Mountain Recovery (☎ 406-838-2040) AAA-endorsed and the people to call if you have a breakdown. Montana fishing licenses are available.
Chamber of Commerce (☎ 406-838-2495; www .cookecitychamber.com) A helpful place that is trying to

realize a new visitor center in the south of town that will include public restrooms and a small museum.

Silver Gate General Store (☎ 406-838-2371) In the nearby town of Silver Gate, this store sells topo maps and rents spotting scopes for $20 per day.

Sinclair Gas Station Offers pricey internet access.

Soda Butte Lodge Has a public laundromat.

Sights & Activities

Sightseers are going to be stumped in Cooke City. The historic 1886 **Cooke City General Store** (www.cookecitystore.com; ☽ 8am-7pm) retains an old-time feel and is a fun browse. It sells park fishing permits and topo maps. Kids will like the animal exhibits in the **Yellowstone Trading Post** (admission $2), next to the Beartooth Café (the admission price can be spent in the store).

The tiny **Cooke City Bike Shack** (☎ 406-838-2412) is the epicenter of an outdoorsy crowd who come to hike, bike or ski in the immediate area. It has a good inventory of equipment (from freeze-dried food to pepper spray) and maps, and the owner is a longtime local who is tremendously helpful with trail suggestions.

In winter the network of mining roads northeast of town are favorites of Nordic skiers and snowmobilers. Near Colter Campground, the unpaved Lulu Pass–Goose Lake Rd, the Goose Lake Track (No 3230) and trails to Aero Lakes are all popular, as is snowmobiling the Beartooth Hwy. There are several snowmobile rental outfits in town (that switch to ATV rentals in summer), and the Cooke City Bike Shack can arrange one-way snowmobile shuttle drops for skiers.

In tiny Silver Gate, 2 miles from Cooke City, **Silvertip Mountain Center** (☎ 800-863-

0807, 406-838-2125; www.silvertipmountaincenter.com) rents cross-country ski and ice-climbing gear and is a good source of local climbing information.

Sleeping

Soda Butte (27 sites), Colter (18 sites) and Chief Joseph (six sites) are Gallatin National Forest **campgrounds** (sites $; ☽ mid-Jul–mid-Sep). They're 1.5 miles, 2 miles and 4 miles from town respectively.

High Country Motel (☎ 406-838-2272; www.cookecityhighcountry.com; d $$) has a mix of good-value cabins and motel-style rooms, some with kitchenettes (extra $10), and is open year-round. Across the road, **Hoosier's Motel** (☎ 406-838-2241; d/q $$/$$; ☽ closed winter) offers 12 clean motel-style rooms. No pets.

Other similar choices include the motel-style **Alpine Motel** (☎ 406-838-2262; www.cookecityalpine.com; d $$; ☽ year-round; ▣) and the cozy **Elkhorn Lodge** (☎ 406-838-2332; www.elkhornlodgemt.com; d $$; ☽ year-round; ▣), with rooms in the main building and pricier cabins, all with microwave and fridge.

Antlers Lodge (☎ 406-838-2432; www.cookecityantlerslodge.com; cabins $$) is a slightly ram-shackle series of 18 piney cabins of all shapes and sizes, some with kitchenettes, that can sleep up to six. The antler horn chandeliers in the main lodge are a bit too *Psycho* for us.

Soda Butte Lodge (☎ 406-838-2251; www.cookecity.com; d $$-$$$; ▣) from the outside looks like the most upscale of Cooke City's hotels, but its flower has definitely faded and the rooms are plain. There are Jacuzzi suites, a hot tub and family rooms with three beds.

There are also several good places in even smaller Silver Gate, 2 miles west of Cooke City, including good-value motel rooms at the **Grizzly Lodge** (☎ 406-838-2219; www.yellowstonelodges.com; r $$; ☽ May-Sep) and cozy log cabins at **Pine Edge Cabins** (☎ 406-838-2371; www.pineedgecabins.com; cabins $$-$$$; ☽ year-round).

Eating

Grizzly Pad Grill (mains $) At the north end of town, this grill is friendly and serves up honest portions of burgers, fries and malts, plus evening pizza.

Prospector Restaurant (☎ 406-838-2251; mains $-$$$; ☽ from 7am) This restaurant in the Soda Butte Lodge has reasonably priced

AROUND YELLOWSTONE

GRASSHOPPER GLACIER

For years one of the region's natural oddities has been Grasshopper Glacier, high in the mine-stained hills above Cooke City. The glacier takes its name from the millions of now extinct grasshoppers that were entombed in the ice when a freak snowstorm enveloped a swarm centuries ago. An early victim of global warming, recent thawing has sadly exposed and decomposed most of the grasshoppers, so if you do decide to hike out here, do it for the scenery, not the grasshoppers.

breakfasts and lunches. Dinner mains are standard mountain fare – steak and trout – and surprisingly pricey, and there's a children's menu. Joan's pies sell for $3 per slice and are well worth the investment.

ourpick **Beartooth Café** (☎ 406-838-2475; www .beartoothcafe.com; lunchtime sandwiches $, dinner mains $$-$$$; �} 11am-10pm, closed winter) A bright place for lunch sandwiches (such as a buffalo burger, a 'funk burger' or lighter portobello sandwich) served on the pleasant front deck, washed down by a fine selection of 130 local microbrews. Dinner mains like ribs, trout and hand-cut steaks are more expensive. Breakfast is served weekends only.

Bistro (☎ 406-838-2160; breakfast & lunch $, dinner mains $$-$$$; �} from 7am) A popular place for breakfast, come nightfall the homey Bistro transforms into a demi-French restaurant with dishes like escargot in garlic butter and lamb Provençal.

For the best espresso, make a beeline for the Cooke City Bike Shack (p179).

In sleepy Silver Gate, the **Log Cabin Café** (☎ 406-838-2367; lunch $, dinner $$; �} closed winter) is an unexpectedly hip place, serving falafel and hummus sandwiches and trout dinners, plus a weekend brunch. The cozy cabin dates back to 1937.

BEARTOOTH ROUTE

BILLINGS
☎ 406 / pop 92,988 / elev 3300ft

Montana's largest city has more in common with the dusty plains of eastern Montana than the celebrated Rocky Mountain scenery to the west of the state, and its conservative roots lie in oil and ranching. It shouldn't be a priority on a Yellowstone itinerary, but it's not a bad place to stay a night before heading to the park or catching a flight back home.

Ernest Hemingway brought some excitement to Billings in November 1930 when he crashed his car on the way home from Yellowstone National Park. Hemingway broke his right arm and had to spend seven weeks in the town's St Vincent's Hospital.

Information
Base Camp (☎ 406-248-4555; 1730 Grand Ave) The place for last-minute outdoor gear, topo maps and that lost widget for your stove.

Billings Visitor Center (☎ 406-245-4111, 800-735-2635; www.itsinbillings.com, http://billingscvb.visitmt .com; 815 S 27th St) Can help with hotel reservations.
Custer National Forest (☎ 406-657-6200; 1310 Main Street) Information on the Beartooth Mountains.

Sights
If you have some time in Billings, pop into the **Western Heritage Center** (☎ 406-256-6809; www.ywhc.org; 2822 Montana Ave; adult/senior $3/2; �} 10am-5pm Tue-Sat) for changing exhibits and an outstanding artifact collection representing the various cultural traditions of Yellowstone Valley.

The **Yellowstone Art Museum** (☎ 406-256-6804; www.artmuseum.org; 401 N 27th St; adult/child/senior $7/3/5; �} 10am-5pm Tue-Sat, noon-5pm Sun, to 8pm Thu) combines a collection of Western art with visiting exhibitions on the site of the 1916 Yellowstone County Jail.

Drive up to the **Rims**, near the airport, for a fine overview of the city as far as the distant Beartooth Mountains and to visit the grave of Yellowstone Kelly, an early scout and guide.

The best Billings day trip is to the **Little Bighorn Battlefield** (☎ 406-638-3204; www.nps .gov/libi; admission per vehicle $10; �} 8am-8pm), site of Custer's Last Stand and just an hour's drive (65 miles) east of town.

Sleeping
Billings KOA (☎ 406-252-3104; tent & RV sites $, cabins $; �} mid-Apr–mid-Oct; ▯ ☎), America's first KOA campground, is in a scenic spot by the Yellowstone River, 0.5 miles south of I-90.

The best motel buys downtown are at the good-value **Cherry Tree Inn** (☎ 406-252-5603, 800-237-5882; 823 N Broadway; r $$) and the quieter **Rimview Inn** (☎ 406-248-2622; www.rimviewinn.com; 1025 N 27th St; r $$; ▯ ☎).

The **Dude Rancher Lodge** (☎ 406-259-5561, 800-221-3302; 415 N 29th St; d $$) has groovy ranch oak furniture dating back to the 1940s and is a characterful choice if you prefer nostalgia over cleanliness.

Most rooms at the well-run and updated **Riverstone Billings Inn** (☎ 406-252-6800; www .riverstone-inns.com; 880 N 29th St; r $$) include a microwave, refrigerator and breakfast.

For those who prefer a more convivial experience, **Josephine's Bed & Breakfast** (☎ 406-248-5898; www.thejosephine.com; 514 N 29th St; r $$$) is down-home and attentive. All five rooms come with private bathroom.

The town's prime address (and the city's tallest building) is the **Crowne-Plaza** (☎ 406-252-7400; 27 N 27th St; d $$$-$$$$; 🖥)), formerly the Sheraton, right in the heart of the downtown area.

Eating & Drinking

McCormick Café (☎ 406-255-9555; 2419 Montana Ave; mains $; 🕑 7am-4pm Mon-Fri, 8am-3pm Sat, 9am-1pm Sun; 🕑) For espresso, French-style crêpes, good sandwiches and lively atmosphere, stop by here.

Caramel Cookie Waffles (☎ 406-252-1960; www .caramelcookiewaffles.com; 1707 17th St W; mains $; 🕑 7am-5pm, closed Sun & Mon; 🖥) Better known as the Dutch Brothers, this place bustles at lunch with superb soups, European pastries and the eponymous *stroopwafels*. It's worth arranging your entire Yellowstone itinerary around their weekly seafood bisque.

Montana Brewing Company (☎ 406-252-9200; 113 N Broadway; mains $) Popular with the 30-something crowd, this place pulls its own microbrews (try a Whitetail Wheat) and serves a standard menu of salads, wood-fired pizzas, burgers and appetizers, with pleasant outdoor seating.

Walkers Grill (☎ 406-245-9291; www.walkersgrill .com; 2700 1st Ave N; tapas $, mains $$-$$$; 🕑 5-11pm) The classiest place in town offers grill and tapas menus, Sunday jazz and sophisticated Western decor.

Some locals claim that **The Rex** (☎ 406-245-7477; www.therexbillings.com; 2401 Montana Ave; mains $$-$$$) serves the best steak in town, and others only eat beef at **Jake's** (☎ 406-259-9375; www.jakes.tv; 2701 1st Ave N; mains $$).

Entertainment

A magnet for all of eastern Montana, the **Alberta Bair Theater** (☎ 406-256-6052; www .albertabairtheater.org; 2801 3rd Ave N) is Billings' cultural jewel, with productions ranging from world music to symphony concerts.

RED LODGE

☎ 406 / pop 2280 / elev 5555ft

A quaint historic mining town lined with fun bars, restaurants, interesting shops and art galleries, and with great hiking, camping and skiing nearby, Red Lodge is the kickoff point for the scenic Beartooth Hwy and well worth a stop in its own right. The town gets its name from the painted red tepees of local Crow (Absaroka) Indians.

The early town grew up around the coal mines from the 1884, and by 1910 the town's largely immigrant population was twice its current size. The hard-drinking, fist-fighting, bootlegging town must have been pretty rough-edged to have required one Jeremiah 'Liver Eatin' Johnson as its deputy sheriff, but this was perhaps spurred more by the 1897 robbery of the central bank by Butch Cassidy's partner, the Sundance Kid. Most of the mines were closed by 1932 after years of depression and mine disasters, and the Beartooth Highway opened four years later, just in time.

The town's cosmopolitan early Scottish, Scandinavian and Slavic population is celebrated in the annual **Festival of Nations** (www.festivalofnations.us) in August. If you're here on the busy 4th of July weekend follow locals to the fairgrounds for the **Home of Champions Rodeo** (www.redlodgerodeo.com), one of the biggest amateur rodeos in Montana.

Orientation & Information

On the west bank of Rock Creek, Red Lodge is 60 miles south of Billings and 65 miles northeast of Cooke City and the north entrance to Yellowstone National Park. US 212 runs north-south through town as Broadway Ave, the main street, and becomes the Beartooth Hwy south of town.

Coffee Factory Roasters (☎ 406-446-3200; 6-1/2 S Broadway) Free wi-fi with your latte.

Red Lodge Area Chamber of Commerce/Visitor Center (☎ 888-281-0625; www.redlodge.com; 601 N Broadway Ave; 🕑 8am-6pm Mon-Fri, 9am-5pm Sat & Sun) On the north edge of town, it's one of the region's best, with an RV dump station and road conditions on the Beartooth Hwy.

Red Lodge Books (☎ 406-446-2742; www.redlodge books.com; 16 N Broadway) Stocks USGS topo maps.

Sights

Set aside a few hours for browsing the shops and galleries along Broadway Ave, making sure to stop in at the tap room of **Red Lodge Ales** (☎ 406-446-4607; www.redlodgeales.net; 417 N Broadway Ave; 🕑 2-8pm summer, 4-8pm winter) for a tasting and brewery tour (it's a small operation). Order the beer sampler ($3.75) to taste the six most popular brews. The kids will love the old-style **Montana Candy Emporium** (7 S Broadway).

The **Carbon County Museum** (☎ 406-446-3667; www.carboncountyhistory.com; 224 N Broadway;

adult/student $3/2; ⊙ 10am-5pm Mon-Sat summer, 10am-5pm Tue-Sat, 11am-3pm Sat winter) has a terrific antique-gun collection but is better known for its coverage of local rodeo and mining lore.

The old railroad depot on Eighth St, one block west of Broadway Ave, is now the **Carbon County Arts Guild Gallery** (☎ 406-446-1370; www.carboncountydepotgallery.org; ⊙ 10am-5pm Mon-Sat, noon-5pm Sun), where local artists exhibit painting, sculpture and mixed media.

Beartooth Nature Center (☎ 406-446-1133; www .beartoothnaturecenter.org; 615 2nd St E; adult/child $6/2.50; ⊙ 10am-5pm May-Sep, 10am-2pm Oct-Apr) is a nonprofit refuge for 75 animals that can't be returned to the wild, including bears, cougars, eagles, a sandhill crane (called Niles), a wolf and a lynx. There are plans to move location so call ahead.

Activities
WINTER

Six miles southwest of downtown, **Red Lodge Mountain** (☎ 800-444-8977, ski reports 406-446-2610; www.redlodgemountain.com; lifts adult $45, child $15-39; ⊙ end Nov–early Apr) has a 2400ft vertical drop, serviced by eight lifts. The higher temperatures and longer days of February and March, plus a higher base elevation (7400ft) than any other Montana ski hill, give Red Lodge Mountain some of Montana's best spring skiing. Full rentals and instruction packages are available, as are guided snowshoe trips.

The **Red Lodge Nordic Center** (☎ 406-425-1070; www.beartoothtrails.org; trail fee adult/child $5/3), 2 miles west of Red Lodge on Hwy 78, is Red Lodge's top cross-country resource and a good place for beginning skiers or those who want to ski on well-maintained tracks. See the website for other local trails.

HIKING

A mile south of Red Lodge, just north of the Ranger Station, West Fork Rd turns southwest off US 212 and continues for a bumpy 12 miles to the West Fork Rock Creek Trailhead at road's end. The **West Fork Trail** follows the creek 4 miles to Quinnebaugh Meadows, a popular day-hike picnic spot, good for wildflower viewing in early July. From here you can take a steep 1-mile trail up to **Lake Mary** or continue along the main trail.

An excellent three-day, 21-mile hike continues past May Lake and on to Sundance Lake and over **Sundance Pass** to the numerous lakes of Lake Fork Valley. The trail takes you into some very scenic and rugged country and offers plenty of side trips and lake fishing but is often snowed in until mid-July. You'll have to arrange a car shuttle between the two valleys.

Another good day hike is up the **Timberline Lake Trail**, which starts on the south side of West Fork Rd, 2 miles before road's end. This trail climbs 4½ miles along Timberline Creek and gains 2000ft to Gertrude and Timberline Lakes, both good for trout fishing.

Alternatively, **Basin Lakes National Recreation Trail** (trail No 61), with its trailhead just east of Basin Campground, heads up 3.8 miles and 2000ft to the two scenic Basin Creek lakes. Nearby **Wild Bill Lake** is a wheelchair-accessible trail to a lake with accessible fishing.

A rugged option is the short but strenuous 3.2-mile return trail to **Glacier Lake**, hidden high up in a glacial valley. Hikers have the option of continuing another mile to **Little Glacier** and **Emerald Lakes**. Glacier Lake is clearly visible from the Beartooth Highway. The trailhead is 7.8 miles southwest of

---

WACKY RACES

Southeast Montana is a proud home to some of the state's more surreal sports. Red Lodge hosts the national **ski-joring finals**, a not-quite-yet Olympic sport that involves a horse towing a skier around an oval speed track. It's like water skiing. On snow. Except with a horse.

Equally silly is the annual **Running of the Sheep** at nearby Reed Point. Inspired by Pamplona's marginally more famous Running of the Bulls, the significantly less dangerous herd of sheep thunder down six blocks of Main St every year during the first weekend in September.

Finally, summer weekend evenings (Thursday to Sunday) see hi-octane **pig racing** at the Bear Creek Saloon, 7 miles east of Red Lodge. Make a bet, urge your porker over the finish line and round off the evening with a bacon sandwich. Proceeds go to charity.

Limber Pine Campground on rough gravel Rock Creek Road (Forestry Road No 421). You need fairly high clearage to attempt this road.

The **Lake Fork Trail** accessed from the end of Lake Fork Road (turn off right about 2 miles before Parkside Campground) offers excellent longer day hikes to Lost Lake (5 miles one way) and 1.5 miles further to Keyser Brown Lake.

Sleeping

South of Red Lodge on US 212 are 10 USFS campgrounds, open May to September. The nearest are small Sheridan and Rattin, 6 miles and 8 miles from Red Lodge and on the east side of the river. A little further, and with shady creekside locations, are the nicer Parkside, Limber Pine and Greenough Lake Campgrounds. All these **campgrounds** (sites $) are run by the concessionaire Gallatin Canyon Campgrounds, and are reservable through **www.recreation.gov** (☎ 877-444-6777).

The cheapest motel in Red Lodge is the family-owned **Eagle's Nest Motel** (☎ 406-446-2312; 702 S Broadway Ave; d $$). The **Yodeler Motel** (☎ 406-446-1435; www.yodelermotel.com; 601 S Broadway Ave; d $$; 🖵 🐾), at the corner of 17th St, has smallish upper-level rooms with balconies and in-room steam baths, coffeemaker and fridge.

A fun and elegant place to stay is the **Pollard** (☎ 406-446-0001; www.thepollard.net; 2 N Broadway Ave; d with breakfast $$$-$$$$), Red Lodge's first brick building, dating from 1893. Its cozy lobby and restaurant are hubs of local activity. Check the website for midweek and activity specials.

The most upscale of Red Lodge's accommodations is **Rock Creek Resort** (☎ 406-446-1111; www.rockcreekresort.com; d/ste $$$/$$$$; 🖵 🐾). It is 4.5 miles south of town off US 212.

Eating & Drinking

our pick **Red Box Car** (☎ 406-446-2152; 1300 S Broadway; meals $; 🕙 May-Sep) Without doubt the Yellowstone region's best fast food, served out of a century-old railroad car at the south end of town. The malts and homemade onion rings are unbeatable.

Bridge Creek Backcountry Kitchen and Wine Bar (☎ 406-446-9900; www.eatfooddrinkwine.com; 116 S Broadway; lunch $-$$, dinner $$-$$$; 🖵) Fresh

mountain cuisine complements the modern bistro vibe here. Smoked trout cakes and a huckleberry salad join the three esses for lunch (soup, salad and sandwiches) and dinner is heavier fare, with wine suggestions tailored to each dish.

Dining Room (☎ 406-446-0001; mains $$-$$$) This romantic restaurant at the Pollard (left) has won national acclaim for its wine list, fresh fish and lobster, and creative pasta dishes, and is the place to splash out.

For home-style Western cookin' and hearty breakfasts, head back in time 20 years to the **Red Lodge Café** (☎ 406-446-1619; 16 S Broadway; mains $-$$; 🕙 from 6am). **Bogart's Restaurant** (☎ 406-446-1784; 11 S Broadway Ave; mains $-$$) is popular for margaritas and Mexican food, and **Red Lodge Pizza Co** (☎ 406-446-3333; www.thepizzaco.com; 115 S Broadway; pizza $$) makes good pies and calzones and serves by the slice.

A young, outdoorsy crowd congregates for drinking and dancing (to live bands on weekends) at the **Snowcreek Saloon** (124 S Broadway Ave), while the **Snag Bar** (107 S Broadway Ave) entertains a leather-faced crowd wearing cowboy hats and boots.

BEARTOOTH HIGHWAY

The breathtaking Beartooth Hwy (US 212) connects Red Lodge to Cooke City and Yellowstone's northeast entrance along a soaring 68-mile road built in 1932. An engineering feat, and the 'most beautiful drive in America' according to the late journalist Charles Kuralt, this 'All-American' road is a destination in its own right and easily the most dramatic route into Yellowstone National Park.

Covering 1474 sq miles, the Absaroka-Beartooth Wilderness stretches along Montana's border with Wyoming (a small section on its east side lies inside Wyoming) and crosses through Gallatin, Custer and Shoshone National Forests. The wilderness area takes in two distinct mountain ranges: the Absarokas and the Beartooth Plateau (the Beartooths). The Beartooths are composed of uplifted three-billion-year-old granite – some of the oldest rock in North America. Steep, forested valleys and craggy peaks characterize the Absarokas, while the Beartooths are essentially a high plateau dotted with more than 1000 lakes and tarns.

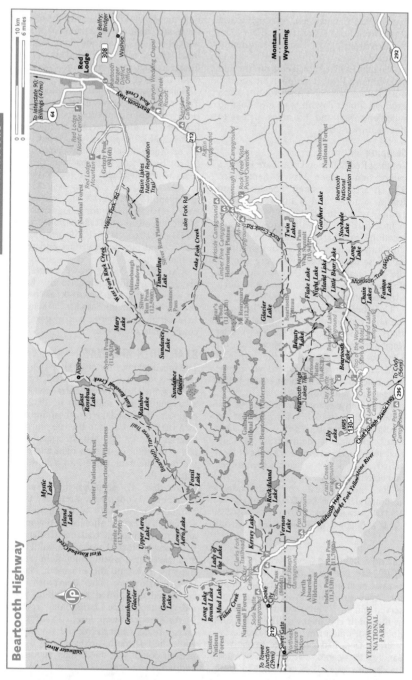

Beartooth Highway

Most of the wilderness consists of high plateau above 10,000ft. Alpine tundra vegetation is the only thing that grows up here (where snow can last from October to mid-July), lending the landscape a desolate, otherworldly look. In fact, unless you are an outdoorsy type who makes frequent forays above 10,000ft, it probably is another world – you can't usually reach this kind of terrain by car. To really experience the surroundings, you must get out of the car, even if it's just for a few minutes, to suck in the thin, cold air.

The highway has a short driving season and is usually closed between mid-October and mid- to late May. For information on weather conditions, hikes and bear sightings pull into the **Beartooth Ranger District office** (☎ 406-446-2103), just south of Red Lodge on Hwy 212. There's gas at Red Lodge, Cooke City and, less reliably, along the highway at the Top of the World store. For more details, see www.beartoothhighway.com.

The political landscape of the highway is as convoluted as the landscape. The highway starts and ends in Montana but dips into Wyoming en route. If you are fishing, you'll need to know exactly where you are so that you have the correct state fishing license.

If you just want a taste of the plateau from Yellowstone National Park, **Xanterra** (☎ 307-344-7311; www.travelyellowstone.com) offers a Beartooth Alpine Adventure guided day tour (adult/child $87/29) from most park junctions.

DRIVING THE BEARTOOTH HIGHWAY

Route Red Lodge to Cooke City
Distance 68 miles (3 hours)
Speed Limit Officially 70 mph, but more like 35mph

From its starting point at Red Lodge, the highway climbs Rock Creek Canyon's glaciated valley before dramatically ascending the valley wall via a series of spaghetti-loop switchbacks, gaining an amazing 5000ft in elevation in just a few miles.

A parking area at **Rock Creek Vista Point Overlook** (9160ft), 20 miles from Red Lodge,

has toilets and a short walk (wheelchair accessible) to superb views. The road continues up onto the high plateau, past 'Mae West Curve' and into Wyoming.

In another 7 miles the road passes **Twin Lakes**, where a parking area offers good views of the cirque and the ski lift that carries the daring to an extreme ski run in spring. Another 1.3 miles further along is **Gardner Lake**. After 0.7 miles, at the start of a series of switchbacks, look northwest across Rock Creek for views of the Hellroaring Plateau and the jagged **Bear's Tooth** (11,612ft; 'Na Piet Say' in the local Crow language), which lends the range its name. A mile later you'll crest the **Beartooth Pass West Summit**, the highest point at 10,947ft. You'll likely pass 15ft-deep snowbanks here as late as June (even July some years).

From this halfway point the road descends past Frozen Lake, Long Lake, Little Bear Lake (the last two with excellent fishing) and then the Chain Lakes (on the left) to the Island Lake and Beartooth Lake Campgrounds. Both of these offer excellent opportunities for a picnic, day hike or a canoe paddle. Between the campgrounds is the Top of the World Store, which is worth a stop for a reviving coffee (and a fishing license if you need one).

As the road descends, you'll see **Beartooth Butte**, a huge lump of the sedimentary rock that once covered the Beartooths. Two miles beyond Beartooth Lake Campground, 42 miles from Red Lodge, turn right up a 2.5-mile dirt road to the former fire watchtower at **Clay Butte Overlook** (open July and August; no RVs or trailers). The views from here are fantastic: look for the effects of the 1988 Clover Mist fire and the 'Reef,' a snaking line of sedimentary rock that follows the entire valley, proof that this lofty region was once underwater.

Back on the main road a mile further on is an **overlook** offering views of Index Peak (11,313ft) and jagged Pilot Peak (11,708ft). Next up is the Clarks Fork Overlook (with toilets) and then a small turnout by Lake Creek Falls. Less than a mile from here, forestry road 130-1 leads 2 miles north to secluded **Lily Lake**, where you'll find a canoe ramp, good fishing and several free campsites.

The turnoff left is for Chief Joseph Scenic Hwy (see p187), which leads 62 miles to Cody

AROUND YELLOWSTONE

and accesses Yellowstone's east entrance via the Wapiti Valley. The Beartooth Hwy descends to several excellent fishing areas on the Clarks Fork and reenters Montana. Not far from Chief Joseph Campground is **Clarks Fork Trailhead**, a fine place for a picnic, a day hike and a look at the flume of the former mining power station. From here it's 4 miles to Cooke City, via the almost imperceptible Colter Pass (8066ft).

HIKING & BACKPACKING

You can gain about 4000ft of elevation by car and begin your hike right from the Beartooth Hwy, but it's important to allow some time to acclimatize. Also be aware that the barren terrain offers little shade, shelter or wood. In order to protect the fragile alpine vegetation, hikers should not light campfires above the tree line. Grizzly and black bears are not that common in the wilderness; hikers have a better chance of seeing bighorn sheep, mountain goats or elk.

August is the best month to hike the Beartooths. Snow remains in many places above tree line at least until the end of July and starts to accumulate again after mid-September. Localized afternoon thunderstorms, with hail, are common in the Beartooths during June (the wettest month) and July. During early summer, you'll also need lots of bug repellent and waterproof shoes to cope with swampy trails. Don't be put off; just be forewarned. With proper preparation, the plateau offers some of Greater Yellowstone's very best hiking.

From Island Lake Campground you can take a wonderful and easy hour-long stroll along the **Beartooth High Lakes Trail** (Trail No 620) to Island Lake and beyond to Night Lake and Flake Lake. All lakes are popular fishing areas. If you can arrange a shuttle, continue downhill to Beauty Lake and then left (south) to Beartooth Lake for a fine half-day hike.

From Beartooth Lake Campground you can make a wonderful half-day 8-mile loop via **Beauty Lake**. Head up Beartooth Creek (trail No 619) and then bear right, passing five lakes, including Claw Lake (trail No 620), to the junction with the Beartooth High Lakes Trail. From here descend right past Beauty Lake (trail No 621) back to Beartooth Lake. Parking is limited at the trailhead.

A longer, preferably overnight, option is the 11-mile **Beartooth National Recreation Trail** (No 613), loop hike accessed from the highway at Gardner Lake. The trail drops from the lake and loops around Tibbs Butte, initially along Little Rock Creek, past turnoffs to Deep Lake, Camp Sawtooth and Dollar Lake to arrive at Stockade Lake, a fine campsite. From here, continue around the loop past Losecamp Lake back to Gardner Lake, or cut east from Losecamp Lake for 3 miles past Hauser Lake to the Beartooth Highway by a pullout overlooking Long Lake (requires a shuttle).

Another easy day hike is the 6-mile return ramble to **Rock Island Lake**, which begins from the Clarks Fork Trailhead, about 4 miles east of Cooke City and across from the Chief Joseph Campground. After about 15 minutes be careful to continue along the hikers trail (signposted Russell Creek Trail No 567) and *not* turn left along horse trail (signposted Broadwater Trail). The trail brushes Kersey Lake and branches right up to Rock Island Lake. An alternative hike branches right 1.3 miles from the trailhead up to Vernon Lake (trail No 565).

The Clarks Fork Trailhead is also the start of the exciting multiday **Beartooth Traverse** that runs along Russell Creek Trail to Fossil Lake and then across plateau trail No 15 to Rosebud Lake. You'd need to be well equipped and experienced for this remote wilderness trek.

The contoured 1:100,000 *Absaroka Beartooth Wilderness* map by Beartooth Publishing and the USFS 1:63,360 *Absaroka Beartooth Wilderness* map are both excellent. *Hiking the Absaroka-Beartooth Wilderness* and *Easy Day Hikes in the Beartooths*, both published by Falcon Press and written by Bill Schneider, are also useful resources.

SLEEPING

There are 13 basic **USFS campgrounds** (sites $) along the Beartooth Hwy between Red Lodge and Cooke City, most charging $8 to $15. The most accessible from US 212 are Island Lake (20 sites) and Beartooth Lake (21 sites), both open July to early September. Further west on the plateau are the Crazy Creek (16 sites) and Fox Creek (34 sites) campgrounds, the former with a small cascade nearby. Fox Creek comes with electricity hookups and is double the price of the other sites These sites come under the **Clarks Fork Ranger district** (☎ 307-527-6921) of the Shoshone National Forest.

Closer to Cooke City, Chief Joseph (six sites), Colter (23 sites) and Soda Butte (27 sites) campgrounds are 4 miles, 2 miles and 1 mile east of town, respectively; all open mid-July to end September. Contact the **Gallatin National Forest Gardiner District Office** (☎ 406-848-7375; www.fs.fed.us/r1/gallatin) for details on these.

Top of the World Motel (☎ 307-899-2482; www .topoftheworldresort.com; RV sites & r $), on the highway about 1 mile east of the Island Lake turnoff, offers four basic rooms and some cramped RV sites, but you are better off camping.

CHIEF JOSEPH SCENIC HIGHWAY

The wild and scenic Clarks Fork of the Yellowstone River runs along much of the Chief Joseph Scenic Hwy (Hwy 296), linking Cody (via Hwy 120 north) with the Beartooth Hwy and Yellowstone National Park's northeast entrance, 62 miles away. It's a very scenic route that joins the equally stunning Beartooth Hwy to make several potential loop itineraries. The highway is named for Chief Joseph of the Nez Percé tribe who eluded the US army and escaped through Clarks Fork here in 1877 (see p83).

The paved highway is open year-round from Cody to the Beartooth Hwy and about 5 miles west to Pilot Creek, though not as far as Cooke City. The Beartooth Hwy itself is closed mid-October to late May. Fall colors are particularly lovely here.

The 47-mile Chief Joseph Scenic Hwy (Hwy 296) starts 16 miles north of Cody, enters the Shoshone National Forest after 8 miles and climbs to a spectacular viewpoint at **Dead Indian Pass** (8048ft). Indians used to ambush game that migrated through the pass between summer mountain pastures and winter ranges down in the plains. The pass is named for a Bannock Indian killed here in skirmishes with the army in 1878.

As you descend from the pass, just 0.3 miles before Dead Indian Campground a dirt road leads a couple of hundred yards to a trailhead parking lot that offers an excellent short hike to view the 1200ft deep

Clarks Fork Canyon. The trail leads north for 2 miles to a scenic overlook; watch for the cairns marking the spot shortly after you first see the gorge. The views of the 1200ft granite gorge and **Dead Indian Creek waterfall** are breathtaking. The canyon effectively separates the 50-million-year-old volcanic rock of the Absaroka Range from the two-billion-year-old granite of the Beartooth Plateau. The trail continues for another 3 miles right down to the canyon floor, but the 700ft descent and then ascent makes for a considerably more strenuous hike.

Back on the road, USFS Rd 101 branches southwest into the beautiful **Sunlight Basin**, whose upper branches end at a wall of peaks forming the boundary of Yellowstone National Park. Writer Ernest Hemingway spent time grizzly hunting here in the 1930s and wrote an article on the subject for *Vogue* magazine.

Where Hwy 296 crosses Sunlight Creek is the terrific **Sunlight Bridge**, the highest in Wyoming. You can park and walk across the bridge for hair-raising views into the gorge (acrophobes beware!), though better overviews can be had 0.5 miles north on the highway.

Just north of Crandall Creek (named after a pioneer miner who was beheaded by Indians), around Swamp Lake, are half-a-dozen ponds where you might spot sandhill cranes and trumpeter swans among others.

Hwy 296 continues northwest to the crossbar junction of US 212, where the Beartooth Hwy leads northwest to Cooke City and Yellowstone Park or northeast to Red Lodge and Billings.

Backpacking Routes

Trailheads north and south of Crandall Creek ranger station offer several hiking routes either side of Hurricane Mesa (11,064 ft). One ambitious backpacking route leads up Papoose Ridge and over **Miller Pass** 18 miles to join Yellowstone National Park's Miller Creek and Lamar Valley Trails. Trails in this area go through areas badly affected by the fires of 1988.

From upper Sunlight Valley trails head south to connect with the **Pahaska-Sunlight Trail**. A longer wilderness trail heads west and then climbs north up to the high ridge overlooking the Yellowstone Park's **Hoodoo**

Basin, finally dropping down to join the Miller Creek Trail and Lamar Valley Trail as above.

Both of these long wilderness routes are snowbound into mid-July, and go through prime grizzly area so you need to be very experienced to consider what are really mini-expeditions. Contact the USFS ranger stations at Sunlight Creek and Crandall Creek for current conditions.

SLEEPING

Shoshone National Forest campgrounds include lovely, forested, six-site **Lake Creek** (sites $; ☽ late Jun-early Sep) and nine-site **Hunter Peak** (sites $; ☽ end May-early Oct), 1.3 and 5 miles respectively from the junction with the Beartooth Highway. Further south, at a bend in the highway, is 10-site **Dead Indian Campground** (sites $; ☽ year-round). Contact the **Clarks Fork Ranger District** (☎ 307-527-6921; www.fs.fed.us/r2/shoshone) in Cody for more details.

You can reserve Hunter Peak through the **Recreation.gov Reservation Service** (☎ 877-444-6777, TDD 877-833-6777; www.recreation.gov).

Just off Hwy 296, 24 miles from Yellowstone, are **Hunter Peak Ranch** (☎ 307-587-3711; www.hunterpeakranch.com; cabin/ste $$$/$$$$) and, 28 miles from Yellowstone, the family-run **K Bar Z Guest Ranch** (☎ 307-587-4410; www.agonline.com/kbarz; d cabin $$), both of which offer plenty of summertime horseback riding and winter skiing.

7D Ranch (☎ 888-587-9885; www.7dranch.com; weekly rates $$$$$; ☽ Jun–mid-Sep) has a fabulous location 8 miles up the Sunlight Valley, with only 11 cabins and excellent horseback and fishing opportunities. Early September is kid-free and has discounted rates.

WAPITI ROUTE

CODY

☎ 307 / pop 9000 / elev 5095ft

Arrive at sundown and you'll find costumed gunslingers midbrawl, flanked by Jezebels toiling under a career in false eyelashes. The spirit of showman Buffalo Bill still thrives in the town that he himself promoted with real-estate speculator George Beck in 1901. Beck and his backers milked Cody's fame to promote settlement, attract the railroad and lobby for a massive dam on the Shoshone

River. But it's more than farce. Despite the goofy cowboy themes, Cody feels like the real West, where graduation photos adorn shop counters, folks chat in doorways and real cowpokes sip silty cups of joe.

Situated 51 miles east of Yellowstone's east entrance and connected to the park by the scenic Wapiti Valley, Cody rivals Jackson as Wyoming's premier summer tourist town. Rather than erecting new faux-Western facades, local businesses have retained or restored their original storefronts, giving a veneer of greater authenticity.

Access to the great outdoors from Cody is excellent, as are winter sports such as ice climbing and cross-country skiing. But the town's ultimate blessing is its proximity to Yellowstone National Park. **Yellowstone Regional Airport** (☎ 307-587-5096; www.flyyra.com) is 1 mile east of Cody and offers daily nonstop fights to Salt Lake City and Denver.

INFORMATION

BLM Cody Resource Office (☎ 307-578-5900; 1002 Blackburn Ave; ☽ 8am-4:30pm Mon-Fri)

Cody Library (☎ 307-527-8820; 1057 Sheridan Ave; ☽ 9am-4pm Mon-Sat)

Cody Newsstand (☎ 307-587-0030; 1121 13th St) Stocks maps and local guides.

Shoshone National Forest Main Office (☎ 307-527-6241; 808 Meadow Ln) For information on Clarks Fork and other area, come here, next to the Olive Glenn Golf Course. Ask for a recreation guide.

Shoshone National Forest Wapiti Ranger District Office (☎ 307-527-6921; www.fs.fed.us/r2/shoshone; 203A Yellowstone Ave) Distributes information on the forest surrounding Wapiti Valley. Ask for a recreation guide.

Visitor Center & Chamber of Commerce (☎ 307-587-2777; www.codychamber.org; 836 Sheridan Ave; ☽ 8am-6pm Mon-Fri, 9am-5pm Sat, 10am-3pm Sun high season) Housed in a 1927 lodgepole cabin, the friendly center helps with trip planning; the website is especially useful.

SIGHTS

Buffalo Bill Historical Center

While the nickname 'Smithsonian of the West' exaggerates a wee bit, this five-museum complex is still a must-see. Entry to the **center** (☎ 307-587-4771; www.bbhc.org; 720 Sheridan Ave; adult/child over 6/student/senior $15/4/6/13; ☽ 8am-8pm May–mid-Sep) is valid for two consecutive days.

The original collection began in 1927 with the **Buffalo Bill Museum**, which presents

Cody

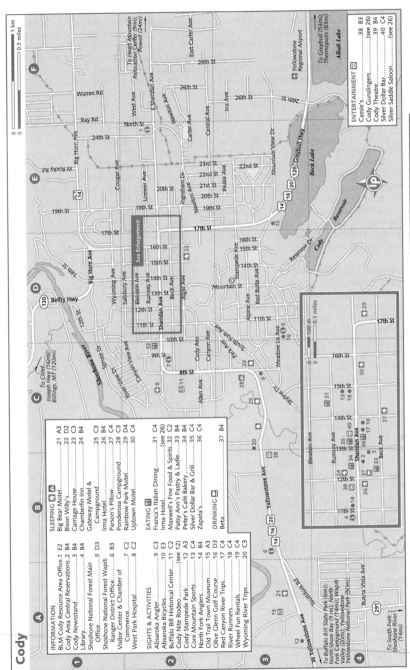

INFORMATION

BLM Cody Resource Area Office..1	E2
Cody Area Central Reservations..2	B4
Cody Newsstand.........................3	B4
Library.....................................4	B4
Shoshone National Forest Main	
Office......................................5	D3
Shoshone National Forest Wapiti	
Ranger District Office...............6	B3
Visitor Center & Chamber of	
Commerce................................7	C2
West Park Hospital....................8	C2

SIGHTS & ACTIVITIES

Absaroka Angler........................9	C3
Absaroka Bicycles....................10	E3
Buffalo Bill Historical Center....11	(see 12)
Cody Nite Rodeo......................12	A3
Cody Stampede Park.................13	C4
Core Mountain Sports..............14	B4
North Fork Anglers...................15	A3
Old Trail Town Museum...........16	D3
Olive Glenn Golf Course..........17	C4
Red Canyon River Trips............18	C4
River Runners...........................19	C4
Wheel Fun Rentals..................20	C3
Wyoming River Trips................	

SLEEPING

Big Bear Motel.........................21	A3
Bison Willy's............................22	D2
Carriage House........................23	B4
Chamberlin Inn........................24	B4
Gateway Motel &	
Campground...........................25	C3
Irma Hotel...............................26	B4
Parson's Pillow.........................27	C4
Ponderosa Campground............28	C3
Rainbow Park Motel..................29	D4
Uptown Motel..........................30	C4

EATING

Franca's Italian Dining.............31	C4
Irma Hotel...............................(see 26)
Maxwell's Fine Food & Spirits..32	C2
Patsy Ann's Pastry & Ladle......33	B4
Peter's Café Bakery..................34	B4
Silver Dollar Bar & Grill............35	C4
Zapata's..................................36	C4

DRINKING

Beta...37	B4

ENTERTAINMENT

Cassie's...................................38	B3
Cody Gunslingers....................(see 26)
Cody Theatre...........................39	B4
Silver Dollar Bar......................40	C4
Silver Saddle Saloon...............(see 26)

a wealth of fascinating, if uncritical, information on the life of William F Cody and his Wild West shows. The **Plains Indian Museum** explores Native American culture and history through its artistry. Displays detail Native American ceremonies such as the Sun Dance (which honors the buffalo spirit) and explain the symbolism of tepee designs. Accounts of life on the reservation are conspicuously absent.

With a powerhouse collection including Remington, Russell and NC Wyeth, the **Whitney Gallery of Western Art** introduces Western art through the powerful and energetic landscapes and wildlife scenes from the masters. Most who are not gun fanatics politely rush through the **Cody Firearms Museum**. The newest addition, the **Draper Museum of Natural History**, gives visitors an overview of Greater Yellowstone ecology.

Old Trail Town Museum

The hideouts of Butch Cassidy, Kid Curry and the Sundance Kid comprise this unique **museum** (☎ 307-587-5302; www.museumoftheoldwest .org; 1831 DeMaris Dr; adult/child over 12 $6/2; a collection of late-19th-century wooden buildings relocated here from all over Wyoming. Look for the bullet holes in the door of the Rivers Saloon and the grave of mountain man Jeremiah 'Liver Eating' Johnson.

Buffalo Bill State Park

This scenic state park (day use $5) centers on the Buffalo Bill Reservoir and Dam, 6 miles west of Cody. When Buffalo Bill and his associates acquired water rights to irrigate 266 sq miles in the Bighorn Basin, but lacked the capital to develop adequate storage, they simply convinced the US Bureau of Reclamation to build the 328ft Shoshone Dam. Upon its completion in 1910, it became the world's highest dam. Now the reservoir is a hot spot for fishing, windsurfing and boating. Boat launches dot the north and southeast shores. The **visitor center** (☎ 307-527-6076; www.bbdvc.org), just west of the dramatic Shoshone Canyon, offers interpretive exhibits.

ACTIVITIES

An excellent base for outdoor pursuits, Cody is not just for cowboys. Anglers can visit Tim Wade's **North Fork Anglers** (☎ 307-527-7274; www.northforkanglers.com; 1107 Sheridan Ave) for great information, flies and guided trips. The website has current fishing conditions. **Absaroka Angler** (☎ 307-587-5105; 754 Yellowstone Ave) is another option.

Just outside of town, the North Fork of the Shoshone River has excellent class II–IV white-water and scenic float trips with best conditions in mid-June. Bighorn sheep hang out on the cliffs, and eagles and moose are sometimes spotted. Prices range from $37 for lower canyon trips to $67 for a half-day on the North Fork. Reputable companies include **Red Canyon River Trips** (☎ 307-587-6988, 800-293-0148; 1374 Sheridan Ave), **Wyoming River Trips** (☎ 307-587-6661, 800-586-6661; www.wyomingrivertrips.com; 233 Yellowstone Ave) and **River Runners** (☎ 307-527-7238, 800-535-RAFT; 1491 Sheridan Ave).

Aspiring climbers should check out **Core Mountain Sports** (☎ 307-527-7354, 877-527-7354; www.coremountainsports.com; 1019 15th St), a family-run adventure shop with an indoor climbing wall that's great for kids. In addition to rafting, it offers fly-fishing, guided climbing, mountaineering and backpacking (the latter through Jackson Hole Mountain Guides). The two-hour kids' camp ($75) puts kids ages four and up on the ropes to climb and learn to belay.

Cody offers some of the best ice climbing in the United States. Check out www .coldfear.com or Bison Willy's website (www .bisonwillys.com) for more information.

Mountain bikers can find trails of all levels inside the city – Beck Lake Park, Red Lakes and Paul Stock Nature Trail – and in the Shoshone National Forest and the McCullough Peaks on Bureau of Land Management lands. Consult **Absaroka Bicycles** (☎ 307-527-5566; 2201 17th St, K-mart Plaza; ☼ Mon-Sat 10am-6pm) for tips, rentals and repairs. **Wheel Fun Rentals** (☎ 307-587-4779; 1390 Sheridan Ave) rents all kinds of fun family bikes from $11 per hour, plus kayaks.

For something totally different, **Red Canyon Wild Mustang Trips** (☎ 800-293-0148; www .wildmustangtours.com) leads van tours (adult/child $24/21) and photo safaris to the McCullough Peaks Wild Horse Range, a new refuge designated for these 142 wild mustangs whose range is ever-shrinking. For more information on the horses, check out the nonprofit **FOAL** (www.friendsofalegacy.org).

FESTIVALS & EVENTS

Steep yourself in the sheer madness of steer wrestling and bronc riding at the prestigious **Cody Stampede Park** (www.codystampederodeo.com; 519 West Yellowstone Ave; admission $20; ☼ July 1-4) or at Cody's smaller **Cody Nite Rodeo** (www .codyniterodeo.com; adult/child 7-12 $17/8; ☼ 8pm), held summer-long in the self-proclaimed Rodeo Capital of the World. In mid-June the **Plains Indians Powwow** (Buffalo Bill Historical Center; adult/youth 7-17 $6/3) gathers native dancers, drummers and artisans in a fantastic celebration of traditions.

The **Cowboy Poetry & Range Ballads Festival** takes place the second week of April. The **Yellowstone Jazz Festival** takes over the city park and the Buffalo Bill Historical Center in mid-July.

SLEEPING

Summertime rates listed here are 50% higher than shoulder-season rates; many places close in winter. Reservations are recommended in summer, but campgrounds usually have sites available. Call **Cody Area Central Reservations** (☎ 888-468-6996; ☼ 9am-5pm weekdays) for assistance.

ourpick **Chamberlin Inn** (☎ 307-587-0202; www.chamberlininn.com; 1032 12th St; r $$$; ☒ ☐) Recently restored and stunning, Chamberlin Inn conjures up the mystique of the original onsite 1904 boarding house, with French tile paintings, embossed tin ceilings, clawfoot tubs and crushed-satin bedcovers. The old register claims Hemingway crashed in room 18 on a 1932 fishing trip. Truth or marketing?

Tent sites and RV hookups are available at the **Gateway Campground** (☎ 307-587-2561; 203 W Yellowstone Ave; sites $) and **Ponderosa Campground** (☎ 307-587-9203; 1815 Yellowstone Ave; sites $) in town. Ponderosa edges out the competition with immaculate showers, laundry and friendly service.

Skip town for more scenic option along the banks of the Buffalo Bill Reservoir. The roadside **North Shore Bay and North Fork Campgrounds** (☎ 307-587-9227; sites $), 6 miles west of Cody, are exposed and shadeless but offer lovely sunsets over the lake. Sites are open year-round, with pit toilets and no RV hookups.

The sole hostel in town is **Bison Willy's** (☎ 307-587-0629, 877-587-0629; www.bisonwillys .com; 1625 Alger Ave; dorm/r $/$$; ☒ ☐) with a full kitchen, washer and dryer, and dog kennel. Hut master Kenny Gasch can guide guests through the local outdoor options; the place serves as a hub for winter ice-climbing.

Several classic motels have rooms starting under $50: the pet-friendly **Uptown Motel** (☎ 307-587-4245; 1562 Sheridan Ave; r $-$$), pet-friendly **Big Bear Motel** (☎ 307-587-3117; 139 W Yellowstone Ave; ☐ ☒) and **Rainbow Park Motel** (☎ 307-587-6251, 800-341-8000; 1136 17th St; ☒ ☐), with some kitchen units. Uptown and Big Bear are open year-round.

The frilly **Carriage House** (☎ 307-587-2572/3818, 800-531-2572; www.carraigehousevillas.com; 1816 8th St; cabin/6-person ste $$/$$$; ☒) offers pristine, white nonsmoking cabins and bungalows in a suburban setting. The rustic cabins at **Gateway Motel** (☎ 307-587-2561; 203 W Yellowstone Ave; r $$-$$$) are pet-friendly, bordered by grassy spaces perfect for Fido and a frisbee. Both are open June to September.

Built for Buffalo Bill's daughter in 1902, the atmospheric **Irma Hotel** (☎ 307-587-4221, 800-745-4762; www.irmahotel.com; 1192 Sheridan Ave; r $$-$$$) offers charming original rooms with big windows and clunky dressers, and less-inspired options in the dowdy modern annex. The hallways and public areas tend to be smoky.

The only local B&B boasting a bell tower, former Episcopalian church **Parson's Pillow** (☎ 307-587-3622, 800-377-2348; www.parsonspillow .com; 1202 14th St; r $$-$$$) has sweetly decorated rooms and a southwestern bunk-bed room

---

THE IRMA

Buffalo Bill got his name from slaughtering bison to lay track for the Kansas Pacific Railroad. But how did his hotel get christened? In 1902 he bought the lavish spread in downtown Cody for his youngest daughter Irma, calling it 'just the swellest hotel that ever was.' He kept two suites and an office for his personal use, and his ghost is said to still frequent the creaking corridors. The original front lobby has since been converted into the Silver Saddle Lounge.

The hotel's most famous feature is the 50ft-long imported French cherrywood bar, in what is now the dining room. Presented to Bill by Queen Victoria, it was transported by stagecoach from Red Lodge and, at $100,000, cost more than the hotel itself.

ideal for kids. Pecan waffles, fresh fruit and coffee start your day right. It's pet-friendly and open year-round.

EATING & DRINKING

Peter's Café Bakery (☎ 307-527-5040; 1191 Sheridan Ave; meals $; ☺ 6am-10pm) pleases wolfish appetites with its low-carb breakfasts of two eggs, two bacon strips and two sausage patties; the griddle also serves up buffalo burgers and overstuffed sandwiches. **Patsy Ann's Pastry & Ladle** (☎ 307-527-6297; 1243 Beck Ave; sandwiches $) bakes pastries and makes homemade soups and sandwiches.

Zapata's (☎ 307-527-7181; 1362 Sheridan Ave; meals $-$$; ☺ closed Sun; ☺) serves up spinach enchiladas, green chili and chips with homemade salsa in comfy booths. The margaritas are a highlight. For bistro dinners, **Maxwell's Fine Food & Spirits** (☎ 307-527-7749; 937 Sheridan Ave; meals $-$$) is a family favorite, with a diverse selection of salads, sandwiches and pizza.

Slow-roasted prime rib and meatloaf are signature dishes at the **Irma** (☎ 307-587-4221; 1192 Sheridan Ave; meals $-$$), where the abundant breakfast/lunch buffets are also popular. Try the deck at **Silver Dollar Bar & Grill** (1313 Sheridan Ave; meals $) for monster burgers, buckets of Bud, and Snake River microbrews on tap.

Sweet smells of fresh focaccia, handmade ravioli and Italian sausage intoxicate diners at **Franca's Italian Dining** (☎ 307-587-5354; 1421 Rumsey Ave; meals $$-$$$$; ☺ dinner Wed-Sun), set in Franca Facchetti's cozy home. Reservations are a must at this romantic nook, known for its extensive wine list, fixed multicourse dinners and pasta mains.

Join hip locals for chai or espresso at the **Beta** (1132 12th St; ☺ 7am-6pm Mon-Fri, 7am-4pm Sat & Sun; ☺) coffee shop. Check the bulletin board for local yoga, hikes and outings.

ENTERTAINMENT

Squeeze among real wranglers and faux-cowboys in 10-gallon hats for the Irma Hotel's Silver Saddle Saloon happy hour – a blast after the gunslingers' mock shoot-out on the porch at 6pm daily except Sunday (June to September).

Catch live music on weekends at the **Silver Dollar Bar** (☎ 307-587-3554; 1313 Sheridan Ave; ☺ to 1:30am), where locals shimmy to rock and roll. Penny pinchers show up in throngs for quarter beer night held Thursdays.

Cassie's (☎ 307-527-5500; 214 Yellowstone Ave) hosts heavy swilling and swingin' country-and-western tunes. Bobby Bridger, a descendent of mountain man Jim Bridger, performs Western ballads summer evenings at the **Old Trail Town Museum** (☎ 307-587-5302; 1831 Demaris Dr; shows $12). Check the website www.bbridger.com for schedules.

The **Cody Theater** (☎ 307-587-2712; 1171 Sheridan Ave) is a 1950s movie house now showing blockbuster hits.

Wapiti Valley

Deemed the 'most scenic 52 miles in the United States' by Teddy Roosevelt, **Buffalo Bill Scenic Byway** (US 14/16/20) traces Wapiti Valley and the North Fork of the Shoshone River from Cody to the East Entrance of Yellowstone National Park. You will find yourself twisting to gape at the volcanic Absaroka Range, a rugged canyon of eroded badlands that gives way to alpine splendor.

The naming of these areas is about as rich as its surroundings. Wapiti Valley translates as 'pale white rump' from Algonquin Indian. Rather than being a jab at homesteaders' wives, the term distinguishes the lighter-colored elk, or wapiti, from darker-colored moose. The North Absaroka Wilderness Area sits to the north and the Washakie Wilderness Area (named after a revered Shoshone warrior

---

HOMELAND SECURITY IN HISTORY

Nearly 11,000 Japanese-Americans were interned in **Heart Mountain Relocation Center** (www.heartmountain.us; Rd 19 off Hwy 14A; admission free), making it Wyoming's third-largest city after the Japanese bombing of Pearl Harbor. Recently added to the National Register of Historic Places, this walking trail 9 miles from Cody explores how – seized by xenophobia – the US failed its own citizens 60 years ago. Taking only what they could carry, Japanese-Americans relocated to these flimsy tar-paper rooms from West Coast homes and made the best of years of confinement there. Today, monuments and fascinating educational displays cover the bare grounds and an interpretive learning center is in the works.

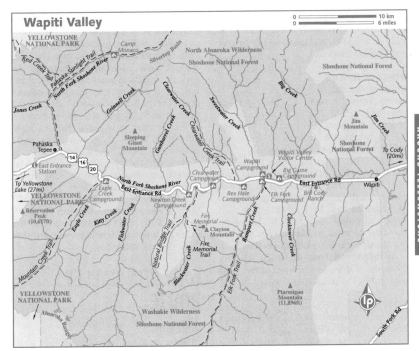

Wapiti Valley

and peacemaker) to the south. This vast wilderness is home to grizzlies, black bears, deer, elk, moose, bighorn sheep and a few bison. The extensive network of trails, easy access to Yellowstone National Park's lake region and a selection of the region's best dude ranches make the valley an excellent route into or out of the park.

Six miles west of Cody, US 14/16/20 emerges from the dramatic **Shoshone Canyon** and tunnel to views of the **Buffalo Bill Reservoir**. Past the settlement of Wapiti, Wyoming's high desert landscape and open ranchland closes in as the road enters Shoshone National Forest and becomes Buffalo Bill Cody Scenic Hwy. The **Wapiti Valley Visitor Center** (☎ 307-587-3925; ☑ 8am-8pm Mon-Fri & 8:30am-5pm Sat & Sun Memorial Day-Labor Day), has a 3D map of the region, as well as information on grizzly sightings.

From here on, the Wapiti Valley is lined with eerie buttes and hoodoos as spectacular as any sight in the nearby parks, with overimaginative names like Four Bobsledders and Holy City. National Forest campgrounds, trailheads and guest

ranches crop up every few miles as the scenery becomes increasingly alpine.

Two miles before the east entrance to Yellowstone is the gas station, store, restaurant and corrals of **Pahaska Tepee** (☎ 307-527-7701; 183 Yellowstone Hwy) resort, a good place to refuel. Staff leads free tours of the original lodge, built by Buffalo Bill in 1904 as a hunting lodge. Pahaska was Bill's Indian name and means 'Longhair' in the Sioux language, a reference to Cody's long white hair and extravagant goatee.

HIKING & BACKPACKING
The gradual ascent of the **Elk Fork Trail** (trail No 760) is particularly popular with horse packers. The trail starts at 6000ft and follows Elk Creek, leading 21 miles up to Rampart Creek and Overlook Mountain (11,869ft), but you don't have to go the whole way. A pleasant round-trip day hike takes you 3 miles up the Elk Fork to where the trail fords the river.

Explorations up Kitty Creek, Fishwater Creek or Clearwater Creek will doubtless turn up other great hikes. For details about these and other hikes in the region see Falcon Press' *Hiking Wyoming's Teton & Washakie Wilderness Areas*, by Lee Mercer and Ralph Maughan.

OTHER ACTIVITIES

Most of the valley's guest ranches offer **horseback riding** (per hour from $25), horse-packing trips and cookouts trips to nonguests in addition to guests. Outstanding **fly-fishing** is easily accessed via the national forest and wilderness areas and campgrounds.

The North Fork Shoshone River is a favorite of **white-water rafting** aficionados. Elk, bighorn sheep and moose are often seen from the river. The rafting season is mid-May to mid-September in the Red Rock and Lower Canyons, and Memorial Day (last Monday in May) to late July for the North Fork. See p190 for details.

North Fork Nordic Trails (☎ 307-527-7701) offer 25 miles of groomed cross-country trails adjacent to Pahaska Tepee resort.

SLEEPING

Nine very economical USFS campgrounds line the Wapiti Valley, starting from 29 miles west of Cody. Overflow from Yellowstone fills up the grounds in July and August, so try to arrive before late afternoon. Most are open June to late September. Call the **Shoshone National Forest North Zone** (☎ 307-577-6921) for details. The following **campgrounds** (all sites $) are listed from east to west and all have bear-resistant food storage.

Big Game Campground is small but spacious and private, whereas Wapiti Campground offers more campsites but allots little space for each. Elk Fork Campground is cramped and sometimes has no water but is popular as a base for hiking and horse-packing trips. Clearwater Campground has water and some groups sites. Rex Hale Campground is more exposed but has six sites with electrical hookups and is slightly pricier than area campgrounds. Newton Creek Campground is woodsy and pleasant, with 31 campsites. Eagle Creek and Three Mile Campgrounds are available to hard-sided campers only due to grizzly activity.

All campgrounds border the river, offering easy access to trout fishing. Most campgrounds are open mid-May to

September (a few into October), but can be closed at any time due to grizzly activity.

Wapiti Valley's lodges make a great base for exploring Yellowstone National Park or Cody. Most offer fishing, hiking, rock climbing and guided horseback rides. Luxury in proximity to the park doesn't come cheap, but discounted rates are the norm before May and after September.

The historic year-round **Pahaska Tepee** (☎ 307-527-7701, 800-628-7791; www.pahaska.com; 183 Yellowstone Hwy; cabins Jun-Aug $$$, Sep-May $$) lodge is closest to the park and one of the best deals, offering cross-country skiing, trout fishing and horseback riding.

Lodges East of Yellowstone Valley (☎ 307-587-9595; www.yellowstone-lodging.com; PO Box 21, Wapiti, WY 82450) provides information on the valley's numerous family-owned member dude ranches and lodges.

GALLATIN VALLEY ROUTE

BOZEMAN

☎ 406 / pop 32,000 / elev 4700ft

The hip college town of Bozeman, only an hour's drive north of Yellowstone, is regularly voted one of America's best outdoor towns, and with good reason. With excellent restaurants and shops, one of the region's best museums and outdoor opportunities that beckon from every direction, the town is well worth a stop en route to the more rustic delights of the parks. The town is named after John Bozeman, who guided settlers here along his namesake Bozeman Trail, a spur of the Oregon, from 1864.

To plug into the local scene pick up the free local paper **Tributary** (www.bozemandtributary.com). Highlights of the cultural year include the independent film and arts festival **Hatchfest** (www.hatchfest.org) in October and the traditional **Sweetpea Festival** (www.sweetpeafestival.org) in August.

Information

Bangtail Bikes (☎ 406-587-4905; www.bangtailbikes; 508 W Main St) Bozeman's best shop for buying and renting bikes and cross-country skis.
Barrel Mountaineering (☎ 406-582-1335; www.barrelmountaineering.com; 240 E Main St) For all-purpose information, maps, and climbing and skiing gear.

Bozeman Public Library (☎ 406-582-2400; www
.bozemanpubliclibrary.com; 626 E Main St; ⏰ 10am-8pm
Mon-Thu, 10am-5pm Fri & Sat) Free internet access and
wi-fi, opposite Montana Ale Works.
Cactus Records (☎ 406-587-0245; 29 W Main St) Visit
the region's best music store for the lowdown on musical
happenings.
Country Bookshelf (☎ 406-587-0166; 28 W Main St)
This community institution hosts readings by local authors
like Tim Cahill and Jim Harrison.
Downtown Bozeman Visitor Information (☎ 406-
586-4008; www.historicbozeman.com; 224 E Main St)
Gallatin National Forest Bozeman Ranger District
(☎ 406-522-2520; 3710 Fallon, Ste C) Located to the
west of town.
Northern Lights (☎ 866-586-2225; 1716 West
Babcock) Good but pricey outdoor-gear store offering
demos and rentals.

Sights & Activities

Arguably Montana's most entertaining
museum, the **Museum of the Rockies** (☎ 406-
994-3466; www.museumoftherockies.org; cnr S 7th
Ave & Kagy Blvd; adult/child $9.50/6.50; ⏰ 8am-8pm
Memorial Day-Labor Day, 9am-5pm Mon-Sat, 12:30-5pm
Sun rest of year) offers some of the most jaw-
dropping dinosaur displays you'll ever see,
including the world's largest T Rex skull
(truly awesome). There are also displays
on native cultures of the Northern Rockies
(look for the fabulous 1904 photo of
Geronimo driving a Cadillac!) and weekly
lectures. Add on a show at the **planetarium**
and a taste of homestead life at the next
door **Living History Farm** (summer only) and
you have to count on at least half a day

here; the entry fee gives admission for two
days. The museum is in the south of town,
next to Montana State University (MSU).
You'll be greeted at the door by 'Big Mike,'
a life-sized bronze T Rex.

Known around town as 'the Emerson,'
the nonprofit **Emerson Cultural Center**
(☎ 406-587-9797; www.theemerson.org; 111 S Grand
Ave; ⏰ most galleries closed Mon) is the place to
plug into Bozeman's art scene, with retail
galleries, exhibits, studios and a fine café/
restaurant.

The **Pioneer Museum** (☎ 406-522-8122; www
.pioneermuseum.org; 317 W Main St; adult/child under
12 $3/free; ⏰ 10am-5pm Mon-Sat Memorial Day-Labor
Day, 11am-4pm Tue-Sat rest of year), in the old jail
building, does a good job presenting local
history and famous residents (including
one Gary Cooper).

Hone your climbing skills on the indoor
wall at **Spire Climbing Center** (☎ 406-586-0706;
www.spireclimbingcenter.com; 13 Enterprise Blvd; day
pass $13; ⏰ 11am-10pm Mon-Fri, 10am-6pm Sat & Sun)
before heading off to tackle Grand Teton.
Private lessons and weekly classes are
offered.

Sleeping

There are three **USFS campsites** (all sites $)
southeast of town near the Hyalite Reservoir: Langhor (11 miles from Bozeman),
Hood Creek (14 miles) and Chisholm (15
miles). Take Forestry Road No 62 from
south Bozeman.

Sites can be reserved through **www.recrea
tion.gov** (☎ 877-444-6777).

MONTANASAURUS REX

It's amazing how much drama you can find in a single 50-million-year-old slab of rock at Bozeman's Museum of the Rockies (MOR). From the group of teenage diplodocus who suffocated
when their legs became stuck in river mud, or the dinosaur skeleton surrounded by the shed
teeth of the pack of predators that devoured it, these are fossils that come alive before your
eyes. I challenge you to stare at the terrifying claws of a deinonychus without feeling a slight
shiver run down your spine.

Like all good museums, MOR also shatters preconceptions, reminding you that many dinosaurs
were in fact clad in feathers and that sharks once swam the tropical seas covering current-day
Montana. This is mind-boggling stuff. Then there's the scale of the beasts – 9ft-long rib bones
stand in the corner near huge 20ft-tall reconstructions of horned torosaurus and Montanaceratops
(we kid you not).

Even the curator is larger than life; paleontologist Jack Horner is widely believed to have
been the model for the character Dr Alan Grant in the book *Jurassic Park* and served as technical
adviser to the film. And yes, they *are* extracting soft tissue from tyrannosaur thigh bones, right
here in Bozeman.

Bozeman KOA (☎ 406-587-3030; tent & RV sites $, cabins $; 🏊 🖥) Off I-90, 8 miles west of Bozeman, this is the only campground in the area open year-round.

Bear Canyon Campground (☎ 800-438-1575; www.bearcanyoncampground.com; tent & RV sites $; 🕑 May–mid-Oct; 🖥 🏊) Three miles east of Bozeman, also off I-90 (exit 313), this has a heated outdoor pool, laundry facilities and a store.

Bozeman Backpacker's Hostel (☎ 406-586-4659; www.bozemanbackpackershostel.com; 405 W Olive St; dm & d $) Two blocks south of Main St, this relaxed and Bohemian hostel is in an old Victorian house (once home to Gary Cooper) and serves a young, outdoorsy, international clientele. There are 12 bunk beds and two double rooms.

Royal 7 Budget Inn (☎ 800-587-3103; www.royal 7inn.com; 310 N 7th Ave; d $$; 🖥) This little inn really tries. Dated but very spacious rooms offer large TVs, microwave, fridge, continental breakfast, laundry service and a handful of DVDs for rent. Swings are set up in a grassy space for the kiddies.

Lehrkind Mansion Bed and Breakfast (☎ 406-585-6932; www.bozemanbedandbreakfast.com; 719 N Wallace Ave; d with breakfast $$$; 🖥) Plunked down in a neighborhood of dilapidated buildings, this sophisticated Victorian B&B was built by a Swiss-German master brewer and is steeped in fine antiques and history. (We're told the 7ft Regina music box is one of only 25!) Lush gardens and verandas welcome you. Grab a cup of Earl Grey and quiz the owners, ex-Yellowstone Park rangers, on the park's hidden spots. The eight beautifully appointed rooms have private baths. Alternatively, soak up the stars in the hot tub out back.

The best chain hotel in town is the new **Hilton Garden Inn** (☎ 406-582 9900; www .hiltongardeninn.com; 2023 Commerce Way; d $$$; 🖥 🏊 ♿), out on the edge of town.

Eating

Only Jackson can compete with Bozeman's range of excellent restaurants. This is not a place to self-cater.

La Parrilla (☎ 406-582-9511; 1624 W Babcock St; mains $; 🕑 11am-9pm) Pop in for a great lunch of gourmet California-style fish tacos, burritos and exotic wraps, strong on the cilantro and wasabi, served up by bright and hip staff.

Starky's Deli (☎ 406-556-1111; http://starkysdeli .com; 229 E Main St; mains $; 🕑 7am-5pm Mon-Fri, 8am-5pm Sat, 9am-2pm Sun) Possibly the best New York–style deli west of Queen's. Come here for cheese blintzes, matzoh ball soup and corned beef and pastrami sandwiches.

Dave's Sushi (☎ 406-556-1351; www.davessushi .com; 115 N. Bozeman Ave; sushi $-$$) If ordering sushi scares you silly, try this unpretentious place, offering the best rolls and freshest fish for miles around. It's 1½ blocks north of Main St.

our pick **John Bozeman's Bistro** (☎ 406-587-4100; www.johnbozemansbistro.com; 125 W Main St; mains $$-$$$; 🕑 closed Sun & Mon) Simply put, this is Bozeman's best restaurant, with a great tapas menu and Thai, Creole and pan-Asian slants on the dinner steak and fish.

The best places for breakfast are the quirky **Cateye Café** (☎ 406-587-8844; www .cateyecafe.com; 23 N Tracy; mains $; 🕑 7am-2:30pm Fri-Mon & Wed, 5-9:30pm Thu-Sat), with its eyebrow-raising opening hours, and the country-style **Main Street Overeasy** (☎ 406-587-3205; 9 E Main St; mains $; 🕑 7am-2:30pm Tue-Sun), the latter consistently voted best breakfast in town.

Drinking

A catchall for food, beer, pool and people-watching is **Montana Ale Works** (☎ 406-587-7700; www.montanaaleworks.com; 611 E Main St). The staff are happy to let you taste any of the 30 microbrews on tap, including the local Bozone brew, and if you find a favorite, you can take some home in a growler.

For a sophisticated Pinot Noir, accompanied by a decadent selection of chocolates or a spicy ceviche, put on your best shirt and head to **Plonk** (☎ 406-587-2170; 29 E Main St), where DJs add a club vibe on Friday nights.

Most nights bring live music to the **Zebra Lounge** (☎ 406-585-8851; 321 E Main St), half a block north of Main on Rouse Ave S; shows start around 10pm. College hangouts include the **Haufbrau** (22 S 8th Ave) and the next-door Molly Brown.

GALLATIN VALLEY

A broad ribbon snaking through big valleys, the Gallatin River leaves its headwaters in the northwest corner of Yellowstone National Park to cascade through the narrow, craggy Gallatin Valley. US 191 traces its path, eventually meeting the

ROCKY MOUNTAIN BREWS

The Yellowstone states of Wyoming and Montana are fast developing a reputation among beer hounds for hosting some of the country's best microbreweries.

Snake River Brewing (www.snakeriverbrewing.com) in Jackson is the region's most popular brewpub. Flagship beers include the Austrian-style Snake River Lager, the crisp Snake River Pale Ale, the dark and creamy Snake River Zonker Stout, and numerous other brews; see also p248.

Teton Valley's **Grand Teton Brewing Company** (www.grandtetonbrewing.com) uses local spring water to produce its Old Faithful Ale, Teton Ale and Moose Juice Stout. Its Teton Huckleberry Wheat is one of several popular regional fruit beers.

The so-called 'Yellowstone Ale' for sale in the park's Yellowstone General Stores is actually a repackaged variety of German-style Dead Man Ale, brewed in Portland, Oregon.

Missoula's **Bayern Brewing** (www.bayernbrewery.com) is the only German microbrewery in the Rockies, serving up amber, pilsner, Killarney and Hefeweizen beers. **Big Sky Brewing** (www.bigskybrew.com), also of Missoula, produces Montana's best-selling microbrew, Moose Drool, a creamy brown ale. The English-style Scape Goat pale ale is also excellent.

Yellowstone Valley Brewing (www.yellowstonevalleybrew.com) in Billings names all its beers after fishing flies, including the amber-colored Wild Fly Ale, the dark, malty Renegade Red Ale, the clear Grizzly Wulff Wheat and the full-flavored Black Widow Oatmeal Stout. Pop into the **Brewhouse Garage Pub** (☎ 406-245-0918; 2123 1st Ave N; 🕑 4-8pm Mon-Sat) in Billings for a sample, before heading to nearby **Angry Hank's** (☎ 406-252-3370; 2405 1st Ave N) for more excellent Billings brews (the Head Trauma India Pale Ale is recommended).

If you are headed along the Beartooth Hwy, drop into **Red Lodge Ales** (www.redlodgeales.net) en route for a brewery tour and sample of their refreshing German-style Glacier Ale or full-bodied porter; see also p181. In Bozeman, head for the excellent Montana Ale Works (opposite) to try the region's best brews, including a Bozone beer from **Bozeman Brewing** (www.bozemanbrewing.com; 504 N Broadway). Livingston offers the small **Neptune's Brewery** (☎ 406-222-7837; 802 E Park St), though the ales here can be a little weak.

Other Yellowstone beers worth tracking down, if only to say their names out loud ('a pint of Old Stinky's, please'), are Monkey's Dunkel, Powder Hound, Trout Slayer, Custer's Last Ale and, yes, Old Stinky's.

Madison, Jefferson and Missouri Rivers at Three Forks. Sandwiched between the scenic Madison and Gallatin Ranges, this route – first forged by Lewis and Clark – is peppered with enough trailheads to make return hikers and skiers arthritic. The commercial heart of the valley is the broad opening connecting Big Sky Ski Resort.

On a clear day, look for a distinct cluster of summits exceeding 10,000ft rising sharply out of the silhouette of the Gallatin Range, west of US 191. These are the Spanish Peaks, the valley's premier hiking and backcountry ski destination and part of the Lee Metcalf Wilderness.

Big Sky

Commercial development hits hyperdrive near the turnoff to Big Sky, Gallatin Valley's main attraction, 18 miles north of Yellowstone and 36 miles south of Bozeman. This world-class winter and summer resort attracts a cosmopolitan crowd more partial to organic

wine than canned pilsner. As multi-million-dollar homes sprout up like milkweed, other prices join the upscale trend.

For a calendar of events, the fishing report or maps contact the **Big Sky Chamber of Commerce** (☎ 406-995-3000, 800-943-4111; www.bigskychamber.com) at West Fork Meadows. **Big Sky Resort** (☎ 800-548-4486; www.bigskyresort.com) also has information.

Big Sky spreads from US 191 to the base of Lone Mountain in four areas: Gallatin Canyon, West Fork Meadows, Meadow Village and Mountain Village. Meadow Village and West Fork Meadows offer the bulk of the services; all are connected by a free shuttle service in summer and winter.

Big Sky Resort is comprised of Andesite Mountain (8800ft) and Lone Mountain (11,166ft), with a 4350ft vertical drop and 3800 acres of skiable terrain, a 15-passenger tram, a gondola and multiple high-speed lifts. Tickets are $75/65 per full/half day; children under 10 ski free.

Gallatin & Paradise Valleys

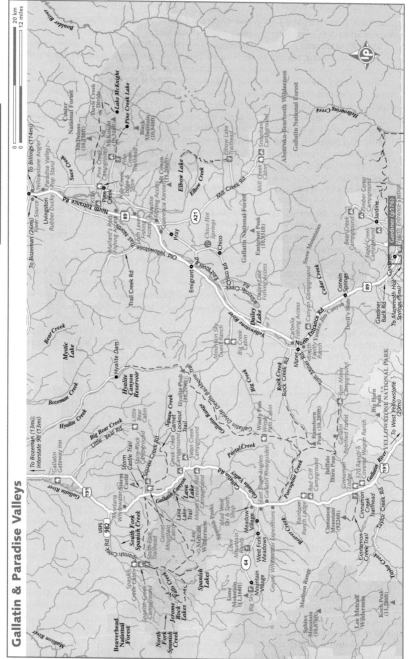

Among the many rental shops around Big Sky, **Mad Wolf Ski & Sport Shop** (☎ 406-995-4369), 100yd south of the Big Sky turnoff on US 191, tends to have the best prices, with ski rentals for around $16 per day.

A gondola shuttles people and bikes to 10,000ft (9:30am to 4:30pm, June to October) for $18 ($29 for unlimited use); buy tickets at Big Sky Sports at the base of the mountain. Serious hikers can bag Lone Mountain (11,166ft) from here, and mountain bikers have a dozen great downhill rides.

A fantastic skiing or snowboarding alternative is **Moonlight Basin** (www.moonlight basin.com), 1.2 miles past Big Sky Mountain Village. Powder is plentiful on Lone Mountain's northern slopes (also accessible via Big Sky); experts covet its double-diamond chutes and bowls. Terrain includes 2000 skiable acres with 4500ft of vertical drop. Tickets are $51/39 full/half day; children under 10 ski free.

Inquire about condominium, cabin or house rentals in Big Sky through **East West Resorts** (☎ 877-845-9817; www.eastwestresorts.com) or **Big Sky Central Reservations** (☎ 800-548-8846); ski packages are available throughout the winter season.

Tucked into the sagebrush meadows, spectacular **Lone Mountain Ranch** (☎ 406-995-4644, 800-514-4644; www.lmranch.com) is one of the country's top Nordic resorts, with 47 miles of groomed cross-country trails and a full-service, high-end lodge. Day trail passes cost $19; it's free for kids 12 and under. It also offers guided hiking, fly-fishing and horseback riding into Yellowstone or the Spanish Peaks. In winter, check out the dinner sleigh rides ($78).

Hiking & Backpacking

Hiking trails – all open to mountain biking – head into the mountains along numerous creek drainages from both sides of US 191. Trails are marked on the *Lee Metcalf Wilderness* and *West Yellowstone Vicinity* USFS maps, available at ranger stations or local sports stores.

A favorite dining and hiking combo is to hike up to the fire lookout at the top of the **Cinnamon Creek Trail**, then have lunch or dinner at the Cinnamon Lodge, near the trailhead on US 191.

The most popular hikes are in the north half of the valley. The popular 6-mile round-trip hike to **Lava Lake** offers decent trout fishing. The trailhead is at tight turnoff at a dangerous curve in I-191. The trail climbs about 1600ft, crossing Cascade Creek several times to meadows and then continues up more switchbacks. Good campsites flank Lava Lake's northeast shore, but fires are banned within 0.5 miles of the lake.

A trailhead on Squaw Creek Rd accesses several trails. The 1.5-mile climb to the top of the **Storm Castle Trail** (No 92) offers great views, but the climb is unrelenting, with the last quarter-mile, across loose scree, especially strenuous and tricky.

The equally demanding 8-mile round-trip **Garnet Lookout Trail** (No 85) leads off in the opposite direction, gaining 2850ft to the top of Garnet Peak, where there is a USFS lookout tower that can be rented as a cabin.

One of the most popular points to access the **Spanish Peaks** area is Spanish Creek Campground at the end of USFS Rd 982, about 22 miles south of Bozeman. Camping is allowed at the trailhead, and there's a USFS cabin nearby. Most routes are overnighters or multiday loops. A popular loop leads up Falls Creek to the **Jerome Rock Lakes** (8 miles) and then back down the South Fork. Longer loops take in the **Spanish Lakes** (8.5 miles from the trailhead) or **Mirror Lake** (7.5 miles) and return via Indian Ridge and Little Hellroaring Creek.

For an ambitious multiday backcountry adventure, hike the **Gallatin Divide Devils Backbone Trail**, which follows the ridgeline of the Gallatin Range.

Other Activities

Scenes from the film *A River Runs Through It* were filmed on the beautiful Gallatin River, where local anglers swear that the sweet spot is anywhere you cast a line. You will also find fishing access sites at Greek Creek, Moose Creek Flat and Red Cliff Campgrounds.

East Slope Anglers (☎ 406-995-4369; www.east slopeanglers.com), 100yd south of the Big Sky turnoff, has a store full of equipment for rent or sale and offers guided fly-fishing trips with instruction, as does **Gallatin Riverguides** (☎ 406-995-2290; www.montanaflyfishing.com), 0.5 miles south of the Big Sky turnoff.

Gallatin Valley offers the best white-water rafting around Yellowstone – most exciting during June's high water. For inspiration, check out the 'mad mile' of white-water visible from the main road after the Cascade Creek bridge. **Geyser Whitewater Expeditions** (☎ 406-995-4989; www.raftmontana.com), on US 191 one mile south of the Big Sky turnoff, offers **white-water rafting** (full/half day $84/48) and **kayaking** (half-day $61). **Montana Whitewater** (☎ 406-995-4613; www.montanawhitewater.com; Hwy 191 mile marker 64; full/half day $79/47) has similar trips.

For a guided mountain biking or backpacking adventure, Big Sky–based **Ayres Adventures** (☎ 406-993-2255; www.mountain ayresadventures.com), run by adventure couple Ryan and Morgan, does it all – from half-day vehicle-assisted trips to multiday adventures in remote areas as well as Yellowstone National Park.

A number of outfitters offer horseback-riding trips, including **Jake's Horses** (☎ 406-995-4630; www.jakeshorses.com), **Diamond K Outfitters** (☎ 406-580-0928) and **Big Sky Stables** (☎ 406-995-2972). The cost is about $34 per hour, $80 for a half day and $136 for a full day.

Sleeping

Numerous **USFS campgrounds** (all sites $) snuggle up to the base of the Gallatin Range along US 191. Open mid-May to mid-September, all have potable water and vault toilets. Reserve campsites and cabins in advance through **www.recreation .gov** (☎ 877-444-6777).

About 48 miles South of Bozeman, Red Cliff Campground has ample availability with 65 sites. Moose Creek Flat is on the riverside with some fishing, but very close to the road. Swan Creek Campground, 32 miles south of Bozeman and 0.5 miles east on paved Rd No 481, is secluded and popular, backing onto Swan Creek. A mile north, Greek Creek Campground doubles

as a fishing access site. Sites are on both sides of the highway; western riverside sites fill early. Away from the road is secluded Spire Rock Campground, 26 miles south of Bozeman, then 2 miles east on Squaw Creek Rd No 1321.

The USFS operates four sweet little cabins in the valley: Little Bear, Spanish Creek, Garnet Mountain and Windy Pass. The last three are hike-, ski- or snowmobile-accessible only. Contact the **Bozeman district office** (☎ 406-522-2520, 1-877-444-6777) to reserve. Great value for groups, most cabins are available year-round for $30 per night, sleep four and are equipped with stoves, firewood, cooking supplies and blankets.

LODGES & GUEST RANCHES
Cinnamon Lodge (☎ 406-995-4253; r $$, cabins with kitchens $$$) The roadside establishment attracts a hodgepodge of seniors in RVs, families, and serious hunters and fly-fishers. The Western bar and Mexican café serves excellent food from 7am to 9pm. It is on the Gallatin River about 10 miles south of the Big Sky turnoff.

320 Ranch (☎ 406-995-4283, 800-243-0320; www .320ranch.com; cabins from $$$) This historic ranch occupies a beautiful swath of the Gallatin, 12 miles south of Big Sky by the Buffalo Horn Creek Trailhead. Guests stay in rustic log cabins with access to a fishing shop, hot tub and saloon. Winter activities include sleigh rides and snowmobiling, with attractive ski packages at the local resorts.

Covered Wagon Ranch (☎ 406-995-4237; www .coveredwagonranch.com; 34035 Gallatin Rd; room & board $$$) Three miles from Yellowstone near Taylors Fork, this 1925 ranch feels more rugged than some of the rhinestone-cowboy ranches around. With a strong emphasis on riding, a top offer is the small pack trips into Yellowstone.

Gallatin Gateway Inn (☎ 406-763-4672; www.gallatin gatewayinn.com; r $$$; 🏊) At the north end of the valley, the Gallatin Gateway is an elegant retreat with soothing atmosphere and spacious quarters. Built by the Milwaukee Railroad in 1927 as the Yellowstone line terminus, its later incarnations included an antique-cars showroom and a women's mud-wrestling arena. With tennis courts, a heated pool and a great restaurant, it's worth a stop or stay. Live music at the bar on weekends attracts Bozeman's outdoorsy 30-somethings.

GOURMET GROCERY GRAB

If a good cabernet and hot made-to-order paninis would spice up the picnic, check out Big Sky's **Hungry Moose Market** (209 Aspen Leaf Dr, West Fork Meadows; ⏰ 6:30am-9pm), a favorite post-ride or pre-ski stop. There are also hot breakfasts, espresso, smoothies, bulk food and groceries leaning toward the organic and natural. Take your order to go or sit out on the patio.

We hope the ghosts of mud-wrestlers past have been put to rest by the tinkling of the baby grand.

Rainbow Ranch Lodge (☎ 406-995-4132, 800-937-4132; www.rainbowranch.com; r $$$-$$$$) Rustic and ultra-chic, Rainbow Ranch offers quiet accommodations on the pond or river with roaring stone fireplaces and an outdoor hot tub. Its upscale slow-food restaurant ($$$$$) has sumptuous offerings, including mesquite-grilled elk tenderloin and gnocchi with organic basil, coupled with Montana's largest wine list. It's hard to beat. The lodge is 5 miles south of the Big Sky turnoff and 12 miles north of Yellowstone.

HEBGEN LAKE AREA

If the Yellowstone park boundary had been drawn differently, this broad lake valley in hills thick with pines would be mobbed with tourists. As it is, most visitors with a mind to meander will find wild and beautiful backcountry with an air of solitude. The Hebgen area's mountains, lakes and trails offer a slew of fine recreational opportunities.

A useful road tour of the region runs west from West Yellowstone along Hwy 20 over the Targhee Pass to Henry's Lake, and then northwest along Hwy 87 to the junction with Hwy 287, near the turnoff to Cliff and Wade Lakes, to return east via Quake Lake.

CLIFF & WADE LAKES

Those willing to wander astray will be justly rewarded by these gems, located 6 miles up a dirt road that branches south 1 mile west of the junction of Hwys 287 and 87. The lakes can also be reached by an easily missed dirt road off Hwy 87. These spring-fed lakes run along a geologic fault line and are home to prolific wildlife including ospreys, bald eagles and beaver. It's a good spot for families, with abundant boating and fishing options as well as some pleasant trails nearby.

USFS campgrounds (all sites $) are at Wade Lake, Cliff Point and Hilltop. Cliff Point is the smallest and a favorite of kayakers. Wade Lake has lakeside tent-only sites. Call the **Beaverhead-Deerlodge Forestry Service** (☎ 406-683-3900) for details.

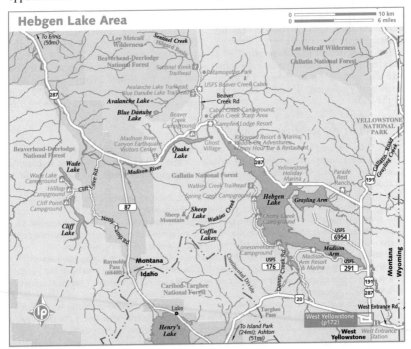

Hebgen Lake Area

QUAKE LAKE

Built atop part of the Madison landslide, the **Madison River Canyon Earthquake Area Visitors Center** (☎ 406-646-7369; admission $3) has a working seismograph and material about the 1959 quake, which was the strongest ever recorded in the Rockies. Walk or drive up to the interpretive trail for a vista of the dramatic slide area and a memorial boulder inscribed with the names of 28 campers killed in the slide. A dock at Quake Lake allows boaters to glide past the surreal submerged treetops of Quake Lake.

The **Cabin Creek Scarp Area** highlights a 21ft-tall scarp that opened up along the Hebgen Lake fault line. One campsite actually straddled the fault; you can still see the picnic table above the scarp and the fire ring 21ft below.

At **Ghost Village** you can see the remains of half-a-dozen cabins stranded in the plain by the post-earthquake flood. To get here turn off the highway toward Campfire Lodge and then branch right down a dirt road. The cabins are on the other side of the river. Rangers lead a 1.5-mile guided walk here Thursdays at 10am (mid-July to mid-September). Call ☎ 406-682-7220 for details.

Ten miles further east along Hwy 287 a road leads off to a parking area and a short trail that leads down to Hebgen Lake and three partly submerged cabins destroyed by the slide.

Cabin Creek and Beaver Creek Campgrounds are two scenic concession-run **USFS campgrounds** (sites $). Call the **Hebgen Lake Ranger District** (☎ 406-823-6961) for information. Just across from Cabin Creek is **Campfire Lodge Resort** (☎ 406-646-7258; RV site/cabin $/$$), offering cabins that sleep up to seven, plus RV sites, laundry and showers.

HEBGEN LAKE

Connected to Quake Lake by a scenic stretch of the Madison River, Hebgen Lake merits a few days of hiking, angling and boating. Motorboats are permitted, and are available for rent at the Madison Arm Resort & Marina on the south shore and the Yellowstone Holiday and Kirkwood Resort marinas on the north shore.

Between the visitor center and the dam, Beaver Creek Rd turns north off the highway. The road follows Beaver Creek, through an area notorious for grizzly sightings, 3 miles to the **Avalanche Lake/Blue Danube Lake Trailhead** (trail 222/152). Both Avalanche (11-mile round-trip) and Blue Danube (12.5-mile round-trip) Lakes make excellent day-hike destinations; the trail splits 4.5 miles from the trailhead.

Further along Beaver Creek the road finishes at Potamogeton Park and the trailhead for an excellent overnight trip up Sentinel Creek to the dozen or so alpine lakes of the **Hilgard Basin** (trail 202/201). Budget a day to make the 7-mile and 2700ft elevation gain to the lakes, a day to explore

---

THE NIGHT THE MOUNTAINS MOVED

Just before midnight on August 17, 1959, an earthquake measuring 7.5 on the Richter scale ripped the landscape of the Upper Madison Valley. As two huge fault blocks tilted and dropped, a massive 80-million-ton landslide pulverized two campgrounds and even rose halfway up the opposite valley wall.

The slip caused the lake's north shore to drop 18ft, flooding lakeshore houses and lodges. Gaps opened up in highways, and cars crashed into the gaping holes.

Hurricane force winds caused by the slide then rushed down the valley, tearing off campers' clothes and creating a huge wave on the lake. Mini tsunamis sloshed up and down the lake for the next 12 hours, pouring over the Hebgen Lake Dam, which, amazingly, held firm.

The slide had blocked the Madison River, and the waters of newborn Earthquake Lake soon started to fill, rising 9ft a day as engineers worked around the clock to cut a spillway and avoid a second catastrophic flood. In a final gesture, several hundred of Yellowstone's thermal features simultaneously erupted.

After the dust settled, it was discovered that 28 people had been killed, mostly in the Rock Creek campsite. Nineteen bodies were never found, presumably entombed under the slide. The quake had been felt in California, and water tables were affected as far away as Hawaii.

KAYAKING AT DUSK

What better way to explore the Hebgen Lakes than from the cockpit of a kayak? **Paddle On Adventures** (☎ 406-209-7452; www.paddleonadventures.com; Kirkwood Marina; guided 3hr trip $45) advertises 'an out of car experience,' but what it delivers is much more. Pete, the enthusiastic owner, transports paddlers through pristine wilderness via meandering waterways and clear lakes flanked by osprey, blue heron, cormorants and moose. Kids and adults alike will have a blast. The most popular tours run at sunset and full moon, when calm waters mean waltzing the kayak through late-afternoon's glassy waters in search of rustling creatures.

the basin and a day to return. This hike takes you into the Lee Metcalf Wilderness, so wilderness-use rules apply (see p42).

Along the northwest shore of Hebgen Lake, a couple of miles past Spring Creek Campground, is the trailhead for Watkins Creek and the 10-mile round-trip day or overnight hike to **Coffin Lakes** (trail 215/209). You can take mountain bikes on this trail, which gains 1700ft in elevation.

The useful 1:63,360 USFS *Lee Metcalf Wilderness and West Yellowstone Vicinity* map marks these and many other trails in the region.

Sleeping & Eating

On the southwest side of Hebgen Lake, three remote **USFS campgrounds** (sites $) serve boaters and anglers. Four miles down a tarmac road, Lonesomehurst is the most accessible, with lovely lake views, potable water and a boat ramp. Another 2 miles and 8 miles, respectively, down a dirt road that turns to rough washboard are lakeshore Cherry Creek and Spring Creek, both primitive sites (no fee) with pit toilets but no drinking water. Reach these by turning north off Hwy 20 about halfway between Targhee Pass and West Yellowstone on Denny Creek Rd (USFS Rd 176). Call the **Hebgen Lake Ranger District** (☎ 406-823-6961) for information.

A superb base for hiking, **Beaver Creek Cabin** (cabin $; ☯ year-round) offers bunk beds sleeping four, a stove, utensils, firewood

and an ax. Contact the ranger station in **Gallatin National Forest Service Headquarters** (☎ 406-646-7369) for reservations.

Though lacking in shade, the comparatively pricey **Madison Arm Resort & Marina** (☎ 406-646-9328; sites $), 5 miles west of US 191/US 287, is well suited to tenters, and there's a marina with a swimming beach and boat rentals.

Ten miles from Yellowstone, and northeast of Hebgen Lake, **Parade Rest Ranch** (☎ 406-646-7217, 800-753-5934; www.paraderestranch .com; 7979 Grayling Creek Rd; day per person $178) offers horseback riding by the hour ($35) or an all-inclusive stay. Daily rates include cabin lodging, meals, horseback riding, and fly-fishing on Graying Creek. Discounted and room-only rates are available in spring and fall.

Grab nachos or a steak at the **Happy Hour Bar & Restaurant** (☎ 406-646-5100; Hwy 287 at mile 4; meals $$; ☯ 11am-midnight), a colorful slice of Montana with a deck overlooking Hebgen Lake. Drawing locals, fly-fishermen, bikers and travelers, the bar hops when patrons launch into moose head karaoke.

PARADISE VALLEY ROUTE

LIVINGSTON

☎ 406 / pop 6800 / elev 4503ft

In the late 1880s the Northern Pacific Railroad laid tracks across the Yellowstone River and began building Livingston as the primary jumping-off point for Yellowstone National Park. Visited by Clark (of Lewis and Clark fame) and at one point a temporary home to whip-crackin' Martha Canary (otherwise known as Calamity Jane), Livingston is an excellent departure point for rafting and fly-fishing trips on the Yellowstone River.

Bozeman's overflow has brought upscale restaurants, antique shops and art galleries to Livingston's picturesque old buildings, as well as a growing community of writers and artists, but generally the Livingston retains its small-town feel. The saloons that Calamity Jane and Kitty O'Leary frequented remain relatively unchanged.

Livingston is at the north end of Paradise Valley, where I-90 meets US 89; the latter heads south to Gardiner and Yellowstone National Park, 53 miles away.

Information

Chamber of Commerce (☎ 406-222-0850; www .livingston-chamber.com; 303 E Park St) Has a very useful website. Try also www.livingstonmontana.com.

Gallatin National Forest Livingston Ranger District (☎ 406-222-1892; 5242 Hwy 89 South) One mile south of town on I-90.

Timber Trails (☎ 406-222-9550; 309 W Park St) For maps and outdoor gear, including rentals.

Sights & Activities

The **Fly Fishing Discovery Center** (☎ 406-222-9369; 215 E Lewis St; adult/child 7-14 $3/1; ☺ 10am-6pm Mon-Sat, noon-5pm Sun) has beautiful displays of hand-tied flies (over 10,000!), rod and reel prototypes, and aquatic habitats. On Tuesday and Thursday summer evenings from 5pm to 7pm staff give casting lessons free of charge; equipment is provided.

Built on a legacy of Goofus Bugs, Humpy Flies, Trudes, Green Drakes and Hair Wing Rubber Legs (to name but a few), **Dan Bailey's Fly Shop** (☎ 800-356-4052; www.dan-bailey .com; 209 W Park St) is one of the world's best fly-fishing shops.

The original Northern Pacific Railroad Depot, built in 1902 by the architects who designed New York's Grand Central Station, is now home to a railroad history and arts museum called the **Depot Center** (☎ 406-222-2300; www.livingstondepot.org; 200 W Park St; adult/senior/child $3/2/2; ☺ 9am-5pm Mon-Sat, 1-5pm Sun late May-early Sep).

From June to August, the revamped **Yellowstone Gateway Museum** (☎ 406-222-4184; 118 W Chinook St; adult/child $4/2; ☺ 10am-5pm mid-May–Aug, 10am-4pm Tue-Sat Sep) displays local historical and archaeological treasures in an old schoolhouse. Exhibits include an early Yellowstone stagecoach. For details on all three museums see www .livingstonmuseums.org. Livingston is also home to over a dozen galleries ('13 galleries; 3 stop lights') – for details see www.livingstongalleries.com.

If you are looking for that special souvenir, **White Buffalo Lodges** (☎ 1-866-358-8547; www.whitebuffalolodges.com) sells authentic Sioux, Blackfeet and Crow teepees for $2000 a pop.

For fun on the Yellowstone River rent a canoe, raft or kayaks from **Rubber Ducky**

River Rentals (☎ 406-222-3746; www.riverservices .com) or **River Source** (☎ 406-223-5134; www .riversourcerafting.com), the latter on the southern outskirts of town.

George Anderson's Yellowstone Angler (☎ 406-222-7130; www.yellowstoneangler.com; Hwy 89), one mile south of Livingston, is another good fly-fishing store with equipment rental and guide service.

Sleeping

The nearest Forestry Service campground is Pine Creek (p207), 15 miles south in the Paradise Valley.

Osen's RV Park & Campground (☎ 406-222-0591; www.montanarvpark.com; 20 Merrill Lane; RV & camping sites $; ▣), just south of I-90, has laundry and showers and is open year-round

Central to Livingston's history, **Murray Hotel** (☎ 406-222-1350; www.murrayhotel.com; 201 W Park St; r/ste $$/$$$; ▣), built in 1904, is the place to bed down with the ghosts of gunslinger Calamity Jane and director Sam Peckinpah (who lived in the top-floor suite for over a year, occasionally shooting holes in the ceiling). The ancient hand-crank lift and creaky wood floors set the tone, but the 30 rooms are all modernized, most with galley kitchens. The Peckinpah suite is a six-sleeper treat if you can swing it.

Halfway between I-90 and downtown is the acceptable **Parkway Motel** (☎ 406-222-3840; 1124 W Park St; d $$; ▣). The rooms with two queens are much bigger than the singles and well worth the extra $10. Rooms come with coffee maker, fridge and microwave. Winter discounts of 30%.

Eating

our pick **2nd St Bistro** (☎ 406-222-9463; 123 N 2nd St; mains $$; ☺ from 5pm) Our personal favorite, with a superb range of appetizers and draft beers (including from the local Neptune Brewery), this is a relaxed bistro with an emphasis on quality food. From the Moroccan lamb 'cigarettes' to the European-style mussels and fries, you simply can't go wrong with this great menu, and there's more vegetarian fare than the average Montana restaurant.

Livingston Bar & Grille (☎ 406-222-7909; 130 N Main St; mains $$-$$$) The restaurant at artist Russell Chatham's establishment is the most distinguished address in town. If nothing else, come for a sophisticated aperitif at the small-on-space, huge-on-style back bar, which came from St Louis by wagon train around 1910 and got considerable use from Calamity Jane.

Mark's In and Out (☎ 406-222-7744; cnr Park & 8th Sts; ☽ Mar-Nov) If your tastes are less Merlot and more chocolate milk, come here. Mark's has been churning out quality never-frozen burgers and malts since 1954, with rollerskating carhops laying on an extra slice of nostalgia on summer weekend evenings.

The Sport (☎ 406-222-9500; 114 S Main St; mains $$) has been running strong since 1909. It's a fun place to go for hot sandwiches, steaks and Mexican food. For a light lunchtime panini and espresso try **Chadz** (☎ 406-222-2247; 104 N Main; snacks $; ☽ 6am-2:30pm, to 9pm Fri; ▣), which has comfy sofas and free wi-fi.

For a top-shelf picnic, combine a fabulous ciabatta sandwiche, gourmet salad or pork vindaloo from **Mustang Catering** (☎ 406-222-8884; www.mustangcatering.com; 215 W Lewis St; dishes $; ☽ 11am-6pm Mon-Fri) with a wine grab from the Gourmet Cellar (next to Livingston Depot) and dine al fresco at the picnic tables by Depot Center or, even better, in the Paradise Valley en route to the park.

PARADISE VALLEY

With Livingston as a railroad stop, Paradise Valley became the first travel corridor to Yellowstone National Park. Gardiner, 50 miles south of Livingston and just north of the Mammoth Hot Springs entrance to Yellowstone, is still one of the park's most popular entry points. The valley is still mostly ranchland but also includes such famous residents as Peter Fonda, Jeff Bridges, Dennis Quaid, Tom Brokaw and the Church Universal & Triumphant (CUT), which borders on Yellowstone National Park. And yes, a river, the Yellowstone, does run through it.

US 89 follows the Yellowstone River through this broad valley, flanked by the Gallatin Range to the west and the jagged Absaroka Range to the east. If you have time, the scenic East River Rd offers a parallel and quieter alternative to busy US 89. Amazingly in retrospect, plans were afoot in the 1960s to dam the Yellowstone River and flood much of the lovely valley.

For a rundown on the valley's various accommodations, restaurants and support

services, go online at www.paradisevalley montana.com.

Chico Hot Springs

Thirty miles from Yellowstone National Park, at the mouth of Emigrant Canyon, **Chico Hot Springs** (☎ 406-333-4933; www.chicohotsprings.com; r $$-$$$, cabins $$$) was established in 1900 as a luxurious getaway for local cattle barons. The Victorian elegance has been restored with great attention to rustic detail. It's worth a visit just to poke around and take a plunge in the large outdoor **pool** (adult/child 7-12 $6.50/4.50; ☽ 8am-11pm), fed from hot springs at a toasty 104°F.

Smallish and creaking rooms in the main lodge with no telephone and shared bath are the cheapest options, with motel-style fishermen's cabins and modern high-ceilinged rooms with a porch around double these rates. Chalets up the hill have mountain views and mostly sleep four to six. Suites with private Jacuzzi are a great luxury.

Chico's activity center offers **horseback riding** (1hr/half-day rides $30/80) and raft trips down the Yellowstone. It also rents mountain bikes and cross-country skis. There's a full spa attached to help you recover. Dogsled tours are operated from Thanksgiving to Easter through **Absaroka Dogsled Treks** (www.extrememontana.com; from per person $110).

our pick **Chico Inn Restaurant** (mains $$$, Sunday brunch $$) is renowned throughout the region, though there's slim pickings for vegetarians. The beef Wellington ($$$$ for two) gets rave reviews, as does the Sunday brunch, which is available between 8:30am and 11:30am.

The Poolside Grill is cheaper and more casual, with sandwiches, pizza and ribs. The rollicking attached saloon has live music on Friday and Saturday nights.

Tom Miner Basin

Tom Miner Rd heads west of US 89, 17 miles north of Gardiner and 35 miles south of Livingston, into one of the prettiest pockets of land in the area. The washboard road ends 12 miles west of the highway at secluded 16-site **Tom Miner Campground** (sites $; ☽ Jun-Oct), which has potable water and toilets.

Several trails start at the campground, including a 3-mile loop (trail No 286)

AROUND YELLOWSTONE

through the **Gallatin Petrified Forest**, where remnants of 35- to 55-million-year-old petrified wood are scattered among the Absaroka's volcanic rocks. Some of the trees were buried where they grew, but most were deposited by a great mudflow caused by nearby volcanic eruptions about 50 million years ago.

A 0.5-mile interpretive trail winds around volcanic bluffs of fused ash (bear right where a sign says 'Hiker Trail Only') and peters out by a remarkable piece of petrified wood that is lodged in the roof of a small cave. Visitors are allowed to keep one small piece of petrified wood (maximum 20 cu inches) with a free permit available at the Gardiner, Bozeman or Livingston ranger offices.

Southern Paradise Valley

South of the Tom Miner turnoff, US 89 winds through Yankee Jim Canyon, a narrow gorge cut through folded bands of extremely old rock (mostly gneiss) that look a bit like marble cake. Yankee Jim George hacked out a toll road through the canyon in the 19th century and made a living from Yellowstone-bound stagecoaches until the railroad put him out of business. The stretch of the Yellowstone River running through Yankee Jim Canyon is a popular white-water spot.

A couple of miles further toward Yellowstone look for the roadside hot springs, which were once channeled into an elegant, turn of the century resort at nearby Corwin Springs. Across the river is the headquarters of the Church Universal & Triumphant (CUT), which built a huge underground nuclear shelter here in the 1980s after their leader Elizabeth Prophet predicted the end of the world. The church butted heads with Yellowstone Park several times in the '80s and '90s but finally added a large chunk of their land to the park in 1998.

Further south, a pullout signposted 'wildlife viewing' offers fine views of the **Devil's Slide**, a superbly named salmon-pink landslide area consisting of 200-million-year-old rock.

Hiking & Backpacking

Paradise Valley's most popular trail is the 10-mile round-trip hike to **Pine Creek Lake**. The trail starts from the Pine Creek Campground parking area and leads 1.2 miles to Pine Creek Falls and then another 3.8 miles to Pine Creek Lake, gaining around 3000ft en route. Budget at least four hours for the return.

Further south, down Mill Creek Rd, is the trailhead for **Elbow Lake**, 3500ft above the trailhead at the base of 11,206ft Mt Cowen, the highest peak in the Absaroka Range. The strenuous 18-mile, round-trip hike (along trails No 51 and 48) is possible as a long day hike, but it's better to overnight at the lake. From the lake you can continue northeast to a second lake and ascend the ridge on the left for views of Mt Cowen.

Further south, there are more hiking opportunities on the east side of the Gallatin Range. A popular day hike from Tom Miner Campground takes you 2.5 miles up Trail Creek to meadows at **Buffalo Horn Pass**. A viewpoint five minutes' walk south offers excellent views of the Gallatin Valley; Ramshorn Peak (10,289ft) beckons to the north.

The USFS *Gallatin Forest East Half* map (scaled 1:126,720) provides a good overview of the valley's routes but lacks contours.

Other Activities

The Yellowstone River winds past 19 **fishing** access sites along Paradise Valley, most of which have boat ramps. Experienced anglers can pit themselves against challenging private spring creeks such as Nelson's, Armstrong's and Depuy's. For bookings (recommended) and fishing conditions contact Livingston's fishing shops (p204).

The Montana Department of Fishing, Wildlife & Parks runs **campgrounds** (sites $5, without a Montana fishing license $10) at the Mallard's Rest, Loch Leven and Dailey Lake fishing access sites. Overnight camping is permitted free of charge at the BLM Carbella and Paradise fishing access areas, but the limited and primitive sites get snapped up quickly. All other access areas are day-use only.

Bearpaw Outfitters (☎ 406-222-6642; www.bearpawoutfittersmt.com; 136 Deep Creek Rd), 8 miles south of Livingston, organizes horse-pack trips in the Absaroka-Beartooth Wilderness (half day $75) and day rides in Yellowstone Park ($200), plus fly-fishing in Yellowstone's Slough Creek.

Try **mountain biking** along the paved East River Rd from the junction with Hwy 89 to Chico Rd and Chico Hot Springs. It's a scenic and smooth ride of 24 miles. For something more rugged, try the 17-mile gravel Gardiner Back Rd between Gardiner and Tom Miner Rd. This route follows the old stagecoach and railroad road from Yellowstone and takes you past the Devil's Slide and the narrows of Yankee Jim Canyon. To shorten the ride, turn off at Corwin Springs after 8 miles. Combine these two routes, and you'll get a complete traverse of the valley.

Sleeping & Eating

There's a beautifully situated **KOA** (☎ 406-222-0992; www.livingstonkoa.com; Pine Creek Rd; tent & RV sites $; May-Oct;) between US 89 and the East River Rd, 10 miles south of Livingston, with an indoor heated pool and laundry room.

Two miles further east, on East River Rd, **Pine Creek Lodge & Store** (☎ 406-222-3628; cabins $$) has four homey cabins in a peaceful location and a cozy café-restaurant (open 9am to 2pm and 5:30pm to 9pm) with a big outside patio.

There are several **campgrounds** (all sites $) in Paradise Valley. About 2 miles further south on East River Rd, Luccock Park Rd heads 3 miles east to 25-site Pine Creek Campground, with pit toilets, water and hiker/biker sites. Both this and the 11-site Snowbank Campground, 17 miles south down Mill Creek Road, serve as springboards to local hikes and are open May to September. (Snowbank closes first,

early in September.) Call the **Livingston Ranger District** (☎ 406-222-1892; www.fs.fed.us/r1 /gallatin) for information.

The roadside, 18-site Canyon Campground in Yankee Jim Canyon, 16 miles from Yellowstone, is waterless but does have picnic tables, fire rings and an accessible toilet. Open year-round.

Mountain Sky Guest Ranch (☎ 406-333-4911, 800-548-3392; www.mtnsky.com; weekly rates $$$$$;), 30 miles from Yellowstone, is a professionally run ranch on the west flanks of the valley, 4.5 miles up Big Creek Rd. Activities include dawn horseback rides to catch the sunrise over Emigrant Peak, fishing, tennis, a pool, a sauna, a hot tub and good kids' programs. There's a one week minimum stay June to August.

For a cheaper option, the USFS operates the year-round **Big Creek Cabin** (☎ reservations 406-222-1892; cabin $$). The cabin sleeps 10 and is set a half-mile from the ranch in the Gallatin National Forest. There's also **Mill Creek Cabin** (cabin $), which sleeps four, on the east side of the valley, 12 miles up E Mill Creek Rd, near Snowbank Campground. It has an electric stove and lights but no mattresses. Reserve either at **www.recreation .gov** (☎ 877-444-6777).

The **Paradise Valley Pop Stand** (☎ 406-222-2006; mains $; 6am-9pm, closed Mon), 2.5 miles south of Livingston, is a 1950s-style joint serving up hand-dipped malts, burgers and homemade pie (with free coffee), the former created with locally made Wilcoxon's ice cream. After a few days in the park, you deserve it.

Grand Teton National Park

Leave it to a French-Canadian fur trapper to christen these majestic spires as colossal teats. True, the Tetons jut abruptly over the sunken valley, the granite fantasy of climbers everywhere. Sharp, steep and spectacular, they are a sight to behold. These glacier-carved, 12,000ft-plus summits lord it over hundreds of alpine lakes and fragrant forests trodden by bear, moose, grouse and marmot. For flatlanders, a look upward invites vertigo. But if you're a mountain enthusiast, you'll crave the challenges of this sublime and crazy terrain, and its crowning glory, the dagger-edged Grand (13,770ft).

Just south of Yellowstone National Park, Grand Teton National Park stretches 40 miles along the compact, 15-mile-wide range. Its western boundary merges with the Jedediah Smith Wilderness within Targhee National Forest. The Bridger-Teton National Forest sits east. The steep eastern flank overlooks Jackson Hole valley, where Jackson Lake catches the Snake River flowing south from its source in Yellowstone National Park. On the western side of the range, Idaho's Teton Valley features more gradual slopes.

You might notice that Grand Teton is a strange sort of park. Trophy homes and ranches dot the landscape, a major airport sits within its borders, open elk-hunting season comes in fall and powerboats buzz its main lake, Jackson Lake, which is dammed. These unsightly concessions helped make the park's 1950 expansion possible.

While the park is dwarfed by Yellowstone, it offers visitors a more immediate intimacy with the landscape. Hikers, climbers, boaters, anglers and other outdoor enthusiasts will find plenty to do. For lovers of alpine scenery, the Tetons' visual impact far exceeds Yellowstone's. Whichever trails you wander, the Tetons' spires will exercise a magnetic attraction on your gaze.

Though not strictly part of Grand Teton National Park, John D Rockefeller Jr Memorial Parkway is administrated by the park, so it is listed in this section.

HIGHLIGHTS

- Hiking and huckleberry hunting in the wilds around **Two Ocean Lake** (p221)
- Climbing to the coveted summit of the **Grand Teton** (p231) with a local outfitter
- Exploring the islands and inlets of **String and Leigh Lakes** (p233) in a canoe
- Pedaling past pronghorn on the backroads of historic **Mormon Row** (p229)
- Floating **Snake River** (p233) at sunset in search of moose

FAST FACTS

- **Area** 484 sq miles
- **Highest elevation** 13,770ft
- **Average high/low January temperature** 26°F/1°F
- **Average high/low July temperature** 80°F/41°F

When You Arrive

To drive on Teton Park Rd, park entrance permits are required. They are valid for seven days for entry into both Grand Teton and Yellowstone National Parks; the fee is $25 per vehicle, $20 per motorcyclist and $12 for cyclists or hikers on foot. Winter day use costs $5. An annual pass to both parks costs $50. For details of other regional park passes, see p27.

There is no charge to transit the park on Hwy 26/89/191 from Jackson to Moran and out the east entrance to the Togwotee Pass. This area encompasses the access road to Jackson Hole Airport.

Visitors receive a free orientation map and copy of the park newspaper, *Teewinot*, which details the extensive program of ranger-led activities, road closures and park news.

Orientation

The park begins 4.5 miles north of Jackson. Three main roads lead to the park: US 26/89/191 from Jackson to the south, US 26/287 from Dubois to the east and US 89/191/287 from Yellowstone National Park to the north.

The least-used entry is the very rough gravel Grassy Lake Rd from Ashton, Idaho, to Flagg Ranch in the Rockefeller Memorial Parkway. This route is not recommended for RVs. There is no entry station along this road, so you will eventually find yourself in the park for free, though there is an entry station on the way north into Yellowstone Park.

Entrance Stations

The park has three entrance stations: one at Moose (south) on Teton Park Rd west of Moose Junction, another 3 miles inside the park at Moran (east) on US 89/191/287 north of Moran Junction and a third (southwest) a mile or so north of Teton Village on the Moose-Wilson road.

Main Regions

Jackson Lake dominates the northern half of the park with the Tetons to the west. The popular central Teton peaks, ringed by alpine lakes, are concentrated in the southwest. The most remote and least-visited area of the park is the northwest region, accessible only by multiday backpacking. This is the Tetons' prime grizzly habitat, although sightings have extended south through other parts of the park.

Before crossing into Idaho, the Snake River winds through flat glacial deposits on the south side of the park. The quieter, less-visited east side is bordered by the forested hills of the Bridger-Teton National Forest and the remote trails of the Teton Wilderness.

Major Roads

The main north–south route through the park is US 26/89/191, contiguous with the east bank of the Snake River between Jackson and Moran Junction. At Moran Junction US 89/191 joins US 287 heading north along Jackson Lake to

GRAND TETON NATIONAL PARK

DITCH THE CROWDS

Parking lots at popular trailheads and areas such as Jenny Lake, String Lake, Lupine Meadows and Granite Canyon are often packed before 11am. The Death Canyon Trailhead parking stays full since overnight backpackers leave cars for multiple days. Cascade Canyon hums with day-trippers to Solitude Lake in August. Get an alpine start on your hike (leave before most of your neighbors think of breakfast) to beat the crowds.

Jenny Lake Campground is perennially full, and Signal Mountain Campground fills up early in the day. You can avoid the campground crowds by choosing less popular campgrounds like Lizard Creek or Gros Ventre. Two Ocean and Emma Matilda Lakes, in the northeast section of the park, offer excellent hiking without the crowds.

Grand Teton National Park

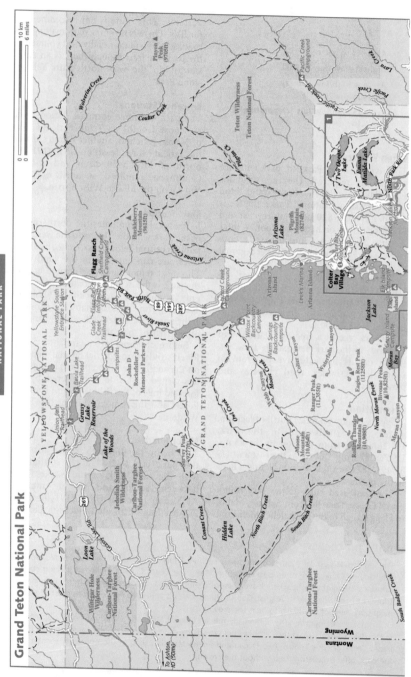

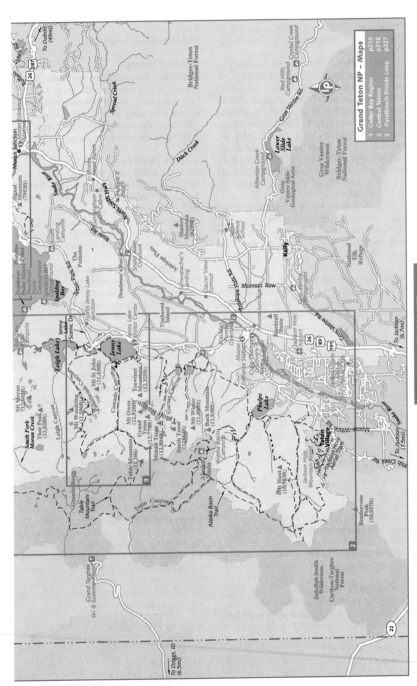

Grand Teton NP – Maps
1	Colter Bay Region	p215
2	Central Tetons	p218
3	Paintbrush Divide Loop	p227

the Rockefeller Memorial Parkway; US 26 joins US 287 heading east to Dubois via Togwotee Pass.

Teton Park Rd links Moose Junction to Jackson Lake Junction and US 89/191/287 via Jenny and Jackson Lakes. The 5-mile Jenny Lake Scenic Drive connects North Jenny Lake and South Jenny Lake Junctions; the road is two-way to Jenny Lake Lodge and one-way south of it. Gros Ventre Rd heads east from US 26/89/191 at the south end of the park to Kelly and out of the park into the Gros Ventre Valley. Antelope Flats Rd is 1 mile north of Moose Junction, east of US 26/89/191.

Moose-Wilson Rd is a partially paved route (its southernmost 3 miles are gravel) that connects Teton Village to Moose. RVs and trailers are not allowed on this road inside the park.

Visitor Service Hubs

Colter Bay hosts the highest concentration of visitor services, with a visitor center, gas station, grocery store, restaurants, laundromat, showers, campground, RV park and marina.

Further south, Jackson Lake Lodge has shops and restaurants. Down Teton Park Rd, Signal Mountain offers accommodations, a restaurant, a gas station and grocery store.

Moose is the national park's southern hub, with a new visitor center, a gas station, accommodations, restaurants, groceries and equipment rental.

Information

Three park concessionaires operate various accommodations, restaurants, marinas and activities:

Dornan's (☎ 307-733-2522; www.dornans.com)
Grand Teton Lodge Company (GTLC; ☎ 307-543-3100, 800-628-9988; www.gtlc.com)
Signal Mountain Lodge (☎ 307-543-2831; www .signalmtnlodge.com)

BOOKSTORES

Grand Teton Natural History Association
(☎ 307-739-3403) This nonprofit organization sells books and maps at all park visitor centers.

INTERNET ACCESS

Dornan's (☎ 307-733-2522; www.dornans.com; Moose Village; per hr $5) Provides internet access.

POST

Post office (Moose Village)

TOURIST OFFICES

Jackson Hole & Greater Yellowstone Visitor Center
(☎ 307-733-3316; www.jacksonholechamber.com; 532 N Cache St, Jackson; ☾ 8am-7pm summer, 8am-5pm winter) Although always willing to help, it's common for volunteer staffers, many of whom aren't locals, to point you to a stack of brochures or a phone book with your queries.

VISITOR CENTERS

Colter Bay Visitor Center (☎ 307-739-3594; ☾ 8am-5pm early May–mid-May, 8am-7pm Jun–early Sep, 8am-5pm Sep–early Oct) On US 89/191/287, 6 miles north of Jackson Lake Lodge. Issues backcountry permits and offers crafts demonstrations and tours of its Indian Arts Museum (p214). Newcomers can get their bearings at 'Teton Highlights,' a daily 30-minute ranger talk at 11am at the auditorium.

Craig Thomas Discovery & Visitor Center (☎ 307-739-3300; ☾ 8am-5pm year-round, 8am-7pm peak summer season, closed Christmas day) Inaugurated in 2007 to replace the Moose Visitor Center, this $21-million center on Teton Park Rd, half a mile west of Moose Junction, is open year-round. Backcountry, climbing and boating permits are available here, as is information on weather, road and avalanche conditions. Excellent interactive displays include working models that demonstrate glacial movement and animal migration. An auditorium is slated to be added.

Flagg Ranch Information Station (☎ 307-543-2327; ☾ 9am-4pm Jun–early Sep, closed for lunch) Provides park information, rest rooms and a small bookstore. Located 2.5 miles from Yellowstone's South Entrance.

Grand Teton National Park Headquarters (☎ 307-739-3600; www.nps.gov/grte; Box 170, Moose, WY 83012) Shares the building with the Craig Thomas Discovery & Visitor Center. For general visitor information call ☎ 307-739-3300. For weather information contact the 24-hour recorded message at ☎ 317-739-3611.

Jenny Lake Visitor Center (☎ 307-739-3343; ☾ 8am-4:30pm early May–early Jun, 8am-7pm Jun–early Sep, 8am-4:30pm Sep–early May) On Teton Park Rd, 8 miles north of Moose Junction. Facilities include a store, lockers, geology exhibits, a relief model, rest rooms and telephones. With in-depth information on backpacking and trails, it's also the meeting place for guided walks and talks, with activity schedules posted.

RANGER STATIONS/BACKCOUNTRY OFFICES

There are backcountry offices at **Colter Bay Visitor Center** (☎ 307-739-3595) and **Craig Thomas Discovery & Visitor Center** (☎ 307-739-3309). **Jenny**

GRAND TETON NATIONAL PARK IN...

Two Days

Start the day with a satisfying breakfast burrito at **Signal Mountain Lodge** (p239). At the adjacent marina, take a half-day on **Jackson Lake** (p232) with an expert guide for your best chance at snagging a monster trout.

Pop your tent at **Jenny Lake Campground** (p237). Gather around the camp circle for a ranger-led twilight talk before bedding down under the stars.

The next day, get an early start. Ride the ferry to the Cascade Canyon Trailhead and get upward bound! The hike to **Lake Solitude** (p223) is stunning but demanding.

Four Days

Follow the two-day itinerary. On your third day start slowly by browsing the exhibits at the new **Craig Thomas Discovery & Visitor Center** (opposite).

Restless yet? Roll through the sagebrush with fat tires on the **Snake River Rd** (p229) ride, keeping an eye out for eagles, osprey and bison. The vintage Old West murals at Jackson Lake Lodge's **Mural Room** (p238) stir up a romantic backdrop for dinner for two.

The windswept walk up the peninsula to **Hermitage Point** (p221) is the perfect way to cap a visit. For more ideas, see the Itineraries chapter (p31).

Lake Ranger Station (☎ 307-739-3343; ☼ summer only) also offers backcountry permits and climbing information.

Park Policies & Regulations

BACKCOUNTRY PERMITS

Backcountry permits are required for all overnight backcountry trips in Grand Teton. Permits are free and given on a first come, first served basis, 24 hours in advance, from the backcountry offices at Craig Thomas and Colter Bay Visitor Centers or Jenny Lake Ranger Station. For best results, apply early in the morning the day before your intended departure. A notice board at Craig Thomas Discovery & Visitor Center indicates which backcountry sites are full that day.

About a third of the backcountry sites can be reserved from January 1 to May 15 by mail (Grand Teton National Park, PO Box 170, Moose, WY 83012), fax (☎ 307-739-3438) or in person at Craig Thomas Discovery & Visitor Center, for a nonrefundable $25 fee.

Backcountry camping is restricted to camping zones. Hikers (with backcountry permits) can choose their own sites inside many of these areas, but in the most heavily used zones all sites are designated (indicated by marker posts). Fires are prohibited, except at some lakeshore sites, so bring a camp stove. Campsites must be at least 200ft from waterways.

BOATING

All private craft must obtain a permit, which costs $20/40 per week/year for motorized and $10/20 for nonmotorized craft (rafts, canoes or kayaks). The Craig Thomas and Colter Bay Visitor Centers and Buffalo Fork Ranger Station at Moran Junction issue permits. Display yours on the port (left) side of the vessel at the rear. Permits for Yellowstone are good for Grand Teton (and vice versa) but must be registered at either Moose or Colter Bay Visitor Centers.

Motorized craft (maximum 7.5 horsepower) are allowed only on Jackson, Phelps and Jenny Lakes. On Jenny Lake, crafts with over 10 horsepower (HP) are prohibited. Hand-propelled nonmotorized craft are permitted on Jackson, Two Ocean, Emma Matilda, Bearpaw, Leigh, String, Jenny, Bradley, Taggart and Phelps Lakes, as well as the Snake River 1000ft below Jackson Dam. Sailboats, water skis and sailboards are permitted only on Jackson Lake. Jet skis are not allowed in the park.

Floating is prohibited within 1000ft of Jackson Lake Dam. Only hand-powered rafts, canoes and kayaks are allowed on the Snake River. Watercraft are forbidden on other rivers.

On Jackson Lake, fires are forbidden along the east shore from Spalding Bay to Lizard Creek and otherwise permitted only below the high-water mark.

GRAND TETON NATIONAL PARK

See the park's *Boating* and *Floating the Snake River* brochures.

FISHING

Anglers must carry a valid Wyoming fishing license. Fishing licenses are issued at Moose Village store, Signal Mountain Lodge and Colter Bay Marina. Jackson Lake is closed to fishing in October. The Snake, Buffalo Fork and Gros Ventre Rivers are closed November 1 to March 31. In general anglers are limited to six trout per day, with varying size limitations. Get a copy of the park's fishing brochure for details.

Dangers & Annoyances

Though people are the greater nuisance, black bears and a growing population of grizzlies live in the park. For advice on encounters (and their prevention) see p278.

Mid-October to early December is elk-hunting season in areas east of US 26/89/191, west of US 26/89/191 along the Snake River between Moose and Moran Junctions, and the Rockefeller Memorial Parkway. If you must venture into these areas during hunting season, exercise caution: don a bright orange vest and avoid elk-like behavior.

The National Park Service (NPS) *Elk Ecology & Management* pamphlet offers more details and a map.

Getting Around

DRIVING

The speed limit on US 26/89/191 is 55mph; elsewhere it's generally 45mph. Gas stations are open year-round at Moose (24 hours, credit card only 8pm to 8am) and Flagg Ranch Resort, and summers only at Colter Bay, Signal Mountain and Jackson Lodge.

ORGANIZED TOURS

GTLC runs half-day tours of Grand Teton (adult/child 3–11 $5/18), full-day tours of Yellowstone ($65/40) and a tour combining both parks ($90/50) daily from Jackson Lake Lodge (p237). Make arrangements at the hotel activities desk.

Gray Line runs all-day tours from Jackson to Grand Teton National Park ($80) or Yellowstone ($95), park entry not included.

Flagg Ranch (☎ 800-443-2311; www.flaggranch.com) calls its full-day tours of Teton (adult/child $170/150) or Yellowstone ($190/170) 'wild-life safaris.' Entrance fee for the parks is not included. Also see wildlife-viewing tours, p267.

PUBLIC TRANSPORTATION

Grand Teton Lodge Company (GTLC; ☎ 800-628-9988; www.gtlc.com) operates several buses a day in summer between Jackson, Jenny Lake Lodge, Jackson Lake Lodge and Colter Bay. The service is free for guests but no longer available to the public.

Gray Line (☎ 800-443-6133; www.graylinejh.com) provides airport shuttles to Jackson (one way/round-trip $15/28).

SIGHTS

COLTER BAY REGION

The road south from Yellowstone drops off the Yellowstone plateau at the end of the Rockefeller Parkway where a startling view of the Tetons soaring above Jackson Lake comes into play. Past Lizard Creek Campground several beaches tucked into nooks offer some of the park's best picnic areas.

Jackson Lake is a natural glacial lake that has been dammed, so water levels fluctuate, dropping considerably toward the end of the summer. Mt Moran (12,605ft), named after landscape painter Thomas Moran, dominates the north end of the park. After Moran first traveled this way with Hayden's geological survey in 1871 his grand depictions forever became synonymous with the area.

Two Ocean and Emma Matilda Lakes sit east of Jackson Lake, tucked into the hills. Visitor services are concentrated at Colter Bay Village.

Colter Bay

At Colter Bay Visitor Center, the **Indian Arts Museum** (admission free; ☾ 8am-5pm May, 8am-8pm Jun-early Sep, 8am-5pm Sep) displays artifacts from the collection of David T Vernon, including beautiful beadwork, bags and photographs. It's well worth browsing; pick up a spiral-bound museum guide for a self-guided tour, or take the daily guided tour offered at 9am and 4pm. The visitor center offers books on Native American history and lore. There are frequent craft demonstrations, and videos are shown all day on subjects ranging from wildlife to Native American art.

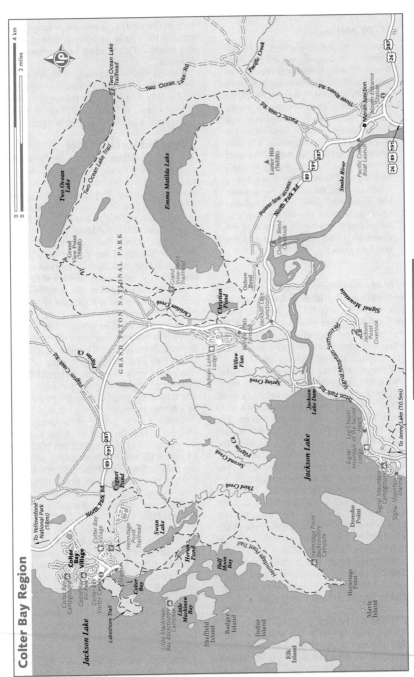

Colter Bay Region

TETON NAMES

Impressions are everything... French Canadian fur trappers named the three Tetons – South, Middle and Grand – 'les Trois Tetons' (the three breasts), most likely in a lonely moment of Western wandering and reflection. Trapper Osborne Russell claimed their Shoshone moniker was 'Hoary Headed Fathers.' Teewinot means 'Many Pinnacles' in Shoshone – it now describes the range as well as Teewinot Mountain. The Snake River gets its name from the local Shoshone, or Snake, Native American tribe, though the name Snake was mistakenly given to the Shoshone when the weaving sign for the Shoshone (who called themselves the people of the woven grass huts) was confused with the sign for a snake.

South of the visitor center is the marina and trailhead for **hikes** to Swan Lake and Hermitage Point (p221). A popular picnic and **swimming area** sits just north of the visitor center, though there's countless other secluded swimming and sunbathing spots dotted around Jackson Lake.

For a nice evening or early morning stroll, try the 45-minute **Lakeshore Trail**, which traces a figure eight across a causeway onto a small island. Take the forest trail that dips onto the beach or just walk along the shore. The trail starts on a paved road beside Colter Bay Marina, or you can access it from the amphitheater next to the visitor center. Finish the hike at the amphitheater by 7pm or 9pm to catch the evening ranger talk.

Grand Teton Lodge Company (GTLC; ☎ 307-543-3111) offers guided fishing trips on Jackson Lake for $65 per hour for three people, plus full-day, guided fly-fishing trips ($425 for two people). Regular fishing boats depart from Colter Bay Marina. GTLC also runs scenic floats (adult/child 6–11 from $49/29), as well as lunch and dinner trips – make bookings at the activity desks in Colter Bay or Jackson Lake Lodge.

RANGER ACTIVITIES

An entertaining way to see how forest fires and glaciers sculpted the landscape is to take the **Fire & Ice boat cruise** (☎ 307-543-2811; adult/child 3–11 $21/10) on Jackson Lake. As long as the weather is good, this ranger-led activity runs daily at 1:30pm from Colter Bay Marina. Tickets must be purchased in advance.

Ask at the visitor center about early morning bird-watching walks. Rangers also lead a daily morning walk from Colter Bay Visitor Center to Swan Lake (3 miles, three hours) and a lakeside stroll at 4:30pm.

Around Jackson Lake Lodge

The elegant Jackson Lake Lodge is worth a stop, if only to gape at the stupendous views through its 60ft-tall windows. In cold weather the cozy fireplaces in the upper lobby are blazing. In summer you can drink in fine Teton views and a cold Snake River Lager while sitting outdoors.

Rangers answer questions on the back deck of Jackson Lake Lodge daily from 6:30pm to 8pm, and there is a free talk on the history of the lodge every Sunday at 8pm.

The willow flats below the hotel balcony are a top spot to catch a glimpse of moose, which flock to willow as a critical food source, particularly in winter. The nearby **Willow Flats turnout** offers views of Mt Moran, Bivouac Peak, Rolling Thunder Mountain, Eagles Rest Peak and Ranger Peak.

A short walk from the lodge, **Christian Pond** is a good place to spot riparian birdlife. The trail to the pond crosses the main road by a bridge just south of the lodge.

About a mile north of Jackson Lake Lodge a rough dirt road branches east off the main road to a trailhead, from which it's a 1 mile walk one way (with a steep climb at the end) to **Grand View Point** (7586ft), which offers fine views of both the Tetons and Two Ocean Lake. You can also visit the viewpoint as part of the Two Ocean Lake hike (p221).

One of the most famous scenic spots for wildlife-watching is **Oxbow Bend**, 2 miles east of Jackson Lake Junction, with the reflection of Mt Moran as a stunning backdrop. Early morning and dusk are the best times to spot moose, elk, sandhill cranes, ospreys, bald eagles, trumpeter swans, Canada geese, blue herons and white pelicans. The oxbow was created as the river's faster water eroded the outer bank while the slower inner flow deposited sediment.

Heading south on Teton Park Rd, you'll find interpretive displays along the west shoulder near **Jackson Lake Dam**. Built in 1916, the dam raises the lake level by 39ft and was paid for by Idaho farmers who still own the irrigation rights to the top 39ft of water. The dam was reinforced between 1986 and 1989 to withstand earthquakes.

South of here is the **Log Chapel of the Sacred Heart**, a pleasant picnic area.

Signal Mountain Summit Road

This 5-mile paved road (no RVs) east of Teton Park Rd winds up to the top of **Signal Mountain** for dramatic panoramas from 800ft above Jackson Hole's valley floor. Below, the Snake River, the valley's only drainage, runs a twisted course through cottonwood and spruce. Abandoned dry channels demonstrate the changing landscape.

Views are superb at sunrise, but the best vistas are actually from three-quarters of the way up at **Jackson Point Overlook**, a short walk south from a parking area. William Jackson took a famous photograph from this point in 1878, when preparing a single image could take a full hour, using heavy glass plates and a portable studio.

The mountain's name dates from 1891, when Robert Ray Hamilton was reported lost on a hunting trip. Search parties lit a fire atop Signal Mountain after he was found a week later, floating in Jackson Lake. A 6-mile round-trip hiking trail leads to the summit from Signal Mountain Campground, through groves of scrumptious huckleberries.

In winter Signal Mountain Rd offers a great Nordic skiing route, with stunning views and a fun 5-mile downhill return run. To get to the turnoff, ski 1 mile south from Signal Mountain along a snowmobiling trail.

CENTRAL TETONS

South of Signal Mountain, Teton Park Rd passes The Potholes, sagebrush flats pockmarked with craterlike depressions called kettles. The kettles were formed slowly by blocks of orphaned glacial ice that were stranded under the soil, left by receding glaciers. Just south is the Mt Moran turnout.

Jenny Lake Scenic Drive

Seven miles south of Signal Mountain, the Jenny Lake Scenic Dr branches west to offer the park's most picturesque drive.

The **Cathedral Group turnout** boasts views of the central Teton spires, known as the Cathedral Group. Interpretive boards illustrate the tectonic slippage visible at the foot of Rockchuck Peak, named for its resident yellow-bellied marmots. **String Lake** is the most popular picnic spot, with dramatic views of the north face of Teewinot Mountain and Grand Teton from sandy beaches along its east side. The road becomes one way beyond String Lake, just before exclusive Jenny Lake Lodge.

Perched on the lake's glacial moraine, **Jenny Lake Overview** offers good views of the Tetons, tall Ribbon Cascade to the right of Cascade Canyon, and shuttle boats headed for Inspiration Point. Be careful not to miss the turnout, as you can't back up on this one-way road.

Jenny Lake

The scenic heart of the Grand Tetons and the epicenter of Teton's crowds, Jenny Lake was named for the Shoshone wife of early guide and mountain man Beaver Dick Leigh. Jenny died of smallpox in 1876 along with her children.

The visitor center (p212) is worth a visit for its geological displays and 3D map of Jackson Hole. The cabin was once in a different location as the Crandall photo studio.

From the visitor center a network of trails leads clockwise around the lake for 2.5 miles to Hidden Falls and then continues

GRAND TETON NATIONAL PARK

WHAT WILDNESS MEANS *Jack Turner*

If the parks and wilderness areas must preserve anything, even at the cost of unpopularity, it must be this: the possibility of contact with wild forms of beings. This requires two things. First, we must preserve those other beings as freely existing, self-organizing nations in their own right. Second, we must preserve true contact with them; simple, unmediated contact, contact with our bodies, or senses, contact where what we experience is their presence. We evolved together. In many ways, we are wired, intellectually and emotionally, for one another's presence, and it would be a tragedy if in the future we were to find this age-old reciprocity had vanished.

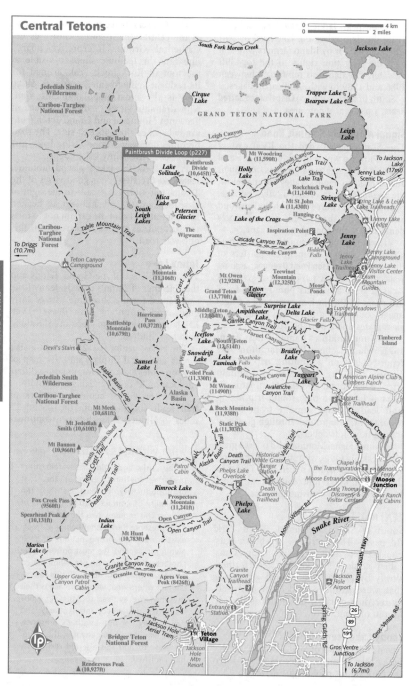

Central Tetons

for a short uphill run to fine views at **Inspiration Point**. Once you're here, it's worth continuing up **Cascade Canyon** for as long as you can, as you've already sacked most of the hard climb. From here you can return the way you came or continue clockwise to the String Lake Trailhead to make a 6-mile circle around the lake. If you're on the Jenny Lake Trail in the early morning or late afternoon, detour approximately 15 minutes (about 0.5 miles) from the visitor center to **Moose Ponds** for a good chance of spotting moose.

Alternatively, **Jenny Lake Boating** (☎ 307-734-9227; www.jennylakeboating.com) runs **shuttles** (adult/child 7-12 round-trip $9/5, one way $5/4; ☺ 8am-6pm Jun-late Sep) across Jenny Lake between the east-shore boat dock near Jenny Lake Visitor Center and the west shore boat dock near Hidden Falls, offering quick (12-minute) access to Inspiration Point and the Cascade Canyon Trail. Shuttles run every 15 minutes, but expect long waits for return shuttles between 4pm and 6pm.

Rangers lead hikes (2 miles, 2½ hours) from Jenny Lake Visitor Center at 8:30am to Inspiration Point via the Jenny Lake ferry. Numbers are limited to 25, and places are first come, first serve; arrive at the visitor center by 8am to secure a spot.

Canoes, kayaks and boats with motors less than 8HP are allowed on Jenny Lake. The put-in is by the east-shore boat dock and is accessed by a separate road that branches off the Lupine Meadows Trailhead road. Jenny Lake Boating rents kayaks and canoes ($12/60 per hour/day). They also offer hour-long scenic Jenny Lake cruises ($14/7) throughout the day. Inquire at the dock or call to reserve.

Jenny Lake also offers good **fishing** and is stocked with lake, brown, brook and Snake River cutthroat trout.

South of Jenny Lake

Just south of Jenny Lake, Teton Park Rd passes the turnoff to the Lupine Meadows Trailhead, for hikes to Surprise Lake and Garnet Canyon. On the east side of the road watch for **Timbered Island**, an enclave of forested glacial soils stacked atop poorly drained sedimentary soils.

Two miles south of here, Teton Glacier turnout offers some of the best views of **Teton Glacier**, the largest in the park. The Taggart Lake Trailhead is 1.5 miles further on.

A short trail and the homestead cabin of William Menor sit half a mile north of Moose Village, off a paved road. Menor was alone on the west bank of the Snake River for 10 years, building a pontoon raft that provided a vital crossing for mule teams and riders who hunted, picked mushrooms and berries, and cut lumber on the Teton side. In 1910 he sold the property to entrepreneur Maude Noble, who started charging a then-brazen $1 to locals and $2 for those with out-of-state plates to cross. Today you can cross in a replica of **Menor's Ferry** (early July to August). Old photographs, restored buggies and the original settlers' wagon offer insight into the lives of early settlers. Stop by the obligatory old-fashioned period **store** (☺ 9am-4:30pm).

The nearby **Chapel of the Transfiguration** (1924) has aspen pews and views of the Tetons through the altar window. In summer Episcopal services are held on Sundays.

Just beyond is Moose Entrance Station and the new **Craig Thomas Discovery & Visitor Center** (p212), offering interpretive displays and the largest selection of books in the park. The park's southern hub, Moose also offers accommodations, restaurants and shops, and serves as the jumping-off point for many park activities. It also serves as the center for wintertime park activity.

THE EASTERN SLOPES

Highway 26/89/191 traverses the park's eastern flank for about 25 miles from the Moran Junction to the park's southern gate past sagebrush flats and the occasional ranch – always with the Tetons' sharp spires diverting your gaze westward. The hardscrabble lives of Jackson Hole's early homesteaders are reflected in the valley's characteristic lodgepole buck and pole fences.

GRAND TETON NATIONAL PARK

DIAL-A-TOUR

The mass return of the holster to the west doesn't herald gunfights. Grand Teton is tapping into technology addictions by offering **cell-phone tours**. The two- to three-minute messages cover subjects such as park history, geology and the homesteading lore of Menor's Ferry. There's no charge except for the minutes used. Look for the tour map with phone number at any visitor center or at Menor's Ferry.

Moran to Blacktail Butte

Ranchers Pierce and Margaret Cunningham, an early major supporter of Grand Teton National Park, cultivated a cattle ranch at **Cunningham Cabin** in 1890, 6 miles south of Moran Junction. The property is one of the best surviving examples of a homestead cabin; a short trail elucidates local homesteading.

Four miles south, the **Snake River Overlook** offers good panoramas of the Tetons and opportunities for wildlife-watching, though forest growth means the photo ops aren't quite as good as when Ansel Adams immortalized the shot.

A better place for photos is **Schwabacher's Landing**, a popular rafting put-in 4 miles further south. The jagged Tetons reflected in the meandering river ranks as some of the park's most sublime scenery. Access the landing via a short dirt road.

East of Blacktail Butte, an unpaved road great for biking (p229) connects Antelope Flats Rd to the north with Gros Ventre Rd to the south (when not washed out). Its scenic collection of ranches with pioneer barns and cabins is known as **Mormon Row**, where 10 settlers took up residence in the 1890s. A resident bison herd, gorgeous post-dawn light and superb Teton views make this area exceptionally popular with photographers. Two barns sit north of the junction and two south, including one that has evolved into a photogenic state of near-collapse.

TOP FIVE SPOTS TO SPY WILDLIFE

Hunker down at dusk or dawn with a spotting scope or binoculars to feast your eyes at the following sites:

■ **Oxbow Bend** (p216) A scenic river bend populated with moose, elk, sandhill cranes, ospreys, bald eagles, trumpeter swans, Canada geese, blue herons, white pelicans and – oh, yeah – abundant mosquitoes.

■ **Willow Flats** (p216) A freshwater marsh home to birds, moose, elk and beavers.

■ **Blacktail Ponds** (p230) Features ospreys, eagles and moose.

■ **Antelope Flats** (p229) Bison and pronghorns at home on the range.

■ **Swan Lake** (p216) The spot to spot beavers, trumpeter swans and geese.

Gros Ventre Rd leads east to the Gros Ventre Slide (p252).

JOHN D ROCKEFELLER JR MEMORIAL PARKWAY

This NPS-managed parkway is a 7.5-mile corridor linking Yellowstone and Grand Teton National Parks. Congress recognized Rockefeller's contribution to the creation of Grand Teton National Park by designating this 24,000-acre parkway in his honor in 1972. Here, the Tetons taper to a gentle slope, and rocks from volcanic flows in Yellowstone line the Snake River. A transitional zone between the two national parks, the area combines characteristics of both, though it's less spectacular than either. Activities focus around historic Flagg Ranch, which was established as a US Cavalry post in 1872.

North–south US 89/191/287 is the main road through the parkway. The turnoff to Flagg Ranch Rd is 2 miles south of Yellowstone's South Entrance Station and 15 miles north of Colter Bay Village. The turnoff to Grassy Lake Rd, which leads west to Ashton, Idaho, is just north of Flagg Ranch.

The **Flagg Ranch Information Station** (☎ 307-543-2401; ☺ 9am-6pm Jun-Sep) is near the Grassy Lake Rd turnoff. **Flagg Ranch Resort** (☎ 307-543-2861, 800-443-2311; www.flaggranch.com) offers parkway accommodations, dining, gas and activities. Once a popular winter launch pad into Yellowstone National Park, the resort now closes in winter since stricter snowmobiling regulations have been put in place. Winter trails can still be accessed here.

No permits are required for backcountry camping in the parkway, though campers must keep a minimum of 1 mile from roads and 100ft from water sources. Fires are generally allowed, but check current regulations at the information station. No bikes or pets are permitted on trails.

Grassy Lake Road

The 52-mile, east–west Grassy Lake Rd links US 89/191/287 to US 20 at Ashton, Idaho, offering an infrequently used 'back way' into the national parks. The road follows an old Native American trade and hunting route. Numerous lakes and streams – and endless fishing, hiking and camping options – lie hidden in the Jedediah Smith Wilderness south of Grassy Lake Rd and in the Winegar Hole Wilderness north of it. Grassy Lake Rd is also a good mountain-biking route.

Shortly after crossing the Polecat Creek Bridge, the pavement ends and the graded gravel road parallels the north bank of the Snake River. Camping along this corridor is restricted to designated sites, which are popular with anglers, hunters and folks headed west along the rough Reclamation Rd (USFS Rd 261) to the Cascade Corner in Yellowstone's lush Bechler region.

The road is open until snow conditions warrant its closure in late fall, when snowmobiles take over.

HIKING

The Tetons' extreme verticality means the hikes in this park follow a different standard; with the steep terrain, flat and easy rambles are few. The easy–moderate day hikes following are suitable for families and most walkers. Hikers should adjust the distance they walk to their satisfaction. For more information on hike classifications, see p40.

Paved wheelchair accessible trails include the Jenny Lake shoreline, String Lake shoreline and Colter Bay Lakeshore Trail (next to the marina) and the southern edge of Jackson Lake Dam.

DAY HIKES
Colter Bay Region
Bids, animals and wildflowers all feature in the popular section of the park.

HERMITAGE POINT

Duration 4 hours (shorter loop 1¾ hours)
Distance 9.2 miles (shorter loop 3 miles)
Difficulty easy–moderate
Elevation Change negligible
Start/Finish Hermitage Point Trailhead (Map p215)
Nearest Town/Junction Colter Bay Village
Summary A wild and windswept point with outstanding views of the multi-fanged Mt Moran.

From the Colter Bay Visitor Center follow the parking lot to the southern end. At first

the trail's signage may seem a little unclear, but throughout the hike the junctions are well marked. The trail itself starts by a sign that reads 'Foot Trail Only, No Road.' The trail follows a former road for less than 10 minutes, turns right, and then turns right again to climb up to the **Jackson Lake Overlook**.

The trail descends and passes along the left (eastern) side of lily-filled **Heron Pond**, where you can look for moose, trumpeter swans and cranes. It branches right then right again for 2.2 miles to the cairn marking **Hermitage Point** (4.4 miles, 1¾ hours).

This lesser-hiked leg is densely forested and without views. Be sure to announce your presence approaching blind corners in case of bears. The return leg (4.8 miles, two hours) loops back, taking a right to **Third Creek** and then a left past **Swan Lake**. Keep a watchful eye out for beavers munching on lily pads.

If you don't have the time to tackle the entire Hermitage Point loop, then turn left at the southeast end of Heron Pond to Swan Lake and back for a 3-mile, 1¾-hour loop, which is commonly used by horseback riders and ideal for families with small children.

It's also an easy and enjoyable destination for overnight backpacking. Reserve ahead backcountry campsite No 9 at Hermitage Point.

TWO OCEAN LAKE & GRAND VIEW POINT

Duration 3½ hours
Distance 6.4 miles
Difficulty easy–moderate
Elevation Change 400ft
Start/Finish Two Ocean Lake Trailhead (Map p215)
Nearest Town/Junction Jackson Lake Junction
Summary On this unique hike views take a backseat to the beauty of Two Ocean Lake and the lush surrounding forest.

The park's wildflowers peak in July, when abundant huckleberries and chokeberries make the area prime black bear territory. The tall grass makes long trousers a good idea. Set out by 8am to take advantage of a calm lake and great bird-watching opportunities.

To reach the trailhead turn north onto the smooth, gravel Pacific Creek Rd around 1 mile west of Moran Junction. After 2 miles turn left onto the rougher Two Ocean Lake Rd and follow it for 2.5 miles to the parking area.

Follow a clear trail counterclockwise around **Two Ocean Lake** through lovely meadows with aspens and Teton views. At the west end of the lake (1¼ hours from the trailhead) the trail branches off to the right; at the next junction, turn left to continue around the lake. Another option is to take the right branch and then a left branch for 1.3 miles uphill to **Grand View Point** (7586ft).

The second hill boasts the best views of Mt Moran, as well as Two Ocean and Emma Matilda Lakes. Return to the main lake trail via the same route.

From the lake junction take a right turn and continue around Two Ocean Lake. Sometimes the trail follows the lakeshore and sometimes it's through conifer forest and open meadow. It's about an hour to the trailhead.

Central Tetons

There's something for everyone here: lakes, waterfalls, glaciers, canyons and viewpoints.

LEIGH & BEARPAW LAKES

Duration 3½ hours
Distance 7.4 miles
Difficulty easy–moderate
Elevation Change negligible
Start/Finish Leigh Lake Trailhead (Map p218)
Nearest Town/Junction North Jenny Lake Junction
Summary A fun, flat family outing skirting forest-clad, crystal-clear swimming holes.

The Leigh Lake Trailhead is at the end of the side road off Jenny Lake Dr; don't confuse it with the String Lake Trailhead. Try to get an early start on this trail, as it's very popular, particularly with young families. Canoeing these lakes (with short portages) is an excellent option on a hot summer's day. Always keep track of your picnic food, since bears are frequently spotted here.

The trail quickly joins **String Lake**. After around 20 minutes a trail branches left across the outlet to Paintbrush Canyon (and a possible loop of String Lake). Instead, take the right branch and then turn right again to **Leigh Lake**. You may see people carrying their canoes over this portage area.

As you continue north along Leigh Lake, your surroundings open up to fine views of Mt Moran and its Falling Ice and Skillet Glaciers. The dark central stripes in both Mt Moran and Middle Teton consist of 1.5-billion-year-old lava-injected rock called diabase, which extends 7 miles west into Idaho.

Continue past the lovely lakeside campsites 12A (group site), 12B and 12C, which make easy camping destinations for families with small children. Ten minutes further along the trail you'll pass a picturesque beach, with views of Mystic Island and, from left to right, Rockchuck Peak, Mt Woodring, Mt Moran and Bivouac Peak.

After an hour (about 2 miles) of Leigh Lake views, the trail heads into forest to a meadow junction; take the central path to the west side of **Bearpaw Lake** and campsites 17A and 17C. The trail then veers away from the lake for 0.5 miles to **Trapper Lake**. Before you descend too far on the trail back to Bearpaw Lake, watch for a faint path that veers off to the left. This drops through forest and over a log bridge to campsite 17B, looping back to join the earlier junction. Return to String Lake the way you came.

Several backcountry campsites are outstanding. On Leigh Lake the most popular sites are 12B and 12C – you'll need to reserve these well in advance. Remoter sites 13 and 15 are accessible by foot on an unmaintained trail that leads north from the bridge over Leigh Lake outlet. The nicest site at Bearpaw Lake is 17B, which has fine views of Rockchuck Peak. Site 17A is on the lakeshore below the path; 17C is more private but a bit uphill. Trapper Lake offers the quietest site (18A). These sites are among the few in Teton where campfires are allowed (in fire grates only).

LAKE SOLITUDE

Duration 6–7 hours
Distance 14.4 miles with boat shuttle, 18.4 miles without
Difficulty moderate–difficult
Elevation Change 2240ft
Start/Finish Jenny Lake Boat Shuttle (Map p218)
Nearest Town/Junction South Jenny Lake Junction
Summary This ultra-popular hike scales to a mountain lake via a gradual climb.

SURPRISE & AMPHITHEATER LAKES

Duration 5–6 hours
Distance 9.6 miles (10.2 miles with Glacier Overlook extension)
Difficulty difficult
Elevation Change 3000ft
Start/Finish Lupine Meadows Trailhead
Nearest Town/Junction South Jenny Lake Junction (Map p218)
Summary One of the park's oldest, this trail is a classic leg-burner. Expect company: great views and accessibility make it very popular.

Thanks to wide patronage, this rewarding trail (particularly its beginning) lacks the elixir of its moniker but still provides a rewarding challenge. Though a long hike with an elevation gain of 2240ft, it is not especially tough since the grade is quite gradual. Gear up for steep sections at the beginning near Inspiration Point and just before Solitude Lake. Moose and bear frequent the area.

Taking the boat shuttle will shave 4 miles off. The Cascade Canyon (west) dock meets a network of trails. Head left to pass **Hidden Falls** after 0.2 miles and ascend to **Inspiration Point** in another 0.5 miles. Climbers complete the scenery – Exum Guides uses this area for training. Soon afterward, the horse trail from String Lake joins from the right.

The Cascade Canyon Trail continues straight, past a lovely beach and a high cascade, with fine views. About two hours (4.5 miles) from the dock the valley splits. The left branch leads to South Fork and Hurricane Pass. Turn right and climb gently for 30 minutes to enter the **Cascade Camping Zone** (12 sites), which stretches for the next 30 minutes. From the zone's end it's 10 minutes up to the lake, past a small cascade and a hitch rail marking the end of the line for horses. It's about three hours (7.2 miles) from here back to the dock.

Rimmed by fir and pines and sporting ice until midsummer, **Lake Solitude** (9035ft) is a great spot to loll around (but probably not to swim). To the northeast, the diagonal slash leading up the hillside leads to **Paintbrush Divide**. Camping is prohibited at the lake.

Return to the boat dock the way you came. The terrain, shaded most of the afternoon, is all downhill, affording full views of Mt Owen and Grand Teton.

Even before cubicle fever existed, two 1920s businessmen built this trail. The route should be free of snow by late June. Bring plenty of water since none is available between the trailhead and the two lakes near the top of the climb.

There are three designated campsites at Surprise Lake for those who want to stay overnight, though due to heavy use, some areas are off-limits for regeneration.

The well-worn trail gently winds through pine forest until it mounts a shoulder and the ascent begins in earnest. A junction with the Taggart and Bradley Lakes Trail lies atop the shoulder, 1.7 miles (40 minutes) from the start. Keep right and tackle the series of switchbacks up the flank of **Disappointment Peak**. The route offers views over Taggart Lake and Jackson Hole. About 1½ hours (3 miles) from the trailhead there is a signed junction with the Garnet Canyon Trail (p224).

The switchbacks ease shortly before the lakes, and after 2¼ hours of solid climbing, you'll finally reach the inviting, gemstone waters of **Surprise Lake**. Set in a hollow beneath jagged white rocks and cliffs, it is a resplendent payoff for your efforts. The slightly bigger and starker **Amphitheater Lake** lies just 0.2 miles further along the trail.

SIDE TRIP: EXTENSION TO TETON GLACIER OVERLOOK

To reach the **Teton Glacier Overlook**, follow the trail around the northeast shore of Amphitheater Lake, staying right at several indistinct forks. Climb between the rocks to the top of a shoulder for breathtaking views into the valley, sweeping down from the Grand Teton. A shattered ridgeline between the razor-sharp spires of Teewinot and Mt Owen to the north contrast with the flatlands visible between sheer valley walls south. Vertigo sufferers beware!

Retrace your steps to the trailhead.

GARNET CANYON

Duration 9 hours
Distance 12 miles (approx)
Difficulty difficult
Elevation Change 4800ft
Start/Finish Lupine Meadows Trailhead
Nearest Town/Junction South Jenny Lake Junction (Map p218)
Summary This climbers' route hauls hikers into the world of rock and ice. You must be fit and well acclimatized.

It's possible to hike this trail in a day, but it's best done as an overnighter, camping at either the Meadows or South Fork sites. Set off at first light since afternoon weather is notoriously fickle up here.

For the first 3 miles follow the Sunrise & Amphitheater Lakes hike description (p223). At the trail junction branch left instead of right. From this junction the trail curves around the hillside to dramatic views of Garnet Canyon and Middle Teton (12,804ft). Just over a mile from the junction the maintained trail stops and the sometimes-indistinct **climbers' path** continues over boulder fields for 20 minutes to the Meadows campsite. If you aren't confident with bouldering and trail finding, this spot makes a good terminus (8.4 miles round-trip, five hours).

The path splits right to **Spalding Falls** and the base camp for **Grand Teton** and left through indistinct boulder fields to switchback up to a small saddle, where you'll find a couple of campsites. From here the trail traverses a small snowfield (present until August) and heads up the valley over a series of false saddles.

With several indistinct trails at your disposal, finding the right one involves some guesswork and bouldering. About 2 miles from the meadows you'll finally reach the **saddle** between Middle and South Teton, with fabulous views down to Iceflow Lake and across to The Wall and Hurricane Pass.

You will likely meet groups of climbers heading to Middle Teton.

From the saddle it's a 3½- to four-hour return the way you came. Take great care on the rocks and snowfields as you return, as you'll be tired; this is no place to sprain an ankle or worse.

TAGGART & BRADLEY LAKES

Duration 3 hours
Distance 5.9 miles
Difficulty easy–moderate
Elevation Change 560ft
Start/Finish Taggart Lake Trailhead (Map p218)
Nearest Town/Junction Moose Junction
Summary An easy amble, this pair of glacial lakes sits at the base of the Tetons, surrounded by grassy areas thick with summer wildflowers or fragrant pine forest.

These lakes were named after surveyors of the 1872 Hayden Expedition. The terrain is open from earlier fires, so it's a bit easier to spot wildlife, particularly moose. The trails here offer several easy loop options ranging from 3 to 5 miles total. Plan an early start in summer since much of the trail lacks shade. Don't forget the bathing suit.

The **Taggart Lake Trailhead** is just off Teton Park Rd, 5 miles north of Moose. Follow the trail northwest, past horse corrals, and take the first left at a marked signpost after 0.2 miles. Although this trail is only slightly longer, it receives far less traffic than the other option. After another 1.4 miles, turn right and climb open slopes to a point on the moraine wall overlooking the beautiful rusty-green **Taggart Lake**. Descend the short distance to the lakeshore and use a wooden footbridge to cross the outlet creek. A small, rocky outcropping makes a fine point to swim. The views of the Tetons are fantastic.

The trail winds around the east shore of Taggart Lake, passing a signposted trail junction for the parking area (a shortcut back if you're tired) to your right. Climb steadily away from Taggart Lake and crest the moraine wall separating Taggart and Bradley Lakes. Descend through the trees to reach the thickly forested shores of **Bradley Lake**. You'll reach a junction just before the trail reaches the shores of Bradley Lake. Turn right to begin the trip back to the parking area or forge ahead to explore the perimeter of Bradley Lake before returning to this junction. The campsite at Bradley Lake is reserved for hikers on multiday loops of the Valley Trail.

If it's still early and you're brimming with energy, consider forging on to Avalanche Canyon and Lake Taminah (below). You might want to combine your hike with the ranger-led wildflower and naturalist walks that depart every morning from the Taggart Lake Trailhead.

AVALANCHE CANYON & LAKE TAMINAH

Duration 6–7 hours
Distance 11 miles (approx)
Difficulty difficult
Elevation Change 2300ft
Start/Finish Taggart Lake Trailhead (Map p218)
Nearest Town/Junction Moose Junction
Summary This challenging hike runs the gamut of good stuff: lake swims, waterfalls and killer views.

Park at the **Taggart Lake Trailhead**, where there's a convenient toilet. Take the shortest route to Taggart Lake, branching right initially then left after 1.1 miles. At Taggart Lake branch right toward **Bradley Lake**.

Curving around the north side of Taggart Lake, you'll lose sight of the lake shortly before the faint left hand turnoff to Avalanche Canyon – if you start to climb the moraine hill to **Bradley Lake**, you've gone too far.

The trail heads up **Avalanche Canyon**, past steep fern-thick inclines, with views ahead to 11,490ft Mt Wister. As the trail becomes increasingly wet, you'll first hear and then see **Taggart Creek**. There's a good chance of spotting moose here. At the head of the valley, about 2½ hours from the trailhead, look for the waterfalls up both branches of the valley – you are headed right for **Shoshoko Falls**.

The trail winds up a steep talus slope to the right of the falls and, once you have gained most of the elevation, swings left up a small gully to meet remote **Lake Taminah**. Approach the falls to get great views down the valley. The ascent takes about 3½ hours.

Return the way you came. At the junction with the main Taggart-Bradley Lake Trail, you can head back to the trailhead, though it's worth detouring to **Bradley Lake** on the Bradley Lake Trail – this only adds an extra 0.7 miles (30 minutes) and it provides more secluded swim spots. From Bradley Lake it's 2 miles back to the trailhead.

DEATH CANYON

Duration 5 hours
Distance 8–10 miles
Difficulty moderate
Elevation Change 1360ft
Start/Finish Death Canyon Trailhead (Map p218)
Nearest Town/Junction Moose Junction
Summary Lesser-known Death Canyon offers moderate hiking up an ethereal river valley flanked by granite climbing walls.

To reach the Death Canyon Trailhead, take the turnoff 3 miles south of Moose on Moose-Wilson Rd. Go right 1.6 miles down a narrow dirt track, which is in poor condition. The small parking area is often crowded with climbers' and backpackers' vehicles. Nearby, the **White Grass Ranger Station** was once an outfitters' cabin.

The trail climbs 0.9 miles to **Phelps Lake Overlook** (elevation 7200ft) and then descends 0.7 miles through lovely aspen forest to a junction; go right here. As you enter the towering gorge, the ascent kicks in – a relentless uphill over rocky switchbacks that quickly joins the river, which cascades over large boulders. After a hard slog of about 1.5 miles the path flattens out. Devoid of the river's roar, the valley seems impressively serene.

The trail hits a junction by an old patrol cabin, 3.7 miles from the trailhead. The right branch climbs steeply to **Static Divide**; if you have the energy, switchback up the trail to the treeline for great views of the peaks and plains (a two-hour detour). Or continue straight on the main trail up **Death Canyon**, through riverside willows in prime moose habitat. The trail crosses a log bridge and enters a lush forest filled with berries, which indicate bear territory. The campsites

GRAND TETON NATIONAL PARK

of the Death Canyon Camping Area pop up occasionally, as do views of the **Death Canyon Shelf**, an impressive layer of sedimentary rock atop harder granites and gneiss. You can continue along this trail as long as you wish, perhaps using one of the campsites as a picnic spot, though a good turnaround point comes where the trail crosses the stream.

To exit, retrace your steps. Consider descending to the pine-rimmed **Phelps Lake** for a dip before the final grind, a 1.6-mile hike back up the moraine hill, which somehow seems a lot longer at the day's end.

OTHER HIKES

Another day-hike loop starts from the top of the tram down the South Fork into **Granite Canyon** and back to Teton Village (13 miles). For more area hikes from Jackson and the Idaho side, check out p243 and p253.

BACKCOUNTRY HIKES
Central Tetons

This is the good stuff. Don your pack and hit the high country.

PAINTBRUSH DIVIDE

Duration 2–3 days
Distance 17.8-mile loop
Difficulty moderate
Elevation Change 3775ft
Start/Finish String Lake Trailhead (Map p218)
Nearest Town/Junction North Jenny Lake Junction
Summary This pretty grind lifts you up into the alpine scenery above tree level.

This is the Teton's most popular backpacking trip. If you like some social atmosphere with your backcountry, make sure you reserve a campsite in advance or keep an open itinerary. Uber-athletes could zip through on an epic day hike.

DAY 1: STRING LAKE TRAILHEAD TO HOLLY LAKE
4 hours, 6.2 miles, 2540ft ascent

From the String Lake parking lot take the trail that curves south around String Lake. It climbs gently until the left-hand junction with **Paintbrush Canyon**, 1.6 miles in. This steeper but moderate trail borders a stream flowing over granite boulders, passing

through the Lower Paintbrush Camping Zone and some stock campsites. It reaches an upper basin surrounded by snowy peaks. The first lake isn't Holly, continue right of it to reach **Holly Lake**. There are two shady designated campsites at the lake's southeast corner. If these sites are booked, camp in the Upper Paintbrush Canyon Camping Zone.

DAY 2: HOLLY LAKE TO NORTH FORK CASCADE CAMPING ZONE
3 hours, 3.2 miles, 1235ft ascent

Ascend steeply to join the main trail; it's one hour to **Paintbrush Divide** (10,645ft). The pass may be snowy into early July – consult a ranger before going. An ice tool could come in handy here. Enjoy the outstanding views before descending along broad switchbacks to reach **Lake Solitude** after another hour or so. Camp in the nearby North Fork Cascade Camping Zone or continue down Cascade Canyon to either the String Lake Trailhead or to Jenny Lake via the shuttle boat (details in the Lake Solitude hike, p223).

MARION LAKE & DEATH CANYON

Duration 2 days
Distance 18 miles (or 23.5-mile loop)
Difficulty moderate
Elevation Change 600ft, 3650ft descent (from tram to Death Canyon Trailhead)
Start/Finish Teton Village/Death Canyon Trailhead (Map p218)
Nearest Town/Junction Teton Village
Summary Downhill but not a downer, this hike gets you steeped in the backcountry quickly by the tram shortcut.

DAY 1: JACKSON HOLE AERIAL TRAM TO MARION LAKE
4 hours, 6.6 miles, 4139ft descent

This hike starts with a considerable boost: after reopening in 2008, the Jackson Hole Aerial Tram to the top of Rendezvous Mountain gains 0.8 miles of elevation. From the tram, descend to a junction at the park boundary and turn right to descend into the South Fork of Granite Canyon. Take a left at the next junction and then a right at the next two junctions to descend into the North Fork of **Granite Canyon**. From here it's a short climb to lovely **Marion Lake**, 6.6 miles

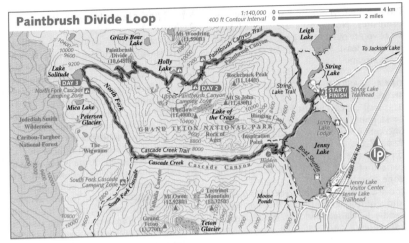

from the trailhead, where you'll find three designated campsites.

DAY 2: MARION LAKE TO DEATH CANYON TRAILHEAD
6 hours, 11.3 miles, 2450ft descent

Today it's 2.3 miles up to **Fox Creek Pass**, then it's all downhill for 9 miles through the forests of Death Canyon to Phelps Lake Overlook and the Death Canyon Trailhead (p225). To avoid a car shuttle, hike south at the junction before Phelps Lake along the Valley Trail to Teton Village (5.5 miles).

By choosing to hike in the opposite direction you can save a few bucks (the downhill tram ride is free of charge), but you'll gain much more elevation.

TETON CREST TRAIL

Duration 4 or 5 days
Distance 31.4 or 39.9 miles
Difficulty moderate–difficult
Elevation Change 6000ft
Start/Finish String Lake/Granite Creek Trailhead or Teton Village (Map p218)
Nearest Town/Junction North Jenny Lake Junction
Summary This epic takes hikers rambling over the lofty spine of the Tetons for jaw-dropping views and a fair share of high exposure.

This classic route is one to remember. Dipping in and out of the neighboring Jedediah Smith Wilderness, the route has numerous outs – the canyons and passes that access the trail on either side. The following is only a suggested itinerary. Hikers must arrange for a shuttle here or have two cars to leave at the start and end points. Bring plenty of sunscreen – there is almost no shade.

DAYS 1 & 2
Day one is the same as the Paintbrush Divide loop (p226). Day two continues to follow this route until the junction between the North and South Forks of Cascade Canyon, where the trail branches up the South Fork to the **South Fork Cascade Camping Zone** (19 campsites). You can start the hike from Jenny Lake and spend night one at the South Fork Camping Zone after hiking up Cascade Canyon Trail; this shaves off a day.

DAY 3: SOUTH FORK CASCADE CAMPING ZONE TO ALASKA BASIN
3–3½ hours, 6.1 miles, 1992ft ascent

The trail climbs up to **Avalanche Divide** junction: head right (southwest) to **Hurricane Pass** (10,372ft), which has unsurpassed views of Grand, South and Middle Tetons. (An excursion from the Avalanche Divide junction leads 1.6 miles to the divide, a scenic overlook above Snowdrift Lake.) From the pass the trail descends into the Jedediah Smith Wilderness, past Sunset Lake, into the **Basin Lakes** of the Alaska

GRAND TETON NATIONAL PARK

Basin, where you'll find several popular campsites. No permits are needed here since you're outside the park, but you must camp at least 300ft from lakes and 50ft from streams.

DAY 4: ALASKA BASIN TO MARION LAKE
4½ hours, 8.2 miles

The trail crosses South Fork Teton Creek on stepping stones and switchbacks up the Sheep Steps to the wide saddle of **Mt Meek Pass** (9726ft) to re-enter the park. The trail dips for the next 3 miles into stunning plateau of **Death Canyon Shelf** and camping zone. Past the turnoff to Death Canyon, the trail climbs to **Fox Creek Pass** (9560ft) and continues southwest over a vague saddle to **Marion Lake** and its designated campsites.

DAY 5: MARION LAKE TO TETON VILLAGE
5 hours, 9.7 miles

The trail descends into the Upper Granite Canyon Camping Zone and continues past the Upper Granite Canyon patrol cabin to the junction with the Valley Trail. From here continue south to the Granite Canyon Trailhead or straight on to Teton Village.

OTHER COMBINATIONS

The Teton Crest Trail can be accessed from the east by several steep canyons. Trailheads (south to north) are: Granite Canyon, Death Canyon, Taggart Lake, Lupine Meadows, Jenny Lake and String Lake/Leigh Lake. Hike canyon-to-canyon to make a combination hike of any length. Options include the following:

Open Canyon to Granite Canyon One-night 19.3-mile loop from the Granite Creek Trailhead.

Granite Canyon to Death Canyon A two- to three-night 25.7-mile loop via the Teton Crest Trail.

Death Canyon to Open Canyon A 24.7-mile loop from the Death Canyon Trailhead.

OTHER HIKES

Other good options for overnighting include camping at **Marion Lake** (13-mile round-trip) from the Jackson Hole Aerial Tram. For an easy overnighter, check out the Hermitage Point hike (p221) or the Leigh & Bearpaw Lakes hike (p222). Also check out Alaska Basin from the Idaho side (p254).

John D Rockefeller Jr Memorial Parkway

Polecat Creek offers a pleasant stroll if you're staying overnight at Flagg Ranch. The trail leads across Grassy Lake Rd from the main parking lot, passing two turnoffs to the right and an employee-housing loop before branching right to peaceful Oxbow Meadows. From here you can take a left at the next junction over a small creek to **Huckleberry Hot Springs**. The NPS advises against bathing here due to high radiation levels in the water (caused by naturally occurring radon), but this hardly deters locals who come here for post-work alfresco soaks. You can also get to the springs from a parking lot 1 mile west of Flagg Ranch, though you need to ford Polecat Creek on this route, so bring waterproof shoes. This former road led to a hot springs resort that was torn down in 1983.

A fairly interesting hiking trail also runs beside the volcanic walls of **Flagg Canyon**, northeast of Flagg Ranch. Get the brochure *Flagg Ranch Area Trails* from the Flagg Ranch information station.

Along Grassy Lane Rd, 2.2 miles west of Flagg Ranch, is the **Glade Creek Trailhead**, which accesses the rarely visited northwest corner of the park and its Berry Creek and Moose Creek Trails. For more hikes in the Grassy Lake Rd area, see p256.

BIKING

Cyclists are in less danger from motorists in the Tetons than in Yellowstone because the roads are wider and more open, but it is still best to venture out early to avoid traffic. Grand Teton National Park gets little traffic from September to early October, and the cool temperatures make for pleasant pedaling. In April, Teton Park Rd is open only to cyclists and pedestrian traffic. This is a great time to bike if the snow has cleared. For tips on biking with traffic and wildlife, see p284.

If you are on a road bike, check out the various Driving Routes (p230) options. The biking tours listed following require mountain-bike treads, but only Shadow Mountain is steep and may require suspension.

MORMON ROW

Duration 2–2½ hours
Distance: 16-mile loop
Difficulty easy
Elevation Change 230ft
Start/Finish Gros Ventre Junction (Map pp210–11)
Nearest Town/Junction Jackson, Wyoming
Summary Discover the heritage of Jackson Hole on a mellow mountain-bike ride.

This relaxed ride is a bikers' favorite. And it's no wonder – the scenery is the only thing to take your breath away. Parts of this ride on **Gros Ventre Rd** and **Antelope Flats** are paved, but **Mormon Row** is unpaved.

SNAKE RIVER ROAD

Duration 2–3 hours
Distance 15 miles one way
Difficulty easy–moderate
Elevation Change negligible
Start/Finish Riverside Rd at Cottonwood Creek/Signal Mt Rd (Map pp210–11)
Nearest Town/Junction Moose Junction
Summary Explore the incredible riparian landscape on a short mountain-bike ride.

This trail follows an abbreviated version of the Hole in One driving loop (p230). Start at Gros River Junction. Go right at the turnoff, heading northeast with Blacktail Butte to your north. Take a left at Mormon Row, another left at Antelope Flats Rd. It ends at Hwy 191; take the highway south to return to the start.

The gravel River (RKO) Rd parallels the west side of the **Snake River** between Signal Mountain and Cottonwood Creek. Those doing the ride one-way can park at the turn-out near **Cottonwood Creek**. There is no shade here and it gets quite hot in summer, so bring plenty of water or bike early. Wildlife is prolific, especially bison. Maintain a safe distance of 300ft and never pass through them. Wait until they move away or bike around.

Be prepared for a bumpy, uneven ride. The road parallels braided channels of the scenic Snake River, one of the most heavily used rivers in the west. Binoculars would

be useful here: the river is critical habitat for beaver and river otter. Osprey and eagle are here too, fishing for cutthroat trout, and moose and deer frequent the willows. The track rejoins **Teton Park Rd** just south of the Signal Mountain Rd turnoff. Arrange a vehicle shuttle or be prepared to cycle the 12 miles south on the paved Teton Park Rd back to Cottonwood Creek.

SHADOW MOUNTAIN

Duration 2½–3 hours
Distance 6-mile loop
Difficulty difficult
Elevation Change 1300ft
Start/Finish Antelope Flats Rd (Map pp210–11)
Nearest Town/Junction Moose Junction
Summary Challenge yourself with this strenuous but quick ascent and descent.

Just east of the park in Bridger-Teton National Forest, the forested **Shadow Mountain** offers a strenuous 6-mile round-trip loop. Set off along a gravel road from the parking lot at the end of paved Antelope Flats Rd. A steady climb, the road is rutted and rocky at points. Open sections offer excellent Teton views. Just over 0.5 miles past the summit there's a single-track path to the left. It splits, but your best option is to stay left, although all trails do lead to the bottom. Be alert as fallen logs cross the path in places. After this exciting downhill run join the fire road. Watch for muddy conditions, which make this section a lot trickier. A webbed network of trails here means it is easy to get turned around. For topographical maps, visit Hoback Sports (p243).

HOLE IN ONE

Duration 5 hours
Distance 33-mile loop
Difficulty moderate
Elevation Change 340ft
Start/Finish Jackson (Map pp210–11)
Nearest Town/Junction Jackson, WY
Summary Scoot past Jackson Hole highlights on this fun loop with long, flat stretches.

This trail follows an abbreviated version of the Hole in One driving loop; for a more detailed description, see below. Start in Jackson and head north on Hwy 191 to **Moose Junction**. Go left here and left again to the narrow and winding Moose-Wilson Rd. While it is paved there are some deep potholes, so stay alert. Horned owls nest along this section. Approaching **Teton Village**, the road becomes smooth and stays that way. Continue on the flats of Moose-Wilson Rd until you hit a juncture with Hwy 22; turn left here. There will be a lot of car traffic on Hwy 22.

An early start will help you avoid traffic on the narrows of Moose-Wilson Rd.

DRIVING

It's sweeping views, park history and wildlife aplenty on these four-wheeled sojourns.

HOLE IN ONE

Route Jackson to Hwy 191 to Moose-Wilson Rd via Hwy 191
Distance 40-mile loop
Speed Limit 15–45mph

You could say **Gros Ventre Butte** ruined it for Jackson – there are no Teton views from the park's main hub due to the blockage created by this oversized hump. But this driving tour, not suitable for RVs or other oversized vehicles, is just the remedy.

Head out of Jackson on Hwy 191. First stop: the **National Museum of Wildlife Art** (p241). You ask, why do this when you have the real thing? Just look. The way these masters envisioned this landscape will change the way you see it yourself.

Continue north on Hwy 191. At the Gros Ventre Junction, take a right and drive along Gros Ventre Rd, skirting the **Gros Ventre River**, which is lined with cottonwoods, juniper, spruce and willows. The river ecology contrasts sharply with the dry sagebrush flats north of it, where pronghorn can often be seen, bounding at speeds up to 60mph (officially, that's faster than you should be going here). At the next junction, take a left to drive north on **Mormon Row**, a picturesque strip that includes a rambling barn left from the hard days of the Mormon settlement. At the end of the row loop left on **Antelope**

Flats Rd, from which you may be able to see bison and more pronghorn. It soon meets Hwy 191 again. Go left, then right at Moose Junction.

Before the park entrance gate, take a left on the small **Moose-Wilson Rd**. Squeeze to the side when you face oncoming traffic: this is why oversized vehicles are explicitly banned. Mind the blind curves, twisting through dense foliage. You will pass a dirt road to Death Canyon Trailhead and later the Granite Canyon Trailhead, both on your right. If you're keen on a swim, detour to the latter, which will take you to **Phelps Lake** (but it will take a few hours). This short section of the road is unpaved but even.

The road spills out near **Teton Village**, where you can take a gondola to the top for views or grab lunch at the Mangy Moose Saloon (p251). Follow the Moose-Wilson road south to Hwy 22. Go left to return back to Jackson.

PLAINS & PANORAMAS

Route Hwy 191 to Teton Park Rd
Distance 45 miles
Speed Limit 30–45mph

This scenic loop offers fantastic views of the Teton Range from the flats of Jackson Hole Valley. Wildlife is prolific along this route; with some luck, you will spot pronghorn, deer or moose. Each year animals are killed on this road, so drive cautiously and watch for animals bounding across the road.

Begin the tour 8 miles north of Jackson at the Moose Junction. Follow Hwy 191 north past **Blacktail Ponds Overlook** and Glacier View Turnout. Seven miles after Moose Junction, **Snake River Overlook** has views of the braided channels of the Snake. Dense cottonwoods, willows and Englemann Spruce provide an excellent habitat for moose and deer. Spotted sandpipers should be easy to pick out.

Make a stop at **Cunningham Cabin**, the site of an 1892 shootout when a band of self-deputized locals sought to root out rumored horse thieves.

At Moran Junction bear left (continuing on 191). The hulking peak of **Mt Moran** looms to the west, bearing five glaciers. Stop about 3.5 miles later at **Oxbow Bend** to look for fishing eagles and ospreys, and trumpeter swans. Long-legged great blue herons stalk the shallows. Head south along Teton Park Rd at Jackson Lake Junction. The **Chapel of the Sacred Heart** follows. On your left you will see a sign for **Signal Mountain** road, a 5-mile climb. You can detour here or continue on.

Turn on the one-way **Jenny Lake Scenic Drive**, twisting through a forested area with the spires of the Tetons just above you. It will deposit you again on Teton Park Rd. On your left you will see **Menor's Ferry** historic area. The brainchild of Bill Menor, the ferry provided the only transportation across the river. In late summer, when tourists crossed the river to pick berries, Menor charged them 'Huckleberry Rates.' The log **Chapel of the Transfiguration**, built in 1914, still holds church services. Detour slightly for these. Return to the main road and follow it until it exits the park at Moose Junction.

OTHER ACTIVITIES

ROCK CLIMBING & MOUNTAINEERING

Garnet Canyon is the gateway to the most popular scrambles to Middle and South Teton and the technical ascent of Grand Teton. These nontechnical climbs can be handled as day hikes from bases at the Meadows, South Fork, Caves or Moraine campsites, but you need to know what you're doing and be with someone familiar with the routes.

The Grand Teton is a classic climb cherished by climbers. It starts with a strenuous hike up Garnet Canyon (4000ft-plus) and making camp. Day two requires an alpine start. The Owen-Spaulding route is the most popular, but there are lots of variants to choose from. The climb itself consists of 2700ft of elevation gain, fun scrambling, three easy 5th-class pitches and an exciting rappel from high on the mountain. Views from above are unparalleled. Ah, and then there's getting down...Very fit nonclimbers

GRAND TETON
NATIONAL PARK

THE CLIMBERS' RANCH

An affordable place for mountaineers and climbers to meet and stay, the Climbers' Ranch gives off a strong tribal vibe. Lonely Planet chatted with Ranch Manager Drew Birnbaum and guests about the strange subculture of rock jocks – who happen to have a lot in common with shoestring travelers.

How do you manage a ranch with no livestock?
Drew: It's like herding cats when you try to ranch climbers.

For those who might walk in one day and think it's a cult...
Drew: The Climbers' Ranch essentially is created to create a space for climbers to hang out in one of the great climbing ranges of North America.
Brian: It is just a wonderful discovery for a climber.
Jimmy: Where is the Kool-Aid?

And for someone who's not into climbing?
Drew: It wasn't created for non-climbers, but it has become a hostel for outdoor pursuits of any kind: backpacking, hiking, cycling, fishing.

Let's look at a typical specimen.
Jimmy: I'm 23 and a high-school history teacher from Boone, North Carolina. I've been here one month. Just do the [volunteer] work week the first week of June and that will allow you to stay free for the month. After that, eat out of the free food box! You can score anything – from dried fruit to candy bars, hair spray, ketchup. This is a really good month. I've got so much mac and cheese right now, it's incredible.
Brian: I'm 62 and having a hoot. I develop friendships here that have lasted for a long, long time. I don't know of any place that I've gone to with that sense of community. People that come here should participate in that.

What's the essence of this place?
Drew: The mountains bring about a certain strain of honesty because when you're up there you can't be lying to yourself about what you'll be able to do. It helps people with the greater questions in life about who they are and what they want to do.

can complete the climb with an outfitter and some training beforehand.

Day climbers don't need to register, but those staying overnight need a backcountry use permit (see p213). Call ☎ 307-739-3604 for recorded climbing information.

Ground zero for climbing information, **Jenny Lake Ranger Station** (☎ 307-739-3343; ☽ 8am-6pm Jun-Sep) sells climbing guidebooks and provides information. A board shows campsite availability in Garnet Canyon.

An excellent resource and the spot to meet outdoor partners in crime, American Alpine Club **Climbers' Ranch** (☎ 307-733-7271; www.americanalpineclub.org; Teton Park Rd; ☽ summer only) has been a climbing institution since it opened its doors (see the boxed text, p231). The inexpensive summer **dormitory** (bunks member/nonmember $8/16; ☽ mid-Jun–mid-Sep) features a large cook shelter, extensive climbing library, and men's and women's shower houses. Volunteers for June's work week can stay the rest of the month for free. The ranch is just south of the Teton Glacier turnout.

For instruction and guided climbs contact **Exum Mountain Guides** (☎ 307-733-2297; www.exumguides.com) at Jenny Lake or **Jackson Hole Mountain Guides** (☎ 307-733-4979, 800-239-7642; www.jhmg.com; 165 N Glenwood St, Jackson). Exum runs climbing schools at Hidden Falls on Jenny Lake's west shore and has a base camp at Grand Teton's Lower Saddle (11,600ft). It's also the slightly more expensive of the two.

HORSEBACK RIDING

Colter Bay corral offers 1½- and 2½-hour trail rides around Swan Lake for $33/48. Children are charged the same rates and must be eight years old. There are also breakfast and dinner rides, either on horseback or (cheaper) wagon. Dinner horseback rides cost $63/53 per adult/child; dinner wagon rides cost $43/33. Make reservations at the **activities booth** (☽ 7am-8pm) next to the Colter Bay grocery store, preferably a couple of days in advance.

Jackson Lake Lodge offers **guided horseback rides** (per 2hr $48) that loop around the local trails, as well as breakfast and dinner rides by horseback or wagon.

Flagg Ranch runs hour-long **horseback riding trips** ($35) hourly from June to September.

BOATING
Colter Bay Region

Next to the lodge, **Signal Mountain Marina** (☎ 307-543-2831; ☽ 7am-7:30pm mid-May–early Sep) rents canoes ($13.50/73 per hour/day), kayaks ($12/66), motorboats ($28/165) and pontoon cruisers ($65/385). Reservations are accepted for larger boats only and depend on lake levels. Ten-mile **scenic floats** (adult/child 6–12 $51/32) on the Snake River offer good wildlife-watching opportunities.

Busy **Colter Bay Marina** (☎ 307-543-2811; ☽ 8am-5pm, no rentals after 3pm) provides fishing gear and licenses, as well as motorboat rentals ($27/155 per hour/day) and rowboat, and canoe rentals ($11 to $13 per hour). Don't expect anything too adventurous here, as canoes aren't allowed more than 0.25 miles from the shore.

Grand Teton Lodge Company (GTLC) arranges daily scheduled **lake cruises** (adult/child aged 3–11; $21/10) from Colter Bay, including breakfast ($33/21) and steak dinner ($55/33) cruises to Elk Island. GTLC operates an **activities booth** (☽ 7am-8pm) next to the Colter Bay grocery store.

Leek's Marina (☎ 307-543-2494), north of Colter Bay Junction, is a simpler affair, with a gas dock and overnight buoys.

Canoes and kayaks rented at the marinas are not supposed to be taken beyond Colter Bay or Half Moon Bay (from Colter Bay) or Dornan's Island (from Signal Mountain).

TRIP OPTIONS

Backcountry campsites flank Jackson Lake at Deadman Point, Bearpaw Bay, Grassy Island, Little Mackinaw Bay, South Landing, Elk Island and Warm Springs. Book these sites in advance, especially on summer weekends when the lake is chock-a-block with powerboats, sailboards, sailboats and canoes. There is a maximum three-night stay.

Outfitter **OARS** (Outdoor Adventure River Specialists; ☎ 209-736-4677, 800-346-6277; www.oars .com) guide trips kayaking around Jackson Lake (overnight adult/child $240/194) with instruction for beginners and multiday rafting trips on the Snake River (two days adult/child $406/338).

With dramatic close-ups of the toothy Mt Moran, Moran Bay is the most popular destination from Colter and Spalding Bays. While boating you can stop at Grassy Island

SNAKE RIVER FLOAT GUIDE

Ansel Adams immortalized images of the Snake as a luminous ribbon retreating from sharp snowbound peaks. With outstanding wildlife-watching, this iconic river is a prime spot for boating. For white-water-rafting options, see p244.

Commercial trips

Float trips (averaging adult/child $52/32) start after Jackson Lake Dam and meander through park wilderness; the wildest white-water flows south of the town of Jackson. Usually kids must be six years or older to participate. Contact the following:

Barker-Ewing Float Trips (☎ 307-733-1800; www.barker-ewing.com; Moose) Offers float trips from Deadman's Bar to Moose.

Flagg Ranch Float Trips (☎ 307-543-2861, 800-443-2311; www.flaggranch.com) Runs floats on the upper Snake River, three-hour scenic float trips and one-hour mild white-water trips through Flagg Canyon from mid-June to early September.

Signal Mountain Lodge (☎ 307-733-5470; www.signalmtnlodge.com) Runs scenic three-hour floats in the early morning and evening from mid-May to mid-September.

Solitude Float Trips (☎ 888-704-2800, 307-733-2871; www.solitudefloattrips.com; Moose) Runs Deadman's Bar–Moose trips and sunrise trips, plus shorter 5-mile floats.

Triangle X Float Trips (☎ 888-860-0005; www.jackson-hole-river-rafting.com) Offers dawn, daytime and sunset floats, plus a four-hour early evening float and cookout.

Do it Yourself

The easiest do-it-yourself float is the 5 miles from just below Jackson Lake Dam to Pacific Creek Landing. Pacific Creek to Deadman's Bar and Flagg Ranch to Lizard Creek are considered intermediate floats. Anything south of Deadman's Bar is considered advanced. Deadman's Bar to the Moose landing is the most commonly offered commercial white-water trip and is considered Class II. Southgate (at Yellowstone's south entrance) to Flagg Ranch via Flagg Canyon is considered advanced Class III white-water. You'll find boat put-ins near Oxbow Bend, at Pacific Creek, Deadman's Bar, Schwabacher's Landing and Moose.

Early trappers didn't name the Snake the 'Mad River' for nothing! The highest water levels are in spring. Independent floaters should have all the required safety equipment (including life jackets and throw bag) and know how to use it. For information on Snake River flows call ☎ 800-658-571.

Save your inner tubes and air mattresses for the lake – they are explicitly banned.

en route. The following sample distances start from Signal Mountain: Hermitage Point (2 miles), Elk Island (3 miles) and Grassy Island (6 miles); from Colter Bay to Little Mackinaw Bay is 1.5 miles.

Alternatively, you can paddle from Lizard Creek Campground to remote backcountry trails on the northwest shore. Wilcox Point backcountry campsite (1.25 miles from Lizard Creek) provides backcountry access to Webb Canyon along the Moose Basin Divide Trail (20 miles). For a longer intermediate-level trip, paddle the twists and turns of the Snake River from Flagg Ranch to Wilcox Point or Lizard Creek.

Predominant winds from the southwest can be strong, especially in the afternoon,

when waves can swamp canoes. Morning is usually the best time to paddle.

Jenny Lake Scenic Drive

String Lake is perfect for a family canoe trip or even just a splash about. The canoe-only put-in is at the end of a turnoff just before the Leigh Lake Trailhead parking lot.

Particularly suited to families, **Leigh Lake** offers the most scenic day and overnight paddles. Getting there requires a 120ft portage between paddling sections. Six beautiful backcountry campsites flank the lakeshore, three of which three (16, 14A and 14B) are only accessible by boat. It is 3 miles one way from the portage point at the outlet of Leigh Lake to furthest campsite (16). Leigh Lake also offers quality **fishing**.

GRAND TETON NATIONAL PARK CAMPGROUNDS

Campground	Location	No of Sites	Elevation	Open
Colter Bay	Colter Bay	350	6820ft	mid-May–mid-Sep
Colter Bay RV Park	Colter Bay	112	6820ft	mid-May–mid-Sep
Flagg Ranch	Rockefeller Parkway	175	6300ft	late May–late Sep
Gros Venture	Central Tetons	372	6783ft	late April–mid-Oct
Jenny Lake	Central Tetons	51	6803ft	mid-May–late Sep
Lizard Creek	Central Tetons	60	6768ft	early Jun–early Sep
Signal Mountain	Colter Bay	86	7593ft	early May–mid-Oct

*Reservations through **Flagg Ranch** (☎ 800-443-2311)

 Fireplace   Drinking Water   Flush Toilets   Ranger Station Nearby   Wheelchair Accessible   Grocery Store Nearby   RV Dump Station

John D Rockefeller Jr Memorial Parkway

At Flagg Ranch Resort, Flagg Ranch Rafting offers three-hour scenic **floats** (adult/child 6-12 $50/30) plus a three-hour **white-water trip** (adult/child $46/34) from mid-June to early September.

FISHING
Colter Bay Region

Cutthroat, brown and lake trout cruise the waters of Jackson Lake. For fishing excursions, Signal Mountain Marina guides up to two people ($72/250 per hour/half day) on the lake. Your catch can be cleaned and served up at the restaurant. Colter Bay Marina charges $65 per hour (minimum two hours) for guided lake fishing, plus fly-fishing day trips for $425 for two people.

WINTER ACTIVITIES

Craig Thomas Discovery & Visitor Center (☎ 307-739-3300; ☉ 8am-5pm year-round, 8am-7pm peak summer season, closed Christmas Day) in Moose is the focus of winter activities and the place to get information on ski trail, weather, road and avalanche conditions. Teton Park Rd is plowed from Jackson Lake Junction to Signal Mountain Lodge and from Moose to the Taggart Lake Trailhead.

From late December to mid-March rangers lead free 1.5-mile (two-hour) **snowshoe hikes** (☎ reservations 307-739-3399) These hikes depart several times a week from the Visitor Center. Snowshoes are provided, and children over eight years of age can take part.

Never walk or snowshoe on ski trails – skiers will thank you for preserving the track! Also, be aware that the NPS does not always mark every trail: consult at the ranger station to make sure that the trail you plan to use is well tracked and easy to follow.

TETON WINTER FACILITIES

In Teton National Park, only private accommodations are available in winter. **Spur Ranch Log Cabins** (☎ 307-733-2522; www.dornans.com) sits close to the Discovery Center, the hub for winter activities.

On the eastern edge of the national park, **Triangle X Ranch** (☎ 307-733-2183; www .trianglex.com) has wood cabins at discount winter rates. All park campgrounds are closed in winter.

The **Craig Thomas Discovery & Visitor Center** (☎ 307-739-3300; ☉ 8am-5pm) stays open in winter except for Christmas Day.

Reservations	Facilities	Description	Page
no		Enormous but wooded, with ready conveniences; buzzing with activity	236
no		RV zones are separate with electrical connections	236
yes*		Features dining & conveniences nearby but not a haven for tenters	238
no		Spacious & shady, with plenty of ample spaces; tent sites are on separate loops	237
no		The most coveted camp spot amid boulders & trails; tenters only	236
no		A secluded spot with shade & lake access	236
no		Close to shops & restaurants, with lake access & forest shade	236

Payphone   Dogs Allowed (On Leash)

Recommended spots include the Moose–Wilson Rd, the Polecat Creek Loop at Flagg Ranch, the Swan Lake-Heron Pond Loop at Colter Bay and Teton Road.

Those interested in cross-country skiing or snowshoeing can download the park brochure for these activities at www.nps.gov/grte/planyourvisit/upload/xcski.pdf.

Cottonwood Creek makes a quality snowshoe outing. Follow its winding course through the relatively flat terrain between Taggart and Jenny Lakes.

John D Rockefeller Jr Memorial Parkway

In winter (roughly mid-December to early March) the Flagg Ranch Resort offers guided **snowmobile tours** to Old Faithful and the Grand Canyon of the Yellowstone, departing at the bushy hour of 6:30am.

Day tour rates start at around $100 for a passenger and $230 for a driver. The tour price covers gas and outer clothing, although the winter park entrance fee ($20) is separate.

You'll find **Nordic skiing** around Polecat Creek and rentals in Jackson. Since the resort is closed, Flagg Ranch offers hotel pickups in Jackson for its snowmobilers. Flagg Ranch information station does stay open in winter for those using the trails.

SLEEPING

Most campgrounds and accommodations are open from early May to early October, depending on the weather conditions. Camping inside the park is permitted in designated campgrounds only and is limited to 14 days (seven days at popular Jenny Lake). The NPS operates the park's six **campgrounds** (☎ 800-628-9988) on a first come, first served basis.

Demand for campsites is high from early July to Labor Day, and most campgrounds fill by 11am (checkout time). Jenny Lake fills by about 8am, followed by Signal Mountain. Colter Bay is a large site and fills later; Gros Ventre fills last, if at all.

Signal Mountain is probably the easiest place to base because of its central location. Colter Bay and Jenny Lake have tent-only sites reserved for backpackers and cyclists.

Group sites (for up to 75 people) available at Gros Ventre and Colter Bay Campgrounds can be reserved only by calling park concessionaire **Grand Teton Lodge Company** (GTLC; ☎ 800-628-9988). Reservations are only taken for groups, up to one year in advance.

COLTER BAY REGION
Camping

Colter Bay Campground (Map p215; US 89/191/287; sites $; ⊗ mid-May–mid-Sep) The merits and detractions of this large, noisy campground (350 sites) on the east shore of Jackson Lake, 3 miles north of Jackson Lake Junction, relate to its size. It should always have available spots and there's a separate RV park, a grocery store, a laundromat and hot showers available at nearby Colter Village. Propane is available, and there's a dumping station.

Colter Bay RV Park (Map p215; ☎ reservations 307-543-2811, 800-628-9988; sites $; ⊗ mid-May–mid Sep) Sewer, electrical, and water connections are perks at these long pull-though sites (112 total). There's a surcharge for vehicles over 38ft.

Lizard Creek Campground (Map pp210–11; ☎ 800-672-6012; US 89/191/287; sites $; ⊗ early Jan–early Sep) Snug in a forested peninsula along Jackson Lake's north shore, about 8 miles north of Colter Bay Junction, these secluded woodsy sites (60 total) are a great option. Register early since it's popular with boaters. Vehicle length limited to 30ft.

Signal Mountain Campground (Map p215; ☎ 800-672-6012; Teton Park Rd; sites $; ⊗ early May–mid-Oct)

This popular campground with 86 sites looks out on lovely sunsets on Jackson Lake from 5 miles south of Jackson Lake Junction. Sites can be cramped but are convenient: a restaurant, bar, grocery store and marina are nearby. Vehicle size is limited to 30ft. There's a dump station for RVs.

Lodging

Colter Bay Village, Jackson Lake Lodge and Jenny Lake Lodge are all operated by **Grand Teton Lodge Company** (GTLC; ☎ advance reservations 307-543-3100, 800-628-9988, same-day reservations 307-543-2811; www.gtlc.com; PO Box 240 Moran, WY 83013).

Colter Bay Village (Map p215; tent cabins $, r with shared bathroom $, cabins $$–$$$) Half a mile west of Colter Bay Junction, Colter Bay Village offers two types of accommodations. Tent cabins (June to early September) are very basic log and canvas structures sporting all the charm of a Siberian gulag. Expect bare bunks, a wood burning stove, picnic table and outdoor grill. Bathrooms are separate and sleeping bags can be rented. At these prices, you're better off camping. The log cabins, some original, are much more comfortable and a better deal; they're available late May to late September.

UNDERCOVER CAMPGROUNDS

You might have seen these pinpricks on the map, but don't underrate their charms. These lesser-known, first come, first served sites near the park (see Map p210–11) offer respite for self-sufficient campers who could care less about flushing johns or a paved path to their tent. Best of all, they have openings when NPS campgrounds are bursting and charge a third to half of the price.

Hidden **Sheffield Creek Campground** (Map pp210–11; sites $; ⊗ late Jun–Nov) is a five-site USFS campground 2.5 miles south of Yellowstone's South Entrance and just south of Flagg Ranch, across the Snake River Bridge, then a half-mile east on a rough dirt road from a subtly signed turnoff.

Eight free, minimally developed, first come, first served campgrounds are strung out along the bumpy unpaved **Grassy Lake Rd**, which begins just west of the parking lot at Flagg Ranch. The first (and most popular) campground is 1.6 miles along the road and has four riverside campsites. Each of the next three riverside campgrounds, in the 1.5-mile stretch past Soldiers' Meadow, has two sites. The last four campgrounds, spaced out along the next 3.5 miles, are useful for hikes into Yellowstone's southern reaches (see Grassy Lake Rd, p256). All sites have toilets and trash service but no potable water. Camping is only allowed in designated sites.

Hidden, eight-site **Pacific Creek Campground** (Map pp210–11; free; ⊗ mid-Jun–Dec) is 12 miles up the graveled Pacific Creek Rd (USFS Rd 30090) from Grand Teton's Moran Ranger/Entrance Station. It's generally used as a base for backpacking trips into the Teton Wilderness.

Several free dispersed campsites sit on **Shadow Mountain**, on the east edge of the valley. This spot has a dedicated following, so show up early. Don't expect water or toilets, and there's a two-day maximum stay. It's a rough drive anywhere, but you'll be rewarded with stunning dawn views of the Tetons.

Jackson Lake Lodge (Map p215; ☎ 307-543-2811; r/ste/cottage $$$/$$$$$/$$$$; ☻ mid-May–early Oct; ☐ ☒ ☒) This lodge perches on a bluff overlooking the Tetons and Jackson Lake, 1 mile north of Jackson Lake Junction. With soft sheets, meandering trails for long walks and enormous picture windows framing the luminous peaks, it's the best spot to woo that special someone (though you can save your $100 and catch the views off the patio). The 348 cinder-block cottages – lifted straight out of the suburbs – are generally overpriced, though some offer private balconies with a view. The duplex walls can be very thin. Amenities include a business center, a heated outdoor pool and a nearby medical clinic.

Signal Mountain Lodge (Map p215; ☎ 307-543-2831; www.signalmtnlodge.com; cabins $$$-$$$$, r $$$; ☻ mid-May–mid-Oct) While these lakeside lodgings beg for a thorough update, they have one thing clear: location, location, location. Smack in the middle of the park, accommodations range from motel rooms to cabins, bungalows and lakefront retreats. Extras can include a kitchenette, gas fireplace and lake views. All units have electric heat, while perks include self-service laundry and dryers, and a TV and games room. Pets lodge too with a $10 fee. Look for early-season discounts. Located on Teton Park Rd, 2 miles southwest of Jackson Lake Junction.

CENTRAL TETONS
Camping

Jenny Lake Campground (Map p218; Teton Park Rd; sites $; ☻ mid-May–late Sep) This congenial and popular tent-only campground (51 sites) sits among the evergreens and glacial boulders 8 miles north of Moose Junction. Convenient to many trailheads, it is almost always full. Only vehicles less than 14ft-long are allowed and trailers are prohibited.

Gros Ventre Campground (Map p218; Gros Ventre Rd; sites $; ☻ late Apr–mid-Oct) This sprawling but secluded 372-site campground sits near the Gros Ventre River, 4.5 miles northeast of US 26/89/191/287 and 11.5 miles from Moose. Closer to the Gros Ventre Mountains than to many park attractions, it tends to fill up later in the day. The more private sites west of the loops fill quickly. There's an RV dump but no hookups.

Lodging

Spur Ranch Log Cabins (Map p218; ☎ 307-733-2522; www.dornans.com; 1-room cabins $$-$$$, 2-room cabins $$$; ☻ year-round) Gravel paths running through a broad wildflower meadow link these tranquil duplex cabins on the Snake River in Moose. Lodgepole pine furniture, Western stylings and down bedding create a homey feel, but the views are what make it. Cabins equipped with a kitchen, a porch and an outdoor grill can sleep up to six. There are only 12, so reserve at least six months in advance. It is an excellent winter base for those interested in Nordic skiing or snowshoeing – you can make tracks right out the door. High-season rates run from the end of May to the end of September (with a three-night minimum); the shoulder season offers deep discounts.

Jenny Lake Lodge (Map p218; ☎ 307-733-4647; cabins & ste $$$$$; ☻ early Jun-early Oct; ☒) Worn timbers, down comforters and colorful quilts imbue this elegant lodging off Teton Park Rd with a cozy atmosphere. The 37 log cabins sport a deck but no TVs or radios (phones available on request). Rainy days are for hunkering down at the fireplace in the main lodge with a game or book from the stacks. The retreat doesn't come cheap, but rates include breakfast, a five-course dinner, bicycle use and guided horseback riding on nearby trails. Reservation lines open November 1 for the following year.

MORAN TO BLACKTAIL BUTTE
Ranches

Triangle X Ranch (Map pp210-11; ☎ 307-733-2183; www.trianglex.com; 2 Triangle X Rd, Moose, WY 83012; weekly all-inclusive $$$$$, winter cabins per night $$$; ☻ year-round) With the gorgeous backdrop of the jagged Tetons, this ranch on the eastern flanks of the park was started in 1926 by the Turner family, who still run it now. Cabins with wood interiors are immaculate, and activity options – from square dancing to trout fishing to Dutch oven cookouts – keep guests out enjoying the fresh air. Summer visits require a weeklong minimum (double occupancy with riding and meals $1670). Kids get special attention with their own dining hall and a 'Little Wrangler' program, featuring horseback riding, swimming and crafts.

Moose Head Ranch (Map pp210-11; ☎ 307-733-3141; weekly all-inclusive $$$$$; ☻ Jun-Aug) Families rave about this ranch, which has modern log cabins, friendly young staff, a varied and tasty menu, and a slew of activities for adults and kids alike. Rides are for all abilities. Visits require a five-night minimum (single occupancy with riding and meals $2700). It's located between the Tetons and Yellowstone, 18 miles north of Jackson at 6800ft.

JOHN D ROCKEFELLER JR MEMORIAL PARKWAY

The parkway is a handy place to stay en route between Yellowstone and Grand Teton National Parks; see the Grand Teton map (Map pp210–11). For additional camping options, see the boxed text, p236.

Flagg Ranch Campground (Map pp210-11; tent & RV sites with full hookup $; ☽ May-early Oct) Among the most expensive campsites around, it features pull-through sites, propane for sale, 24-hour showers, laundry and a nightly campfire program. Sites are generally available the same day, but RV campers should reserve a week or more in advance.

Flagg Ranch Resort (Map pp210-11; ☎ 307-543-2861, 800-443-2311; www.flaggranch.com; PO Box 187 Moran WY 83013; campsite/d $/$$$; ☽ mid-May–mid-Oct; ♿) Since its occupation by the US Cavalry, this 1910 resort has been gussied up: walkways lead to prim log duplexes with phones, coffeemakers and patio rockers. While less rugged than a mountain hideaway, the grounds still provide solitude for a short break. Pet-friendly ($10 extra), it's popular with families and couples; most stay a night or two between parks. The lodge offers upscale dining, a minimarket and an activities desk. Shuttles go to Jackson and the Jackson Hole Airport.

EATING & DRINKING

Visitors may dine in the park for the convenience or the stunning views, but not for the food. In general, the quality is not outstanding or even notable. The better restaurants face the challenge of getting chefs on a seasonal basis – the quality of your meal will depend largely on their success. For foodies, it's worth a trip to nearby Jackson.

Other options include taking a Jackson Lake dinner and breakfast cruise (p232) or packing a picnic basket with five-star goodies. Dornan's in Moose offers an impressive selection of wines.

COLTER BAY REGION
Colter Bay

For the cheapest nearby picnic fixings, hit the deli counter at the Colter Bay grocery store across the road.

Leek's Pizzeria (☎ 307-733-5470; meals $; ☽ 11am-10pm) Pizza and draft beer on the patio at Leek's is a fine way to end an active day. North of Colter Bay Village, this casual but cozy eatery also serves soup, salad and sandwiches. There is a basic kids menu. Open-mike nights are on Mondays, and live bands play every two weeks.

John Colter Café Court Pizza & Deli (meals $; ☽ 11am-10pm) An airy, plain cafeteria offering salads, burritos, picnic takeout and grill staples. Kids will like this place. The service is friendly and the grilled free-range chicken tacos are tasty but they get you with pricey canned and bottled drinks.

Chuckwagon Steak and Pasta House (meals $$-$$$; ☽ 7:30am-9pm May-Sep) A more formal setting (meaning tablecloths), where you can gorge on an all-you-can-eat breakfast pre-hiking. At dinnertime the exotic dishes tend to disappoint – go for beef tenderloin or pasta instead.

Jackson Lake Lodge

Pioneer Grill (meals $-$$; ☽ 6am-10:30pm) A casual classic diner with leatherette stools lined up in a maze, the Pioneer serves up wraps, burgers and salads. A Mt Owen – an oversized profiterole topped with ice cream, hot fudge and whipped cream – takes the burn off hikes up Cascade Canyon. Pioneer has a takeout window, boxed lunches (order before 9pm for the next day) and room service pizza for pooped hikers (5pm to 9pm).

Poolside Barbecue (☎ 307-543-2811; meals $$; ☽ 6-8pm Sun-Fri Jul-Aug) Reservations are required for this all-you-can-eat BBQ buffet with live music.

Mural Room (☎ 307-543-3100; meals $$$-$$$$) The ambiance could hardly be heightened: in addition to stirring views of the Tetons and moose ambling in the willow flats, the dining room walls are adorned with the romantic Rendezvous Murals, depictions of 19th-century life by Carl Roters. Gourmet selections include game dishes and imaginative creations like trout wrapped in sushi rice with sesame seeds. Breakfasts are very good; dinner reservations are recommended.

The Blue Heron recaffeination station serves lattes and espressos from 6am and alcohol and appetizers from 11am to midnight; occasionally you'll hit on live music. To fully appreciate the outdoor patio, sip a huckleberry margarita while watching the alpenglow on Mt Moran.

Signal Mountain

Signal Mountain Lodge (☎ 307-543-2831; meals $-$$$) With an encyclopedic menu, the Trapper Grill should please each picky member of the family, offering a range from burgers and Mexican to gourmet sandwiches and ribs. The hot breakfasts, with sides of ham, bacon or buffalo sausage, are gut busters. Next door, the Peaks Restaurant serves selections of cheese and fruit, local free-range beef and organic polenta cakes. While the indoor ambiance is rather drab, the patio seating, starring sunsets over Jackson Lake, gets snapped up early. Simpler palettes will be happy with a Philly steak and a pint of Snake River Lager at Deadman's Bar, named after the site of an unsolved murder in 1886.

Jenny Lake Lodge Dining Room (☎ 307-733-4647; meals $$$$) Leave your hiking boots in the car; men must wear jackets at the park's premier restaurant. Pasta, an excellent wine list and strip steak in soy glaze are some of the offerings. While we love the idea of a five-course meal in the wilderness, some diners report that the service and food could benefit from more attention. Dinner reservations are required. Lunch is a more causal affair, with lighter meals (try the smoked trout), but reservations are still a good idea.

CENTRAL TETONS
Moose

Dornan's Grocery Store (☎ 307-733-2415; Moose Village) The park's best-quality selection, with an excellent deli, sandwich and espresso counter and a wildly popular frozen-yogurt machine. The Wine Shoppe offers 1700 selections as well as monthly wine tasting, as per its motto – life is too short to drink cheap wine. Salud!

Dornan's Chuckwagon (☎ 307-733-2415 ext 213; Moose Village; breakfast & lunch $, dinner $$; ☺ noon-3pm & 5-9pm Jun–mid-Sep) Dinner doesn't get any more casual than these picnic tables scattered in the open air, but the views are simply grand. At this family favorite, breakfast means sourdough pancakes and eggs off the griddle while lunchtime means light fare and sandwiches. At dinner time the Dutch ovens are steaming with steak dinners and Mexican dishes, along with a bottomless salad bar. The bar boasts zinging margaritas and Snake River Lager on tap.

Pizza Pasta Company (meals $-$$; ☺ noon-9pm) Packed with crowds nightly, this unpretentious pizza parlor is simple yet so satisfying. Crusty pizza, pastas and nachos are offered with beer, wine and snappy service. The 2nd-floor terrace serves up a fun evening atmosphere, lovely Teton views and occasional live music.

JOHN D ROCKEFELLER JR MEMORIAL PARKWAY

Bear's Den (☎ 800-443-2311; lunch $, dinner from $$-$$$) Hungry travelers flock to this eatery at Flagg Ranch, the area's sole dining option. Breakfast and lunches are casual at this handsome lodge while dinner goes Western with grilled steaks, meatloaf and chicken potpie. Whiskey and local brews are served at the Burnt Bear Saloon. The adjoining minimart has a deli (open 1:30pm to 5:30pm).

Around Grand Teton

As rich in character and as scenic as the park itself, the areas surrounding Grand Teton National Park merit expanding your vacation beyond park boundaries – and we don't just mean giddying-up to the local brew pub (although we hear the organic wheat beer is mighty fine). Hiking Bridger-Teton or Jedediah Smith National Forests offers off-the-beaten-track adventure, if not in the Tetons then with supreme views of their adulated peaks. Plus, outside park boundaries the rules are looser and the possibilities broader. Bring your pup on a hike, break in your Stetson on a dude ranch, ride or paddle the curvaceous Snake River – opportunities abound.

Visitors will find that the down-home vibe of Idaho's Teton Valley contrasts sharply with the Western worldliness of Jackson. Those after a buzzing social scene or browsing for Western baubles should seek out the stimulation of Jackson. But if you came here to embrace every scrap of solitude, a trip west across the divide might be in order.

One of the best times to visit this region is in winter, when Jackson Hole and Grand Targhee serve up soft powder that spells heaven to snowboarders and skiers. Lodges light roaring fires and the surrounding wilderness becomes a haven for dogsledding, snowshoeing, Nordic touring and winter fun.

HIGHLIGHTS

- Riding through the wildflower meadows to explore Idaho's **Teton Valley** (p256) on horseback
- Tearing down singletrack trails on mountain bikes only to catch your breath on the gondola ride up at **Jackson Hole** (p250)
- Crossing streams and cresting lofty ridges on the trail to **Table Mountain** (p253)
- Luxuriating in **Rock Spring Yurt** (p251) in a guided overnight trek to the backcountry
- Soaking in **Granite Hot Springs** (p252) pool after a hard day on the hoof

JACKSON

☎ 307 / pop 9000 / elev 6234ft

Technically this is Wyoming, but you'll have a hard time believing it. With a median age of 32, this Western town has evolved into a mecca for mountain lovers, hardcore climbers and skiers, many of whom spend years living out of their trucks for lack of a better option. Once a diamond in the rough, Jackson is now undergoing some laborious polishing: the county boasts the highest construction expenses per capita in the US, McMansions spread like brucellosis and service jobs attract a sizeable immigrant community with nowhere to live.

This new confluence of locals – the ranchers, rhinestone cowboys and the service army – must come to grips with tensions between the evolving community and wilderness, since 97% of Teton County is, in fact, public land.

The upswing of being posh and popular? Jackson is abuzz with life: trails and outdoor opportunities abound, fresh sushi is flown in daily and generous purse-strings support a vigorous cultural life. Skip the souvenirs and remember why you came to Jackson in the first place: to visit its glorious backyard called Grand Teton National Park.

Orientation & Information

The town of Jackson marks the intersection of Hwy 22 (heading west to Teton Pass) and US 26/89/191. The main drag follows east–west Broadway into the downtown area, where it turns north onto Cache Dr at the town square, the heart of the pedestrian-oriented commercial district.

The exclusive community of Wilson is 5 miles west of Jackson on Hwy 22, just west of the junction with Hwy 390 (Moose-Wilson Rd), which leads north 7 miles to Teton Village.

Tune to 90.3 FM (NPR), 93.3 (KJAX) or 96.9 (KMTN) for the local lowdown. Free newspapers include the *Jackson Hole Daily* (liberal) and the *Daily Guide* (conservative).

Bank of Jackson Hole ATMs (990 W Broadway, cnr E Broadway & S Cache)

Jackson Hole & Greater Yellowstone Visitor Center (☎ 307-733-3316; www.jacksonholechamber .com; 532 N Cache St; ☽ 8am-7pm summer, 8am-5pm winter) Provides information, books, rest rooms, an ATM and a courtesy phone for free local calls.

Jackson Ranger District (☎ 307-739-5450; www .fs.fed.us/btnf; 25 Rosencranz Lane; ☽ 8am-4:30pm Mon-Fri) Side-by-side with the USFS Bridger-Teton National Forest Headquarters.

Soap Opera Laundromat (☎ 307-733-5584; 850 W Broadway)

St John's Medical Center (☎ 307-733-3636; 625 E Broadway)

Teton County Library (☎ 307-733-2164; www.tclib .org; 125 Virginian Lane; ☽ 10am-9pm Mon-Thu, 10am-5pm Fri & Sat, 1-5pm Sun;) Free internet and wireless connection.

USFS Bridger-Teton National Forest Headquarters (☎ 307-739-5500; www.fs.fed.us/btnf; 25 Rosencranz Lane) Office in the Jackson Ranger District; information available at the visitor center.

Valley Bookstore (☎ 307-733-4533, 800-647-4111; 125 N Cache St in Gaslight Alley) Books, guides and maps.

Wyoming Game & Fish Department (☎ 307-733-2321; 420 N Cache St; ☽ 8am-5pm Mon-Fri) For fishing licenses.

Sights

If you visit only one area museum, make it the **National Museum of Wildlife Art** (☎ 307-733-5771; www.wildlifeart.org; 2820 Rungius Rd; adult $10, child free with adult; ☽ 9am-5pm), with major works by Bierstadt, Rungius, Remington and Russell that will make your skin prickle. The discovery gallery has a kids' studio for drawing and print rubbing that adults plainly envy. Check the website for summer film series and art-class schedules. The on-site **Rising Sage Café** (☎ 307-733-8649) is superb. The 51,000-sq-ft Arizona sandstone facility blends into the landscape overlooking the National Elk Refuge, three miles north of town on the west side of US 26/89/191.

The beautiful new **Center for the Arts** (☎ 307-734-8956; www.jhcenterforthearts.org; 240 S Glenwood S) is one-stop shopping for culture, attracting big-name concert acts and featuring theatre performances, classes, art exhibits and events. Check the calendar of events online. Students get discounts on performances.

The **Jackson Hole Museum** (☎ 307-733-2414; www.jacksonholehistory.org; 105 N Glenwood St; adult/child/senior/family $3/1/2/6; ☽ 9:30am-6pm Mon-Sat, 10am-5pm Sun) explores local lore from hunter-gatherers to the present epoch. Look online for current programs and events, which include a 'Hollywood in the Hole' film series.

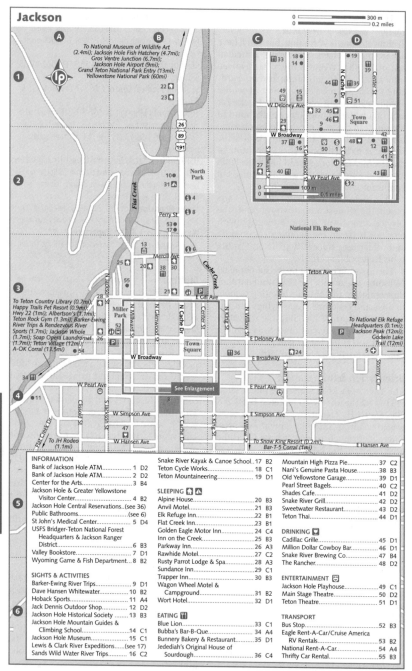

Jackson

INFORMATION
Bank of Jackson Hole ATM................... 1 D2
Bank of Jackson Hole ATM................... 2 D2
Center for the Arts.............................. 3 B4
Jackson Hole & Greater Yellowstone
  Visitor Center.................................. 4 B2
Jackson Hole Central Reservations..(see 36)
Public Bathrooms..........................(see 6)
St John's Medical Center.................... 5 D4
USFS Bridger-Teton National Forest
  Headquarters & Jackson Ranger
  District... 6 B3
Valley Bookstore.............................. 7 D1
Wyoming Game & Fish Department.... 8 B2

SIGHTS & ACTIVITIES
Barker-Ewing River Trips..................... 9 D1
Dave Hansen Whitewater.................. 10 B2
Hoback Sports................................ 11 A4
Jack Dennis Outdoor Shop............... 12 D2
Jackson Hole Historical Society 13 B3
Jackson Hole Mountain Guides &
  Climbing School........................14 C1
Jackson Hole Museum...................... 15 C1
Lewis & Clark River Expeditions......(see 17)
Sands Wild Water River Trips.......... 16 C2

Snake River Kayak & Canoe School...17 B2
Teton Cycle Works........................... 18 C1
Teton Mountaineering..................... 19 D1

SLEEPING
Alpine House.................................. 20 B3
Anvil Motel.................................... 21 B3
Elk Refuge Inn................................ 22 B1
Flat Creek Inn................................ 23 B1
Golden Eagle Motor Inn................... 24 C4
Inn on the Creek............................ 25 B3
Parkway Inn................................... 26 A3
Rawhide Motel............................... 27 C2
Rusty Parrot Lodge & Spa................ 28 A3
Sundance Inn................................. 29 C1
Trapper Inn.................................... 30 B3
Wagon Wheel Motel &
  Campground................................ 31 B2
Wort Hotel.................................... 32 D1

EATING
Blue Lion...................................... 33 C1
Bubba's Bar-B-Que.......................... 34 A4
Bunnery Bakery & Restaurant.......... 35 D1
Jedediah's Original House of
  Sourdough................................. 36 C4

Mountain High Pizza Pie.................. 37 C2
Nani's Genuine Pasta House............. 38 B3
Old Yellowstone Garage................... 39 D1
Pearl Street Bagels.......................... 40 C2
Shades Cafe................................... 41 D2
Snake River Grill............................. 42 D2
Sweetwater Restaurant.................... 43 D2
Teton Thai.................................... 44 D1

DRINKING
Cadillac Grille................................ 45 D1
Million Dollar Cowboy Bar................ 46 D1
Snake River Brewing Co................... 47 B4
The Rancher................................... 48 D2

ENTERTAINMENT
Jackson Hole Playhouse................... 49 C1
Main Stage Theatre......................... 50 D2
Teton Theatre................................ 51 D1

TRANSPORT
Bus Stop....................................... 52 B3
Eagle Rent-A-Car/Cruise America
  RV Rentals................................. 53 B2
National Rent-A-Car........................ 54 A4
Thrifty Car Rental........................... 55 B3

The affiliated **Jackson Hole Historical Society** (☎ 307-733-9605; 105 Mercill Ave; admission free; ⏰ 8am-5pm Mon-Fri Jun-Sep), housed in a historic log cabin, maintains an extensive research library of Western Americana.

Among a herd of kitsch and souvenir shops in downtown Jackson, you'll find the **Alaska Fur Gallery** (☎ 307-733-4772; 135 N Cache Dr), where you can pick up a toasty beaver pelt jockstrap (a best-seller) for your sweetie – but don't expect to see Bridget Bardot shopping there.

About 7000 Rocky Mountain 'welfare' elk (and a few hungry wolves) winter on alfalfa hay pellets at the **National Elk Refuge** (☎ 307-733-9212; 675 E Broadway; admission free) when snow covers the native grasses October through May. Access these 25,000 acres northeast of Jackson via Elk Refuge Rd, an extension of E Broadway. Bundle the kids up for the refuge's one-hour winter **sleigh ride** (adult/child 5–12 $16/12), departing from the National Museum of Wildlife Art mid-December through early April. It's interesting to note that elk provide the 'raw materials' for the **antler arch** on Jackson Town Square (also see p245).

Just north of the refuge, the **Jackson National Fish Hatchery** (☎ 307-733-2510; 1500 Fish Hatchery Rd; admission free; ⏰ 8am-4pm) offers daily tours.

Activities

The cowboy myths may have gone to pasture, but Jackson remains paradise for outdoor enthusiasts. Options are only limited by your lack of gear or imagination, so consult the following shops for rentals or trip suggestions.

The nearby Gros Ventre Mountains offer superb day hikes with expansive views and wildlife. Call ☎ 307-690-5646 for details about car shuttles run by Taxi Service Rent-a-Raft. Hikers can warm up on the nearby Jackson Peak hike (right).

HIKING

A renowned local hike practically unknown to outsiders, this is one of the closest summits to Jackson offering a distinct view of the Tetons across the valley. Since this is national forest, entry is free and dogs are OK. On the 4th of July locals flock to this spot to enjoy great views of the local fireworks displays.

GOODWIN LAKE & JACKSON PEAK

Duration 5 hours
Distance 9 miles
Difficulty moderate
Elevation Change 2380ft
Start/Finish Jackson Peak Trailhead
Nearest Town/Junction Jackson, Wyoming
Summary Dog-friendly and a great warm-up for bigger hikes; convenient to Jackson, with panoramas of the Tetons.

To get here, drive east on East Broadway until it ends, turning left into the National Elk Refuge. The road switchbacks. Bear right at Curtis Canyon for Goodwin Lake (after 9.2 miles) and drive 2.7 miles to the parking lot. The trailhead is on the left.

The trail climbs steadily through a field of wildflowers, topping out on a level hilltop, passing through fragrant forests of Douglas fir. Approach the forested shores of **Goodwin Lake** (880ft), named for a fur trapper who spent his solitary winters here. Stop here for an easy, 6-mile, round-trip hike. It's a nice spot for a swim or trout fishing, but picnicking might be a challenge since it's also popular with mosquitoes.

The bare, pointed summit of **Jackson Peak** sits directly above the lake. Its most secure approach winds left up a more gradual saddle. Continue past Goodwin Lake heading southeast, crossing an open field. Take a right at a well-worn but narrow trail marked with cairns. The trail climbs steeply to the ridge, crossing snow patches and rocky outcrops (but nothing too tricky here) to the peak. A large **cairn** marks the summit. Enjoy the expansive views of the valley and Gros Ventre Wilderness. Return via the same route.

MOUNTAIN BIKING

Teton Cycle Works (☎ 307-733-4386; 175 N Glenwood St) is a superb full-service shop that also offers rentals. The helpful **Hoback Sports** (☎ 307-733-5335; 520 W Broadway Ave; ⏰ 9am-7pm) offers bike rentals ($20 to $40 per day), tours (from $45), repairs and maps of area biking trails.

Popular rides include Cache Creek, southeast of Jackson into the Gros Ventre; Game Creek, along USFS Rd 30455 east off US 26/89/191; and Spring Gulch Rd, west of and parallel to US 26/89/191 between

Hwy 22 and Gros Ventre Junction. Hard-core riders can try Old Pass Rd, the old route over Teton Pass, south of Hwy 22.

ROCK CLIMBING & MOUNTAINEERING

With world-class climbing at your nubby fingertips, Jackson is an ideal center for instruction or guided climbs. The reputable standbys are **Exum Mountain Guides** (☎ 307-733-2297; www.exumguides.com) and **Jackson Hole Mountain Guides & Climbing School** (☎ 307-733-4979, 800-239-7642; www.jhmg.com; 165 N Glenwood St). Exum runs climbing schools in Grand Teton National Park and at the upper cliffs at the Jackson Hole Mountain Resort, accessed by the aerial tram (p250).

Singles seeking climbing partners swear by the bulletin board at **Teton Mountaineering** (☎ 307-733-3595; 170 N Cache St), which stocks a good range of books and outdoor gear. **Teton Rock Gym** (☎ 307-733-0707; 1116 Maple Way) offers a wide variety of indoor sport climbs.

WHITE-WATER RAFTING & FLOATING

A splashy paddle down the class-III **Snake River Canyon**, south of Jackson along US 89/26 between Hoback Junction and Alpine, is a popular summer pastime. Wildlife includes ospreys and eagles nesting along the river. Half-day trips (from $48) put in at West Table Creek and take out at Sheep Gulch (8 miles). Full-day trips (from $80) put in at Pritchard Creek, upstream from West Table Creek, and take out at Sheep Gulch (16 miles). The rafting season runs May to Labor Day, but the best white-water is in June. July and August are crowded, so reserve ahead.

Half-day **scenic float trips** on a 13-mile section of the swift-flowing Snake River put in south of Grand Teton National Park and take out north of Hoback Junction, passing through the Jackson Hole wetlands, which are rich with bird and wildlife-viewing opportunities. For more information on boating the Snake, see p233.

Reputable Jackson-based outfitters:

Barker-Ewing River Trips (☎ 307-733-1000, 800-448-4202; www.barker-ewing.com; 45 W Broadway)

Dave Hansen Whitewater (☎ 307-733-6295, 800-732-6295; www.davehansenwhitewater.com; 515 N Cache St)

Lewis & Clark River Expeditions (☎ 307-733-4022, 800-824-5375; www.lewisandclarkexpeds.com; 335 N Cache St)

Sands Wild Water River Trips (☎ 307-733-4410, 800-358-8184; www.sandswhitewater.com; 110 W Broadway)

CANOEING & KAYAKING

Rendezvous River Sports & Jackson Hole Kayak School (☎ 307-733-2471, 800-733-2471; www.jhkayakschool.com; 945 W Broadway) offers kayak rentals and instruction, as does **Snake River Kayak & Canoe School** (☎ 307-733-9999, 800-529-2501; www.snakeriverkayak.com; 365 N Cache St), which also offers multiday paddling trips to Yellowstone Lake.

REEL & FLY-FISHING

Native whitefish and cutthroat, as well as lake and brown trout, abound in most area waterways. Fishing is subject to Wyoming state regulations. Purchase a license at an outdoor shop or the visitor centers.

For guided fly-fishing and casting instruction, check out **Jack Dennis Outdoor Shop** (☎ 307-733-6838; www.jackdennis.com; 50 E Broadway, Jackson), also a pro fly shop. See p234 for services in the park.

HORSEBACK RIDING

In Jackson, day-long, evening, supper and hourly trail rides depart from **Snow King Stables** (☎ 307-733-5200; ☉ Memorial Day-early Sep), behind Snow King Resort. The meat of the program for **Bar-T-5 Corral** (☎ 307-733-5386, 800-772-5386; www.bart5.com; 812 Cache Creek Dr; adult/child 5-12 $40/33) is chuck-wagon supper shows, located east of Jackson in the Cache Creek drainage. **A-OK Corral** (☎ 307-733-6556; 9550 S Henry Rd), on US 26/189/191 just north of Hoback Junction, offers guided rides and full-day excursions. All three offer cookouts and evening excursions.

OTHER SUMMER ACTIVITIES

For stunning views of five mountain ranges, take the scenic 20-minute **Snow King Chairlift** (adult/child $10/6) ride up to 7751ft. Follow the nature trail at the top through wildflower fields and aspen groves. The lift operates 9am to 6pm mid-May to early September, with extended summer hours.

The resort's meandering 2500ft **Alpine Slide** (☎ 307-733-7680; adult/child $15/12) is open late May to mid-September. Other diversions include **indoor ice skating** and **minigolf**.

The **Wyoming Balloon Co** (☎ 307-739-0900; www.wyomingballoon.com; per person $275) offers the ultimate float trip in the form of hour-long flights over the Tetons. The season runs from early June to mid-September. Flights are weather-dependent. Still not high enough? **Jackson Hole Paragliding** (☎ 307-739-2626, 307-690-7555; www.jhparagliding.com; tandem flight $225) offers tandem rides from several local peaks (no experience necessary), meeting at the Jackson Hole gondola.

SKIING & SNOWBOARDING

The only ski resort where you can sling the skis over your shoulder and walk to from town, the 400-acre **Snow King Resort** (☎ 307-733-5200, 800-522-5464; www.snowking.com; 400 E Snow King Ave) sits on the south edge of the town grid at a base elevation of 6237ft.

In this tiny area, three lifts serve ski and snowboard runs with a vertical drop of 1571ft (15% beginner, 25% intermediate, 60% advanced). Full-day lift tickets are $35/25 per adult/child, while half-day tickets (good after 1pm) are $23/15. The ski season runs from Thanksgiving to March. **Night skiing** (adult/child $15/10; ☽ 4:30-8:30pm Mon-Sat) and **tubing** (per ride $5) are also popular. This north-facing slope catches less snow than other resorts but is convenient and well suited to children and families.

The best values are packages such as the 'Ski All Three' deal, which includes three nights' lodging, daily breakfast, two full-day lift tickets good at Snow King, Jackson Hole Mountain Resort and Grand Targhee, and transfers to and from the airport and between the ski hills. (The regular season price per person for three nights and two days skiing is $400.)

See p250 for details on nearby ski areas.

Festivals & Events

For the scoop on Jackson's annual events see local newspaper listings. If an ungulate rack would provide the finishing touch to your home decor, check out **ElkFest & Antler Auction**, which takes place every May around the town square. Boy scouts collect and sell the shed antlers during the festival to raise money to buy pellet winter feed for the elk – thus the elk financially support themselves during the winter. The **Teton County Fair** takes over the Teton County Fairgrounds (Snow King Ave and Flat Creek Rd) in late July. Also held at the fairgrounds, the **JH Rodeo Company** (☎ 307-733-2805) saddles up at 8pm

Wednesdays and Saturdays June through August. September's **Jackson Hole Fall Arts Festival** features live auctions, artist talks and samples of local chefs' culinary wizardry.

Kids shouldn't dodge what's considered the longest running **shoot out** (☽ 6:15pm Memorial Day-Labor Day) in the country, on the Jackson Town Square, where the good guys and bad guys face off on a daily basis.

Sleeping

Unfortunately, budget lodgings in Jackson have gone the way of the stagecoach. The best deals come during the shoulder seasons (from October 1 until the opening of ski season in late November and after spring snowmelt in early April until Memorial Day), when rooms are as much as 50% less than high-season prices quoted here. Those on a tight budget should plan to camp or stake out the bargain off-season ski lodgings over the pass in Idaho.

Advance reservations are essential during holiday periods. Options are listed below – for more, contact **Jackson Hole Central Reservations** (☎ 888-838-6806; www.jacksonholewy .com), which has listings for the town of Jackson as well as Teton Village.

Rates quoted here are for doubles with private bathroom, since single rates are often not available. Walk-in rates can be up to 20% lower than rack rates, especially during slow periods when it pays to shop around. Check online for special seasonal package deals.

CAMPING

Wagon Wheel Campground (☎ 307-733-4588, 800-323-9279; 435 N Cache Dr; tent & full RV hookup $) The basic and in-town Wagon Wheel is cramped but popular with climbers.

Snake River KOA (☎ 307-733-7078, 800-562-1878; tent & full RV hookup $) Grassy Snake River is 12 miles south of town off US 26/89/191 near Hoback Junction. Cheaper, recommended public US Forest Service (USFS) campgrounds are outside town.

Curtis Canyon Campground (sites $; ☽ late May-Sep 30) Conveniently located, this popular 12-site campground, on gravel USFS Rd 30440 (off Elk Refuge Rd), sits 7 miles northeast of Jackson at 6900ft, with splendid views of the Tetons.

Cabin Creek Campground (sites $; ☽ late May-Sep 30) The roadside, 10-site Cabin Creek is 19 miles south of Jackson and 7 miles west

AROUND GRAND TETON

of Hoback Junction off US 26/89 in Snake River Canyon at 5800ft.

Elbow Campground (sites $; ☻ late May-Sep 30) Three miles further along on the south side of US 26/89 is the scenic, nine-site Elbow, 22 miles south of Jackson.

East Table Campground (sites $; ☻ late May-early Sep) Two windy miles further along toward Idaho on the southeast side of US 26/89 is the roadside, 18-site East Table, 24 miles south of Jackson at 5900ft.

Hoback Campground (sites $; ☻ early Jun–mid-Sep) Along the Hoback River, 8 miles east of Hoback Junction and 22 miles southeast of Jackson (6600ft), is the shady, 14-site Hoback.

Kozy Campground (sites $; ☻ late May-Sep 30) Five miles further along on the east side of US 189/191 is riverside, seven-site Kozy, 30 miles southeast of Jackson at 6500ft.

Granite Creek Campground (sites $; ☻ late May-Sep 30) The signed turnoff for 52-site Granite Creek is 1 mile north of Kozy Campground. The campground itself is 35 miles from Jackson, since it's 9 miles northwest of US 189/191 up (often washboard) gravel USFS Rd 30500, nestled deep in the Gros Ventre Mountains at 6900ft.

Station Creek Campground (sites $; ☻ late May-Sep 30) One mile further west along the Snake River is 16-site Station Creek, 25 miles south of Jackson at 5900ft.

For more information on campgrounds in the Jackson Ranger District call ☎ 1-800-342-CAMP.

LODGING
Midrange
Sundance Inn (☎ 307-733-3444, 888-478-6326; www .sundanceinnjackson.com; 135 W Broadway; d $$$; ✸) Let's start with the homemade cookies, baked by the desk person's mom, that accompany afternoon lemonade. Simply a well-run motel, the Sundance distinguishes itself with good service and tidy rooms. Perks include an outdoor Jacuzzi and continental breakfast.

Anvil Motel (☎ 307-733-3368, 800-234-4507; www .anvilmotel.com; 215 N Cache Dr; d $$$; ✸) Friendly and well scrubbed, the Anvil offers good value, is centrally located and has an outdoor Jacuzzi. The popular hostel is no longer available.

Wagon Wheel Motel (☎ 307-733-2357, 800-323-9279; www.wagonwheelvillage.com; 435 N Cache Dr; cabins

$$$) It's a shame mountain men didn't live to see the day: these sprightly log cabins are equipped with in-room Jacuzzis, fireplaces and kitchenettes, in addition to cable TVs and phones. Don't mind the stuffed elk – it's part of the rustic ambiance.

Golden Eagle Motor Inn (☎ 307-733-2042; 325 E Broadway; d $$$) Just far enough out of the fray, this refurbished motel with friendly hosts is a reliable choice in the center.

Rawhide Motel (☎ 307-733-1216, 800-835-2999; www.rawhidemotel.com; 75 S Millward St; d $$$) New Berber carpets and pine furniture spruce up these typical motel rooms. The staff is friendly and there is no smoking or pets allowed.

Flat Creek Inn (☎ 307-733-5276, 800-438-9338; www.flatcreekinn.com; 1935 N US 89; d $$$; ✸) More motel than inn, this inn offers 72 standard, king rooms and suites with microwave, cable TV, mini-fridge and coffeemakers. Just outside of town, it offers prime views of the National Elk Refuge. Continental breakfast is included.

Elk Refuge Inn (☎ 307-733-3582, 800-544-3582; www.elkrefugeinn.com; 1755 N US 89; d $$$; ✸) Similar to the Flat Creek Inn, this nonsmoking roadside motel seems a bit cozier, with balconies, soft lighting and muted colors. Family rooms sleep five and kids under 12 stay free.

Trapper Inn (☎ 307-733-2648, 888-771-2648; www .trapperinn.com; 235 N Cache Dr; d $$$; ✸ ✸) The modern makeover outside (think corrugated tin and stone) masks what are really simple courtyard motel rooms with screw-on headboards and chintzy furniture. If you can, splurge on the upscale new rooms. Perks include a Jacuzzi and indoor pool.

Parkway Inn (☎ 307-733-3143, 800-247-8390; www.parkwayinn.com; 125 N Jackson St; d $$$$) You may feel like you're spending the weekend at grandma's (except the wolf remains in Yellowstone). This Victorian-themed hotel offers ample suites decked in chintz with quilted brass beds. Perks include a well-stocked continental breakfast, indoor lap pool, hot tub and fitness facility.

Top End
ourpick Alpine House (☎ 307-739-1570, 800-753-1421; www.alpinehouse.com; 285 N Glenwood St; d with breakfast $$$-$$$$; 💻) Two former Olympic skiers infused this downtown home with sunny Scandinavian style and personal

touches like great service and a cozy mountaineering library. Amenities include plush robes, down comforters, a shared Finnish sauna and an outdoor Jacuzzi. Save your appetite for the creative breakfast options like poached eggs over ricotta toast with asparagus or multi grain French toast.

Inn on the Creek (☎ 307-739-1565, 800-669-9534; www.innonthecreek.com; 295 N Millward St; d $$$$; 🖳) Elegant and intimate, this stone inn offers nine handsome rooms. Details include recessed fireplaces, beds fluffed with down comforters, an outdoor Jacuzzi and views of a gurgling creek out back. It's wedged into the edge of town, handy to restaurants and shopping.

Wort Hotel (☎ 307-733-2190, 800-322-2727; www .worthotel.com; 50 N Glenwood St; d $$$$; 🖳) Western themes run amok at this historic 1940s English Tudor gussied up with lodgepole pine beds, cowboy-motif sheets, full-sized baths and Jacuzzis. It's ideal for those who like to be in the thick of it. Attached is the popular Silver Dollar bar and restaurant, featuring an antique S bar encrusted with silver dollars and painted bordello scenes.

Snow King Resort (☎ 307-733-5200, 800-522-5464; www.snowking.com; 400 E Snow King Ave; summer d $$$, condos $$$$) This expanding resort offers a variety of options ranging from condominiums to luxury suites, with the advantage of being slope-side. Inquire about their attractive seasonal package deals.

Rusty Parrot Lodge and Spa (☎ 888-739-1749; www.rustyparrot.com; 175 N Jackson St; d with breakfast $$$$$) This kind of place will make you the envy of the office mates you left behind. Excruciating in its luxury, this new lodging pampers with in-room Jacuzzis, well-tended bedroom fireplaces and a plush teddy bear on the bed. The gourmet restaurant prepares innovative international cuisine. Those who don't ski will get distracted at the spa, where the arnica sports massages and rose and honey wraps are pure hedonism.

Eating

Jackson's fare boasts sophistication – even if that means garnishing your burger with a basil leaf. Those hungry for exotic options won't come away disappointed: all manner of game and international cuisine are present, particularly if you're willing to pony up. Pick up a free *Jackson Hole Dining*

Guide, found in shops and hotel lobbies, for menus.

Travelers who plan to pack a cooler can shop at grocery stores **Jackson Whole** (☎ 307-733-0450; 974 W Broadway), emphasizing the local and organic, or **Albertson's** (105 Buffalo Way; 🖳). Both are at the west end of town off Broadway.

BUDGET

Pearl Street Bagels (☎ 307-739-1218; 145 W Pearl Ave; meals $; ⏰ 6:30am-6pm; 🖳) Cheap and cheery: the bagels are baked onsite and there are good sandwiches, fast service and espresso.

Bunnery Bakery & Restaurant (☎ 307-733-5474; 130 N Cache St; meals $; ⏰ 7am-3pm & 5-9pm summer) Lunch and breakfast at this buzzing café offer an assortment of hearty fare, including all-day eggs and great vegetarian options. The dessert case tempts with mammoth chocolate cake slices, pecan pie and caramel cheesecake.

Shades Cafe (☎ 307-733-2015; 75 S King St; meals $; ⏰ 7am-4pm) A recommended lunch spot: lounge around the shady deck and choose from leafy greens, espresso drinks, panini sandwiches and sides like white bean salads. Breakfasts range from muesli to spicy steamed eggs.

MIDRANGE

Teton Thai (☎ 307-733-0022; 135 N Cache St, Stage Stop Mall; meals $-$$; ⏰ 11:30am-3pm & 5:30-9pm Tue-Sun) Supremely satisfying, this crowded deck sandwiched between strip malls is the locals' longtime favorite. Get your curry 'Thai hot' for a religious experience. Diners BYOB.

Bubba's Bar-B-Que (☎ 307-733-2288; 515 W Broadway; meals $-$$; ⏰ 6:30am-10pm summer, to 8:30pm winter) Vegetarians may shrink from the smokehouse odors, but this casual eatery is wildly popular (the word has it a waitress refused to seat the Schwarzenegger party ahead of other waiting customers, earning kudos from townsfolk). Expect big biscuit breakfasts, succulent brisket and BBQ beans. Kids are well looked after.

Jedediah's Original House of Sourdough (☎ 307-733-5671; 135 E Broadway; breakfast & lunch $, dinner $$; ⏰ 7am-2pm & 5:30-9pm summer) A 30-year institution. For diner food it's a bit overpriced, but the sourjacks satisfy, and the sourdough's is the eatery's very own.

Mountain High Pizza Pie (☎ 307-733-3646; 120 W Broadway; meals $-$$; ⏰ 11am-11pm) A skier's favorite, with trough-sized salads, fresh garlic topping and the option of wheat crust.

Sweetwater Restaurant (☎ 307-733-3553; 85 S King St; meals $$-$$$; ⏰ 11:30am-3pm & 5:30-10pm) A 30-year local staple, Sweetwater's aim is elegant comfort food. Think chicken and blue cheese sandwiches, wyomato salad (featuring Wyoming tomato), rainbow trout and blackened prime rib. There's deck seating, but it doesn't get more romantic than the historic log cabin setting.

TOP END

Blue Lion (☎ 307-733-3912; 160 N Millward St; dinner $$-$$$; ⏰ from 6pm) In a precious cornflower-blue house, the Blue Lion offers outdoor dining under grand old trees on the deck. It creatively combines Thai and French influences in dishes such as beef tenderloin au bleu and green curry prawns.

Nani's Genuine Pasta House (☎ 307-733-3888; 242 N Glenwood St; meals $$-$$$$; ⏰ from 5pm) Boasting gratifying regional cuisine, this cozy house cooks up pastas, risottos and hormone-free Wyoming beef. Those dining *pranzo* (Italian-style) get aperitifs, a fish course, wine, salad, cheese, fruit and nuts. Reservations are a good idea.

our pick **Old Yellowstone Garage** (☎ 307-734-6161; 175 Center St; meals $$$) Slow-cooked lamb shank, fresh fish and tortellini in broth: your mouth starts watering just reading the menu. When hardworking locals splurge, this elegant Piemontese eatery is where they

come. And given the town's many eating options, that says something.

Snake River Grill (☎ 307-733-0557; 84 E Broadway; dinner $$$-$$$$; ⏰ from 5:30pm) With a roaring stone fireplace and snappy white linens, this grill creates notable American haute cuisine. Grilled elk chops and wild mushroom pasta show a tendency toward the earthy. Sample the extensive wine list and the homemade ice cream or soufflé for dessert.

Drinking

Cadillac Grille (☎ 307-733-3279; 55 N Cache) Locals in fleece and Carharts pile around the island bar of this upscale restaurant for lively two-for-one happy hours from 5pm to 7pm, complemented by a Billy Burger served from next door. Those feeling fancy will appreciate the tantalizing martini menu and calamari and oyster appetizers.

Snake River Brewing Company (☎ 307-739-BEER; 265 S Millward; ⏰ 11:30am-midnight) With an arsenal of 22 microbrews made on spot, some award-winning, it is no wonder that this is a favorite rendezvous spot. While the food (wood-fired pizzas and pasta) doesn't compare to a nutty, fresh OB-1 (organic brown ale), that's not why you came here. Right? Happy hour is from 4pm to 6pm.

Million Dollar Cowboy Bar (☎ 307-733-4790; 25 N Cache St; cover $5; ⏰ noon-late) Most can't wait to plunk their hind quarters on a saddle stool in this dark chop house, an obligatory stop on the Western tour. Weekends get

---

THE NEW FOOD OF THE WEST *Joe Ray*

Food of the West was once cowboy grub: baked beans, boiled spuds and chewy steak. In the eighties, the budding tourist town of Jackson Hole may have out-powdered Aspen, but as journeyman Western chef Richard Bellingham says, food-wise, 'Mediocrity was everywhere.' Most local restaurants essentially built reputations on a view.

Migrating chefs are now bringing their regional traditions from around the country and abroad, melding modern Western food in a culinary hodgepodge that can be surprisingly good. There's a big emphasis on creativity and freshness: since price isn't an objection, what isn't local is simply flown in express. Jackson's Snake River Grill (above) roams from main courses like a classic stuffed chicken breast to pecan-crusted Idaho trout with watercress, shaved apple and horseradish crème fraîche.

But that elk you presumed was bagged by some plaid-clad local hunter? It probably grew up on a farm in Canada or even New Zealand. Wild game such as deer and buffalo can be very good, but much of it travels further than sushi to get to your plate.

Welcome to the new Wild West.

Paris-based journalist Joe Ray covers food from around the world.
He can be reached via www.joe-ray.com.

lively when the dance floor sparks up and karaoke drones.

The Rancher (☎ 307-733-3886; 20 E Broadway) This pool hall is a local happy-hour favorite.

Entertainment

The free weekly *Jackson Hole Weekend Guide* appears Friday and reviews local entertainment options, as does the *Stepping Out* insert.

Snow King Resort's popular **Lounge** (☎ 307-733-5200) features live acid jazz on Saturday nights.

Local theater troupes stage Broadway-style musical comedies and provide dinner at the **Jackson Hole Playhouse** (☎ 307-733-6994; www.jhplayhouse.com; 145 W Deloney Ave) and **Main Stage Theatre** (☎ 307-733-3670; cnr W Broadway & Cache Dr).

The 1941 sandstone **Teton Theatre** (120 N Cache Dr) is the best place to catch a flick; ring the **Jackson Movieline** (☎ 307-733-4939) for a rundown of what's showing at all three of Jackson's movie houses.

Getting There & Away

Actually within Grand Teton National Park, **Jackson Hole Airport** (☎ 307-733-7682; www .jacksonholeairport.com; ☐) is 7 miles north of Jackson off US 26/89/191. Always packed, the airport yearns to expand but is limited by a 50-year agreement with the National Park Service (NPS).

For shuttle service, **Alltrans' Jackson Hole Express** (☎ 307-733-1719, 800-443-6133; www .jacksonholebus.com) goes to Jackson (one way/round-trip $15/28) and Teton Village (one way/round-trip $23/42). Shuttles run daily from Jackson to Idaho Falls (one way/round-trip $40/70, 2½ hours), Salt Lake City (one way/round-trip $75/140, 4½ hours) and points in between. Reservations are recommended. Jackson pickup is at Maverick, on the corner of South Park Loop Rd and Broadway, just south of the US 26/89/191 and Hwy 22 junction. In winter they offer packages with lift tickets to Grand Targhee Ski Resort. Idaho Falls-based **CART** (☎ 208-354-2240) offers bus service between Jackson and Idaho Falls via Teton Valley.

Jackson is bisected by US 26/89/191, 4 miles south of the south entrance to Grand Teton National Park. US 26/89/191 leads north to Moran Junction (31 miles), where US 89/191/287 continues north to Yellowstone's South Entrance (57 miles). US 26 heads east over Togwotee Pass (9658ft) to Riverton (168 miles) via Dubois and the Wind River Indian Reservation, and south to Alpine (35 miles) at the Wyoming–Idaho border. US 89 leads north through Grand Teton and Yellowstone parks to Gardiner and southwest to Salt Lake City (270 miles). US 191 goes south to Hoback Junction (12 miles) and Rock Springs (178 miles) on I-80.

Getting Around

Southern Teton Area Rapid Transit (START; ☎ 307-733-4521; www.startbus.com) runs a free around-town shuttle and two routes (Red Line and Workers' Special) between Jackson and Teton Village. One-way fares are free within town limits and $1 to $2 outside of town; exact change is required. Check maps and timetables posted at stops for current routes and schedules.

Car rental agencies **Alamo** (☎ 307-733-0671, 800-327-9633; www.alamo.com), **Avis** (☎ 307-733-3422, 800-331-1212; www.avis.com), **Budget** (☎ 307-733-2206, 800-527-0700; www.budget.com) and **Hertz** (☎ 307-733-2272, 800-654-3131; www.hertz.com) all have desks in the Jackson airport. In town are **Eagle Rent-A-Car/Cruise America RV Rentals** (☎ 307-739-9999, 800-582-2128; www.cruiseamerica .com; 375 N Cache St), **National Rent-A-Car** (☎ 307-733-0735, 800-227-7368; 345 W Broadway) and **Thrifty** (☎ 307-739-9300, 800-367-2277; 220 N Millward St).

Call **A-1** (☎ 307-690-3900), **All-Star** (☎ 307-733-2888, 800-378-2944) or **Alltrans** (☎ 307-733-3135, 800-443-6133) for a taxi. For shuttle service to trails, try **Taxi Tim** (☎ 307-690-4141).

JACKSON HOLE

Now clad in faux-fur, Stetsons and trophy homes, it's hard to remember that the first settlers to Jackson Hole wrangled with harsh winters and a short growing season, not to mention the horse thieves, poachers and elk tuskers that roamed the rural valley. Dubbed 'hole' by early European visitors, the broad valley is bounded by the Gros Ventre (*grow*-vant: 'big belly' in French) and Teton Ranges to the east and west, respectively, and the Yellowstone lava flows and Hoback and Wyoming Ranges to the north and south. The communities of Jackson, Teton Village, Kelly, Moose and Wilson, as well as much of south Grand Teton National Park, lie within the Hole.

AROUND GRAND TETON

This is one of the most breathtaking destinations in the country. Moose, elk and bison roam the valley floor against the rugged backdrop of the Tetons. Eagles and osprey fish the cold, crystalline streams and lakes. Surrounding the valley, the mountainous 3.4-million-acre Bridger-Teton National Forest is the second-largest forest in the lower 48.

Downhill skiing rules winter, but summertime visitors find no shortage of things to do. The **Grand Teton Music Festival** (☎ 307-733-1128; www.gtmf.org; adult $20-50, student $5-10) offers nightly symphony concerts in summer. For details on rafting, mountain biking and horseback riding in the valley, see p243.

Teton Village & Jackson Hole Mountain Resort

Long runs, deep powder and a screeching 4139ft vertical drop may have earned it infamy, but Jackson Hole has quickly become the pet resort of a tony, jet-setting crowd. Continually expanding to keep its status, this modern year-round resort is at the foot of Rendezvous Mountain, 12 miles northwest of Jackson. There are real athletes here, though, and those with any inkling to play outdoors can revel in the fair-weather pursuits of hiking, biking, white-water rafting, fly-fishing, mountain biking and faux cowboying.

The **Jackson Hole Guest Service Center** (☎ 307-739-2753, 800-450-0477) is near the tram ticket office in the Clock Tower Building in Teton Village. Contact **Jackson Hole Mountain Resort** (☎ 307-733-2292, 888-333-7766; www.jacksonhole.com) for a free visitor guide. The resort also has an in-town **office** (☎ 307-733-4005; 140 E Broadway).

The **Kids' Ranch** (307-739-2788; ☺ 9am-5pm) provides child care, with activities for bigger kids and teens like hikes, field trips and rock climbing.

JACKSON HOLE AERIAL TRAM & BRIDGER GONDOLA

This scenic **tram** was under renovation at the time of research. It re-opens in December 2008. Until then, summer hikers can take the Bridger Gondola to the headwall area to get a head-start on hikes. The new 100-passenger tram will extend 2.5 miles to the top of Rendezvous Mountain (10,450ft),

offering great views of Jackson Hole and providing a high-altitude piggyback to Grand Teton National Park's high-country trails. From the summit, hikers can either descend Granite Canyon Trail or choose from a series of shorter trails: the 0.5-mile **Summit Nature Loop**, 3-mile **Cody Bowl Trail** or the 4.25-mile Rock Springs Bowl.

The **Bridger Gondola** (adult/child 6-14 $15/7; ☺ 9am-5pm summer, to 9pm Thu-Sat) offers unlimited rides to the headwall (which is 1355ft lower than Rendezvous Mountain). Most of the aforementioned hikes can be accessed here; check with operators for details.

SKIING & SNOWBOARDING

'The Hole' is all about vertical: boasting a continuous vertical rise of 4139ft – beaten only by Big Sky by 41ft (we're sure that some front loader is poised to adjust this injustice). Among the world's top ski destinations, the resort has 2500 acres of ski terrain blessed by an average of 380in of snow annually. The runs (10% beginner, 40% intermediate and 50% advanced) are served by six lifts, an aerial tram, two high-speed quads and the Bridger gondola. Full-day lift tickets are $77/63/39 for adult/young adult/child; half-day tickets (after 12:30pm) are $58/48/29. Ski season runs from December to early April. The free *Jackson Hole Mountain Map & Guide*, available at the guest service center, depicts Teton Village.

If you want downhill or snowboard lessons, check out the **Jackson Hole Mountain Sports School** (☎ 800-450-0447, 307-733-4505). The school's top-dollar draw is skiing with Olympic gold medalist Tommy Moe. **Jackson Hole Nordic Center** (☎ 307-739-2629) offers 20 miles of groomed track and wide skating lanes with rentals and instruction. **High Mountain Heli-Skiing** (☎ 307-733-3274; www.heliskijackson.com) delivers advanced skiers and snowboarders to ungroomed backcountry powder.

Several Teton Village shops rent and sell downhill gear: **Jackson Hole Sports** (☎ 307-739-2687), **Teton Village Sports** (☎ 307-733-2181) and **Wildernest Sports** (☎ 307-733-4297). For Nordic gear, try **Skinny Skis** (☎ 307-733-6094; 65 W Deloney Ave) in Jackson. Jackson's **Boardroom of Jackson Hole** (☎ 307-733-8327; 225 W Broadway) is the snowboarder's alternative.

SUMMER ACTIVITIES

Bill & Scott's Jackson Hole Trail Rides (☎ 307-733-6992; 1-/2-hr rides $35/50; end of May-Sep) take would-be cowboys on the trails around the ski area. Early morning rides offer cool temperatures while late-day rides tend to spot wildlife.

Jackson Hole Sports and Wildernest Sports rent mountain bikes and can offer the low-down on area **rides**. Get a ticket to ride the Teewinot Chair and gain access to 7 miles of single track and 15 trails. Tickets are available at the **Bridger Center** (☎ 307-739-2654).

Fishing at Crystal Springs Pond is free for kids under 14. Rent a pole at the pond building.

The **Mountain Dew Climbing Wall** has routes for beginners and experienced climbers, open at 9am daily. **Disc Golf** is free to all guests; purchase discs at Jackson Hole Sports. Visit Guest Services for information on area hikes.

SLEEPING

As in the rest of Jackson Hole, rates here vary widely and seasonally; some hotels also levy a resort fee. Quoted rates are for high-season doubles; figure up to 50% off during low season. (Visitors will find the lowest rates in autumn and springtime, typically when it is too warm to ski but too muddy to mountain-bike!) Try **Jackson Hole Central Reservations** (☎ 888-838-6306; www.jacksonholewy.com) for off-season specials and package deals.

Teton Village KOA Campground (☎ 307-733-5354; tent sites & full RV hookups $; May-Oct) Jackson Hole's only West Bank camping option is this full-service campground 2 miles north of Hwy 22 on Hwy 390. Tenters might prefer the more affordable sites in the surrounding national forest.

Hostel X (☎ 307-733-3415; www.hostelx.com; d $$; closed during shoulder seasons;) Teton Village's only budget option, this old ski lodge offers private doubles and bunk-bed rooms for up to four in cramped and dowdy spaces. The spacious lounge with fireplace is ideal for movies or Scrabble tournaments and there's a playroom for tots. Guests can use a microwave and outdoor grill, coin laundry and a ski-waxing area.

ourpick Alpenhof Lodge (☎ 307-733-3242; www.alpenhoflodge.com; d $$$$) The classic Tyrolean Alpenhof offers upscale accommodations in an easygoing atmosphere. Gable rooms feature hand-painted furniture and cozy wood paneling.

Rock Spring Yurt (☎ 888-333-7766, 307-739-2779; up to 8 people $$$$) If you're craving a wilderness experience without the hassle, come here for a modified Central Asian–style tent equipped with a wood-burning stove and gas lamps. An expert guide cooks your food and does the dishes (but you tell the bedtime stories yourself). The hut is reached via a 2.5-mile hike from Teton Village in summer.

Ski-in, ski-out, slope-side options include **Crystal Springs Lodge** (☎ 800-329-9205; condo $$$$) above Teton Village Sports and studio rooms with kitchen facilities at the **Village Center Inn** (☎ 307-733-3155, 800-735-8342; d $$$$).

Jackson Hole Resort Lodging (☎ 307-733-3990, 800-443-8613; www.jhrl.com; 3200 W McCollister Dr) manages Teton Village rental properties ranging from studio condos ($245 per night) to two-bedroom town homes (from $420) as well as multiple-bedroom houses (from $530).

EATING

For a quick-fix, try the smoothies and hoagies at **Café 6311** (meals $; 11am-5pm) in the lower level of the Bridger Center.

The **Mangy Moose Saloon** (☎ 307-733-4913; music hotline 307-733-9779; dinner $$; 5-9pm) is a rockin' steak-and-seafood joint (with a good salad bar) that doubles as a spirited nightspot featuring big-name live music.

In the Teton Mountain Lodge, **Cascade Grill House & Spirits** (☎ 307-732-6932; meals $$$; 7am-10pm) is a popular stop for cocktails, but the upscale menu of steaks, and new Western cuisine might tempt you, too.

With a lovely summer deck, the **Alpenhof Bistro** (☎ 307-733-3242; meals $$-$$$; 7am-10pm), next to the clock tower, specializes in wild game and schnitzel.

With a sterling reputation, the reservations-required **Masa Sushi** (☎ 307-732-2962; meals $$-$$$; 5:30-9:30pm Tue-Sun) serves the Teton's freshest raw fish at the Inn at Jackson Hole.

In a renovated 1905 church just north of Vista Grande, **Calico Italian Restaurant & Bar** (☎ 307-733-2460; Hwy 390; meals $$; from 5pm) serves pizzas, hearty pastas and rich desserts around an open kitchen. A good wine list and cheap kids' menu are bonuses.

Next door, the upscale **Q's Roadhouse** (☎ 307-739-0700; Hwy 390; meals $$) serves ribs and cold microbrews in a sleek modern setting. Vegetarians can try the BBQ tofu, steamed greens and corn bread.

We know it's corny, but all who visit **Bar J Ranch** (☎ 307-733-3370; Hwy 390; adult/child $18/8; ⏰ 7pm Memorial Day weekend-Sep) rave about the sing-along chuck-wagon suppers, featuring BBQ beef, biscuits and beans. Dinner is followed by an hour of stories and songs from the wranglers. Lap-sized kids go free. Reservations are recommended.

Gros Ventre Slide Area

On June 23, 1925, a vast slide of 50 million cu yards of rock, one of the world's largest recent movements of earth, plummeted 2000ft down the side of the Gros Ventre Mountains to form a 225ft-high dam, creating a lake atop the Gros Ventre River. Two years later when the dam suddenly gave way, it created a monster wave that killed six and washed away the downstream town of Kelly.

Today the **Gros Ventre Slide Geological Area** offers a 0.5-mile interpretive trail with views over the slide. Amazingly, some trees survived the fall, 'surfing' the slide to reroot on the valley floor. The resulting Upper and Lower Slide Lakes attract anglers and boaters. The turnoff to the slide area is 1 mile north of Kelly. Not far from the junction is the **Kelly Warm Spring**, an undeveloped pool of warm (80°F) water.

The slide sits outside Grand Teton National Park, but is most easily accessed through it by taking Gros Ventre Rd east off Hwy 26/89/191. Three very attractive and economical **USFS campgrounds** (☎ Jackson Ranger District 307-739-5400; sites $; ⏰ early Jun-Sep 30) are spread out along Gros Ventre Rd beyond the Gros Ventre Slide Geological Area (18 to 23 miles northeast of Jackson). Sites have pit toilets and water but no RV hookups. Twenty-site Atherton Creek Campground, 5.5 miles along Gros Ventre Rd at Lower Slide Lake, at the end of the paved road, has a boat dock. If your car can take rough roads, check out the five-site Red Hills Campground, 4.5 miles further east, fronting the Gros Ventre River; the six-site Crystal Creek Campground is 0.5 miles further east. A 7-mile round-trip day hike heads up to Grizzly Lake from near Red Hills Campground.

Granite Hot Springs

The signed turnoff for the developed **Granite Hot Springs Swimming Pool** (☎ 307-733-6318; www.granitehotsprings.net; adult/child $6/4; ⏰ daylight hr year-round) and **Granite Creek Campground** (☎ Jackson Ranger District 307-739-5400; sites $; ⏰ Jun-Sep) is 35 miles southeast of Jackson on Hwy 189/191, 1 mile before Kozy Campground. Free camping is allowed along the road to the hot springs, but not within 2 miles of the hot springs. In winter, the hot springs (a delicious 112°F) are accessible by snowmobile or skiing only. In summer the water temperature drops to 93°F. The route south through Hoback Canyon affords views of the stunning south face of the Gros Ventre Mountains.

The campground bumps up against the **Gros Ventre Wilderness** and offers good hiking up Granite Creek. Within walking distance of the campground is the undeveloped **Granite Falls Hot Springs**, accessed from the dirt parking area just below the falls. Reaching the hot springs (on the east bank of the creek) requires an often tricky and always chilly ford, and water levels only allow for soaking from around late May until spring snowmelt submerges the pool, with winter access by snowmobile or cross-country skis. Please respect the place and enjoy one of Wyoming's best natural soaks.

Wilson

Big barns and open range make this little outpost 13 miles from Jackson feel more like cowboy country, even though the median home price pushes a cool million. Accommodations are scarce, but you will find worthwhile eateries and a kicking saloon. Wilson's roadside attractions are a typical feeding stop before that last push over the pass to Idaho, or after, especially for cyclists and backcountry and downhill skiers going to Grand Targhee Ski Resort.

A popular mainstay of live music, mingling cowboys with rhinestone cowgirls, hippies and hikers, Wilson's **Stagecoach Bar** (☎ 307-733-4407; 5755 W Hwy 22) is worth the short drive. 'Mon-day' means reggae, Thursday is disco night and every Sunday the house band croons country-and-western favorites until 10pm. Attached is **Pica's Mexican Taqueria** (⏰ lunch & dinner), serving big salads and tasty grilled tacos on the deck and at a lively community table.

Local institution **Nora's Fish Creek Inn** (☎ 307-733-8288; 5600 W Hwy 22; breakfast & lunch $, dinner $$; 🕑 6am-9:30pm) reels 'em in with heaping country breakfasts, including tasty green chili huevos rancheros. Morning rush hour means dining bottlenecks: bring a newspaper to pass the time. Lunch features prime rib and a selection of fresh fish and sandwiches.

For carbs and caffeine, hit the Wilson branch of **Pearl Street Bagels** (☎ 307-739-1261; 1230 Ida Lane; 🕑 9am-6pm Mon-Sat, 9am-2pm Sun; 🖥) for the same swift service as its Jackson counterpart. The creek-side picnic area out back proves ideal for those traveling with dogs or children.

UPPER WIND RIVER VALLEY

Part of the Wyoming Centennial Scenic Byway, US 26/287 climbs east from Grand Teton National Park's Moran Junction up the slopes of Bridger-Teton National Forest to Togwotee Pass (*Toe*-ga-tee; 9658ft), before dropping into the upper Wind River Valley. To the north is the 914-sq-mile Teton Wilderness; to the south is the more distant Gros Ventre Wilderness. Dubois is the only town in the upper valley, east of which the landscape yields to the semi-arid red sandstone Dubois badlands.

The Bridger-Teton National Forest **Buffalo Ranger District Blackrock Ranger Station** (☎ 307-543-2386, 307-739-5600), 8 miles east of Moran Junction, has general information and free maps of the region.

MORAN JUNCTION TO TOGWOTEE PASS

About 3 miles east of Moran Junction, the paved Buffalo Valley Rd forks off the main highway to offer a 4-mile detour northeast up the Buffalo Fork to the Turpin Meadow Recreation Area, a popular launching pad for local outfitters.

There's a USFS campground here and lots of dispersed camping. The road loops south as the unpaved USFS Rd 30050 to rejoin US 26/287.

Three miles from this junction, just past Togwotee Cowboy Village, a short detour to the left leads to a **scenic overlook** with fine views back to the Tetons. A second viewpoint, the **Togwotee Pass Vista View**, is 5 miles further along; the actual pass is another 12 miles from here. The pass, named for a Shoshone medicine man who led the US Army Corps of Engineers here in 1873, marks the Continental Divide. Just by the pass, the lovely **Wind River Lake** makes a perfect picnic spot.

Six miles downhill, the turnoff to Falls Campground offers access to pretty **Brooks Lake Creek Falls**, with fine views up to the breccia (lava and ash) cliffs of the Pinnacle Buttes.

Across from Falls Campground, unpaved Brooks Lake Rd (USFS Rd 515) winds uphill for 5 miles to gorgeous **Brooks Lake**, a popular base for camping, canoeing, fishing and hiking set at the base of dramatic Pinnacle Buttes. The road passes Pinnacle Campground before it descends to Brooks Lake Campground, a boat ramp and a trailhead. From the Brooks Lake turnoff it's 23 miles to Dubois, or 31 miles back to Grand Teton. For **campground** (sites $) information call the **Wind River Ranger District** (☎ 307-455-2466).

IDAHO'S TETON VALLEY

The west face of the mighty Teton Range soars above this broad valley, which is warmer, sunnier and more tranquil than its well-known Wyoming neighbor, Jackson Hole. Here the Teton River descends the west side of the Teton Range and flows northwest, joining Henry's Fork of the Snake River near Rexburg, Idaho. Mountains surround the valley on three sides: the Targhee National Forest, and the Teton Range to the west, the Snake River Range to the south and the Big Hole Mountains to the southwest.

TABLE MOUNTAIN	
Duration 5 hours	
Distance 12 miles	
Difficulty difficult	
Elevation Change 4100ft	
Start/Finish Table Mountain Trailhead	
Nearest Town/Junction Driggs	
Summary A hearty challenge with just rewards: the Grand Teton front and center. Terrain varies between river crossings, steep sections and wildflowers, with wildlife such as moose and marmots.	

This outstanding hike offers solitude, wildflowers galore and stunning high-alpine scenery without the crowds on the eastern side. While it is a long haul, it is not especially difficult for experienced hikers. If you are inexperienced, the stream crossings and steep sections make it advisable for you to go with an experienced hiker. The trail is optimal after snow pack has melted (early July through September). The final scramble onto Table Mountain can be slippery – tread carefully.

To get here, heading north through Driggs, take a right at the traffic light (toward Targhee Ski Resort). Take a right onto a gravel road (6.5 miles) when the road forks toward Teton Campground. Just past the campground there are two parking lots. Park in the first and follow the trail for Table Mountain. The Teton Campground next door provides a good base for day hikes.

The first section is a thigh-burner – you will ascend a steep forested trail to a lovely **wildflower meadow** dotted with aspens. The next part of the hike is more mellow, with a slow ascent that requires crossing the north fork of **Teton Creek** several times. There are primitive log bridges, but you may have to wade once or twice. Hiking poles and sandals are a great help here. After the last stream crossing, the trail winds through a tall pine forest giving way to the open cirque below Table Mountain. Here you ascend steeply – the trail zigzags with breathtaking views of the valley below and the Jedediah Smith Wilderness. You may have to cross a few patches of snow, so step carefully.

Once you achieve the ridge, the rounded knob of Table Mountain appears so close! But it will take you about an hour and a half to reach its summit. Follow the trail as it bends left toward Table Mountain. Once there, ascend the steep, crumbly rock with care, using the least steep path.

The flat-top summit of **Table Mountain** (11,106ft) affords great gawping views of the Grand Teton, Alaska Basin and the western slope of the peaks. Make sure you save time to drink it all in. This was the famous viewpoint from which photographer William H Jackson took the first photos of the Grand Teton during the Hayden Survey in 1872. Head down at a reasonable hour since snowmelt will increase the runoff in the streams and make the crossing more challenging as the day goes on.

Moose and bear frequent this trail.

DEVIL'S STAIRCASE TO ALASKA BASIN

Duration 9 hours
Distance 15.7 miles
Difficulty moderate–difficult
Elevation Change 2900ft
Start/Finish Alaska Basin Trailhead
Nearest Town/Junction Driggs
Summary Much of this outstanding loop hike has a gradual gradient. The high alpine scenery, reminiscent of Alaska, stuns with wildflower meadows, lakes, great panoramas of peaks and the chance to spot Dall sheep.

Get ready for an epic trek. This one is stunning – savor it best by overnighting in Alaska Basin. This loop can be done in either direction, but by hitting it counterclockwise you will encounter fewer people in the early leg of the hike and quickly achieve stunning views after ascending the Devil's Staircase.

To get to the trailhead, follow the driving directions in the Table Mountain hike, but park instead in the second parking lot with pit toilets. Bring water tablets or a purifier, sandals for river crossings and ample sunscreen – there is little shade on this high trek.

The first 2.7 miles follow an old jeep track at a mellow grade through fir and lodgepole pine. The south fork of Teton Creek parallels the trail. The trail forks for Alaska Basin and Devil's Staircase. Take the right-hand fork, which quickly gets steep. After a few switchbacks, you end up on a gently up-sloping high meadow with views. Heading toward **Mt Meek Pass**, look for Dall sheep on the cliffs that tower to the right. A gurgling brook parallels most of this section, steeped in wildflowers.

The trail splits with the right fork heading toward Mt Meek Pass and the left dropping down the Sheep Steps into Alaska Basin. Savor the views of Mt Meek, Buck Mountain (11,938ft) and South Teton (12,514ft). Take the fork to **Alaska Basin**.

This high-alpine area resembles the open tundra regions of Alaska. If you are settling in for the night, take advantage of the extra time to explore the Basin Lakes. There are many good campsites. Make sure you have a permit and camp at the required distance from waterways.

The rest of the hike follows the valley downhill through switchbacks and stream crossings (either shallow or with stepping stones or a bridge). The polished rock outcrops abutting the trail show evidence of glacial movement. This rocky and sometimes steep forested section can be somewhat tough on the knees. From Alaska Basin to the signed junction with Devil's Staircase it is 5 miles. Continue toward the parking lot via the way you entered. If you're hot and sweaty, there are a couple of great swimming holes off short paths to the creek.

Teton Valley

Teton Valley (6200ft) was first frequented by Blackfoot, Bannock, Shoshone, Nez Percé and Crow Indian tribes as a summer hunting ground. Lewis and Clark expedition member John Colter stumbled upon it in 1808 while hunting for beaver, finding them in abundance. The valley soon became known as Pierre's Hole, a favored mountain man rendezvous, until a violent battle with a band of Blackfoot in 1832 caused the fur company's abandonment. The trade totally fell when beaver hats fell out of fashion (although some await their return with anticipation).

Farming has been the valley's mainstay since Mormon families settled here in the late-19th century, but these once-sleepy ranching towns are now a year-round mecca for outdoor adventure and summer music festivals, with fabulous skiing, hiking, mountaineering and mountain biking. North of Driggs, however, the classic Fords and antique grain silos hark back to days of yore.

Most of the valley lies in Teton County, Idaho, though a small portion (up to the Teton crest) is in Teton County, Wyoming. In Jackson it's dubbed the 'Tetons' backside,' while in Idaho it's dubbed the 'sunny side.'

You know you've found a small town when asking directions causes locals to ponder the street names. A friendly feel, the great outdoors and a smattering of good restaurants make **Victor**, Idaho a growing

draw, especially for those who work in Jackson and can't afford to live there. Grab groceries at the **Victor Valley Market** (☎ 208-787-2610; 5 S Main St). Next door, the friendly **Victor Valley Cafe** (☎ 208-787-2632; 16 W Center St; ☼ 6am-2pm Tue-Sat, 8am-1pm Sun) serves up sandwiches, whopping breakfast burritos and coffee, with a patio seating.

For frantic fun, the **Knotty Pine** (☎ 208-787-2866; 58 S Main St) cranks out an eclectic summer music line-up that gets crowds on their feet. It is known for its burgers, microbrews and relaxed local vibe. If you need outdoor gear, check out used items and seconds at **Victor Outdoors Seconds** (☎ 208-787-2887; ☼ 10am-6pm, closed Sun) or hip bike shop **Habitat** (☎ 208-787-7669; www.ridethetetons.com; 170 N Main St), also featuring ski and snowboard gear.

Between Victor and Driggs (look for the monstrous potato on the back of the vintage flatbed), the **Spud Drive-In Theatre** (☎ 208-354-2727; www.spuddrivein.com; 231 S Hwy 33; ☼ Mon-Sat summer) is a classic shot of Americana. Grab a malt and fries and get the kids in their jammies for the full experience.

Rapidly growing Driggs (population 1100) is the valley's tourist nerve center. Located just minutes from the ski slopes, **Alta Lodge B&B** (☎ 307-353-2582; 590 Targhee Towne Rd; d $$) offers outstanding views and a cozy atmosphere. To get there take Ski Hill Rd 5 miles east of the main road, then go north on State Line Rd for half a mile. The **Targhee National Forest Teton Basin Ranger District** (☎ 208-354-2312; 525 S Main St) has information on trails and campgrounds, and offers free travel-planner maps. For online information visit the **Teton Valley Chamber of Commerce** (www.tetonvalleychamber.com).

Grand Targhee Ski & Summer Resort

On the west side of the Teton Range, **Grand Targhee Ski & Summer Resort** (☎ 307-353-2300, 800-827-4433; www.grandtarghee.com) is revered for its incredible powder stashes (more than 500in of snow falls each winter), its high-elevation location and its easygoing vibe. Base elevation is 8100ft, and four high-speed lifts to the top of Fred's Mountain (10,200ft) access 1500 acres of runs, with a total vertical drop of 2200ft in 3.2 miles. The runs are suited for families and intermediate-level skiers.

The ski season runs from mid-November to mid-April. Targhee **lift tickets** (adult/child

6-12 full-day $59/36, half-day $41/29) are a bargain compared with the competition. Performance **demos** (ski/snowboard per day $40/42), where you get to sample the newest gear, and **rentals** (ski/snowboard per day $32/34) are available. The ski and snowboard schools offer private and group instruction, as well as telemark and skate clinics.

Wilderness **snowcat powder skiing** (half-/full-day $349/259) leads intermediate and advanced skiers to Peaked Mountain (10,230ft), for breathless powder runs that average 2000 vertical feet. There are 10 miles of groomed **Nordic trails** (adult/child $10/5) and skating tracks. Other winter activities include snowshoeing, tubing, skating and dogsledding.

When the snow melts, and muddy trails then wildflower fields replace it, the valley becomes a haven for hiking, climbing and biking. The mountain offers **scenic chairlift rides** (adult/child 6-14 $10/5; ☒ late Jun–early Sep) to the summit of Fred's Mountain; **horseback riding** (half-day $89) and lift-served **mountain biking** (day pass/bike rental $18/$40). Horseback riding takes advantage of the stunning scenery at Grand Targhee. Riders amble the dusty trails rimmed by wildflowers in the shadow of the Tetons. Pack trips and lessons on Western and English riding are also available. A one-hour hike affords a spectacular vista of Grand Teton itself, ride the lift down for free.

Frisbee fans take note: there's also free **disc golf**, plus a **climbing wall** ($6), **ropes course** (1st/2nd person $30/20) and **cable zip line ride** ($10). The staff naturalist provides excellent **campfire programs** (☎ 307-353-2300 ext 1384; free; ☒ 7:30pm Fri) at the amphitheater behind Teewinot Lodge and day-long **field outings** (free; ☒ full-day Sat) on topics ranging from wolves to botany and geology. Outings are only available to the first 20 people to sign up.

Amenities include a full spa, kids' programs and day care. A fabulous summer music festival series includes **Rockin' the Tetons** in mid-July, the **Blues & Microbrew Fest** in late July, and the **Grand Targhee Bluegrass Music Festival** in early August.

SLEEPING & EATING
Rates vary seasonally; contact **Targhee Resort** (☎ 800-827-4433; www.grandtarghee.com) about off-season specials and package deals. Kids under 15 stay for free. All lodgings have access to an indoor and outdoor hot tub, pool and wireless internet. Options include the following:

Sioux Lodge Condos (q summer/winter $$$/$$$$$; ☐ ☒) A steal in summer, these are recently remodeled, bright, four-person studios and eight-person two-bedroom units with flat-screen TV, microwave, mini-fridge and full bath. Ideal for families and groups.

Targhee Lodge (d summer/winter $$/$$$$; ☐ ☒) Standard rooms slope-side with two queen-sized beds, full bath, TV and phone.

Teewinot Lodge (d summer/winter $$$/$$$$$; ☐ ☒) Snug and luxuriant, with deluxe doubles, flat-screen TV, phone, huge indoor Jacuzzi and ski-in location.

GETTING THERE & AWAY
From Driggs head 4 miles east on USFS Rd 025 (toward Alta) to the Idaho–Wyoming state line and continue east 8 miles to Targhee. From the second switchback en route to the resort you get the first glimpse of Grand Teton and an overlook of the Teton Basin. Sunset colors are wonderful from here.

Resort **shuttles** (☎ 800-827-4433; 1-way per person $50) between Targhee and airports in Idaho Falls and Jackson, Wyoming, can be booked for two or more people. **Targhee Express** (☎ 800-443-6133; round-trip with lift ticket skiers/nonskiers $73/35; ☒ daily) operates winter bus service between Jackson, **Teton Village** (☎ 307-733-3101) and Targhee. Reservations are required.

Grassy Lake Road
This back route into the parks bumps and grinds for 52 miles to Flagg Ranch in the Rockefeller Memorial Parkway. As soon as you enter Targhee National Forest, the road degenerates into gravel and then gets progressively worse – it's the kind of road you're glad you've taken once it's over, but you wouldn't want to take again. Don't consider this route if you're in a hurry and take particular care if there has been heavy rain.

Sandwiched between the Winegar Hole and Jedediah Smith Wildernesses, this region is peppered with lakes, of which the most accessible are the roadside **Indian Lake** and **Loon Lake**, 1 mile down a bumpy track. Further east is the turnoff for the rough road down to stunning **Lake of the Woods**, site of the Boy Scouts' Loll Camp. A mile further east is the 0.5-mile detour south to

Tilley Lake. Beyond here is the expansive **Grassy Reservoir**, which is popular for its boating, fishing and dispersed campsites. Just after the reservoir the road enters the Rockefeller Parkway. For details of the eight free campsites further along Grassy Lake Rd (USFS Rd 261), see p236.

At the west end of Grassy Reservoir, by the dam, trailhead 9K5 is the start of the 15.5-mile round-trip hike to **Union Falls**, one of the most spectacular in the national park. After a mile the trail branches right, fords Cascade Creek and then branches left (right leads to the Pitchstone Plateau Trail). After another 4 miles the trail fords Proposition Creek and then a mile later branches right onto the Union Falls Trail for another 2 miles. Feathery Union Falls are the second highest in Yellowstone National Park.

At the east end of Grassy Reservoir a pullout marks the trailhead for the 6-mile round-trip hike northeast to **Beula Lake** inside Yellowstone National Park. The trail crosses the South Boundary Trail en route.

For information on hikes in the Bechler region, see p143 and p152.

Directory

CONTENTS

Accommodations	258
Business Hours	262
Climate Charts	263
Courses	263
Discount Cards	263
Festivals & Events	264
Food & Drink	264
Holidays	264
Insurance	264
International Visitors	264
Internet Access	265
Money	265
Post	265
Showers & Laundry	265
Telephone	266
Time	266
Tourist Information	266
Tours	267
Travelers with Disabilities	267
Volunteering	268
Women Travelers	268
Work	269

ACCOMMODATIONS

For hotels in the park and for gateway towns, peak season generally means June to September, with discounts normally available in the shoulder months of May and October.

Low season runs from November to April (Christmas excluded). It may come as no surprise that rates for accommodations are noticeably higher in the Yellowstone region than in the surrounding areas of Wyoming, Idaho and Montana, particularly in the mad months of July and August. Still, you'll find a wide range of places to stay, from the excellent National Park Service (NPS) and US Forest Service (USFS) campgrounds to private RV parks, simple motels, B&Bs and five-star luxury hotels, as well as that uniquely Western institution, the guest or dude ranch. You should be able to find something reasonably priced in most areas.

Yellowstone itself remains the biggest headache, with noncamping accommodations limited to a handful of pricey lodges or cookie-cutter cabins, both of which get booked up months in advance, despite there being almost 2200 rooms in the park.

Outside the parks you can normally find somewhere to stay if you just roll into town, but it's still a good idea to make a reservation at least a day or two in advance. The more popular hotels fill up a month or two in advance of the summer. Winter is also a prime season in Cooke City and West Yellowstone.

In this guide we use the following price ratings: $ (budget; under $50), $$

PRACTICALITIES

- Video systems are NTSC standard (not compatible with PAL or SECAM).

- Electrical current is AC 110V; you'll need an AC adapter and probably a voltage converter to run most non-US electronics. Plugs have flat prongs.

- The US uses the imperial system; ie miles, yards, pints and quarts. A US gallon is slightly larger than an imperial gallon and the US ton is slightly heavier than a metric tonne. To convert weights, liquid measures and distances to the metric system, see the inside back cover.

- The area's main newspapers are the *Jackson Hole News and Guide* (www.jhnewsandguide.com) and the *Billings Gazette* (www.billingsgazette.com). You can get these and *USA Today* inside the parks. The *Yellowstone Journal* has useful information on the park's wildlife and ecology.

- National Public Radio is available through **Yellowstone Public Radio** (www.ypradio.org) in Yellowstone National Park (104.9 FM), Bozeman (102.1 FM), Livingston (88.5 FM) and Red Lodge (89.1 FM); or **Wyoming Public Radio** (www.wyomingpublicradio.com) in Jackson (90.3 FM), Cody (90.1 FM) and elsewhere.

(midrange; $50 to $100), $$$ (top end; $101 to $200), $$$$ (deluxe; $201 to $500) and $$$$$ (royalty and rock stars; over $500).

Camping

Camping is the cheapest, and in many ways the most enjoyable, approach to a Yellowstone vacation. Toasting marshmallows over an open fire, stargazing in the crisp mountain air and taking in an evening ranger talk are essential parts of the national park experience.

Most campsites in Yellowstone and all sites in Grand Teton are on a first come, first served basis. In July and August campsites get snapped up quicker than you can find them on the map. Establish your campsite in the morning before you head off sightseeing, and once you have a site that you like, hold onto it and use it as a base to visit neighboring sights.

If you have a tight itinerary and will be moving around a lot, try to plan at least a few overnight stays at Yellowstone's concession (Xanterra) campgrounds, where you can make site reservations in advance. Gamblers should remember that even if you manage to score a same-day site at a Xanterra campground, you may have to move out the next day if your spot is booked that night. Concessionaire campsites are around 50% pricier than the park service sites.

If all else fails, you'll find some great USFS campsites outside the park, but even these fill up early in summer.

Generators are generally only allowed between 8am and 8pm, and no generators are allowed at any time at Yellowstone's Indian Creek, Lewis Lake, Pebble Creek, Slough Creek and Tower sites. Fishing Bridge in Yellowstone, Colter Bay in Grand Teton and Flagg Ranch in the John D Rockefeller Jr Memorial Parkway are the only places with full hookups, though a couple of grounds have RV dumps.

XANTERRA CAMPGROUNDS

Yellowstone's concessionaire, **Xanterra** (☎ 307-344-7311; www.travelyellowstone.com), runs five campgrounds, where sites can be reserved in advance. Reservations can be made over the phone or from other Xanterra campgrounds or facilities in the park. When you make a phone booking, you

must pay by credit card and then receive a booking reference number. You'll need to show that credit card when you turn up at the campground. Xanterra doesn't take checks. A full refund of your deposit is possible if you cancel more than 48 hours in advance.

Be careful to specify the type of site you want: tent or nontent site, reverse-in or pull-through site, and even the length of the site. If your site requirements change, you'll need to change the reservation.

Xanterra campgrounds take credit cards and cash between around 8am and 9pm and can book campsites and accommodation across the park. If you arrive late without a reservation, look on the notice board to see which sites are vacant and pay the next morning before 10am.

NATIONAL PARK SERVICE CAMPGROUNDS

Yellowstone and Grand Teton campgrounds usually have flush toilets (cheaper sites have vault toilets), drinking water, garbage disposal, fire pits (or charcoal grills) and picnic benches. Most sell boxes of firewood ($7) and kindling and most hold some kind of nightly campfire talk. Days, times and topics are prominently posted and are listed in the park newspapers.

The process of picking a site varies with the campground, but generally involves picking up an envelope, driving around the various loops until you find an available site you like, marking the site with either the tab from the envelope, some camp furniture, or the most agreeable family member, and then filling out the envelope and depositing it with the correct fee back at the entrance. Don't dally trying to find the world's best campsite – by the time you get back, the earlier one you liked may well have been snapped up. Some grounds ask you to keep the receipt tab displayed on your car windshield; others ask you to tag it to the campsite post. Rangers often come around at night to check receipts against vehicle number plates.

A 'site occupied' sign can be useful to mark your turf, and these are for sale in most campsites. In larger campgrounds such as Colter Bay in Teton and in all concession grounds in Yellowstone, you register and pay at the entrance and are computer-assigned a spot, so there's no need to mark your site.

NPS campsites generally do not accept checks or credit cards (with the exception of Signal Mountain in Grand Teton) and are self-service so make sure you bring plenty of $1 and $5 bills. Golden Age and Golden Access Passports give 50% reductions on most camping fees in national parks and national forests.

When choosing a site, discerning campers scrutinize its proximity to a bathroom, trash and water supply, whether the ground is level and, most importantly, the neighbors (a scattering of kids' toys or beer cans can be a very bad sign). In general, back-in sites offer a little more privacy; parallel sites are little more than car parks by the side of the road. A campground's outer loops are usually the most private.

OUTSIDE THE PARKS

USFS campgrounds are generally less developed than NPS campgrounds; some don't have drinking water and require you to pack out all trash. A few of these sites are free. Many turn off the water supply about mid-September and then either close or run the site for a while at half-price. At any rate, it's always a good idea to bring a few gallons of water when camping.

Sites can be reserved in certain USFS campgrounds in the Gallatin Valley, Targhee National Forest and Custer National Forest (around Red Lodge) through the reservation service at **Recreation.gov** (☎ 877-444-6777, TDD 877-833-6777; www.recreation.gov). It's possible to select and reserve specific campsites online. Sites need to be booked no less than three days and no more than eight months in advance.

Free dispersed camping (meaning you can camp almost anywhere) is permitted in some public backcountry areas. Sometimes you can pull off a dirt road and into a small layby where you can camp, especially in Bureau of Land Management (BLM) and national forest areas. In other places, you must be 0.25 miles from a developed campground and often not within 0.5 miles of a major highway. Check with the local district ranger office.

Private campgrounds outside the park are mostly designed with RVs in mind; tenters can camp, but fees are quite a bit higher than in public campgrounds, and sites are normally crushed together to maximize profits. Facilities can include hot showers, coin laundry, a swimming pool, full RV hookups with phone and

---

CAMPSITE RULES

Some rules to remember from the NPS and the USFS:

▪ Camping in pullouts, trailheads, picnic areas or anywhere except designated campgrounds is illegal.

▪ Wash dishes, hair, teeth etc away from the spigot. Camp wastewater must be disposed of in waste sinks, restroom sinks (no grease) or the toilet, not chucked into your neighbor's site.

▪ Campfires must be in established grates. Never leave a fire unattended.

▪ Cutting trees or shrubs for firewood is prohibited.

▪ Don't build trenches around campsites.

▪ Checkout time is 10am.

▪ Camping in Yellowstone is limited to 14 consecutive nights.

▪ A maximum of six people and two cars are allowed at each site (some USFS sites charge extra for a second car).

▪ No food, ice chests, food containers, utensils or camp stoves may be left outside or unattended. If you are tenting, store all food and containers in bear boxes. Don't dispose of food in the camp area; put it in a bag or container and dispose of it in the trash. Don't put trash in the toilets.

▪ Pets must be physically controlled at all times. Please pick up after your pet.

▪ Bear restrictions require that only hard-sided campers (no pop-ups) can occupy sites at Fishing Bridge in Yellowstone and certain USFS grounds in the upper Wapiti Valley.

satellite TV, games area, playground and a convenience store.

Kampgrounds of America (KOA; ☎ 800-562-7540; www.koa.com; sites $18-35) is a vast national network, based in Billings, Montana, which has grounds at Billings, Bozeman, Red Lodge, Livingston, and outside West Yellowstone and Jackson Hole.

Lodging

If you aren't camping, accommodations in Yellowstone and Grand Teton are limited to concession-run park lodges and cabins. Lodges are often grand reminders of a bygone era, but the rooms have usually been renovated and are generally quite comfortable. Not all rooms are equal, and there's often a vast range of different room permutations available.

Cabins are generally remnants from the 1950s, almost always jammed in a small area and resembling anything from an affluent suburb to a military barracks. The cheaper cabins haven't been renovated for 30 years but contain a modicum of rustic charm. The pricier cabins have modern interiors but are pretty charmless. Lodges in Grand Teton are generally more modern.

There are no TVs or radios in park accommodations (don't panic!), so bring a book. Children under 12 usually stay free.

In general, park accommodations are overpriced but not outrageously so. Lodge accommodations start around $80 for a double without bathroom and $105 for a double with bathroom. Cabins start at $60 for a double without bathroom, and $90 with bathroom. Room rates listed are without tax.

Most places offer discounts in the park-accommodation shoulder seasons, which are May and from mid-September to October. Early bird specials of up to 40% are available for May bookings (each hotel has slightly different dates), and there are sometimes discounts of up to 20% for advance bookings in fall (late September and early October) and early winter (book before November 1 for mid-December). Check the website www.travelyellowstone.com for occasional internet specials.

In winter you'll save money by signing up for a joint accommodations and activities (normally snowmobile rental) package.

HISTORIC BLOWOUTS

The following hotels rank as the region's most historic lodgings and are worth the splurge:

■ The Pollard (p183), Red Lodge
■ Irma Hotel (p191), Cody
■ Old Faithful Inn (p166), Yellowstone National Park
■ Gallatin Gateway Inn (p200), near Bozeman
■ Lake Yellowstone Hotel (p165)

RESERVATIONS

Park accommodations are in great demand, and many lodges are fully booked months in advance, especially during the high season and around holidays, so reserve as soon as your plans are set. Many people book their July accommodations at least six months in advance, or at the very least by March.

The main reservation lines are **Xanterra Parks & Resorts** (☎ 307-344-7311; www.travelyellowstone.com) and **Grand Teton Lodge Company** (☎ advance reservations 307-543-3100, 800-628-9988, same-day reservations 307-543-2811; www.gtlc.com). See also the boxed text, p262.

If you find yourself without a reservation, any of the parks' accommodations can tell you exactly what's available parkwide on the spot and can make bookings for up to two days ahead. If you are desperate, keep heading back to check, as cancellations open up a limited number of accommodations every day.

Make sure to let the hotel know if you plan on a late arrival – many places will give your room away if you haven't arrived or called by 6pm. Cancellation policies vary; inquire when you book.

OUTSIDE THE PARKS

Accommodations outside the parks offer much greater variety, from hostels to top-of-the-line dude ranches and fly-fishing lodges.

USFS cabins are an interesting option, particularly during winter, when you can either snowshoe or snowmobile into a cabin equipped with a woodstove, cooking utensils and bunk beds. See the Around Yellowstone chapter for cabins in the

DIRECTORY

vicinity of Cooke City, Hebgen Lake and Paradise Valley.

Houses or condos are available for rent in ski-resort areas and can be a good value for a large group or family, as they almost invariably include a kitchen and living room.

There are several B&Bs scattered around the gateway corridors to the parks. Some offer rooms in the owner's house, while others offer stand-alone accommodations. The website of the **Montana Bed & Breakfast Association** (www.mtbba.com) offers a good listing of places close to the park, as do the sites www.wyomingbnb-ranchrec.com and www.jacksonholebnb.com.

Some places, especially B&Bs and some cabins, don't accept credit cards.

BUSINESS HOURS

Banks, post offices and government offices are generally open between 9am and 5pm weekdays, with a half day on Saturday. Park visitor centers are generally open from 8am to 7pm in summer. Convenience stores within the parks are normally open to around 9:30pm.

Opening hours for all facilities are very seasonal. Outside of the high season from Memorial Day to Labor Day you can expect opening hours to be shorter by an hour or two. The park newspapers detail exact opening hours and dates. Reviews in this book don't include business hours unless they deviate from the standard hours quoted in this section. Restaurants hours are typically 7am to 10:30am, 11am to 2:30pm and 5pm to 9pm, while shops open 9:30am to 5:30pm.

CLIMATE CHARTS

Weather extremes are the norm in Yellowstone and Grand Teton National Parks, with topography being the key factor in temperature and rainfall variations across the parks. Snow in the middle of summer, warm winds midwinter and freak storms at any time means you need to be prepared for anything, particularly if you're heading into the backcountry.

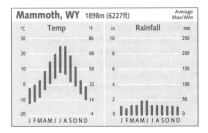

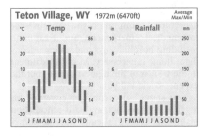

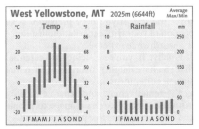

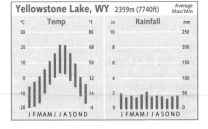

COURSES

Established in 1907, the nonprofit **Yellowstone Institute** (☎ 307-344-2293; www .yellowstoneassociation.org/institute) conducts an educational field program offering one- to five-day outdoor courses in everything from identifying mammal tracks and wild edible plants to wolf behavior and Yellowstone's colorful history. It also runs multiday backpacking and horsepack trips, kayaking, fly-fishing for teens and women, and backcountry and Leave No Trace courses, as well as courses on photography and wildlife-watching. 'Lodging and Learning Programs' are four- to five-day packages that include food and park accommodation. These are particularly popular in winter.

The institute's headquarters is at the historic Buffalo Ranch in Yellowstone's Lamar Valley, where most courses are conducted from late May to late September (plus some in January and February). Courses start at $80 per day, excluding food and accommodations. Buffalo Ranch's self-catering log-cabin bunkhouses cost $25 per person. Ask for a summer or winter catalogue or view it online.

The highly regarded **Teton Science School** (☎ 307-733-4765; www.tetonscience.org) in Kelly runs twice weekly natural-history seminars (from $65/35 for adult/child per day) for families, plus weeklong programs. It also houses the free Murie Natural History Museum; call for an appointment to visit.

If all of that sounds too much like school, try a fly-fishing course at the **Yellowstone Fly Fishing School** (☎ 406-220-5234; www.yellowstonefly fishingschool.com; 271 Old Clyde Park Rd, Livingston, MT). Women-only courses and two-hour clinics are available.

DISCOUNT CARDS

Always ask for some kind of discount, whether it be AAA, Good Sam, seniors, off-season, shoulder season, multiday or any other even half-credible reason you can imagine. Rates are notoriously flexible in the Yellowstone region. **American Automobile Association** (AAA; www.aaa.com) members often get a discount on hotel rates. Holders of senior and access park passes get a 50% discount at park campsites. Student cards are of little use.

FESTIVALS & EVENTS

The Yellowstone region has some interesting festivals, from cowboy rodeos to fat-tire races – for the highlights see p26. State tourism websites offer a comprehensive list.

FOOD & DRINK

Food in Yellowstone is generally more functional than fun, though you shouldn't have difficulty finding somewhere to eat whatever your budget. The parks offer a multitude of fast-food outlets and sandwich bars, as well as the occasional need-to-eat-something-different gourmet restaurant.

Outside the tourist-driven eateries in the parks, local cuisine is a stick-to-your-ribs diet of biscuits and gravy, chicken-fried steaks, turkey loaf and mashed potatoes, plus table-shaking half-pound burgers and bloody steaks. One local 'delicacy' that always gets foisted (with a grin) on tourists is Rocky Mountain Oysters – deep-fried bison testicles, normally served in pairs.

If you plan on sticking to a strict vegetarian diet while traveling in Greater Yellowstone, you'll have to get used to two things: baked potatoes and grudging looks from local ranchers.

Convenient snack bars, delis and grocery stores are never far away in the parks, but you'll find a wider selection in the gateway towns and the cheapest prices at supermarkets in larger towns like Cody and Jackson.

Predictably, given the lovely locations and abundant picnic areas, picnicking is a popular option. A cooler is an invaluable piece of equipment during the heat of summer, and overpriced ice is available at most park junctions. The majority of campers bring a dual-burner stove (Coleman is the most popular brand) to speed along cookouts. At the end of the day, even the blandest can of beans tastes like heaven when cooked over an open fire and under a blanket of stars.

In this book we use the following definitions: $ (budget; meals under $10), $$ (midrange; meals $10 to $19), $$$ (top end; meals $20 to $30) and $$$$ (deluxe; meals over $30). This is for a main course, not including tips or drinks.

In general breakfast is served from 7am to 10:30am; lunch from 11am to 2:30pm; and dinner from 5pm to 9pm.

HOLIDAYS

On the following national public holidays, banks, schools and government offices (including post offices) are closed, and transportation, museums and other services operate on a Sunday schedule. Holidays falling on a weekend are usually observed the following Monday. (For more planning information, see p23.)

January 1 New Year's Day
Third Monday in January Martin Luther King Jr Day
Third Monday in February Presidents' Day
Last Monday in May Memorial Day
July 4 Independence Day (or the Fourth of July)
First Monday in September Labor Day
Second Monday in October Columbus Day
November 11 Veterans' Day
Fourth Thursday in November Thanksgiving
December 25 Christmas Day

INSURANCE

Foreigner visitors to the US should take out adequate travel insurance, purchased before departure. At a minimum, you need coverage for medical emergencies and treatment, including hospital stays and an emergency flight home if necessary. Medical treatment in the USA is of the highest caliber, but the expense could kill you.

You should also consider coverage for luggage theft or loss, and trip cancellation insurance. If you already have a home-owner's policy, see what it will cover and consider getting supplemental insurance to cover the rest. If you have prepaid a large portion of your trip, cancellation insurance is a worthwhile expense.

Finally, if you're driving it's essential that you have liability insurance. Car-rental agencies offer insurance that covers damage to the rental vehicle and separate liability insurance (which covers damage to people and other vehicles). See p273 for details.

Worldwide travel insurance is available at www.lonelyplanet.com/travel_services. You can buy, extend and claim online anytime – even if you're already on the road.

INTERNATIONAL VISITORS
Entering the Country

If you have a non-US passport, you must complete an arrival/departure record (form I-94) before you reach the immigration desk. It's usually handed out on the plane along with the customs declaration.

The Department of Homeland Security's registration program – called **US-VISIT** (www .dhs.gov/us-visit) – is now almost completely phased in. It includes every port of entry and every foreign visitor to the USA. For most visitors, registration consists of having your photo taken and having electronic (inkless) fingerprints made of each index finger; the process takes less than a minute. The same registration procedure is followed when you exit the USA.

No matter what your visa says, US immigration officers have absolute authority to refuse admission to the USA or impose conditions on admission. They will ask about your plans and whether you have sufficient funds; it's a good idea to list an itinerary, produce an onward or round-trip ticket and have at least one major credit card.

Passports & Visas
Most visitors from Western Europe, Australia, New Zealand, Japan and Singapore can enter the US for stays of 90 days or less on a visa waiver program (VWP).

To qualify for this, your passport must meet one of the following conditions: your passport was issued before October 26, 2005, but is 'machine readable' (with two lines of letters, numbers and <<< at the bottom); it was issued on or after October 26, 2005, and includes a digital photo as well as being machine readable; or it was issued on or after October 26, 2006, and contains a digital photo and 'biometric data,' such as digital iris scans and fingerprints. Confirm with your passport issuing agency that your passport meets current US standards; otherwise you'll need a visa. If it doesn't, you'll be turned back, even if you belong to a VWP country.

For more details see the **US State Department** (www.travel.state.gov, www.unitedstatesvisas.gov).

INTERNET ACCESS
There is currently no public internet access in Yellowstone National Park. Most hotel rooms inside the park don't even have a telephone connection. Dornan's (p212), at Moose in Grand Teton, has internet access at $5 per hour. An internet icon has been used in this book where internet access and/or wi-fi is available.

Most hotels in the gateway towns offer wireless connections, as does the West Yellowstone Chamber of Commerce (p171) and Teton County Library (p241) in Jackson. In fact most libraries (West Yellowstone Public Library, p171, for example) offer free internet access for short durations. Most bookstores, cafés and even MacDonald's in the neighboring towns offer wi-fi internet access. Search www.wifiareas.com to find one near you.

For information on internet resources, see p29.

MONEY
Yellowstone has 24-hour ATMs at almost all hotels and general stores – see p93 for a rundown. The front desks of all park accommodations exchange foreign currency 9am to 5pm weekdays.

In Grand Teton, look for 24-hour ATMs at Dornan's and Jackson Lake Lodge and other ATMs at Colter Bay grocery store and Signal Mountain.

Foreign currency travelers checks can only be cashed in banks in the gateway towns, so do yourself a favor and bring US-dollar checks. They are by far the easiest to change and many businesses will simply accept them as cash.

Accommodation tax ranges from 4% to 8% and varies from county to county, even inside the parks. Sales tax is 4% in Wyoming (plus up to 2% county tax). There is no statewide sales tax in Montana, though a few places like Red Lodge and Cooke City impose a local 'resort' tax.

Bear in mind that tipping (around 15%) is generally expected on horse-packing and rafting trips and stays at dude ranches.

POST
The only year-round post office in Yellowstone is at Mammoth Hot Springs. Seasonal post offices are at Canyon, Lake and Grant Villages, and Old Faithful. Opening hours are 8:30am to 12:30pm and 1:30pm to 5pm weekdays only.

In Grand Teton you'll find post offices at Colter Bay (summer only) and Kelly, Moose and Moran Junctions.

SHOWERS & LAUNDRY
In Yellowstone Canyon Village, Fishing Bridge RV Park and Grant Village provide laundry and showers; Old Faithful Lodge and Roosevelt Lodge offer showers only; and

Lake Lodge has laundry only. All facilities close in winter. Showers cost $3.25.

In Grand Teton, Colter Bay Village provides public showers and laundry service. Flagg Ranch RV Park also has public showers and laundry.

TELEPHONE

Cell phone coverage is good in Grand Teton (except for the canyons) but patchy in much of Yellowstone. Bring yours along, but don't rely on it for emergency communications.

There are pay phones at most junctions but they can be expensive, especially for collect calls. It's best to bring a prepaid phonecard, but make sure it has a toll-free access number from pay phones.

Useful Numbers

YELLOWSTONE NATIONAL PARK
Albright Visitor Center (☎ 307-344-2263)
Backcountry office (☎ 307-344-2160)
Fire information (☎ 307-344-2580)
Lost & found (☎ 307-344-2109, for items lost in accommodations or restaurants 307-344-5387)
Mammoth clinic (☎ 307-344-7965)
Old Faithful clinic (☎ 307-545-7325)
Old Faithful Visitor Center (☎ 307-545-2750)
Park road updates (☎ 307-344-2117)
Recorded campground & accommodation information (☎ 307-344-2114)
Xanterra (☎ 307-344-7311, TDD 307-344-5395, same-day reservations 307-344-7901)
Yellowstone National Park (☎ 307-344-7381, TDD 307-344-2386)

GRAND TETON NATIONAL PARK
Grand Teton Lodge Company (☎ 307-543 3100, same-day reservations 307-543-2811)
Grand Teton National Park (☎ 307-739-3300)
Jackson Hole & Greater Yellowstone Visitor Center (☎ 307-733-3316)
Recorded campground information (☎ 307-739-3603)
Recorded weather (☎ 317-739-3611)

GREATER YELLOWSTONE
Recreation.gov reservation service (☎ 1-877-444-6777)
State road & weather conditions (☎ Wyoming 307-772-0824, Montana 800-226-ROAD, Idaho 208-336-6600)

TIME

All areas covered in this guide operate on US Mountain Time, which is -7 hours GMT.

GETTING HITCHED

Thinking of getting married in the region? You certainly won't have far to travel for your honeymoon! Consider the following:

- The lovely, classic English-style church (p101) at Mammoth, for a $100 reservation fee.

- Church of the Transfiguration (p219) at Moose, a tiny chapel with huge Teton views.

- The gazebo or riverside site at the **Canyon Wedding Chapel** (www.canyonweddingchapel.com) in Red Lodge, in full view of the Beartooth Mountains.

- Lake Butte Overlook (p116) outside Mammoth; weddings in the park require a $50 permit.

America subscribes to daylight savings time (DST): on the first Sunday in April, clocks are set one hour ahead (spring ahead). Then on the last Sunday of October, clocks are turned back one hour (fall back).

TOURIST INFORMATION
Tourism Organizations

Montana's statewide tourist board, **Travel Montana** (☎ 800-VISIT-MT, 800-847-4868; www.visitmt.com), offers free publications, including the *Montana Vacation Guide, Montana Winter Guide* and *Yellowstone County*. The website is particularly useful. For winter activities see the branch site www.wintermt.com.

The **Wyoming Division of Tourism** (☎ 307-777-7777, 800-225-5996; www.wyomingtourism.org) produces the very helpful seasonal *Wyoming Travelers' Journal* package, which includes a state highway map and a winter guide. You can get it online or through the post. The website is useful, as is www.state.wy.us.

The **Idaho Travel Council** (☎ 208-334-2470, 800-VISIT-ID, 800-635-7820; www.visitid.org) supplies the *Official Idaho State Travel Guide*, the useful *Idaho RV & Campground Directory*, and either a summer or winter activity package.

Useful county tourism boards include the following:
Custer Country (☎ 800-346-1876, 406-323-3544; http://custer.visitmt.com)
Wyoming's Yellowstone Country (☎ 307-587-2297, 800-393-2639; www.yellowstonecountry.org)

Yellowstone County (☎ 800-736-5276, 406-556-8680; www.yellowstone.visitmt.com)

Chambers of Commerce & Communities

Big Sky (☎ 800-943-4111, 406-995-3000; www
.bigskychamber.com)
Bozeman (☎ 800-228-4224, 406-586-5421; www
.bozemanchamber.com)
Cody (Map p189; ☎ 307-587-2777; www.codychamber.org)
Cooke City (☎ 406-838-2495; www.cookecity
chamber.com)
Gardiner (Map p176; ☎ 406-848-7971; www.gardiner
chamber.com)
Jackson Hole (☎ 307-733-3316; www.jacksonhole
chamber.com)
**Jackson Hole & Greater Yellowstone Visitor
Center** (Map p242; www.fs.fed.us/jhgyvc)
Livingston (☎ 406-222-0850; www.yellowstone
-chamber.com)
Paradise Valley (www.paradisevalleymontana.com)
Red Lodge (☎ 406-446-1718, 888-281-0625; www
.redlodge.com)
Teton Valley (☎ 208-354-2500; www.tetonvalley
chamber.com)
West Yellowstone (Map p172; ☎ 406-646-7701;
www.westyellowstonechamber.com)

National Forests

The following national forests offer information on campsites, hiking routes and other recreational use:
Beaverhead-Deerlodge National Forest (☎ 406-683-3900; www.fs.fed.us/r1/b-d)
Bridger-Teton National Forest (www.fs.fed.us/r4
/btnf) headquarters (Map p242; ☎ 307-739-5500;
Jackson); Jackson ranger office (☎ 307-739-5400); Moran/
Hatchet ranger office (☎ 307-543-2386); Pinedale ranger
office (☎ 307-367-4326)
CaribouTarghee National Forest (www.fs.fed.us/r4
/caribou-targhee) headquarters (☎ 208-524-7500; Idaho
Falls); Ashton ranger office (☎ 208-652-7442); Driggs ranger
office (☎ 208-354-2312); Idaho Falls ranger office (☎ 208-
523-1412)
Custer National Forest (www.fs.fed.us/r1/custer)
headquarters (☎ 406-657-6200; Billings); Red Lodge ranger
office (☎ 406-446-2103)
Gallatin National Forest (www.fs.fed.us/r1/gallatin)
supervisor's office (☎ 406-587-6701; Bozeman);
Bozeman ranger office (☎ 406-522-2520); Livingston
ranger office (☎ 406-222-1892); Gardiner ranger office
(Map p176; ☎ 406-848-7375); Hebgen Lake ranger office
(☎ 406-823-6961)
Shoshone National Forest Main Office (Map p189;
☎ 307-527-6241; www.fs.fed.us/r2/Shoshone; 808
Meadow Lane, Cody, WY)

TOURS

The Yellowstone concessionaire **Xanterra** (www.travelyellowstone.com) runs a huge range of coach tours, from wildlife viewing to photography tours, as well as transport and accommodation packages. New for 2007 is the return of the classic Old Yellow Bus. See p99 for details.

The **Grand Teton Lodge Company** (☎ 800-628-9988; www.gtlc.com) runs half-day tours of Grand Teton, and full-day tours of both Yellowstone and a combination of the two parks. **Flagg Ranch** (☎ 800-443-2311; www
.flaggranch.com) also offers full-day tours of Grand Teton or Yellowstone. See p214 for details.

The following independent outfitters offer bus tours from the park's gateway towns at slightly higher rates:
Buffalo Bus Co (Map p172; ☎ 406-646-9353, 800-
426-7669; www.yellowstonevacations.com/buffalo.htm;
415 Yellowstone Ave, West Yellowstone, MT) Northern or
southern loops of Yellowstone cost around $55.
Gray Line of Jackson Hole (☎ 307-733-4325, 800-
443-6133; www.graylinejh.com; 1580 W Martin Lane,
Jackson) Full-day park tours cost between $80 and $95.

Wildlife Tours

If you have a particular interest in watching wildlife then consider a private day or multiday trip in the company of a naturalist from the Yellowstone Institute (p263) or **Teton Science School** (☎ 888-945-3567, 307-733-2623; www.wildlifeexpeditions.org; Jackson). Both have a range of programs and safaris, starting at around $100 per person per day.

Specialized private companies such as **Yellowstone Wildlife Safari Co** (☎ 800-SAFARIS; www.safariyellowstone.com) in Livingston, and **Yellowstone Safari Co** (☎ 866-586-1155; www
.yellowstonesafari.com) and **Off the Beaten Path** (☎ 800-445-2995; www.offthebeatenpath.com), both in Bozeman, all offer summer and winter wildlife-watching.

TRAVELERS WITH DISABILITIES

Yellowstone has many accessible boardwalks and trails, and several wheelchair-accessible backcountry campsites, including Goose Lake in Geyser Country and Ice Lake on the Norris-Canyon road, which is half a mile from the trailhead and has a wheelchair-accessible vault toilet.

The pamphlet *Visitor Guide to Accessible Features in Yellowstone National Park* lists accessible sights and facilities, and is available online at the park website or by writing to the **Park Accessibility Coordinator** (☎ 307-344-2017; PO Box 168, Yellowstone National Park, WY 82190-0168). In Yellowstone there are wheelchair-accessible campsites at Bridge Bay, Canyon, Grant Village, Madison and Mammoth, and even a wheelchair-accessible riverside fishing spot on the Madison River.

Deaf visitors can get information at TDD ☎ 307-344-2386 (Yellowstone) or TDD ☎ 307-739-3400 (Grand Teton). The park will provide sign language interpreters if booked three weeks in advance – call ☎ 307-344-2251.

Wheelchair-accessible trails in Grand Teton include the 6-mile paved trail along String Lake. Accessible accommodations are available at several campsites and all lodging facilities. For more details view the Accessibility brochure on the park's website or contact the Accessibility Coordinator, Grand Teton National Park, PO Drawer 170, Moose, WY 83012.

Blind and permanently disabled people can get a free lifetime access pass, good for all federal parks. Get one at the park entrances.

Access Tours (☎ 208-787-2338; www.accesstours .org; PO Box 1320, Driggs, ID 83422) runs tours in Grand Teton and Yellowstone for those with physical disabilities.

VOLUNTEERING

The NPS runs a Volunteer in Parks (VIP) program. See the website www.nps.gov /volunteer for details.

The USFS accepts a wider range of volunteers, from trail maintenance to campground hosts, and normally supplies rooms and board with a subsistence wage. Visit the websites www.fs.fed.us/fsjobs /volunteers.html or www.volunteer.gov.

The **Student Conservation Association** (www .thesca.org) places student volunteers in the parks.

Youth Conservation Corps (YCC; www.nps.gov /yell/parkmgmt/yccjobs.htm) offers an eight-week program for 30 teenagers (aged 15 to 19), who work in the park on jobs like trail construction, often in the backcountry. You'll receive minimum wage but the cost of food and accommodation is deducted from this, so you won't get rich, but you will

have the chance for recreational activities. Only 30 spots are available, chosen from a random draw. It's funded by the excellently named Loyal Order of the Moose.

For details of Grand Teton's volunteer program, contact the **Park Volunteer Coordinators** (☎ 307-739-3397, 739-3656; www.nps.gov /grte/supportyourpark/volunteer.htm). Available are 14- to 16-week placements as a park-ranger naturalist intern, three times a year. You get free accommodation and $120 a week for expenses.

Other volunteering options in the region:

Community Foundation of Jackson Hole (☎ 303-739-1026; www.volunteerjacksonhole.org) Lists opportunities with dozens of local agencies, from therapeutic riding to art and wilderness organizations.
Continental Divide Trail Alliance (☎ 888-909-2382; www.cdtrail.org; PO Box 628, Pine, CO 80470)
Continental Divide Trail Society (☎ 410-235-9610; www.cdtsociety.org; 3704 N Charles St, Suite 601, Baltimore, MD 21218)
Wilderness Volunteers (☎ 928-556-0038; www .wildernessvolunteers.org) Weeklong trips helping maintain America's parks and wild lands.
Yellowstone Association (☎ 307-344-2293; www .yellowstoneassociation.org; volunteer@yellowstone association.org) Volunteers at the Buffalo Ranch center assist with courses for summer or winter seasons.

WOMEN TRAVELERS

Women traveling solo or in groups in the national parks rarely experience any problems. Sexism on the trail is a pretty rare thing and, especially within the parks, women regularly hike alone. In national forest areas outside the park, where you'll find hunters, off-roaders and fishermen (ie large groups of beer-swilling males), women may feel less comfortable, justifiably.

Many women feel reluctant about solo overnight backpacking. Although the *fear* of spending the night alone in the wilderness is obviously a different beast for women than it is for men, women are generally just as safe. The notion that a menstruating woman attracts bears is a myth. However, used tampons and pads should be sealed up and stored in a bear-proof food canister or poop tube, just like anything else that's scented.

There are some good books out there to help prepare for a trip. Check out Thalia Zepatos' *Adventures in Good Company:*

The Complete Guide to Women's Tours and Outdoor Trips and Adrienne Hall's *Backpacking: A Woman's Guide.*

WORK

Occasional seasonal jobs (for US citizens only) are available as rangers or laborers with the National Park Service, though competition for these jobs is fierce; check for openings at www.sep.nps.gov or www .nps.gov/personnel. Yellowstone has an overview of job options at www.nps.gov /yell/parkmgmt/ynpjobs.htm, or call ☎ 307-344-7381. The government website www .usajobs.gov is also worth a look.

Your first stop should be **Coolworks** (www .coolworks.com), which is an excellent clearing house for jobs both in and around the parks. The page www.coolworks.com/yell .htm deals specifically with the Yellowstone region.

The main Yellowstone Concessionaire, **Xanterra** (☎ human resources 307-344-5324, 24hr application request line 307-344-5627; www.yellowstonejobs .com for online applications), employs 3000 people in summer and 300 in winter, who do everything from making beds to making soup. Pay starts at about $6 per hour and employee morale generally seems pretty low. Employee housing and food cost around $70 per week (RV sites $30 to $40 per week). Apply in December for summer jobs and in August/September for winter positions. Staff are a mix of students, overseas workers (who need to arrange their own work visas) or retirees living in their RVs.

Other opportunities are available from the following:

DNC Parks and Resorts (☎ 406-586-7593 in Bozeman; www.visityellowstonepark.com) Runs the Yellowstone General Stores and employs around 800 people a year.

Yellowstone Park Medical Services (☎ 800-654-9447, ext 462; 707 Sheridan Ave, Cody, WY 82414) Fills a small number of professional and nonprofessional positions at its park medical clinics.

Yellowstone Parks Service Stations (www.cool works.com/ypss) The third Yellowstone concessionaire, with clerical as well as automotive technicians.

For job opportunities in Grand Teton contact the following:

Dornans (http://dornans.com/employment)

Flagg Ranch (www.flaggranch.com/employment.html)

Grand Teton Lodge Company (☎ 800-350-2068; www.gtlc.com/employ.aspx)

Signal Mountain Lodge (www.coolworks.com /signalmt)

The **Association of National Park Rangers** (ANPR; www.anpr.org/publications.htm) publishes the booklet *Live the Adventure: Join the National Park Service* ($6), which gives advice on how to get a job as a park ranger.

Transportation

CONTENTS

Getting There & Away	**270**
Air	270
Bus	272
Car & Motorcycle	272
Getting Around	**273**
Train	273
Bicycle	274
Bus	274
Car & Motorcycle	274
Hitchhiking	275

TRANSPORTATION

GETTING THERE & AWAY

The main gateways (and airports) nearest to Yellowstone National Park are Jackson (56 miles), Cody (52 miles), Bozeman (65 miles), Billings (129 miles) and Idaho Falls (107 miles). Grand Teton National Park sits right outside Jackson (13 miles). Depending on your direction of travel, it may be cheaper to land in Salt Lake City (390 miles) or Denver (563 miles) and rent a car there.

Flights, tours and rail tickets can be booked online at www.lonelyplanet.com /travel_services.

AIR
Airports
Jackson Hole Airport (JAC; ☎ 307-733-7682; www .jacksonholeairport.com), 8.5 miles from Jackson, is actually 4 miles inside Grand Teton National Park. There are frequent flights between Jackson Hole and Salt Lake City (Delta/SkyWest), Atlanta (Delta), Denver (United), Dallas and Chicago (American Airlines). Inquire about a possible future nonstop service to New York City. If flying into Jackson, the seats on the right side of the plane normally offer the best views.

West Yellowstone's **Yellowstone Airport** (WYS; ☎ 406-646-7631) is the closest airport to Yellowstone National Park, with three daily

---

CLIMATE CHANGE & TRAVEL

Climate change is a serious threat to the ecosystems that humans rely upon, and air travel is the fastest-growing contributor to the problem. Lonely Planet regards travel, overall, as a global benefit, but believes we all have a responsibility to limit our personal impact on global warming.

Flying & Climate Change

Pretty much every form of motorized travel generates CO_2 (the main cause of human-induced climate change), but planes are far and away the worst offenders, not just because of the sheer distances they allow us to travel, but because they release greenhouse gases high into the atmosphere. The statistics are frightening: two people taking a return flight between Europe and the US will contribute as much to climate change as an average household's gas and electricity consumption over a whole year.

Carbon Offset Schemes

Climatecare.org and other websites use 'carbon calculators' that allow travelers to offset the level of greenhouse gases they are responsible for with financial contributions to sustainable travel schemes that reduce global warming – including projects in India, Honduras, Kazakhstan and Uganda.

Lonely Planet, together with Rough Guides and other concerned partners in the travel industry, support the carbon offset scheme run by climatecare.org. Lonely Planet offsets all of its staff and author travel. For more information, check out our website: www.lonelyplanet.com.

summer flights (June through September) to and from Salt Lake City (SkyWest, with connections on Delta). Due to snow conditions, the airport closes in winter (approximately November to May).

Billings' **Logan International Airport** (BIL; ☎ 406-247-8609; www.flybillings.com) has connections to and from Salt Lake City (Delta Airlines), Denver (Continental, Frontier and United Airlines), Minneapolis (Northwest Airlines), Seattle (Horizon) and other Montanan destinations (Big Sky Airlines).

Bozeman's **Gallatin Field** (BZN; ☎ 406-388-8321; www.gallatinfield.com) has flights to and from Denver (United), Detroit (Northwest), Minneapolis (Northwest), Salt Lake City (Delta), Seattle (Horizon) and other Montanan destinations (Big Sky Airlines).

Cody's **Yellowstone Regional Airport** (COD; ☎ 307-587-5096; www.flyyra.com) has flights to and from Salt Lake City (SkyWest and Delta) and Denver (SkyWest, Mesa and United Express).

The **Idaho Falls Regional Airport** (IDA; ☎ 206-612-8221; www.idahofallsairport.com) has flights to and from Boise (Horizon), Minneapolis (Northwest Airlines), Salt Lake City (SkyWest-Delta) and Denver (United Express).

Private planes can land at Jackson Hole Airport and several small airstrips, including Driggs and Mission Field, east of Livingston, Montana.

Airlines

The following airlines service the regional airports around the parks:

American Airlines (☎ 800-433-7300; www.aa.com)
Big Sky Airlines (☎ 800-237-7788; www.bigskyair.com)
Continental (☎ 800-523-FARE; www.continental.com)
Delta-Skywest (☎ 800-221-1212; www.delta.com)

Horizon-Alaska (☎ 800-252-7522; www.horizonair.com)
Mesa (☎ 800-MESA-AIR; www.itn.net/cgi/get?itn/air/mesaair/index)
Northwest (☎ 800-225-2525; www.nwa.com)
Skywest (☎ United connections 800-221-6903, Delta connections 800-325-8244; www.skywest.com)
United-Skywest (☎ 800-864-8331; www.united.com)

Flights from USA & Canada

Discount travel agents (consolidators) are your best bet for booking cheap flights within the USA. For online bookings, check out the following:

Cheap Tickets (www.cheaptickets.com)
Expedia (www.expedia.com)
Kayak (www.kayak.com)
Orbitz (www.orbitz.com)
STA Travel (www.sta.com) For travelers under the age of 26.
Travelocity (www.travelocity.com)

Flights from UK & Ireland

Travelers coming from the UK or Ireland can expect at least one layover, usually two. **British Airways** (www.britishairways.com) flies to Denver and US carriers complete the flight to Jackson Hole (11 hours plus layover time); this is probably the most direct route. Also consider American, United, Delta, Northwest, Continental and Virgin Atlantic. Check out the following:

EBookers.com (☎ 0871-223-5000; www.ebookers.com)
Flight Centre (☎ 0870-499-0040; www.flightcentre.co.uk)
STA Travel (☎ 0870-163-0026; www.statravel.co.uk)
Travelocity (☎ 0870-273-3273; www.travelocity.co.uk)

Flights from Australia & New Zealand

Those coming from Australia or New Zealand will have to touch down in Los Angeles or San Francisco before continuing on to airports closer to Yellowstone and Grand Teton.

If going via the Pacific route, expect the first leg to be 12 to 14 hours. Flying through Asia probably means spending a night or considerable layover time in a connecting city. Check out the following:

Flight Centre Australia (☎ 133-133; www.flightcentre.com.au); New Zealand (☎ 0800-243-544; www.flightcentre.co.nz)
STA Travel Australia (☎ 134-782; www.statravel.com.au); New Zealand (☎ 0800-474-400; www.statravel.co.nz) Agency for travelers under the age of 26.
travel.com.au (☎ 1300-130-482; www.travel.com.au)

TRANSPORTATION

AMERICA'S MOST SCENIC AIRPORT

Brimming with controversy, the Jackson Hole Airport is the only US airport inside a national park, and sports one of the shortest commercial runways in the nation. As Jackson's popularity booms, its public periodically goes up in arms over wildlife disturbance and planes that occasionally overshoot the tarmac. Traffic in the past decade was further bogged down with the comings and goings of Air Force Two shuttling Dick Cheney to his vacation home.

Boosters want the runway extended, but airport expansion is currently restricted under a 50-year agreement signed by the airport and the National Park Service (NPS) in 1983. Moves by local Jackson businesses to subsidize (and thus guarantee) flights from major US airports like Chicago, New York and Atlanta only aggravates the problem. One option is to move the airport to Idaho Falls, 100 miles away.

In the meantime, put your seat in its upright and locked position, hold onto your Stetson and enjoy the free scenic view of Grand Teton National Park.

BUS

Unfortunately, long-distance bus services are a slow, somewhat infrequent and highly inconvenient way to get to Yellowstone and Grand Teton National Parks. But they will get you to major cities from which you could then rent a car or bicycle or book a local shuttle service.

Greyhound (☎ 800-231-2222; www.greyhound.com) is the major long-distance bus company, with routes to Cody, Wyoming, and Bozeman, Montana. Greyhound's **Discovery Pass** (www.discoverypass.com) can be a good deal if you are planning to travel throughout the US and Canada. Passes are valid for anything from one week to two months. Consider purchasing two short-term passes if planning to stay in one destination a while.

Competing with Greyhound, **Rimrock Trailways** (☎ 800-255-7655; www.rimrocktrailways .com), a division of Trailways, travels to Billings, Montana.

Most baggage must be checked. Make sure you label it clearly. Call the bus company to see if there is an extra charge for bringing skis or a bicycle.

Reservations

Tickets for Rimrock Trailways may only be purchased immediately prior to departure. Greyhound bus tickets may be purchased over the phone or on the internet with a major US credit card (international cards are only accepted in-person); tickets purchased with a 10-day advance may be mailed to you, otherwise pick them up at the terminal with proper identification. Greyhound terminals also accept traveler's checks and cash. All seating is first come,

first serve, so go early (one hour prior to departure).

CAR & MOTORCYCLE

The quintessential American road trip is practically a right of passage. Despite high fuel costs, this is the way to see the parks. Be aware that soft-shelled vehicles (like Jeeps) do not provide safe storage for food in bear country. Car and motorcycle drivers will need the vehicle's registration papers, liability insurance and an international driving permit or domestic license.

Distances to Yellowstone (West Entrance)

Atlanta	1950 miles
Boston	2500 miles
Kings Canyon National Park	967 miles
Miami	2600 miles
New York	2300 miles
Salt Lake	325 miles
San Francisco	950 miles
Seattle	750 miles
Sequoia National Park	948 miles
Washington DC	2200 miles

Automobile Associations

These organizations offer 24-hour roadside assistance, free maps and trip planning help. The **American Automobile Association** (AAA; ☎ 800-874-7532; www.aaa.com) is the main US auto club, with reciprocal membership agreements with several international auto clubs (check with AAA and bring your membership card). The smaller alternative, **Better World Club** (☎ 866-238-1137; www.better worldclub.com), donates 1% of earnings to environmental cleanups and offers ecologically sensitive choices for services. They also have roadside assistance for cyclists.

Driver's License

Visitors can legally drive in the USA for up to 12 months with their home driver's license. However, it is recommended that you also get an International Driving Permit (IDP); this will have more credibility with US traffic police, especially if your home license doesn't have a photo or is in a foreign language. Your automobile association at home can issue an IDP, valid for one year, for a small fee. You must carry your home license together with the IDP.

To ride a motorcycle you need a US state motorcycle license or an IDP appropriate for motorcycles. Helmets are required in most states.

Rental

CAR RENTAL

Car rental rates in the towns around Yellowstone vary considerably throughout the year, with summer weekends bringing the highest rates. See the individual towns in the Around Yellowstone (p169) and Around Grand Teton (p240) chapters for car rental company contact details.

Jackson, Billings, Bozeman and Cody have the best selection of rental companies and thus slightly lower rates. All the airports have car rentals. The major companies are **Hertz** (☎ 800-654-3131; www.hertz.com), **Avis** (☎ 800-331-1212; www.avis.com), **Thrifty** (☎ 800-THRIFTY; www.thrifty.com) and **National** (☎ 800-CAR-RENT, 800-227-7368; www.nationalcar.com).

RV RENTAL

It is hard not to see the irony of visiting America's greatest remaining wilderness in a manner that causes the greatest environmental impact possible. Most RVs get between five to 10 miles per gallon. In addition, many plug into power grids at campsites, causing greater energy consumption (and we thought the idea of camping was to get away from it all…). While money may be saved in accommodations and dining out, at least consider the costs of gas, higher RV campsite fees and environmental impact when calculating travel expenses. The choice is ultimately yours.

Cruise America (☎ 800-671-8042; www.cruiseamerica .com) rents a range of RVs through local dealers in Salt Lake City and Jackson. Renters face a three-day minimum, and costs for one week starting at $1155 for the smallest RV in high season (mid-June to mid-August), not including mileage fees. Summer rentals should be reserved well in advance.

Insurance

Don't put the key in the ignition if you don't have auto insurance. In most states it is compulsory; moreover, you risk financial ruin if you have an accident without insurance. If you already have auto insurance, make sure it covers a rental car where you will be driving. Rental companies provide limited insurance, usually charging extra for collision damage. Check to see if your credit card covers collision damage coverage for rental cars; most do and it will save you a bundle of money.

Road Rules

Most US natives know that cars drive on the right side of the road, but bear this mind if you're from the UK, Australia, New Zealand or Japan. The use of seatbelts and child safety seats is required in every state. The speed limit is generally 65mph to 75mph on western highways, 25mph in cities and 15mph in school zones. Littering can bring a fine of up to $1000. Most states don't allow you to transport open containers of alcohol, and penalties for driving under the influence of drugs or alcohol (DUI) are severe.

TRAIN

In its heyday the *Union Pacific* pulled right into West Yellowstone and Gardiner; now this social event is preserved as a quaint memory by the local historical society. If you are not intimidated by the fact that the closest passenger trains to this region service destinations over 300 miles away (Denver and Salt Lake City), contact **Amtrak** (800-USA-RAIL; www.amtrak.com) for more information.

GETTING AROUND

It's almost impossible to visit Yellowstone without your own vehicle. There's no public transportation of any kind inside the park and only minimal transportation in the gateway corridors. What's surprising is that despite the volume of traffic trundling through the park, there appears to be little movement in the direction of a mass transit system inside the park.

BICYCLE

Touring by bicycle is popular, although traveling through Yellowstone National Park presents its own special challenges. Specifically, many riders report that cycling can be very unpleasant due to narrow roads jammed with RVs – whose side mirrors and wide loads present a real danger to the little guy. For more on safe biking, traffic and road conditions, see the Health & Safety chapter (p284).

Cyclists using national-park campgrounds usually pay the same fee as walk-ins, which can be considerably lower than the fee for a vehicle. Mountain biking in areas around the national parks is outstanding; however, bike travel on national-park trails is severely limited and wilderness areas may also have restrictions. Ask at bike shops for the favorite local rides.

The best resource for cyclists is the **League of American Bicyclists** (LAB; ☎ 202-822-1333; www.bikeleague.org), which lists bike regulations by airline and offers general advice on the website. The **Better World Club** (☎ 866-238-1137; www.betterworldclub.com) offers a bicycle roadside assistance program.

Rental

Long-term bike rentals are easy to find; recommended rental shops are listed throughout the guide. Rates run from $100 per week and up, and a credit-card authorization for several hundred dollars is usually necessary as a security deposit.

Buying a bike and reselling it before you leave may be a more economical option. Check out local yard sales or message boards in local coffee shops for used bikes, and be sure to tune up your ride before hitting the road.

BUS

Although some long-distance touring companies visit the parks, there is no public bus service. **Xanterra** (☎ 307-344-7311; www.travelyellowstone.com) runs interpretive tours that leave from the visitor centers. The Yellowstone in a day tour ($62 adults/$31 children), which starts in Mammoth or Gardiner, is free for kids under eight years old. The **Old Yellow Bus tours** (☎ 866-439-7375; 1hr adult/child $12/8; 🕑 Jun-Sep) reinstate classic vintage vehicles for tours ranging from one hour to all day. Both services should be reserved in advance; see p99.

Jackson has a free town shuttle that runs every 20 to 30 minutes and the **Start Bus** (www.startbus.com) public service to Teton Village. For regional shuttle service, Alltrans' **Jackson Hole Express** (☎ 307-733-1719, 800-443-6133; www.jacksonholebus.com) shuttles daily from Jackson to Idaho Falls (one way/round-trip $40/70, 2½ hours), Salt Lake City (one way/round-trip $75/140, 4½ hours) and points in between. Reservations are recommended. Idaho Falls–based **CART** (☎ 208-354-2240) offers bus services between Jackson and Idaho Falls via Teton Valley.

CAR & MOTORCYCLE

While drivers in this region tend to be lead-foots on the interstate, traffic in the park is exasperatingly slow, typified by lumbering RVs wheezing over the Continental Divide. At the slightest whiff of a bison or moose, traffic slams to a halt. For this reason, it pays be extra-attentive when driving.

Fuel & Spare Parts

Gas prices inside the park are slightly higher than elsewhere in Wyoming and Montana. Prices rise as you get closer to the park, peaking at Red Lodge and Cooke City. Most gateway towns have an auto-parts store (Napa or Checker) and bicycle shop. Yellowstone has a car-repair garage in Bridge Bay, next to the gas station, but if your car is struggling, it is best to take it to a shop outside the park.

Road Conditions

Harsh winter conditions create frost heaves and potholes that mar even recently repaved roads. Grand Teton National Park's roads are generally in better condition than Yellowstone's. At Yellowstone, there's usually one section of the Grand Loop under construction, causing delays of up to an hour. Sometimes sections of road are closed between certain hours; see the parks' newspapers or websites for current road conditions.

For road closures and conditions outside the parks, contact www.fhwa.dot.gov/trafficinfo/index.htm or state agencies:

Idaho (☎ 208-336-6600, in-state only 888-IDA-ROAD; www2.state.id.us/itd/ida-oad/index.ap)
Montana (☎ 800-226-ROAD, in-state only 406-444-6339; www.mdt.state.mt.us)
Wyoming (☎ 307-772-0824, in-state only 888-WYO-ROAD; http://wyoroad.info/travinfo)

Road Rules

Practice courteous driving etiquette. If you're driving a slow vehicle, use one of the numerous pullouts to let faster traffic pass. If you don't want your open driver's side door torn off by a passing bus, pull fully off the road when watching wildlife. Wildlife always has the right of way.

Speed limits in the park are generally 45mph, dropping to 25mph or less at popular pullouts or junctions. Hwy 191 in Grand Teton National Park has a limit of 55mph. Roads outside the park generally have limits between 55mph and 65mph, with highways up to 65mph or 75mph.

The use of seat belts and child-safety seats are required. On motorcycles, helmets are required for anyone under 18 in Montana and Idaho or under 19 in Wyoming.

Road Hazards

Every year hundreds of wild animals meet their fate on the grill of a car. Keep an eye out for crossing animals and drive with particular care at night.

Higher-risk areas have signs marked with a deer, though all areas, even those outside the park, may have animals crossing. Bison should be passed very carefully – they are not nearly as passive as cattle.

HITCHHIKING

Hitchhiking is potentially dangerous and not recommended. While it is prohibited on highways, you'll see more people hitchhiking (and stopping) on rural roads, especially near hiking trailheads.

If you are hiking a long loop, it's sometimes difficult to count on a ride for those last few road miles, although the most popular trailheads should be easy to find a ride from.

You can check ride-share boards at ranger stations and in hostels. You might get lucky at **Planet Carpool** (www.autotaxi.com), an online ride-share bulletin board.

TRANSPORTATION

Health & Safety

CONTENTS

Before You Go	**276**
Medical Checklist	276
Internet Resources	277
Further Reading	277
In the Parks	**277**
Medical Assistance	277
Infectious Diseases	278
Environmental Hazards	278
Safe Hiking	**283**
Crossing Streams	283
Fire	283
Lightning	283
Rockfall	283
Rescue & Evacuation	283
Safe Biking	**284**
Traffic in the Parks	284
Road Conditions	284

Keeping healthy while on vacation in the national parks depends on your predeparture preparations, your daily health care while traveling and how you handle any medical problems that develop. While the potential problems can seem frightening, in reality few visitors experience anything worse than a skinned knee. The sections that follow are not intended to alarm but are worth reading before you go.

For suggestions on hiking safely, see the Activities chapter (p46).

BEFORE YOU GO

If you are a little out of shape, the best preparation for a hiking vacation is to embark on some regular, dedicated exercise at least three weeks prior to travel. To lessen your chances of getting sore shoulders, blisters and foot fatigue, wear in your boots thoroughly by undertaking long walks with a loaded pack. This will also allow you to try out different pack adjustments, socks and footwear.

Those coming from sea level should wait several days after arriving before undertaking any strenuous activity at altitude. Prepare your metabolism for acclimation to the higher elevations by drinking more water and laying off the alcohol.

No special vaccinations are required for the Rocky Mountain region (or even to enter the US, although evidence of cholera and yellow fever vaccinations may be required if arriving in the US from an infected area). However, it's a good idea to make sure you are up to date with routine vaccinations such as diphtheria, polio and tetanus. It's particularly important that your tetanus is up to date – the initial course of three injections, usually given in childhood, should be followed by boosters every 10 years.

MEDICAL CHECKLIST

- Acetaminophen (paracetamol) or aspirin
- Adhesive or paper tape
- Antibacterial ointment for cuts and abrasions
- Antibiotics
- Anti-diarrhea drugs (eg loperamide)
- Anti-inflammatory drugs (eg ibuprofen)
- Antihistamines (for hay fever and allergic reactions)
- Bandages, gauze swabs, gauze rolls and safety pins
- Insect repellent with DEET
- Iodine tablets or water filter (for water purification)
- Non-adhesive dressing
- Oral rehydration salts
- Paper stitches
- Pocket knife
- Reverse syringe (for snakebites)
- Scissors, safety pins, tweezers
- Sterile alcohol wipes
- Steroid cream or cortizone (for allergic rashes)
- Sticking plasters (Band-Aids)
- Moleskin (to prevent chafing of blisters)
- Sunscreen and lip balm
- Thermometer

EMERGENCIES

In an emergency of any sort dial ☎ 911. If you need to contact friends or family, emergency messages can be posted at the parks' entry stations and at visitor centers.

COMMON AILMENTS

Fatigue

A simple statistic: more injuries of whatever nature happen toward the end of the day than earlier, when you're fresher. Although tiredness can simply be a nuisance on an easy hike, it can be life-threatening on narrow, exposed ridges or in bad weather. You should never set out on a hike that is beyond your capabilities for that day. If you feel below par, have a day off – write in your journal or watch the grass grow. To reduce the risk, don't push yourself too hard – take rests every hour or two and build in a good half-hour lunch break. Towards the end of the day, take down the pace and increase your concentration. You should also eat properly throughout the day to replace the energy used up. Things like nuts, dried fruit and chocolate are all good energy-giving snack foods. Remember to breathe deeply, as oxygen is another important kind of body fuel.

Blisters

Blisters *can* be avoided. Make sure that your hiking boots or shoes are well worn in before your trip. At the very least, wear them on a few short hikes before tackling longer outings. Your boots should fit comfortably with enough room to move your toes; boots that are too big or too small will cause blisters. The same applies for socks – be sure they fit properly, and wear socks specifically made for hikers. Wet and muddy socks can cause blisters, so even on a day hike pack a spare pair of socks. Keep your toenails clipped but not too short. If you do feel a blister coming on, treat it sooner rather than later. Apply a simple sticking bandage, or preferably one of the special blister bandages (look for Second Skin or Band-Aid Blister Block) and follow the maker's instructions.

Knee Pain

Many hikers feel the judder on long steep descents. When dropping steeply, reduce the strain on the knee joint (you can't eliminate it) by taking shorter steps which leave your legs slightly bent and ensure that your heel hits the ground before the rest of your foot. Hiking poles are very effective in taking some of the weight off the knees.

INTERNET RESOURCES

The following are health-issue websites useful to Rocky Mountain hikers:

Centers for Disease Control & Prevention (www.cdc.gov) Represents US government agencies with a vast amount of relevant information.

International Society for Infectious Diseases (www.isid.org) A world organization representing agencies and individuals that work in infectious disease research.

Lonely Planet (www.lonelyplanet.com/weblinks) Has links to the World Health Organization (WHO) and many other useful sites.

Wilderness Medical Society (www.wms.org) A nonprofit organization dedicated to promoting outdoor and emergency knowledge and research.

FURTHER READING

If you're hiking in remote areas, consider the following detailed health guides:

- *Medicine for the Backcountry* by Buck Tilton and Frank Hubbell prepares you for just about any major or minor medical emergency in the outdoors.
- *Medicine for the Outdoors* by Paul Auerbach is a general reference with brief explanations of many medical problems and practical treatment options.
- *Wilderness 911* by Eric A Weiss is a step-by-step guide to first aid and advanced care in remote areas with limited medical supplies and no professional help.

IN THE PARKS

MEDICAL ASSISTANCE

Yellowstone National Park

Yellowstone Park Medical Services operates three clinics:

Lake Hospital (☎ 307-242-7241; 🕑 8:30am-8:30pm mid-May–mid-Sep) Has a 24-hour emergency service.

Mammoth Hot Springs Clinic (☎ 307-344-7965; 🕑 8:30am-1pm Mon-Sun, 2-5pm Mon-Tue & Thu-Fri)

Old Faithful Clinic (☎ 307-545-7325; 🕑 8:30am-5pm mid-May–mid-Oct)

NPS emergency medics (☎ 307-344-2132) are on call 24 hours a day, year-round. First aid is available at visitor centers and ranger stations. In an emergency call ☎ 911.

Emergency messages can be left on boards at park entrances and visitor centers.

Grand Teton National Park

The **Grand Teton Medical Clinic** (☎ 307-543-2514, 307-733-8002; ☻ 10am-6pm mid-May–mid-Oct) is near the Chevron station at Jackson Lake Lodge.

INFECTIOUS DISEASES
Amoebic Dysentery

Fluid replacement is the mainstay of management for serious diarrhea. Weak black tea with a little sugar, soda water or soft drink allowed to go flat and 50% diluted with water are all good. With severe diarrhea, a rehydrating solution is necessary to replace minerals and salts. Commercially available oral rehydration salts (ORS) are very useful. You should stick to a bland diet as you recover.

Lyme Disease

A bacterial infection, in the Rocky Mountains Lyme disease is mainly transmitted by the deer (wood) tick. Although the number of cases reported in the US has skyrocketed during the last two decades, Lyme disease remains relatively uncommon over large parts of the Rockies. The early symptoms, which may take months to develop, are similar to influenza – headaches, stiff neck, tiredness and painful swelling of the joints. If left untreated, complications such as meningitis, facial palsy or heart abnormalities may occur, but fatalities are rare. A safe vaccination is not yet available, but Lyme disease responds well to antibiotics.

West Nile Disease

These infections were unknown in the United States until a few years ago, but have now been reported in almost all 50 states. The virus is transmitted by culex mosquitoes, which are active in late summer and early fall, and generally bite after dusk. Most infections are mild or asymptomatic, but the virus may infect the central nervous system, leading to fever, headache, confusion, lethargy, coma and sometimes death. There is no treatment for West Nile virus. For the latest update on the areas affected by West Nile, go to the **US Geological Survey website** (http://westnilemaps .usgs.gov/).

ENVIRONMENTAL HAZARDS
Altitude

In the thinner atmosphere of the Rockies, a lack of oxygen may cause headaches, nausea, nosebleeds, shortness of breath, physical weakness and other symptoms. These can lead to serious consequences, especially if combined with heat exhaustion, sunburn or hypothermia. Most people adjust to altitude within a few hours or days, but you need to be careful (especially with children) when driving and overnighting on the Beartooth Plateau, where altitudes reach 10,000ft. In mild cases of altitude sickness, everyday painkillers such as aspirin may relieve discomfort. If symptoms persist, descend to lower elevations.

Bears

Travelers in the region need to be bear aware, whether camping in a developed site or hiking in the backcountry.

It's helpful to learn the difference between grizzly bears and black bears, since the two model different behaviors (adult grizzlies, for example, can't climb trees very well, but black bears can). You can't rely on color alone – black bears also come in various shades of brown, and some grizzly bears look almost black. Instead, look for the distinguishing

---

WATER PURIFICATION

As a rule, don't drink any snowmelt, stream, lake or ground water without filtering it with a filter at 0.5 microns or smaller, or treating with water tablets. The stubborn pest you want to avoid is *Giardia lamblia*, a microscopic, waterborne parasite that causes intestinal disorders, with notable symptoms such as chronic diarrhea, bloating and appalling gas. Treatment requires a course of antibiotics. Boiling water for 10 minutes is effective against most microbes except giardia.

Seek medical advice if you think you have giardiasis. Symptoms, which can appear weeks after exposure to the parasite, include stomach cramps, nausea, a bloated stomach, watery, foul-smelling diarrhea and frequent gas.

For more information on water treatment, see p287.

BEAR NECESSITIES

Yellowstone's intact wilderness offers hikers a unique opportunity, inspiring what author Paul Schullery in his book *Mountain Time* calls 'that hackle-raising humility that comes from knowing one is in the presence of a superior predator.'

When hiking in grizzly country, always stay alert and make plenty of noise on the trail. Never hike after dusk. While grizzlies have a highly acute sense of smell, they may not catch your scent if you approach from downwind. Some hikers wear 'bear bells' on their packs to announce their approach, but bears are better able to hear deeper sounds like shouting or clapping. The human voice is effective: while some prefer a medley of show tunes, many shout, 'Hey Bear!' when approaching a blind corner.

If you happen to encounter a bear at close range:

- Do not run – bears can easily outrun humans and will instinctively pursue a fleeing animal.
- Do not drop your pack as a decoy – this may teach the bear that threatening humans is a good way to get food.
- Back away slowly, talking soothingly to the bear while avoiding direct eye contact.

Bears very often 'bluff charge' an intruder, veering away at the last instant. Using a pepper spray (see p280) may deter a charging bear, but if an attack does ensue:

- If the attack is imminent, play dead.
- Lie down and pull your knees against your chest, and (if not wearing a large backpack) pull in your head and shield your neck with your hands.
- In most cases the bear will eventually leave the scene once assured that you present no danger.

In extremely rare cases, grizzly bears with clear predatory intent have attacked humans. Such attacks tend to occur around campsites at dusk or during the night, and are the only time when you should fight back against an aggressive grizzly.

HEALTH & SAFETY

hump on the grizzly's shoulder as well as long claws. Grizzlies have rounded ears, a dish-shaped face and tend to be quite a bit bigger than black bears.

Bears live a sedentary life and will typically avoid contact if given sufficient warning of an approaching individual. The main causes of human–bear conflict include the animal's instinctual protection of its young, the presence of food and surprise encounters. To learn more about bears, see p69.

BEARS & FOOD
Bears are obsessed with food and rarely 'unlearn' knowledge acquired in finding it. In the past, Yellowstone's bears were regularly fed and given access to garbage dumps while tourists watched in grandstand seating. While this tradition no longer continues, visitors are unnecessarily careless and the problem persists. Conditioned to associate humans with food, large numbers of 'habituated' bears have harassed picnickers

or aggressively raided camps. Nowadays, even mildly troublesome bears are usually destroyed.

Don't let your carelessness result in the death of one of these magnificent creatures. Never leave food unattended, even in your backpack. Use the bear boxes at developed campgrounds or lock food in your car. Never store food or eat in your tent, and don't sleep in clothes worn while fishing or cooking. Make sure you are not camping downwind of your food stash.

Backcountry campers must hang food and scented items such as garbage, toothpaste, soap and sunscreen at least 12ft above the ground and 200ft from their tents. Carry a robust stuff-sack attached to a 50ft length of rope. First weight the sack with a rock and throw it over a high, sturdy limb at least 4ft from the tree trunk. Gently lower the sack to the ground with the rope, stash everything with food smells and perfumes, and then pull the sack back

---

PEPPER SPRAYS

Pepper sprays contain the severe irritant oleoresin capsicum. Their effectiveness in deterring charging or attacking bears remains controversial, but many backcountry travelers now carry pepper spray as a last line of defense. Rangers recommend a minimum size of 7.9oz (225g) and a concentration of 1.4% to 1.8% capsaicin (such as those made by UDAP). It costs around $40 and is widely available in backpacking stores. The spray jet can reach up to 30ft. When spraying, wait for the bear to be in close range and aim toward the ground. Be aware which way the wind is blowing, since you don't want to be downwind. Pepper spray must be carried within easy and immediate reach – not in your pack. Remember that carrying pepper spray is not a substitute for vigilance or other safety precautions. Never use it as a repellent.

---

up close to the tree limb. Finally, tie off the end of the rope to another trunk or tree limb well out of the way. Backcountry campgrounds in Yellowstone and Grand Teton invariably supply a food pole, which simplifies the process.

Bison, Moose, Mountain Lions & Wolves

One of the memorable sights in Yellowstone is watching an amateur photographer encourage their loved one to edge toward a seemingly tame, fuzzy bison for an exclusive photo-op. These two-ton creatures can sprint at 30mph and have actually harmed more visitors than bears have.

Moose usually flee intruding humans but if a moose feels cornered or otherwise threatened, it may suddenly charge. Moose cows with calves are especially dangerous, as they will aggressively defend their young. Moose can inflict severe injuries by striking out with their powerful front hoofs.

Although your chances of encountering an aggressive mountain lion remain extremely small, as humans encroach on their territory, attacks appear to be on the increase. Avoid hiking alone in prime mountain lion habitats. Keep children within view at all times. If you happen to encounter a mountain lion, raise your arms and back away slowly. Speak firmly or shout. If attacked, fight back fiercely.

There have been no reliable documented cases of fatal wolf attacks on humans for more than a century. Attacks on humans by wild wolves are believed to be attributable to either rabies infection or habituation – when a wolf has lost its fear of people.

If you stay aware and keep a respectful distance from all wildlife, most encounters will be avoided.

Bites & Stings

LEECHES

Sometimes present in lakes, leeches attach themselves to your skin to suck your blood. Salt or a lit cigarette end will make them fall off. Do not pull them off, as the bite is then more likely to become infected. Clean and apply pressure if the point of attachment is bleeding.

MOSQUITOES

Mosquitoes can be a major irritant in early and midsummer (until around mid-August), so remember to carry mosquito repellent. The most effective sprays contain DEET (the higher the percentage of DEET, the more effective the spray). DEET is powerful stuff and should be kept away from plastics. Citronella is a kinder (to the skin at least) alternative.

SNAKES & SPIDERS

In the history of the park there have been only two recorded snakebites. The prairie rattlesnake is the only poisonous snake in the region, found in the driest and warmest river areas of Yellowstone. If someone is bitten by a rattlesnake, the best first aid is to immediately apply a reverse syringe (Sawyer Extractor) to slow the poison's spread. Keep the victim calm and still, wrap the bitten limb tightly (as you would for a sprained ankle) and then attach a splint to immobilize it. Tourniquets and sucking out the poison by mouth are now comprehensively discredited. Get the victim to a doctor as soon as possible. There are some spiders with dangerous bites but antivenins are usually available.

TICKS

Always check all over your body if you have been walking through a potentially tick-infested area, as ticks can cause skin infections and other more serious diseases. Ticks are most active from spring to autumn, especially where there are plenty of sheep or deer. They usually lurk in overhanging vegetation, so avoid pushing through tall bushes if possible.

If a tick is found attached to the skin, press down around the tick's head with tweezers, grab the head and gently pull upwards. Avoid pulling the rear of the body as this may squeeze the tick's gut contents through its mouth into your skin, increasing the risk of infection and disease. Smearing chemicals on the tick will not make it let go and is not recommended.

Cold

HYPOTHERMIA

This occurs when the body loses heat faster than it can produce it and the core temperature of the body falls.

It is frighteningly easy to progress from very cold to dangerously cold due to a combination of wind, wet clothing, fatigue and hunger, even if the air temperature is above freezing. If the weather deteriorates, put on extra layers of warm clothing: a wind and/or waterproof jacket, plus a wool or fleece hat and gloves are all essential. Have something energy-rich to eat and ensure that everyone in your group is fit, feeling well and alert.

Symptoms of hypothermia are exhaustion, numb skin (particularly toes and fingers), shivering, slurred speech, irrational or violent behavior, lethargy, stumbling, dizzy

---

GETTING INTO HOT WATER

You'll see plenty of signs warning you to stay on existing boardwalks and maintain a safe distance from all geothermal features. Thin crusts of earth can break, giving way to boiling water. Even warm springs can be dangerous; temperatures often fluctuate, sometimes dramatically, so what is safe one day may not be safe the next. About 20 people have died in Yellowstone's hot springs since the 1880s; some have backed into hot springs while taking photos, and more than one pet has jumped gleefully into a boiling pool.

The park service warns that spring waters can cause a rash and that thermophilic amoebas in the water can transmit amoebic meningitis (though there has apparently never been a recorded case of this). If you do swim in any of the areas mentioned in this guide, keep your head above the surface and don't take in any water.

---

spells, muscle cramps and violent bursts of energy. Irrationality may take the form of sufferers claiming they are warm and trying to take off their clothes.

To treat mild hypothermia, first get the person out of the wind and/or rain, remove their clothing if it's wet and replace it with dry, warm clothing. Give them hot liquids – not alcohol – and some high-energy, easily digestible food. Do not rub victims: instead, allow them to slowly warm themselves. This should be enough to treat the early stages of hypothermia. The early recognition and treatment of mild hypothermia is the only way to prevent severe hypothermia, which is a critical condition.

FROSTBITE

This refers to the freezing of extremities, including fingers, toes and the nose. Signs and symptoms of frostbite include a whitish or waxy cast to the skin, or even crystals on the surface, plus itching, numbness and pain. Warm the affected areas by immersion in warm (not hot) water or with blankets or clothes, only until the skin becomes flushed. Frostbitten parts should not be rubbed. Pain and swelling are inevitable. Blisters should not be broken. Get medical attention right away.

WATER

Water from even the wildest mountain lakes and streams may contain harmful pathogens (especially those causing giardiasis and amoebic cysts) and should always be properly treated. Spring water – ie water gushing straight out of the ground – is usually free of pathogens if taken directly from the source. Don't collect water downstream from abandoned mines or other human infrastructure, such as ski resorts, as it may contain toxic impurities that cannot be removed by standard methods of purification. It is advisable not to rely on just one method of water purification.

HEALTH & SAFETY

Heat

DEHYDRATION & HEAT EXHAUSTION

Dehydration is a potentially dangerous and generally preventable condition caused by excessive fluid loss. Sweating combined with inadequate fluid intake is one of the commonest causes of dehydration in trekkers, but other important causes are diarrhea, vomiting and high fever – see Amoebic Dysentery (p278) for more details about appropriate treatment in these circumstances.

The first symptoms are weakness, thirst and passing small amounts of very concentrated urine. This may progress to drowsiness, dizziness or fainting on standing up, and, finally, coma.

It's easy to forget how much fluid you are losing via perspiration while you are trekking, particularly if a strong breeze is drying your skin quickly. You should always maintain a good fluid intake – a minimum of 3L a day is recommended.

Dehydration and salt deficiency can cause heat exhaustion. Salt deficiency is characterized by fatigue, lethargy, headaches, giddiness and muscle cramps; salt tablets are overkill; just adding extra salt to your food is probably sufficient.

HEATSTROKE

This is a serious, occasionally fatal, condition that occurs if the body's heat-regulating mechanism breaks down and the body temperature rises to dangerous levels. Long, continuous periods of exposure to high temperatures and insufficient fluids can leave you vulnerable to heatstroke.

The symptoms include feeling unwell, not sweating very much (or at all) and a high body temperature (102°F to 106°F or 39°C to 41°C). Where sweating has ceased, the skin becomes flushed and red. Severe, throbbing headaches and lack of coordination will also occur, and the sufferer may be confused or aggressive. Eventually the victim will become delirious or convulse.

Hospitalization is essential but in the meantime get victims out of the sun, remove their clothing, cover them with a wet sheet or towel and then fan continually. Give fluids if they are conscious.

Snow Blindness

This is a temporary painful condition resulting from sunburn of the surface of the eye (cornea). It usually occurs when someone walks on snow or in bright sunshine without sunglasses.

Treatment is to relieve the pain – cold cloths on closed eyelids may help. Antibiotic and anesthetic eye drops are not necessary. The condition usually resolves itself within a few days and there are no long-term consequences.

Sun

Protection against the sun should always be taken seriously. Sunburn occurs rapidly in the rarified air and deceptive coolness of the mountains. Slap on the sunscreen and a barrier cream for your nose and lips, wear a broad-brimmed hat and protect your eyes with good-quality sunglasses with UV lenses, particularly when walking near water, sand or snow. If, despite these precautions, you get yourself burnt, calamine lotion, aloe vera or other commercial sunburn relief preparations will soothe.

WALK SAFETY – BASIC RULES

- Allow plenty of time to accomplish a walk before dark, particularly when daylight hours are shorter.
- Study the route carefully before setting out, noting the possible escape routes and the point of no return (where it's quicker to continue than to turn back). Monitor your progress during the day against the time estimated for the walk, and keep an eye on the weather.
- It's wise not to walk alone. Always leave details of your intended route, the number of people in your group and the expected return time with someone responsible before you set off; let that person know when you return.
- Before setting off, make sure you have a relevant map, compass and whistle, and that you know the weather forecast for the area for the next 24 hours.

OGLE WITH CAUTION!

For some reason, perfectly reasonable adults lose all their sense when sighting wildlife: it's happened to us and it will probably happen to you. Rubbernecking at wildlife doesn't just cause traffic jams; along with speeding, it's the main cause of more than 600 annual vehicular accidents in Yellowstone. Trust us when we tell you, the bear, bison or moose you're stalking won't be the last one you see in the park. If you absolutely must get that rutting elk snapshot, pull completely off the road. If there's no room to park, just wait for a better opportunity.

Also, vehicles dispatch about 100 animals a year in Yellowstone, so watch your speed and the road, especially at dusk.

SAFE HIKING

CROSSING STREAMS

Sudden downpours are common in the mountains and can speedily turn a gentle stream into a raging torrent. If you're in any doubt about the safety of a crossing, look for a safer passage upstream or wait. If the rain is short-lived, it should subside quickly.

If you decide it's essential to cross (late in the day, for example), look for a wide, relatively shallow stretch of the stream rather than a bend. Take off your trousers and socks, but keep your boots on to prevent injury. Put dry, warm clothes and a towel in a plastic bag near the top of your pack. Before stepping out from the bank, unclip the chest strap and belt buckle of your pack. This makes it easier to slip out of your backpack and swim to safety if you lose your balance and are swept downstream. Use a walking pole, grasped in both hands, on the upstream side as a third leg, or go arm in arm with a companion, clasping at the wrist, and cross side-on to the flow, taking short steps.

FIRE

Fire danger in the Rockies varies from year to year, but is often extreme in July and August. Local park and USFS offices can advise hikers about forest fires, and fire warnings are usually posted at wilderness access points. Always check with a ranger station or visitor center before embarking on a hike. For fire updates contact the parks at ☎ 307-739-3300 or check out their websites. Or contact the **National Interagency Fire Center** (☎ 208-387-5050; www.nifc.gov).

LIGHTNING

Getting struck by lightning during a summer afternoon storm is a real possibility. Your best bet is to undertake long hikes early. If you do get caught out during a lightning storm, steer clear of exposed ridges, open areas, lone trees, the base of cliffs, and shallow caves or depressions. Move away from bodies of water or beaches. If camping, sit on a foam mattress in a crouched position, your arms around your knees.

ROCKFALL

Even a small, falling rock could shatter your hand or crack your skull, so always be alert to the danger of rock fall. Trail sections most obviously exposed to rock fall pass below cliffs fringed by large fields of raw talus – don't hang around in such areas. If you accidentally let a rock loose, loudly warn other hikers below. Mountain goats and bighorn sheep sometimes dislodge rocks, so animal watchers should be especially vigilant.

RESCUE & EVACUATION

Hikers should aim to manage emergency situations themselves – self-evacuation should be your first consideration. However, even the most safety-conscious hikers may be involved in a serious mountain accident requiring urgent medical attention. If a person in your group is injured or falls seriously ill, leave someone with them while others seek help. If there are only two of you, leave the injured person with as much warm clothing, food and water as it's sensible to spare, plus a whistle and flashlight (torch). Mark the position with something conspicuous – a bright bivvy-bag or perhaps a large stone cross on the ground. Remember, the rescue effort may be slow, perhaps taking some days to remove the injured person. Also keep in mind that search-and-rescue operations are expensive and often require emergency personnel to risk their own welfare.

HEALTH & SAFETY

ROUTE FINDING

While accurate, our maps are not perfect. Inaccuracies in altitudes are commonly caused by air-temperature anomalies. Natural features such as river confluences and mountain peaks are in their true position, but sometimes the location of villages and trails is not always so. This may be because a village is spread over a hillside, or the size of the map does not allow for detail of the trail's twists and turns. However, by using several basic route-finding techniques, you will have few problems following our descriptions:

- Be aware of whether the trail should be climbing or descending.
- Check the north-point arrow on the map and determine the general direction of the trail.
- Time your progress over a known distance and calculate the speed at which you travel in the given terrain. From then on, you can determine with reasonable accuracy how far you have traveled.
- Watch the path – look for boot prints and other signs of previous passage.

SAFE BIKING

TRAFFIC IN THE PARKS

Bicycles are subject to the same traffic rules as cars. While cycling is permitted on established public roads, parking areas and designated routes, it is prohibited on backcountry trails and boardwalks.

Sadly, this is not an easy place to bike. Road shoulders are slim and many a cyclist has been threatened by an encroaching RV mirror. Cyclists must be very aware. For this reason, it's best to bike early in the morning or after 6:30pm when traffic thins out. Drivers sometimes pass on hill crests, blind curves or in oncoming traffic. Wearing a helmet and using high-visibility clothing and mirrors is essential. Never use headphones while cycling.

Bison may be a hazard to cyclists. If you come upon some, dismount your bike and walk far around them or wait for a vehicle to drive through (the bison will follow it).

Visitor centers will have additional information. For more biking suggestions, see p47.

ROAD CONDITIONS

Use extreme caution when cycling in the park; roads are winding and narrow, and shoulders are either narrow or nonexistent. Vehicle traffic is heavy most of the time. There are no bicycle paths along roads.

Road elevations range from 5300ft to 8860ft, and services and facilities are relatively far apart – typically 20 to 30 miles.

Cyclists should take advantage of shoulder seasons. A great time to bike is between October and mid-November, when there is little traffic and less wind. Springtime cyclists can enjoy some roads closed to motorized vehicles. While roads are plowed and summer preparations are made, cycling is permitted between the West Entrance and Mammoth Hot Springs from about mid-March (weather allowing) through to the third Thursday in April. Note that high snowbanks from April to June can make travel more dangerous. August is typically the windiest month.

General road closures are posted at www.nps.gov/yell/planyourvisit/open_close dates.htm.

Clothing & Equipment

CONTENTS

Clothing   285
Equipment   285
Buying & Renting Locally   287

It takes a masterful plan to sort out what clothing and equipment is indispensable for a trip and what will become only a needless addition to an already brimming backpack. Those overnighting on the trail should pay special mind to dividing their belongings into necessities and luxuries. Weigh the benefits of a freshly laundered shirt versus an achy back and you will see why most experienced backpackers choose to harmonize with the riper smells of nature.

Make sure you devote adequate time to this phase of trip planning. Using a checklist can help ensure you get the important stuff in your pack. Spending some time sampling the load will keep it streamlined and you a happy camper.

CLOTHING
Layering
When traveling in the mountains, layering is essential. Be prepared for changeable weather, including flash thunderstorms and frosts even in the middle of summer. Base layers of synthetic fabrics (not cotton) are most effective in wicking moisture from the body. Heavy denim jeans take forever to dry.

Bring several layers of light clothing that you can adjust as you warm up or cool down. For the upper body, the base layer is typically a synthetic shirt that wicks moisture away from the body. The insulating layer retains heat next to your body, and is usually a fleece jacket or wool sweater. The outer shell should be waterproof and protect against wind, rain and snow.

For summer hiking, shorts or loose-fitting trousers are usually adequate. Sturdy cotton or canvas pants are good for hiking through brush. Have sweats or thermal pants to wear around camp or at night. Depending on the weather, thermal underwear, wind pants or waterproof shell pants (for winter conditions) may be appropriate.

If you are headed up a peak, prepare for wind and cooler temperatures. Even on a cloudless summer day, it's smart to pack a shell jacket and a knit cap.

Waterproof Shells
Raingear should be light, breathable and waterproof. A rain jacket and rain pants are recommended for fall through spring conditions; summer travelers can probably get away with a having a sturdy shell. Check for sealed seams, and contoured hoods that won't obscure your vision.

Footwear & Socks
Light to medium hiking boots are recommended for day hikes, while sturdy boots are necessary for extended trips with a heavy pack. Most important, they should be well broken-in and have a good nonslip (such as Vibram) sole. Waterproof boots are preferable in spring and early summer. Running or hiking shoes will work for hikes graded easy or moderate in this book. However, you'll probably appreciate the support and protection provided by boots for demanding hikes, uneven terrain and overnight backpacking.

Don't fail to break in your boots before your trip – even if it means clodhopping to the grocery store. Buy boots in warm conditions or go for a walk while trying them on, so that your feet can expand slightly, as they would while walking. Most hikers carry a pair of sandals to ford rivers and wear at night.

Synthetic and wool-blend hiking socks are the most practical option. They should be free of ridged seams in the toes and heels.

EQUIPMENT
Backpacks & Daypacks
For day hikes, a day-pack (30L to 40L) will usually suffice, but for multiday hikes you will need an internal frame pack (45L to 90L). Even if the manufacturer claims your pack is waterproof, use heavy-duty liners or a trash bag.

EQUIPMENT CHECKLIST

The following is meant to be a general guideline. Know yourself and what special things you may need on the trail.

- Boots
- Binoculars
- Extra footwear – flip-flops, sandals or running shoes are best for wearing around camp and crossing streams
- Raingear
- Hat – wool or fleece is best for cold weather, and a brimmed cap protects against the sun
- Sunglasses – it is easy to burn your eyes at altitude, especially in the snow
- Bandana or handkerchief
- First-aid kit – include self-adhesive bandages, disinfectant, antibiotic salve or cream, gauze, small scissors, tweezers and compact heat blanket
- Camera and binoculars – don't forget to precharge digital camera batteries
- Small towel
- Insect repellent – solutions with DEET protect against West Nile virus
- Sundries – water containers, toilet paper, sealable plastic bags, sunscreen, lip balm and mole-skin for foot blisters
- Topographical maps in a zip-lock bag and compass
- Gloves – for early/late season conditions
- Empty plastic bags – to carry out trash
- Swimsuit – to visit hot springs or lakes

Campers should consider the following:

- Stove, pots and cooking utensils
- Water purifier – either tablets such as Potable Aqua or Aquamira, liquid iodine or a filter
- Waterproof matches or lighter
- Headlamp or flashlight, spare batteries
- Pocket knife
- Hiking poles – useful on steeper terrain and for fording rivers
- Sleeping bag
- Sleeping mat
- A fold-up chair and cooler for car camping

Tents & Tarps

A three-season tent will suffice in most conditions. The floor and the outer shell, or fly, should have taped or sealed seams and covered zips to stop leaks. The weight can be as low as 1kg for a stripped-down, low-profile tent, and up to 3kg for a roomy, luxury, four-season model.

Dome- and tunnel-shaped tents handle blustery conditions better than flat-sided tents.

If you expect to encounter rain, it is a good idea to bring a tarp and short lengths of rope to make a covered cook shelter.

Sleeping Bag & Mat

Goose-down bags are warm, lightweight and compact but useless if they get wet. Synthetic bags are cheaper and better in the wet, but they are bulky, unless you get a compression sack. Mummy-shaped bags prove best for weight and warmth. The given figure (-5°C, for instance) is the coldest temperature at which a person should feel comfortable in the bag. Liners purchased separately can increase the warmth of your bag.

Self-inflating sleeping mats work like a thin air cushion between you and the ground; they also insulate from the cold. Foam mats are low-cost, but less comfortable than blow-up mats like a Therm-A-Rest.

Stoves & Fuel

When buying a stove, think lightweight and easy to operate. Most outdoors stores sell and rent propane or butane stoves. Multifuel stoves are versatile but need pumping, priming and lots of cleaning. In general, liquid fuels are efficient and cheap, while gas is more expensive, cleaner and a reasonable performer. However, the gas canisters can be awkward to carry and are a potential litter problem. Be sure to pack yours out.

Stoves using butane gas are the easiest to operate. True, butane doesn't win many environmental points, but it is much easier to come by than liquid fuels. It is available from outdoor gear shops and, in some remote areas, from small supermarkets.

Liquid fuel such as white gas can be found at outdoor gear shops, hardware stores and some supermarkets. Look for high-performance, cleaner-burning fuel.

Airlines prohibit the carriage of any flammable materials and may well reject empty liquid-fuel bottles or even the stoves themselves.

Water Purifiers & Tablets

Mountain streams may look crystal clear, but with the prevalence of bacteriological contamination, sipping from the source has become a thing of the past. Boiling water rapidly for 10 minutes is effective, but uses fuel that's precious to campers. The advantage of using a filter over iodine tablets is clear: it tastes better. But it also is extra weight to carry and a greater expense.

When buying a filter, pay attention to the type of organisms it filters out. The particle size (in microns) indicates the size of microorganism it can handle. While you may not need a filter whose particle rating is 0.004 microns, if you plan on traveling in developing countries later it may come in handy. Giardia is filtered out by a filter with

a rating of 1.0 to 4.0 microns and *E Coli* is filtered out with a microfilter rating 0.2 to 1.0 microns. When filtering, go for clear water in the current of a stream instead of stagnant water and avoid silty water.

The two-step iodine tablets come with a neutralizing tablet that improves the taste considerably. If you don't plan to be in the backcountry often, these tablets are the most convenient solution.

For more on water purification, see the Health & Safety chapter (p278).

BUYING & RENTING LOCALLY

Don't wait until you get into the park to evaluate what you need. The bandanas, Band-Aids and snow globes sold at souvenir shops will be of little use on a hike. As a hotbed for outdoor gear innovation and consumption, the Rocky Mountain area offers products generally designed and manufactured to high standards. If you can't afford new gear, some shops sell used clothing and equipment. It is not unheard of to find decent nontechnical gear for a song at a church rummage sale in Jackson or a neighborhood garage sale.

If you plan on visiting a winter resort, all have good rental shops with ski, snowboard and Nordic equipment. Most have a program to 'demo' new models with the cost of the rental subtracted from the price if you later decide to buy. Ski festivals often have a free demo booth offered by manufacturers. The same resorts usually rent mountain bikes in summer.

More listings can be found in town sections.

Grand Teton National Park & Around

Adventure Sports (☎ 307-733-3307; Moose Village, WY; ☷ 9am-6pm) At Dornan's, Adventure Sports rents mountain and road bikes ($10/32 per hour/day), kids' bikes ($7/18) and racks ($7/20). It also offers a range of spare tires, a repair shop and info on local trails. Lake boaters can rent canoes ($10/46) and kayaks ($10/46), with discounts for weekly rental. Ask about shuttles. Winter rentals include Nordic skis, snowshoes and sleds.

Colter Bay Marina (☎ 307-543-2811; ☷ 8am-5pm) Rents motorboats ($155/27 per day/hour), rowboats and canoes ($11 to $13 per hour).

Hoback Sports (☎ 307-733-5335; 520 W Broadway Ave, Jackson, WY; ☷ 9am-7pm) Rents road bikes and full-suspension mountain bikes ($20 to $40 daily), skis, snowboards, trailers, racks, hiking poles and kids' bikes.

CLOTHING & EQUIPMENT

NAVIGATION EQUIPMENT

Maps & Compass

You should always carry a good map (see p28) of the area in which you are walking, and know how to read it. Before setting off, familiarize yourself with the contour interval, the map symbols and the magnetic declination (difference between true and grid north), plus the main ridge and river systems in the area and the general direction in which you are heading. On the trail, try to identify major landforms such as mountain ranges and valleys, and locate them on your map.

Compasses require some practice. The attraction of magnetic north varies in different parts of the world, so compasses need to be balanced accordingly. Compass manufacturers have divided the world into five zones: have yours balanced for your destination zone. The 'universal' compasses on the market can be used anywhere in the world.

1	Base plate
2	Direction of travel arrow
3	Dash
4	Bezel
5	Meridian lines
6	Needle
7	Red end
8	N (north point)

How to Use a Compass

This is a very basic introduction to using a compass and will only be of assistance if you are proficient in map reading. For simplicity, it doesn't take magnetic variation into account. Before using a compass we recommend you get further instruction.

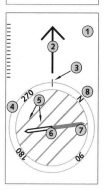

Reading a Compass

Hold the compass flat in the palm of your hand. Rotate the bezel (4) so the red end (7) of the needle (6) points to the N (north point; 8) on the bezel. The bearing is read from the dash (3) under the bezel.

Orienting the Map

To orient the map so that it aligns with the ground, place the compass flat on the map. Rotate the map until the needle is parallel with the map's north–south grid lines and the red end is pointing to north on the map. You can now identify features around you by aligning them with labeled features on the map.

Taking a Bearing from the Map

Draw a line on the map between your starting point and your destination. Place the edge of the compass on this line with the direction of travel arrow (2) pointing towards your destination.

Moosely Seconds (☎ 307-733-6094; Moose Village, WY; ☼ 9am-6pm) At Dornan's, Moosely sells used clothing and mountaineering and camping equipment. Rentals include sleeping bags ($7 per day), tents ($10), ice axes ($6) and crampons ($10), with discounted weekly rates.

Rendezvous River Sports & Jackson Hole Kayak School (☎ 307-733-2471, 800-733-2471; www .jhkayakschool.com; 945 W Broadway, Jackson, WY; ☼ 8am-7pm) White-water and sit-on-top kayaks, and canoe rentals ($35 to $45).

Signal Mountain Marina (☎ 307-543-2831; ☼ 7am-7:30pm mid-May–early Sep) Rents canoes ($13.50/73 per hour/day), kayaks ($12/66), motorboats ($28/165) and pontoon cruisers ($65/385).

Skinny Skis (☎ 307-733-6094; www.skinnyskis.com; 65 W Deloney Ave, Jackson, WY; ☼ 9am-7pm Mon-Sat, 10am-6pm Sun) The best spot for Nordic ski and skate gear, with a knowledgeable staff, a great selection of women's outdoor clothing and products, and children's gear as well.

Snake River Angler (☎ 307-733-3699, 800-998-7688; Moose Village, WY; ☼ 8am-4:30pm) Sells and rents equipment and offers fishing licenses and guided trips.

Yellowstone National Park & Around

Absaroka Bicycles (☎ 307-527-5566; 2201 17th Street, K-mart Plaza, Cody, WY; ☼ 10am-6pm Mon-Sat) Offers riders tips, rentals and repairs.

Bear Den Bike (Old Faithful Snow Lodge, Yellowstone National Park) This small booth inside the hotel's giftshop at Old Faithful rents out kids' and adults' bikes during the summer, and snowshoes, skis and other equipment in the winter.

Rotate the bezel until the meridian lines (5) are parallel with the north–south grid lines on the map and the N points to north on the map. Read the bearing from the dash.

Following a Bearing

Rotate the bezel so that the intended bearing is in line with the dash. Place the compass flat in the palm of your hand and rotate the base plate (1) until the red end points to N on the bezel. The direction of travel arrow will now point in the direction you need to walk.

Determining Your Bearing

Rotate the bezel so the red end points to the N. Place the compass flat in the palm of your hand and rotate the base plate until the direction of travel arrow points in the direction in which you have been walking. Read your bearing from the dash.

GPS

Originally developed by the US Department of Defense, the Global Positioning System (GPS) is a network of more than 20 earth-orbiting satellites that continually beam encoded signals back to earth. Small, computer-driven devices (GPS receivers) can decode these signals to give users an extremely accurate reading of their location – to within 10m, anywhere on the planet, at any time of day, in almost any weather. The cheapest hand-held GPS receivers now cost less than $100 (although these may not have a built-in averaging system that minimizes signal errors). When purchasing, also consider a GPS receiver's weight and battery life.

A GPS receiver is useful only when used with an accurate topographical map. The receiver gives your position, which you must then locate on the local map. GPS receivers only work properly in the open. The signals from a crucial satellite may be blocked (or bounce off rock or water) directly below high cliffs, near large bodies of water or in dense tree cover and give inaccurate readings. GPS receivers are more vulnerable to breakdowns (including dead batteries) than the humble magnetic compass – a low-tech device that has served navigators faithfully for centuries – so don't rely on them entirely.

Altimeter

An altimeter gives one piece of information: the elevation. Newer watch altimeters can be easier to use than traditional models with a needle and dial. With one you can keep track of your progress and pinpoint your location on the map. By making note of the elevation of points along the way, this information can help you find these unmarked places again. It is also useful to note progress: if in the first hour you gained 800ft and only 500ft in the second, you can predict your pace for the next 1000ft of a steady slope with better accuracy. And if you summit a peak in the clouds, it's one way to be sure you've truly arrived!

Cooke City Bike Shack (☎ 406-838-2412; Cooke City) A good inventory of rental equipment, winter ski shuttles and information on the best runs in the region.

Flying Pig Camping Store (☎ 406-848-7510; http://flyingpigrafting.com/store.cfm; 511 Scott St West, Gardiner) Decent range of gear, often on sale, and rafting and horse-riding trips in the area.

Free Heel & Wheel (☎ 406-646-7744; www.freeheel andwheel.com; 40 Yellowstone Ave, West Yellowstone, MT; ☽ 9am-8pm Mon-Sat, 9am-7pm Sun) Rents mountain bikes ($25 per day), skis ($20 per day) and snowshoes ($15), and offers touring, skate-ski lessons and free women's rides.

Paddle On Adventures (☎ reservations only 406-209-7452; www.paddleonadventures.com; Kirkwood Marina,

West Yellowstone area) Rents canoes and sit-on-top kayaks with lifejackets and paddles.

Sierra Trading Post (☎ 307-578-5802; www .sierratradingpost.com; 1402 8th St, Cody WY; ☽ 9am-7pm Mon-Sat, noon-6pm Sun) This nationally known discount outlet sells clothing, gear and sports footwear at reduced prices, including bear spray.

Wheel Fun Rentals (☎ 307-587-4779; 1390 Sheridan Ave, Cody WY) Rents bikes from $11 per hour and kayaks.

Yellowstone Adventures (☎ 307-242-7551; www .visityellowstonepark.com; Canyon Village; ☽ 9am-6pm mid-Apr–late Oct) The only outdoor gear store in the park sells Columbia and North Face clothing, along with camp items, bear spray and fishing flies.

Glossary

AAA – American Automobile Club of America; usually called 'triple-A'
ATV – all terrain vehicle

backcountry – anywhere more than a couple of hundred yards from roads, boardwalks or other park infrastructure
basalt – a hard, dense and very common volcanic rock; solidified lava
blaze – stripe of paint on a tree or rock serving as a trail marker
BLM – Bureau of Land Management
breccia – fragments of jagged rock embedded in finer grained rock or silt
bugle – high-pitched cry of a male elk during the *rut*
butte – a prominent hill or mountain standing separate from surrounding ranges

caldera – large crater caused by volcanic explosion and/or the collapse of a volcanic cone
chinook – dry, warm, westerly wind on the east side of the *Continental Divide*
comfort station – toilet
concessionaire – private business or service provider permitted to operate inside the parks by the park service
Continental Divide – major watershed separating east-flowing (to the Atlantic) from west-flowing (to the Pacific) streams

dude ranch – a ranch or farm that caters for paying guests

erratic – a boulder carried by glacial ice and deposited some distance from its place of origin

fumarole – steam vent

glissading – to slide in a standing or squatting position down a snow-covered slope without the aid of skis
GPS – global positioning system; an electronic, satellite-based network that allows for the calculation of position and elevation using a hand-held receiver/decoder

hatch – fishing term relating to the hatching of certain insect larvae
hazing – use of noise and distractions to prevent animals such as elk and bison from leaving park territory
hole – valley, as in Jackson Hole
hoodoo – fantastically shaped rock formation produced by weathering

hookup – facility at a campsite for giving an *RV* water and/or electricity

kettle hole – deep, kettle-shaped depression in glacial drift
KOA – Kampgrounds of America; a private chain of campgrounds throughout the USA
krummholz – wind-twisted, stunted trees found near treeline

Labor Day – national holiday that falls on the first Monday in September
lower 48 – the 48 contiguous states of the continental USA; all states except Alaska and Hawaii

Memorial Day – national holiday that falls on the last Monday in May
mud pot – acidic hot spring that has broken down the local rock to become bubbling mud

NPR – National Public Radio; a noncommercial, listener-supported national network of radio stations, which are notable for news, classical music and cultural programming
NPS – National Park Service

obsidian – a black, glassy volcanic rock commonly used by Native Americans to make cutting tools
out-and-back – a hike that backtracks to its starting point from its destination
outfitter – supplier of guides, equipment and/or transport for fishing, canoeing, hiking, rafting or horseback trips

quad – short for 'quadrangle'; topographical map in the USGS 1:24,000 series

RV – recreational vehicle; also called a motor home or camper
rhyolite – tough granite-like volcanic rock
rut – Autumn mating season for elk

saddle – low place in a ridge
shuttle hike – a destination hike where it is necessary to leave a vehicle at both trailheads
sinter – silica-rich mineral deposited by geysers and hot springs, also known as geyserite
snag – dead, downed tree
snowcoach – coach adapted with tracks for over-snow use
solfatara – acidic thermal area

talus – slope of rock boulders or debris

TDD – Telecommunications Device for the Deaf; abbreviation that prefaces phone numbers; using this number, the TDD machine converts sound to screen words and vice versa

thermophile – bacteria that lives in the very high temperatures of Yellowstone's hot springs

travertine – light-colored calcium carbonate deposited by mineral springs in the Mammoth region

USFS – United States Forest Service, which manages the nation's system of national forests

USGS – United States Geological Survey; the national cartographic organization

Behind the Scenes

THIS BOOK

This 2nd edition of *Yellowstone & Grand Teton National Parks* was researched and written by Bradley Mayhew, Carolyn McCarthy and David Lukas. The 1st edition was written by Bradley Mayhew, Andrew Dean Nystrom and Amy Marr.

This guidebook was commissioned in Lonely Planet's Oakland office, and produced by the following:

Commissioning Editor Heather Dickson
Coordinating Editors Simon Williamson, Pete Cruttenden
Coordinating Cartographer Helen Rowley
Coordinating Layout Designer Cara Smith
Senior Editor Sasha Baskett
Managing Cartographer Alison Lyall
Managing Layout Designer Adam McCrow
Assisting Cartographer Alissa Baker
Cover Designer Amy Stephens
Color Designer Margie Jung
Project Managers Bronwyn Hicks, Glenn van der Knijff

Thanks to Helen Christinis, Melanie Dankel, Barbara Delissen, Andrea Dobbin, Ryan Evans, Jennifer Garrett, Suki Gear, Michelle Glynn, Brice Gosnell, James Hardy, Corey Hutchison, Lisa Knights, Adriana Mammarella, Raphael Richards, Lyahna Spencer, Emily K Wolman, Celia Wood

THANKS
Bradley Mayhew

Thanks to Heather Dickson for offering me a guidebook-writing job that didn't involve me flying half-way across the world, and for answering endless emails all through the production process.

Cheers to coauthor Carolyn McCarthy, who was a joy to work with. Thanks to Bill Sampson for his generous help tracking down rooms at the Old Faithful Lodge. Thanks also to my father-in-law John Hahn, who got the whole trip started by fixing up my dying van. And cheers to all the professional rangers throughout the park who offered advice and information. Love and thanks to Kelli, as always, without whom I would never have come to call Montana home.

Carolyn McCarthy

Exploring Yellowstone and the Tetons in summer is truly a dream job. Sincere thanks to Heather Dickson for giving me the opportunity to reconnect with the west and coauthor Bradley Mayhew for his help with the project.

On the road, many offered thoughtful contributions. They include Rob and Mary Weller, Kristen Schnepp, Jeff Brown, volunteers at the Yellowstone Association, Norm Bishop, Pete Owens and the

---

THE LONELY PLANET STORY

Fresh from an epic journey across Europe, Asia and Australia in 1972, Tony and Maureen Wheeler sat at their kitchen table stapling together notes. The first Lonely Planet guidebook, *Across Asia on the Cheap*, was born.

Travelers snapped up the guides. Inspired by their success, the Wheelers began publishing books to Southeast Asia, India and beyond. Demand was prodigious, and the Wheelers expanded the business rapidly to keep up. Over the years, Lonely Planet extended its coverage to every country and into the virtual world via lonelyplanet.com and the Thorn Tree message board.

As Lonely Planet became a globally loved brand, Tony and Maureen received several offers for the company. But it wasn't until 2007 that they found a partner whom they trusted to remain true to the company's principles of traveling widely, treading lightly and giving sustainably. In October of that year, BBC Worldwide acquired a 75% share in the company, pledging to uphold Lonely Planet's commitment to independent travel, trustworthy advice and editorial independence.

Today, Lonely Planet has offices in Melbourne, London and Oakland, with over 500 staff members and 300 authors. Tony and Maureen are still actively involved with Lonely Planet. They're traveling more often than ever, and they're devoting their spare time to charitable projects. And the company is still driven by the philosophy of *Across Asia on the Cheap*: 'All you've got to do is decide to go and the hardest part is over. So go!'

Climbers' Ranch. Boulder friends Louise Ross, Joce-lyn Turnbull and Bjorn Johns were kind enough to lend me a workspace. Special thanks to Dave Mencin for two spectacular flights and to Joe, who lost his luggage but not his sense of humor. Various creatures came forth to prove that wilderness indeed survives in America, in spite of all we do to it. Thank you.

OUR READERS

Many thanks to the travelers who used the last edition and wrote to us with helpful hints, useful advice and interesting anecdotes:

Laura Gwinn, J Hauer, Andie Lueders, Nicola Ostler, Barry Prager, Leslie Richter, Jayna Rutz, Maria Sieve, Larry Spinelli

ACKNOWLEDGMENTS

Many thanks to the following for the use of their content:

Internal photographs by Tom Mareschal/Getty p12 (#2); Tania Hopkins/Flickr p14 (#2); Dick Zambrano/Flickr p15 (#5). All other photographs by Lonely Planet Images, and by Rob Blakers p16, Richard Cummins p10 (#1); Wade Eakle p3; John Elk III p5 (#3), p8 (#1 & #2), p9 (#4 & #5), p10 (#3), p14 (#1); Lee Foster p13 (#4); Christer Fredriksson p7 (bull bison, top right; bull moose, bottom right), p10; Holger Leue p6 (top), p11 (#2); Andrew Nystrom p7 (young black bear #3); Carol Polich p4 (#1), p5 (#4), p6 (bottom); Cheyenne Rouse p11 (#6), p15 (#6); Stephen Saks p13 (#2); David Thomlinson p5 (#5); Jim Wark p4 (#2), p12 (#6).

All images are the copyright of the photographers unless otherwise indicated. Many of the images in this guide are available for licensing from Lonely Planet Images: www.lonelyplanetimages.com.

SEND US YOUR FEEDBACK

We love to hear from travelers – your comments keep us on our toes and help make our books better. Our well-traveled team reads every word on what you loved or loathed about this book. Although we cannot reply individually to postal submissions, we always guarantee that your feedback goes straight to the appropriate authors, in time for the next edition. Each person who sends us information is thanked in the next edition – and the most useful submissions are rewarded with a free book.

To send us your updates – and find out about Lonely Planet events, newsletters and travel news – visit our award-winning website: **www.lonelyplanet.com/feedback**.

Note: we may edit, reproduce and incorporate your comments in Lonely Planet products such as guidebooks, websites and digital products, so let us know if you don't want your comments reproduced or your name acknowledged. For a copy of our privacy policy visit www.lonelyplanet.com/privacy.

Index

See also separate subindex for Hikes (p308).

A

Absaroka (people) 82, 109
Absaroka-Beartooth Wilderness
    183, 206
Abyss Pool 113
accommodations 258-62, see also
    individual locations
    accommodation tax 265
    camping 259-61
    dude ranches 262
    Grand Teton National Park 235-8
    lodging 261-2
    reservations 261
    Yellowstone National Park 160-6
activities 39-55, see also individual
    activities
acute mountain sickness, see altitude
    sickness
air travel 270-1
Alaska Basin 227, 254
altimeters 289
altitude 289
altitude sickness 278
amoebic dysentery 278
Amphitheater Lake 223
Anemone Geyser 123
Angel Terrace 101
animals 69-76, 275, see also individual
    animals, birds, pets, travel with
Antelope Creek 107
Antler Arch 243, 11
Appolinaris Spring 103
area codes, see inside back cover
art galleries, see museums
Artemisia Geyser 123
Artist Paint Pots 118
Artist Point 110
arts festivals 245
ATMs 265
Atomizer Geyser 123
Aurum Geyser 123
automobile associations 272
Avalanche Canyon 225
avalanche conditions 52
Avalanche Peak 141

B

backcountry skiing, see cross-country
    skiing
backpacks 285
bald eagles 75
ballooning 244
Bannock (people) 82, 102, 128, 255
Basin Lakes 182
Batchelder Column 153
bathrooms 45
beargrass 79
Bearpaw Lake 222
bears 69, 7
    Grand Teton National Park 214
    safety 98, 278-80
    Yellowstone National Park 98
Bear's Tooth 185
Beartooth Butte 185
Beartooth Hwy 183-7, 184
Beartooth Nature Center 182
Beartooth Pass West Summit 185
Beartooth Plateau 183
Beauty Lake 186
Beauty Pool 123
Beaver Lake 103
Bechler Falls 143
Bechler Region
    accommodations 166
    hiking 143, 152
    sights 127-8
Bechler River 152
Beehive Geyser 123
beer
    brewpubs 197
    tours 181
Beryl Spring 118
Beula Lake 257
Big Sky 197-9, 13
Bighorn Pass 136
bighorn sheep 74
Bijou Geyser 123
Billings 180-1
birds 74-6, see also individual species
bird-watching
    Bechler Meadows & Falls Trail 143
    Hayden Valley 111
    Hermitage Point 221
    Jackson Lake Lodge 216
    Norris Meadows Picnic Area 118

Oxbow Bend 216
Pelican Valley 116
Snake River Rd 229
Swan Lake (Yellowstone National
    Park) 103
Two Ocean Lake & Grand View
    Point Trail 221
Yellowstone Lake 112
Birnbaum, Drew 231
Biscuit Basin 124
Biscuit Basin Overlook 131
bison 72, 280, 7
black bears, see bears
Black Canyon of the Yellowstone
    143-6, 145
Black Dragon's Cauldron 112
Black Growler Steam Vent 117
Black Pool 113
Black Sand Basin 124
Blackfoot (people) 82, 255
Blacktail Butte 220
Blacktail Deer Creek 136
Blacktail Ponds 102
Blacktail Ponds Overlook 230
blisters 277
Blue Star Spring 122
blueberries 78
Blues & Microbrew Fest 256
boating, see also canoeing &
    kayaking, rafting & floating
    Colter Bay Region 232
    Grand Teton National Park
        213, 232
    Jenny Lake 219
    John D Rockefeller Jr Memorial
        Parkway 234
    Leigh Lake 233
    licenses & permits 97-8, 213-4
    Shoshone Lake 158
    String Lake 233
    tours 158, 232-3
    Yellowstone Lake 157-8
    Yellowstone National Park 97
bobcats 74
Boiling River 101
books 27-8
    canoeing 49
    children, travel with 56, 58
    fishing 28, 49, 177
    geology 67

INDEX

geysers 147
health 277
hiking 41
history 85
Bozeman 194-6
Bradley Lake 224, 225
Bridger, Jim 84, 106
Bridger Gondola 250
Brock, Dr Thomas 90
Brooks Lake 253
brucellosis 73
Buffalo Bill 191
Buffalo Bill Historical Center 188, 10
Buffalo Bill Reservoir 193
Buffalo Bill Scenic Byway 192
Buffalo Bill Stampede 59
Buffalo Bill State Park 190-4
Buffalo Byway 155
Buffalo Horn Pass 206
Buffalo Ranch 106
Bunsen Peak 102, 134
Bunsen Peak Rd 154
bus travel
    to/from the parks 272
    within the parks 274
bushwalking, *see* hiking
business hours 262, *see also inside
    back cover*

C
Cabin Creek Scarp Area 202
Cache Lake 135
Calamity Jane 203
Calcite Springs Overlook 106
camping 259-61, *see also* accommo-
    dations, *individual locations*
    camp programs 58
    Grand Teton National Park 234-5,
        236-7
    permits 96, 213
    responsible camping 43, 260
    Yellowstone National Park 161-6
Canary Springs 101
canoeing & kayaking 49, *see also*
    boating, rafting & floating
    books 49
    Cody 190
    Colter Bay Region 232
    courses 263
    Gardiner 176
    Hebgen Lakes 203
    Jackson 244
    Jenny Lake 219
    Livingston 204
    permits 97-8, 213

rental 287-9
Sedge Bay 116
Shoshone Lake 158
String Lake 233
tours 176, 200, 203
Yellowstone Lake 157-8
Canyon Country **108**
    accommodations 164
    cycling 154
    food 167
    hiking 138, 149
    sights 107-12
Canyon Village 107, **110**
Canyon Visitor Education Center 107
car travel, *see also* driving routes,
    motorcycle travel
    automobile associations 272
    driver's licenses 273
    insurance 273
    rental 273
    road distances 272
    road updates 266
    to/from the parks 272-3
    within the parks 98, 274-5
Carbon County Arts Guild Gallery 182
Carbon County Museum 181
carbon offset schemes 270
Cascade Canyon 219
Cascade Lake 139-40
Cassidy, Butch 181
Castle Geyser 123
Cathedral Group turnout 217
Cave Falls 143
Celestine Pool 125
cell phones 266
Center for the Arts 241
Central Tetons **218**
    accommodations 237
    food 239
    hiking 226-8
    sights 217-19
chambers of commerce 267
Chapel of the Sacred Heart 217
Chapel of the Transfiguration 219, 231
Chico Hot Springs 204, 205
Chief Joseph Creek 156
Chief Joseph Scenic Hwy 187-8
children, travel with 56-60, *see also*
    safety
    books 56, 58
    camp programs 58
    child-friendly hikes 57, 15
    climbing 58
    hiking difficulty 40
    ranger programs 44, 57, 113, 216

Chinese Spring 121
Chittenden, Hiram 107
Christian Pond 216
Chromatic Pool 123
Churning Cauldron 112
Cinnamon Creek 199
cinquefoil 78
Cistern Spring 118
Clarks Fork Canyon 187
Clark's nutcracker 76
Clay Butte Overlook 185
Clear Lake 140
Clepsydra Geyser 125
Cliff Geyser 124
Cliff Lake 201
climate 23, 263
climate change 270
clothing 285
Cody 188-94, **189**, 14, 15
Cody Firearms Museum 190
Cody Nite Rodeo 191
Cody Stampede Park 191
Coffin Lakes 203
Colonnade Falls 153
Colter, John 83
Colter Bay Region **215**
    accommodations 236-7
    boating 232
    fishing 216, 234
    food 238-9
    hiking 221-2
    sights 214-17
Columbia Pool 151
columbines 78
Comet Geyser 123
common loons 76
compasses 288
Congress Pool 117
Constant Geyser 117
Continental Divide Trail 40
Cooke City 178-80
corn lilies 79
costs 26, 264, *see also inside back
    cover*
Cottonwood Creek 229
cougars 74
courses 263
    canoeing & kayaking 263
    fishing 263
    rock climbing 232, 244
    wildlife 263
Cowboy Poetry & Range Ballads
    Festival 191
coyotes 71, 6
Crackling Lake 117

Craig Pass 127
Craig Thomas Discovery & Visitor Center 219
Crested Pool 123
cross-country skiing 53-4, *see also* downhill skiing
  Cooke City 179
  Gallatin Valley 199
  Grand Targhee 256
  Grand Teton National Park 234
  Jackson Hole 250
  rental 287-9
  snow conditions 52
  tours 159, 161
  Wapiti Valley 194
  weather services 266
  West Yellowstone 173, 13
  Yellowstone National Park 160, 161
Crow (people) 82, 109
Crystal Falls 110
Cunningham Cabin 220, 230
currency exchange 265
cycling 47-8, *see also* mountain biking
  Grand Teton National Park 228
  rental 274
  safety 284
  tours 47, 171
  Yellowstone National Park 153-6

D

Daisy Geyser 123
daypacks 285
Dead Indian Creek Waterfall 187
Dead Indian Pass 187
Death Canyon 225
Death Canyon Shelf 228
Deckard Flats 145
dehydration 282
Delacy Creek 132
Depot Center 204
Devil's Slide 206
Devil's Staircase 255
digital resources 29
disabilities, travelers with 267
discount cards 263
dogsledding 55, 205
Doublet Pool 123
Douglas fir 77

000 Map pages
000 Photograph pages

downhill skiing 52-3, *see also* cross-country skiing
  Beartooth Hwy 185
  Gallatin Valley 197-9
  Grand Targhee 255
  Grand Teton National Park 234-5
  Jackson 245
  Jackson Hole 250
  Red Lodge 182
  rental 287-9
  snow conditions 52
  tours 159
  weather services 266
  West Yellowstone 173
  Yellowstone National Park 159, 161
Dragon's Mouth Spring 112
Draper Museum of Natural History 190
drinks 264, *see also* beer
driver's licenses 273
driving routes, *see also* car travel, motorcycle travel
  Beartooth Hwy 183, 185
  Buffalo Bill Scenic Byway 192
  Chief Joseph Scenic Hwy 187
  Firehole Lake Dr 125
  Gallatin Valley 196-7
  Grand Teton National Park 230-1
  Grassy Lake Rd 220
  itineraries 31-8, **31-8**
  Jenny Lake Scenic Dr 217, 231
  John D Rockefeller Jr Memorial Parkway 220
  Paradise Valley 203-7
  Signal Mountain Summit Rd 217
  West Yellowstone 173
  Yellowstone National Park 98, 125, 156-7
Duck Lake Trail 142
dude ranches 262
Dunraven Pass 106

E

earthquakes 202
Eastern Slopes 219-20
Echinus Geyser 118
Elbow Lake 206
electricity 258
Elephant Back Mountain 133
elk 72, 6
Elk Park 118
ElkFest & Antler Auction 245
Emerald Pool 124
Emerald Spring 117
emergencies 276

Emerson Cultural Center 195
Engelmann spruce 77
entrance fees 27, 92, 209
environment 63-80
  internet resources 63
environmental issues 79-80
  carbon offset schemes 270
  climate change 270
  internet resources 79
  recycling 80
  snowmobiling 80
  wildfires 79, 144
equipment 285-9
evacuation 283
events, *see* festivals & events
Everts, Trumen 102
Excelsior Pool 124

F

Fairy Falls 129-30, 156, **130**
Fan Geyser 123
fatigue 277
fauna, *see* animals
Fawn Pass 135
Ferris Fork Hot Springs 153
Festival of Nations 181
festivals & events 26
  arts 245
  Blues & Microbrew Fest 256
  Buffalo Bill Stampede 59
  Cody Nite Rodeo 191
  Cowboy Poetry & Range Ballads Festival 191
  ElkFest & Antler Auction 245
  Festival of Nations 181
  Grand Targhee Bluegrass Music Festival 256
  Grand Teton Music Festival 256
  Jackson Hole Fall Arts Festival 245
  Mountain Man Rendezvous 26
  music 26, 256
  Native American 26, 191
  Plains Indians Powwow 191
  Rockin' the Tetons 256
  Running of the Sheep 182
  Teton County Fair 245
  Yellowstone Jazz Festival 191
  Yellowstone Ski Festival 173
film 28
fire 283
Firehole Canyon Dr 126
Firehole Falls 126
Firehole Lake 125
Firehole Lake Dr 125
Firehole Swimming Area 126

fireweed 78
first aid 277-8
fish 76, *see also individual species*
fishing 49-50
  books 28, 49, 177
  Cody 190
  Colter Bay Region 216, 234
  courses 263
  Gallatin Valley 199
  Grand Teton National Park 214, 216, 234
  Jackson 244
  Jackson Hole 251
  licenses & permits 50, 97, 214
  Lily Lake 185
  Paradise Valley 206
  Wapiti Valley 194
  West Yellowstone 172
  Yellowstone National Park 97, 158, 160, 9
Fishing Bridge 113
Fishing Cone 113
Flat Cone 131
floating, *see* rafting & floating
Floating Island Lake 102
flora, *see* plants
Fly Fishing Discovery Center 204
Folsom-Cook-Peterson expedition 84
food 264
footwear 285
Fort Yellowstone 99-101
Fountain Flat Dr 126
Fountain Freight Rd 156
Fountain Paint Pot 125
Fox Creek Pass 227
foxes 71
frostbite 281
fumaroles 65

G
Gallatin Petrified Forest 206-7
Gallatin Valley 196-201, **198**
Gardiner 175-8, **176**
Garnet Canyon 224
gentians 78
geology 63-9
George, Jim 206
Geyser Country **120**, 14
  accommodations 165-6
  cross-country skiing 160
  cycling 155-6
  fishing 160
  food 167
  hiking 129-33, 146
  sights 119-27

Geyser Hill 121
Geyser Trail 156
geysers 64-5
  Anemone Geyser 123
  Atomizer Geyser 123
  Aurum Geyser 123
  Beehive Geyser 123
  Bijou Geyser 123
  books 147
  Castle Geyser 123
  Clepsydra Geyser 125
  Cliff Geyser 124
  Comet Geyser 123
  Constant Geyser 117
  Daisy Geyser 123
  Echinus Geyser 118
  Giant Geyser 123
  Giantess Geyser 122
  Grand Geyser 123
  Great Fountain Geyser 125
  Grotto Geyser 123
  Heart Lake Geyser Basin 150
  Imperial Geyser 130
  Jelly Geyser 125
  Jewel Geyser 124
  Lion Geyser 123
  Lone Star Geyser 127, 132, 155
  Minute Geyser 118
  Monument Geyser 142
  Mortar Geyser 123
  Mud Volcano 112, 155
  Norris Geyser Basin 117, 5
  Old Faithful 119-37, 4
  Pearl Geyser 118
  Pink Cone Geyser 125
  Plume Geyser 123
  Pocket Basin Geyser 126
  Porkchop Geyser 118
  Queen's Laundry Geyser 131
  Riverside Geyser 123
  Rustic Geyser 151
  Sawmill Geyser 124
  Shell Geyser 124
  Shoshone Geyser Basin 147, 5
  Solitary Geyser 121
  Spasmodic Geyser 124
  Spray Geyser 130
  Turban Geyser 124
  Vault Geyser 122
  Vent Geyser 124
  West Thumb Geyser Basin 113
  Whirligig Geyser 117
  White Dome Geyser 125
Ghost Village 202
Giant Geyser 123

Giantess Geyser 122
giardia 278
Gibbon Falls 118
Glacier Lake 182
glacier lilies 79
glaciers 68
  Grasshopper Glacier 179
  Teton Glacier 219, 223
Global Positioning System 289
golden eagles 75
Goodwin Lake 243
GPS 289
Grand Canyon of the Yellowstone 66, 107-11, 12
Grand Geyser 123
Grand Prismatic Spring 124, 130, 4
Grand Targhee Bluegrass Music Festival 256
Grand Targhee Ski & Summer Resort 255-6
Grand Teton Music Festival 256
Grand Teton National Park 208-39, **210-11**, 12
  accommodations 235-8
  backcountry permits 213
  boating 213, 232
  bookstores 212
  Central Tetons 217-19, **218**
  Colter Bay Region 214-17, **215**
  cross-country skiing 234
  cycling 228
  downhill skiing 234-5
  drinking 238-9
  driving routes 230-1
  Eastern Slopes 219-20
  entrance fees & passes 27, 209
  entrance stations 209
  equipment rental 287-8
  fishing 214, 216, 234
  food 238-9
  geology 67
  hiking 221-8
  horseback riding 232
  internet access 212
  itineraries 20, 33, 35-8, 213, **33**, **35-8**
  medical services 278
  opening dates 25
  postal services 212
  ranger stations 212-13
  rock climbing 231-2
  safety 214
  sights 214-21
  snowmobiling 235
  snowshoeing 234

Grand Teton National Park
   continued
   surrounding region 240-57
   tourist offices 212
   tours 214
   travel to/from 270-3
   travel within 214, 273-5
   visitor centers 212
   wildlife-watching 220
Grand View Point (Grand Teton
   National Park) 216
Grand View Point (Yellowstone
   National Park) 109
Granite Canyon 226
Granite Hot Springs 252
Grants Pass 146
Grasshopper Glacier 179
Grassy Lake Rd 220, 256-7
Grassy Reservoir 257
great blue herons 75
Great Fountain Geyser 125
great horned owls 75
Grizzly & Wolf Discovery Center 171
grizzly bears, *see* bears
Grizzly Fumarole 112
Gros Ventre (people) 82
Gros Ventre Butte 230
Gros Ventre River 230
Gros Ventre Slide Area 252
Grotto Geyser 123
guided hikes, *see* hiking, tours
Gumper, the 112

H
Handkerchief Pool 124
Harlequin Lake 126
Hayden Expedition 85
Hayden Survey 254
Hayden Valley 111-12, 155
health 276-84
   books 277
   internet resources 277
   medical assistance 277-8
Heart Lake Geyser Basin 150
Heart Mountain Relocation Center 192
Heart Spring 123
heat exhaustion 282
heatstroke 282
Hebgen Lake Area 201-3, **201**
Hellroaring Creek 145
Hellroaring Trailhead 102

Hemingway, Ernest 187
Hermitage Point 221
Heron Pond 221
herons 75
Hidden Falls 223
hiking 39-46, *see also* Hikes *subindex*
   backcountry 42
   books 41
   child-friendly hikes 57, 15
   difficulty levels 40
   Grand Teton National Park 221-8
   guided hikes 141
   internet resources 52
   Jackson 243
   maps 28-9
   permits 96, 213
   ranger-led 219
   responsible hiking 42-3
   safety 283
   Yellowstone National Park 128-53
Hilgard Basin 202
history 81-90
   books 85
   European contact 82
   exploration 84
   gold rush 85
   internet resources 86, 89, 90
   mass tourism 87
   Native Americans 81-4
   park creation 86
   park management 89
hitching 275
Hole in One 229
holidays 264
Holly Lake 226
Home of Champions Rodeo 181
Hoodoo Basin 187
hoodoos 102
horseback riding 48
   Absaroka-Beartooth Wilderness
      206
   Chico Hot Springs 205
   equestrian facilities 62
   Gallatin Valley 200
   Gardiner 177
   Grand Taghee 256
   Grand Teton National Park 232
   Jackson 244
   Jackson Hole 251
   permits 96-7
   tours 62, 157
   Wapiti Valley 194
   West Yellowstone 172
   Yellowstone National Park 96-7, 157
Hot Lake 125

hot springs 50, 65, 101, *see also*
   swimming
   Abyss Pool 113
   Beauty Pool 123
   Beryl Spring 118
   Black Dragon's Cauldron 112
   Black Pool 113
   Blue Star Spring 122
   Canary Springs 101
   Celestine Pool 125
   Chico Hot Springs 205
   Chinese Spring 121
   Chromatic Pool 123
   Churning Cauldron 112
   Cistern Spring 118
   Doublet Pool 123
   Dragon's Mouth Spring 112
   Emerald Pool 124
   Emerald Spring 117
   Excelsior Pool 124
   Ferris Fork Hot Springs 153
   Firehole Lake 125
   Fishing Cone 113
   Flat Cone 131
   Grand Prismatic Spring 124, 130, 4
   Granite Hot Springs 252
   Grizzly Fumarole 112
   Gumper, the 112
   Handkerchief Pool 124
   Heart Spring 123
   Hot Lake 125
   Huckleberry Hot Springs 228
   Hymen Terrace 133
   Kelly Warm Spring 252
   Mammoth Hot Springs 101, 5
   Morning Glory Pool 123, 5
   Mound Spring 131
   Mustard Spring 124
   Ojo Caliente 156
   Ojo Caliente Hot Spring 126
   Opal Spring 101
   Palette Springs 101
   Pocket Basin 126
   Ragged Spring 124
   Rainbow Pool 124
   Sapphire Pool 124
   Sour Lake 112
   Steady Geyser 125
   Steep Cone 131
   Sulfur Cauldron 112, 155
   Terrace Spring 118
   Thumb Paint Pots 113
   Washburn Hot Springs 149
   Whale's Mouth 117
hotels, *see* accommodations

000 Map pages
000 Photograph pages

Huckleberry Hot Springs 228
Hymen Terrace 133
hypothermia 281

I

ice climbing 190
Ice Lake 119
ice skating 159, 244
Idaho's Teton Valley 253-7
Imperial Geyser 130
Indian Arts Museum 214
Indian hellebore 79
Indian Lake 256
Indian paintbrush 79
Inspiration Point (Grand Teton
    National Park) 216
Inspiration Point (Yellowstone
    National Park) 109
insurance
    travel 264
    vehicle 273
international visitors 264
internet access 265
internet resources 29-30, *see also*
    inside back cover
    environment 63
    environmental issues 79
    health 277
    hiking 52
    history 86, 89, 90
    photography 88
    wildlife 72
Iris Falls 153
Irma Hotel 191
Isa Lake 127
itineraries 31-8
    Grand Teton National Park 20, 33,
        35-8, 213, **33, 35-8**
    Yellowstone National Park 19,
        31-2, 34-7, 93, **31-2, 34-7**

J

Jackson 241-9, **242**
Jackson, William H 254
Jackson Hole 249-53
Jackson Hole Aerial Tram 226,
    250
Jackson Hole Airport 272
Jackson Hole Fall Arts Festival 245
Jackson Hole Museum 241
Jackson Lake Dam 217
Jackson Lake Lodge 216
Jackson Lake Overlook 221
Jackson National Fish Hatchery 243
Jackson Point Overlook 217

Jedediah Smith Wilderness 220,
    227, 254
Jelly Geyser 125
Jenny Lake 217, 219, 233
Jenny Lake Overview 217
Jenny Lake Scenic Dr 217, 231
Jewel Geyser 124
John D Rockefeller Jr Memorial
    Parkway
    accommodations 238
    boating 234
    food 239
    hiking 228
    sights 220-1
Johnson, Jeremiah 'Liver Eatin' 181, 190

K

kayaking, *see* canoeing & kayaking
Kelly Warm Spring 252
Kepler Cascades 127, 132
knee pain 277
Knowles Falls 145
Kuralt, Charles 183

L

Lacktail Plateau Dr 102
Lake Butte Overlook 116
Lake Country **114-15**
    accommodations 165
    cycling 155
    food 168
    hiking 133, 140, 142, 150
    sights 112-16
Lake Mary 182
Lake of the Woods 256
Lake Solitude 223
Lake Taminah 225
Lake Village 113
lakes
    Amphitheater Lake 223
    Bearpaw Lake 222
    Bradley Lake 224, 225
    Elbow Lake 206
    Goodwin Lake 243
    Holly Lake 226
    Ice Lake 119
    Jenny Lake 217, 219, 233
    Lake Mary 182
    Lake of the Woods 256
    Lake Solitude 223
    Lake Taminah 225
    Lava Lake 199
    Leigh Lake 222, 233
    Lily Lake 185
    Loon Lake 256-7

Lost Lake 129
Marion Lake 226, 228
North Twin Lake 103
Nymph Lake 103
Phantom Lake 102
Phelps Lake 226
Pine Creek Lake 206
Riddle Lake 142
Rock Island Lake 186
South Twin Lakes 103
Sportsman Lake 136
String Lake 217, 226
Surprise Lake 223
Swan Lake (Grand Teton National
    Park) 221
Swan Lake (Yellowstone National
    Park) 103
Taggart Lake 224
Timberline Lake 182
Trout Lake 105
Two Ocean Lake 221
Wild Bill Lake 182
Lamar River 136
Lamar Valley 105
laundry 265
Lava Lake 199
leeches 280
Lehardy's Rapids 113
Leigh Lake 222, 233
Lewis & Clark Corps of Discovery 82
Liberty Cap 101
licenses & permits
    boating 97-8, 213-4
    camping 96, 213
    canoeing & kayaking 97-8, 213
    driver's licenses 273
    fishing 50, 97, 214
    hiking 96, 213
    horseback riding 96-7
Lily Lake 185
Lion Geyser 123
literature, *see* books
Little Bighorn Battlefield 180
Livingston 203-5
lodgepole pine 77
Log Chapel of the Sacred Heart 217
Lone Star Geyser 127, 132, 155
Lookout Point 109
lookouts, *see* viewpoints
Loon Lake 256-7
Lost Creek Falls 129
Lost Lake 129
Lower Geyser Basin 125
Lyme disease 278
lynxes 74

M

Madison Valley 126
magazines 258
Mammoth Country **100**
  accommodations 161-2
  cross-country skiing 160
  cycling 154
  food 167
  hiking 133-7, 143
  sights 99-103
Mammoth Hot Springs 101, 5
Mammoth Junction 99
Mammoth Visitor Center Museum 99
maps 28-9, see also navigation
Marion Lake 226, 228
marriage 266
Mary Bay 116
measures 258, see also inside back
  cover
medical services 277, see also health
Menor's Ferry 219, 231
menstruation 268
metric conversions, see inside back
  cover
Mexican War 84
Middle Teton 224
Midway Geyser Basin 124
Miller Creek 136
Miller Pass 187
Minerva Spring 101
Minute Geyser 118
mobile phones 266
money 26, 263, 265, see also inside
  back cover
Monument Geyser 142
moose 73, 280, 7
Moose Ponds 219
Mormon Row 220, 229, 230
Morning Glory Pool 123, 5
Mortar Geyser 123
mosquitoes 280
motorcycle travel, see also car travel,
  driving routes
  driver's licenses 273
  driving distances 272
  insurance 273
  road updates 266
  to/from the parks 272-3
  within the parks 274-5
Mound Spring 131
Mt Holmes 136

Mt Meek 228
Mt Meek Pass 254
Mt Sheridan 150
Mt Washburn 107, 138, 8
Mt Wister 225
mountain biking 47-8, see also cycling
  Cody 190
  Gallatin Valley 200
  Grand Targhee 256
  Jackson 243
  Jackson Hole 251
  Paradise Valley 207
  West Yellowstone 171
mountain chickadees 76
mountain goats 74
mountain lions 74
Mountain Man Rendezvous 26
mountaineering, see rock climbing &
  mountaineering
mud pots 65, 112
Mud Volcano 112, 155
Murphy, Tom 148
Museum of the National Park Ranger
  116
Museum of the Rockies 195, 11
Museum of the Yellowstone 171
museums
  Beartooth Nature Center 182
  Buffalo Bill Historical Center
    188, 10
  Carbon County Arts Guild
    Gallery 182
  Carbon County Museum 181
  Center for the Arts 241
  Cody Firearms Museum 190
  Depot Center 204
  Draper Museum of Natural History
    190
  Emerson Cultural Center 195
  Heart Mountain Relocation Center
    192
  Indian Arts Museum 214
  Jackson Hole Museum 241
  Mammoth Visitor Center
    Museum 99
  Museum of the National Park
    Ranger 116
  Museum of the Rockies 195, 11
  Museum of the Yellowstone 171
  National Museum of Wildlife
    Art 241
  Norris Museum 117
  Old Trail Town Museum 190
  Pioneer Museum 195
  Plains Indian Museum 190

  Western Heritage Center 180
  Whitney Gallery of Western Art 190
  Yellowstone Art Museum 180
  Yellowstone Gateway Museum 204
  Yellowstone Heritage & Research
    Center 176
music festivals 26, 256
Mustard Spring 124
Mystic Falls 131

N

National Elk Refuge 243
National Forest organizations 267
National Museum of Wildlife Art 241
Native Americans 81-2
  Bannock 82, 102, 128, 255
  Blackfoot 82, 255
  Crow (Absaroka) 82, 109, 255
  festivals 26, 191
  Gros Ventre 82
  history 81-4
  lore 105, 138
  museums 180, 190, 214
  Nez Percé 83, 156, 187, 255
  Shoshone 216, 255
  sites 103
  Tukudika 82, 103
Natural Bridge 142, 155
navigation 288
New Blue Spring 101
newspapers 258
Nez Percé (people) 83, 156, 187, 255
Nordic skiing, see cross-country skiing
Norris **108**
  accommodations 162
  hiking 142
  sights 116-19
Norris Geyser Basin 117, 5
Norris Meadows Picnic Area 118
Norris Museum 117
North Absaroka Wilderness Area 192
North Shoshone Lake 146
North Twin Lake 103
Nymph Lake 103

O

Observation Hill 121
Observation Peak 139
Obsidian Cliff 103
Ojo Caliente 156
Ojo Caliente Hot Spring 126
Old Faithful 119-37, 4
Old Faithful Inn 124, 10
Old Trail Town Museum 190
O'Leary, Kitty 203

INDEX

INDEX

Opal Spring 101
opening hours 262, *see also inside back cover*
Orange Spring Mound 101
Osprey Falls 135, 154
ospreys 75
overlooks, *see* viewpoints
Oxbow Bend 216, 231

P

Paintbrush Canyon 226
Palette Springs 101
Paradise Valley 205-7, **198**
paragliding 245
passports 265
Pearl Geyser 118
Pebble Creek 136
Peckinpah, Sam 204
Pelican Valley 116, 140, 141
pepper sprays 280
permits, *see* licenses & permits
petrified forests 67
Petrified Tree 102
pets, travel with 60-2
Phantom Lake 102
Phelps Lake 226, 230
Phelps Lake Overlook 225
phonecards 266
photography 51, 88, 148
pig racing 182
Pine Creek Lake 206
Pink Cone Geyser 125
Pioneer Museum 195
Plains Indian Museum 190
Plains Indians Powwow 191
planning 23-30, *see also itineraries*
    children, travel with 56-60
    clothing & equipment 285-9
    discount cards 263
    health 276-7
    pets, travel with 60
plants 76-9, *see also individual species*
Plume Geyser 123
Pocket Basin 126
Point Sublime 111
Porcelain Basin 117
Porcelain Terrace Overlook 117
Porkchop Geyser 118
postal services 265
pumas 280

Q

Quake Lake 202
quaking aspen 77
Queen's Laundry Geyser 131

R

radio 258
rafting & floating 48-9, *see also boating, canoeing & kayaking*
    Chico Hot Springs 204
    Cody 190
    Gallatin Valley 199-200
    Gardiner 176-7
    Jackson 244
    John D Rockefeller Jr Memorial Parkway 234
    Livingston 204
    rental 289
    Snake River 233, 8
    tours 233
    Wapiti Valley 194
Ragged Falls 153
Ragged Spring 124
Rainbow Pool 124
raingear 285
ranger programs 44, 57
    Grand Teton National Park 216
    Yellowstone National Park 113, 141
ranger stations
    Bridger-Teton National Forest 253
    Gallatin National Forest 203
    Grand Teton National Park 212-3
    Shoshone National Forest 188
    West Yellowstone 171
    Yellowstone National Park 93-6
rangers 44, 46
rattlesnakes 280
recycling 80
Red Lodge 181-3
Red Lodge Ales 181
Red Lodge Mountain 182
Red Rock 109
Red Spouter 125
red-capped sandhill cranes 75
red-naped sapsuckers 76
rescue 283
responsible travel 42-3, 260, 270
Ribbon Lake Trail 140
Riddle Lake 142
Rink of the Lower Falls 109
Riverside Geyser 123
road distances chart 272
road rules 273, 275
road updates 266
Roaring Mountain 103
rock climbing & mountaineering 46-7, *see also ice climbing*
    Bozeman 195
    Cody 190

courses 232, 244
    Grand Teton National Park 231-2
    Jackson 244
    Jackson Hole 251
Rock Creek Vista Point Overlook 185
Rock Island Lake 186
Rockefeller, John D 88
rockfalls 283
Rockin' the Tetons 256
Rocky Mountain juniper 78
rodeos 26, 59
    Cody 191, 14
    Gardiner 175
    Jackson 245
    Red Lodge 181
Roosevelt, Franklin D 88
Roosevelt, Theodore 103
Roosevelt Arch 176
Roosevelt Country **104**
    accommodations 163-4
    cross-country skiing 160
    fishing 160
    food 167
    hiking 128, 136, 137-8
    horseback riding 97, 157
    sights 103-7
Roters, Carl 238
rucksacks 285
Running of the Sheep 182
Rustic Falls 102
Rustic Geyser 151
RVs 273, *see also* car travel

S

safety 46
    bears 98, 278-80
    children, travel with 59-60
    cycling 284
    evacuation 283
    first aid 277-8
    GPS 289
    Grand Teton National Park 214
    hiking 283
    hitching 275
    water 45, 278, 281, 283, 287
    winter activities 159
    women 268
    Yellowstone National Park 98
sagebrush 78
Sapphire Pool 124
Sawmill Geyser 124
Schwabacher's Landing 220
Sedge Bay 116
Sentinel Meadows 131
Sevenmile Hole 149-50

Shadow Mountain 229
Sheepeater Canyon 135
Sheepeater Cliffs 103
Sheepeaters (people), *see* Tukudika
(people)
Shell Geyser 124
Sheridan, General Philip 86
Shoshoko Falls 225
Shoshone (people) 216, 255
Shoshone Canyon 193
Shoshone Geyser Basin 147, 5
Shoshone Lake 146, 158
showers 265
Signal Mountain 217, 231
Signal Mountain Summit Rd 217
Silver Cord Cascade 109, 140, 150
Silver Gate 179
skiing, *see* cross-country skiing,
downhill skiing
ski-joring 182
sleeping bags 286
sleeping mats 286
Slough Creek 136
Snake River 233, 8
Snake River Overlook 220, 230
Snake River Rd 229
snakes 280
snow blindness 282
snow conditions 52
Snow King Chairlift 244
Snow Pass 135
snowboarding 52-3
Gallatin Valley 199
Grand Targhee 255-6
Jackson 245
Jackson Hole 250
rental 287-9
snow conditions 52
snowcoach tours 55
snowmobiling 54
Cooke City 179
environmental issues 80
Grand Teton National Park 235
regulations 159
snow conditions 52
weather services 266
West Yellowstone 173
Yellowstone National Park 159
snowshoeing 54
Grand Targhee 256
Grand Teton National Park 234

rental 287-9
snow conditions 52
tours 159, 161
weather services 266
West Yellowstone 173
Yellowstone National Park 159-60,
161, 234
Soda Butte 105
Solitary Geyser 121
Sour Lake 112
South Fork Teton Creek 228
South Rim 110
South Rim Trail 110
South Twin Lakes 103
Southern Paradise Valley 206
Spalding Falls 224
Spanish Peaks 199
Spasmodic Geyser 124
Specimen Ridge 136
spiders 280
Spire Climbing Center 195
Sportsman Lake 136
Spray Geyser 130
stagecoach rides 157
Steady Geyser 125
Steamboat Geyser 118
Steamboat Point 116
Steep Cone 131
Steller's jay 76
stoves 287
String Lake 217, 226, 233
subalpine fir 77
Sulfur Cauldron 112, 155
sunburn 282
Sundance Kid 181
Sundance Pass 182
Sunlight Basin 187
Sunlight Bridge 187
Surprise Lake 223
sustainable travel 80
Swan Lake (Grand Teton National
Park) 221
Swan Lake (Yellowstone National
Park) 103
swimming 50-1, *see also* hot springs
Boiling River 101
Bradley Lake 225
Cave Falls 143
Colter Bay 216
Fairy Falls 130
Firehole Swimming Area 126
Goodwin Lake 243
Granite Hot Springs 252
Leigh Lake 222
Pelican Valley 141

Phelps Lake 230
Taggart Lake 224
Sylvan Lake 116
Sylvan Pass 116

T
Table Mountain 253-4
Taggart Lake 224
taxes 265
telephone services 266, *see also inside
back cover*
tents 286
Terrace Spring 118
tetanus 276
Teton County Fair 245
Teton Glacier 219
Teton Glacier Overlook 223
Teton Science School 263
Teton Valley 255
Teton Village & Jackson Hole
Mountain Resort 250
Thumb Paint Pots 113
ticks 280
Timbered Island 219
Timberline Lake 182
time 266
world time zones 310-11
Togwotee Pass Vista View 253
toilets 45
Tom Miner Basin 205-6
tourism organizations 266
tourist information 266-7
tours 267
boating 158, 232-3
brewery 181
canoeing & kayaking 176, 200,
203
cell-phone 219
cross-country skiing 159, 161
cycling 47, 171
dogsled 205
downhill skiing 159
Grand Teton National Park 214
guided hikes 141
horseback riding 62, 157
rafting 233
snowcoach 55
snowshoeing 159, 161
stagecoach 157
wildlife 190, 267
Yellowstone National Park 98, 113,
173, 177
Tower Fall 106
train travel 273
transportation 270-5

travel insurance 264
travelers checks 265
travertine terraces 66
trees 77-8, *see also individual species*
trekking, *see* hiking
trout 49, 76, 97
Trout Lake 105
trumpeter swans 75
Tukudika (people) 82, 103
Turban Geyser 124
turkey vultures 75
Twin Buttes 129
Twin Lakes 185
Two Ocean Lake 221
Two Ribbons Trail 127
tying the knot 266

U
Undine Falls 102
Union Falls 257
Upper Falls Viewpoint 109
Upper Geyser basin 121-4, **122**
Upper Wind River Valley 253

V
vacations 264
vaccinations 276
Varley, Nathan 111
Vault Geyser 122
vegetarian travelers 264
Vent Geyser 124
video systems 258
viewpoints
    Artist Point 110
    Biscuit Basin Overlook 131
    Blacktail Ponds Overlook 230
    Calcite Springs Overlook 106
    Cathedral Group turnout 217
    Clay Butte Overlook 185
    Grand View Point (Grand Teton
        National Park) 216
    Grand View Point (Yellowstone
        National Park) 109
    Inspiration Point (Grand Teton
        National Park) 216
    Inspiration Point (Yellowstone
        National Park) 109
    Jackson Lake Overlook 221
    Jackson Point Overlook 217
    Jenny Lake Overview 217
    Lake Butte Overlook 116
    Lookout Point 109
    Mt Washburn 138, **8**
    Observation Hill 121
    Observation Peak 139

Phelps Lake Overlook 225
Point Sublime 111
Porcelain Terrace Overlook 117
Rink of the Lower Falls 109
Rock Creek Vista Point Overlook 185
Signal Mountain 217
Snake River Overlook 220, 230
Table Mountain 254
Teton Glacier Overlook 223
Togwotee Pass Vista View 253
Upper Falls Viewpoint 109
Washburn Hot Springs Overlook 107
Willow Flats 216
Virginia Cascade 118
visas 265
visitor centers 93-6, 212
volunteering 268

W
Wade Lake 201
walking, *see* hiking
Wapiti Valley 192-4, **193**
Washakie Wilderness Area 192
Washburn Bear Management Area
    138
Washburn Hot Springs 149
Washburn Hot Springs Overlook 107
Washburn-Langford-Doane
    expedition 85
water 278
    safety 45, 281, 283, 287
waterfalls
    Bechler Falls 143
    Cave Falls 143
    Colonnade Falls 153
    Crystal Falls 110
    Dead Indian Creek Waterfall 187
    Fairy Falls 130, 156
    Firehole Falls 126
    Gibbon Falls 118
    Grand Canyon of the Yellowstone
        107, **12**
    Hidden Falls 223
    Iris Falls 153
    Kepler Cascades 127, 132
    Knowles Falls 145
    Lost Creek Falls 129
    Mystic Falls 131
    Osprey Falls 135, 154
    Ragged Falls 153
    Rustic Falls 102
    Shoshoko Falls 225
    Silver Cord Cascade 109, 140, 150
    Spalding Falls 224
    Tower Fall 106

Undine Falls 102
Union Falls 257
Virginia Cascade 118
Wraith Falls 102
weather services 266
websites, *see* internet resources
weddings 266
weights 258
West Nile disease 278
West Thumb Geyser Basin 113
West Yellowstone 170-5, **172**
Western Heritage Center 180
Whale's Mouth 117
Whirligig Geyser 117
White Dome Geyser 125
White Elephant Back Terrace 101
White Grass Ranger Station 225
whitebark pine 77
white-water rafting, *see* rafting &
    floating
Whitney Gallery of Western
    Art 190
Wild Bill Lake 182
wildfires 79, 144
wildflowers 78-9, 144, **16**
    Avalanche Peak 141
    DeLacy Creek Trail 132
    Elephant Back Mountain 133
    Fossil Forest Trail 137
    Goodwin Lake 243
    Lost Lake 129
    Mammoth Country 102
    Table Mountain 253-4
    Two Ocean Lake 221
wildlife 69-76, *see also* animals, plants
wildlife-watching 70, *see also*
    bird-watching
    Bechler Meadows & Falls Trail 143
    Cache Lake Trail 135
    courses 263
    Delacy Creek Trail 133
    Elk Park 118
    Grand Teton National Park 220
    Harlequin Lake Trail 127
    Hayden Valley 111, 155
    Hermitage Point 221
    Jackson Lake 216
    Lamar Valley 105
    Mammoth Country 103
    Pelican Valley 141
    Red Lodge 182
    road hazards 275
    Roosevelt Country 107, 136
    Snake River 233
    Snake River Rd 229

INDEX

wildlife-watching *continued*
tours 190, 267
Wapiti Valley 193
Yellowstone Lake 112-13
Yellowstone National Park 99
Willow Flats 216
Willow Park 103
willows 78
Wilson 252-3
Wind River Lake 253
Witch Creek 151
wolves 70, 105, 280
women travelers 268
work 269
Wraith Falls 102

X
Xanterra 267

Y
Yellowstone Act 86
Yellowstone Art Museum 180
Yellowstone Fly Fishing School
263
Yellowstone Gateway Museum 204
Yellowstone Heritage & Research
Center 176
Yellowstone IMAX Theater 171

Yellowstone Institute 263
Yellowstone Jazz Festival 191
Yellowstone Lake 66, 112-13
boating 157-8
fishing 158
Yellowstone Lake Overlook 142
Yellowstone National Park 91-168,
94-5
accommodations 160-6
backcountry permits 96
Bechler region 127-8
boating 97, 157-8
bookstores 93
Canyon Country 107-12, **108**
cross-country skiing 160, 161
cycling 153-6
downhill skiing 159, 161
drinking 166-8
driving 98
driving routes 156-7
entrance fees & passes 27, 92
entrance stations 92
equipment rental 288-9
fishing 97, 158, 160, 9
food 166-8
geology 63-9
Geyser Country 119-27, **120**, 14
hiking 128-53

history 126
horseback riding 96-7, 157
itineraries 19, 31-2, 34-7, 93,
31-2, 34-7
Lake Country 112-16, **114-15**
laundry 93
Mammoth Country 99-103, **100**
medical services 93, 277
money 93
Norris 116-19, **108**
opening dates 25
postal services 93
ranger stations 93-6
regulations 96
Roosevelt Country 103-7, **104**
safety 98
showers 93
sights 99-128
snowmobiling 159
snowshoeing 159-60, 161, 234
surrounding region 169-207,
170
tours 98, 113, 141, 173, 177
travel to/from 270-3
travel within 98, 273-5
visitor centers 93-6
wildlife-watching 99
Yellowstone Ski Festival 173

HIKES

Avalanche Canyon & Lake Taminah
225
Avalanche Lake 202
Avalanche Peak 141-2
Basin Lakes National Recreation
Trail 182
Beartooth High Lakes 186
Beartooth Hwy 186
Beartooth National Recreation Trail
186
Beartooth Traverse 186
Beaver Ponds Trail 133-4
Bechler Meadows & Falls 143
Bechler River Trail 152-3, **152**
Bighorn Pass 136
Black Canyon of the Yellowstone
143-6, **145**
Blacktail Deer Creek 136
Blue Danube Lake 202
Bunsen Peak (& Osprey Falls) 134-5

Cache Lake 135, 137
Cascade Lake & Observation Peak
139-40
Cinnamon Creek Trail 199
Coffin Lakes 203
Death Canyon 225-6
Delacy Creek Trail 132-3
Devil's Staircase to Alaska Basin 254-5
Duck Lake 142
Elbow Lake 206
Elephant Back Mountain 133
Elk Fork 193
Fairy Falls & Twin Buttes 129-30, **130**
Fawn Pass 136
Forces of the Northern Range
Trail 102
Fossil Forest Trail 137-8
Fountain Paint Pot Nature 125
Gallatin Divide Devils Backbone
199
Gallatin Petrified Forest 206
Gallatin Valley 199
Garnet Canyon 224
Garnet Lookout 199
Glacier Boulder 109

Glacier Lake 182
Goodwin Lake & Jackson Peak 243
Harlequin Lake 126
Heart Lake & Mt Sheridan
150-1, **151**
Hebgen Lake 202
Hermitage Point 221
Hilgard Basin 202
Ice Lake 119
Lake Fork Trail 183
Lake Solitude 223
Lakeshore Trail 216
Lamar River 136
Lava Lake 199
Leigh & Bearpaw Lakes 222
Lone Star Geyser 132
Lost Lake 129
Marion Lake & Death Canyon
226-7
Miller Creek 136
Monument Geyser Basin Trail 142-3
Mt Holmes Trail 136
Mt Washburn 138-9, 8
Mt Washburn & Sevenmile Hole
149-50, **149**, 8

000 Map pages
000 Photograph pages

INDEX

Mystic Falls & Biscuit Basin 130-1
Natural Bridge 142
North Rim Trail 109
North Shoshone Lake & Shoshone
    Geyser Basin 146-9, **147**
Pahaska-Sunlight 187
Paintbrush Divide 226, **227**
Paradise Valley 206
Pebble Creek 136
Pelican Valley 140-1
Pine Creek Lake 206
Red Lodge 182

Ribbon Lake 140
Riddle Lake 142
Sentinel Meadows & Queen's Laundry
    Geyser 131-2, **130**
Slough Creek 136
Specimen Ridge 136
Sportsman Lake 136
Storm Castle 199
Storm Point 116
Sundance Pass 182
Surprise & Amphitheater Lakes 223-4
Table Mountain 253-4

Taggart & Bradley Lakes 224-5
Teton Crest Trail 227-8, 9
Timberline Lake 182
Two Ocean Lake & Grand View
    Point 221-2
Two Ribbons 127
Wapiti Valley 193
West Fork Trail 182
Wild Bill Lake 182
Yellowstone Lake Overlook 142
Yellowstone River Picnic Area
    Trail 128-9

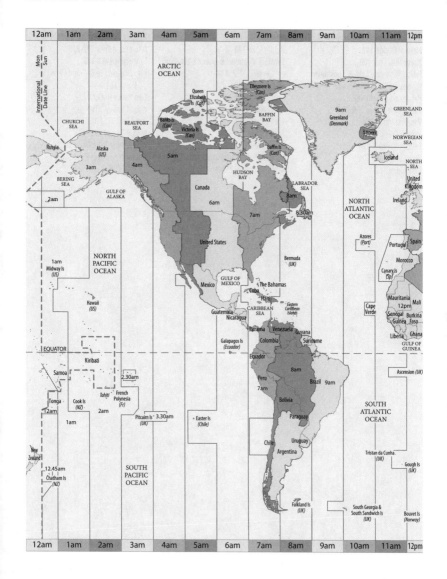